15

Pat Donaldson
P.O. Box 43
Georgetown, Ok 4512

WEST VIRGINIA ESTATE SETTLEMENTS

An Index to Wills, Inventories,
Appraisements, Land Grants, and Surveys to 1850

Compiled by

ROSS B. JOHNSTON

GENEALOGICAL PUBLISHING CO., INC.

Baltimore   *1988*

Excerpted from
West Virginia History,
Volumes XVII-XXIV, 1955-1963

Reprinted with permission of
the West Virginia Department
of Archives and History

Genealogical Publishing Co., Inc.
Baltimore, 1977, 1978, 1985, 1988

Library of Congress Catalogue Card Number 76-53168
International Standard Book Number 8063-0755-2

Made in the United States of America

CONTENTS

West Virginia Estate Settlements

In 1936 and 1937, the West Virginia Commission on Historic and Scenic Markers, the Works Progress Administration, and the Federal Emergency Relief Administration compiled court records of the various counties, such as Births, Deaths, Marriages and Wills. Under Wills were grouped subjects pertaining to Estate Settlements, including Wills, Inventories and Appraisements. Copies of these county records were filed at the Department of Archives and History, Charleston, the Library of West Virginia University, Morgantown, and the DAR Library, Washington.

Believing that there would be particular interest on the part of the general public in the Estate Settlements in the older counties, the West Virginia Historical Society has undertaken to abstract the Estate Settlement Records, as filed in the State Department of Archives and History, and offer them for publication in the *West Virginia History Quarterly*. (No responsibility can be assumed as to the accuracy of the copies made from the original county records.)

There are 13 counties which were formed prior to 1800, and it has been agreed to arrange these counties in chronological order, and to print their records from the earliest date to 1850. The formation dates of these counties are as follows: Hampshire—1753; Berkeley—1772; Monongalia—1776; Ohio—1776; Greenbrier—1778; Harrison—1784; Hardy—1786; Randolph—1787; Pendleton—1788; Kanawha—1788; Brooks—1797; Wood—1798 and Monroe—1799.

Hampshire County, Formed 1753

Abbreviations used in this material include: Adm.—administrator; Agr.—agreement; App.—appraisement; Bro.—brother; Dau.—daughter; Dev.—devisees; Divn.—division; Ind.—indenture; Inv.—inventory; L. G.—land grant; Obl.—obligation; S. B.—sale bill; Set.—settlement; Sis.—sister; and Sur.—Survey.

ABERNATHEY, JOHN, App., 10-17-1803.

ABERNATHEY, WM., App., 6-18-1810.

ABERNATHY, JOHN, Will, 1-18-1830.
Dev.: Hannah, wife; John, Thom., James, William Robt., sons; Virg. Currency, Elinor, Marg., Martha, Hannah, dau.

ABERNATHY, JOHN, App., 3-19-1830.

ABERNATHY, SAM, Will, 3-23-1815.
Dev.: Sam., Wm., John, James, sons; Eliz., Elenor, Susan, dau.

ABERNATHY, SAM, Will, 3-23-1840.
Dev.: Sam, Wm., John, James, sons; Eliz., Elianor, Susan, dau.

ABRASAM, JOHN, App., 12-16-1790.

ACTON, RICH, Bond, 5-23-1791.

ADAM, JOHN, S.B., 12-10-1799.

ADAMS, CATH., Will, 4-20-1807.
Dev.: Jacob, son; Cath. Daniels, Rachel, dau.

ADAMS, CATH., App., 9-14-1807.

ADAMS, CATH., S.B., 9-14-1807.

ADAMS, JOHN, App., 12-10-1794.

ADAMS, JOHN, S.B., 12-10-1794.

ADAMS, LYDIA, Will, 12-22-1834.
Dev.: Wm., son; and others.

ADEMS, WILL, Will, 8-18-1828.
Dev.: Elinor, wife; Geo., son; other children. ,

AIKMAN, JOHN, Will, 4-14-1806.
Dev.: Mary, wife; Adam, son.

AITON, JOHN, Sur., 5-15-1791.

AITON, RUTH, Sur., 5-16-1791.

ALEXANDER, JAS., Will, 5-11-1773.
Dev.: Sarah, wife; Eliz., sis.; and others.

ALLEN, JAMES, Set., 5-27-1833.

ALLEN, JAMES, Set., 6-24-1833.

ALLEN, ROBT., Will, 3-18-1816. ,
Dev.: Isebelle, wife; Wm., Sam., sons; Iney, dau.

ALLEN, SAM., Will, 8-28-1843.
Dev.: Sarah Allen, Marg. Colven, Eliz. Burkett, Ann Vandergrift, Mary Cunningham, Jane Zane; Isaac Garret, nephew.

ALLEN, THOMAS, App., 3-20-1822.

ALLEN, WILL, Will, 2-15-1830.
Dev.: Wife; Sam., bro.

ALLEN, WM., App., 3-15-1830.

ALLENDER, WILL, Will, 6-14-1815.
Dev.: Crestene, wife; Crestene, dau., Geo., Wm., Jacob, James, sons.

ALLENSON, JOHN, Sur., 3-7-1798.

ALLOWAY, WILL, Will, 12-18-1828.
Dev.: Jane, Hannah, dau.; and others.

ALLOWAY, WM., App., 12-14-1829.

ALLOWAY, WM., S.B., 12-14-1829.

AMBLER, JACQUILIN, Bond, 3-10-1784.

ANDERSON, ALEX., L.G., 12-2-1796.

ANDERSON, DAVID, L.G., 12-24-1783.

ANDERSON, GAR., L.G., 5-11-1780.

ANDERSON, JESSE, Sur., 3-15-1798.

ANDERSON, JESSE, Sur., 2-2-1802.

ANDERSON, WM., Will, 4-9-1794.
Dev.: Nancy, wife; Rachael, Cath., Sarah, Hannah, dau.; Thomas, son.

ANDERSON, WILL, Will, 6-19-1815.
Dev.: Margaret, wife; Will Philip.

ANDREW, JOHN, App., 7-17-1804.

ANDREW, JOHN, Set., 12-16-1807.

ANETT, CHRIS., Set., 4-18-1814.

APENDALE, PETER, Set., 3-18-1785.

ARJALOU, PRICE, Bond, 10-15-1799.

ARMSTRONG, ANN, App., 9-19-1829.

ARMSTRONG, ANN, S.B., 9-19-1829.

ARMSTRONG, ANN, S.B., 4-17-1830.

ARMSTRONG, ANN, Set., 6-22-1831.

ARMSTRONG, DAN, Set., 4-22-1839.

ARMSTRONG, DAVIS, App., 11-26-1836.

ARMSTRONG, WM., L.G., 10-4-1788.

ARMSTRONG, WM. & RANDOLPH, CAPT., Sur., 7-22-1797.

ARMSTRONG, WM., TO KING, ALEX., Sur., 4-13-1801.

ARMSTRONG, WM., Set., 2-20-1832.

ARNOLD, ANDREW, Will, 4-22-1844.
Dev.: Mary, wife; Lettice, Sarah, Rebecca, Mary, dau.; John, Archibald, sons; and others.

ARNOLD, ARCH, Will, 10-27-1836.
Dev.: Mary, wife; Louisa, Rebecca, Mary, Frances, dau.; Lewis, Elias, Andrew, Lemuel, Jos., sons.

ARNOLD, DAN., Will, 9-24-1849.
Dev.: Eliz., wife; Sol., Sam., Emmanuel, Dan., Michael, John, sons; Christina, Ann, Cath., Eliz., Magdelina, Susan, dau.; and others.

ARNOLD, DAVID, Set., 12-24-1849.

ARNOLD, JACOB, Will, 7-18-1828.
Dev.: Sarah, wife; Sam., son; Barbary, Mary, Susana, Cath., Lydia, Willian, dau.; and others.

ARNOLD, JACOB, Set., 3-15-1828.

ARNOLD, JACOB, Set., 2-20-1832.

ARNOLD, JOHN, Will, 6-14-1819.
Dev.: Hannah, wife; Sarah Hort, Phebe Grove, Anrilla Wall, dau.; John, Rich., Andrew, Levi, sons; and others.

ARNOLD, JNO., App., 3-18-1822.

ARNOLD, JNO., S.B., 3-1822.

ARNOLD, JOHN, Sur., 11-17-1824.

ARNOLD, JOSIAH, S.B., 3-14-1763.

ARNOLD, LEVI, App., 3-15-1830.

ARNOLD, LEVI, S.B., 3-15-1830.

ARNOLD, LEVI, Set., 5-27-1834.

ARNOLD, LEVI, Inv., 12-26-1836.

ARNOLD, LEVI, S.B., 1-28-1837.

ARNOLD, RICH., Will, 12-12-1758.
Dev.: Eliz., dau.; and others.

ARNOLD, SAM., Set., 2-20-1832.

ARNOLD, SAM., App., 4-23-1832.

ARNOLD, SAM., S.B., 1-23-1837.

ARNOLD, SAMUEL, Set., 10-28-1833.

ARNOLD, WM., S.B., 8-24-1835.

ARNOLD, WM., App., 8-24-1835.

ARNOLD, WM., Set., 9-28-1835.

ARNOLD, ZACH., App., 8-17-1829.

ARNOLD, ZACH., S.B., 11-15-1829.

ARNOLD, ZACH., Set., 9-19-1831.

ARNOLD, ZACH., Set., 2-24-1834.

ARRETE, CHRIS., S.B., 11-16-1812.

ASBERY, JOSEPH, App., 3-14-1825.
ASBURN, GEO., Set., 7-16-1789.
ASBURY, HENRY, S.B., 4-16-1822.
ASBURY, JEREMIAH, Will, 9-18-1826.
Dev.: Ruth, wife; Jos., son; other children.
ASBURY, JOSEPH, App., 3-14-1825.
ASBURY, JOS., Set., 9-24-1832.
ASHBEY, BENJ., Will, 9-17-1804.
Dev.: Hannah, wife; Jermich, son; Lottie, Eliz., dau.
ASHBROOK, JOHN, S.B., 3-15-1775.
ASHBROOK, JOHN, Divn., 8-8-1780.
Dev.: Ester, wife; Aron, son; and others.
ASHBROOK, LEVI, S.B., 10-15-1794.
ASHBROOK, LEVI, App., 10-15-1794.
ASHBROOK, LEVI, Inv., 10-15-1794.
ASHBROOK, LEVI. S.B., 8-14-1815.
ASHBROOK, MOSES, L.G., 12-31-1793.
ASHBURY, HENRY, Deed, 5-15-1809.
ASHBY, ED., & HOMLS, DAULA, L.G., 5-7-1789.
ATHEY, MARTHA, Set., 3-19-1830.
ATHEY, THOM., Sur., 4-26-1791.
AUGHINEY, ANN, Will, 4-15-1795.
Dev.: Nancy Rector, Mary Ann Kirkpatrick, Abegil Lyal, Wineford Newl, dau.; Sam, Oldhum, son; and others.
AUGHNEY, DARBEY, Will, 10-19-1795.
Dev.: Anne, wife; and others.
AUZHEY, DARBY, App., 2-15-1796.

BABB, CHAS., Sur., 3-10-1798.
BAILEY, BENJ., S.B., 10-17-1831.
BAILEY, BENJ., Set., 11-14-1831.
BAILEY, BENJ., Set., 1-15-1833.
BAILEY, BENJ., Set., 2-25-1833.
BAILEY, EDWARD, Will, 1-18-1828.
Dev.: Elinor, Eliz., Alice Steman, Mary Clark, dau.; John, Edward, Benj., Wm., sons.
BAILY, BENJ., Will, 4-19-1830.
Dev.: Ed., Mary, Wm., Eliz. Baily, John, Eliz. Kelley; and others.
BAKER, JACOB, Sur., 5-13-1795.
BAKER, JOHN, App., 6-11-1794.
BAKER, JONATHAN, App., 1-18-1808.
BAKER, JOS., L.G., 12-8-1795.
BAKER, JOSEPH, S.B., 7-24-1837.
BAKER, JOS., Will, 4-26-1847.
Dev.: Rebecca, dau.
BAKER, PERGINE, App., 11-26-1849.
BAKER, PERGINE, S.B., 11-26-1849.
BAKER, SAM., App., 5-7-1836.
BAKER, SAM., App., 1-22-1840.
BAKER, SAM., S.B., 1-27-1840.
BAKER, THES., App., 11-26-1849.
BAKER, THES., S.B., 11-26-1849.
BAKER, THOM., Will, 2-26-1844.
Dev.: John, Thom., sons; Nancy, dau.; and others.
BANES, JESSE, Will, 10-17-1831.
Dev.: Alex., Jesse, Geo., sons; Nancy Chamberlain, dau.
BANES, JESSE, App., 7-25-1833.
BANKS, HENRY, L.G., 12-24-1783.
BANKS, WM., App., 4-15-1823.

BANKS, WM., S.B., 3-14-1825.
BANKS, WM., Set., 3-17-1825.
BARBER, JAMES, App., 2-18-1805.
BARBER, JAMES, S.B., 2-18-1805.
BARKALORE, JAMES, Will, 9-19-1796.
Dev.: Eliz., wife; Benj., Johnson, sons; Sarah, Mary, Seanah, Anna, dau.
BARKELOW, JAS., App., 1-16-1797.
BARKLOW, JOHNSON, App., 9-19-1808.
BARRE, JESSE, App., 2-25-1833.
BARRET, JOHN, Will, 12-15-1823.
Dev.: Rhoda, wife; Jonathan, David, sons; Edeth, dau.
BARRETT, JOHN, Inv., 3-15-1824.
BARRETT, JOHN, App., 3-15-1824.
BARRICK, GEO., Will, 3-22-1841.
Dev.: Cath., wife; children.
BARRICK, JACOB, App., 3-26-1832.
BARRICK, JACOB, S.B., 3-26-1832.
BARRICK, JACOB, Set., 2-24-1834.
BARRS, JOHN, Will, 12-14-1818.
Dev.: Sarah, wife; Sarah Racey, sis.; and others.
BARTLOW, ELIZ., Will, 3-14-1818.
Dev.: Sarah, dau.; Leonora Beatty.
BARTNIFF, AND., App., 8-22-1836.
BARTNIFF, AND., S.B., 8-22-1836.
BARTRUFF, AND., S.B., 5-22-1837.
BARTRUFF, JOHN, S.B., 5-22-1837.
BARTRUFF, LAVINA, S.B., 5-22-1837.
BARTUFF, JOHN, Set., 8-24-1840.
BASLEY, JAMES, Will, 3-24-1834.
Dev.: John, James, Wm., sons; Elinor, Eliz., Mary Roberts, Arbella Aranholt, Priscilla Evans, dau.; and others.
BATH, JAMES, Sur., 10-13-1791.
BAUL, JESSIE, Will, 10-17-1831.
Dev.: Alex., Jesse, Geo., sons; Nancy Chamberlain.
BEAL, GEO., S.B., 10-17-1800.
BEALL, BENJ., Will, 8-13-1765.
Dev.: Mary, wife; Nancy, Nelean, Cephas, dau.; Shoyd, son.
BEALL, BENJ., S.B., 11-11-1777.
BEALL, ELISHA, Sur., 5-13-1795.
BEALL, ELISHA, Set., 2-1805.
BEALL, GEO., Sur., 5-15-1795.
BEALL, GEO., Will, 9-18-1797.
Dev.: Prudence, wife; Ann, dau.; Elisha, Ely, sons.
BEALL, GEO., App., 12-18-1797.
BEALL, GEO., Set., 4-16-1804.
BEALL, THOMAS, Set., 2-20-1832.
BEALLS, MEIZER, S.B., 8-1-1840.
BEARD, GEO., Will, 9-17-1821.
Dev.: Martha Thompson.
BECKDOLE, JOHN, App., 4-28-1836.
BECKDOLL, JNO., S.B., 4-23-1838.
BEELER, ROBT., Sur., 2-2-1779.
BEERY, JOS., Will, 10-18-1802.
Dev.: Sarah, wife; Evin, Amnasia, children.
BEGGANS, JOHN, App., 1-8-1795.
BEGGERSTAFF, WM., Will, 4-18-1803.
Dev.: Wm., son; Rebecca Hortley, dau;. and others.

4   West Virginia Estate Settlements

BEGGINS, JOHN, S.B., 6-15-1795.
BELL, ROBT., S.B., 4-12-1774.
BENNETT, SYL., Set., 8-18-1809.
BENNETT, SYL., S.B., 11-21-1820.
BENNETT, SYL., Set., 9-22-1834.
BENNICK, GEO., S.B., 2-13-1787.
BERRY, JOHN, App., 3-22-1824.
BERRY, JOHN, App., 4-20-1824.
BERRY, JOHN, S.B., 9-20-1824.
BERRY, JOHN, Set., 9-20-1824.
BERRY, JOHN, S.B., 7-18-1825.
BERRY, JOS., App., 4-20-1807.
BERRY, WM., OR BERRY, JOHN,
App., 5-17-1824.
BETHELL, GEO., Will, 8-15-1814.
Dev.: Jane, wife; Geo., Joshua, Ed.,
sons; Mary Ann Engle, Nancy, Mary,
Ruth Asberry, dau.
BEVER, JOHN, S.B., 2-6-1768.
BIGGERSTAFF, WILL, Will, 5-15-1809.
Dev.: Wife; Nancy, Mary, Rachael,
Sarah, Alice, Susana, Plesant, dau.;
and others.
BIGGINS, JOHN, S.B., 10-5-1799.
BISBY, WM., Set., 2-14-1825.
BISER, JACOB, Will, 8-18-1823.
Dev.: Eliz., wife; children.
BISER, JACOB, App., 3-18-1824.
BISER, JACOB, S.B., 6-25-1825.
BISHOP, JOHN, Sug., 5-3-1791.
BIZZERSTAFF, W., Will, 5-15-1809.
Dev.: Rachel, wife; Friend, Hugh,
sons; Mary, Nancy, Sarah, Alice,
Susana, Plesent, dau.
BLACKMORE, SMITH, App., 1-19-1824.
BLAIR, MATILDA, Set., 2-24-1834.
BLEAKMAN, SMITH, App., 1-19-1823.
BLUE, GARRETT, Will, 3-23-1835.
Dev.: Mary, wife; Elenor Monroe,
Nancy Chambers, Hannah Magualin,
dau.
BLUE, GARRETT, App., 5-25-1835.
BLUE, GARRETT, S.B., 5-25-1835.
BLUE, GARRETT, S.B., 4-24-1837.
BLUE, GARRETT, Set., 10-22-1849.
BLUE, JOHN, Will, 8-14-1770.
Dev.: Cath., wife; John, Uriah, Ab-
raham, sons.
BLUE, JOHN, S.B., 3-10-1772.
BLUE, JOHN, Will, 4-14-1791.
Dev.: Marg., wife; Uriah, Peter,
John, David, Jacob, Michael, Gar-
ret, Benj., Wm., Abraham, Jesse,
sons; Eliz., Hannah, Marg., dau.
BLUE, JOHN, Inv., 9-11-1793.
BLUE, JOHN, App., 9-11-1793.
BLUE, JOHN, L.G., 4-28-1794.
BLUE, JOHN, S.B., 7-15-1822.
BLUE, JOHN, Set., 7-15-1822.
BLUE, JOHN, App., 3-19-1830.
BLUE, JOHN, S.B., 5-17-1830.
BLUE, MARY, Set., 10-22-1849.
BLUE, MICHAEL, Will, 3-28-1842.
Dev.: Wife; Mich., Thom., John, Lau-
son, Garrett, sons; Hannah Kuyken-
dall, Charity, dau.
BLUE, URIAH, App., 1-16-1815.

BOGART, GUSBERT, Will, 8-11-1778.
Dev.: Eliz., wife; Cornelius, Ezekeel,
sons; Warner, bro.; Charity Riche,
Hannah Bresrt, Phebe More, Grizinia
See, dau.
BOGEL, ANDERSON, Sur., 6-8-1808.
BOMGARDNER, RUD., Set., 9-17-1810.
BOMEROTZ, LEO., Will, 9-17-1827.
Dev.: Eleanor, wife; Wm., son; and
others.
BONCROTZ, LENORD, Set., 11-16-
1829.
BOND, JOHN, App., 8-17-1829.
BOND, THOM., Will, 5-16-1814.
Dev.: Spelman, wife; John, Thom.,
sons; Ann Dawson, Winfred, Mary,
Eliz., dau.
BOOKHART, MUHIAL, Sur., 6-11-1788.
BOSER, JACOB, Will, 11-10-1778.
Dev.: Basbery, wife; Chas., Jacob,
Thom., sons; Mary, Eliz., Basbery,
Rosalind, Martah, dau.
BOSLEY, JAMES, Will, 3-24-1834.
Dev.: John, James, Jacob, Wm.,
sons; Eleanor, Eliz., Mary, Arbella,
Andrew, Ann, Priscillia, Nancy, El-
eanor, dau.; and Thomas Burgas.
BOSLEY, JAMES, App., 1-25-1836.
BOSLEY, JAMES, S.B., 1-25-1836.
BOSLEY, JAMES, Set., 2-25-1836.
BOSLEY, WM., S.B., 2-14-1825.
BOSLEY, WM., Sur., 12-11-1826.
BOURK, MITCHAEL, Will, 11-18-1811.
Dev.: Eliz., wife; children; and
others.
BOWELL, WM., S.B., 5-13-1772.
BOWMAN, ANDREW, Will, 2-22-1847.
Dev.: Nellie, wife; children.
BOXWELL, WM., Set., 3-15-1830.
BOYCE, RICH., Sur., 12-23-1788.
BOYCE, RICH., Will, 2-10-1791.
Dev.: Rich., Nicholas, John, Robt.,
James, sons; Sarah, wife; Ann, dau.
BOYCE, RICH., Set., 6-12-1793.
BOYCE, RICH., S.B., 6-12-1793.
BRANSON, JOS., Will, 8-9-1780.
Dev.: John, son; Basbery, Cath.,
Susanna.
BRANSON, JOS., Inv., 2-13-1781.
BRANSON, JOS., Will, 8-8-1781.
Dev.: John, son; and others.
BREEZE, LAWRENCE, Set., 10-15-1798.
BREEZES, MARG., Will, 10-19-1807.
Dev.: Mary Knight, sis.; and others.
BREEZES, MARG., App., 5-16-1808.
BREEZES, MARGARET, Set., 5-11-1810.
BREEZES, SAM., App., 12-18-1797.
BRELSFORD, BERN., Will, 6-26-1844.
Dev.: Jesse, son; Eliz. Higgins, Mary
Harper, Leah Starnes, Rachael, Sa-
ran, Phebe, Marg., Mahaly, dau;
and others.
BRESLFORD, MARY, Will, 8-23-1847.
Dev.: Ann; John, son; and others.
BRIGGS, JOS., Will, 8-8-1823.
Dev.: Viletta, wife; Ann Crable,
dau.; others.
BRILL, HENRY, App., 8-27-1832.
BRILL, HENRY, S.B., 8-27-1832.

BRILL, HENRY, Set., 9-22-1834.
BRILL, HENRY, S.B., 7-24-1837.
BRILL, JANE, Set., 12-22-1834.
BRINK, HYBERT, Will, 5-12-1778.
Dev.: Huselty, wife; Philip, Issac, Hybert, John, sons; Huselty, dau.
BRINK, HYBERT, S.B., 11-10-1785.
BRINK, HYBERT, Set., 11-10-1785.
BRINKER, HENRY, Will, 3-27-1838.
Dev.: John Brady, Hannah Lamberger.
BROOKHEART, MICH., App., 12-18-1808.
BROOM, BRAXTON, S.B., 10-22-1838.
BROWN, ALEX., Will, 9-16-1816.
Dev.: Adam, Sam., Isaac, Mathew, John, sons; Jane, Polly, Eliz., dau.; and others.
BROWN, BAXTER, S.B., 9-24-1838.
BROWN, DAN., Will, 5-10-1780.
Dev.: Frances, wife; Dan, Thom., sons; Sarah, Ann, Mary, dau.
BROWN, DAN., Inv., 8-8-1780.
BROWN, DAN., S.B., 2-10-1791.
BROWN, DAN., Set., 12-10-1791.
BROWN, ISSAC, L.G., 11-3-1797.
BROWN, JOHN, Sur., 3-19-1798.
BRUCE, ANDREW, Will, 10-22-1832.
Dev.: Susanna, dau.; Normond, Wm., Dan., Andrew, sons.
BRUCE, JOS., Inv., 8-12-1783.
BRUCE, JOSEPH, Set., 10-11-1787.
BRUCE, RICH., Inv., 6-16-1791.
BRUCE, THOM., S.B., 10-11-1787.
BRUE, NORMAND, Sur., 10-18-1798.
BRUIN, BRYON, Sur., 7-9-1780.
BRUIN, BRYN, L.G., 9-18-1792.
BRUNER, ELIZ., Set., 6-20-1831.
BRUNER, ELIZ., Set., 3-25-1833.
BRUNER, HENRY, Set., 6-14-1830.
BRUNER, HENRY, Set., 12-22-1834.
BRYON, JAMES, Set., 1-19-1818.
BUBBER, SAMLERD, Will, 5-10-1774.
Dev.: Cath., wife; Hummel Buzzard.
BUCK, ROBT., App., 12-11-1793.
BUFFINGTON, RICH., Will, 6-14-1817.
Dev.: Sister Mary's children; Brother David's children; Pete Davis.
BUFFINGTON, WM., Will, no date.
Dev.: Mary, wife; Thom., Wm., Joel, David, Jonathan, Rich., sons; Ruth Collins, Susannah, Mary, dau.
BUFFINGTON, WM., Will, 8-10-1781.
Dev.: Thom., Wm., Joel, Jonathan, sons; Ruth Collins, Susannah Sullivan, dau.; Mary, wife.
BUFFINGTON, WM., Inv., 7-11-1784.
BUFFINGTON, WM., Set., 10-12-1784.
BUFFINGTON, WM., Will, 7-11-1786.
Dev.: Mary, wife; Rich., Wm., sons.
BUFFINGTON, WM., App., 7-11-1786.
BUFFINGTON, WM., S.B., 10-12-1787.
BUFFINGTON, WM., Will, 6-20-1825.
Dev.: David, bro.; Mary Black, sis.; and others.
BUFFINGTON, WM., Set., 2-16-1833.
BUFFINGTON, WM., Set., 3-1-1833.
BUFFINGTON, WM., Set., 10-26-1835.

BUMGARDNER, RUDOLPH, Will, 12-16-1805.
Dev.: Agness, wife; Ruben, son; Rebecca, dau.
BUMGARDINER, R., S.B., 2-16-1807.
BUMGARDINER, R., App., 2-16-1807.
BUNGONER, RUD., Set., 7-17-1810.
BUPORT, LAMBERT, S.B., 8-12-1777.
BURCH, JONATHAN, Sur., 9-9-1818.
BURTON, MESHACK, App., 11-18-1811.
BURWELL, ELIZ., Bond., 5-7-1760.
BUSBEY, JOHN, Will, 11-19-1810.
Dev.: Marg., wife; Wm., John, Mathew, Sam, Benj., Hamilton, sons; Eliz., dau.
BUSBY, JOHN, Set., 2-18-1811.
BUSBY, JOHN, Set., 4-15-1811.
BUSHBEY, JOHN, S.B., 4-15-1811.
EUSHBY, JOHN, App., 2-18-1811.
BUSLEY, JAMES, S.B., 2-14-1825.
BUSLEY, JOHN S., Set., 2-15-1825.
BUSLEY, WM., Set., 2-14-1825.
BUSLEY, WM., S.B., 2-14-1825.
BUSLEY, WM., S.B., 7-18-1825.
BUTCHER, JOHN, App., 9-11-1788.
BUTCHER, JOS., Sur., 10-2-1791.
BUYEW, JACOB & PENNENGITER, RICH., Article agreement, 9-4-1782.
BUZZARD, FRED., Will, 1-18-1816.
Dev.: Eliz. Mouser, Madaline Regin, Barbary Luttrell, Ester Kiter, Susan Cowgill, dau.; John, Fred., Jacob, sons; and others.
BUZZARD, FRED., App., 8-19-1823.
BUZZARD, FRED., Set., 2-15-1825.
BUZZARD, FRED., S.B., 2-15-1825.
BUZZARD, FRED., Set., 3-15-1825.
BUZZARD, FRED., S.B., 12-19-1825.
BUZZARD, FRED., Set., 4-23-1832.
BUZZARD, JOHN, App., 6-14-1813.
BUZZARD, MARY, App., 10-22-1832.
BUZZARD, MARY, S.B., 11-26-1832.
BYSER, JACOB, Will, 8-18-1823.
Dev.: Eliz., wife; children.

CADDIS, WM., Will, 3-9-1773.
Dev.: Prisilla, wife; John, son.
CALDWELL, CHAS., Will, 12-28-1840.
Dev.: Wife; Sam., son; Eliz., dau.
CALMES, FIELDING, Will, 5-14-1804.
Dev.: Isabella Beneon, sis.
CALMES, FIELDING, App., inv., 7-16-1804.
CALMES, GEO., App., 3-23-1835.
CALMES, GEO., App., 1-25-1836.
CALMES, GEO., S.B., 1-25-1836.
CALMES, GEO., Set., 3-28-1836.
CALMES, WM., Will, 12-24-1849.
Dev.: Catherine, wife.
CALSTON, JOHN, Set., 12-8-1785.
CALSTON, MARG., Sur., 12-23-1783.
CALVIN, LUTHER, AND JOHNSON, JOHN, Sur., 8-5-1818.
CAMBELL, ELIZ., Will, 6-16-1812.
Dev.: Sam., Henry, John, Andrew Heinzman, grandsons.
CAMBELL, JOHN, Inv., 6-10-1790.

CAMBELL, WM., Inv., 8-31-1802.
CAMPBELL, JAMES, Sur., 4-1-1783.
CAPSEY, JOHN, App., 9-24-1849.
CARDER, ALLEY, S.B., 4-23-1838.
CARDER, GEO., Inv., 3-15-1830.
CARDER, GEO., S.B., 3-15-1830.
CARDER, GEORGE, App., 3-15-1830.
CARDER, GEO., Set., 10-18-1830.
CARDER, GEO., Will, 9-19-1831.
 Dev.: Mary Ann, wife.
CARDER, WM., Sur., 11-15-1777.
CARLILE, WM., L.G., 12-13-1804.
CARLISLE, JONATHAN, Sur., 9-12-1818.
CARMES, FIELD, Inv., 9-7-1804.
CARSWELL, JOHN, Will, 8-20-1807.
 Dev.: Abigal, wife; Robt. Slocom,
 John Slocom, step-sons.
CARSWELL, JOHN, Inv., 12-14-1807.
CARTER, ALLEY, Set., 6-24-1839.
CASGROUS, CORNELIOUS, App.,
 6-14-1824.
CASGROVE, CORNELIS, Set., 11-16-1824.
CASGROVE, CORNELIS, S.B., 11-16-1824.
CASLER, MICHAEL, Will, 3-19-1810.
 Dev.: Sarah Johnson, dau.; and
 others.
CAUDY, DAVID, Inv., 3-26-1832.
CAUDY, JAMES, Will, 3-9-1781.
 Dev.: Ann Dulain, Marg. Wood, Mary
 Kinner, Sarah Kinner, dau.; and
 others.
CAUDY, JAMES, Inv., 5-11-1784.
CAUDY, JAMES, Set., 6-11-1789.
CAUDY, JAMES, S.B., 12-20-1824.
CAUDY, JAMES, Set., 3-14-1825.
CAWAN, ROBT., Will, 9-14-1795.
 Dev.: wife; Wm., son.
CHADWICK, CATH., Set., 5-25-1835.
CHADWICK, ELIZ., & ZILER, Set.,
 5-25-1835.   ----
CHADWICK, J. F., Set., 4-22-1833.
CHADWICK, JER., App., 12-14-1829.
CHADWICK, JER., S.B., 8-16-1830.
CHADWICK, JER., Set., 3-25-1833.
CHANDLEY, STEAPHEN, App.,
 10-15-1794.
CHAPMAN, CHARITY, App., Inv.,
 4-17-1797.
CHAPMAN, WM., Will, 2-15-1796.
 Dev.: Cattran, wife; Wm., son; Feby,
 Eliz., Dorothy, dau.
CHAPMAN, WM., App., 7-10-1796.
CHAPMAN, WM., S.B., 4-15-1799.
CHAPMAN, WM., S.B., 12-20-1813.
CHAPMAN, WM., Set., 6-9-1829.
CHAPMAN, WM., Set., 4-18-1831.
CHAUDER, STEPHEN, Set., 9-1-1797.
CHENOWITH, JOHN, Will, 9-14-1812.
 Dev.: Elanor, wife; Absalom, John,
 James, Elias, Wm., sons; Eliz., El-
 eanor Ashbrook, Mary Ashbrook,
 Rachael Ashbrook, dau.
CHENOWITH, JOHN, App., 5-17-1813.
CHENOWITH, JOHN, S.B., 5-17-1813.

CHESER, JOHN, App., 11-19-1829.
CHESER, JOHN, S.B., 11-19-1829.
CHESHIRE, BARD., Will, 10-19-1829.
 Dev: Sam., Uriah, Sam., Obadiah,
 Job., sons; Sarah Kisner, Rebecca
 Emmert, dau.; others.
CHESHIRE, BARB, App., 11-16-1829.
CHESHIRE, BARD, Set., 11-14-1831.
CHESHIRE, ERN., Inv., 6-20-1796.
CHESHIRE, JOHN, Inv., 12-19-1825.
CHESHIRE, SAM., Inv., 4-16-1810.
CHESHIRE, SAM., Set., 1-18-1812.
CHESHIRE, SAMUEL, App., 4-16-1810.
CHESHIRE, SAMUEL, S.B., 5-14-1810.
CHEW, ROBT., Sur., 8-6-1783.
CLALK, JAMES, Inv., 5-11-1784.
CLARK, GEO., L.G., 1-29-1780.
CLARK, STEPHEN, Inv., 4-1802.
CLARK, WM., L.G., 2-27-1822.
CLARK, WM., S.B., 3-17-1822.
CLARK, WM., Inv., 3-24-1822.
CLARK, WM., Sur., 11-18-1822.
CLEAVER, WM., App., 6-11-1789.
CLEAVER, WM., Set., 6-11-1789.
CLUTTER, JACOB, Sur., 4-27-1788.
COAKLY, ELIJAH, Set., 10-22-1832.
COBBENS, THOM., Inv., 12-17-1804.
COCKREL, THOM., L.G., 2-11-1817.
COCKREL, SAM., L.G., 1-28-1818.
COCKRILL, SAM., Sur., 3-19-1798.
CODDY, JOHN, L.G., 12-13-1813.
COKELEY, ELIJAH, Set., 4-23-1832.
COKELY, ANDREW, Set., 8-5-1833.
COKELY, EDMOND, Set., 8-5-1833.
COKELY, EDMOND & ANDREW, Set.,
 4-25-1836.
COKELY, ELIJAH, Set., 8-5-1833.
COLEMAN, ROBT., Sur., 8-9-1794.
COLESHERE, JOHN, App., 12-19-1825.
COLLINS, JOHN, Set., 4-10-1788.
COLLINS, THOM., L.G., 4-30-1790.
COLLINS, THOM., Bond, 9-17-1798.
COLLINS, THOM., Will, 2-16-1824.
 Dev.: Eliz., wife; Dan., John, Thom.,
 sons; Jenny Jones, Casonder, Colli-
 hau, dau.
COLLINS, THOS., App., 6-14-1824.
COLLINS, THOM., Set., 11-17-1830.
COLLINS, THOM., Set., 4-22-1833.
COLLINS, THOM., Will, 11-25-1833.
 Dev.: Eliz., wife; John, Daniel, sons;
 Casondra, Jenny, dau.
COLSTON, JOHN, Inv., 5-10-1784.
COLSTON, JOHN, Will, 8-10-1791.
 Dev.: Marg., wife; and others.
COMBS, JOHN, Bond, 11-2-1793.
COMBS, JONAS, App., 12-24-1832.
COMBS, JONAS, Inv., 12-24-1832.
COMBS, JONAS, Set., 1-22-1836.
COMBS, THOM., Will, 10-13-1791.
 Dev.: Martha, wife; Mary White,
 dau.; Jonas, Jonathan, David, Dan.,
 Francis, Thom., Alloses, John, sons.
COMBS, THOM., Inv., 12-15-1791.
COMBS, THOM., Set., 9-20-1802.

CONNARD, JAMES, Will, 4-18-1796.
Dev.: James, son; and others.
CONRAD, JAMES, Inv., 4-17-1797.
CONNELLY, BRIDGET, Set., 4-22-1839.
CONNELLY, PATRICK, Set., 4-22-1839.
COOL, HERBERT, App., 10-16-1834.
COOL, HERBERT, S.B., 2-25-1836.
COOL, PHIL., Inv., 6-15-1795.
COOLE, HERBERT, Will, 6-23-1834.
Dev.: Wm., Harbert, sons; Nancy,
Polly, Rebecca, Caty Hamilton, dau.;
and others.
COOLE, HERBERT, Bond, 6-22-1840.
COOPER, ANDREW, Bond, 11-20-1794.
COOPER, ANDREW & MITCHELL,
JOHN, TO FLEMINGS, JAMES,
Deed, 11-16-1803.
COOPER, GEO., Will, 6-19-1809.
Dev.: Mary, wife; Christian, Andrew,
John sons; Eliz. Millslagel, Caty,
dau.
COOPER, GEORGE, App., 11-20-1809.
COOPER, GEORGE, S.B., 11-20-1809.
COOPER, GEO., Inv., 11-20-1809.
COOPER, HAMILTON, L.G., 10-4-1788.
COOPER, HAMILTON, Bond, 8-12-1790.
COOPER, JOB, App., 10-20-1823.
COOPER, THOM., Will, 12-16-1799.
Dev.: Rebecca, wife; Jos., Joul,
Thom., sons; Mary, Rachel, Marg.,
Elener, Eliz., Katie, Sallie, Rebecca,
dau.
COOPER, THOM., Inv., 4-14-1800.
COOPPER, JOB, Set., 11-17-1828.
COPERLAND, WM., L.G., 3-28-1788.
COPLAND, CHAS., Deed, 8-2-1793.
COPREY, JOHN, Sur., 3-7-1798.
CORBIN, DAVID, L.G., 1-15-1802.
CORBIN, DAVID, App., 11-15-1829.
CORBIN, DAVID, Inv., 11-15-1829.
CORBIN, DAVID, S.B., 4-19-1830.
CORBIN, DAVID, Set., 8-17-1830.
CORBIN, DAVID, Set., 1-28-1839.
CORBIN, WM., Sur., 10-17-1791.
CORLINE, ANDREW, Inv., 7-14-1800.
CORN, ANDREW, Inv., 4-14-1791.
CORN, ANDREW, App., 4-14-1791.
CORNWELL, ENOCH, Inv., 5-12-1779.
COUL, PHILIP, Will, 4-20-1795.
Dev.: Cath., wife; Paul, Jacob,
Philip, Herbert, sons; Lindia, dau.
COULSHINE, EARNEST, Will,
4-18-1796.
Dev.: Eliz., wife; Henry, John, sons;
Latty, dau.
COWAN, ROBT., Inv., App., 9-19-1796.
COWPER, WM., & MITCHELL, JOHN,
L.G., 3-28-1788.
CRAGM, JAMES & CHRESTMAR,
JACOB, L.G., 4-7-1794.
CREASAP, MICH., Set., 10-30-1782.
CREASAP, MICH., Bond, 3-14-1786.
CREASAP, THOM., Inv., 10-11-1787.
CREASOP, MICH., Set., 10-30-1792.
CRESAP, MICH., Will, 4-14-1791.
Dev.: Mary, wife; James, son; Mary,
Eliz., Sarah, dau.
CRESAP, MICHAEL, Inv., 9-16-1790.

CRESAP, THOM., Sur., 3-15-1760.
CRESAPS, MICH., Sur., 12-9-1766.
CRESOP, LUTHER, Set., 2-14-1831.
CRESOP, MICHAEL, Will, 6-28-1774.
Dev.: Mary, wife; James, son; Mary,
Eliz., Sarah, dau.
CREVEY, HOMER, Sur., 2-2-1789.
CRITCHFIELD, AMOS, Set., 8-12-1783.
CRITTON, WM., Sur., 8-10-1818.
CROCK, GEO., Will, 7-19-1802.
Dev.: Barb., wife; Eliz., dau.
CROCK, GEO., Inv., 7-16-1804.
CROPS, JOSHWAY, L.G., 11-4-1819.
CROSBY, ABEL, Will, 10-11-1791.
Dev.: Johanna, wife; John, son.
CROSLEY, ABEL, Will, 9-11-1793.
Dev.: Joanna, wife; John, son.
CROSLEY, ABEL, Inv., 10-8-1793.
CROSTON, FRANCIS, App., 3-23-1840.
CRUTON, ISAAC, Deed, 4-7-1790.
CUNDIFF, BENJ., Will, 12-16-1822.
Dev.: Alecy, wife.
CUNDIFF, JOHN, Sur., 11-2-1818.
CUNNINGHAM, JAMES, Sur.,
8-15-1805.
CUNNINGHAM, JESSE, App.,
3-11-1783.
CUNNINGHAM, JESSE, Set., 8-12-1783.
CURLETT, WM., Inv., 1-28-1833.

DAILEY, JAMES, Bond, 2-18-1799.
DAILEY, JAMES, L.G., 6-7-1819.
DAILEY, JAMES, App., 1-17-1825.
DAILEY, JAMES, S.B., 1-17-1825.
DAILEY, JAMES, Set., 5-17-1830.
DAILEY, S. W., Will, 4-14-1791.
Dev.: Hugh Bailey, bro.
DAILEY, WM., Set., 8-27-1832.
DALEY, JAMES, Set., 7-18-1825.
DANIAL, EVERETT, Will, 3-17-1823.
Dev.: Ezekiel, Dan., Asa, Enos,
Moses, sons; Sarah, Eliz., Fanny,
dau.
DANIELS, NANCY, Set., 7-27-1835.
DAPSON, WM., Will, 10-15-1798.
Dev.: Wife, Marg., dau; and others.
DAUESON, ABR., Inv., 3-25-1805.
DAUGHERTY, CON., Inv., 10-8-1765.
DAUGHERTY, CON., Bond, 8-13-1768.
DAVALT, ANDREW, Set., 12-19-1814.
DAVIDSON, WM., L.G., 1-26-1799.
DAVIS, ELI, Set., 6-20-1833.
DAVIS, ELI, Set., 7-22-1833.
DAVIS, ELIJA, Will, 11-15-1813.
Dev.: Ann, wife; David, Elija, Thom.,
Absalom, sons; Eliz., Ann Simmons,
Miriam Secrist, dau.
DAVIS, ELY, App., 1-19-1824.
DAVIS, ELY, S.B., 1-19-1824.
DAVIS, JOHN, Sur., 8-21-1794.
DAVIS, JOHN, Sur., 9-25-1794.
DAVIS, JOS., Set., 8-14-1819.
DAVIS, JOS., Set., 10-16-1820.
DAVIS, REBECCA, Bond, 8-27-1832.
DAVIS, RICH., Set., 5-28-1832.

DAVIS, RUBEN, L.G., 12-9-1819.
DAVIS, S. B., Will, 5-25-1840.
Dev.: Ann, wife; Nancy, Sarah, Matilda, dau.; Jethro, son.
DAVIS, SAM., Sur., 2-9-1789.
DAVIS, SAM., L.G., 11-2-1826.
DAVIS, THOM., App., 3-24-1834.
DAVIS, THOM., S.B., 3-24-1834.
DAVIS, THOM., Set., 5-23-1836.
DAVIS, THOM., S.B., 5-22-1837.
DAVIS, THUPILUS, Bond, 2-14-1750.
DAVIS, THUPILUS, Inv., 2-14-1759.
DAVIS, THUPILUS, Bond, 4-15-1767.
DAWSON, A., S.B., 7-19-1805.
DAWSON, ABRAHAM, Will, 2-18-1805.
Dev.: Isaac, Abraham, Israel, sons; Betsey, Ary, Fanny, dau.
DAWSON, ABRAHAM, Set., 3-18-1807.
DAWSON, ABRAHAM, Set., 7-19-1813.
DAWSON, ANN, ELMIRA, JOHN & JESSE, Set., 11-25-1833.
DAWSON, JESSE, Set., 11-23-1835.
DAWSON, JOHN, S.B., 3-17-1821.
DAY, ANORY, L.G., 11-29-1802.
DEAKINS, FRANCIS, Will, 4-22-1833.
Dev.: Eleanor, wife; and others.
DEAN, THOM., Will, 4-17-1809.
Dev.: Jane, wife; John, Thom., Henry, Wm., Dan., Nathan, sons; Eliz., Mary, Marg., Elinor, Anna, dau.
DEAN, THOM., Inv., 5-1-1809.
DEAN, THOMAS, App., 5-15-1809.
DEAVER, ALEX., App., 4-25-1836.
DEAVER, ALEX., S.B., 4-26-1836.
DEAVER, RICH., Sur., 8-6-1818.
DEAVERS, WM., App., 8-16-1813.
DEAVERS, WM., S.B., 8-16-1813.
DECKER, LUKE, Inv., 2-14-1758.
DECKER, LUKE, Sale, 2-10-1761.
DECKER, LUKE, Inv., 4-15-1767.
DELLOYZEAS, ED., Bond, 10-9-1763.
DELLOYZEAS, JAS., App., 12-13-1763.
DELLOYZEAS, JAS., Adm., 9-13-1786.
DENTEN, ROBT., Will, 5-12-1778.
Dev.: Jane, wife; Robt., Jacob, John, Thom., sons; and others.
DENTON, ROBT., Inv., App., 8-11-1778.
DEVAULL, ANDREW, App., 2-15-1813.
DEVER, RICH., Inv., 8-19-1823.
DEVER, RICH., S.B., 8-19-1823.
DEVOLTS, ANDREW, S.B., 12-19-1814.
DEW, SAM., Sur., 3-15-1791.
DEW, SAM, L.G., 12-22-1798.
DEW, SAM, Set., 6-15-1829.
DEW, SAMUEL, Set., 2-23-1835.
DICK, DAN., Sur., 8-29-1804.
DIVER, RICH., Set., 6-25-1832.
DIVOLL, JOHN, Sur., 12-15-1781.
DIXON, EDMOND, S.B., 8-24-1840.
DIXON, ED., App., 8-24-1840.
DOBBINS, THOM., Will, 9-17-1804.
Dev.: Thom., Sam., John, sons; Ann Wolf, dau.; and others.
DOBBINS, THOM., Set., 8-2-1805.

DOBBINS, THOM., Will, 9-15-1805.
Dev.: Sam., John, bro.; Esabel, sis.; and others.
DOBSON, WM., S.B., 11-7-1800.
DOLL, JACOB, Will, 5-23-1836.
Dev.: Cath., wife; Abraham, Jacob, Phil., Dan., Geo., sons; Cath., Mary, Marg., dau.
DOLL, JACOB, App., 1-22-1838.
DOLL, JACOB, S.B., 1-22-1833.
DOLL, JACOB, Set., 12-24-1839.
DOLSON, WM., Inv., 7-15-1799
DOMAN, HENRY, App., 12-28-1835.
DOMAN, JACOB, Set., 6-22-1821.
DONALDSON, DON., App., 6-18-1810.
DONALDSON, JOHN, Sur., 5-16-1794.
DONALDSON, WM., L.G., 9-16-1783.
DONALDSON, WM., Bond, 12-10-1794.
DONTHIT, JOHN, Will, 12-19-1803.
Dev.: Marg., wife; Thom., John, Silas, Sol., Caleb, David, Dan., sons; Rebecca Cooper, Cath., Tuncle, Mary, Sarah, Christina, dau.
DORAN, ALEX., Will, 4-27-1846.
Dev.: Sarah, Eliz., dau.; Jos., Wm., James, Joseph, Peter, Wm., sons.
DORAN, WM., L.G., 11-18-1822.
DOUGLAS, MALINDA, App., 1-19-1824.
DOUGLAS, MALINDA, S.B., 3-14-1825.
DOUGLAS, MALINDA, Set., 3-15-1825.
DOWDEN, JOHN, Sur., 2-8-1790.
DOWMAN, HENRY, S.B., 10-23-1837.
DREW, PEREZ, Will, 9-18-1797.
Dev.: Mary, wife; and others.
DREW, PEREZ, Inv., 12-18-1797.
DREW, SAM., L.G., 11-4-1817.
DUGGAN, WM., Sur., 10-2-1791.
DULEY, WM., Will, 11-25-1839.
Dev.: Wm., Collins, Edmond, Achilles, Elijah, sons; Nancy, Ruth Dean, Saraham Dean, dau.; and others.
DULING, WM., App., 3-23-1840.
DULING, WM., S.B., 3-23-1840.
DUNLAP, JAS., L.G., 9-4-1782.
DUNN, LEWIS, S.B., 8-28-1837.
DWAMAN, PETER, Sur., 1-8-1795.
DYER, ED., Set., 5-18-1822.
DYER, EDWARD, S.B., 5-20-1822.
DYER, ELIZ., S.B., 5-20-1822.
DYER, ELIZ., App., 5-20-1822.
DYER, NATH., Inv., 12-15-1804.

EARNEST, MICHAEL, Will, 3-10-1785.
Dev.: Eliz., wife; Jacob, John, Geo., Leanest, and Peter Harness, sons; Elizabeth Yoker, Barbara See, Sihenue Hornbeck, Dorthea Hornbeck, Margeretha Frunbo, dau.; and others.
EARSOM, JOHN, Will, 4-15-1790.
Dev.: Christana, wife; Simon, John, sons; Barb., Mary, Susanah, dau.
EARSOM, MARY, S.B., 2-24-1834.
EARSOM, SEMAN, Will, 6-20-1796.
Dev.: Jacob, John, sons; and others.
EARSOME, JOHN, Set., 2-14-1831.
EARSOME, JOHN, S.B., 2-14-1831.
EARSOME, MARY, App., 3-26-1832.

EARSOME, MARY, Set., 11-27-1834.
EARSON, JOHN, Will, 4-15-1790.
Dev.: Christina, wife; Simon, John, sons; Barb., Mary, Susanna, dau.; and others.
EARSON, JOHN, Set., 3-11-1794.
EARSON, JOHN, Set., 12-10-1794.
EARSON, SIMON, Deed, 9-19-1808.
EASTER, PETER, App., 6-17-1822.
EASTER, PETER, S.B., 6-18-1822.
EATON, ALICE, Set., 2-25-1833.
ECKSTINE, LEO., Set., 10-14-1805.
EDMINDSON, THOS., App., 6-14-1824.
EDMINSON, THOS., S.B., 6-15-1824.
EDMONDSON, THOM., Set., 11-26-1832.
EDWARD, JOS., Will, 2-17-1782.
Dev.: Joseph, Thom., sons; and others.
EDWARD, THOMAS, App., 6-20-1813.
EDWARD, THOMAS, S.B., 6-20-1813.
EDWARDS, DAVID, Inv., 5-11-1772.
EDWARDS, JOHN, App., 3-17-1822.
EDWARDS, JOHN, S.B., 3-17-1822.
EDWARDS, JOS., Inv., 3-11-1783.
EDWARDS, JOS., S.B., 6-10-1790.
EDWARDS, JOS., Set., 6-10-1790.
EDWARDS, THOM., Will, 7-14-1791.
Dev.: Mary, wife; Thom., David, Jeff., Andrew, sons; Sarah, Ann, Naomi, Marg., dau.
EDWARDS, THOM., Set., 9-20-1819.
ELIZIE, WM., L.G., 11-28-1795.
ELLIS, JOEL, Sur., 6-10-1820.
ELLSEY, THOM., Sur., 12-4-1788.
ELLSWICK, JOHN, Bond, 11-13-1759.
ELLSWICK, JOHN, Inv., 11-11-1760.
ELLSWICK, JOHN, Inv., 10-8-1765.
ELSWICH, JOHN, Will, 11-13-1759.
Dev.: Rachell, wife; Rachell, dau.; Thom., John, sons; and others.
ELZEY, THOWEZIN, L.G., 9-15-1789.
EMERSON, THOM., Sur., 5-3-1789.
EMERY, GEO., L.G., 6-7-1790.
EMMART, JACOB, Set., 8-16-1820.
EMMIT, WM., L.G., 3-24-1823.
ENGLE, PETER, Will, 11-2-1792.
Dev.: Eliz., wife; Justinius, Peter, sons; Charlett, dau.; and others.
ENGLE, PETER, App., 9-11-1794.
ERSOME, JOHN, Inv., 12-16-1790.
ESKELY, EDMONS, Set., 9-23-1833.
ESKRIDGE, GEO., S.B., 3-27-1838.
ETHEY, THOM., Will, 10-16-1826.
Dev.: Martha, wife; Sam., Jos., sons; Nancy, Martha, dau.
EVANS, JOHN, Set., 6-16-1819.
EVERETT, DAVIS, Deed, 10-28-1817.
EVERETT, MOSES, App., 11-22-1840.
EVERETT, MOSES, S.B., 11-23-1840.

FAHS, JOHN, App., 12-22-1834.
FAHS, JOHN, Set., 8-24-1835.
FAHS, JOHN, S.B., 4-27-1835.
FALLIS, BASWON, Sur., 10-9-1792.

FARLEY, THOM., Will, 5-14-1782.
Dev.: Wife; John, Andrew, David, sons; Mary, Marg., Elinor, dau.
FARLEY, THOM., App., 11-12-1782.
FARMER, WM., Set., 5-19-1800.
FARRLY, JOHN, Sur., 6-20-1791.
FELLING, CATH., App., 1-19-1824.
FELLING, CATH., S.B., 1-19-1824.
FELLING, CATH., Set., 7-18-1825.
FERRIS, CORN., Bond, 3-27-1792.
FERRIS, CORN., Sur., 5-27-1795.
FINK, FRED., L.G., 1-9-1817.
FINK, FRED., Will, 12-25-1837.
Dev.: Sam., son; Cath., dau.
FINK, FRED., S.B., 1-22-1838.
FINK, FRED., Set., 6-24-1839.
FINK, FRED., App., 1-22-1840.
FINLEY, THOM., App., 11-12-1782.
FISHER, ADAM, Will, 3-11-1783.
Dev.: Christine, wife; Adam, Jacob, John, Geo., Mich., Sol., sons.
FISHER, ADAM, Inv., 11-11-1783.
FISHER, ADAM, Inv., 9-12-1783.
FISHER, ADAM, Divn., 11-10-1784.
Dev.: wife.
FISHER, ADAM, Set., 11-10-1784.
FITZGERALD, ED., Will, 6-12-1793.
Dev.: Ann, wife; Maria, dau.
FITZGERALD, THOM., S.B., 10-18-1825.
FITZGERALD, THOM., Set., 9-26-1836.
FITZPATRICK, JOS., Bond, 3-8-1768.
FITZPATRICK, PAT., Bond, 12-12-1758.
FITZPATRICK, PAT., Inv., 5-8-1759.
FLANIGAN, SAM., App., 1-18-1830.
FLANIGAN, SAM., S.B., 3-15-1830.
FLANIGAN, SAM., Set., 5-28-1832.
FLEMING, PAT., Will, 10-22-1838.
Dev.: James, Ed., sons; Cath., Ann Shurby, Christine Kline, dau.; and others.
FLEMING, PAT., S.B., 1-27-1840.
FLOOD, JOHN, S.B., 6-26-1832.
FLOOD, JOHN, App., 12-26-1832.
FLOOD, JOHN, App., 4-22-1833.
FLOOD, JOHN, Set., 4-22-1833.
FLOOD, JOHN, S.B., 4-23-1838.
FLOYD, WM., Sur., 11-13-1819.
FOLEY, WM., Set., 9-15-1829.
FOREMAN, ELIZ., Bond, 3-6-1765.
FOREMAN, SAM., Sur., 6-8-1818.
FORMAN, JOHN, Bond, 11-12-1782.
FORMAN, JOHN, Bond, 5-20-1784.
FORMAN, JOHN, Set., 9-1-1810.
FORMAN, THOM., App., Inv., 6-12-1765.
FORMAN, WM., App., 5-11-1779.
FOSTER, JOHN, L.G., 10-3-1794.
FOUT, JACOB, Set., 9-15-1829.
FOX, GABRIAL, Sur., 4-12-1780.
FOX, JERMIAH, App., 11-15-1825.
FOX, JERMIAH, Set., 3-19-1830.
FOX, THOM., L.G., 3-6-1782.
FOX, WILLIAM, S.B., 2-14-1825.
FOX, WM., S.B., 2-13-1793.

FOX, WM., App., 6-17-1822.
FOX, WM., S.B., 6-17-1822.
FOX, WM., Adm., 2-14-1825.
FOX, WM., Set., 11-26-1832.
FOX, WM., S.B., 11-26-1832.
FRANKLIN, LEWIS, L.G., 12-13-1783.
FRENCH, JAMES, Will, 11-9-1773.
Dev.: Mary, wife; Robt., Wm., sons.
FRENCH, JAMES, Bond, 3-9-1774.
FRENCH, JAMES, App., Inv., 3-14-1775.
FRENCH, JOHN, Will, 11-15-1830.
Dev.: Mary, wife; children.
FRENCH, JOHN, App., 11-27-1832.
FRENCH, JOHN, S.B., 11-27-1832.
FRENCH, JOHN, Set., 1-28-1839.
FRENCH, ROBT., Sur., 7-23-1795.
FRENCH, ROBT., Will, 5-18-1829.
Dev.: Elinor, wife; Wm., James,
John, Robt., sons; Nancy Corbin,
Eliza., Sarah, Mariah, Kath., dau.
FRENCH, ROBT., App., 10-18-1830.
FRENCH, ROBT., Set., 3-14-1831.
FRENCH, ROBT., Set., 2-20-1832.
FRENCH, WM., Set., 3-24-1834.
FRENCH, WM., Set., 10-26-1840.
FRY, BENJ., App., 4-1-1840.
FRY, HENRY, App., 10-19-1812.
FRYE, BENJ., Will, 2-24-1840.
Dev.: Mary, wife; Henry, Benj.,
Abraham, Isaac, sons; Nancy, Jane,
Sarah, Susan Littler, Lucy Doran,
Fanny Moon, dau.; and others.
FRYE, BENJ., S.B., 4-27-1840.
FRYE, HENRY, S.B., 5-17-1824.
FRYE, HENRY, Set., 2-14-1825.
FULKAMORE, JOHN M., Inv., 12-16-1822.
FULLER, STEPHEN, Sur., 3-31-1818.

GANOE, STEPHEN, Will, 9-18-1809.
Dev.: Stephen, son; and others.
GANOE, STEPHEN, App., 3-16-1812.
GANOE, STEPHEN, S.B., 3-16-1812.
GANOE, STEPHEN, App., 3-18-1823.
GANOE, STEPHEN, S.B., 2-20-1826.
GARRETT, CHRIS., App., 10-10-1812.
GARRETT, CHRIS., S.B., 11-16-1812.
GASTON, DAN., Sur., 5-4-1789.
GEAFEO, ELIZ., Inv., 3-13-?
GEORGE, ELLIS, Will, 4-16-1810.
Dev.: Lydia, wife; James, Rich.,
sons; Salley Barret, Rebecca Lup-
ton, Rachael Barret, dau.
GEORGE, ELLIS, App., 9-16-1811.
GEORGE, MATHEW, Inv., 8-12-1783.
GEORGE, MATHIEW, Will, 5-14-1782.
Dev.: James King, Mathiew, sons.
GEORGE, MATHIEW, Set., 2-14-1788.
GEORGE, MATT., S.B., 1-17-1778.
GEORGE, MATT., S.B., 12-27-1782.
GEORGE, RICH., Will, 9-20-1821.
Dev.: Mary, wife; Ellis, Rich., Geo.,
Henry, sons; Ruth, Rachel, Sarah,
Mary, Lydia, dau.
GEORGE, RICH., App., 1-28-1825.
GEORGE, RICH., Set., 3-15-1825.

GEULICK, ELISA, Sur., 1-14-1819.
GEULICK, F., App., 4-1-1837.
GIBSON, JOHN, Deed, 9-20-1802.
GILLIPIN, GEO., Sur., 8-31-1795.
GILMER, JOHN, Will, 8-10-1773.
Dev.: Marg., wife; Mary, Marg., Eli-
nor, Ann, Eliz., Jane, dau.
GILMOR, MATHIEW, App., 3-11-1783.
GILMORE, JOHN, Bond, 8-7-1773.
GILMORE, JOHN, Inv., 4-25-1774.
GILPIN, GEO., L.G., 10-3-1794.
GINEVAN, WM., App., 4-16-1827.
GINNEVAN, MATHISA, Set., 2-20-1832.
GINNEVAN, MATHIAS, Sur., 8-4-1818.
GLASGOW, ELIZA., Bond, 12-13-1763.
GLASS, SARAH, Will, 11-30-1837.
Dev.: Mary, Hester, Evaline, Ann,
Susan, Sidney, sis.; others.
GLAZE, ANDREW, Deed, 12-11-1793.
GLAZE, CONRAD, Will, 6-21-1831.
Dev.: Andrew, Conrad, sons; others.
GLAZE, CONRAD, App., 5-28-1832.
GLAZE, CONRAD, S.B., 5-28-1832.
GLAZE, CONRAD, Set., 11-24-1834.
GLAZE, CONRAD, Set., 10-26-1835.
GODDIS, WM., Inv., 8-10-1773.
GOOD, ABRAHAM, Will, 9-28-1840.
Dev.: Sarah, wife; Peter, bro.; Ann
Smith, sis.
GOOD, JACOB, Will, 5-9-1780.
Dev.: Susanna, wife; Peter, Abra-
ham, Isaac, sons.
GOOD, JACOB, App., 8-8-1780.
GOOD, PHILIP, L.G., 3-3-1824.
GOODSON, ANDREW, L.G., 6-3-1779.
GRAHAM, JAMES, App., 8-4-1823.
GRAHAM, JAMES, S.B., 12-15-1823.
GRAHAM, JAMES, S.B., 3-21-1827.
GRAHAM, JAMES, Adm., 6-22-1827.
GRAPES, DAVID, Inv., 9-19-1826.
GRAPES, DAVID, S.B., 9-11-1827.
GRAPES, HANNAH, Sur., 1-3-1827.
GREENWALT, JOHN, Sur., 3-27-1819.
GREENWELL, ELIJAH, App., 11-16-1829.
GREENWELL, ELIJAH, Set., 12-14-1829.
GREENWELL, ELIJAH, Set., 2-16-1833.
GREENWELL, ELIJAH, Set., 3-25-1833.
GREGG, JOSHUA, Set., 8-26-1834.
GRIGG, JOSHUA, Set., 3-25-1833.
GRIGG, JOSHUA, Set., 9-38-1835.
GRIGGS, JOSHUA, Set., 11-15-1830.
GRIGGS, JOSHUA, Inv., 10-17-1831.
GROVE, SIMON, Set., 9-2-1835.
GROVES, SIMON, App., 9-28-1835.
GROVES, SIMON, Set., 10-21-1835.
GROVES, SIMON, Set., 10-26-1835.
GROVES, SIMON, Set., 11-23-1835.
GULARD, CAP., Sur., 4-9-1793.
GULICK, FERD,, Sur., 4-18-1797.
GULICK, FERD., Will, 3-27-1837.
Dev.: Stephen, Amos, Elisha, sons;
Polly, dau.

GULICK, FERD., S.B., 6-25-1838.
GUNOE, JAMES, S.B., 4-23-1838.
GUSE, JACOB, App., 3-26-1832.
GUSTIN, ROBT., L.G., 10-24-1803.
GYMUS, JAMES, App., 4-23-1838.

HACK, ABRAHAM, Set., 10-18-1830.
HACKHOUSE, JOHN, App., 9-13-1759.
HAFF, CORN., Will, 9-12-1786.
Dev.: Eliz., wife; Eliz., Rachel, dau.;
Cornelius, John, sons.
HAFF, CORN., Inv., 10-10-1786.
HAFF, CORN., Set., 4-9-1794.
HAFF, LAWRENCE, Inv., 11-17-1783.
HAFF, LAWRENCE, Will, 11-11-1788.
Dev.: Sarah, wife; Lawrence, Paul,
Luke, Abram, sons; others.
HAGERTY, JOHN, S.B., 6-20-1796.
HAGGAID, WM., Will, 11-12-1771.
Dev.: Eliz., wife.
HAGGAN, THOM., S.B., 1-13-1806.
HAGGAN, THOM., S.B., 2-17-1806.
HAGGARDS, WM., Inv., 3-10-1772.
HAGGARTY, JOHN, App., 6-14-1787.
HAGGARTY, THOM., Deed, 10-23-1821.
HAGGERTY, JOHN, Inv., 6-14-1787.
HAGLER, JACOB, Inv., 3-12-1760.
HAINES, ADAM, Sur., 11-8-1788.
HAINES, BENJ., Will, 11-13-1771.
Dev.: Dan., John, Henry, bro.; Lydia,
Eliz., sis.; others.
HAINES, BENJ., Bond., 11-14-1771.
HAINES, GEO., Sur., 3-30-1818.
HAINES, HENRY, App., 11-25-1839.
HAINES, JOHN, Set., 2-14-1831.
HAINES, THOM., App., 2-28-1824.
HAINES, THOMAS, App., 5-17-1824.
HAINES, WM., S.B., 11-26-1832.
HALL, JOS., Will, 3-9-1785.
Dev.: Mary, wife; and others.
HALL, JOS., Inv., 8-9-1785.
HALLIDAY, RICH., S.B., 7-19-1830.
HALLIDAY, RICH., Set., 8-27-1832.
HALLIDAY, RICHARD, App., 3-15-1830.
HALTEMAN, ABRAM, S.B., 3-6-1783.
HAMBELTON, HARRY, Set., 4-16-1810.
HAMILTON, HENRY, App., 7-18-1808.
HAMMACK, HARRIET A., Set., 10-22-1839.
HAMMACK, HARRIET, Set., 9-28-1840.
HAMMACK, SAM., Set., 10-24-1836.
HAMMAR, JON., Inv., 12-31-1768.
HAMMERECK, SAM., Will, 9-24-1822.
Dev.: Jane, wife; Wm., son; Mary,
Harriet, dau.
HAMMOCK, SAM., App., 9-12-1832.
HAMMOCK, SAM., S.B., 9-23-1833.
HAMMOCK, SAM, Set., 11-24-1834.
HAMMOCK, SAM, Set., 1-22-1836.
HAMPTON, NOAH, Bond, 5-9-1775.
HAMPTON, NOAH, Inv., 4-14-1778.
HAMRICK, LEWIS, Will, 11-23-1835.
Dev.: Jacob Doll.

HANEY, PETER, Inv., 5-12-1767.

HANEY, THOM., Set., 6-26-1792.
HANKS, JOHN, Bond, 6-11-1766.
HANKS, JOHN, Inv., 11-13-1766.
HANNAS, WM., Will, 3-27-1840.
Dev.: Daniel, son.
HARD, MALDELAN, Will, 3-12-1776.
Dev.: Eliz., dau.
HARNESS, ADAM, Bond, 2-14-1759.
HARNESS, CON., Inv., 5-11-1763.
HARNESS, CON., Bond, 12-?-1757.
HARNESS, CONRAD, S.B., 3-10-1772.
HARNESS, GEO., L.G., 11-16-1781.
HARNESS, MICH., Bond, 2-14-1758.
HARNESS, MICH., Inv., 6-11-1765.
HARNESS, MICH., S.B., 1-8-1782.
HARNESS, MICH., Set., 2-12-1782.
HARNESS, MICHAEL, Inv., 7-11-1786.
HARRIS, WM., App., 11-26-1832.
HARRIS, WM., S.B., 11-26-1832.
HARRIS, WM., Set., 12-28-1833.
HARRISON, ELIZ., S.B., 7-15-1800.
HARRISON, THEADORE, L.G., 8-3-1822.
HART, MAGADILINE, S.B., 5-12-1778.
HART, STEPHEN, Bond, 4-12-1774.
HARTEY, JOHN, Inv., 8-10-1784.
HARTLEY, JOHN, Will, 3-9-1784.
Dev.: Mary Wilson, Marg. Hartley,
Eliz., Ann Harding, Hannar Peascelle,
Eleanor Houghland, dau.; and others.
HARTLEY, JOHN, Inv., 8-10-1784.
HARTLEY, JOHN, S.B., 9-10-1789.
HARTLEY, JOHN, Set., 9-10-1789.
HARTMAN, ANTHONY, App., 9-20-1824.
HARTMAN, HENRY, Will, 6-16-1823.
Dev.: Mary, wife; Peter, Anthony,
Dan., Geo., sons; Caty, Marg., dau.;
others.
HARTMAN, HENRY, S.B., 8-18-1823.
HARTMAN, HENRY, App., 9-15-1825.
HARTMAN, HENRY, S.B., 6-22-1835.
HARTMAN, HENRY, App., 10-26-1835.
HARTON, JOS., S.B., 6-14-1776.
HARTS, MADLINE, Inv., 8-13-1776.
HAUKER, PHIL., Bond, 5-11-1763.
HAUKER, PHIL., Inv., 12-11-1764.
HAUSE, JOHN, Inv., 10-8-1761.
HAUSE, PAUL, Will, 5-12-1792.
Dev.: Wife; Leon., Rudolph, sons;
Barb., Eliz., Lilla, Magdiline, dau.
HAUSE, PETER, Inv., 8-13-1776.
HAWKINS, DAVID, App., 9-14-1829.
HAYDEN, WM., Sur., 9-12-1785.
HAYWISE, JOHN, Bond, 2-15-1758.
HAZEL, HENRY, Sur., 6-7-1791.
HAZEL, RICH., Bond, 5-14-1760.
HAZEL, RICH., Inv., 2-10-1761.
HEAD, JAMES, S.B., 10-27-1834.
HEAD, JAMES, Set., 8-24-1835.
HEATH, HENRY, L.G., 9-15-1788.
HEATH, JON., Bond, 11-10-1772.
HEATH, JON., Bond, 11-15-1775.
HEATH, JONATHAN, Bond, 11-11-1773.

HEATH, JONATHAN, Bond, 5-14-1782.
HEATH, MICH., App., 6-20-1796.
HEATH, MICH., S.B., 4-15-1805.
HEATOR, MICHAEL, Will, 4-18-1796.
Dev.: Moseley, wife; Sol., Philip, Michael, sons; Basbery, Mary, Marg., dau.
HEDGE, SOL., Bond, 9-8-1761.
HEGGONS, THOM., App., 4-15-1801.
HEIR, LEONARD, Bond, 6-13-1778.
HEISKELL, ADAM, App., 8-18-1823.
HEISKELL, PETER, App., 9-28-1833.
HEISKELL, PETER, S.B., 2-24-1834.
HEISKELL, SAM., App., 6-20-1834.
HEISKILL, ADAM, Will, 8-19-1822.
Dev.: John, Christopher, Sam., Isaac, Peter, sons; others.
HELMICK, ADAM, Will, 11-11-1777.
Dev.: Children.
HELMICK, ADAM, Bond, 11-11-1777.
HELMICK, ADAM, Inv., 4-14-1778.
HENDERSON, ELIZ., Dower, 12-19-1831.
HENDERSON, JOHN, Set., 2-20-1826.
HENDERSON, SAMP., S.B., 2-12-1825.
HENDERSON, SAMP., App., 2-14-1825.
HENDERSON, SAMP., Set., 3-15-1825.
HENDERSON, THOM., L.G., 11-20-1810.
HENDERSON, THOM., Set., 2-20-1826.
HENKLE, JACOB, Will, 5-11-1779.
Dev.: Barbra, wife; Benj., Moses, Jos., John, Paul, sons; Eliz.; Christine, dau.
HENKLE, JACOB, App., 5-10-1780.
HENRY, PEER & ARMSTRONG & ARMSTRONG, Deed, 1-20-1840.
HERRIOTT, EPHRIAM, Will, 7-14-1800.
Dev.: Wm., John, Ephriam, sons; Uresela Wicuf, Sarah Blue, Isabella Blue, dau.
HERRIOTT, WM., App., 7-20-1807.
HERRIOTT, WM., Set., 2-18-1811.
HESS, CORN., Will, 9-12-1786.
Dev.: Eliz., wife; Cornelius, John, sons; Eliz., Rachel, dau.
HESS, LAURANCE, Will, 5-13-1782.
Dev.: Sarah, wife; Laurance, Paul, Luke, Abram, sons; others.
HETH, WM., Will, 10-28-1833.
Dev.: Eliz., wife; Wm., John, Andrew, Sam., sons.
HICKEY, JOHN, App., 10-28-1839.
HICKLE, STEPHEN, L.G., 2-23-1828.
HIDER, MICH., Inv., 2-14-1758.
HIDER, MICH., S.B., 8-11-1772.
HIERS, LEO., Bond, 5-12-1772.
HIET, EVAN, Will, 2-26-1815.
Dev.: Sarah, wife; Jos., John, Jonathan, Jerimiah, sons; Marg., Eliz., Ann, Sarah, Martha, Mary, dau.
HIGGINS, JACOB, S.B., 12-11-1788.
HIGGINS, JOHN, Will, 4-20-1807.
Dev.: Jane, wife; James, Jos., John, Thom., Jonathan, sons; Helly French, Mary Rucket, Ann Plummer, Rachael Springs, Martha, dau.
HIGGINS, JOHN, App., 7-18-1808.
HIGGINS, JOHN, S.B., 7-18-1808.

HIGGINS, JOHN, S.B., 9-17-1810.
HIGGINS, JOHN, Set., 9-17-1810.
HIGGINS, JOHN, L.G., 5-22-1819.
HIGGINS, JOHN, S.B., 3-3-1829.
HIGGINS, JOHN, S.B., 7-22-1833.
HIGGINS, JOHN, Set., 1-26-1835.
HIGGINS, JOS., App., 1-6-1826.
HIGGINS, JUDIA, Inv., 5-13-1783.
HIGGINS, JUDIAH, Will, 6-20-1796.
Dev.: Matilda, wife; Sarah, dau.; Archibal, son; Kessial Osborne, sis.; John Higgins, bro.
HIGGINS, JUDIAH, S.B., 7-15-1805.
HIGGINS, JUDITH, Set., 12-11-1787.
HIGGINS, JUDITH, App., 6-19-1797.
HIGGINS, THOM., Bond, 8-20-1762.
HIGGINS, THOM., Inv., 6-10-1767.
HIGGINS, THOM., S.B., 8-12-1772.
HIGH, HENRY, Will, 2-24-1834.
Dev.: Susanah, wife; Geo., Jacob, Jonathan, Henry, sons; Eliz., Mary Ludwick, Cath., Emily, Sarah Ann, dau.
HIGH, HENRY, App., 6-24-1834.
HIGH, HENRY, S.B., 1-25-1835.
HIGH, HENRY, Set., 8-22-1836.
HIGH, WM., Sur., 9-2-1791.
HILL, ADAM., Sur., 6-16-1791.
HILL, GEO., Sur., 3-24-1818.
HILLYER, THOM., L.G., 9-7-1802.
HINDSMAN, HENRY, S.B., 6-13-1769.
HINES, JAMES, Ind., 6-11-1826.
HINKLE, JACOB, Inv., 5-10-1780.
HINSMAN, HENRY, Bond, 3-8-1768.
HITE, ABRAHAM, Bond, 11-13-1760.
HITE, ABRAHAM, Bond, 12-8-1761.
HOFF, CORNELIUS, Will, 7-20-1795.
Dev.: Eliz., wife; John, Jacob, Andrew, sons; Cath., Hannah, dau.
HOFFMAN, CHRIS., Inv., App., 3-23-1835.
HOFFMAN, CHRIST., App., 3-23-1835.
HOFFMAN, CONRAD, Set., 3-16-1830.
HOGAN, THOM., Will, 8-26-1833.
Dev.: Mary, Susanah, dau.; and others.
HOGAN, THOM., Set., 11-23-1835.
HOGAN, THOM., S.B., 9-24-1838.
HOGANS, THOM., Inv., App., 7-26-1835.
HOGES, ISRAEL, App., 4-20-1807.
HOGES, JOHN, L.G., 6-1-1818.
HOGGAN, WM., Bond, 11-12-1771.
HOGUE, SOL., L.G., 3-24-1802.
HOLLENBACK, DAN., S.B., 5-28-1838.
HOLLENBACK, MARG., App., 4-15-1822.
HOLLENBACK, THOS., Sur., 9-30-1791.
HOLLENBACK, WM., S.B., 7-23-1832.
HOLLENBACK, WM., App., 7-23-1832.
HOLLENBACK, WM., Set., 6-22-1835.
HOLLEWAY, RICH., Set., 4-27-1835.
HOLLIDAY, RICH., Inv., 7-19-1830.
HOLLINBACK, DAN., L.G., 2-5-1820.

HOLLINBACK, DAN., Will, 5-23-1836. Dev.: Wife; Caroline, dau.; and other dau.; and others.

HOLLINBACK, MARG., Set., 6-24-1839.

HOLLINBACK, THOM., App., 10-14-1805.

HOLLINBACK, WM., S.B., 7-19-1826.

HOLLINBACK, WM., S.B., 7-23-1832.

HOLLINBACK, WM., Inv., 7-23-1832.

HOLMES, EB., Bond, 3-14-1775.

HOLMES, EB., Inv., 11-11-1775.

HOLTEMAN, ABRAM, Sur., 8-4-1791.

HOMES, EBENEZER, Will, 3-14-1775. Dev.: Susanah, dau.; and others.

HOOFMAN, CHRIS., Will, 4-20-1807. Dev.: Jos., Lawson, sons; Mary Harris, dau.

HOOK, MARY, Set., 11-23-1835.

HOOK, WM., Will, 5-24-1837. Dev.: Mary, wife; Thom., Wm., Sam., Jos., Josiah, Robt., sons; Eliz., Mary, Hetty, dau.

HOOP, WM., App., 5-4-1837.

HOPKINS, JOHN, Sur., 8-22-1749.

HORN, GEO., Will, 4-14-1800. Dev.: Mary, wife; Geo., Andrew, Philip, sons; Eve Breslsfud, dau.; and others.

HORN, HENRY, Deed, 9-14-1807.

HORNBACK, ABRAM, Bond, 12-13-1757.

HORNBACK, ABRAM, Inv., 2-14-1758.

HORNBACK, DAN., Bond, 3-14-1775.

HORNBACK, DAN., Inv., 4-14-1776.

HORNBACK, DAN., Will, 9-8-1784. Dev.: James, Abraham, sons; wife.

HORNBACK, JOHN, Bond, 3-8-1768.

HORNBACK, JOHN, Inv., 8-11-1778.

HORNBACK, JON., Bond, 12-14-1758.

HORNBACK, JON, Inv., 2-14-1758.

HORSE, PETER, Will, 3-12-1776. Dev.: Marg., Mary, Eliz., dau.; and others.

HORSE, PETER, Bond, 3-12-1776.

HORSE, PETER, S.B., 11-12-1776.

HORTAGUE, WM., Bond, 5-11-1762.

HORTZIPILLER, P., Inv., 8-13-1782.

HOTHAM, JOHN, Inv., 3-11-1783.

HOTHMAN, JOHN, Set., 4-14-1791.

HOTSENPILLER, HENRY, Set., 9-24-1832.

HOTSENPILLER, P., Inv., 5-14-1782.

HOTSENPILLER, PETER, S.B., 6-1-1788.

HOTSENPILLER, PETER, Will, 5-14-1782. Dev.: Ann, wife; John, Henry, Jacob, Abraham, sons.

HOTSINPILLER, PETER, App., 8-13-1782.

HOTT, JOHN, Sur., 7-30-1783.

HOTZENBURGER, PETER, Will, 5-14-1782. Dev.: Ann, wife; Jacob, Honory, Jacob, Abraham, sons.

HOUGES, JACOB, Bond, 2-13-1759.

HOUSE, JOHN, Bond, 8-13-1765.

HOUSE, JOHN, Sur., 6-20-1791.

HOUZARE, LEWIS, S.B., 2-24-1840.

HOWARD, WM., Will, 10-22-1849. Dev.: Mary Howard, Marg., Eliz., Lucy.

HOWDLE, JER., S.B., 3-14-1831.

HOWELL, JEMIMA, Will, 9-20-1830. Dev.: Hannah Anderson, Lucreasy Anderson, Anna Johnson, dau.; others.

HOWELL, JEMIMA, Set., 10-22-1832.

HOWELL, JER., Inv., App., 2-14-1831.

HOWZARS, LEWIS, Will, 2-24-1840. Dev.: Thom., John, Jacob, sons; Lysanda, Charlotta, Capanda, dau.; others.

HOYE, JOHN, L.G., 11-18-1841.

HUCKHOUSE, JOHN, Bond, 5-8-1759.

HUFF, JOHN, Sur., 12-23-1783.

HUFFMAN, CHRISTIAN, Will, 2-23-1835: Dev.: Eliz., wife; Dan., son; and others.

HUFFMAN, CONRAD, App., 8-20-1829.

HUFFMAN, CONRAD, S.B., 8-20-1829.

HUGHES, HUGH, Bond, 5-10-1763.

HUGHES, HUGH, Inv., 12-13-1763.

HUGHES, WM., Bond, 6-9-1767.

HUGHS, WM., Inv., 8-11-1767.

HULL, BENJ., Will, 9-18-1809. Dev.: Jemima, wife; Martin, Silas, Benj., Stephen, Isaac, Wm., Jacob, sons; Eliz. Barnes, Mary Moon, Ann Hull, dau.

HUMA, ANDREW, S.B., 11-16-1812.

HUME, ANDREW, S.B., 9-14-1812.

HUME, ANDREW, S.B., 9-14-1812.

HUME, ANDREW, Set., 11-16-1812.

HUMES, ANDREW, App., 2-19-1810.

HURITES, MOSES, L.G., 6-6-1794.

HUTTA, CHRESTINA, Will, 7-28-1834. Dev.: Cath., Eliz., dau.; Christian, son; and others.

HYTON, WM., Sur., 3-16-1799.

West Virginia Estate Settlements

In 1936 and 1937, the West Virginia Commission on Historic and Scenic Markers, the Works Progress Administration, and the Federal Emergency Relief Administration compiled court records of the various counties, such as Births, Deaths, Marriages, and Wills. Under Wills were grouped subjects pertaining to Estate Settlements, including Wills, Inventories and Appraisments. Copies of these county records were filed at the Department of Archives and History, Charleston; the Library of West Virginia University, Morgantown; and the DAR Library, Washington.

Believing that there would be particular interest on the part of the general public in the Estate Settlements in the older counties, the West Virginia Historical Society has undertaken to abstract the Estate Settlement Records, as filed in the State Department of Archives and History, and offer them for publication in the *West Virginia History Quarterly*. (No responsibility can be assumed as to the accuracy of the copies made from the original county records.)

There are 13 counties which were formed prior to 1800, and it has been agreed to arrange these counties in chronological order, and to print their records from the earliest date to 1850. The formation dates of these counties are as follows: Hampshire—1753; Berkeley—1772; Monongalia—1776; Ohio—1776; Greenbrier—1778; Harrison—1784; Hardy—1786; Randolph—1787; Pendleton—1788; Kanawha—1788; Brooks—1797; Wood—1798; and Monroe—1799.

Hampshire County, Formed 1753 (concluded)

Abbreviations used in this material include: Adm.—administrator; Agr.—agreement; App.—appraisement; Bro.—brother; Dau.—daughter; Dev.—devisees; Divn.—division; Ind.—indenture; Inv.—inventory; L. G.—land grant; Obl.—obligation; S. B.—sale bill; Set.—settlement; Sis.—sister; and Sur.—survey.

INNIS, ENOCH, Bond, 5-10-1780.
INNIS, ENOCH, Inv., 11-12-1783.
INNIS, ENOCH, App., 11-12-1783.
INNIS, ENOCH, S.B., 12-12-1783.
INSKEEP, ABRAHAM, App., 8-17-1829.
INSKEEP, ANDREW, Set., 10-24-1836.
INSKEEP, ELIZ., Sur., 10-17-1825.
INSKEEP, JAS., App., 6-9-1767.
INSKEEP, JASP., Set., 3-14-1786.
INSKEEP, JOHN, L.G., 1-15-1822.
INSKEEP, JOHN, Will, 2-16-1824.
Dev.: Sarah, wife; John, Henry, sons.
INSKEEP, JOHN, App., 6-20-1825.
INSKEEP, JOHN, S.B., 6-20-1825.
INSKEEP, JOHN, App., 9-19-1827.
INSKEEP, JOHN, Set., 8-21-1833.
INSKEEP, JOS., S.B., 3-7-1785.
INSKEEP, JOS., S.B., 3-14-1786.
INSKEEP, JOS., Set., 4-23-1832.
INSKEEP, JOS., Will, 5-22-1837.
Dev.: none.
INSKEEP, JOS., App., 8-27-1838.
INSKEEP, JOS., S.B., 5-27-1839.
INSKEEP, JOS., Set., 6-24-1839.
JACK, JOHN, Sur., 8-21-1797.
JACK, JOHN, L.G., 2-2-1816.
JACK, JOHN, Will, 10-23-1837.
Dev.: Rebecca, wife; and others.
JACK, JOHN, App., 11-25-1839.
JACK, JOHN, Set., 12-23-1839.
JACOB, JOHN, Bond, 8-14-1811.
JACOB, JOHN, Will, 5-27-1839.
Dev.: Susan, wife; John, son; Julia, dau.; and others.
JACOB, JOHN, App., 11-25-1839.
JACOBS, JOHN, L.G., 6-16-1783.
JACOBS, JOHN, Bonds, 9-14-1812.
JAMES, ISAAC, Sur., 11-6-1818.
JANEY, WM., Sur., 11-25-1792.
JANNY, ELIZ., App., 11-25-1839.
JANNY, WM., App., 1-17-1825.
JEMMEY, WELE, Sur., 2-11-1779.
JENKINS, ISAAC, App., 12-19-1825.
JENKINS, JACOB, Will, 9-14-1795.
Dev.: Eliz., wife; Evan, Michael, Jacob, John, sons; Sarah, Mary, Ann, Ruth, Eliz., Rachell, dau.; and others.
JENKINS, JACOB, App., 12-14-1795.
JENKINS, JACOB, L.G., 1-29-1803.
JENKINS, JACOB, Will, 12-15-1823.
Dev.: Mary, wife; Fred., John, Geo., sons; Mary Wilina, Betsy, Lousanna Marie, dau.
JENKINS, JACOB, App., 12-19-1825.
JENKINS, JACOB, Set., 8-19-1829.
JENKINS, JACOB, Set., 3-16-1830.
JENKINS, JONATHAN, Inv., 8-10-1784.
JENKINS, JONATHAN, Set., 6-14-1787
JENKINS, JOS., S.B., 4-14-1828.
JENNEY, WM., S.B., 2-17-1825.
JENNINGS, WM., App., 5-12-1778.

JENNINGS, WM., App., 2-13-1789.
JENNY, MARY, Bond, 9-23-1839.
JENNY, WM., App., 1-21-1825.
JOHN, ALLEN, Inv., 12-4-1785.
JOHN, FOSTER, L.G., 10-3-1794.
JOHNSON, ABRAM, Sur., 9-21-1791.
JOHNSON, ABR., Sur., 7-25-1795.
JOHNSON, BENJ., S.B., 6-20-1825.
JOHNSON, BENJ., App., 3-20-1822.
JOHNSON, BENJ., Set., 6-22-1835.
JOHNSON, CATH., App., 9-19-1803.
JOHNSON, JOHN, Will, 12-18-1809.
Dev.: Dinah, wife; James, John, sons; Mary House, dau.
JOHNSON, JOHN, S.B., 3-3-1832.
JOHNSON, JOHN, App., 3-25-1833.
JOHNSON, JOHN, S.B., 3-25-1833.
JOHNSON, JOHN, Set., 6-23-1834.
JOHNSON, JOS., App., 10-14-1799.
JOHNSON, JOS., Will, 2-19-1810.
Dev.: Nancie, wife; Pool, Jos., Wm., John, James, sons; Deborah, Nancy, dau.
JOHNSON, JOS., App., 4-16-1810.
JOHNSON, OKEY, Will, 10-16-1780.
Dev.: Wife and sons.
JOHNSON, OKEY, App., 6-11-1789.
JOHNSON, OKEY, Bond, 9-17-1810.
JOHNSON, OKEY, Will, 4-14-1815.
Dev.: Jonathan, Abraham, Nathaniel, sons; and others.
JOHNSON, R. P., S.B., 6-27-1759.
JOHNSON, THOM., Will, 4-15-1811.
Dev.: Susanna, wife; Deborah, dau.
JOHNSON, THOM., App., 8-19-1811.
JOHNSON, THOM., Sur., 9-18-1818.
JOHNSON, THOM., L.G., 11-1-1833.
JOHNSON, WM.. Will, 12-10-1794.
Dev.: Eliz., wife; Wm., John, Thom., sons; Eliz., Mary, Nancy, Abagail, dau.
JOHNSON, WM., Sur., 6-2-1795.
JOHNSON, WM., App., 7-20-1801.
JOHNSON, WM., Set., 2-18-1805.
JOHNSTON, JOSHUA, Sur., 5-30-1795.
JOHNSTON, SARAH ELIZ., ISAAC, & JOHN, Set., 10-22-1839.
JONES, DAN., L.G., 5-19-1795.
JONES, DAN., Sur., 9-2-1795.
JONES, ELIAS, S.B., 11-26-1849.
JONES, JOHN, Will, 10-15-1792.
Dev.: Cath., wife; Abel, Sam., Kesiah, David, Sol., Aaron, Abr., Dan., John, Joshua, sons; Cath., Marg., Natty, dau.; and others.
JONES, JOHN, Will, 10-15-1794.
Dev.: Cath., wife; Peter, David, Sol., Aaron, Abraham, Daniel, John. Joshau, sons; Cath. Williams, Mary Rogers, Marg., dau.; and others.
JONES, JOHN, App., 6-15-1795.
JONES, JOHN, App., 8-21-1810.
JONES, JOHN, S.B., 8-20-1810.
JONES, JOSHUA, App., 6-17-1811.
JONES, JOSHUA, S.B., 6-17-1811.

JONES, JOSHUA, S.B., 6-17-1813.
JONES, JOSIAH, App., 6-17-1811.
JONES, PETER, Will, 10-19-1795.
Dev.: David, Isaac, John, Moses,
Peter, Aron, Jacob, sons; Ruth, Sarah, Susannah, dau.
JONES, ROBT., Will, 7-27-1835.
Dev.: Nancy Neall, Sarah Darling,
Lucy Harrison, sisters; Dan., Wm.,
Elias, bro.; and others.
JONES, SAM., App., 7-18-1808.
JONES, SOL., App., 6-11-1789.
JONES, SOL., App., 12-11-1793.
JORDAN, JESSE, Sur., 12-14-1782.
JUDY, MARTIN, Inv., 3-11-1783.
JUDY, MARTIN, App., 3-11-1783.
JUDY, MARTIN, Will, 8-9-1785.
Dev.: Rosanna, wife; Jacob, Henry,
Michael, John, sons; Eliz., Marg.,
dau.; and others.
JUDY, MARTIN, App., 2-13-1787.
JUDY, MARTIN, Set., 4-14-1791.
JUNIS, ENOCH, JR., Will, 7-12-1783.
Dev.: Sarah, wife; Mother, Father,
James, bro.; Sisters.
KABRICK, SARAH, Set., 5-17-1830.
KAIL, GEO., S.B., 10-16-1797.
KAIL, JOHN, App., 8-25-1824.
KALE, GEO., S.B., 5-19-1806.
KALER, ADAM, App., 1-16-1832.
KARBRICK, PETER, L.G., 8-30-1824.
KARSKADEN, THOM., L.G., 2-22-1828.
KAYLOER, GEO., Inv., 10-16-1797.
KAYLOR, WM., Inv., 4-19-1803.
KEASMAN, JACOB, Inv., 7-16-1810.
KEASNER, JACOB, S.B., 7-16-1810.
KELLER, JOHN, Inv., 4-22-1805.
KELLER, JOHN, S.B., 4-22-1805.
KELLER, JOHN, S.B., 2-16-1812.
KELLER, JOHN, Set., 8-21-1822.
KELLER, MARY, JOHN, JAMES,
ELIZ., & CHAS., Set., 7-27-1835.
KELLEY, ARIONOH, App., 11-26-1840.
KELLY, ED., & KELLY, MARY, Deed,
9-17-1821.
KELLY, JOHN & KELLY, FRANCIS,
Sur., 7-24-1826.
KELLY, PATRICK, App., 3-6-1822.
KENNER, JOHN, Inv., 1-18-1802.
KENNER, JOHN, S.B., 1-10-1802.
KENT, ABRAHAM, S.B., 3-16-1769.
KERCHIVALL, J. S., Will, 7-27-1840.
Dev.: Emily, wife; John, Andrew,
sons; Mary, dau.; and others.
KERN, JACOB, App., 10-28-1839.
KERNS, JACOB, App., 3-19-1827.
KERNS, JACOB, S.B., 10-28-1839.
KESLAR, JOHN, Sur., 5-29-1826.
KESSELER, JOHN, L.G., 2-12-1821.
KEYES, FRANCIS, Inv., 7-10-1800.
KEYES, JAMES, Inv., 9-18-1797.
KEYES, JAMES, S.B., 7-15-1800.
KEYGER, GEO., S.B., 9-14-1807.
KEYTON, JOHN, S.B., 8-10-1773.

KIDWELL, HAWKINS, Set., 12-24-1849.
KIDWELL, JOHN, L.G., 5-15-1824.
KIELER, SUSAN, Set., 7-27-1835.
KIGER, DAN., Sur., 4-7-1796.
KIGER, GEO., Sur., 4-7-1796.
KILE, HANNAH, Set., 6-16-1814.
KILE, ROBERT, App., 3-15-1814.
KILE, ROBERT, S.B., 3-15-1814.
KILSOE, ELEANOR, Set., 12-22-1834.
KILSOE, MARGARET, Set., 12-22-1834.
KILSOE, WM., Set., 12-22-1834.
KING, ALEX., Agr., 12-12-1789.
KING, ALEX., Sur., 12-29-1793.
KING, ALEX., S.B., 4-11-1806.
KLINE, ABR., L.G., 4-19-1804.
KNOTTS, ED., Sur., 11-23-1818.
KUKENDALL, IDA, Sur., 6-1-1821.
KUYKENDALL, ABR., Set., 11-13-1783.
KUYKENDALL, HEN., Deed, 4-10-1793.
KUYKENDALL, ISAAC, L.G., 12-8-1808.
KUYKENDALL, JOHN, App., 5-13-1783.
KUYKENDALL, NAT., L.G., 11-2-1826.
KYGAR, GEO., S.B., 4-15-1799.
KYGEN, GEO., Inv., 4-15-1799.
LAFOLLETE, BARTHOLAMEW, Will,
2-27-1837.
Dev.: Elinor, wife; and children.
LAFOLLETT, B., App., 5-22-1839.
LAIRMORE, JOS., S.B., 9-16-1822.
LAISMORE, JOS., Inv., 9-16-1822.
LAMBERT, DAVID, L.G., 3-10-1783.
LANE, RACHEL, Set., 2-14-1831.
LANGFETTE, PHILIP, L.G., 3-10-1812.
LANGHAM, ELIAS, Sur., 11-10-?
LANTZ, DAN., L.G., 4-17-1802.
LAREW, SOMBERT, L.G., 2-17-1826.
LARGENT, JACOB, Will, 4-19-1813.
Dev.: Margery, wife; John, son;
Marg. Lane, Mary Lane, dau.
LARGENT, JAMES, App., 12-20-1813.
LARGENT, JAMES, S.B., 12-20-1813.
LARGENT, JAS., Deed, 4-15-1779.
LARGENT, JOHN, S.B., 1-16-1809.
LARGENT, JOHN, L.G., 12-17-1826.
LARGENT, THOM., Will, 9-19-1831.
Dev.: Lewis, Sam., Randle, Thom.,
sons; Susan Deavers, Nancy, Grace,
Ellender, dau.
LARGENT, THOM., Set., 2-25-1833.
LARGENT, THOS., Set., 3-25-1833.
LARNE, JACOB, Will, 5-8-1785.
Dev.: Abraham, Thom., sons; Three
daughters.
LARNE, JOHN, Inv., 4-10-1796.
LARUE, JOHN, S.B., 3-18-1811.
LARUE, NOAH, Set., 3-15-1830.
LARUE, RACHEL, App., 8-18-1830.
LARVE, ISAAC, Sur., 8-15-1821.
LARVE, PETER, Set., 6-21-1825.
LAUGHLIN, DAN., S.B., 3-37-1837.
LAWSON, HANNAH, App., 8-17-1811.

LAWSON, HANNAH, Inv., 8-19-1811.
LAWSON, HANNAH, Set., 1-18-1812.
LAWSON, HANNAH, S.B., 1-18-1812.
LAWSON, MOSES, App., 6-12-1793.
LAWSON, MOSES, S.B., 7-20-1795.
LAWSON, MOSES, S.B., 9-15-1800.
LAWSON, THOM., Inv., 2-20-1797.
LAWSON, THOM., Set., 9-18-1797.
LAYON, DAN, L.G., 12-1-1812.
LAYONS, DAN., L.G., 2-12-1816.
LAYONS, DAN., L.G., 3-26-1812.
LEATHERMAN, ART., Sur., 10-3-1802.
LEATHERMAN, PETER, App., 2-25-1836.
LEATHERMAN, PETER, S.B., 2-25-1836.
LEATHERMAN, PETER, S.B., 7-23-1838.
LEAWRIGHT, E. M., App., 1-28-1839.
LEAWRIGHT, E. M., S.B., 1-28-1839.
LEE, CHAS., L.G., 12-12-1793.
LEEK, CHRIS., App., 8-13-1782.
LEEK, CHRIS., Set., 8-13-1782.
LEEPER, ELIZA, Will, 12-15-1823.
Dev.: Martha Walker, Eloner Swaney, Rebecca Stewart, sis.
LEIPER, ELIZ., App., 4-19-1824.
LEP, JOHN, Sur., 7-21-1789.
LESSE, JACOB, S.B., 3-26-1832.
LESSE, JACOB, Set., 10-25-1835.
LESSE, JACOB, Set., 11-23-1835.
LETCHFIELD, AMOS, Set., 8-12-1783.
LEVAN, WM., Sur., 5-16-1795.
LEWIS, PETER, S.B., 6-21-1825.
LEWIS, SAM., L.G., 6-16-1783.
LEWIS, WM., App., 6-1-1824.
LINDSEY, THOM., Sur., 11-22-1754.
LINTHICUM, ARCH., App., 1-18-1812.
LINTHICUM, ARCH., S.B., 1-18-1812.
LINTHICUM, ARCH., Set., 4-25-1836.
LOCK, JACOB, Inv., 8-9-1785.
LOCKHART, JOS., L.G., 9-11-1824.
LOCKHEART, ANDREW, App., 4-10-1763.
LONG, DAVID, Sur., 9-16-1791.
LONG, DAVID, App., 3-15-1813.
LONG, DAVID, S.B., 3-15-1813.
LONG, JACOB, Will, 11-19-1810.
Dev.: Mary Ann, wife; Dan., Sam., Wm., David, sons.
LONG, JACOB, App., 2-17-1812.
LONG, JACOB, Inv., 10-17-1812.
LONG, JACOB, S.B., 12-20-1813.
LONG, MARY, Set., 11-16-1824.
LONG, MARY ANN, Inv., 10-13-1821.
LOTTEN, SAM., S.B., 9-25-1837.
LOTTON, SAM., Will, 5-23-1836.
Dev.: James, John, sons.
LOWE, HANNAH, S.B., 3-18-1811.
LOWE, JACOB, Inv., 3-9-1785.
LOWERS, JOHN, L.G., 12-7-1807.

LUNSFORD, LEWIS, Will, 6-16-1823.
Dev.: Sisters.
LUPTON, ASA, Inv., 12-15-1806.
LUPTON, HANNAH, Inv., 9-19-1808.
LUTHER, ELIZ., Set., 5-16-1825.
LUTHER, GEORGE, Set., 5-16-1825.
LUTHER, HENRY, Set., 5-16-1825.
LYLE, JOHN, App., 10-13-1807.
LYLE, JOHN, Set., 2-14-1825.
LYNN, ROBT., App., 2-16-1795.
LYNN, ROBT., S.B., 8-4-1800.
LYONS, DAN., L.G., 8-1-1807.
LYONS, DAN., L.G., 4-24-1813.
LYONS, DAN., L.G., 2-2-1816.
LYONS, DAN., L.G., 1-3-1817.
LYONS, ELIJAH, App., 9-24-1849.
LYONS, ELIJAH, S.B., 9-24-1849.
LYONS, ELISHA, Set., 2-25-1833.
LYONS, ELISHA, Set., 9-22-1834.
McARTY, ED., Deed, 8-21-1821.
McBRIDE, ALEX., Inv., 3-26-1832.
McBRIDE, ARCH., Inv., 7-12-1782.
McBRIDE, ELIZ., Will, 8-18-1821.
Dev.: James, Stephen, bro.; Mary Yeats, Sarah Chinowith, Eleonor Lyons, Hannah, sis.; others.
McBRIDE, ELIZ., App., 5-16-1824.
McBRIDE, JAMES, App., 4-2-1818.
McBRIDE, JAS., App., 12-20-1830.
McBRIDE, JOHN, Will, 7-20-1829.
Dev.: Sam., John, Andonivan, Elijah, sons; Bersheba Cowen, Rhoda, Eliza, Marie, Matilda White, Zilpha, dau., others.
McBRIDE, JOHN, S.B., 11-16-1830.
McBRIDE, JNO., App., 11-16-1830.
McBRIDE, JOHN, Set., 7-27-1835.
McBRIDE, MARY, Inv., 11-15-1830.
McBRIDE, THOM., Sur., 4-22-1818.
McCALISTER, JAMES, S.B., 5-18-1808.
McCALISTER, JAS., S.B., 4-15-1811.
McCALLEYS, ADDISON, Sur., 4-30-1818.
McCARMASK, SAM., App., 11-26-1849.
McCARTHY, ED., L.G., 2-17-1817.
McCARTY, ED., Set., 11-15-1830.
McCARTY, PAT., S.B., 11-10-1768.
McCARTY, PAT., S.B., 2-24-1834.
McCARTY, PAT., S.B., 1-23-1837.
McCARTY, PATRICK, App., 2-24-1834.
McCARTY, RUTH, Set., 3-15-1830.
McCAULEY, ELIAS, Set., 12-22-1834.
McCAULEY, GEO., App., 8-14-1815.
McCAULY, ELIAS, S.B., 12-22-1834.
McCAULY, ELIAS, S.B., 8-28-1837.
McCLAREY, JAS., App., 4-19-1824.
McCLEARY, JOHN, L.G., 1-23-1801.
McCRAKIN, WM., S.B., 4-17-1789.
McCRAKIN, WM., Set., 7-14-1799.
McCRAKINS, JANE, Bond, 10-14-1767.
McCUELY, JOHN, Bond, 3-12-1776.
MacCUBBIN, THOM., Bond, 3-11-1790.

McDAIMELS, JOHN, Bond, 1-13-1768.
McDONALD, ANGUS, Set., 5-20-1820.
McDONALD, ANGUS, S.B., 6-18-1822.
McDONALD, ANGUS, L.G., 1-16-1830.
McDONALD, ANN., Set., 7-28-1834.
McDONALD, ANNA, App., 2-24-1834.
McDONALD, ANNA, S.B., 2-24-1834.
McDONALD, DONALD, S.B., 6-20-1810.
McDONALD, DONALD, Set., 11-15-1813.
McDONALD, NANCY, S.B., 6-17-1822.
McDONALD, THOMPSON, S.B., 5-19-1823.
McDONALD, THOMPSON, Set., 9-22-1824.
McDONALD, THOMPSON, App., 5-16-1831.
McDOUGAL, PETER, Will, 10-16-1796.
Dev.: Sisters; and others.
McDOUGAL, PETER, Set., 11-15-1810.
McDOUGLE, MARY, Will, 5-17-1824.
Dev.: Marg. Olby, James & Jos. Sheperd.
McDOUGLE, MARY, App., 7-19-1824.
McGEE, JOHN, Inv., 3-11-1777.
McGEE, JOHN, S.B., 11-10-1778.
McGUIRE, ELIZ., Will, 7-12-1786.
Dev.: Wm., stepson.
McGUIRE, MILLICENT, Will, 8-25-1835.
Dev.: Chariety Johnson, Susan Naylor and her children, and others.
McGUIRE, MILLICENT, App., 1-25-1836.
McGUIRE, WM., Will, 2-11-1790.
Dev.: Rachel, wife; Robt., Thom., James, sons; Frances, dau.
McGUIRE, WM., Inv., 7-16-1790.
McGUIRE, WM., L.G., ?-24-1798.
McKEAVER, PAUL, Sur., 5-2-1795.
McKEEVER, PAUL, S.B., 6-21-1834.
McKEERMAN, JENNETT, Inv., 1-14-1822.
McKEVER, PAUL, Set., 4-23-1832.
McKEY, JOS., L.G., 5-15-1815.
McKIERMAN, JANET, Set., 11-19-1829.
McLAUGHLIN, DAN., Will, 2-15-1830.
Dev.: Dan., Wm., Berryman, sons; Ann, Mary Collins, Eliz. Chopman, dau.
McLAUGHLIN, DAN., S.B., 2-14-1831.
McNARY, EBENEZER, Set., 6-23-1831.
McNEIL, STROWDER, Set., 1-28-1833.
McQUAWN, JOHN, L.G., 2-4-1804.
McVICKER, JOHN, Sur., 6-10-1820.
McVIKER, WM., S.B., 8-14-1815.
McVIKER, WM., App., 8-14-1816.
McVION, DUNCAN, Sur., 5-1-1795.
MACHIR, ELIZ., Will, 8-27-1832.
Dev.: Jane Baraugh, sis.; others.
MADDEN, ELIZ., S.B., 9-25-1837.
MADDEN, ELIZ., App., 9-25-1837.
MAKEN, WM., App., 9-13-1787.
MALCOLM, PETER, S.B., 8-12-1832.
MALCOLM, PETER, App., 7-28-1834.

MALCOLM, PETER, S.B., 8-20-1834.
MALCOLM, PETER, S.B., 7-28-1834.
MALONE, HUGH, App., 8-17-1829.
MALONE, HUGH, S.B., 8-17-1829.
MANNAU, WM., Sur., 4-28-1796.
MANNOCK, SAM., Set., 2-25-1839.
MARCH, HENRY, Inv., 8-17-1789.
MARCH, HENRY, Set., 6-26-1792.
MARLOW, ANN, Will, 4-9-1794.
Dev.: Sarah, dau.
MARTCH, HENRY, Will, 4-13-1787.
Dev.: Christian, wife; Christiana, dau.; and others.
MARTIN, ANNIE, S.B., ---1816.
MARTIN, GEO., Sur., 3-8-1798.
MARTIN, GEO., S.B., 10-15-1810.
MARTIN, GEO., Inv., 5-18-1818.
MARTIN, H O U S E, A N D M I L L S, JOHN, Sur., 3-8-1798.
MARTIN, JOHN, Will, 5-16-1831.
Dev.: Mary Baker, dau.; others.
MARTIN, JOHN, App., 6-27-1832.
MARTIN, JOHN, S.B., 8-27-1832.
MARTIN, STEPHAN, App., 3-12-1765.
MARUNE, JOHN, L.G., 2-12-1827.
MATTHEW, LEVI, L.G., 11-17-1807.
MATTHEWS, GEO., Will, 5-14-1782.
Dev.: Wife; James, Geo., Matt., King, sons.
MAURY, JAMES, L.G., 11-10-1783.
MAURY, JAMES & LEWIS, JOHN, L.G., 1-20-1789.
MAUZY, GEO., App., 3-27-1838.
MAUZY, GEO., Set., 7-22-1839.
MAUZY, PETER, Will, 8-24-1835.
Dev.: Eliz., wife; Henry, Peter, John, Geo., Wm., sons; Nancy Allen, Polly, Susan, Eliz. Sommerville, dau.
MAUZY, PETER, App., 10-24-1836.
MAUZY, PETER, S.B., 4-23-1838.
MAYNER, ED., Sur., 5-17-1791.
MEANS, ANN, App., 10-25-1833.
MEANS, ANN, App., 10-28-1833.
MEANS, ISAAC, Set., 2-25-1833.
MEANS, ROBT., Sur., 7-15-1795.
MEANS, ROBT., App., 3-1-1830.
MEANS, ROBT., S.B., 2-24-1834.
MEANS, ROBT., Set., 9-26-1836.
MEEKINS, JAMES, Will, 11-15-1830.
Dev.: Jos., James, sons; Milley Gulick, dau.; others.
MEEKINS, JAMES, App., 8-27-1832.
MEEKINS, JAMES, Set., 2-24-1834.
MEEKINS, JAS., S.B., 4-23-1832.
MENS, ISAAC, S.B., 3-14-1831.
MENSON, CONRAD, App., 4-23-1832.
MENTZER, CONRAD, Set., 6-25-1832.
MESSHIE, BENJ., Inv., 6-16-1791.
MICHAEL, EARNEST, Will, 3-8-1785.
Dev.: Eliz., wife; Jacob, John, Geo., Sam., Peter Harness, sons; and others.
MICHAEL, GEO., Inv., 10-13-1791.

MICHAEL, JAMES, Will, 9-16-1822.
Dev.: Eliz. Mitchell, granddau.; and others.
MICHAEL, JOHN, Sur., 10-14-1783.
MIELISON, WM., Set., 7-22-1839.
MILBORN, WM., Sur., 7-24-1795.
MILCH, ISAAC, S.B., 10-22-1837.
MILES, JOSEPH, S.B., 7-27-1840.
MILES, JOS., App., 7-27-1840.
MILLER, GEORGE, App., 12-18-1809.
MILLER, HENRY, L.G., 12-12-1788.
MILLER, ISAAC, Will, 6-11-1794.
Dev.: Geo., Henry, Mich., bro.; and others.
MILLER, JOHN H., Will, 10-30-1790.
Dev.: Eliz., wife; Mary, dau.; Jacob, Rubin, Wm., sons.
MILLER, JOHN H., App., 9-11-1793.
MILLER, MICH., 1-19-1819.
MILLER, PETER, App., 5-2-1820.
MILLER, SILAS, S.B., 9-19-1829.
MILLER, SILAS, Set., 11-15-1830.
MILLER, THOM., Inv., 8-4-1781.
MILLER, WM., App., 6-16-1829.
MILLER, WM., Set., 2-20-1832.
MILLESON, JOHN, App., 3-20-1815.
MILLESON, PHEBE, App., 1-22-1836.
MILLISON, PHEBE, Will, 11-24-1834.
Dev.: Hannah Snapp, Harriett, dau.; Silas, John, sons.
MILLISON, PHOBEY, S.B., 4-23-1838.
MILLS, WM., Sur., 4-22-1818.
MITCHEL, JOHN, S.B., 3-3-1789.
MITCHELL, JOHN, Bond, 4-10-1788.
MITCHELL, JOHN, L.G., 3-6-1795.
MITCHELL, JOHN, Sur., 10-14-1798.
MONROE, ALEXANDRA, L.G., 6-26-1800.
MONROE, FRANCIS, S.B., 2-23-1835.
MONROE, JAMES, App., 2-18-1822.
MONROE, JOHN, Sur., 12-2-1782.
MONROE, JOHN, Will, 9-20-1821.
Dev.: Lucy, wife; James, Wm., John, James, Jeremiah, Geo., Marques, Jesse, sons; Anna, Eliza Arnold, dau.; others.
MONROE, JOHN, App., 3-14-1825.
MONROE, JOHN, Set., 1-25-1836.
MONROE, LUCY, App., 12-20-1824.
MONROE, LUCY, S.B., 12-19-1825.
MONROE, LUCY, Set., 3-15-1830.
MOORE, ELI, Sur., 11-4-1818.
MOORE, FRANCIS, S.B., 2-23-1835.
MOORE, FRANCIS, Set., 10-26-1840.
MOORE, JOS., App., 8-20-1792.
MOORE, PHIL., S.B., 5-11-1773.
MOORE, PHIL., S.B., 11-14-1781.
MOORE, PHILIP, Set., 11-14-1781.
MOORE, REESE, App., 10-18-1830.
MOORE, REESE, S.B., 6-24-1833.
MOORE, ROSE, S.B., 10-1-1830.
MOORE, RUTH, Set., 11-26-1849.

MORE, SAM., Will, 11-18-1823.
Dev.: Eliz., wife; Jerimah, son, Ann, dau.
MOREGRELMAN, CHRIS., Sur., 2-30-1791.
MORELAND, WM., App., 3-18-1822.
MORRISON, JAMES, Inv., 5-17-1824.
MORRISON, JAMES, Inv., 5-5-1824.
MORRISON, JAMES, Will, 2-15-1825.
Dev.: Agnes, wife; John, son; Mary, Nancy, Iona, dau.; others.
MORRISON, JAS., Set., 3-19-1830.
MORRISON, JOHN, S.B., 11-10-1778.
MORTHA, EDWARD, App., 8-17-1829.
MORTIN, JAMES, Bond, 12-16-1790.
MOSELEY, JAMES, L.G., 11-2-1812.
MOSELY, JAMES, Set., 8-21-1829.
MOTT, ADAM, Sur., 9-3-1795.
MULLIN, CHAS., Sur., 5-10-1791.
MURPHEY, FRANCIS, App., 9-18-1809.
MURPHEY, FRANCIS, App., 8-19-1812.
MURPHEY, FRANCIS, S.B., 8-19-1812.
MURPHEY, FRANCIS, Set., 11-17-1825.
MURPHEY, JAMES, S.B., 7-16-1810.
MURPHEY, JAMES, Set., 8-8-1810.
MURPHEY, JAS., App., 1-20-1802.
MURPHEY, JOHN, App., 11-18-1811.
MURPHY, HENRY, S.B., 3-14-1825.
MURPHY, HENRY, App., 3-15-1825.
MURPHY, JOHN, Deed, 2-17-1779.
MURPHY, MARY, Will, 5-27-1823.
Dev.: Wm., Robt., sons; Sally, dau.; others.
MURPHY, SALLY, Set., 11-17-1825.
MYERS, CATH., S.B., 9-25-1837.
MYERS, JACOB, Sur., 8-25-1818.
MYERS, JACOB, Set., 2-20-1832.
MYTINGER, SARAH, Set., 2-20-1832.
NAYLOR, WM., L.G., 1-18-1794.
NAYLOR, WM., L.G., 2-2-1816.
NAYLOR, WM., Sur., 9-16-1818.
NAYLOR, WM., L.G., 12-14-1833.
NEFF, ABR., App., 1-17-1803.
NEFF, ABR., S.B., 1-17-1803.
NEFF, JOHN, Inv., 5-22-1835.
NEFF, JOHN, App., 5-25-1835.
NEPTUNE, JOHN, S.B., 7-20-1802.
NEPTUNE, JOHN, App., 9-19-1803.
NESBETT, JAMES, L.G., 9-12-1783.
NESBIT, JOHN, Will, 6-16-1823.
Dev.: Eliz., wife; John, nephew.
NESBIT, JOHN, App., 4-19-1824.
NESBIT, JOHN, S.B., 4-19-1824.
NEVILL, JOS., Bond, 1-8-1782.
NEVILL, JOS., Bond, 5-14-1782.
NEWMAN, GEO., App., 2-18-1805.
NEWMAN, ISAAC, App., 12-20-1802.
NEWMAN, ISAAC, Set., 12-16-1805.
NEWMAN, JOHN, Sur., 5-11-1792.
NEWMAN, JOHN, Set., 6-22-1831.
NEWMAN, SOL., App., 7-15-1805.
NEWMAN, SOL., S.B., 7-15-1805.

NEWMANS, ELIZ., S.B., 11-19-1829.
NEWMONS, DAVID, Sur., 5-9-1791.
NIXON, GEO., Will, 4-10-1783.
Dev.: Rachel, wife; Geo., Wm., Jos.,
Jonathan, sons; Rhoda Thomas,
Eliz., Webb, Nancy Nixon, dau.; and
others.
NIXON, GEO., Set., 2-19-1790.
NIXON, GEO., App., 9-11-1793.
NIXON, GEO., S.B., 11-11-1793.
NIXON, WM., Set., 6-15-1795.
NOCORBY, ED., Sur., 4-18-1796.
NORMAN, JOHN, Inv., 11-11-1783.
NORRIS, SAM., Sur., 7-31-1795.
NOTEMAN, JAMES, Inv., 9-3-1785.
OATS, JACOB,. App., 10-28-1833.
OATS, JACOB, Set., 4-27-1835.
OATS, JACOB, S.B., 7-3-1835.
OBER, PETER, Will, 3-12-1782.
Dev.: Capt. Wm. Vause.
OBER, PETER, Inv., 12-11-1782.
OGG, ALEX, App., 4-20-1801.
O'HANO, DANIEL, Set., 9-16-1822.
O'HARRA, DAN., Set., 8-28-1833.
O'HARRO, DANIEL, S.B., 9-16-1822.
O'HERRA, DANIEL, Set., 3-15-1825.
OLDHAM, JOHN, S.B., 2-27-1769.
ONEAL, ABRAM, S.B., 3-14-1769.
O'QUEEN, JAS., App., 5-15-1809.
O'QUEEN, JAMES, S.B., 6-18-1810.
ORR, ANTHONY, App., 8-27-1833.
OSBORN, GEO., Will, 11-11-1783.
Dev.: Hannah, wife; Josiah, Isaac,
Sol., Francis, sons; and others.
OSBORN, GEO., Inv., 5-11-1784.
OSBURN, GEO., Set., 7-16-1789.
OSMAN, ELIZ., Will, 11-9-1784.
Samuel, son; Rebecca, Rhoda Dailey,
Catherine Lafferty, dau.
OSMAN, ISAAC, Will, 11-9-1784.
Dev.: Eliz., wife; Sam., son.
OSMOND, ELIZ., Inv., 5-10-1785.
OSMOND, ELIZ., Set., 4-12-1787.
OSMOND, JABEZ, Inv., 11-13-1783.
PACKMORTON, W., L.G., 2-19-1823.
PAINE, RICH., Bond, 8-13-1770.
PALMER, DAN., Bond, 5-13-1777.
PALMER, MARY, Bond, 2-14-1778.
PANCAKE, ANDREW, BY ELIZ., HIS
WIFE, Will, 11-11-1793.
Dev.: Eliz., wife; John, Abraham,
Geo., sons; Hannah, Mary, Agnes,
dau.; and others.
PANCAKE, HENRY, Set., 9-19-1814.
PANCAKE, JOHN, S.B., 9-15-1801.
PANCAKE, JOS., S.B., 9-15-1801.
PANCAKE, JOS., App., 7-20-1805.
PANCAKE, JOS., Set., 10-14-1805.
PANCAKE, JOS., Set., 2-19-1809.
PANCAKE, JOSEPH, S.B.. 9-19-1814.
PARK, ANDREW, App., 4-14-1791.
PARK, ANDREW, Set., 9-15-1791.
PARK, JOHN, Set., 12-28-1835.

PARK, JOHN, S.B., 3-27-1837.
PARKE, ANDREW, Will, 4-15-1790.
Dev.: Ruth Patten, Rachel Nekson,
Lorah Shire, Hannah, dau.; Sam.,
John, Amos, sons.
PARKE, ANDREW, App., 9-11-1791.
PARKER, BENJ., App., 2-20-1809.
PARKER, BENJ., Set., 2-16-1813.
PARKER, BENJ., L.G., 12-15-1821.
PARKER, CLAWSON, Set., 7-19-1813.
PARKER, GEO., Inv., 9-6-1750.
PARKER, GEO., Bond, 12-14-1757.
PARKER, GEO., Bond, 5-8-1759.
PARKER, GEO., S.B., 11-15-1769.
PARKER, GRACE, Deed, 11-29-1824.
PARKER, HANNAH, S.B., 7-19-1813.
PARKER, HANNAH, Set., 7-1-1815.
PARKER, JACOB, L.G., 5-24-1811.
PARKER, JACOB, Will, 12-22-1834.
Dev.: Sarah, wife; Susannah, dau.
PARKER, JACOB, App., 8-24-1835.
PARKER, JACOB, S.B., 6-26-1837.
PARKER, JOHN, Bond, 11-11-1760.
PARKER, JOHN, S.B., 3-12-1765.
PARKER, JOHN, Set., 7-17-1815.
PARKER, JOHN, S.B., 12-22-1834.
PARKER, JOHN, S.B., 12-28-1835.
PARKER, MARGARET, App., 10-18-
1824.
PARKER, MARTHA, Set., 12-24-1849.
PARKER, NAT., Sur., 2-3-1783.
PARKER, PETER, Set., 9-24-1832.
PARKER, RICH., Set., 7-17-1815.
PARKER, RICH., S.B., 7-19-1813.
PARKER, ROBT., Bond, 3-14-1775.
PARKER, ROBT., Will, 2-20-1809.
Dev.: Grace, wife; John, Wm., sons;
Mary, dau.
PARKER, ROBT., S.B., 1-20-1817.
PARKER, ROBT., Set., 6-19-1820.
PARKER, SAM., L.G., 1-24-1802.
PARKER, SAM., Set., 1-19-1818.
PARKER, SOL., Inv., 3-28-1836.
PARKER, SOL., App., 3-28-1836.
PARKER, SOL., Set., 10-24-1836.
PARKES, ROGER, Bond, 11-9-1773.
PARKS, ANDREW, Inv., 4-14-1791.
PARKS, DAN., Inv., 3-12-1782.
PARKS, DAN., App., 3-12-1782.
PARKS, ROBT., Set., 5-20-1807.
PARKS, ROGER, Inv., 5-9-1775.
PARKS, ROGER, S.B., 5-19-1775.
PARLER, THORNTON, S.B., 2-27-
1837.
PARLER, THORNTON, App., 2-27-1837.
PARRELL, ED., Set., 2-15-1830.
PARRILL, ED., Set., 5-17-1830.
PARRILL, JOHN, App., 4-19-1813.
PARSONS, ELIZ., Set., 5-17-1830.
PARSONS, ELIZ., Set., 3-17-1831.
PARSONS, ISAAC, App., 2-20-1797.

PARSONS, JAMES, Will, 2-22-1847.
Dev.: James, Isaac, David, sons; Sarah Blue, Eliz. Shobe, Rebecca Fairfax, dau.; and others.
PARSONS, THOM., Inv., 5-9-1775.
PARSONS, THOM., S.B., 5-12-1779.
PASTON, ELIAS, Bond, 3-13-1788.
PATTEN, JAMES, S.B., 2-9-1762.
PATTERSON, ALEX., Sur., 1815.
PATTERSON, JAS., Bond, 12-14-1757.
PATTERSON, JAMES, Will, 5-18-1812.
Dev.: Tennet, wife; John, James, Alex., Robt., Alec., sons.
PATTERSON, JAS., App., 1-18-1812.
PATTERSON, JAS., S.B., 1-18-1812.
PATTERSON, JAS., Set., 5-18-1819.
PATTERSON, JOHN, Set., 2-14-1831.
PATTERSON, JOHN, App., 3-25-1833.
PATTERSON, JOHN, Set., 3-25-1833.
PATTERSON, MARY, S.B., 10-26-1835.
PATTERSON, MARY, Set., 11-23-1835.
PATTERSON, ROBT., S.B., 7-24-1837.
PATTIN, JAMES, S.B., 3-9-1762.
PATTONS, JAMES, S.B., 3-9-1762.
PAUGH, NICH., Inv., 8-9-1785.
PAUGH, NICH., Set., 3-14-1786.
PEARCELL, BIRITHIN, Bond, 8-9-1774.
PEARSALL, PETER, Bond, 11-13-1770.
PENNINGTON, ELIJAH, Will, 5-25-1835.
Dev.: John, Wm., Thom., James, Enoch, Adam, Henry, sons; Nancy, Charlotte Caughy, Fiavy Miller, Eliz. Emmet, Fanny Lafolet, dau.
PENNINGTON, WM., Sur., 3-16-1798.
PEPERMAN, DAN., Set., 2-15-1796.
PEPPER, JOHN, Set., 1-19-1829.
PEPPER, JOHN, Set., 3-28-1836.
PEARCELL, JOHN, Bond, 8-4-1770.
PERCEALL, JOHN, Will, 11-18-1811.
Dev.: Hannah, wife; and others.
PERCELL, JOHN, S.B., 8-12-1777.
PERRE, AIJALON, Sur., 10-2-1791.
PERRY, GEO., L.G., 3-19-1782.
PERSALL, HANNAH, Will, 8-19-1822.
Dev.: Elenor Lyons, niece; others.
PETER, PETER, Bond, 5-11-1773.
PETERS, THOM., Sur., 8-28-1795.
PETERS, TUNIS, Sur., 8-28-1795.
PETERSON, JACOB, S.B., 9-25-1787.
PETERSON, JACOB, S.B., 12-16-1790.
PETERSON, PETER, S.B., 11-12-1782.
PETTIT, MOSES, S.B., 6-26-1837.
PETTIT, MOSES, App., 6-26-1837.
PETTIT, MOSES, Set., 3-26-1839.
PEYTON, TIM., L.G., 12-23-1783.
PHILIP, JAMES, Sur., 6-20-1791.
POLAND, COMFORT, Dower, 4-27-1840.
POLAND, JOHN, Set., 12-16-1822.
POLAND, JOHN, Set., 12-22-1834.
POLAND, KATH., Set., 6-20-1828.

POLING, AMOS, App., 8-26-1839.
POLING, JOHN, S.B., 11-24-1834.
POLING, ROBT., L.G., 10-29-1816.
POOL, HENRY, Set., 1-19-1829.
POOL, HENRY, Set., 6-20-1831.
POOL, WM., App., 5-15-1809.
POOLE, HENRY, ROBT., GEO., Set., 6-22-1840.
POPE, LAWRENCE, Inv., 6-9-1761.
POPERMAN, DAN., App., 6-12-1793.
POSSINAN, DAN., App., 6-12-1793.
POSTMAN, JOHN, Set., 8-26-1833.
POSTON, BRANSON, App., 8-27-1833.
POSTON, BRANSON, Set., 7-22-1835.
POSTON, BRONSON, S.B., 8-22-1835.
POSTON, ELIAS, Bond, 3-13-1788.
POSTON, ELIAS, App., 7-19-1803.
POSTON, JAMES, & WM., Set., 2-25-1839.
POSTON, SAM., L.G., 8-21-1815.
POWELL, JAMES, Sur., 4-29-1818.
POWELL, JOS., Inv., 3-10-1772.
POWELL, ROBT., L.G., 11-18-1824.
POWELL, WM., App., 3-15-1824.
POWELL, WM., S.B., 2-14-1825.
POWELLSON, CHAS., App., 6-24-1833.
POWELLSON, CHAS., S.B., 7-22-1833.
POWELLSON, THOM., Sur., 10-30-1800.
POWELSON, CORN., Will, 12-25-1837.
Dev.: Eliz., wife.
POWELSON, EVE, Will, 1-18-1813.
Dev.: Conrad Powelson.
POWELSON, ISAAC, S.B., 8-16-1813.
POWELSON, JOHN, L.G., 2-24-1826.
POWELSON, JOHN, Set., 7-14-1828.
POWELSON, JOHN, Set., 8-20-1833.
POWELSON, LENA, Will, 9-15-1806.
Dev.: Eva, dau.; others.
POWELSON, RINEAR, App., 6-25-1838.
POWELSON, RINIEE, Will, 5-28-1838.
Dev.: Eliz., wife; John, Riniee, sons; Eliza, Rosanna, dau.
POWER, HAZELLS, Bond, 8-14-1770.
FOWERS, JOS., Bond, 11-12-1791.
POWERS, MICH., Bond, 2-14-1758.
FOWERS, MICH., Inv., 12-12-1758.
POWERS, MICH. , Inv., 2-10-1761.
POWERS, MICH., S.B., 5-12-1779.
POWNALL, JAMES, S.B., 7-27-1834.
POWNELL, ELIAS, App., 12-25-1837.
POWNELL, ELISHA, Will, 7-28-1837.
Dev.: Abigail, wife; Jonathan, Isiah, Ruben, sons; Rachael, Sarah, dau.
POWNELL, ELISHA, S.B., 12-25-1837.
POWNELL, GEO., S.B., 10-18-1830.
POWNELL, GEO., Set., 10-18-1830.
POWNELL, ISAAC, Set., 8-18-1810.
POWNELL, ISAAC, App., 8-15-1813.
POWNELL, JAMES, Sur., 9-23-1791.
POWNELL, JAMES, L.G., 6-7-1819.
POWNELL, JOHN, and ISAAC, Sur., 6-12-1818.

POWNELL, JON., App., 1-27-1834.
POWNELL, JON., S.B., 1-27-1834.
POWNELL, JON., App., 7-27-1834.
POWNELL, JON., S.B., 7-27-35.
POWNELL, JON., Set., 8-24-1835.
POWNELL, ROBT., L.G., 11-1-1833.
POWNELL, RUBEN, App., 4-23-1838.
POWNELL, RUBEN, S.B., 4-28-1838.
PRATHER, SILAS, L.G., 1-2-1826.
PRICE, ARELINA, Set., 6-16-1823.
PRICE, ED., Set., 8-27-1832.
PRICE, ED., Set., 9-24-1832.
PRICE, ED., Set., 8-26-1833.
PRICE, ED., Set., 9-23-1833.
PRICE, ELMIRA, Set., 6-16-1823.
PRICE, EVALINA, Set., 6-16-1823.
PRICE, EVALINA, Set., 7-19-1830.
PRICE, EVELINA, Set., 9-23-1833.
PRICE, JOHN, L.G., 3-3-1801.
PRICE, SILAS, Set., 6-1-1823.
PRICE, SILAS, Set., 9-24-1832.
PRICE, SILAS, Set., 8-26-1833.
PRICE, SILAS, SILAS, EDMOND, & EVELINA, Set., 4-25-1836.
PRICE, WM., Inv., 5-10-1785.
PRICE, WM., Sur., 2-27-1794.
FRICHARD, JOHN, App., 8-16-1813.
PRINGLE, HENRY, Will, 1-19-1821.
Dev.: Mary, wife; Wm., John, Geo., sons; Eliz., Mary, Jeddiah, Odaiah, Malenda, Pernina, dau.
PRITCHARD, JOS., Inv., 5-10-1768.
PRITCHARD, SAM., Bond, 5-13-1777.
PRITCHARD, SAM., Inv., 3-9-1779.
PRITCHARD, SAM., Sur., 4-1-1801.
PRITEFORD, GEO., L.G., 6-26-1801.
PROTZMAN, BARBARA, App., 8-17-1829.
PROTZMAN, JOHN, Set., 7-22-1833.
PROTZMAN, JOHN, S.B., 3-28-1836.
PRUKENHUFF, SAM., Sur., 11-7-1759.
PUGH, BETHEL, Will, 1-14-1822.
Dev.: Rebecca, wife; Jacob, son; children.
PUGH, DAN., Sur., 10-10-1791.
PUGH, DAN., Will, 11-10-1794.
Dev.: Sarah, wife; Hannibal, son; Amy, Juliana, dau.
PUGH, DAN., App., 7-20-1795.
PUGH, JESSE, Sur., 6-___-1788.
PUGH, JESSE, App., 9-19-1831.
PUGH, JESSE, S.B., 3-26-1832.
PUGH, JESSE, Set., 9-28-1835.
PUGH, JON., App., 2-16-1795.
PUGH, JON., S.B., 2-16-1795.
PUGH, JON., App., 5-25-1835.
PUGH, JON., Set., 9-26-1836.
PUGH, JONA, JR., Will, 3-26-1832.
Dev.: Ann, wife.
PUGH, JONAS, S.B., 6-27-1836.
PUGH, JONATHAN, Will, 10-15-1794.
Dev.: Marg., wife; Jonathan, David, Jefferson, Anmanes, John, sons.

PUGH, JONATHAN, Will, 10-27-1834.
Dev.: Wife; John, son; Lucy, Marie, dau.; and others.
PUGH, MICHAEL, App., 8-27-1838.
PUGH, MICHAEL, S.B., 8-27-1838.
PUGH, ROBT., App., 7-18-1808.
PUGH, ROBERT, Set., 2-15-1825.
PURCELL, ED., App., 3-11-1783.
PURCELL, ED., Inv., 3-11-1783.
PURCELL, JON., App., 2-14-1814.
PURCELL, JON., Set., 3-15-1814.
PURGET, FRED., App., 5-16-1825.
PURGET, HENRY, Will, 3-27-1834.
Dev.: Eliz., wife; Wm., Henry, Geo., Fred., sons; Mary Racer, Eliz. Shoemaker, dau.
PURGETT, FRED., Set., 11-14-1831.
PURGETT, JACOB, App., 4-15-1805.
PUTMAN, JACOB, Will, 8-26-1833.
Dev.: Rachel, wife; Jacob, son.
PUTMAN, JACOB, App., 8-24-1835.
PUTMAN, JACOB, S.B., 8-24-1835.
PUTMAN, JACOB, Set., 10-26-1835.
PUTMAN, JOS., S.B., 8-24-1835.
PUTMAN, PETER, Sur., 6-10-1793.
PUTMAN, PETER, App., 6-15-1795.
PUTMAN, PETER, S.B., 9-16-1799.
PUTMAN, PETER, S.B., 4-20-1800.
PUTMAN, PETER, Set., 5-15-1825.
QUEEN, JAMES, App., 5-15-1809.
QUEEN, MARTHA, Will, 11-24-1835.
Dev.: Sarah Smoot, Martha Hott, niece; Abslom Queen.
QUEEN, MARTHA, App., 1-22-1836.
QUEEN, MARTHA, S.B., 10-23-1837.
RACE, REBECCA, App., 1-25-1836.
RACE, REBECCA, S.B., 1-25-1836.
RACEY, JOHN, Will, 6-20-1831.
Dev.: Rebecca, wife.
RACEY, JOHN, S.B., 6-24-1833.
RACY, THOM., Will, 9-16-1822.
Dev.: Marg., wife; others.
RAMSEY, MARG., Bond, 12-10-1759.
RANDALL, ABEL, TO JOHNSON, ABR., Indenture, 4-13-1779.
RANKIN, JOHN, L.G., 12-9-1820.
RANKIN, JOHN, L.G., 12-9-1820.
RANNELLS, JAMES, Set., 4-20-1807.
RANNELLS, JAMES, Set., 7-20-1807.
RANNELLS, JAMES, Set., 8-19-1811.
RANNELLS, WM., Will, 10-25-1784.
Dev.: Jane, wife; James, Sam., John, Robt., David, Wm., sons; Nancy Holmes, Marg, dau.; others.
RANNELLS, WM., Will, 10-15-1794.
Dev.: Jane, wife; James, Sam., John, Robt., David, Wm., sons; Nancy Holmes, Marg, dau.; others.
RANNELS, ROBT., App., 12-15-1823.
RATCHLIFFE, DAN., Inv., 3-8-1785.
RATELIFFS, DAN., Inv., 3-8-1785.
RAULINGS, MOSES, Will, 5-15-1809.
Dev.: Floyd, Moses, sons; Nancy, Ann, dau.; and others.

RAVENCRAFT, JOHN, S.B., 2-15-1830.
RAVENCRAFT, SAMUEL, S.B., 2-19-1810.
RAVENSCRAFT, CHAS., Inv., 5-19-1822.
RAVENSCRAFT, CHAS., S.B., 7-14-1823.
RAVENSCRAFT, JAS., App., 2-23-1835.
RAVENSCRAFT, JAS., S.B., 2-23-1835.
RAVENSCRAFT, JAS., Set., 6-22-1840.
RAVENSCROFT, JAMES, S.B., 2-23-1835.
RAVENSCROFT, SAM., L.G., 1-2-1810.
RAWLINGS, BENJ., App., 9-19-1814.
RAWLINGS, COOK, Set., 6-1-1822.
RAWLINGS, MOSAS, App., 6-20-1809.
RAWLINGS, PETER, L.G., 3-26-1819.
RAYNOLDS, CORN., Will, 8-20-1810.
Dev.: John, Corn., sons; Eliz., wife; others.
READ, JOHN, Will, 2-16-1824.
Dev.: Mary, wife; children.
READ, LEO., S.B., 3-14-1769.
READ, PETER, Bond, 5-10-1763.
READ, PETER, Bond, 5-10-1763.
READOR, CONEWAY, Set., 11-15-1825.
REAR, JOHN, App., 2-14-1803.
RECTOR, CONAWAY, Set., 8-14-1838.
RECTOR, CONWAY, Deed, 5-26-1818.
RECTOR, MARY, Will, 3-25-1839.
Dev.: Sarah, Alvekine, Marie, Harriett, dau.; Francis, James, sons.
REDDENBURG, MICH., Bond, 8-17-1758.
REED, ANN, Set., 5-9-1780.
REED, EALNOR, Set., 10-15-1798.
REED, GEO., Set., 6-15-1795.
REED, JACOB, S.B., 2-26-1780.
REED, JACOB, Set., 5-9-1780.
REED, JACOB, Inv., 8-9-1780.
REED, JAMES, Will, 12-16-1811.
Dev.: Nancy, wife; others.
REED, JAMES, App., 9-14-1812.
REED, JER., Sur., 3-12-1798.
REED, JERIMAH, Will, 6-17-1822.
Dev.: Eliz., wife; Jermiah, John, sons; Jane Wilkson, Ann Wilson, Eliz. McKee, Becky Hickle, dau.
REED, JOHN, Set., 6-13-1775.
REED, JOHN, App., 8-12-1777.
REED, JOHN, Set., 5-11-1785.
REED, PETER, Inv., 12-11-1764.
REEDS, PETER, S.B., 10-8-1765.
REES, ASHFORD, Will, 8-26-1833.
Dev.: Susanna, wife; John, Wm., sons; Harriett, Elianor, Susanah, dau.
REES, ASHFORD, App., 12-23-1833.
REES, THOM., S.B., 4-25-1836.
REESE, ASHFORD, S.B., 11-23-1835.
REESE, ASHFORD, Set., 9-26-1836.

REESE, THOM., Will, 7-23-1832.
Dev.: Marg., wife; Wm., John, Geo., Thom., Ashford, Sam., sons; Eliz., Martha, Ellen, Marg., dau.
REESE, THOM., App., 1-26-1835.
REESE, THOM., Set., 6-22-1835.
REESE, THOM., Set., 10-25-1840.
REESE, THOMAS, App., 11-26-1832.
REESE, WM., App., 9-24-1838.
REESE, WM., S.B., 10-22-1838.
REESE, WM., Set., 10-26-1840.
REEVES, BENJ., Bond, 6-14-1787.
REEVES, BENJ., Bond, 10-11-1787.
REGAR, ANTHONY, S.B., 5-11-1779.
REGEAR, HENRY, Inv., 11-10-1778.
REGERS, ANTHONY, Inv., 8-12-1777.
REID, ANN, S.B., 2-26-1780.
REID, ANN, Inv., 5-9-1780.
REID, GEO., App., 6-12-1793.
REID, JOHN, Bond, 11-9-1762.
REID, LEONARD, Bond, 12-14-1787.
RENICK, GEO., Divn., 11-10-1784.
Dev.: Jenny, wife.
RENICK, JAMES, Bond, 5-13-1777.
RENICK, JAMES, Inv., 8-12-1777.
RENNICK, GEO., Set., 2-13-1787.
REVENSCROFT, SAM., L.G., 9-6-1788.
REYNOLDS, CORNEL., App., 8-19-1811.
RICHARD, ANN, Bond, 5-11-1773.
RICHARD, ANN, Inv., 8-10-1773.
RICHMOND, WM., L.G., 2-27-1829.
RIED, JER., Sur., 7-29-1788.
RIGGLE, ELIJAH, App., 3-18-1822.
RIGGLE, ELIJAH, S.B., 3-18-1822.
RIGGS, JOHN, Inv., 11-10-1772.
RILEY, MICH., L.G., 3-16-1795.
ROBINSON, JAS., Bond, 8-12-1766.
ROBINSON, JAS., Set., 4-23-1832.
ROBINSON, JAMES, S.B., 6-22-1835.
ROBINSON, PATIENCE, Bond, 5-9-1759.
ROBINSON, RICH., App., 12-20-1824.
ROBINSON, SAM., App., 3-15-1830.
RODGERS, DAN., 4-15-1805.
ROGER, OWEN, App., 6-18-1812.
ROGERS, ANTHONY, Bond, 5-8-1770.
ROGERS, DAVID, Inv., 8-12-1783.
ROGERS, OWEN, Will, 2-18-1811.
Dev.: Mary, wife; Owen, Robt., sons; Lydia Bevan, dau.; others.
ROGERS, OWEN, S.B., 6-18-1812.
ROGERS, ROBT., Sur., 6-3-1789.
ROGERS, ROBT., App., 8-15-1825.
ROGERS, ROBT., Set., 8-22-1836.
ROSENBERGER, JACOB, S.B., 3-14-1831.
ROSENBERGER, JOHN, Will, 11-14-1831.
Dev.: Eliz., wife; Ausarme, son; Eliz., dau.
ROSENBERGER, JOHN, App., 8-27-1832.

ROSENBERGER, JOHN, S.B., 11-25-1834.
ROSENBERGER, ISSAC, App., 3-16-1831.
ROSENBERGER, MICH., Bond, 12-1-1757.
ROSENBROUGH, MICH., S.B., 9-10-1761.
ROSS, AMANDA, Inv., 9-20-1781.
ROSS, FRANCIS, Bond, 3-10-1762.
ROSS, FRANCIS, S.B., 11-11-1762.
ROSS, FRANCIS, Inv., 5-11-1762.
ROSS, WM., Inv., 5-14-1760.
ROSS, WM., Bond, 3-12-1760.
RUCKMAN, JOHN, Set., 4-25-1833.
RUCKMAN, SAM., L.G., 1-28-1813.
RUCKMAN, SAM., S.B., 6-15-1829.
RUCKMAN, SAM., Set., 6-17-1829.
RUCKMAN, SAM., Set., 6-17-1829.
RUCKMAN, THOS., S.B., 8-14-1809.
RUDDLE, STEPHEN, Bond, 11-14-1780.
RUDDLE, STEPHEN, Bond, 11-15-1780.
RUDDLE, STEPHEN, Bond, 3-13-1781.
RUDDLE, STEPHEN, Bond, 5-14-1782.
RUDOLPH, GEO., App., 10-17-1831.
RUDOLPH, GEO., Set., 12-22-1834.
RUDOLPH, GEO., S.B., 1-23-1837.
RUMSEY, JOHN, Inv., 2-14-1768.
RUST, MATHEW, L.G., 10-14-1783.
RYON, JOHN, Inv., 11-19-1760.
RYON, JOHN, Bond, 5-11-1760.
RYON, JOHN, Inv., 8-13-1760.
SADOWS, ANDREW, App., 4-14-1767.
SAMS, FRED, Set.. 5-18-1818.
SANDUSKEY, ANDREW, App., 3-9-1768.
SARVEL, NOAH, S.B., 8-17-1829.
SAUNDERS, HENRY, Sur., 4-3-1779.
SAVAGE, JAMES, App., 9-19-1814.
SAVAGE, JAMES, Inv., 9-19-1814.
SAVAGE, PAT., Sur., 3-30-1790.
SAVERS, CHAS., App., 10-8-1765.
SAVILLE, JOS., App., 3-17-1828.
SCHOONOW, THOM., App., 8-11-1778.
SCOTT, ANNANIAH, App., 8-11-1767.
SCOTT, RICH., L.G., 4-5-1795.
SCOTT, ROBT., Sur., 3-17-1779.
SCOTT, WM., Inv., 9-13-1768.
SCRELCHFIELD, JOS., App., 9-22-1824.
SCRELCHFIELD, JOS., S.B., 10-8-1824.
SCRODE, JOHN, Sur., 8-3-1818.
SCRUTCHFIELD, AMOS, App., 3-13-1781.
SEARS, JAMES, Will, 5-12-1783.
Dev.: John, Wm., sons; Mary Wilson, Cath. Shook, dau.
SEARS, JAMES, Inv., 12-11-1783.
SEARS, JAMES, App., 12-11-1783.
SEARS, JAMES, Will, 3-9-1784.
Dev.: Wife; John, Wm., sons; Cath., Mary Wilson, dau.

SEATON, ALLEY, Will, 11-15-1830.
Dev.: Hiriam, Geo., Wm., James, sons; Frankey Farmer, Lydia Race, dau.; others.
SEAVER, NICH., Will, 8-10-1784.
Dev.: Eliz., wife; Nich., son; Lydia, Mary Macarty, Ann, Prudence, dau.; Ann Sheppard, sis.; and others.
SEBRINGS, ELIZ., Will, 4-18-1814.
Dev.: Peter, son; Ann Cool, Eliz., Cath. Stephenson, dau.
SECRIST, FRED., Will, 12-22-1834.
Dev.: Rebecca, wife; children.
SECRIST, FRED., S.B., 6-20-1835.
SECRIST, FRED., S.B., 7-24-1837.
SEE, MARG., Bond, 2-14-1758.
SEIVERS, CHAS., Set., 11-15-1769.
SELBY, JOHN, L.G., 1-28-1813.
SERUNGTONE, JAS., L.G., 7-17-1762.
SEVERS, JACOB, S.B., 3-28-1836.
SEVERS, JACOB, Set., 4-25-1836.
SEVERS, NICH., L.G., 6-23-1788.
SEVIORS, JACOB, S.B., 9-20-1830.
SEWEL, JOHN, Inv., 2-16-1818.
SHACKEY, VALENTINE, App., 4-18-1831.
SHACKEY, VALENTINE, S.B., 4-18-1831.
SHAFFER, MARTIN, App., 5-17-1824.
SHAFFER, MARTIN, S.B., 12-20-1824.
SHAFFER, MARTIN, Set., 9-24-1832.
SHANBOUGH, GEO., App., 12-10-1794.
SHANBOUGH, GEO., S.B., 7-20-1795.
SHANHOLTZER, PETER, App., 4-25-1836.
SHANHOLTZER, PETER, S.B., 4-25-1836.
SHANKS, GEO., Inv., 8-14-1815.
SHANNON, HUGH, Will, 8-12-1783.
Dev.: Rachel, wife; Esther, Ruth, dau.; and others.
SHANNON, HUGH, App., 5-11-1784.
SHANNON, HUGH, Inv., 5-11-1784.
SHANNON, HUGH, Set., 4-18-1796.
SHANNON, JOHN, App., 8-11-1778.
SHANNON, THOM., App., 12-14-1812.
SHANNON, THOM., Set., 10-20-1828.
SHANNON, THOS., S.B., 1-13-1812.
SHARFE, GEO., L.G., 1-18-1815.
SHARP, JESSE, L.G., 10-14-1783.
SHEETZ, FRED, L.G., 12-16-1818.
SHEETZ, FRED, L.G., 8-14-1828.
SHEPARD, JOB., Obl., 1796.
SHEPHARD, JOB., App., 4-16-1798.
SHEPLER, HENRY, App., 5-9-1780.
SHEPLER, HENRY, Set., 3-11-1783.
SHERRARD, ROBT., L.G., 4-2-1818.
SHERRARD, ROBT., L.G., 5-1-1823.
SHERRARD, ROBT., L.G., 11-1-1833.
SHERRARD, WM., Will, 1-17-1832.
Dev.: Millicent, wife; Mary Abernathey, mother; Mary Myers, sis.; Jos., bro.; others.
SHERRARD, WM., Set., 6-12-1834.

SHERRARD, WM., App., 3-28-1836.
SHERRARD, WM., S.B., 8-27-1838.
SHIELDS, JOHN, App., 7-24-1837.
SHINGLETON, AB., S.B., 4-14-1828.
SHINGLETON, AB., Set., 2-20-1832.
SHINGLETON, THOM., App., 3-12-1765.
SHINGLETON, THOM., Set., 3-12-1765.
SHINNS, DAVID, Inv., 11-18-1815.
SHIPLER, CONRAD, Set., 9-12-1786.
SHIPLER, WM., App., 3-14-1780.
SHIPLER, WM., Set., 12-11-1788.
SHIPLEY, JACOB, Inv., 11-11-1760.
SHIPLEY, WM., App., 3-14-1780.
SHIPMAN, BENJ., App., 5-18-1796.
SHIPMAN, BENJ., Set., 10-14-1805.
SHIRLEY, JACOB, App., 9-8-1761.
SHISOR, THOM., App., 2-10-1761.
SHOCKEY, VAL., App., 3-31-1831.
SHOCKEY, VAL., S.B., 4-18-1831.
SHOFFE, JACOB, Will, 11-21-1834.
Dev.: Germima, wife; Wm., son.
SHOFFE, JACOB, App., 3-25-1835.
SHOFFE, JACOB, Inv., 3-25-1835.
SHOMAN, JOHN, Set., 5-9-1780.
SHORES, THOM., L.G., 12-29-1818.
SHORT, JACOB, App., 6-16-1791.
SHORT, JACOB, Inv., 6-16-1791.
SHORT, JACOB, Set., 6-26-1792.
SHORT, MICH., App., 1-14-1828.
SHORT, RICH., Sur., 8-16-1824.
SHRIDE, ADAM, Will, 4-14-1791.
Dev.: Charety, wife; Eliz. Pennington, dau.; and others.
SHRIDE, ADAM, App., 6-16-1791.
SHRIDE, ADAM, Inv., 6-16-1791.
SIL, GEO., Inv., 4-18-1814.
SILLER, HENRY, Set., 12-24-1849.
SIMMONS, CHAS., Set., 4-14-1828.
SIMMONS, CHARLES, Set., 6-22-1835.
SIMMONS, SIMON, App., 11-14-1831.
SIMONS, JACOB, App., 8-11-1772.
SIMONS, GEO., Inv., 2-18-1779.
SIMPKINS, GASSAGE, Set., 7-14-1823.
SIMPKINS, GEO., Set., 7-14-1823.
SIMPKINS, GOSSET, S.B., 2-18-1822.
SIMPKINS. SILAS, App., 9-19-1796.
SIMS, DAVID, S.B., 11-16-1818
SINCLAIR, JOHN, L.G., 2-24-1812.
SINCLAIR, ROBT., Will, 4-18-1831.
Dev.: Nancy, wife; Hugh, Dan., Robt., Alex., sons; Jane, Nancy, Marg. King, dau.
SINCLAIR, ROBT., App., 5-16-1831.
SIVER, JOHN, App., 11-25-1839.
SIX, HENRY, App., 4-18-1814.
SLACK, ABR., Inv., 7-18-1823.
SLACK, ABR., Inv., 8-18-1824.
SLACK, JAMES, Will, 5-20-1822.
Dev.: John, Jonathan, Henry, Geo., James, sons; Jane Ruckman, Betsey Hartley, Mary Huddleston, dau.; others.

SLACK, JAMES, Inv., 8-18-1823.
SLACK, JONATHAN, Inv., 8-18-1824.
SLADDERS, STEP., Inv., 3-12-1765.
SLAGEL, CONRAD, Set., 9-12-1786.
SLAGLE, CONRAD, Inv., 5-13-1783.
SLAGLE, JACOB, App., 10-19-1801.
SLANE, ANN, Will, 8-17-1829.
Dev.: Benj., son.
SLANE, ANN, App., 2-15-1830.
SLANE, JAMES, App., 8-16-1831.
SLANE, JOHN, Set., 10-25-1833.
SLANE, JOHN, S.B., 10-30-1833.
SLANE, SARAH, App., 10-26-1840.
SLAUGHTER, GEO., L.G., 5-31-1783.
SLAUGHTER, PHIL., L.G., 2-3-1794.
SLEGAL, CONRAD, Will, 2-12-1782.
Dev.: Christina, Eliz., dau.; Jacob, John, sons.
SLOAN, CHARLOTTE, App., 9-25-1837.
SLOAN, CHARLOTTE, Set., 9-27-1839.
SLOAN, CHARLOTTE, S.B., 7-23-1838.
SLOAN, JOHN, L.G., 10-31-1827.
SLOAN, JOHN, App., 6-25-1833.
SLOAN, JOHN, L.G., 5-19-1849.
SLOAN, RICH., Will, 6-20-1831.
Dev.: Charolete, wife; Mary Arnold, Eliz. Arnold, dau.; others.
SLOAN, RICH., Inv., 6-22-1831.
SLOAN, RICH., App., 11-14-1831.
SLOAN, RICH., Set., 9-23-1839.
SLOAN, RICHARD, Set., 9-25-1833.
SLOCUMB, ROBT., Inv., 5-18-1817.
SLONE, ANN, App., 2-15-1830.
SLONE, ANN, S.B., 8-12-1830.
SLONE, DAN, App., 2-15-1796.
SLONE, JAMES, L.G., 8-14-1799.
SLONE, JAMES, Inv., 8-16-1831.
SLONE, JOHN, App., 3-31-1831.
SLONE, JOHN, L.G., 1-15-1833.
SLONE, JOHN, S.B., 10-30-1833.
SLONE, THOM., V.S., ASBURY, HENRY, Set., 6-19-1828.
SMITH, BENJ., App., 8-27-1832.
SMITH, BENJ., Set., 12-28-1835.
SMITH, CHAS., S.B., 11-18-1815.
SMITH, CHAS., Inv., 6-17-1816.
SMITH, CHAS., S.B., 8-26-1816.
SMITH, CHRIS., App., 11-11-1777.
SMITH, CHRIS., Set., 10-12-1787.
SMITH, GEO., App., 12-11-1798.
SMITH, GEO., S.B., 12-17-1798.
SMITH, GEO., Set., 10-18-1802.
SMITH, ISRAEL, Sur., 6-15-1747.
SMITH, JOHN, Inv., 5-25-1833.
SMITH, JOHN, S.B., 5-25-1835.
SMITH, PHIL., App., 2-13-1759.
SMITH, RICH., Will, 4-16-1789.
Dev.: Mary, wife; James, Rich., Geo., sons; Fanny, dau.
SMITH, RICH., App., 9-10-1789.
SMITH, RICH., Inv., 9-10-1789.
SMITH, ROBT., App., 4-15-1801.

SMITH, WILL, Set., 2-15-1813.
SMITH, WM., Set., 8-12-1777.
SMITH, WM., App., 7-18-1796.
SMITH, WM., L.G., 2-4-1812.
SMOOT, JAMES, L.G., 11-16-1783.
SMOOT, JOHN, App., 5-16-1808.
SMOOT, JOHN, Set., 8-11-1811.
SMOOT, JOHN, S.B., 7-18-1813.
SMOOT, JOHN, S.B., 8-16-1813.
SMOOT, MARY, Dower, 2-20-1809.
SMOOTS, LUCRESY, Inv., App., 8-16-1815.
SNAPP, MARG., S.B., 8-25-1835.
SNAPP, MARG., Set., 9-28-1835.
SNYDER, JOHN, L.G., 2-1-1804.
SNYDER, JOHN, Inv., 2-17-1817.
SNYDER, JOHN, S.B., 8-21-1821.
SNYDER, LETHIAS, Inv., 6-19-1815.
SNYDER, VAL., App., 9-8-1761.
SOUTHERLAND, WM., App., 12-10-1794.
SOUTHERN, GEORGE, Set., 9-20-1813.
SPEARS, MICH., App., 5-14-1760.
SPEELMAN, WM., Set., 8-15-1825.
SPEELMAN, GEO., Set., 10-28-1833.
SPEELMON, GEO., App., 10-18-1830.
SPEELMON, GEO., S.B., 10-18-1830.
SPENCER, JOHN, App., 10-19-1796.
SPILLIMAN, WM., Inv., 12-15-1817.
SPILLIMAN, WM., S.B., 12-15-1817.
SPILLMAN, GEO., App., 10-18-1830.
SPILLMAN, GEO., S.B., 10-18-1830.
SQUIRE, MICH., Set., 12-16-1816.
SQUIRES, MICH., Inv., 2-15-1813.
SQUIRES, MICHAEL, App., 2-15-1813.
STACKEY, FREDERICK, App., 4-15-1809.
STACKEY, T., S.B., 11-17-1817.
STACKEY, T., Set., 12-18-1820.
STAFFORD, C., Set., 6-22-1820.
STAFFORD, CATH., Will, 9-17-1810.
Dev.: Washington, son; Sarah, dau.
STAFFORD, CATH., App., 8-14-1811.
STAFFORD, JOS., Deed, 3-11-1812.
STAFFORD, RICH., App., 2-20-1809.
STAFFORD, RICH., S.B., 2-20-1809.
STAFFORD, RICH., S.B., 12-20-1813.
STAFFORD, RICH., Set., 12-20-1813.
STAFFORD, SALLY, Set., 6-22-1820.
STAGGES, GEO., Sur., 3-20-1818.
STAINE, ANN., Set., 5-16-1825.
STAINE, CHARLES, Set., 5-16-1825.
STAINE, FRED., Set., 5-16-1825.
STAINE, JOHN, Set., 7-18-1825.
STAINE, THOMAS, Set., 5-16-1825.
STALLCUP, INO., Set., 6-15-1818.
STALLCUP, JOHN, App., 12-16-1799.
STARKEY, FRED., App., 1-16-1804.
STARKEY, FRED., S.B., 4-17-1809.
STARN, JACOB, Set., 12-15-1806.
STARNES, FRED., App., 9-19-1814.

STARNES, JACOB, App., 6-19-1777.
STARNES, JACOB, App., 9-19-1797.
ORPHANS OF JACOB STARNES, Set., 12-15-1806.
STARNES, JOHN, L.G., 1-8-1810.
STARNES, JOHN, S.B., 7-14-1828.
STARNES, JOHN, Set., 5-28-1832.
STARNS, FRED., S.B., 9-19-1814.
STARNS, FRED., Inv., 11-19-1814.
STARNS, FRED., Set., 6-19-1816.
STEED, JOHN, App., 5-18-1801.
STEED, JOHN, App., 2-7-1806.
STEENE, ISABELLA, App., 10-1-1808.
STEENE, ISABELLA, S.B., 12-16-1812.
STEIN, ISABELLA, S.B., 12-16-1811.
STEPHENS, CHRIS., Bond, 5-11-1795.
STEPHENSON, THOM., App., 1-17-1808.
STERRETT, WM., L.G., 11-3-1800.
STEWART, JAS., App., 8-8-1775.
STEWART, JAMES, Set., 11-14-1775.
STEWART, JOHN, App., 8-22-1836.
STEWART, JOHN, S.B., 8-22-1836.
STEWART, M., App., 8-5-1829.
STEWART, M., S.B., 8-17-1829.
STEWART, MICH., S.B., 8-17-1829.
STIMMEL, JOST, App., 2-6-1807.
STINEBACK, FRED., App., 5-17-1824.
STOCKEY, MICH., App., 3-11-1783.
STOCKEY, MICH., Inv., 3-11-1783.
STOKER, JOHN, Sur., 8-13-1818.
STONE, JASPER, Sur., 3-22-1791.
STORN, JACOB, Set., 12-15-1806.
STRADDLERS, STEP., Inv., 3-12-1765.
STREET, JOHN, L.G., 11-7-1790.
STUMP, GEO., Guardian, 3-7-1785.
STUMP, JOHN, L.G., 2-18-1812.
STUMP, JOHN, Set., 2-23-1835.
STUMP, MICH., App., 5-15-17?.
STUMP, PETER, Inv., 2-10-1816.
STUMP, PETER, Set., 2-28-1835.
SULLIVAN, GILES, Bond, 8-12-1750.
SULLIVAN, MORRIS, L.G., 8-14-1783.
SULLIVAN, NAT., App., 3-12-1765.
SULLIVAN, SILLES, L.G., 2-15-1816.
SULPIN, GEO., Sur., 8-31-1795.
SUMMERS, WALTER, Inv., 6-19-1815.
SUMMERVILLE, JAS., L.G., 1-31-1826.
SWICK, TUNIS, App., 12-10-1789.
SWIER, JACOB, Will, 5-17-1830.
Dev.: Mary Ann, wife; David, John, Jacob, Geo., Martin, Sam., sons; Eliz., Sarah, Cath. Corbin, Mary Carbauy, dau.; others.
SWISHER, JOHN, S.B., 1-14-1828.
SWISHER, JOHN, S.B., 2-18-1828.
SWISHER, JOHN, App., 3-18-1830.
SWISHER, SAM., Set., 11-26-1849.
SWITZER, V., Set., 10-18-1817.
SYON, JACOB, Inv., 8-10-1808.
TACKER, JOS., App., 2-14-1825.

TAFFEE, JAMES, Inv., 1-14-1783.
TAGGART, FRAN. TO COMBS, THOM., Deed, 8-9-1785.
TAPP, GEO., App., 3-19-1830.
TAPP, GEO., S.B., 6-24-1837.
TAPSCOTE, CHI., S.B., 8-27-1835.
TAPSCOTE, NEWTON, S.B., 9-29-1830.
TAPSCOTT, NEWTON, Set., 9-28-1835.
TAPSCOTT, NEWTON, S.B., 5-22-1837.
TARPLAY, JAMES, Bond, 10-11-1787.
TARPLAY, JAS., Bond, 10-11-1787.
TARPLEY, JAS., Bond, 8-13-1782.
TASKER, G.R., App., 1-26-1839.
TASKER, GEO., L.G., 9-5-1822.
TASKER, GEO., Will, 1-22-1839.
Dev.: Cath., wife; Geo., Benj., sons; Christina, dau.
TASKER, GEO., S.B., 6-22-1840.
TAWBRIDGE, JOHN, App., 1-19-1824.
TAYLOR, CHAS., App., 7-15-1805.
TAYLOR, CHAS., Set., 9-19-1808.
TAYLOR, DAN., App., 8-20-1792.
TAYLOR, EDWARD, App., 10-28-1839.
TAYLOR, ELIZ., S.B., 4-24-1837.
TAYLOR, JACOB, S.B., 8-6-1832.
TAYLOR, JACOB, App., 6-23-1834.
TAYLOR, JACOB, Set., 5-25-1835.
TAYLOR, JAMES, S.B., 3-18-1812.
TAYLOR, JOHN, App., 3-19-1810.
TAYLOR, JOHN, S.B., 3-19-1810.
TAYLOR, JOHN, Set., 1-18-1812.
TAYLOR, JOS., S.B., 3-18-1817.
TAYLOR, JOS., S.B., 6-11-1819.
TAYLOR, MARG., S.B., 4-24-1837.
TAYLOR, REBECCA, S.B., 3-18-1817.
TAYLOR, SALLIE, S.B., 3-18-1817.
TAYLOR, SALLIE, S.B., 6-12-1819.
TAYLOR, SEPTIMUS, App., 8-13-1782.
TAYLOR, SEPTIMUS, Inv., 8-13-1782.
TAYLOR, SIMON, Bond, 11-9-1784.
TAYLOR, SIMON, Bond, 5-9-1775.
TAYLOR, SIMON, Bond, 11-9-1784.
TAYLOR, SIMON, App., 7-11-1788.
TAYLOR, SIMON, S.B., 4-24-1837.
TAYLOR, SUSANAH, S.B., 3-18-1817.
TAYLOR, TARPLAY, Inv., 5-10-1784.
TAYLOR, TARPLAY, Will, 5-11-1784.
Dev.: Silbea, wife; Geo., Wm., John, sons; Nancy, dau.
TAYLOR, TARPLAY, S.B., 12-10-1789.
TAYLOR, TARPLAY, Set., 12-10-1789.
TAYLOR, WM., L.G., 10-12-1782.
TAYLOR, WM., Sur., 3-16-1798.
TAYLOR, WM., L.G., 12-31-1809.
TAYLOR, WM., Inv., 5-15-1815.
TEACHANEEL, MOSES, Sur., 10-1-1788.
THARP, JOHN, Set., 3-19-1831.
THATCHER, SYL. V., Set., 10-29-1808.
THING, ALEX., Sur., 7-28-1795.
THOCKMORTON, CATH., Set., 7-20-1830.

THOCKMORTON, R., L.G., 11-14-1782.
THOCKMORTON, W., Set., 5-19-1828.
THOCKMORTON, W., Set., 12-24-1832.
THOMAS, JOHN, Sur., 7-28-1794.
THOMAS, LAWR., Inv., 5-20-1820.
THOMAS, MOSES, Inv., 1-19-1818.
THOMAS, MOSES, S.B., 3-16-1818.
THOMAS, SAM., Set., 10-23-1833.
THOMPSON, CHAS. & BLUE, JOHN, Sur., 6-1-1824.
THOMPSON, DAVID, Inv., 8-10-1779.
THOMPSON, DAVID, S.B., 8-9-1780.
THOMPSON, DAVID, Divn., 4-14-1791. Dev.: none.
THOMPSON, GEO., L.G., 2-12-1782.
THOMPSON, GEO., Sur., 8-29-1794.
THOMPSON, GEO., Sur., 9-25-1794.
THOMPSON, JER., S.B., 6-18-1817.
THOMPSON, JERMIAH, App., 4-17-1809.
THOMPSON, JOHN, Bond, 4-8-1777.
THOMPSON, JOHN, Sur., 3-5-1789.
THOMPSON, JOHN, S.B., 8-18-1811.
THOMPSON, JOHN, S.B., 6-14-1819.
THOMPSON, JOHN, Set., 8-18-1830.
THOMPSON, JOS., L.G., 7-29-1797.
THOMPSON, JOS., Sur., 2-6-1816.
THOMPSON, MARTHA, Set., 9-15-1828.
THOMPSON, PAT., L.G., 12-22-1787.
THOMPSON, THOM., Set., 4-20-1807.
THOMPSON, WM., S.B., 2-14-1825.
THORN, LAZARUS, Bond, 5-14-1760.
THORN, LAZARUS, Inv., 6-9-1761.
THORN, MARY, Bond, 6-9-1761.
THORN, PETER, Bond, 2-14-1758.
THORN, PETER, Bond, 2-10-1761.
THORN, TOBIAS, Bond, 5-9-1759.
THORN, TOBIAS, Inv., 10-13-1768.
THORNTON, BENJ., App., 2-25-1833.
THORNTON, BENJ., S.B., 1-23-1837.
THORPE, JOHN, Set., 3-14-1831.
THORPE, JOHN, S.B., 3-14-1831.
THORTON, B. B., Will, 1-28-1833. Dev.: Hannah, wife.
THORTON, B. B., S.B., 8-22-1836.
THOUMAZIN, ELZEY, Sur., 9-17-1789.
THROCKMORTON, GABRIAL, and WINTERTON, WM., and ROGERS, ROBT., Sur., 3-12-1798.
THROCKMORTON, WARNER, L.G., 3-8-1816.
THROCKMORTON, WARNER, Set., 9-20-1830.
THROCKMORTON, WARNER, Set., 7-27-1835.
THROCKMORTON, WARNER, S.B., 7-23-1838.
TIDHALL, JAMES, App., 6-27-1832.
TOLTON, SAM., App., 6-27-1836.
TOLTON, SAM., S.B., 6-27-1836.
TORRANCE, JOHN, App., 3-3-1823.
TORRANCE, JOHN, Inv., 4-15-1823.

TORRENCE, JOHN, Set., 11-16-1824.
TOWBRIDGE, JOHN, Will, 11-17-1823.
Dev.: Benj., son; Cath., Mary, Ellen, Eleabeth Nail, dau.; others.
TOWSON, DAVID, Set., 7-9-1780.
TRENTON, WM., App., 9-24-1838.
TRENTON, WM., S.B., 9-24-1838.
TREUET, JOS., Set., 6-22-1833.
TREVET, JAS., Set., 7-22-1833.
TREVETT, JOS., App., 11-26-1832.
TREVETT, JOS., S.B., 11-26-1832.
TROUTTES, RICH., Set., 9-28-1801.
TUCKER, CRASMUS, Set., 2-18-1828.
TUCKER, DAN. & TUCKER, JOHN, Deed, 7-11-1808.
TUCKER, HENRY, Bond, 3-8-1768.
TUCKER, HENRY, S.B., 3-26-1768.
TUCKER, HENRY, Inv., 9-13-1768.
TUCKER, HENRY, S.B., 8-8-1769.
TUCKER, JOHN, Bond, 2-1-1758.
TUCKER, JOS., Inv., 3-17-1817.
TUCKWELL, JOHN, Bond, 6-13-1769.
TUCKWELL, JOHN, Inv., 8-11-1773.
TURNER, DAN., L.G., 11-29-1794.
UMPSTOTT, JACOB, Inv., 2-15-1819.
UMPSTOTT, PETER, Inv., 8-15-1820.
UMPSTOTT, PETER, S.B., 8-15-1820.
URICE, GEO., S.B., 4-23-1835.
URTON, ALFRED, S.B., 3-26-1838.
URTON, ALFRED, Set., 8-26-1839.
URTON, BERSHEBA, Dower, 5-23-1836.
URTON, ELIZ., S.B., 3-26-1838.
URTON, ELIZ., Set., 8-26-1839.
URTON, MARY, S.B., 3-26-1838.
URTON, MARY, Set., 8-26-1839.
URTON, NORMAN, App., 6-23-1834.
URTON, NORMAN, S.B., 7-27-1835.
URTON, NORMAN, S.B., 1-23-1837.
URTON, NORMAN, Set., 2-25-1839.
URTON, SARAH, S.B., 3-26-1838.
URTON, SARAH, Set., 8-26-1839.
URTON, WM., S.B., 3-26-1838.
UTTA, CHRISTIAN, App., 11-25-1834.
UTTA, CHRISTIAN, S.B., 5-25-1835.
UTTA, CHRISTIAN, S.B., 7-24-1837.
VANDERVATER, CORN., Inv., 3-11-1783.
VANDEVANDER, CORN., Set., 10-17-1803.
VANDIVER, ELIZ., Will, 5-15-1815.
Dev.: John, Lewis, Wm., Sam., Jacob, sons; Mary, Eliz., Susanah, Cath., dau. and others.
VANDIVER, JACOB, App., 4-27-1840.
VANDIVER, JACOB, S.B., 5-25-1840.
VANDIVER, JOHN, Set., 3-16-1830.
VANDIVER, JOHN, App., 7-19-1824.
VANDIVER, SAM., Sur., 11-5-1818.
VANDIVER, VINC., L.G., 7-27-1821.
VANDIVER, VINC., L.G., 7-25-1823.
VANDIVER, WM., Inv., 2-17-1806.

VANDIVER, WM., App., 10-28-1833.
VANDIVER, WM., S.B., 5-27-1834.
VANDIVER, WM., Set., 11-23-1835.
VANDIVER, WM., Set., 12-24-1849.
VANDIVER, SAM., Sur., 4-19-1802.
VANHORN, JOHN, App., 5-14-1830.
VANHORN, JOHN, S.B., 6-14-1830.
VANMETER, ABRAM, L.G., 9-4-1821.
VANMETER, ANN, Bond, 9-11-1760.
VANMETER, GAR., Inv., 12-11-1770.
VANMETER, ISAAC, S.B., 2-11-1758.
VANMETER, ISAAC, S.B., 11-15-1759.
VANMETER, WILL, Inv., 8-24-1758.
VARDIN, JAMES, Sur., 3-9-1780.
VAUGHAN, JOHN, Set., 4-28-1834.
VAUGHAN, JOHN, S.B., 5-24-1834.
VAUHION, JOHN, S.B., 6-14-1830.
VAUSE, WM., Inv., 9-16-1790.
VAUSE, WM., S.B., 4-20-1795.
VAUSE, WM., L.G., 1-28-1803.
VINEY, ANDREW, Set., 8-11-1781.
VINEY, ANDREW, App., 8-13-1782.
VINEY, ANDREW, S.B., 11-20-1784.
VONFELT, JACOB, Sur., 7-29-1795.
VOUGHIN, JOHN, Inv., 5-14-1830.
VOWLER, CHAS., Set., 4-15-1805.
VOWLER, HENRY, Sur., 8-1-1783.
WAITT, JAMES, App., 2-14-1831.
WALKER, AND., App., 9-17-1810.
WALKER, ANDREW, Will, 5-14-1810.
Dev.: Robt., father; James, Robt., bro.; Hannah, Jane, Ann, Rebecca, Marg., Sarah, sis.
WALKER, JAMES, Inv., 7-20-1817.
WALKER, JAMES, S.B., 7-20-1817.
WALKER, MARY, L.G., 7-26-1783.
WALLIS, JOHN, Sur., 6-20-1790.
WALLIS, JOHN, Sur., 2-28-1798.
WARD, DAVID, Bond, 8-12-1760.
WARD, DAVID, Inv., 6-9-1761.
WARD, DAVID, S.B., 3-12-1765.
WARD, ISRAEL, Inv., 5-9-1780.
WARD, ISRAEL, Inv., 5-9-1781.
WARD, JESSE, App., 6-26-1837.
WARD, JESSE, S.B., 6-26-1837.
WARD, JOHN, Will, 2-20-1815.
Dev.: Mary, wife; Joel, John, sons; Eliz. Butler, Mary Rinehart, Lydia Rinehart, Hannah Rinehart, Sarah Barret, dau.; others.
WARD, JOHN, Inv., 6-19-1815.
WARD, JOHN, Set., 4-19-1824.
WARD, JOHN, Will, 7-18-1825.
Dev.: Eliz., wife; John, Jesse, Ed., Hester, Joel, sons.
WARDEN, JOHN, S.B., 6-9-1767.
WARDS, JOHN, App., 8-15-1825.
WARNER, ADAM, Bond, 12-13-1757.
WASSON, JAMES, Will, 9-24-1838.
Dev.: Ann, Sally, Isabella, Jean, Hanah, Cath., Martha, Doris, dau.; and others.
WATSON, JOSIAH, Sur., 3-6-1788.

WATTS, THOM., Bond, 12-12-1754.
WATTS, THOM., Inv., 5-8-1759.
WEADLE, PETER, App., 8-19-1811.
WEALTON, JOHN, Inv., 11-11-1772.
WEAVER, ABRAHAM, S.B., 5-27-1834.
WEAVER, ABRAHAM, Set., 6-23-1834.
WEAVER, GEO., Inv., 11-8-1785.
WEBB, FOSTER, L.G., 5-5-1786.
WEDDEL, PETER, S.B., 2-19-1808.
WEDMYER, MICH., L.G., 6-24-1813.
WELCH, DEMCY, Inv., 2-25-1833.
WELCH, DEMECY, Set., 2-23-1835.
WELCH, DEMPSY, S.B., 12-30-1834.
WELCH, SILVESTER, Will, 2-19-1810.
Dev.: Jemima, wife; Demcery, Silvester, Benj., Isaac, sons; Nancy Smith, Luraner, Mary Mott, Eliz. Fleming, dau.; others.
WELCH, SUSAN, Set., 5-25-1835.
WELCH, SYLVISTER, App., 4-16-1810.
WELCH, TAYLOR, S.B., 8-29-1810.
WELTON, JACOB, Bond, 2-11-1777.
WELTON, JACOB, Inv., 11-18-1818.
WELTON, JERMOAH, App., 7-27-1840.
WELTON, JOB, Set., 4-23-1832.
WELTON, JOB, Set., 8-28-1832.
WELTON, JOHN, Bond, 6-9-1767.
WELTON, JOHN, S.B., 8-11-1778.
WELTON, JOHN, S.B., 7-19-1819.
WELTON, NOAH, Will, 5-9-1779.
Dev.: Alse, wife; Andrew, son; Martha, Ann, dau.
WELTON, SOL., Inv., 6-11-1789.
WELTON, SOL., S.B., 9-15-1791.
WESCH, ISAAC, App., 10-23-1837.
WEST, JACOB, Bond, 2-31-1759.
WESTFALL, ABEL, S.B., 11-15-1759.
WESTFALL, ABRAM, Inv., 2-14-1758.
WESTFALL, CORN., Divn., 11-12-1783.
Dev.: Wife.
WESTFALL, CORN., Inv., 8-11-1784.
WESTFALL, CORN., Set., 2-14-1788.
WESTFALL, JOHN, Bond, 12-13-1757.
WESTMILLER, JACOB, Inv., 3-9-1784.
WHEELER, IGNATIUS, Bond, 3-14-1794.
WHITE, FRANCIS, Set., 3-16-1829.
WHITE, FRANCIS, S.B., 3-15-1830.
WHITE, FRANCIS, Set., 7-27-1835.
WHITEMAN, MARY, Inv., 9-30-1823.
WICKHAM, LEVI, L.G., 8-25-1821.
WIDMER, MICH., L.G., 1-19-1807.
WIGGINS, THOM., Inv., 8-11-1778.
WILCH, SUSAN, S.B., 4-13-1835.
WILEY, ELIZ., App., 12-24-1849.
WILEYS, BENJ., Will, 8-28-1833.
Dev.: Betsey Bevers, dau.; and others.
WILKINS, JOHN, Set., 11-19-1810.
WILL, BENJ., Inv., 8-8-1775.
WILLETT, BENJ., Bond, 8-9-1774.
WILLIAMS, CATH., Bond, 6-9-1761.

WILLIAMS, DAVID, Sur., 9-26-1788.
WILLIAMS, ED., Bond, 9-18-1761.
WILLIAMS, ED., Inv., 8-10-1762.
WILLIAMS, ED., Inv., 10-15-1789.
WILLIAMS, JOHN, Inv., 11-13-1759.
WILLIAMS, MECRAKIN, Will, 5-14-1782.
Dev.: Sarah, wife; Virgil, Isaac, Seneca, Wm., Cyras, Ovid, sons; Jane Flint, Sarah Lanclaster, dau.
WILLIAMS, REMEMBERANCE, Inv., 3-9-1763.
WILLIAMS, RICH., App., 2-13-1787.
WILLIAMS, RICH., Will, 6-12-1788.
Dev.: Father; Bro.; Sis.
WILLIAMS, RICH., Inv., 12-10-1789.
WILLIAMS, RICH., S.B., 6-20-1796.
WILLIAMS, ROBT., L.G., 9-8-1804.
WILLIAMS, ROBT., App., 4-25-1836.
WILLIAMS, SAM., Inv., 11-15-1830.
WILLIAMS, THOM., Sur., 11-10-1794.
WILLIAMS, THOM., S.B., 8-11-1820.
WILLIAMS, THOM., S.B., 2-14-1825.
WILLIAMS, THOM., Set., 3-15-1825.
WILLIAMS, VINC., Bond, 2-1-1759.
WILLIAMS, VINC., Inv., 12-12-1768.
WILLIAMS, VINC., S.B., 3-12-1772.
WILLIAMS, WM., Bond, 2-11-1761.
WILLIAMS, WILL, Inv., 5-11-1763.
WILLIAMSON, JOHN, Sur., 5-7-1821.
WILLIAMSON, SAM., App., 8-17-1829.
WILLIAMSON, SAM., Set., 6-25-1832.
WILLIAMSON, THOM., L.G., 5-7-1791.
WILLIAMSON, THOM., Sur., 5-9-1791.
WILLSSONSON, ED., Inv., 10-12-1763.
WILSON, DAN., Inv., 8-11-1772.
WILSON, NATH., Inv., 6-20-1819.
WILSON, ROBT., Set., 11-26-1849.
WILSON, ZEDAKIAH, S.B., 3-28-1833.
WILSON, ZEDIKAH, App., 7-23-1832.
WILTON, JOHN, Inv., 8-18-1807.
WINTER, WM., Sur., 3-12-1798.
WINTERTON, JOHN, App., 3-18-1822.
WINTERTON, JOHN, Inv., 3-18-1822.
WINTERTON, WM., S.B., 12-17-1831.
WIRTMILLER, JACOB, Inv., 3-9-1784.
WISE, ABRAHAM, Inv., 11-15-1780.
WISE, ABRAM, Bond, 3-10-1773.
WISE, GEO., S.B., 7-23-1835.
WISE, GEORGE, App., 11-25-1833.
WISE, JOS., Bond, 2-4-1761.
WOLFORD, JOHN, Sur., 3-20-1811.
WOLFORD, JOHN, Will, 11-26-1849.
Dev.: Henry, Adam, Jacob, John, sons; Eliz., Phebe, Ann, Rosanna, Isabella, Susanna, dau.
WOLVERTON, JOEL, Inv., 4-17-1815.
WOLVERTON, JOEL, Set., 6-15-1822.
WOLVERTON, JOE, S.B., 6-22-1822.
WOLVERTON, SALE., S.B., 6-17-1822.
WOOD, JAMES, Bond, 9-17-1798.
WOOD, JOHN, Bond, 2-14-1758.

WOOD, JOHN, Inv., 12-13-1758.
WOODROW, AND., L.G., 4-26-1791.
WOODROW, AND., Sur., 8-17-1791.
WOODROW, ANDREW, Will, 8-15-1814.
Dev.: Mary, wife; Andrew, Wm.,
sons; Emiley, Eliz., Matilda, dau.;
others.
WOODROW, ANDREW, Set., 6-20-1828.
WOODROW, EMILY J., Set., 1-19-1825.
WOODSON, JOHN, Bond, 8-11-1767.
WORDEN, JOHN, Inv., 8-13-1765.
WORK, ASRON, Inv., 2-28-1789.
WREN, JAMES, App., 3-19-1830.
WREN, JOHN, Will, 8-19-1830.
Dev.: Wm., son; others.
WRICE, GEO., JOHN, PETER, Sur.,
3-23-1818.
WRICE, GEO., Set., 5-25-1835.
WRIGHT, HEZ., Inv., 2-11-1761.
WRIGHT, JOHN, L.G., 2-11-1817.
WRIGHT, SARAH, Bond, 3-11-1760.
YONKUM, JACOB, Inv., 3-13-1781.

YONKUM, JACOB, Inv., 5-8-1781.
YONLEY, JANE, S.B., 9-24-1838.
YONLEY, LOUSEA, S.B., 9-24-1838.
YONLEY, SAM., S.B., 9-24-1838.
YONLEY, THOM., App., 11-26-1833.
YONLEY, THOM., S.B., 5-26-1834.
YONLEY, THOM., S.B., 1-26-1835.
YOOKUM, JOCHOB, Will, 11-14-1780.
Dev.: Eliz., wife; Mich., Geo.,
Jacob, Sol., Mathias, Isaac, sons;
Eliz., Millia, dau.
YOUNEY, THOM., S.B., 5-26-1834.
YOUNEY, THOM., Set., 2-23-1835.
YOUNG, HUGH, L.G., 8-2-1781.
YOUNG, ROBT., Inv., 5-16-1825.
YOUNG, ROBT., S.B., 5-16-1825.
ZIMMERMAN, JACOB, App., 10-28-
1839.
ZIMMERMAN, JACOB, S.B., 10-28-
1839.
ZIMMERMAN, JACOB, Set., 11-25-
1839.

West Virginia Estate Settlements

In 1936 and 1937, the West Virginia Commission on Historic and Scenic Markers, the Works Progress Administration, and the Federal Emergency Relief Administration compiled court records of the various counties, such as Births, Deaths, Marriages and Wills. Under Wills were grouped subjects pertaining to Estate Settlements, including Wills, Inventories and Appraisements. Copies of these county records were filed at the Department of Archives and History, Charleston, the Library of West Virginia University, Morgantown, and the DAR Library, Washington.

Believing that there would be particular interest on the part of the general public in the Estate Settlements in the older counties, the West Virginia Historical Society has undertaken to abstract the Estate Settlement Records, as filed in the State Department of Archives and History, and offered them for publication in the *West Virginia History Quarterly*. (No responsibility can be assumed as to the accuracy of the copies made from the original county records.)

There are 13 counties which were formed prior to 1800, and it has been agreed to arrange these counties in chronological order, and to print their records from the earliest date to 1850. The formation dates of these counties are as follows: Hampshire—1753; Berkeley—1772; Monongalia—1776; Ohio—1776; Greenbrier—1778; Harrison—1784; Hardy—1786; Randolph—1787; Pendleton—1788; Kanawha—1788; Brooks—1797; Wood—1798 and Monroe—1799.

Berkeley County, Formed 1772

(1772-1815)

Abbreviations used in this material include: Adm.—administrator; Agr.—agreement; App.—appraisement; Bro.—brother; Dau.—daughter; Dev.—devisees; Divn.—division; Est.—estate a/c; Ind.—indenture; Inv.—inventory; L. G.—land grant; Obl.—obligation; S. B.—sale bill; Set.—settlement; Sis.—sister; and Sur.—Survey.

ABRELL, JOHN, Will, 6-16-1772.
(Frederick Co.) Dev.: John, Jacob,
sons; Mary Reagan, Eliz. Lindsey,
Sarah Lindsey, Lidy, Hannah. dau.;
Eliz., wife.

ABRELL, JOHN, App., 8-18-1772.

ABRIEL, JAMES, App., 2-23-1795.

ABRIL, JAMES, Will, 9-21-1790.
Dev.: Eliz., wife; John, James. Joseph, Jacob, sons.

AIRISS, JOHN, Will, 4-21-1800.
Dev.: Eliz., wife; others.

AIRISS, JOHN, App., 12-27-1802.

ALEXANDER, WM., Inv., 3-14-1814.

ALLER FRED., Will, 12-16-1788.
Dev.: Mary, dau.; Fred., son.

ALLER, FRED., App., 4-24-1789.

ALLISON, MATHEW, Will, 5-19-1772.
(Frederick Co.) Dev.: Fanny, wife;
children.

ALLISON, MATT., Est., 10-16-1782.

ALSOP, JOHN O.B.. Will, 7-27-1801.
Dev.: Mary, John, Susannah, Caroline McKnight, Esther and Mary
Burr.

AMBROUSE, HENRY, Inv., 5-12-1812.

AMBROUSE, HENRY, Sale, 5-12-1812.

ANDERSON, JAS., Inv., 6-13-1814.

ANDERSON, JAS., Sale, 6-13-1814.

ANDERSON, COL., Est., 10-27-1806.

ANDERSON, COL. COLB., Will, 2-25-1805.
Dev.: Nancy, wife; Colbert, Wm.,
Providence, James, Thom., sons;
Rebecca, Elinor, Mary, Nancy, dau.

ANDERSON, COLBERT, Est., 2-19-1811.

ANDREWS, DAVID, App., 11-20-1781.

ANDREWS, DAVID, Est., 3-22-1783.

ANGEL, MICHAEL, Will, 9-17-1794.
Dev.: Priscilla, wife; John, son.

ARISS, THOMAS, App., 9-21-1779.

ARMSTRONG, ALEX., Will, 9-24-1784.
Dev.: Susannah Johnson and children.

ARMSTRONG, E., Est., 6-22-1807.

ARMSTRONG, ELIZ., Inv., 2-24-1806.

AUTER, JAMES, App., 7-24-1797.

AUTON, JAMES, Est., 4-21-1800.

AX, WM., App., 2-19-1782.

AX, WM., Sale, 2-19-1782.

BABCOCK, WM., App., 9-18-1787.

BADINGER, MAGDALANE, Will, 1-23-1797.
Dev.: Jacob, Solomon, and all other
children.

BAILIFF, DANIEL, App., 8-19-1777.

BAILIFF, DAN., Est., 4-23-1784.

BAKER, JOHN, Will, 6-26-1798.
Dev.: John, son; Ann, Ary, Sucka,
Polly, Pegalie, Elsie, Juliet, dau.

BAKER, JOHN, Est., 2-27-1809.

BAKER, WALTER, Will, 10-17-1786.
Dev.: Eliz., wife; Walter, Carlin,
sons; Eliz., Harriett, dau.

BAKER, WALT., ESQ., App., 12-18-1787.

BALDWIN, WM., Will, 10-18-1785.
Dev.: Jean, wife; Wm., Benj., Joseph,
Jonah, Joshua, James, sons; Mary
Foster, Rebecca, dau.

BALDWIN, WM., Est., 7-26-1802.

BANNER, JOHN, Will, 6-17-1783.
Dev.: Mary, wife; John, son; dau.

BARGES, PETER, Will, 6-15-1790.
Dev.: Barb., wife; John, Jacob, Peter,
sons.

BARNHOUSE, RICH., Inv., 12-23-1805.

BARNISER, CATH., Will, 4-17-1781.
Dev.: John Frink, step-father.

BARNS, JAMES, App., 3-18-1783.

BARNS, STEPHEN, Will, 11-18-1784.
Dev.: Martha, wife; Stephen, Geo.,
sons, Eliz., dau.

BARTLETT, WM., Will, 11-18-1777.
Dev.: Mary, wife; Harry, John, James,
Fred., sons; Eliz., Nancy, dau.

BARTLETT, WM., Est., 2-22-1792.

BATT, THOM., Inv., 2-28-1797.

BAYLEY, TARPLEY, App., 10-22-1798.

BEATTY, ELIZ., App., 1-23-1809.

BEATTY, WM., App., 4-22-1799.

BEATY, WM., Est., 12-23-1799.

BEDINGER, PETER, App., 7-27-1801.

BEIDLER, JACOB, App., 6-19-1787.

BELLER, JACOB JR., Will, 4-27-1801.
Dev.: Ann, wife; Jacob, Eli, Peter,
Isaac, sons; Lydia, Naomi Sagatha,
Mary Neal, Leah Marlatt, Eliz. Shaw,
Rachel Harper, dau.; others.

BELLER, JACOB, Inv., 12-21-1801.

BENNETT, GEO., App., 12-20-1785.

BENNETT, GEO., Est., 6-20-1786.

BERGER, PETER, Est., 6-26-1797.

BESHEARS, ZEPHRIAH, Will, 6-25-1798.
Dev.: Mary, Martha Kean, Agnes
Prather, sis.; Wm., Rezen, bro.; Ed.,
slave; others.

BESORE, BARNEY, Will, 4-21-1800.
Dev.: Cath., wife; Geo., John, Peter,
Mich., sons; Mary, Mary Shively,
Cath., Marg., dau.; others.

BIDLER, JACOB, Est., 9-26-1797.

BILLINGSLY, CHAS., Will, 1-15-1810.
Dev.: James, Moses, Thom., John,
Robt., sons; Eliz. Steel, Prudence
Hanan, dau.; Rachael, wife.

BILLINGSLY, CHAS., Inv., 2-19-1811.

BILLUPS, JOHN, Will, 3-20-1781.
(Caroline Co.)
Dev.: Frances, wife; Clary, John,
sons; Eliz. Burdeck, Molly Burdeck,
Nancy, dau.

BINGAMAN, HENRY, Est., 8-20-1783.

BINGERMAN, HENRY, Will, 5-18-1779.
Dev.: Cath., wife; John, son.

BISHOP, GREENBERRY, Inv., 6-12-1815.

BLACKFORD, BENJ., App., 8-17-1784.

BLACKFORD, BENJ., Sale, 8-17-1784.

BLACKFORD, EB., Est., 4-22-1799.

BLACKFORD, EBENEZER, Inv., 2-22-1796.

BLACKMORE, JAS., App., 12-21-1790.
BLACKMORE, JAS., Est., 10-21-1794.
BLACKMORE, LAWRENCE, App., 1-20-1795.
BLACKMORE, LAWRENCE, Est., 6-24-1799.
BLUE, CATH., App., 4-27-1801.
BLUE, JOHN, App., 9-24-1798.
BLUE, URIAH, Est., 6-27-1796.
BOAKE, JOHN, App., 3-13-1815.
BOGGS, JAMES, Sale, 7-22-1805.
BOGGS, WM., Will, 2-15-1791.
Dev.: Wm., John, sons; Eliz., Mary, Jane, dau.
BOGGS, WM., Inv., 4-16-1791.
BOLEY, BENJ., App., 6-22-1801.
BOLEY, SIMON, Will, 3-21-1786.
Dev.: Mary, wife; Benj., Wamput Connor, Delborah Patterson, sons; Sereham Shoemaker, Mary Kilecoke, dau.
BOLEY, SIMON, App., 9-19-1786.
BORKERT, MARTIN, Will, 9-15-1789.
Dev.: Cath., wife.
BOSWELL, WALTER, Will, 8-18-1778.
Dev.: Eliz., wife.
BOSWELL, WALTER, App., 3-16-1779.
BOWERS, GEO., SR., Will, 6-18-1810.
Dev.: Marg., wife; John, Jacob, Henry, Geo., sons; Cath. Burke (and her heirs), Mary, dau.
BOWERS, GEO., Inv., 1-22-1811.
BOWERS, HENRY, App., 9-16-1788.
BOWLAND, MICH., Est., 6-15-1790.
BOWMAN, AND., Inv., 7-25-1803.
BOWMAN, AND., Est., 2-19-1811.
BOYD, JOHN, SR., Will, 6-23-1800.
Dev.: Sarah, wife; Chas., John, Wm., Elijah, Elisha, sons; others.
BOYD, JOHN, SR., Est., 1-15-1810.
BOYD, SARAH, Will, 1-20-1807.
Dev.: Chas., Elisha, John, sons; Marg. Sutton, Rachel Bayly, dau.; others.
BOYD, SARAH, Est., 1-15-1810.
BOYD, THOM., Inv., 1-13-1791.
BOYD, WM., Will, 5-20-1777.
(Frederick Co.)
Dev.: Jean, wife; Wm., John, sons; Jean Marsh, Hannah Miller, Anna, dau.; Sambo, slave.
BOYD, WM., Est., 12-16-1783.
BOYLE, HENRY, Est., 1-21-1811.
BOYLES, HENRY, App., 6-22-1795.
BRABSON, JOHN, Will, 9-18-1782.
Dev.: Mary, wife; John, Thom., Ephriam, Robt., sons; Eliz., Margaret, dau.; and other children.
BRABSON, JOHN, App., 5-20-1783.
BRASHEARS, ZEPH., App., 12-24-1798.
BRASHEARS, ZEPH., Est., 7-21-1806.
BRISCOE, JAMES, Will, 3-16-1779.
Dev.: Eliz. and Sam., Davis.
BRISCOE, JOHN, Will, 1-20-1789.
Dev.: Ann, wife; Hezekiah, Parmen, John, sons; Sarah Slaughter, Eliz. Baker, Frances Davis, dau.; others.

BRISCOE, DR. JOHN, Inv., 12-20-1791.
BRISCOE, JOHN, Est., 10-12-1812.
BROOKS, SAM., Will, 2-16-1790.
Dev.: Mary, wife.
BROOKS, SAM., Inv., 4-20-1790.
BROOKS, WM., Will, 10-21-1799.
Dev.: James, slave; Dan., bro.; others.
BROOKS, WM., Est., 11-14-1814.
BROUSE, AND., Will, 5-13-1811.
Dev.: Eliz., wife; Adam, John, Fred., Lewis, Mich., sons; Ann, Rebecka, Sarah, Eliz., Mary, Rachal, dau.
BROUSE, JOHN A., Inv., 6-10-1811.
BROWN, ARCHIBALD, App., 3-21-1775.
BROWN, JAMES, Will, 5-21-1776.
Dev.: Ann, wife; Sucky, dau., Joseph, son; other children.
BROWN, JAMES, App., 5-20-1777.
BROWN, JOHN, Will, 9-25-1797.
Dev.: Eliz., wife; Alex., John, David, Joseph, Sam., sons.
BROWN, WM., Will, 9-21-1801.
(Shepherdstown).
Dev.: John, Parry Wash., Shepherd, sons; Eliz., Mary, Sarah, Hannah Matilda, dau.; others.
BUCKELS, JAS., Est., 3-13-1815.
BUCKLES, ABR., Sale, 9-21-1779.
BUCKLES, JAMES, Will, 1-23-1797.
Dev.: Sarah, wife; John, James, Robt., Wm., Abraham, sons; Ann Seamour, Mehitable, Mary, Abigail, Marg., Janes, dau.
BUCKLES, MARY, Will, 6-17-1777.
Dev.: Ann, dau.; John, Robt., Abraham, sons.
BUCKLES, ROBT., Will, 12-21-1790.
Dev.: James, Robt., sons; others.
BUCKLES, ROBT., Est., 9-26-1797.
BULL, ROBT., Will, 9-21-1807.
Dev.: Sarah, wife; Nathan, Jonah, sons; Sarah Merchant, Lydia Brown, dau.; others.
BULL, ROBT., Inv., 4-26-1808.
BUNN, BENJ., Adm., 2-18-1811.
BURGHILL, WM., Est., 6-25-1798.
BURGHILL, WM., App., 6-25-1798.
BURK, JAMES, Inv., 6-19-1809.
BURK, JAMES, Adm., 6-10-1811.
BURK, LUKE, App., 12-26-1796.
BURNER, GASPER, App., 8-17-1779.
BURNER, WM. SR., Will, 1-20-1807.
Dev.: Rebecca, dau.; Geo., Wm., Robt., John, sons; Robt., bro.; others.
BURNER, WM. SR., Est., 8-10-1812.
BURNS, BENJ., App., 6-22-1795.
BURNS, WM., SR., Est., 12-18-1810.
BURR, PETER, Will, 2-23-1795.
Dev.: Peter, James, Moses, William, sons; Mary, Abigal, Sarah, Marian, Jane, Anna, Elizabeth, Hannah, Hester, dau.
BURR, PETER, App., 10-26-1795.
BUTLER, JOHN, Will, 2-27-1809.
Dev.: Deborah, wife; Sam., Doug., sons; Rebecca Fryatt, dau.; others.

BUTLER, JOHN, App., 3-27-1809.
BUTLER, PEARCE, App., 10-17-1786.
BUTLER, SAM., Will, 6-26-1798.
Dev.: John, Wm., bro.; others.
BUTT, ARCH., Est., 6-12-1815.
BUTT, JOSEPH, Will, 4-16-1793.
Dev.: Eliz., wife; Israel, son; infant.
BUTT, JOS., Est., 9-22-1800.
BUTT, RICH., Will, 6-64-1799.
Dev.: Sarah, wife; Isaac, Arch., Rich., sons; Ruth, Susanna, Dinah, Darke, Mary, dau.
BUTT, RICH., Est., 2-21-1803.
BUTT, RICH., Will, 6-18-1810.
Dev.: Mary, wife; others.
BUTT, RICH., Inv., 6-10-1811.
BUTT, RICH., Will, 4-13-1812.
Dev.: Deliah, wife; Sarah, dau.; others.
BUTT, RICH., Est., 3-13-1815.
BUTT, ROBT., Inv., 12-23-1805.
BYERLY, MICH., Will, 10-22-1788.
Dev.: Iva, wife; Ludwick, Mich., sons.
CALDWELL, ANDREW, Will, 1-13-1791.
Dev.: Sarah, wife; mother, others.
CALDWELL, AND., App., 9-20-1791.
CAMPBELL, DEGALL, Will, 5-19-1772.
(Frederick Co.)
Dev.: Andrew, Robt., sons; Francis, Mary, dau.; heirs of Robt. and Andrew; wife.
CAMPBELL, DUGALL, App., 6-16-1772.
CAMPBELL, FRANCES, Will, 6-13-1773.
Dev.: Andrew, Robt., sons; Frances, Mary Andrews, dau.; others.
CAMPBELL, FRANCES, App., 6-18-1773
CAMPBELL, FRANCES, Will, 6-8-1812.
Dev.: Numerous bequests.
CAMPBELL, FRANCES, Inv., 8-10-1812.
CAMPBELL, JACOB, App., 9-21-1807.
CAMPBELL, JAS. W., App., 6-8-1812.
CAMPBELL, JOHN, Will, 10-18-1791.
Dev.: Mother; Patrick, Andrew, bro.
CAMPBELL, ROBT., Will, 9-25-1797.
Dev.; Andrew, bro.; Mary Andrews, Frances, sis.; Robt., Wm., Findley, Davis, Sam., Barton, sons.
CAMPBELL, ROBT., App., 4-27-1801.
CARBY, JOHN, Will, 9-20-1791.
Dev.: Jane, wife; Eliz., Rebecca, Sarah, Phoebe, Jane, Mary, dau.; Jesse, son.
CARBY, JOHN, App., 5-15-1792.
CARNEY, ELIZ., Will, 9-23-1799.
(OR KERNEY)
Dev.: Eliz. White, Susanna Kerney, Mary Hedges, dau.; James, husband; Wm., James, Robert Tabb, Wm. Tabb, Thomas Tabb, sons; others.
CARNEY, JOHN, Will, 4-18-1775.
Dev.: Susanna Branah, John Carney, Thomas Carney; Moses, slave; and children.
CARNEY, JOHN, Est., 1-17-1786.
CARR, JAMES, App., 9-21-1807.
CARR, JAS., Est., 6-19-1810.

CARRINGER, BARB., Will, 4-11-1814.
Dev.: Mary Kulp, dau.; all other children.
CARRINGER, BARB., Est., 8-14-1815.
CARROLL, COLLIN, Inv., 3-9-1812.
CHAMBERLAIN, JONAS, Inv., 1-22-1798.
CHAMPION, JOS., Will, 4-21-1778.
Dev.: Rosanna, wife; Thom., John, bro.; others.
CHAMPION, JOSEPH, Est., 4-15-1783.
CHENOWITH, ABS., Est., 5-18-1779.
CHENOWITH, ABSOLAM, Will, 6-15-1773.
Dev.: Ruth, wife; and others.
CHENOWITH, ISAAC, Est., 1-20-1801.
CHENOWITH, JOS., Will, 10-18-1785.
Dev.: Sarah, wife; Joseph, son; Newly, dau.
CHENOWITH, JOS., App., 2-19-1788.
CHENOWITH, WM., Will, 12-20-1785.
Dev.: Anna, wife; Absolam, Wm., Isaac, sons; Mary, Anne, Hannah, dau.; others.
CHENOWITH, WM., Est., 9-16-1794.
CHEW, JAMES, Est., 1-27-1803.
CHRISTY, ADAM, Will, no date.
Dev.: Wm., And., Sam., Ebenezer, bro.; Sarah Pattan, sis.
CHRISTY, SAM., App., 10-16-1809.
CLARK, ELIZ., Will, 8-18-1772.
(Frederick Co.)
Dev.: Eliz. Owens, Sarah Night, dau.; and others.
CLARKE, WALTER, Est., 12-17-1793.
CLAWSON, JOHN, Will, 11-16-1814.
(Jefferson Co.)
Dev.: Massey, wife; Isaac, Israel, Jacob, Wm., John, sons; Rachel Dunn, Anne Quick, Experience Dunn; dau.; others.
CLAWSON, JOHN, App., 4-12-1815.
CLAWSON, RICH., Will, 11-20-1776.
Dev.: Rachel, wife; Thom., Cataline, sons.
CLISE, JACOB, App., 2-25-1805.
CLISE, JACOB, Sale, 2-23-1807.
COFFINBERGER, GEO., Will, 3-8-1813.
Dev.: Fanny, wife; Mary Newman, Eliz. Custus, Nancy Seybert, Fanny Stipp, Sarah McCasland, Cath. Young, dau.; Jacob, Geo., sons.
COFFINBERGER, GEO., App., 5-1-1813.
COFFMAN, JACOB, App., 2-20-1787.
COFFMAN, JACOB, Est., 4-21-1789.
COFFMAN, JOHN, App., 5-15-1781.
COLE, JACOB, Will, 2-19-1788.
Dev.: Barbary, wife; Marg., Barbary, dau.
COLE, JACOB, App., 4-15-1788.
COLLET, MOSES, Will, 11-19-1782.
Dev.: Eliz., wife; Stephen, Dan., John, Isaac, Aaron, sons; Rachel Spenks, Eliz., Sarah, dau.
COLLET, MOSES, App., 3-19-1783.
COLVIN, THOM., Inv., 6-13-1814.
COMEGYS, JACOB, Inv., 1-27-1806.

COMEGYS, JACOB, Est., 6-19-1810.
CONCLIN, JOHN, Will, 6-23-1800.
Dev.: Abigail, wife; John, son; others.
CONN, JAMES, App., 2-25-1799.
CONNALLY, JENKINS, App., 10-17-1786.
CONNALLY, JENKINS, Est., 4-19-1791
CONOLLY, LAWR., Inv., 2-21-1803.
COOK, GILES, Will, 6-24-1799.
Dev.: Marg., wife.
COOKUS, HENRY, App., 9-19-1786.
COOKUS, HENRY, Will, 6-20-1789.
(Mechlenburg)
Dev.: Cath., wife; Henry, Jacob, sons; Cath., Mary, dau.
COON, ADAM, Inv., 4-20-1790.
COON, ADAM, App., 9-25-1797.
COONTZ, HENRY, Will, 2-21-1787.
Dev.: Cath., wife; Eliz., dau.; and all children.
COOPER, ADAM, App., 5-19-1778.
COOPER, HAZALET, Will, 12-16-1794.
Dev.: Ann, wife; others.
COOPER, ISAAC, App., 1-25-1799.
COPENHAVER, MICH., Will, 10-18-1785.
Dev.: Anne, wife; Henry, son; Eve. Cath., Mary, Eliz., dau.
COPENHAVER, MICH., Est., 2-22-1792.
COUCHMAN, BENDEDICT, Est., 12-22-1801.
COUCHMAN, BENEDICK, App., 9-25-1797.
COUCHMAN, CATH., Inv., 4-26-1802.
COUCHMAN, CATH., Est., 12-21-1807.
COUGLE, JOHN, App., 3-19-1782.
COWAN, THOM., App., 9-20-1780.
COWAN, THOM., Est., 12-20-1785.
COWENHOVER, JOHN, App., 5-19-1778.
COWENOVER, JOHN, Will, 3-17-1778.
Dev.: Lydia, wife; Joseph, Dan., John, sons; Ann, Ruth, Betsy, Polly, dau.
COWN, JAMES, Will, 6-26-1798.
Dev.: Wm. Young, Isaac, Rich., James, Raphel, sons; Elinor Wilson, Ruth, Molly, Sary Deavall, dau.; Ruth, wife.
CRAGG, JONATHAN, Inv., 10-26-1802.
CRAGHILL, JOHN, Will, 9-9-1811.
Dev.: Wife; Slaves freed; numerous other bequests.
CRANE, JAMES, App., 9-17-1793.
CRANE, JAMES, Will, 12-21-1795.
Dev.: Lucy, wife; John, Jos., sons.
CREAMER, JOHN, App., 9-12-1814.
CREAMER, JOHN, Sale, 9-12-1814.
CREIGHTON, JOHN, Est., 3-20-1782.
CREIGHTON, ROBT., Will, 9-25-1797.
Dev.: Susannah, wife; Wm., son; Mary, Isabella Lyle, Agnes Park, Dianna, dau.; Ede, Robin, James, slaves; others.
CREIGHTON, ROBT., Est., 2-28-1799.
CROOK, JACOB, Inv., 10-21-1805.
CROOK, JACOB, Est., 9-26-1808.

CROTHERS, JOHN, Inv., 7-21-1806.
CROTHERS, JOHN, Est., 2-10-1812.
CROW, JOHN, Will, 8-15-1775.
Dev.: Mary, wife; Thomas, son; Esther Grace, Mary Hall, Eliz. Britian, dau.; others.
CROW, JOHN, App., 10-17-1775.
CROWL, HENRY, Inv., 5-13-1811.
CRUMLEY, ADAM, App., 8-21-1781.
CRUMLEY, JOHN, Sale, 12-12-1814.
CRUMLEY, WM., Will, 9-17-1793.
Dev.: Sarah, wife; James, Wm., Catrow, Aaron, Thom., Henry, Stephen, John, sons; Ann, Jane, Sarah, Nany, Eliz., Martha, Rebecca, dau.
CRUMLEY, WM., Est., 12-23-1799.
CUKUS, HENRY, App., 8-19-1777.
CUNNINGHAM, GEO. W., Est., 12-15-1789.
CUNNINGHAM, GEO., Will, 10-14-1811.
Dev.: Ruth, wife; Geo. Geddis, Levi, sons; Lydia, Rhoda Brown, dau.; others.
CUNNINGHAM, GEO., Sale, 8-10-1812.
CUNNINGHAM, JAMES, Will, 3-17-1773.
Dev.: Rebecca, wife; Wm., Geo., Robt., bro.
CUNNINGHAM, JAMES, Est., 11-18-1783.
CUNNINGHAM, ROBT., Will, 5-17-1785.
Dev.: Wm., Slaughter, stepfather; Wm., bro.; mother.
CUNNINGHAM, RUTH, Sale, 8-16-1815.
CUNNINGHAM, RUTH, Inv., 11-14-1815.
CUNNINGHAM, WM., Will, 9-19-1786.
Dev.: Ann Slaughter, mother; Eliz. Holliday, Eleanor Davidson, sis.; others.
CUNNINGHAM, WM., App., 2-20-1787.
CURTIS, JOB, Will, 4-24-1804.
Dev.: Ann Morgan, Rachel Ellis, Rebecca Burris, Martha Dermoss, Sarah, Cath., dau.; Thom., Jonathan, James, Job, Ed., Josh., Seth, David, sons; Mary, wife.
CURTIS, JOB, Est., 2-24-1806.
DALRYMPLE, JOHN, Will, 3-18-1777.
Dev.: Mary Ward, dau.; John and Frances Thustin.
DALRYMPLE, JOHN, App., 5-20-1777.
DAMINE, JOHN, Inv., 4-17-1793.
DANDRIDGE, ALEX. S., Will, 5-17-1785.
Dev.: Anne, wife.
DANDRIDGE, ALEX. S., App., 11-15-1785.
DANIEL, ELIZ., Will, 9-26-1796.
Dev.: Wm. Pendleton.
DANIEL, JOHN, App., 10-27-1800.
DANIEL, JOHN, Est., 4-22-1806.
DAVENPORT, ABRAHAM, Will, 10-20-1789.
Dev.: Mary, wife; Rachel, slave; Stephen, Abraham, Anthony Simm, John, Adrian, Sam., sons; Eliz. Connell, Mary Long (and children), Cath. Orrick, dau.

DAVIS, DAN., App., 4-16-1782.

DAVIS, DAN., JR., Est., 9-18-1783.

DAVIS, DAN., Will, 12-24-1804.
Dev.: Cath., wife; Lewis, son; other.

DAVIS, DAN., Est., 7-27-1807.

DAVIS, JACOB, Will, 11-21-1780.
Dev.: Israel, bro.; Mary Watkins, servant girl; others.

DAVIS, JOHN, Will, 6-27-1796.
Dev.: Eliz., wife; James, Jos., sons; Sarah, Ruth, Drusilla, Mary, dau.

DAVIS, JOHN, App., 12-26-1796.

DAVIS, JOSEPH, Will, 4-22-1799.
Dev.: Sarah Gilliand, Ruth, Mary. Drusilla Grove, Eliz. Gilliland, Anna, sis.; James, John, Jacob, bro.

DAVIS, JOSEPH, App., 10-23-1799.

DAVIS, WM., Will, 11-17-1772.
(Frederick Co.)
Dev.: Wm., Sam., sons; Margaret Sheeley, dau.

DAVIS, WM., App., 6-17-1777.

DAWSON, FRED., Inv., 1-22-1798.

DELL, PETER, SR., Inv., 6-23-1806.

DELL, PETER, SR., Est., 6-23-1806.

DEMOSS, CHAS., Will, 9-19-1786.
Dev.: Rebecca, wife; Peter, Ichance, Andrew, Throckmorton, Chas., Wm., Thom., Lewis, sons; Susannah, Sarah, Cath., dau.

DEMOSS, CHAS., Est., 7-23-1798.

DEMOSS, CHAS., JR., Est., 6-27-1803

DEMOSS, REBECCA, Will, 12-20-1791.
Dev.: Wm., Thom., Throckmorton, sons; Sarah, Cath., dau.

DEMOSS, REBECCA, Est., 7-23-1798.

DERMOSS, THOM., App., 2-25-1800.

DERMOSS, THOM., Est., 6-27-1803.

DEVENPORT, MARMADUKE, App., 4-21-1778.

DICK, HANNAH, App., 3-16-1774.

DIXON, THOM., App., 9-15-1778.

DOWLAN, THOM., Will, 12-26-1808.
Dev.: John, Chris., sons; Rachel, wife.

DOWLAN, THOM., App., 2-27-1809.

DOWNEY, RICH., App., 6-19-1787.

DOWNEY, RICH., Est., 9-23-1799.

DREW, WM., Will, 2-20-1785.
Dev.: Hannah, wife; Benj., son.

DREW, WM., Est., 9-27-1796.

DRUGGETT, ISAAC, App., 8-20-1782.

DRUGGETT, ISAAC, Est., 6-20-1786.

DUFFEY, BARNEY, Inv., 2-25-1805.

DUFFEY, BARNEY, Sale, 2-25-1805.

DUKE, JOHN, SR., Will, 6-16-1789.
Dev.: Marg., wife; Marg., Jane, dau.

DUKE, JOHN, Will, 1-17-1792.
Dev.: James, Wm., John, sons.

DUKE, JOHN, Est., 10-15-1793.

DUKE, MARG., Will, 9-20-1791.
Dev.: Marg., Johnny, dau.; John, son.

DUKE, WM., App., 9-21-1795.

DUNCAN, MATHEW, Will, 4-22-1789.
Dev.: Thom., Joseph, Seth, bro.; Sarah Green, sis.; others.

DUNCAN, MATTHEW, Inv., 9-17-1793.

EADE, ROBT., App., 9-16-1788.

EAKENS, ELIZ., Will, 10-26-1801.
Dev.: Wm., Alex., sons; others.

EAKIN, THOM., App., 9-22-1800.

EAKINS, BENJ., App., 9-18-1809.

EAKINS, ELIZ., App., 9-27-1803.

EAKINS, THOM., Will, 6-23-1800.
Dev.: Eliz., wife; Robt., Wm., Alex., sons; Patt, James, slaves.

EDELIN, CHAS., App., 12-23-1805.

EDELIN, CHAS., Est., 7-21-1806.

EDWARDS, JONATHAN, App., 8-17-1773.

EDWARDS, JOS., SR., Will, 4-24-1797.
Dev.: Sam., John, Jos. Jr., Andrew, sons; Eliz., Feagan, dau.; others.

EDWARDS, JOS., Inv., 9-25-1797.

ELLIOT, JAS., App., 3-27-1809.

ELLIS, ELENOR, App., 12-21-1807.

ELLIS, ELENOR, Adm., 1-21-1811.

ELLIS, ELIZ., App., 12-21-1807.

ELLIS, ELIZ., Adm., 1-21-1811.

ELLIS, ENOS, Will, 6-17-1783.
Dev.: Eliz., wife; Thom., Ellis, Enos, Jonathan, sons; Hannah, Rebecca, Jane, Elenor, dau.

ELLIS, ENOS, App., 11-18-1784.

ELLIS, JACOB, Will, 2-27-1809.
Dev.: Sam., John, Henry, sons; Cath., dau.; others.

ELLIS, JOHN, Will, 4-17-1782.
Dev.: Eliz., wife; Ann, Elenor, dau.; Benj., John, Ellis, sons.

ELLIS, JOHN, App., 6-18-1782.

ELLIS, JOHN, Will, 9-27-1803.
Dev.: Ellis, bro.; Ellinor, sis.; Eliz., mother; other.

ELLIS, JOHN, Adm., 1-21-1811.

ELLIS, MORDEICA, App., 11-15-1785.

ELLIS, WM., Will, 12-15-1772.
Dev.: Eliz., wife.

ELLIS, WM., App., 5-20-1777.

ENTLER, ADAM, Will, 5-20-1777.
(Mechlenburg)
Dev.: Juliania, wife; Marg., Eliz., dau.

ENTLER, ADAM, Est., 4-19-1786.

ENTLER, PHILIP, Will, 6-24-1799.
Dev.: Magdaline, wife; Martin, son; others.

EVANS, ISAAC, Will, 4-17-1793.
Dev.: Martha, wife; Marg. A., Eliz. M., dau.; Robt., John, Isaac, Thom., Wm., sons.

EVANS, ISAAC, Inv., 6-18-1793.

EVANS, JOHN, JR., Will, 1-20-1801.
Dev.: Marg., Martha, Rebekah, Eliz., Ann, dau.; John, Ephraim, Edmond, Washington, Isaac, Jos., sons.

EVANS, JOHN, App., 9-22-1801.

EVANS, JOS. SR., Will, 9-24-1804.
Dev.: Ann, wife; Robt., Isaac, Henry, Sciotha, Jos., sons; Hannah Cooper, Mary, dau.

EVANS, JOS., Est., 4-26-1808.

EVANS, MARG., Adm., 5-15-1811.

EWINGS, THOM., Will, 4-17-1793.
Dev.: Sam., son; Ann, dau.

EWINGS, THOM., Est., 9-26-1808.

FARBER, SEBASTIAN, App., 6-8-1812.

FARRIS, ART., Inv., 4-9-1811.

FAULK, CHRIS., Will, 8-10-1812.
Dev.: Anna Eliz., wife; Abr., John,
sons; Peggy, Susannah, Eliz. Reel,
Polly Lingenfelter, Sarah Gebhart,
Cath. Westenhaver, Hanna Keefer
dau.; widow of son Jacob.

FAULK, JACOB, Will, 4-13-1812.
Dev.: Mary, wife; Eliz., Mary, dau.

FAULK, JACOB, Sale, 4-12-1813.

FIELDS, WILLIAM, Will, 5-17-1774.
Dev.: Charles Pierce.

FIELDS, WILLIAM, App., 8-16-1774.

FILLROY, ANDREW, Will, 11-22-1780.
Dev.: Jannett, Paggy, dau.; others.

FISHER, JACOB, Will, 6-19-1787.
Dev.: Wife; Susannah, dau.; John
Fisher, bro.

FISHER, JACOB, App., 4-15-1788.

FLAGG, THOMAS, Will, 8-18-1772.
Dev.: Ruth Keys, friend.

FLECKNER, PETER, Est., 4-15-1794.

FLEECE, JACOB, App., 9-25-1798.

FLEEK, JOHN G., App., 1-24-1803.

FLEMING, HENRY, Est., 9-23-1805.

FLETCHER, AZEL, Inv., 6-12-1815.

FLETCHER, JOHN, Will, 6-16-1772.
Dev.: Eliz., wife; John, Rich., sons;
Mary, Sarah, dau.

FLETCHER, JOHN, Est., 6-17-1777.

FLETCHER, MARTHA, Will, 10-25-1802.
Dev.: Jacob, Thom., Wm., Azel, sons;
Mary, dau.; others.

FLETCHER, PETER, Will, 12-22-1800.
Dev.: Martha, wife; Mary Dilley,
Eliz., Heaton, dau.; Jacob, Wm.,
Thom., sons; others.

FLETCHER, PETER, Est., 9-26-1808.

FOGLE, GEO., App., 8-14-1815.

FOLAND, GEO., Inv., 4-20-1790.

FOLK, CHRIS., Inv., 5-8-1815.

FOSTER, ISAAC, Inv., 2-18-1790.

FOSTER, THOM., Est., 9-22-1800.

FOX, BRYAN, Est., 7-25-1796.

FRANCEWAY, JOS. SR., Will, 6-23-1806.
Dev.: Pheby, Eliz. Austrim, dau.; Jos.,
son; slaves freed.

FRANCEWAY, JOS. SR., Est., 1-15-1810.

FRANK, BERNARD, Will, 10-15-1782.
Dev.: Cath., wife; Bernard, son;
Mary, dau.; others.

FREDERICK, HENRY, App., 11-21-1775.

FRENCH, JACOB, SR., App., 10-21-1788.

FRENCH, JACOB, Est., 6-18-1794.

FRESHOUR, MARY, Sale, 11-12-1812.

FRESHOUR, MARY, App., 12-11-1713.

FRESHOUR, WINDLE, Will, 10-15-1793.
Dev.: Mother; John, Fred., Geo.,
sons; Mary, Caty, Barb., Lucy, Sphia
[sic] dau.; others.

FRESHOUR, WINDLE, Est., 2-25-1805.

FRIER, ALEX., SR., Will, 12-18-1792.
Dev.: Alez., Humphrey, sons; Mary,
Cath. Grantham, dau.; others.

FRIER, ALEX., Will, 12-18-1792.
Dev.: Ruth, wife; Marg., Sarah, dau.;
Matthew, John, sons.

FRIER, ALEX., JR., Inv., 4-16-1793.

FRIER, ALEX., JR., App., 2-25-1799.

FRITZ, MICH., Will, 6-19-1787.
Dev.: Valentine, son; Mary Wilson,
Cath. Lee, Eliz. Davis, dau., others.

FRITZ, MICH., App., 10-16-1787.

FRY, ABRAHAM, Est., 10-24-1797.

FRY, JACOB, Will, 4-22-1806.
Dev.: Judity, wife; John, Jacob,
Mich., sons; Cath. Trigg, Mary Eccles.
Marg. Clausen, Eliz. Trigg, Ann Hus-
ton, Jane Dilliplane, Rachel Fry, dau.

FRY, JACOB, Est., 10-14-1811.

FRYATT, BART., Will, 12-17-1793.
Dev.: Rosanna, wife; John, Robert,
Edmund, Bartholemew, William, sons;
Margaret, Ann, Mary, Rosanna, Eliz-
abeth, dau.

FRYATT, BARTHOLEMEW, App., 9-16-
1794.

FULTON, DAVID, Est., 2-27-1797.

FULTZ, BOLTZER, Inv., 10-22-1798.

GANO, JAMES, Est., 1-25-1808.

GARRINGER, DAVID, Will, 8-10-1812.
Dev.: Barb., wife; David, John, Jacob,
sons; Sevil, Mary Culp, Eliz. Zenner,
Madelenah Miller, dau.

GAUDY, JAMES, App., 8-21-1782.

GAUNT, J. ED., Will, 5-18-1791.
Dev.: John, bro.; mother, father;
others.

GERRARD, JOHN, Will, 9-18-1787.
Dev.: Mary, wife; David, Nath., Jonathan, Abner, Wm., Justice, sons; Phebe, Nancy, Sarah Buckle, dau.;
others.

GERRARD, JOHN, Est., 9-16-1794.

GERRARD, WM., Est., 12-26-1796.

GERRELL, WM., Est., 3-15-1815.

GILBERT, NATHAN, Will, 13-21-1786.
Dev.: Eliz., wife; Wm., Elias, sons;
Rachel, dau.

GILBERT, NATHAN, Est., 7-17-1792.

GINGAR, GASPAR, App., 6-22-1795.

GLENN, JAMES, Will, 5-17-1774.
Dev.: Martha, wife; Jane, Margaret
Snodgrass, dau.; John, James, Wil-
liam, sons.

GLENN, JAMES, Will, 9-17-1793.
Dev.: Wm. Boyd, John, sons; Anna
Miller, Ann Helm, dau.; others.

GLENN, JANE, Inv., 9-26-1796.

GLENN, JOHN, Will, 9-20-1785.
Dev.: Jean, wife; Jean Glenn, Ann
Maxwell, sis.; others.

GLENN, JOHN, Est., 6-19-1787.

GLENN, MARTHA, Will, 8-15-1775.
Dev.: John, James, Wm., sons; Marg.
Snodgrass, Jane Miller, dau.

GODDART, JOHN, App., 11-18-1777.

GOLD, THOMAS, Will, 10-26-1795.
Dev.: John, James, sons; Jane Bale, dau.; others.

GORDEN, THOM., Est., 7-25-1803.

GORREL, WM., Inv., 2-23-1807.

GORRELL, WM., Will, 12-24-1804.
Dev.: James, Wm., Joseph, Jacob, sons; Mary Chenoeth, Rachel, dau.

GOUDY, JAMES, Est., 7-19-1791.

GOWAN, JOS. DR., Est., 9-26-1808.

GRAHAM, JAMES, Will, 8-19-1777.
Dev.: James, Edmund, John, sons; Sarah, Mary, dau.

GRAHAM, JAMES, Est., 3-18-1783.

GRANT, DAN., App., 11-19-1782.

GRANT, ROBT., Inv., 2-27-1799.

GRANTHAM, WM., Est., 10-27-1806.

GRANTHAM, WM., Inv., 7-26-1802.

GRAY, DAVID, Est., 7-24-1798.

GRAY, DAVID, Est., 6-28-1803.

GRAY, HUGH, Will, 4-17-1787.
Dev.: Alee, wife; James, Wm., sons; Wm., bro.; Sally, Alee, Jane, dau.

GREEN, DINAH, Will, 2-21-1803.
Dev.: Sarah Butt, Dinah Dean, dau.; others.

GREEN, WM., SR., Will, 3-21-1780.
Dev.: Dinah, wife; Regnal, Wm., sons; Sarah, Mary, Keziah, Eliz., Dinah, dau.; Wm., grandson.

GREEN, WM., Est., 3-20-1781.

GREEN, WM., Est., 12-23-1805.

GREER, CHAS., App., 12-18-1787.

GROVE, MICH., Inv., 2-25-1805.

GROVE, MICH., Est., 9-21-1807.

GULEFORD, JOHN, Will, 5-21-1782.
Dev.: Polly, Amy, Lydia, Christiana, dau.

GULLIFORD, JOHN, Est., 8-20-1783.

GWIN, DAN., App., 9-12-1814.

HAINS, HENRY, Will, 12-16-1777.
(Mechlenburg)
Dev.: Cath., wife; Henry, John, Peter, sons; Eliz., Cath., dau.

HAINS, HENRY, Est., 6-19-1787.

HAIR, SAM., Will, 8-19-1782.
Dev.: Nath., Sam., Abraham, Henry, Isaac, Jacob, Joseph, sons; Sarah, dau.

HAIR, SAM., App., 5-20-1783.

HALEY, REUBEN, Will, 1-19-1790.
Dev.: Mother; Cath., sis; Larkin, bro.

HALL, GEO., Will, 3-21-1786.
Dev.: Susannah, wife; Rich., son; others.

HALL, GEO., App., 9-19-1786.

HALL, JOHN, App., 2-20-1787.

HALL, JOS., Will, 2-27-1797.
Dev.: Mary, wife; free all slaves; others.

HALL, JOSEPH, App., 6-26-1797.

HAM, JACOB, App., 4-17-1787.

HAMILL, MICH., App., 11-18-1783.

HAMMON, GEO., App., 7-27-1801.

HAMMOND, JAS., Inv., 5-11-1812.

HAMMOND, JAS., Adm., 7-12-1813.

HAMMOND, VAL., App., 12-24-1804.

HAMMOND, VAL., Est., 2-25-1805.

HANCKES, NICH., Will, 8-19-1777.
(Frederick Co.)
Dev.: John, Wm., sons; Elenor Brownfield, Mary Stonebridge, dau.; others.

HANNA, WM., Adm., 12-18-1809.

HANSILL, MICH., Will, 9-18-1781.
Dev.: Mary, wife; Laurence, Geo., sons; Eliz., Eve, Mary, dau.: and all children.

HANSILL, MICH., Est., 8-19-1784.

HARLAN, JEHU, Inv., 9-22-1806.

HARLAN, JOHN, Will, 4-21-1806.
Dev.: Geo., Dan., Elijah, Silas, Jehu, John, sons.

HARLAN, STEPHEN, Will, 12-26-1796.
Dev.: Mary, wife; Jess, James, sons; Rachel Gibson, Sarah Roads, dau.

HARLAN, STEPHEN, Est., 10-9-1815.

HARMAN, NICK., Will, 7-22-1805.
Dev.: Mich., Geo., son; Marg., Modlin, Susannah, dau.

HARMAN, NICK., App., 9-22-1805.

HARPER, JOHN, Will, 9-18-1793.
Dev.: Margery, wife; John, Wm., James, Alex., Sam., sons; Jean Brown, Mary Burcham, Sarah, dau.; others.

HARPER, JOHN, App., 10-21-1794.

HARPER, ROBT., Will, 10-15-1782.
Dev.: Robt. Griffith, Joseph, Jonas, Hezekiah, and Israel Keen, Robt. and Josiah Harper, nephews; Sarah Harper, niece.

HARPER, ROBT., Est., 1-26-1807.

HARRIS, JACOB, Inv., 6-18-1810.

HARRIS, JACOB, Est., 9-10-1815.

HARRIS, JOS., Inv., 1-25-1797.

HARRIS, JOS., Est., 6-24-1799.

HARRISON, SAM., Will, 6-16-1789.
Dev.: Marg., wife; Sam., James, Wm., John, sons; Mary Hedges, Charity, dau.; others.

HARRISON, SAM., Inv., 4-20-1790.

HART, ANDREW, Est., 6-27-1796.

HART, THOS., Will, 1-20-1795.
Dev.: Ann, wife; Thomas, son; Margaret, Elizabeth, Anne, Esther, Sarah, dau.

HART, THOM., Inv., 6-26-1797.

HAWKINS, WM., App., 12-24-1798.

HAWKINS, WM., Est., 4-21-1800.

HAYS, JOHN, Will, 9-18-1787.
Dev.: Jean, wife; Gabrial, John, Ichnand, Jess, sons; Charity, Grace, Eliz., Suiah Chenowith, Anne Chenowith, dau.

HAYS, JOHN, App., 12-18-1787.

HEDGES, BENJ., Inv., 6-19-1809.

HEDGES, JONAS, Will, 2-27-1804.
Dev.: Agnes, wife; Benj., Sam., sons; all children.

HEDGES, JONAS, App., 4-25-1804.

HEDGES, JOSHUA. Will, 2-16-1790.
Dev.: Eliz., wife; Joshua, Sam., Solomon, Jesse, sons; Mary, Abigail Swim, Anna Robertson, dau.

HEDGES, JOSEPH, Inv., 4-20-1790.

HEDGES, MARY, Will, 6-26-1797.
Dev.: Eliz., King, Eliz. Swain, Eliz. Morgan, Eliz. Robertson, Eliz. Hedges, Phebe Hedges, nieces.

HENDRICKS, JAS., Will, 2-23-1795.
Dev.: Priscilla, wife; James, John. sons; Elizabeth Blue, dau.; others.

HENDRICKS, JAS., Sale, 6-23-1805.

HENDRICKS, JAS., Est., 6-23-1805.

HENDRICKS, JOHN, Will, 4-26-1796.
Dev.: Eliz., wife; Jos., Wm., James, sons; Eliz., Mary, Rebecca, Sarah, dau.

HENDRICKS, JOHN, App., 1-25-1799.

HENRY, MICH., Will, 9-22-1800.
Dev.: Cath., wife; Eliz., dau.; Geo., Mich., Christian, David, sons; others.

HENRY, MICH., Adm., 10-14-1811.

HENRY, DR. ROBT., App., 6-24-1800.

HENRY, DR. ROBT., Est., 6-24-1800.

HENSHAW, ANN, Will, 7-21-1806.
Dev.: Wash., Wm., Uriah, sons.

HENSHAW, ANN, App., 1-26-1807.

HENSHAW, JON., Inv., 1-27-1804.

HENSHAW, JON., Est., 5-8-1815.

HENSHAW, CAPT. WM., Inv., 4-22-1806.

HENTHORN, JAMES, Will, 5-21-1776.
Dev.: Mary, wife; Mary Jackson, Ann Watson, Eliz. Watson, Sarah Collins, Susanna Robb, dau.; Adam, James, Wm., John, sons; James Yellegin, slave; others.

HENTHORN, JAMES, App., 9-17-1777.

HERSHFIELD, FRED., Will, 4-21-1778.
Dev.: Abulan, wife; Henry, John, Fred., sons; Marg., dau.

HERSHFIELD, FRED., Est., 9-17-1783.

HESSE, CHAS., App., 10-15-1782.

HIATT, GEO., Will, 6-19-1787.
Dev.: Eliz., Nancy, Sharity, dau.; Leonard, Levi, Thom., sons.

HICKMAN, EZEKIAL, Will, 2-20-1793.
Dev.: Eliz., wife; Francis, Wm. E., Ezekial T., Lewis, Joshua, sons; Anna Swearingen, dau.; others.

HIETT, GEO., Est., 9-22-1800.

HIETT, SIMON, Will, 6-25-1798.
Dev.: Eliz., wife; Rebecca, Elinor, Lettene, Ann, Sally, Mary, dau.; Simon, Thom., Wm., James, John, sons.

HITE, JACOB, Will, 3-16-1778.
(Frederick Co.)
Dev.: Frances, wife; Betty, Mary, Nelly, Sucky, dau.; John, Thom., James, Geo., sons.

HITE, JACOB, Est., 9-23-1799.

HITE, JOHN, JR., Will, 3-18-1777.
Dev.: Sarah, wife; Jacob O., son; Mary, dau.; Mary, Eliz., sis.; infant unbaptized; others.

HITE, JOHN, JR., App., 11-18-1783.

HITE, THOM., App., 11-18-1783.

HITE, THOMAS, Will, 8-17-1779.
Dev.: Frances, wife; children.

HOFFMAN, JACOB, Inv., 6-21-1802.

HOFFMAN, MICH., Est., 10-27-1806.

HOGLAND, EVERHART, App., 3-20-1781.

HOLLIDAY, JAMES, Sale, 6-23-1805.

HOLLIDAY, JAS., Adm., 3-14-1814.

HOLLIDAY, JOHN, Est., 12-27-1803.

HOLLIDAY, NANCY, Inv., 6-23-1805.

HOLLINBACK, DAN., App., 7-27-1801.

HOLLINGER, CHRISTIAN, Will, 12-27-1802.
Dev.: Eve, wife; Geo., John, Dan., sons; Cath. Unger, Magdaline March, dau.; others.

HOLYDAY, JAMES, Will, 9-27-1802.
Dev.: Robt., Geo., sons; Nancy, Polly, dau.

HOOKE, MARY, Will, 11-17-1778.
Dev.: Eliz., Vogallar, dau.; John A., son; other.

HOOKE, MARY, App., 3-17-1779.

HOOVER, JACOB, App., 4-27-1801.

HOOVER, JACOB, Est., 7-27-1801.

HOOVER, MARTIN, Inv., 10-18-1791.

HOOVER, MARTIN, App., 1-21-1794.

HOUK, JACOB, JR., Inv., 4-24-1804.

HOUK, JACOB, Sale, 4-24-1804.

HOUK, JACOB, Inv., 11-13-1815.

HOUKE, JACOB, Will, 8-14-1815.
Dev.: Marg., wife; Mich., Geo., Sam., Henry, David, sons; Sally, Betsy Thurston, Cath. Keisacre, dau.; others.

HOUSMAN, DAVID, Will, 9-16-1794.
Dev.: Mary, wife; Martins, son; others.

HOUSEMAN, DAVID, Est., 6-18-1810.

HOUSEMAN, MARTIN, Will, 12-23-1805.
Dev.: Maria Eliz., wife; Mary E. Rosenberger, dau.; others.

HOUSEMAN, MARTIN, Est., 2-27-1809.

HOUTE, GEO., Will, 9-20-1786.
Dev.: Cath., wife; Mary, dau.; Jacob, Peter, Mich., Rudolph, sons.

HOUTE, GEO., App., 10-17-1786.

HOWARD, JOHN, App., 6-23-1805.

HOWARD, ROBT., App., 4-20-1779.

HOYLE, JACOB, SR., Will, 8-21-1781.
Dev.: John Rill, Barnett, Jacob, sons; Mary, Mayo, Katy, dau.; wife.

HOYLE, JACOB, App., 6-18-1782.

HUFFMAN, JACOB, Inv., 2-21-1803.

HUFFMAN, JACOB, Est., 7-25-1803.

HUFFMAN, JOHN, Est., 4-27-1807.

HUFFMAN, JOHN, Est., 9-13-1813.

HUFFMAN, MICH., Est., 6-27-1808.

HUGHES, ISAAC, App., 5-21-1776.

HUGHES, ISAAC, Est., 11-16-1784.

HULL, HENRY, App., 4-15-1794.

HULSE, JOSIAH, App., 5-19-1778.

HULSE, JOSIAH, Est., 6-20-1792.

HUM, JACOB, Will, 9-20-1786.
Dev.: Barb, wife; Jacob, Nich., Mich.,
John, sons; Cath. Potts, dau.
HUNTER, HUGH, App., 5-20-1778.
HUNTER, HUGH, Est., 5-19-1779.
HUNTER, MOSES, App., 9-23-1799.
JACK, ANN, Adm., 6-10-1811.
JACK, JAMES, Will, 1-26-1796.
Dev.: Ann, wife; Jeremiah, John,
Wm., Robt., sons; Isabel Barton, Ann,
dau.; others.
JACK, JAMES, Inv., 4-26-1796.
JACK, JAMES, Est., 9-26-1808.
JACK, JEREMIAH, Will, 8-16-1785.
Dev.: Eliz. Pearce, dau.; others.
JACK, JEREMIAH, App., 2-21-1786.
JACK, JOHN, App., 1-24-1803.
JACK, JOHN, Sale, 4-12-1815.
JACK, NATH., Inv., 1-24-1803.
JACK, NATH., Est., 1-24-1803.
JACK, WM., Inv., 7-22-1805.
JACK, WM., Adm., 6-10-1811.
JACKSON, JOHN, SR., Will, 12-18-1787.
Dev.: Ed. Jackson, cousin; John
Smith, nephew.
JACKSON, JOHN, Est., 7-19-1791.
JENNINGS, ED., Inv., 12-22-1806.
JENNINGS, ED., Adm., 10-16-1809.
JOB, THOM., Sale, 10-24-1803.
JOB, THOM., Est., 6-24-1805.
JOHN, SAM., Will, 4-13-1812.
Dev.: Mary, wife; David, son; Isa-
bella, Ann Williamson, dau.
JOHN, SAM., App., 9-14-1812.
JOHN, WM., Est., 12-21-1795.
JOHNSTONE, WM., Will, 6-22-1807.
Dev.: Jane, wife; John, James, Wm.,
Sam., Robt., Jos., Moses, sons; Eliz.,
dau.
JOHNSTONE, WM., Inv., 4-26-1808.
JONES, ELIZ., Will, 3-20-1781.
Dev.: Hannah, sis.
JONES, JAMES, App., 9-21-1779.
JONES, ROBT., Inv., 10-23-1797.
JONES, ROBT., Will, 2-25-1798.
Dev.: Hannah, wife; Robt., Wells,
sons; Ann Rawlings, Hannah, dau.;
others.
JORDAN, THOM., App., 9-21-1801.
KAIN, DAN., Est., 2-26-1799.
KANE, DAN., App., 10-16-1781.
KEATS, ANDREW, App., 9-24-1805.
KELLER, ANDREW, App., 4-28-1795.
KELLY, THOM., Will, 2-25-1805.
(Bath)
Dev.: Mary, wife; Gil., Wm., Thom.,
John, sons; Ann, Sarah, dau.; Eliz.
Jackson, step-dau.
KELLY, THOM., App., 6-22-1807.
KELLY, WM., Will, 9-16-1777.
Dev.: John, son; Susannah, sis.
KELLY, CAPT. WM., Est., 11-15-1785.
KENEDAY, THOM., Will, 12-24-1798.
Dev.: Col. Dan. Keneday, bro.; others.

KENEDAY, THOM., App., 2-25-1799.
KENNEDY, DAN., App., 12-27-1803.
KENNEDY, DAN., Est., 4-21-1806.
KEESACER, CON., App., 3-13-1815.
KEESACKER, JOHN, Will, 4-22-1799.
Dev.: Christiana, wife; Matthias,
Andrew, Aaron, John, Geo.; sons;
Mary, dau.
KERNEY, JOHN, Inv., 8-16-1815.
KERNEY, JOHN, Est., 10-9-1815.
KERNEY, WM., Will, 10-16-1787.
Dev.: Jean, wife; James, John, Wm.,
Ed., Alex., Anthony, sons; Mary
King, Marg. Blue, dau.
KERSNER, JACOB, Inv., 2-29-1804.
KEYES, GERSHAM, Est., 8-19-1783.
KEYES, HUMPHREY, Will, 6-18-1793.
Dev.: Sarah, wife; Francis, John,
Humphrey, Gershom, Thom., sons;
Sarah Wight, Lucrita Piles, Eliz.,
Cath., Ruth, dau.
KEYES, HUMPHREY, Inv., 7-16-1793.
KEYS, FRED., App., 6-22-1801.
KEYS, JOHN, App., 5-20-1777.
KEYS, RUTH, Will, 12-24-1798.
Dev.: Thom. and Jonah Flagg.
KING, MATT., App., 10-22-1808.
KITCHEN, JOB., Inv., 6-12-1815.
KLECKHAM, CONRAD, Will, 8-17-1784.
Dev.: Eliz., wife; Henry, Baltzar,
Conrad, Peter, Fred., John, Geo.,
sons; Christina Carpenter, Charlotte
Bruner, Mary Sophia, dau.
KLECKHAM, CONRAD, App., 9-21-1784.
KLINGER, HENRY, Inv., 6-27-1808.
KNOX, WM., Will, 3-17-1778.
Dev.: Hannah, wife; Wm., John, Geo.,
Enoch, James, Jesse, Moses, sons;
Esther Small, Marg., dau.
KNOX, WM., App., 11-17-1778.
KRUCK, JACOB, Will, 9-22-1795.
Dev.: Elinor, wife; Peter, Jacob,
John, Michael, Henry, Andrew, sons;
Molly Spring, dau.
KRUCK, JACOB, Inv., 2-28-1797.
(OR CROOK)
KYLE, JOSEPH, Will, 3-18-1783.
Dev.: Agnes, wife; Agnes, May,
Marg., Jane, Anne, Eliz. Johnson,
dau.; John, Joseph, Wm., James, sons.
KYLE, JOSEPH, App., 9-16-1783.
KYSER, JOHN, Adm., 9-7-1811.
LACKY, JAMES, Will, 9-15-1798.
Dev.: Cath., wife; Thom., bro.
LADY, CHRISTIAN, Will, 10-24-1803.
Dev.: Jacob, Christian, Henry, David,
sons; others.
LAMON, JOS., Est., 6-24-1800.
LAMON, JOS., Est., 1-26-1807.
LAUGHLAND, JOSH., App., 8-19-1783.
LEE, MAJ. GEN. CHARLES, Will, 4-15-
1783.
Dev.: Sidney, sister; Guisippi Min-
gini, servant; Eliz. Dunn, house-
keeper; others.
LEE, MAJ. GEN. CHAS., App., 5-20-
1783.

LEE, DR. JOHN, Inv., 9-20-1791.

LEE, JOHN, Est., 7-15-1794.

LEESON, JOHN, Will, 2-22-1808.
Dev.: Corn., Tim., bro.; other.

LEMASTER, ABR., App., 9-15-1778.

LEMEN, JAMES, Will, 10-21-1777.
Dev.: Mother; Ruth C., Polly Morgan, dau.; Wm., bro.; others.

LEMEN, JAMES, Est., 5-16-1780.

LEMEN, JOHN, SR., Will, 8-16-1774.
Dev.: wife; John, James, William, sons.

LEMEN, JOHN, Est., 5-15-1781.

LEONARD, NICH., Will, 4-24-1797.
Dev.: Anna, wife; Peter, John, Nich., Wm., sons; Cath., Mary, Eliz., dau.

LEONARD, NICH., Inv., 10-24-1797.

LETMAN, VAL., Will, 6-22-1802.
Dev.: Cath., wife; John, Henry, Peter, sons; Eve Wise, Cath. Neigh, Anna Bedinger, Marg. Kennedy, Magdaline Collins, dau.

LETMAN, VAL., Inv., 2-21-1803.

LEWIS, CHRISTOPHER, App., 3-16-1779.

LEWIS, DAVID, JR., App., 9-17-1793.

LIGHT, PETER, Will, 3-9-1811.
Dev.: John, Peter, Jacob, Jos., Sam., David, sons; Susannah Myers, Eliz. Anderson, Cath. Hoke, Polley, Nancy Thornburg, dau.

LIGHT, PETER, App., 8-11-1812.

LILBURN, FRAN., Est., 9-22-1779.

LILBURN, FRANCES, App., 11-19-1778.

LILBURN, JAMES, App., 5-21-1782.

LILBURN, JOHN, App., 5-19-1778.

LILBURN, JOHN, Est., 10-17-1780.

LINGENFELTER, ABR., Inv., 7-18-1810.

LINGENFELTER, ABR., Adm., 1-12-1813.

LINGENFELTER, VAL., Will, 12-24-1804.
Dev.: Abraham, son; Barb., Magdalena, Rebecca, Caty, Mary, Eliz., Rosannah, dau.

LINGHAMFELTER, VAL., Est., 11-13-1811.

LITTLEJOHN, WM., Will, 9-13-1813.
Dev.: Fabey, wife; Abr., Jos., John, Wm., Moris, Ed., sons; Sarah, Ester, Fabey, dau.

LOCK, RICH., Est., 5-16-1780.

LOCKE, RICHARD, App., 10-17-1775.

LOGAN, JAMES, Will, 4-17-1782.
Dev.: Jane, wife; Thom., son; Mary McDaniel, dau.

LOGAN, JAMES, Est., 10-19-1784.

LONG, COOKSEN, Est., 7-17-1787.

LONG, REBECCA, Sale, 7-17-1787.

LOW, RICH., Inv., 1-27-1803.

LOW, RICH., Est., 10-24-1803.

LOWDEN, WM., Will, 7-28-1795.
Dev.: Elizabeth, wife; William, Thomas, John, Samuel, sons; Sarah Clark, dau.

LOWDEN, WM., Inv., 6-27-1796.

LOWER, PHILIP, Will, 7-20-1779.
Dev.: John, Henry, sons; Eliz., Christiana, Barbary, Cath., dau.

LOWER, PHILIP, Est., 6-19-1787.

LOWMAN, RICH., Will, 7-21-1806.
Dev.: Rachel, wife; James, Geo., Rich., sons; Betsy Lee, dau.; others.

LUCAS, ED., SR., Will, 10-21-1777.
Dev.: Ed., Wm., Robt., Isaac, David, Andrew, John, Job, Benj., sons; Ann Baldwin, Mary, Marg., Hannah, dau.; others.

LUCAS, ED., App., 8-18-1778.

LYLE, HUGH, Will, 10-19-1790.
Dev.: John, Hugh, sons; Mary Watson, Van Morrison, dau.; grandson.

LYLE, CAPT. HUGH, Sale, 2-22-1798.

LYLE, JOHN, Will, 9-24-1798.
Dev.: Abagail, wife; Hugh, John, Wm., sons; Nancy, Sally, Polly, Anne, Betsy, Milly, dau.

LYLE, JOHN, Est., 6-27-1808.

LYLE, ROBT., App., 6-17-1788.

LYLE, ROBT., Est.; 2-27-1798.

MACKEY, WM., JR., App., 12-27-1808.

MACKEY, WM., Will, 11-10-1812.
Dev.: numerous bequests.

MACKEY, WM., App., 2-8-1813.

MAGAW, JOHN, Will, 6-12-1815.
Dev.: John McKee, friend.

MARSHALL, JAMES, App., 6-22-1807.

MARSHALL, JAS., Est., 7-25-1808.

MARTIN, BENJ., App., 4-19-1786.

MASON, JAS., Will, 1-10-1814.
Dev.: Rachel, wife; Wm., son; Eliz., Mary, Marthia, dau.

MASON, RACHEL, Will, 5-9-1814.
Dev.: Wm., son; Eliz. Mary, Martha, dau.

MATTHEWS, JOHN, Will, 5-19-1778.
Dev.: Mary, wife; Mary White, apprentice.

MATTHEWS, JOHN, Est., 9-16-1778.

MATTHEWS, WM., App., 3-17-1778.

MAY, DANIEL, Will, 6-17-1777.
Dev.: Mary, wife.

MAY, DAVID, Est., 11-22-1780.

McABOY, WM., App., 3-27-1809.

McABOY, WM., Adm., 11-8-1813.

McALLISTER, BENJ., Inv., 2-22-1808.

McALLISTER, CHRIS., App., 12-21-1807.

McAYMONS, WM., Will, 5-20-1777. (Frederick Co.)
Dev.: Marg., wife; John, Wm., Robt., James, sons; Mary, Eliz., Jean, Marg., Isabella, dau.

McBRIDE, JAS., App., 12-23-1805.

McCARTNEY, BENJ., App., 8-20-1776.

McCARTNEY, JOHN, Inv., 8-16-1815.

McCARTNEY, SARAH, Will, 3-20-1781.
Dev.: Sarah Vance, niece: others.

McCLEMONS, WM., App., 9-16-1777.

McCOACH, ROBT., Will, 4-28-1807.
Dev.: James, Wm., sons; Matty Borland, Eliz. Borland, dau.

West Virginia Estate Settlements

In 1936 and 1937, the West Virginia Commission on Historic and Scenic Markers, the Works Progress Administration, and the Federal Emergency Relief Administration compiled court records of the various counties, such as Births, Deaths, Marriages and Wills. Under Wills were grouped subjects pertaining to Estate Settlements, including Wills, Inventories and Appraisements. Copies of these county records were filed at the Department of Archives and History, Charleston, the Library of West Virginia University, Morgantown, and the DAR Library, Washington.

Believing that there would be particular interest on the part of the general public in the Estate Settlements in the older counties, the West Virginia Historical Society has undertaken to abstract the Estate Settlement Records, as filed in the State Department of Archives and History, and offered them for publication in the *West Virginia History Quarterly*. (No responsibility can be assumed as to the accuracy of the copies made from the original county records.)

There are 13 counties which were formed prior to 1800, and it has been agreed to arrange these counties in chronological order, and to print their records from the earliest date to 1850. The formation dates of these counties are as follows: Hampshire—1753; Berkeley—1772; Monongalia—1776; Ohio—1776; Greenbrier—1778; Harrison—1784; Hardy—1786; Randolph—1787; Pendleton—1788; Kanawha—1788; Brooke—1797; Wood—1798 and Monroe—1799.

Berkeley County, Formed 1772

(1772-1815)

Abbreviations used in this material include: Adm.—administrator; Agr.—agreement; App.—appraisement; Bro.—brother; Dau.—daughter; Dev.—devisees; Divn.—division; Est.—estate a/c; Ind.—indenture; Inv.—inventory; L. G.—land grant; Obl. —obligation; S. B.—sale bill; Set.—settlement; Sis.—sister; and Sur.—Survey.

Berkeley County, 1772-1815   43

McCONNELL, WM., Will, 9-21-1808.
Dev.: Sally, Martha, Betsy, Ann,
Hannah, Isabel, Janet (or Jenny),
Mary, dau.; Abraham, James, sons.

McCOY, ABSALOM, App., 12-18-1809.

McCOY, ABSOLIM, Will, 12-26-1803.
Dev.: Rebecca Crouch; Thom. and
Geo., Gahex; slaves freed.

McCOY, JOS., Will, 1-21-1805.
Dev.: Ruth, wife; Thom., son; Marg.
Wilson, dau.

McCOY, JOS., Inv., 2-26-1805.

McDONALD, ANDREW, Will, 4-22-1799.
Dev.: Hester, wife; Wm., James, Andrew, sons; others.

McDONALD, BRYAN, Will, 5-13-1811.
Dev.: Sarah, dau.; and her heirs.

McKEEVER, JOHN, Inv., 6-19-1809.

McKELVEY, PAT., App., 6-24-1805.

McKELVEY, PAT., Sale, 6-24-1805.

McKENNEY, JOHN, SR., Will, 9-24-1804.
Dev.: Mary, wife; Wm., son; Marg.,
Sarah, Rachel, dau.

McKERNAN, MICH., Inv., 10-24-1803.

McKIERNAN, MICH., Est., 6-19-1809.

McKINNEY, ED., Will, 2-22-1796.
Dev.: James Coyle, Tulley, Wm.
Coyle, bro.; Mary Coyle, sis.; other.

McKINNEY, JOHN, App., 5-8-1815.

McKINNEY, JOHN, Sale, 5-8-1815.

McKNIGHT, ANN, Will, 3-13-1815.
Dev.: Freed slaves; other bequests.

McKNIGHT, ROBT., Will, 7-25-1808.
Dev.: Ann, wife; others.

McKNIGHT, ROBT., Est., 9-18-1809.

McKOWN, GIL., Will, 12-26-1803.
Dev.: Martha, wife; Sam., Gil., sons;
Eliz. Magill, Rebecca Hair, Ann Mires,
Mary Lamon, Rachell, dau.; Molly,
slave; others.

McKOWN, GIL., Est., 6-27-1808.

McKOWN, JOHN, Inv., 2-26-1805.

McPHERSON, DAN., Will, 4-22-1789.
Dev.: Wife; Wm., John, Dan., sons;
Mary, Ruth, Rebecca, Ann, dau.;
Isaac, son.

McPHERSON, DAN., Inv., 10-20-1789.

McSHERRY, BARNEY, App., 1-23-1797.

McSHERRY, BARNEY, Est., 2-25-1799.

MEDLEY, WM., Will, 1-21-1794.
Dev.: Sarah, wife; Lily, dau.; William, Elijah, sons.

MELICK, PHILIP, Will, 4-25-1797.
Dev.: Mary, wife; David, John, sons;
Fanny, Charlotte, Marg., Cath., Eliz.,
Lenah, dau.

MELICK, PHILIP, App., 7-23-1798.

MENDENHALL, JOHN, Will, 6-15-1773.
Dev.: Mordecai, Stephen, Moses,
James, sons; Martha, wife; others.

MENDENHALL, JOHN, App., 8-17-1773.

MERCER, ED., Est., 12-23-1805.

MERCER, EDWARD, Will, 5-20-1783.
Dev.: Mary, wife; Nich., Ed., sons;
Mary, Jane, Marg., Blanche, Ruth,
Rebecca, Nancy, dau.; grandson.

MERCHANT, ISAAC, Will, 1-14-1814.
Dev.: Nancy, wife; Sarah, Mary,
Nancy, Eliz., dau.; Jacob, Hiram,
Washington, Peter, sons.

MERCHANT, JOHN, Inv., 3-9-1812.

MERCHANT, JOHN, Est., 3-9-1812.

MERCHANT, WM., Will, 6-18-1772.
Dev.: Rebecca Stewart, Rich., Wm.,
Jacob, Isaac, Mary, Frances, Eliz.,
Abraham, John, Priscilla, wife.

MERCHANT, WM., App., 8-18-1772.

MERRIOT, BARB., Will, 3-16-1779.
Dev.: Eliz., dau.; Wm., John, sons.

MERRIOTT, GEO., Will, 3-10-1776.
Dev.: Susannah, wife; John, Wm.,
sons; Eliz., dau.

MERRIOT, GEO., App., 11-20-1776.

MERRITT, BARB., Est., 2-23-1796.

MICHAEL, MICHAEL, App., 9-16-1794.

MICHEL, MICHEL, Will, 12-17-1793.
Dev.: Eva, wife; Peter, Andrew,
Michel, sons; Catherine Sellers, Mary,
dau.

MIDDLETON, ADAM, Inv., 2-21-1792.

MIDDLETON, THOM., Will, 9-14-1812.
Mary, wife; Bethuel, son; four dau.

MIDDLETON, THOM., Est., 9-10-1815.

MILER, RICH., Est., 12-23-1805.

MILES, LOYD, Will, 11-10-1812.
Dev.: Jacob, Jesse, bro.; others.

MILLAN, JOHN, Will, 6-20-1787.
Dev.: Eliz., wife; Jane Lyle, dau.;
slaves freed.

MILLAR, HENRY, Will, 6-23-1806.
Dev.: Marg., wife; Eliz., dau.; Jacob,
son; others.

MILLEN, JOHN, Est., 6-23-1801.

MILLER, ABSOLOM, Inv., 6-27-1808.

MILLER, AGNUS, Will, 3-27-1809.
Dev.: Jos., Alex., sons; Heirs of son
Absalom.

MILLER, CHRIS. SR., Will, 3-29-1809.
Dev.: Wife; John, son; others.

MILLER, DAN., App., 2-23-1801.

MILLER, DAN., Est., 9-27-1802.

MILLER, DAVID, App., 9-17-1782.

MILLER, DAVID, Will, 4-16-1782.
Dev.: Agnes, wife; John, James,
David, Absolam, Joseph, Alex., sons;
Sarah Hewill, Eliz., Mary, dau.; Robt.
Glen, grandson.

MILLER, HUGH, Will, 12-16-1794.
Dev.: Elinor, wife; Mary Snodgrass,
Jennet Hammerly, dau.; Hugh, son;
others.

MILLER, HUGH, Inv., 2-23-1795.

MILLER, JACOB, App., 12-22-1800.

MILLER, JACOB, Est., 9-21-1807.

MILLER, JAMES, Will, 2-22-1796.
Dev.: Easter, wife; David, Wm. D.,
James, sons; Marg., Mary, dau.

MILLER, JAMES, Inv., 4-26-1796.

MILLER, JOHN, Will, 9-20-1791.
Dev.: Hannah, wife; Isaac, Wm., sons;
Jane, dau.

MILLER, MICH., App., 2-27-1809.

MILLER, MICH., Sale, 2-27-1809.

MILLER, PHILIP, Will, 9-24-1798.
Dev.: Molly, wife; Cath., Hannah, Polly, Eliz., Susanna, Rebecca, dau.; Wm., John, sons; Caty Wilson, Mary Grove, step-dau.

MILLER, PHILIP, App., 1-25-1799.

MILLER, ROBT., App., 2-19-1788.

MILLER, ZACH.. Will, 4-26-1796.
Dev.: Cath., wife; John, Zach., Jacob, sons; Sarah, Ann, Cath. Crosen, Susannah, Eliz. Mclean, dau.

MILLER, ZACH., Inv., 6-27-1796.

MILLER. ZACH., Will, 7-12-1813.
Dev.: Barb. wife; Polly, Cath., Eliz. Tabler, dau.; Mich., Geo., Henry, sons.

MOLER, ADAM, SR., Will, 11-18-1783.
Dev.: Adam, John, Fred., Jacob, Henry, Mich., Gasper, sons; Mary, Eliz., Anne, dau.

MOLER, ADAM, App., 8-17-1734.

MOLER, HENRY, Will, 1-26-1801.
Dev.: Mary, wife; Mary, dau.; sons; others.

MOLER, HENRY, Est., 4-10-1815.

MONKS, OWEN, Inv., 12-18-1792.

MOON, JACOB, Will, 6-25-1804.
Dev.: Jane, wife; James, Thom., Simon, sons; Mary How, Nancy Wright, dau.; others.

MOON, JACOB, Est., 4-26-1808.

MOONEY, JOS., App., 6-18-1810.

MOONEY, JOS., Est., 6-12-1815.

MOORE, ARCH., Inv., 2-22-1808.

MOORE, CATO, Will, 7-24-1797. (Shepherdstown)
Dev.: Marg., wife; Henry, son; Dixon, dau.

MOORE, CATO, Sale, 6-25-1804.

MOORE, JOHN, Will, 8-17-1784.
Dev.: Rich., John, sons; Ann, Margaret, dau.; other.

MOORE, JOHN, App., 4-19-1786.

MOORE, JOS., App., 8-21-1781.

MOORE, JOSEPH, Will, 5-15-1781.
Dev.: Mary, wife; Robt., John, sons; Sarah Small, dau.

MORGAN, GEO., Inv., 12-18-1810.

MORGAN, GEO., Est., 12-18-1810.

MORGAN, ISAAC, Will, 11-16-1784.
Dev.: Let, wife; Thom., Rees, John, sons; Thom., bro.

MORGAN, ISAAC, Est., 11-16-1784.

MORGAN, JACOB, Will, 3-21-1780.
Dev.: Jane, wife; Rich., Jacob, sons; Polly, dau.

MORGAN, JACOB, App., 6-20-1780.

MORGAN, MORGAN, Will, 12-28-1797.
Dev.: Mary, wife; Morgan, Tackwell, David, sons; Mary Lewis, Phebe, Cath., Rebecca, dau.

MORGAN, MORGAN, Est., 9-27-1802.

MORGAN, WM., Will, 10-21-1788.
Dev.: Abraham, Rawleith, Ralph, Geo., sons; Elenor, Sarah, Williams, dau.; others.

MORGAN, WM., Inv., 4-20-1790.

MORGAN, WM., Will, 4-28-1795.
Dev.: Priscilla, wife; William, Andrew, sons; Elizabeth Crosen, Margaret, dau.; others.

MORGAN, COL. WM., Est., 4-21-1800.

MORGAN, ZACH., Est., 9-17-1810.

MORGAN, ZACH., Sale, 9-17-1810.

MORLATT, ABR., Will, 3-20-1810.
Dev.: Abraham, Rich., sons; Jane Bodine, dau.; others.

MORLATT, ABR., SR., Inv., 4-9-1811.

MORRISON, ELIZ., App., 9-18-1792.

MORRISON, NAT., Will, 9-22-1806.
Dev.: Wife; Hannah, dau.; Jesse, James, Rich., sons; others.

MORRISON, WM., App., 5-21-1782.

MORRISS, ELIZ., Will, 5-15-1792.
Dev.: Margaret, Elenor, and John McNeal and their children.

MORROW, CHAS., Will, 12-18-1792.
Dev.: Mary, wife; Mary, Mary Barnes, dau.

MORROW, CHAS., Est., 2-28-1797.

MOWLER, GEO. A., Est., 2-20-1793.

MOWLER, HENRY, Est., 1-21-1811.

MULLINER, NAT., App., 10-23-1797.

MURPHY, JOHN, Will, 12-23-1799.
Dev.: Cath., wife; John, David, Ephraim, Abraham, Jacob, sons; Lydia, Nancy, Eliz., Caty, dau.

MURPHY, JOHN, Est., 4-21-1806.

MURPHY, WM., App., 8-20-1782.

MURPHY, WM., Est., 8-16-1785.

MYLES, GEO., App., 3-9-1776.

MYLES, GEO., Sales, 3-9-1776.

NACE, HENRY SR., Will, 1-27-1800.
Dev.: Magdalena, wife; Henry, Geo., Jacob, sons; Cath., dau.; others.

NEWLAND, John, Will, 10-27-1800.
Dev.: John, Jacob, Isaac, Abr., sons; Mary Lindon, Sarah Byers, dau.; others.

NICHOLS, MATHIAS, Inv., 9-17-1810.

NICHOLS, MATHIAS, Est., 9-17-1810.

NICHOLS, MATT., Sale, 12-13-1813.

NOBLE, THOS., Will, 4-15-1794.
Dev.: Joseph Lamon.

NOLAND, WM., Will, 4-25-1804.
Dev.: Joanna, wife; Obed, Wm., Thom., Phil., Henry, Joshua, Pears, sons; Susannah, Mary, dau.

NOLAND, Wm., App., 6-25-1804.

NORMAN, DAVID, Will, 1-9-1815.
Dev.: James and Alex. Grimes.

NOURSE, JAMES, App., 7-19-1785.

NOURSE, JAMES, Est., 1-26-1807.

OBANION, BRIANT, Will, 6-15-1784.
Dev.: Eliz., wife; John, son; others.

OBANION, BRYANT, App., 8-17-1784.

OBURN, JAMES, Will, 3-19-1782.
Dev.: Sarah, wife; Hannah, dau.; Daniel, Thomas, sons.

OBURN, JAMES, Est., 5-20-1783.

OLER, GEO. A., Est. 4-21-1789.

OLLER, FRED., Est., 12-23-1805.

ORRICK, NICH., Will, 3-21-1781.
(Baltimore Co., Md.)
Dev.: John, Nich., Charles, sons;
Mary, wife; Marg., Susanah, Sarah,
Sidney, Ann, dau.; Alex., slave.

ORRICK, NICH., App., 6-20-1786.

ORRICK, WM., Will, 9-24-1804.
Dev.: Mary, mother; Chas., bro.; Sidney, Ann Stephenson, Susanna Butler, sis.; others.

ORRICK, WM., Inv., 6-23-1805.

OTT, NICH., App., 10-27-1800.

OTT, NICH., Inv., 4-26-1802.

OULEBAUGH, JACOB, Adm., 12-18-
1809.

OWEN, THOM., App., 1-27-1800.

OWLURBOUGH, JACOB, Sale, 1-25-
1803.

OZBURN, DAVID, Will, 8-20-1783.
Dev.: Katy, wife; David, Wm., sons;
Thom., grandson.

OZBURN; JONATHAN, Will, 3-16-1779.
Dev.: Jonathan Gerrard, Jonathan
Booth, grandsons; Mary Clark, grand-
dau.; others.

PALMER, JACOB, Will, 5-21-1810.
Dev.: Marthalena, wife; Rachel, Eliz.,
Barb., Catty, Susanna, Mary, Jeany,
dau.; John, Jacob, Chris., Martin,
Sam., sons.

PALMER, THOM., Will 6-26-1797.
(Bath, Va.)
Dev.: Anne, wife; John, Sam., Wm.,
bro.; Mary Parker, sis.; others.

PALMER, THOM., Est., 12-26-1808.

PARK, SAM. SR., Will, 7-23-1798.
Dev.: Elinor Orr, Sarah Eakin, Mary
Wilson, Jane Boyd, dau.; John, Sam.,
Joseph, sons; others.

PARKS, JAMES, Inv., 1-13-1791.

PARKS, JAMES, Est., 2-27-1797.

PARKS, JOHN, Will, 5-18-1784.
Dev.: Mary, wife; James, Wm., sons;
Eliz. Vance, dau.; others.

PARKS, JOHN, App. 6-15-1784.

PATTERSON, WM., Will, 4-17-1782.
Dev.: Eliz. Hannah, Sarah Hannah,
Ann Pendleton, Mary, Hannah, Anna,
Eleanor, dau.; Hannah, wife; Wm.,
David, Hugh Vance, sons.

PATTERSON, WM., Est., 5-20-1785.

PAUL, JOHN, Will, 3-19-1782.
Dev.: Eliz., wife; Mary Porterfield,
dau.; John, nephew.

PAUL, JOHN, App., 5-21-1782.

PAUL, WM., Est. 3-15-1785.

PAULL, WM., Will, 8-17-1779.
Dev.: Eliz., wife; Cath., dau.; Cath.
Finley, sis.

PAYNE, GEO., Will, 2-23-1801.
Dev.: Rachel, wife; Jesse, Geo.,
Henry, sons; Hannah Hazlett, Mary
Manifold, Rachel McCleary, Martha
Smith, Sarah Squibb, dau.; others.

PAYNE, GEO., Est., 9-18-1809.

PEARCE, JEAN, Will, 10-22-1804.
Dev.: Sarah McKain, Ann Orr, sis.;
others.

PEARCEY, JEAN, Inv., 2-25-1805.

PEARSON, ROSANNAH, App., 2-23-
1801.

PEERY, SAM., Will, 10-22-1804.
Dev.: Sam., son of Thom., Sam., son
of John, Sam., son of Wm., all three
are nephews.

PENDLETON, NAT., Will, 9-19-1793.
Dev.: Nat., Wm., Philip, sons; Mary
Williams, Eliz. Tutt, Susannah Wil-
son, dau.

PENDLETON, PHIL., Will, 1-25-1802.
Dev.: Agnes, wife; Eliz. Hunter,
Nancy Kennedy, Sarah, Maria, dau.;
Philip, James, Edmond, Henry, son;
Dan., slave.

PEPPERS, JOSH., Inv., 2-24-1806.

PHILIPAY, CHRISTIAN, Will, 9-17-
1793.
Dev.: Anna M., wife; John, son; all
other children.

PHILIPS, THOM., App., 9-19-1780.

PHILLIPPY, CHRISTIAN, App., 12-17-
1793.

PIKE, MICHAEL, App., 8-15-1775.

PLATNER, JOHN, Est., 1-27-1800.

PLATNER, JOHN, Sale, 1-27-1800.

PLOTNER, JOHN, App., 10-20-1791.

PLOTNER, MORRUS, Will, 6-8-1812.
Dev.: Sarah, wife; all children.

PLUMMER, JOS., Will, 6-23-1806.
Dev.: Jos., Sam., Moses, Aaron, Aza,
sons; Marian Ball, Ann.; Janney,
dau.; others.

PLUMMER, JOS., App., 12-22-1806.

POISAL, PETER, SR., Will, 5-21-1810.
Dev.: Magdalene, wife; Peter, Jacob,
sons; Marg., dau.; all other children.

POLAND, SAM., Will, 10-17-1780.
Dev.: Jamimah, wife; Sam., John,
sons; Margaret Eve, Mary, dau.;
Eliz., Williamson's two sons.

POLAND, SAM., Inv., 11-21-1780.

POLLOCK, ALLEN, Will, 4-23-1798.
Dev.: Sarah, John, Nancy, And.,
James Miller.

PORTERFIELD, ALEX., Will, 7-24-1799.
Dev.: Eliz., wife; Wm., John, Arch.,
sons; Sarah, Martha, Nancy, Rachel,
Polly, dau.

PORTERFIELD, ALEX., App., 10-23-
1799.

PORTERFIELD, MATT., Will, 12-24-
1804.
Dev.: Josiah, Geo., bro.; Rachel
Mason, Mary Harlan, sis.; others.

POTTINGER, ROBT., App., 9-16-1778.

POTTS, JOHN, Will, 7-25-1808.
Dev.: Wife: Peggy Silar, Hannah
Becket, Elenor Cofflin, Eliz. Potts,
dau.; Charles, John, sons.

POTTS, JOHN, Inv., 6-19-1809.

PRICE, IGNATIUS, Will, 7-28-1795.
Dev.: Ann, wife; Richard, bro.; Levi,
Ignatius, sons; others.

PRICE, IGNATIUS, Est., 9-25-1798.

PRICE, JACOB, Will, 6-27-1808.
Dev.: Jane, wife; Ephraim, Jos., Jacob, Dan., sons; Mary, Susannah, Betsy, Hannah, dau.; unborn infant.

PRICE, JACOB, Sale, 2-18-1811.

PULTZ, JACOB, Inv., 2-25-1805.

PULTZ, MICH., Inv., 1-27-1806.

PULTZ, MICH., Est., 4-26-1808.

PYKE, MICHAEL, Will, 3-21-1775.
Dev.: William, son; Stephen, bro.; and others.

PYKE, WM., Will, 11-30-1776.
Dev.: Mary Hurst, Esther Clark, dau.

PYKE, WM., App., 8-19-1777.

PYLES, RICH., App., 8-15-1780.

PYLES, RICH., Sale, 8-15-1780.

QUIGLEY, JOHN, Est., 9-13-1813.

QUINN, JAS., Will, 7-23-1804.
Dev.: numerous bequests.

QUINN, JAMES, Inv., 2-24-1806.

RACOB, JACOB, Will, 9-27-1802.
Dev.: Eliz. Racob, sis.; other.

RACOB, JACOB, Inv., 1-24-1803.

RAMSBERGER, HENRY, Inv., 4-13-1812.

RAMSBERGER, HEN., Sale, 4-13-1812.

RAMSEY, SAM., Will, 10-24-1808.
Dev.: Rachel Ramsey alias Cross; Eley, Rachel, nieces.

RAMSEY, SAM., Sale, 6-18-1810.

RANDALL, JAMES, Est., 1-27-1806.

RANDELS, ROGER, App., 1-10-1815.

RANDOLPH, JOHN, Will, 9-21-1790.
Dev.: Cath., Ann, Marg., dau.; Wm., son; two other children.

RANDOLPH, JOHN, Est., 7-25-1796.

RANKIN, BENJ., Will, 1-16-1787.
Dev.: Judith, wife; Marg. Helm, Molly Rankin, dau.; others.

RAY, LUCUS, App., 1-22-1794.

REAGAR, BURKET, Will, 10-15-1782.
Dev.: Marg., wife; Burket, Leo., Geo., Henry, Anthony, sons; Sarah, Prudance, Marg. Stroop, dau.; other children.

REDMAN, ROBT., App., 2-16-1790.

REES, ENOCK, Will, 6-27-1803.
Dev.: Jacob, David, Ellis, Sam., bro.; Jane Wilson, Lydia, Ross, Mary Rees, Hanna Rees, sis.

REILEY, JOHN, App., 8-17-1779.

RHEINEFELD, JOHN, Will, 5-11-1812.
Dev.: Philipine, wife; Nich. Roush, friend.

RHODES, JOHN, Inv., 4-17-1793.

RHODES, JOHN, Est., 9-26-1797.

RICHARDSON, JOHN, Will, 7-21-1806.
Dev.: Thom., James, sons; Maryburg, Nancy, Sweny, Grace, dau.; others.

RICHARDSON, JOS., Est., 1-19-1790.

RIDENOUR, JOHN, Will, 9-17-1810.
Dev.: Eliz., wife; Geo., son; Eliz., Cath., dau.

RIDENOUR, JOHN, Inv., 4-14-1812.

RIDGEWAY, JOHN, App., 1-21-1794.

RIELEY, JOHN, Will, 10-15-1793.
Dev.: John, Geo., Magnus, and Wm. Tate, half-bro.; others.

RILEY, JOHN, SR., Will, 12-21-1801.
Dev.: Thom., John, Wm., sons; Mary, Mary Kennedy, dau.; Martah, wife; others.

RILEY, JOHN, Inv., 6-21-1802.

RIPPY, JOS., Will, 3-15-1774.
(Frederick Co.)
Dev.: Ellen, wife; Mathew, son; others.

ROACH, ANN, App., 12-18-1809.

ROACH, JAS., App., 12-26-1808.

ROACH, JAMES, Est., 1-21-1811.

ROADS, JOHN, Will, 2-19-1793.
Dev.: Eliz., wife; Dorathia, Mary, dau. '

ROAKE, JOHN, Sale, 4-11-1815.

ROBERTS, HANNAH, App., 9-12-1814.

ROBERTS, HANNAH, Est., 3-13-1815.

ROBERTS, JON., App., 12-18-1809.

ROBERTS, JON., Est., 2-20-1810.

ROBERTS, SAM., Will, 2-25-1799.
Dev.: Dan., Sam., Wm., Abraham, Isaac, John, sons; Hannah, Mary, Rebecca, Ruth, Anny, dau.

ROBERTS, SAM., Est., 1-25-1802.

ROBINSON, ALEX., Inv., 3-9-1812.

ROBINSON, ALEX., Est., 3-14-1814.

ROBINSON, JAMES, Inv., 6-25-1798.

ROBINSON, JAS., Will, 12-22-1806.
Dev.: Hannah, wife; Israel, Thom., Geo., Abraham, James, sons; Sally Milligan, Eliz. Winning, Hannah Cunningham, Lydia, dau.

ROBINSON, JAS., Est., 8-9-1814.

ROCHESTER, ELIZ., Inv., 1-27-1806.

ROMAN, THOM., Will, 9-10-1815.
Dev.: Cath., wife; Thom., Abr., sons; Susanah Hacden, dau.; others.

ROSE, CONRAD, Will, 6-27-1796.
Dev.: Mary, wife; Henry, Chris, bro.; Marg. Nevil, Hannah, sis.

ROSE, CONRAD, Inv., 9-26-1796.

ROSE, JONATHAN, Will, 8-16-1785.
Dev.: Anne or Nancy, wife; others.

ROSE, JONATHAN, App., 11-15-1785.

ROSS, STEPHEN, Will, 5-16-1780.
Dev.: Marg., wife; Lydia, Mary, dau.; Nathan, Gabrill, sons.

ROSS, STEPHEN, App., 3-21-1781.

ROY, RENOLD, App., 5-21-1776.

RUMSEY, JAMES, Will, 9-17-1793.
Dev.: Wife; James, son; Susannah, Clarisa, dau.; others.

RUMSEY, JAS., App., 2-19-1794.

RUMSEY, JAMES, Est., 2-24-1801.

RUSH, ABR., Inv., 12-11-1815.

RUSH, ABR., Sale, 12-11-1815

RUSH, JACOB, Inv., 6-10-1811.

RUSH, LEONARD, Will, 4-15-1788.
Dev.: Ann, wife; Wm., Jacob, Abraham, sons; Mary, Rebecca, Sidney, Eliz., Sarah, Susannah, dau.

RUSSELL, REBECCA, Will, 3-21-1780.
Dev.: Wm., son; Hanna Jones, sis., and her children.

RUSSELL, REBECCA, Est., 8-21-1781.

RUTHERFORD, ROBT., JR., App., 8-16-1785.

RUTHERFORD, ROBT., Est., 2-23-1795.

RUTHERFORD, THOM. JR., Will, 7-25-1796.
Dev.: Mary, wife; Sarah, dau.; Van, bro.

RUTHERFORD, THOM. JR., Inv., 6-26-1797.

RYAN, JOHN, Sale, 9-16-1788.

RYON, JOHN, Will, 2-19-1788.
Dev.: Mary, wife; Sarah, Cloe, dau.; John, Jr., son.

SAVELEY, CATH., Will, 5-8-1815.
Dev.: Jacob, son.

SAVELEY, CATH., Inv., 6-12-1815.

SAVELY, FRED., Inv., 6-22-1807.

SAVLEY, FRED., Est., 10-14-1811.

SCOTT, GEO., Will, 9-16-1788.
Dev.: Angeletta, wife; Wm., Geo. James, sons; others.

SCOTT, GEO., App., 10-22-1788.

SEABURN, GEO., Will, 10-24-1796.
Dev.: Wife; Dan., Theodorur, Peter, David, Wm., sons; Elinor, dau.

SEABURN, GEO., Inv., 1-25-1797.

SEAMAN, JACOMIAH, App., 8-19-1783.

SEAMAN, JACOMIAH, Est., 3-15-1785.

SEAMAN, JONAH, Will, 10-21-1783.
Dev.: John, Jeremiah, Jonah, Chas., sons; Carry, Eliz., Cath., Hannah, Pheba, Susah, Martha, Lydia, dau.

SEAMAN, JONAH, Est., 1-23-1797.

SEAMAN, JONATHAN, Will, 3-15-1785.
Dev.: Phebe Seaman, sis.

SEAMON, PHEBE, Will, 9-21-1807.
Dev.: numerous bequests.

SEEVER, PETER, Will, 11-20-1781.
Dev.: Hannah, wife; Henry, son; Cath., Eliz., Mary, dau.

SEEVER, PETER, App., 9-19-1786.

SEWELL, JOHN, Will, 12-17-1793.
Dev.: Jane, wife; Abigail, Elizabeth, Jane, Ann, dau.; Timothy, David, sons.

SEWELL, JOHN, Est., 4-22-1799.

SHARP, JOHN, Inv., 6-28-1803.

SHARP, THOM. SR., Will, 5-15-1809.
Dev.: Thom., John, sons; Rebecca, dau.; Rachel Hare, housekeeper.

SHARP, THOM., App., no date.

SHAVER, MICH., Est., 4-17-1793.

SHAVER, MICH., App., 3-15-1785.

SHEAR, HENRY, Est., 6-18-1810.

SHEARER, ARCH., App., 6-22-1801.

SHEARER, CAPT. ARCH., Est., 1-26-1807.

SHEARER, HENRY, Inv., 12-23-1805.

SHEARER, HENRY, Sale, 12-23-1805.

SHEARER, JOHN, App., 6-17-1777.

SHEARER, JOHN, Est., 6-16-1778.

SHEARER, SARAH, Inv., 12-23-1805.

SHEARER, SARAH, Sale, 12,23-1805.

SHEARER, THOM., App., 3-8-1813.

SHEARER, THOM., Sale, 3-8-1813.

SHEERER, ARCH., Will, 4-21-1800.
Dev.: John, Thom., James, Harry, Arch., sons; Martha, Mary, Kath., Eliz., Nancy, Sally, dau.; Sarah, wife.

SHEERER, ARCH., Sale, 10-25-1802.

SHEERER, SARAH, Will, no date.
Dev.: Cath., Sarah, Eliz., Marthy Nancy, Mary, dau.; James, Henry. Arch., John, Thom., sons.

SHEETS, PHIL., Will, 2-18-1794.
Dev.: Juliana, wife; Martin, Jacob, sons; Margaret Hanes, dau.; others.

SHEETS, PHIL., Est., 6-23-1800.

SHEPHERD, ELIZ., Will, 6-18-1793.
Dev.: David, son; Susannah, dau.

SHEPHERD, THOM., Will, 10-16-1792.
Dev.: Susannah, wife; Thom., David, John, Joseph, James, sons.

SHEPHERD, THOM. SR., Will, 8-20-1776.
Dev.: Eliz., wife; Wm., Thom., John, Abraham, David, sons; Susanna, Mary, Martha, Sarah, Eliz., dau.; others.

SHEPHERD, THOM., Set., 8-9-1814.

SHEPHERD, THOMAS, Est., 8-18-1779.

SHETFORD, SIMON, Will, 1-21-1783.
Dev.: Eliz., wife.

SHIELDS, JOHN, Inv., 9-26-1808.

SHOAPSTALL, JOHN, Inv., 6-23-1805.

SHOAPSTALL, JOHN, Sale, 6-23-1805.

SHYROCK, LEONARD, App., 3-19-1782.

SIBERT, WINDEL, Will, 10-26-1802.
Dev.: Henry, Christian, Peter, Jacob, Wendel, Fred., Mich., John, sons; Maria, Eliz., Cath., dau.

SIBERT, WENDLE, Inv., 10-27-1806.

SILAR, PETER, App., 12-21-1807.

SILBORN, FRANCES, Will, 3-15-1774.
Dev.: Mary, wife.

SILER, ANDREW, Inv., 6-23-1805.

SILER, ANDREW, Inv., 8-10-1812.

SILER, JACOB, SR., Will, 7-23-1804.
Dev.: Esther, wife; Andrew, Phil., Jacob, John, sons; Esther Tharp, Hanna Elder, Charity Fraise, Eliz., Molly Snyder, dau.

SILER, JACOB, Inv., 1-21-1805.

SIMPSON, WM., App., 1-21-1805.

SKELDING, JOHN, App., 4-22-1789.

SKINNER, WM., Will, 12-18-1793.
Dev.: Rebecca, wife; Joseph, bro.; others.

SKINNER, WM., App., 1-24-1794.

SLIGH, FRED., Will, 1-26-1801.
Dev.: Christiana, wife; Matthias, Henry, Fred., sons; Mary Melvin, Cath. Ager, dau.

SLOAN, JOHN, Inv., 6-16-1789.

SLOCUM, ISAAC, Est., 4-15-1794.

SLOCUM, ISAAC, App., 4-15-1794.

SMALL, ADAM, App., 8-21-1781.

SMITH, ALEX., App., 7-27-1801.

SMITH, JOHN, Will, 6-25-1798.
Dev.: John, Jr., Wm., Rees, Moses, sons; Phebe Fry, Sarah, dau.; Eliz., wife.

SMITH, JOHN, will, 2-24-1800.
Dev.: John, Jr., Rees, Moses, sons; Phebe Fry, Sarah, dau.; others.

SMITH, JOHN, Will, 6-23-1800.
Dev.: Sarah, wife; Elinor, dau.; John, son.

SMITH, THOM., Will, 7-19-1791.
Dev.: Cath. Woolf, Eliz. Droomgoole, Rose Striat, dau.; Thom., John, David, sons.

SMITH, WM., App., 12-19-1786.

SMOOT, ED., Will, 4-23-1798.
Dev.: Jane, wife; Rachel, dau.; Josiah, bro.; others.

SMOOT, ED., App., 10-23-1798.

SNIDER, BALSER, Will, 8-8-1814.
Dev.: Cath., wife; Phil., Paul, sons; Cath., Mary Flatcher, dau.; others.

SNIDER, HENRY, Will, 10-27-1806.
Dev.: Sarah, wife; Sarah, Eliz., Betty, dau., Dan., John, sons.

SNIDER, HENRY, Est., 12-21-1807.

SNIDER, JACOB, Will, 6-15-1790.
Dev.: Marg., wife; David, Joseph, Abraham, Wm., John, Jacob, Dan., Geo., sons.

SNIDER, JACOB, App., 9-21-1790.

SNIVELY, JOHN, Adm., 10-16-1809.

SNODGRASS, JOHN, Will, 2-19-1788.
Dev.: Wm., Benj., James, John, sons; Eliz. Kennedy, Cath., Sarah Eakin, dau.

SNODGRESS, JOHN, App., 6-17-1788.

SNOW, GUY, Est., 4-15-1783.

SNOW, GUY, Est., 12-17-1793.

SNYDER, JACOB, Est., 2-24-1806.

SOPER, FRED., Est., 1-23-1809.

SOPER, FRED., App., 1-23-1809.

SOPER, FRED., Est., 10-9-1815.

SOUDER, JOHN, Est., 4-17-1793.

SOUDER, JOHN, Est., 2-11-1812.

SOUDER, RUDOLPH, App., 9-20-1785.

SOUDER, RUDOLPH, Est., 9-27-1803.

SPAW, THEO., Will, 2-22-1808.
Dev.: Dorathy, wife; John, Henry, Ed., Simon, sons; Nancy, Eliz. Matthews, Cath., Rebecca Meeks, Sarah Sackman, Susannah, Fanny, Ruth, dau.

SPAW, THEO., Est., 9-13-1813.

SPROUL, SAM., App., 11-15-1785.

SPROWL, SAM., Adm., 1-21-1804.

STALEY, JACOB, Will, 10-15-1793.
Dev.: Cath., wife; Jacob, Peter, John, Stephen, Dan., sons; Sarah Fisher, Cath. Strayer, dau.

STALEY, JACOB, App., 1-21-1794.

STANLEY, ISAAC, Will, 12-16-1794.
Dev.: Mary, wife; Mary, Ann, Elizabeth, dau.; Joseph, Isaac, John, Archelous, sons; John, bro.

STANLEY, ISAAC., Est., 9-26-1803.

STARRY, DAN., App., 9-18-1787.

STARRY, DAN., Sale, 9-18-1787.

STEPHENS, RICH., Inv., 10-23-1797.

STEPHENS, ROBT., Will, 12-9-1811.
Dev.: Alex., Adam, sons; Mary, Nancy Gregory, Marg. Kennedy, dau.; others.

STEPHENS, ROBT., Inv., 11-14-1814.

STEPHENSON, HUGH, Will, 11-20-1776.
Dev.: Ann, wife; Wm., John, Marcus, Hugh, sons; Nancy, Betsy, dau.

STEPHENSON, JAS., Will, 2-25-1805.
Dev.: Mary, wife; James, Wm., Benj., sons; Marg. Sterrit, Sarah Kennedy, Isabella Boyd, Maria Boyd, dau.; Cath., Bound girl.

STEPHENSON, RICH., Will, 4-16-1776.
Dev.: Eliz., wife; Sarah, Mary, Effie, Bell, dau.

STEPHENSON, RICH., Will, 9-16-1777.
Dev.: Jane, wife; Rosannah, Ann, Mary, Eliz., Abigail, dau.; Rich., son; others.

STEPHENSON, RICH., Will, 5-21-1782.
Dev.: Ann, wife; Rich., John, sons; Mary, Ruth, Jane, dau.

STEPHENSON, RICHARD, Will, 4-27-1795.
Dev.: John, bro.; Ruth, Jane, sis.

STEWART, GEO., Will, 9-18-1792.
Dev.: Ann, wife; James, bro.; other.

STEWART, GEORGE, Est., 1-20-1795.

STEWART, JOHN, Will, 9-23-1799.
Dev.: Chas., bro.; Marg., wife.

STIP, FRED., Will, 12-26-1808.
Dev.: Fanny, wife; all children.

STIP, FRED., Inv., 6-19-1809.

STIP, PETER, App., 10-15-1782.

STIPP, MARTIN, Will, 10-26-1795.
Dev.: Susannah, wife; Abraham, son; Mary, Eliz., Cath., Sarah, Marg., Susannah, dau.

STIPP, MARTIN, Est., 2-21-1803.

STOCKTON, ROBT., Est., 6-17-1778.

STOKE, AND., Inv., 10-18-1810.

STRAYER, NICH., SR., Will, 4-18-1809.
Dev.: Maria Cath., wife; Mich., Adam, John, sons; Susanna Couchman, dau.; others.

STRAYER, NICH., SR., Sale, 9-13-1813.

STRICKLER, CON., App., 10-22-1804.

STRIDER, ISAAC, Will, 1-22-1794.
Dev.: Christina, wife; Thomas, Samuel, William, John, Henry, Philip, Isaac, Jacob, sons; Charlotte, Sally, Mary, dau.; others.

STRIDER, KILIAN, Will, 11-19-1810.
Dev.: Christiana Hout, dau.

STRIDER, KILIAN, Inv., 5-13-1811.

STRIDER, PHIL., Inv., 2-24-1806.

STRODE, JAS., Will, 4-28-1795.
Dev.: Elizabeth, wife; Susannah Magowan, Elinor Shepherd, Rachel Bedinger, Anna, dau.; James, John, sons; others.

STRODE, JAS., Est., 3-15-1815.

STRODE, JAMES, Inv., 2-22-1796.

STRODE, JER., Est., 6-24-1799.

STRODE, JEREMIAH, Will, 3-15-1785.
Dev.: Marg., wife; Mary Evans, Anne,
dau.; James, Ed., Geo., John, Jeremiah, Wm., sons.

STRODE, JOHN, Inv., 1-26-1804.

STRODE, JOHN, Est., 4-26-1808.

STROOP, ELIZ., Will, 8-21-1781.
Dev.: Cath. Dust, Eliz. Cooper, Barb.
Morritt, dau. Wm., Jacob, Henry,
Milgan, sons; others.

STROOP, ELIZ., Sale, 8-20-1782.

STROOP, HENRY, Will, 12-18-1787.
Dev.: Jenny, wife; John, Wm., sons;
Betsy, Polly, dau.

STROOP, HENRY, App., 4-15-1788.

STROPE, MELEHON, App., 8-20-1782.

STRUP, HENRY, Est., 2-16-1790.

SWEARINGEN, JOS., Est., 12-27-1802.

SWEARINGEN, SARAH, Will, 12-23-
1799.
Dev.: Thom., Andrew, Van, Joseph,
Bennoni, sons; Drusilla Morgan, Elinor Israel, dau.

SWEARINGEN, THOM., Will, 2-20-1786.
Dev.: Thom., Van, Andrew, sons;
Drusilla, Lydia, dau.; Binoni, bro.

SWEARINGEN, THOM., Est., 9-16-1788.

SWEARINGEN, THOM., Will, 7-8-1811.
Dev.: Margery, wife; others.

SWEARINGEN, THOM., Will, 2-14-1814.
Dev.: Thom., Van, And., sons; Drusilla, Lydai, dau.; Benoni, bro.

SWEARINGEN, THOM., Est., 11-14-1815.

SWEARINGEN, VAN, Will, 6-17-1788.
Dev.: Priscilla, wife; Peggy, Susannah Bennett, Drusilla Rutherford,
dau.; Josiah, Hezekiah, sons.

SWEARINGEN, COL. VAN., App., 9-15-
1789.

SWEARINGEN, COL. VAN. Est., 10-16-
1792.

SWEARINGEN, VAN., Will, 7-17-1792.
Dev.: Thom., Andrew, bro.; Lydia
Morgan, sis.; others.

SWEARINGER, THOM., JR., Will, 3-21-
1788.
Dev.: Hannah, wife; Sarah Bennet,
niece.

SWEGAR, JACOB, Est., 5-15-1781.

SWIFT, GODWIN, Will, 4-23-1798.
Dev.: Meade Swift, nephew; Jane
Swift, niece; others.

SWIGAR, JOSEPH, Will, 3-21-1775.
Dev.: wife; George, Jacob, sons; and
others.

SWINGLEY, PETER, Inv., 1-22-1798.

SYBERT, FRED., Will, 11-13-1813.
Dev.: Eve, wife; Mich., Henry, sons.

SYBERT, HENRY, Inv., 4-24-1804.

SYBERT, WENDELL, Will, 12-23-1805.
Dev.: Marg., wife; all other children.

SYLER, JOHN, App., 6-14-1813.

SYLER, JOHN, Sale, 6-14-1813.

TABB, ROBT., App., 5-21-1776.

TABB, ROBT., Est., 8-20-1782.

TAYLOR, ISAAC, App., 11-21-1780.

TAYLOR, JOHN, Will, 2-20-1793.
Dev.: Blanche, wife; Wm., John, Levi,
Sam., sons; Sarah, Susannah Hendricks, Jean Morgan, Mary Brown,
dau.

TAYLOR, JOHN, Est., 6-25-1798.

TAYLOR, SAM., Will, 2-21-1786.
Dev.: Sarah, wife; John, Isaac, Dan.,
Wm., Rich., Jacob, sons; Mary, Sus-
annah, dau.

TAYLOR, SAM., Est., 2-21-1792.

THATCHER, SAM., Will, 11-20-1776.
Dev.: Mary, wife; Thom., Jonathan,
sons.

THATCHER, SAM., Est., 8-19-1779.

THATCHER, STEPHEN, Inv., 12-27-
1803.

THATCHER, STEPHEN, Est., 10-21-
1805.

THOM, GEO., App., 10-25-1796.

THOMPSON, CORN., Will, 5-5-1815.
Dev.: John, bro.; Anna McDonald,
sis.; others.

THOMPSON, CORN., Inv., 12-11-1815.

THORNBERRY, FRANCES, App., 8-17-
1779.

THORNBERRY, THOM., Will, 10-20-
1789.
Dev.: Thom., John, Hezekiah, Joaish,
Wm., Azamah, sons; Mercy, Sarah,
dau.; others.

THORNBOROUGH, THOM., Est., 10-15-
1810.

THORNBROUGH, BENJ., App., 1-23-
1795.

THORNBROUGH, SARAH, Will, 2-23-
1795.
Dev.: Deborah Lee, Sarah Lee,
Thomas Lee, others.

THORNBRUGH, BENJ., Est., 9-25-1797.

THROCKMORTON, JOB, Will, 9-19-
1730.
Dev.: Sarah, Mary, dau.

THROCKMORTON, JOB, App., 8-20-
1782.

THROCKMORTON, JOHN, Will, 8-13-
1775.
Dev.: Elizabeth, dau.; Albion, Robert,
son.

THROCKMORTON, JOHN, Est., 1-21-
1795.

THROCKMORTON, ROBT., Will, 10-24-
1796.
Dev.: John, son; Lucy Moore, dau.

THROCKMORTON, ROBT., Est., 9-27-
1802.

THROCKMORTON, WM., App., 6-26-
1797.

THUMMY, JACOB, Will, 3-18-1783.
Dev.: Hannah Close, dau.; others.

THURSTON, JOHN, Adm., 9-10-1811.

THUSTIN, WM., App., 8-21-1782.

THUSTON, JOHN, App., 5-19-1779.

TILLEY, GEO., App., 6-22-1795.

TILLEY, GEO., Est., 4-26-1796.

TILROY, ANDREW, Est., 7-25-1796.
TINGLE, GEO., Will, 3-18-1777.
Dev.: Mary, wife.
TINGLE, GEO., App., 5-20-1777.
TOOLE, JAMES, Inv., 2-24-1806.
TOOLE, JAMES, Sale, 2-24-1806.
TRAVERS, JOHN M., Will, 4-21-1778.
Dev.: Louisa, wife.
TULLIS, MOSES, Will, 10-21-1777.
Dev.: Mary E., wife; Aaron, son; and children.
TULLIS, MOSES, App., 3-20-1781.
TURNER, JOHN, Inv., 5-15-1792.
TURNER, JOHN, Est., 12-27-1802.
TURNER, JOHN, Will, 9-9-1811.
Dev.: Ruth, wife; Thom., Jos., John, sons; Mary, sis; Eliz., Mary, dau.
TURNER, JOHN, Inv., 5-11-1812.
TURNER, MARY, Will, 11-19-1782.
Dev.: Thom., Joseph, John, sons; Mary, Rebecca Swearingen, dau.; others.
TURNER, MARY, App., 3-18-1783.
TURNER, RUTH, Will, 2-13-1815.
Dev.: Jos., John, Thom., sons; Eliz., Mary, dau.; Phyllis, slave.
TURNER, RUTH, App., 3-13-1815.
TYTES, FRAN., Will, 8-12-1811.
Dev.: Jane, wife; Tunis, son; Mary Dungan, Marg. Prendwick, Ann Carter, Rebeckah Crage, Eliz., dau.; others.
TYTUS, FRAN., App., 4-11-1814.
UNGER, NICH., Will, 4-11-1814.
Dev.: Cath., wife; Mary, Cath., dau.; Nich., Geo., John, Dan., Henry, Washington, sons.
VANARSDALE, CORN., App., 3-20-1782.
VANCE, HUGH, Will, 1-17-1792.
Dev.: Eliz., wife; John, James, John, sons; Sarah, Polly, Eliz., Nancy, Mary, dau.; others.
VANCE, HUGH, Est., 9-25-1797.
VANCE, JOS., Will, 9-23-1799.
Dev.: Rachel, wife; Jane, Rachel, dau.; John, Sam., Joseph, Alex, sons; others.
VANCE, JOS., Est., 6-25-1804.
VANCE, RACHEL, Will, 1-9-1815.
Dev.: John, Sam., Jos., Alex., sons; Rachel Porterfield, dau.
VANMETER, ABRAHAM, SR., Will, 11-18-1783.
Dev.: Dan., John, Joseph, Jacon, Abraham, Isaac, sons; Ruth, Hannah, Rebeccah Spahar, Mary, dau.
VANMETER, HENRY, Will, 12-17-1793.
Dev.: Elizabeth, wife; Hester, dau.; Nathan, Henry, Joshua, sons; other.
VANMETER, HENRY, App., 2-19-1794.
VANMETRE, ABRAHAM, Est., 9-22-1800.
VANMETRE, JACOB, SR., Will, 10-27-1806.
Dev.: Isabella, wife; Magdalen Burns, Isabella Gorrell, Mary Evans, Eliz. Tabb, Ruth Gorrell, Anna Vanmetre,

dau.; Isaac, Abraham, Jos., Jacob, sons.
VANMETRE, JACOB, Sale, 1-23-1809.
VEAL, ISAAC, Inv., 9-23-1805.
VEAL, ISAAC, Est., 2-22-1808.
VERDIER, JAMES, Will, 11-15-1785.
Dev.: Susannah, wife; James, Paul, Adam, sons; Mary Anne, Eliz., Jenny, dau.
VERDIER, JAMES, Est., 10-19-1790.
VERNER, PAUL, Will, 12-11-1815.
Dev.: Anna Maria, wife; Eliz. Dybert, Sarah Spero, Polly Knode, dau.; others.
VESTALL, JOHN, App., 3-9-1776.
VINCENHELLER, PHIL., Est., 6-19-1809.
VINSENHELLER, PHIL., App., 1-27-1800.
VIOLET, LEROY, Est., 4-26-1796.
WAGGONER, CHRIS., Will, 10-21-1794.
Dev.: Mary, wife; others.
WAGGONER, MAJ. AND., App., 1-10-1815.
WAGGONER, MAJ. AND., Sale, 1-10-1815.
WALLS, GEO., Will, 4,19-1788.
Dev.: Mary, wife; Thom., Jacob, Geo., Sam., sons; Ann, Mary, Eliz. Patton, dau.; others.
WARD, AQUILLA, Inv., 9-22-1806.
WARD, AQUILLA, Adm., 12-14-1812.
WARD, JOSEPH, Will, 12-18-1787.
Dev.: Mary, wife; Joseph, Stephen, sons.
WARD, JOSHUA, Inv., 1-17-1792.
WARD, JOSHUA, Est., 7-28-1795.
WASHINGTON, CHAS., Will, 9-23-1799.
Dev.: Mildred, wife; Sam., son.
WASHINGTON, FERD., App., 6-16-1789.
WASHINGTON, SAM., Will, 12-18-1781.
Dev.: Wife; Thornton, John Perrin, Ferdinand, Geo. Steptoe, Lawrence A., sons; Harriett, dau.; John, bro.
WASHINGTON, SAM., Est., 1-26-1807.
WASHINGTON, SUSANNAH, Will, 5-20-1783.
Dev.: John Perrin, son; Nancy and Susannah Holding, dau.; others.
WASHINGTON, MRS. SUSANNAH, App., 8-19-1783.
WASHINGTON, THORN., Est., 1-15-1793.
WASHINGTON, THORNTON, Will, 10-16-1787.
Dev.: Frances T., wife; Sam., son; two sons of former wife; others.
WATSON, JOHN, Est., 5-19-1779.
WATSON, JOHN, SR., Will, 11-15-1785.
Dev.: Agnes, wife; Thom., John, James, sons; Jean, wife; Mary, Jean, dau.; others.
WATSON, THOM., Will, 10-20-1778.
Dev.: John, Sam., Thom., Wm., James, Jacob, sons; Marg., Mary, dau.
WATSON, THOM., Est., 1-25-1796.

WEAVER, CHRIS., Will, 4-15-1788.
Dev.: Eliz., wife; John, Wm., Henry,
Christopher, sons; Mary, Dolly, Eliz.,
dau.
WELCH, JACOB, Est., 1-23-1797.
WELSH, JACOB, Will, 6-19-1787.
Dev.: Barb., wife; Jacob, Henry, son;
Susannah, dau.; other children.
WEST, DAN., App., 1-19-1790.
WHITE, JOHN, App., 7-28-1795.
WHITING, ELIZ., App., 10-26-1795.
WHITING, ELIZ., Est., 6-24-1799.
WHITING, FRANCES, App., 9-15-1778.
WHITING, MATHEW, Est., 6-24-1799.
WHITING, MATTHEW, Inv., 10-16-1792.
WHITMORE, FRED., App., 8-17-1784.
WIGHT, JAMES, Inv., 2-25-1799.
(OR WITE)
WILCOX, HOMER, Inv., 12-10-1811.
WILLIAMS, JEROME, App., 7-17-1792.
WILLIS, RICH., Will, 6-24-1799.
7-22-1799; 4-21-1800.
Dev.: Perrin Willis, nephew; Ann
Rich Willis, niece; others.
WILLIS, ROBT. C., Will, 10-21-1783.
Dev.: Martha, wife; Lewis B., Robt.
C., sons; Eliz., sis.; others.
WILLIS, COL. ROBT. C., App. 11-18-
1783.
WILSON, JAS., Will, 3-13-1815.
Dev.: Jane, wife; James, son; Jane
Roberts, Sarah Newell, Mary Warver,
dau.; others.
WILSON, JAS., Inv., 6-12-1815.
WILSON, JOHN, Will, 4-16-1783.
Dev.: Jane, wife; Ed., Wm., Jacob,
James, Jeremiah, John, Thom., La-
ther, Dan., Isaac, sons; Eliz. Clawson,
Mary Jones, Sarah, dau.
WILSON, JOHN, App., 6-18-1783.
WILSON, JOS., App., 4-21-1778.
WILSON, JOSEPH, Will, 10-27-1795.
(Montgomery Co., Md.)
Dev.: Sarah, Ann Worthington, Mary
Davis, dau.; others.
WILSON, PHIL., Inv., 6-27-1808.
WILSON, PHIL., Sale, 10-12-1812.
WINING, SAM., Will, 6-14-1813.
Dev.: Eliz., wife; all children.
WINING, SAM., Inv., 3-16-1814.
WINNING, ALEX., Will, 10-16-1809.
Dev.: Sam., John, bro.; Marg., Nancy
Cunningham, sis.; others.
WINNING, ALEX., Est., 12-9-1811.
WINNING, JAS., Will, 2-27-1804.
Dev.: Mary, wife; Sam., Jas., John,
Alex., sons; Peggy, Nancy, Eliz., dau.
WINSETT, RICH., App., 5-18-1791.
WINSETT, RICH., Est., 2-23-1792.
WITHERS, WM., Will, 9-20-1785.
Dev.: Rachel, wife; James, Wm., sons;
Eliz. Hoskins, Mary Fleece, dau.;
others.
WITHERS, WM., App., 1-17-1786.
WOLFORD, MARTIN, Will, 3-20-1781.
Dev.: Elnore, wife; Jacob, John, sons;
Eliz., dau.

WOLGAMOTT, DAVID, App., 6-24-1799.
WOLGAMOTT, DAVID, Est., 9-21-1801.
WOLGAMOTT, SUS., Inv., 12-27-1803.
WOLTZ, PETER, Will, 11-15-1785.
Dev.: Eliz., wife; Geo., Peter, sons;
Eliz., Islor, Anne Sheetz, Mary Bish-
op, dau.
WOOLAM, JACOB, Est., 4-19-1786.
WOOLLAM, JACOB, Will, 11-17-1778.
Dev.: Magdaline, wife; Dan., John,
Jacob, Balses, Mathias, Peter, Windle,
Sham, sons; Juliana Shellingand,
Magdaline Morsey, Hannah, dau.
WORM, MICH., Inv., 5-16-1792.
WORM, MICH., Est., 10-15-1793.
WORTHINGTON, EPH., App., 7-26-1797.
WORTHINGTON, EPHRAIM, Will, 6-
26-1797.
Dev.: Effy, wife; Robt., son; Marg.,
Martha, dau.
WORTHINGTON, ROBT., Will, 3-17-
1779.
Dev.: Marg., wife; Ephraim, Wm.,
Robt., Thom., sons; Martha, Mary,
dau.
WORTHINGTON, ROBT., App., 9-19-
1780.
YEATS, ANDREW, Will, 12-24-1804.
Dev.: Thom., Jos., Wm., David, James,
John, Andrew, sons; Mary Finley,
Jane, Eliz., dau.
YEATS, ANDREW, Inv., 2-20-1810.
YINGLING, MARY, Will, 6-23-1806.
Dev.: John, Abraham, James, Benj.,
Jacob, sons; Rachel How, dau.;
others.
YOEL, HENRY, Will, 3-16-1779.
Dev.: Euphemia, wife; Cath., Marg.,
dau.; others.
YOEL, HENRY, App., 4-20-1779.
YOUNG, DAN., App., 7-20-1779.
YOUNG, ELIZ., Will, 5-11-1812.
Dev.: John Fisher, son; others.
YOUNG, HENRY, Inv., 8-15-1815.
YOUNG, JOHN D., Inv., 6-25-1804.
YOUNG, NICH., Will, 6-27-1796.
Dev.: Susannah, wife; Mary M., Eliz.,
Cath., Mary, dau.; Geo., Chris., son.
YOUNG, NICH., Inv., 2-28-1797.
YOUNG, NOAH, Will, 6-27-1796.
Dev.: Mary, Fanny, Eliz., dau.; Wm.,
son.
YOUNG, NOAH, Inv., 2-27-1797.
YOUNG, NOAH, Est., 4-22-1799.
ZEILER, CHRISTIAN, Inv., 6-12-1812.
ZEILER, CHRISTIAN, Sale, 6-12-1815.
ZEILER, PETER, Est., 4-12-1815.
ZEILOR, PETER, Adm., 11-11-1811.
ZIMMERMAN, ADAM, App., 9-15-1789.
ZIMMERMAN, ADAM, Est., 6-24-1800.
ZIMMERMAN, MICH., Inv., 9-10-1815.
ZIMMERMAN, MICH., Sale, 9-10-1815.
ZINN, PETER, Will, 12-22-1800.
Dev.: Jane, wife; Dan., son; others.
ZOMBRO, PETER, App., 12-14-1812.
ZOMBRO, PETER, Set., 6-13-1814.
ZUMBRO, PETER, Will, 2-10-1812.
Dev.: Eve, wife.

WEST VIRGINIA ESTATE SETTLEMENTS

In 1936 and 1937, the West Virginia Commission on Historic and Scenic Markers, the Works Progress Administration, and the Federal Emergency Relief Administration compiled court records of the various counties, such as Births, Deaths, Marriages and Wills. Under Wills were grouped subjects pertaining to Estate Settlements, including Wills, Inventories and Appraisements. Copies of these county records were filed at the Department of Archives and History, Charleston, the Library of West Virginia University, Morgantown, and the DAR Library, Washington.

Believing that there would be particular interest on the part of the general public in the Estate Settlements in the older counties, the West Virginia Historical Society has undertaken to abstract the Estate Settlements Records, as filed in the State Department of Archives and History, and offered them for publication in the *West Virginia History Quarterly*. (No responsibility can be assumed as to the accuracy of the copies made from the original county records.)

There are 13 counties which were formed prior to 1800, and it has been agreed to arrange these counties in chronological order, and to print their records from the earliest date to 1850. The formation dates of these counties are as follows: Hampshire—1753; Berkeley—1772; Monongalia—1776; Ohio—1776; Greenbrier—1778; Harrison—1784; Hardy—1786; Randolph—1787; Pendleton—1788; Kanawha—1788; Brooke—1797; Wood—1798 and Monroe—1799.

Berkeley County, Formed 1772
(1815-1850)

Abbreviations used in this material include: Adm.—administrator; Agr.—agreement; App.—appraisement; Bro.—brother; Dau.—daughter; Dev.—devisees; Divn.—division; Est.—estate a/c; Ind.—indenture; Inv.—inventory; L. G.—land grant; Obl. —obligation; S. B.—sale bill; Set.—Settlement; Sis.—sister; and Sur.—Survey.

ABEL, WM., App., 4-10-1848.

ABEL, WM., Sale, 4-10-1848.

ABELL, BENJ., App., 4-14-1829.

ABELL, BENJ., Est., 3-8-1830.

ABELL, SALLY, Will, 8-11-1846.
Dev.: John Jas., son; Susan McSherry, Jane E. Cleveland, dau.; others.

ALBURTIS, JOHN, Will, 5-14-1827.
Dev.: Nancy, wife; children; slaves.

ALBURTIS, WM., Will, 11-8-1847.
Dev.: Rose, wife; Bertrand, son.

ALEXANDER, ELIZ., Will, 1-14-1828.
Dev.: Mary, dau.

ALEXANDER, ELIZ., App., 6-9-1828.

ALEXANDER, JOS., App., 12-9-1822.

ALEXANDER, JOS., Est., 9-13-1824.

ALEXANDER, WM., Est., 8-13-1827.

ALEXANDER, WM., Est., 3-9-1830.

ALLEBAUGH, JOHN, App., 3-8-1841.

AMBROSE, HENRY, Est., 1815.

AMOS, GEO., Will, 5-12-1828.
Dev.: Barb., wife; Josh., Robt., bro.; slaves; others.

AMOS, GEO., App., 2-9-1829.

ANDERSON, COL., Est., 10-11-1824.

ANDERSON, COL., Est., 10-10-1831.

ANDERSON, ANN, App., 8-8-1825.

ANDERSON, ANN, Est., 2-8-1830.

ANDERSON, JAS., Est., 3-14-1825.

ANDERSON, PROV., App., 5-10-1824.

ANDERSON, PROV., Est., 5-8-1826.

AUSTIN, LEVI, Est., 12-14-1846.

BAKER, LEAKIN, Inv., 12-13-1824.

BAKER, LEAKIN, Est., 12-13-1824.

BAKER, SEAKIN, App., 6-11-1838.

BARNES, TETER, Will, 1-13-1823.
Dev.: Dan., John, Jacob, Henry, sons; Cath. Cramer, Eliz. Ervin, dau.; others.

BARR, JAMES, Will, 9-10-1838.
Dev.: Benj., son.

BARTLESON, CEP., Est., 12-12-1836.

BARTLESON, CEPHAS, App., 9-12-1836.

BARTLESON, JAS., Est., 1-14-1828.

BASHOHR, MICH., Will, 10-12-1829.
Dev.: Marg., wife; Jacob, Henry, John, Mich., sons; others.

BASHORE, MICH., Est., 4-11-1842.

BAST, MICH., Est., 5-8-1848.

BAST, MICHAEL, C., App., 2-8-1847.

BAYLY, SCELAH, Will, 3-12-1827.
Dev.: Eliz. McFarland.

BEALL, ISAAC, Will, 3-11-1816.
Dev. : Marjorie, wife; Anna, Mary, dau.; Alex., Isaac, sons.

BEALL, RICH., Est., 10-14-1839.

BEATTY, LUCY, Est., 11-13-1837.

BEATTY, WM., Est., 6-13-1837.

BEATTY, WM., Est., 3-14-1842.

BEATY, WM., Est., 9-12-1831.

BEESON, ED., Will, 6-9-1817.
Dev.: Jane, wife; Jeppe, Ed., Mieajah, Jas., sons; Martha Ridgeway, Elice Clever, Taee, Charity, dau.; others.

BEESON, ED., Est., 11-8-1824.

BEESON, ED., Est., 2-8-1836.

BELL, JAMES, Will, 9-12-1825.
Dev.: Marg., wife; John, Zeb., Lancelot, Thom., James, Wm., Adam, sons; Isaac, slave.

BELL, JAMES, Est., 7-14-1828.

BELL, JOHN, Will, 12-9-1839.
Dev.: John, Robt., Jos., sons; Prudence, wife; Cath., Mary Evans, Julian Evans, dau.

BELL, JOHN, Est., 9-11-1843.

BELLER, ANNA, Will, 6-13-1825.
Dev.: Eliz. Rush, Rebecca Conine, Sarah McQuilken, Susanna Hill, dau.; others.

BELLER, ANN, Est., 12-8-1828.

BERRY, PETER, App., 1-10-1831.

BERRY, PETER, Est., 2-13-1832.

BILLMIRE, JACOB, App., 4-9-1832.

BILLMIRE, MARG., Will, 5-10-1841.
Dev.: John, Mich., Wm., sons; Jane, Rosan Swartz, Cath. Curtis, Polly Harris, dau.

BILLMYRE, JOHN, Will, 2-10-1845.
Dev.: Eliza, wife; children.

BISHOP, GREEN., Est., 8-13-1827.

BISHOP, JACOB, Est., 2-13-1826.

BISHOP, JACOB, Est., 3-16-1831.

BISHOP, JACOB, Est., 6-10-1839.

BITZER, MICH., Will, 5-18-1822.
Dev.: Cath., wife; Matthias, Martin, Jacob, Geo., John, Mich., sons; Sarah, Nancy, Peggy, Molly, Eve, Mary, Cath., Hanna, Barb., Eliz., Susanna, dau.; others.

BLUE, URIAH, Est., 4-9-1816.

BOAK, JOHN, Est., 3-13-1821.

BOAK, ROBT., App., 2-14-1831.

BOGGS, WM., Will, 7-11-1836.
Dev.: Sarah, wife; Eliz., Jane, dau.; John, son.

BOGGS, WM., App., 6-12-1837.

BOOTH, CALEB SR., Est., 9-9-1822.

BOWERS, ELIZ., Est., 2-14-1842.

BOWERS, ELIZ., Est., 6-10-1844.

BOWERS, HENRY, Will, 9-11-1837.
Dev.: Eliz., wife; Adam, Henry, Wm., sons; slaves; others.

BOWERS, HENRY, App., 10-9-1837.

BOWMAN, AND., Est., 3-13-1826.

BOWMAN, GEO., Est., 8-8-1836.

BOYD, ELISHA, Will, 11-8-1841.
Dev.: Sarah Ann Pendleton, Ann Powell, Mary Faulkner, dau.; John, Andrew, sons; others.

BOYD, ELISHA, Est., 7-9-1849.

BOYD, ELIZ., Will, 4-13-1840.
Dev.: Maria Nichols, sis.; Taylor Byrd, bro.; others.

BOYD, SAM., Will, 10-11-1819.
Dev.: James Stephenson, Alex. Cooper.

BRANNON, ISAAC, App., 2-8-1819.

BRANNON, JOHN, Est., 8-8-1819.

BRAYARLY, RICH., Will, 6-8-1829.
Dev.: Thom., Robt., sons; Hannah Dunbar, dau.; others.

BRENNER, FRED., Est., 12-13-1841.

BRENNER, SUSANNA, Will, 2-10-1845.
Dev.: Abner Snyder, neph.

BROWN, JAMES, Will, 3-12-1844.
Dev.: Marg., wife; Marg., dau.

BROWN, WM., Will, 6-13-1842.
Dev.: Cath. Brown, niece; others.

BRYAN, JOHN, Est., 10-10-1836.

BRYARLY, ANN, Will, 8-8-1825.
Dev.: numerous bequests.

BUCKLES, ABR., Will, 5-11-1840.
Dev.: Eliz., wife; Sarah, dau.; Aaron,
Ephraim, sons; unnamed sons.

BUCKLES, ABR., Est., 10-9-1843.

BUCKLES, LEWIS, Est., 10-12-1846.

BUCKLES, ROBT., Est., 3-8-1819.

BURK, WM., Est., 12-10-1844.

BURNS, GEO., Will, 6-14-1841.
Dev.: Wm., Jos., John, sons; Eliz. Hite,
Nancy Light, Ruth, dau.; others.

BURNS, JOHN, Est., 10-12-1829.

BURNS, JOHN, Est., 5-8-1843.

BURNS, WM. SR., App., 9-9-1822.

BURNS, WM., Est., 9-14-1840.

BURWELL, BACON, Est., 5-12-1828.

BURWELL, BACON, Est., 8-8-1836.

BURWELL, JAS. N., Will, 12-13-1847.
Dev.: Nancy, wife; Margaret Ann,
Rachel Emison, Mary Frances, Mar-
tha Christina, Frances Byron, Nancy
Burwell, dau.

BUTT, ARCH., Est., 9-8-1823.

BUTT, BARRICK, Will, 9-12-1825.
Dev.: Dinah, wife; Benj., Ed., Jos.,
James, sons; Martha Green, Mary,
dau.

BUTT, DELILAH, Est., 3-9-1830.

BUTT, ISAAC, Will, 11-11-1816.
Dev.: Cassander, wife; others.

BUTT, ISAAC, Est., 5-9-1820.

BUTT, JAMES, Will, 9-9-1844.
Dev.: Jos., James, Isiah, Reson, sons.

BUTT, RICH., Est., 9-14-1818.

BUTT, RUTH, Will, 4-12-1847.
Dev.: Zephniah Butt, nephew; others.

BUZZARD, JOHN, Est., 5-13-1839.

CAMPBELL, DOUGAL, App., 3-9-1846.

CAMPBELL, JACOB, Est., 6-12-1822.

CAMPBELL, JAS., Will, 5-13-1817.
Dev.: Sarah, wife; Marg. McFarland,
Ann Orrick, Mary Pollock, dau.; Du-
gall, Wm., sons; others.

CAMPBELL, WM., Est., 5-13-1839.

CARNINE, PHIL., Will, 7-10-1826.
Dev.: Rebecca, wife; others.

CARPER, JACOB, Est., 3-12-1838.

CARPER, JACOB, Est., 9-8-1845.

CARPER, JOHN, Est., 10-14-1839.

CARPER, JOHN, Est., 6-9-1846.

CARPER, PHILIP, Est., 3-10-1845.

CARPER, PHILIP, Est., 9-13-1847.

CARRELL, COLLIN, Est., 11-11-1816.

CHAMBERS, VINC., Est., 9-14-1829.

CHENOWITH, GEO., Est., 5-12-1828.

CHENOWITH, JAMES, Est., 3-12-1832.

CHENOWITH, JAS., Est., 6-12-1820.

CHENOWITH, JOHN, Will, 9-11-1820.
Dev.: Joshua, John, Rich., Art., sons;
Sarah Taylor, Hannah Harris, Ruth
Offut, dau.; other.

CHENOWITH, JOHN, Will, 11-14-1842.
Dev.: Isabella, wife; other.

CHENOWITH, JOS., App., 9-11-1837.

CHENOWITH, PHILLIS, Est., 3-13-1848.

CHENOWITH, RICH., App., 8-11-1824.

CHENOWITH, SAM., Est., 12-10-1844.

CHIDESTER, PETER, Est., 2-9-1829.

CHRISTY, ROBT., Will, 1-8-1838.
Dev.: slaves freed; school for orphans;
others.

CHRISTY, ROBT., App., 10-11-1847.

CLAGETT, RICHARD, Est., 8-10-1830.

CLAIR, GEO., (colored), Will, 5-10-
1830.
Dev.: Catherine, wife; slave, freed.

CLARK, JOS., App., 3-11-1816.

CLAWSON, ISAAC, Est., 5-14-1827.

CLAWSON, JOHN, Est., 11-12-1822.

CLAYCOMB, CON., Will, 9-9-1839.
Dev.: Mary, wife; Eliz. Green, Mary
Myers, Cath. Job, Barb. Myers, dau.;
Fred., son; others.

CLAYCOMB, CON., Est., 11-11-1844.

CLAYCOMB, MARY, Est., 2-14-1842.

CLEMENS, LEO., Est., 10-8-1827.

COCKBURN, ROBT., Will, 9-9-1822.
Dev.: Robt., Adam, sons; others.

COFFENBERGER, GEO., Est., 6-11-1823.

COFFENBERGER, GEO., Est., 7-9-1849.

COLLINS, MOSES, App., 3-9-1818.

COLSTON, JOHN, Will, 1-9-1826.
Dev.: Mary Thomas, Lucy Ann, sis.;
others.

COLSTON, RAWLEIGH, Will, 9-8-1823.
Dev.: Eliz., wife; Ed., J. J. Marshall,
Thom. Marshall, Raleigh T., sons;
Mary Thomas, Lucy Ann, Susan,
dau.; others.

COLSTON, RAWLEIGH, Est., 11-13-1826.

COMPTON, ELIJAH, App., 9-14-1818.

COMPTON, ISAAC, App., 5-8-1826.

CONNELY, BENJ., Will, 8-12-1844.
Dev.: Cath., wife; John, Thom., sons.

COUCHMAN, GEO., Est., 4-10-1837.

COUCHMAN, HENRY, Will, 2-12-1849.
Dev.: Eliz., Sarah Ellis, Marg. Van-
aker, dau.; Wm., David, Benj., Geo.,
Mich., Corn., James, sons; others.

COUCHMAN, MICH., Est., 12-10-1844.

COWENHOVEN, WM., Est., 6-13-1836.

COX, HORACE, Est., 12-14-1846.

COX, HORACE, Est., 3-8-1847.

CRAGHILL, ELIZ., Will, 12-8-1823.
Dev.: Jane Hixon, niece.

CRAGHILL, ELIZ., Est., 11-8-1824.

CRAGHILL, JOHN, Est., 1-10-1825.

CRAGHILL, JOHN, Est., 5-12-1828.

CRISWELL, ABR., Est., 10-14-1839.

CRISWELL, ABR., Est., 2-8-1841.

CRISWELL, JOHN, Est., 4-10-1837.

CRISWELL, JOHN SR., Est., 10-14-1839.

CRISWELL, JOHN, Est., 12-13-1841.

CROMWELL, JOHN, Est., 2-14-1825.

CROMWELL, JOHN, Est., 10-10-1836.
CROSS, BRAZIL, Est., 2-9-1824.
CROSSON, EL., Will, 12-13-1824.
Dev.: Ed., father; others.
CROSSON, EL., Est., 11-14-1825.
CROUCH, REBECCA, Will, 4-14-1828.
Dev.: James Erskine.
CROUCH, REBECCA, App., 8-8-1836.
CUNNINGHAM, GEO., Est., 8-10-1829.
CUNNINGHAM, HUGH, Will, 4-14-1817.
Dev.: Wm., Sam., John, James, Hugh, Robt., sons; Sarah, Nancy, Rosanna, Mary, dau.; others.
CUNNINGHAM, HUGH, Est., 6-10-1822.
CUNNINGHAM, JOHN, App., 1-9-1837.
CUNNINGHAM, JOHN, Est., 3-9-1840.
CUNNINGHAM, RUTH, Est., 8-10-1829.
CUNNINGHAM, SAM., Will, 8-9-1824.
Dev.: Wife; Wm., John, Hugh, Geo., Sam., sons; Dolly Robinson, Jane, dau.
CURTIS, WM., Sale, 1-9-1832.
CUSHWA, DAVID, Est., 1-14-1839.
CUSHWA, DAVID M., Est., 12-8-1845.
CUSHWA, JON., Est., 3-13-1837.
CUSHWA, JON., Est., 7-13-1840.
CUSTARD, JOHN, Sale, 10-13-1823.
CUSTER, JOHN, Est., 3-9-1824.
CUSTER, JOHN, Est., 1-14-1828.
CUSTER, PETER, Will, 3-8-1841.
Dev.: Eliz., wife; John, Geo., Mark, Jacob, Reuben, sons; Marg. Baker, Hannah Hayse, Cath. Hens, dau.
DANIEL, ANN, Est., 3-14-1842.
DANIEL, ROBT., Will, 10-13-1823.
Dev.: Ann, wife; Ann Brown, Eliz. Miller, Polly Stewart, dau.; Robt., son.
DANIEL, ROBT., Est., 3-14-1842.
DAUGHERTY, ALEX., Will, 7-13-1840.
Dev.: Eliz., wife; Cath., Rosanna, Eliz., Mary, dau.; Moses, Alex., Wm., Geo., sons.
DAUGHERTY, ALEX., Est., 12-13-1841.
DAUGHERTY, HUGH, Will, 10-8-1827.
Dev.: Ruth, niece.
DENNISON, THOM., Est., 12-11-1837.
DOLL, JOHN, Est., 3-12-1838.
DOLL, JOHN, Est., 12-12-1842.
DOUGHERTY, JAS., Will, 5-13-1822.
Dev.: Molly, Cath., Jane, sis.; Alex., bro.
DOUGHERTY, MARY, Will, 5-8-1826.
Dev.: Jane Armstrong, Cath. McLaughlin, sis.; Alex., bro.; others.
DOWNING, JOHN, App., 6-12-1848.
DOWNS, CHAS., Will, 12-8-1828.
Dev.: Chas., son; Mary, Fanny, Prisa., dau.; others.
DOWNS, CHAS., Est., 3-16-1831.
DOWNS, HENRY, Will, 2-14-1820.
Dev.: Charles, son; other.
DRISKELL, PAT., Est., 11-?-1848.
DUFFY, PAT., Will, 9-9-1816.
Dev.: Thom., bro.; others.
DUGAN, GEO., Est., 8-8-1836.
DUGAN, GEO., Est., 3-12-1838.

DUNHAM, BENJ., Est., 10-9-1843.
DUNHAM, DAVID, Est., 10-10-1842.
DUNHAM, JAS. C., Est., 4-12-1830.
DUNHAM, SAM., Est., 11-14-1825.
DUNHAM, SAM., SR., Est., 10-10-1842.
DUNKER, JOHN, Will, 5-8-1826.
Dev.: Eliz., wife.
DUNN, WM., Will, 6-14-1830.
Dev.: Catherine, wife; Jos., Wm., David, John, Thos., sons; Ann, Hannah Bell, Jane Mendenhall, Mary, dau.; others.
DUTTON, DAVID, Will, 10-14-1839.
Dev.: Hannah, wife; Wm., Robt., David, Francis, sons; Sarah Watson, Hannah Hensell, Susan Cowarden, Ann Mills, dau.; Asa, son; others.
EAKIN, JAS., Will, 8-14-1820.
Dev.: numerous bequests.
EAKIN, JAS., Est., 1-10-1825.
EAKIN, ROBT., Will, 5-10-1819.
Dev.: Eliz., wife; Polly Lucas, Esther Hatton, dau.; others.
EAKIN, ROBT., Adm., 10-8-1821.
EARLY, ELIZ., Will, 10-13-1823.
Dev.: Mary Forman, dau.; others.
EBBERTS, CHRIS., Will, 3-12-1832.
Dev.: John, son; Phebe Landerkin, dau.
EBERSOL, EMANUEL, Will, 12-10-1827.
Dev.: Cath., Eliz., Nancy, Mary, dau.; Peter, Dan., sons; slaves.
EBERSOLE, EMANUEL, Est., 6-14-1831.
EICHELBERGER, DAVID, Est., 8-10-1830.
ELIOTT, JAS., Est., 5-11-1818.
ELLIOT, ELIJAH, App., 10-12-1830.
ELLIS, ELLIS, Will, 10-14-1839.
Dev.: Mary, wife; John, James, sons; Ellenor, Sarah Ann, Mariah, dau.
ELLIS, ELLIS, Est., 7-10-1848.
ELLIS, JACOB, Est., 5-11-1819.
ELLIS, JAMES, Will, 7-8-1844.
Dev.: Eliz., wife; others.
ELLIS, JAMES, Est., 11-13-1848.
EMERSON, LEO., Est., 11-14-1826.
EMMERT, GEO., Will, 8-11-1823.
Dev.: Marg., wife.
EMMERT, GEO., Est., 2-9-1829.
ENGLE, WM., Inv., 6-10-1823.
ENSMINGER, CHRIS., Est., 2-14-1825.
EVANS, JOHN, Est., 2-11-1828.
EVANS, JOHN, SR., Est., 3-10-1845.
EVANS, MARY, App., 3-13-1843.
EVERSOLE, EMAN., Est., 8-12-1839.
EVERSOLE, JACOB, App., 3-?-1849.
FAULK, JACOB, Est., 11-8-1824.
FAULKNER, JAS., Will, 4-14-1817.
Dev.: James, son; others.
FAULKNER, JAS., Est., 4-12-1824.
FAULKNER, JAS., Est., 9-13-1847.
FEARMAN, SARAH, Will, 5-11-1840.
Dev.: Henry, bro.; other.
FEARMAN, SARAH, Est., 3-8-1841.
FELKER, JOHN, Will, 2-12-1849.
Dev.: Wife; Abr., son; Eliz. Weaver, Cath. Gabrael, dau.; others.

FETTER, LEM., Will, 9-11-1848.
Dev.: Cath., wife; Cath. Staub, Susannah Jones, Sally Fetter, dau.; others.
FILES, JOHN, Will, 6-12-1837.
Dev.: Eliz., wife; John, Thom., sons; Sally Keenes, dau.; others.
FILES, JOHN, Est., 7-8-1839.
FISER, MICH., App., 11-9-1829.
FLEMING, JOHN, Est., 2-11-1828.
FLETCHER, AZEL, Est., 4-12-1830.
FLETCHER, AZWELL, Est., 2-14-1825.
FOGLE, GEO., Est., 2-14-1825.
FOGLE, JOHN, Est., 5-12-1828.
FOILES, JOHN, App., 7-8-1839.
FOLCK, CHRIS., Est., 2-11-1822.
FOLCK, CHRIS., Est., 9-8-1828.
FOLCK, ELIZ., Est., 3-13-1826.
FOLK, JACOB, Est., 11-12-1816.
FORD, HENRY, Est., 2-14-1825.
FORD, HENRY, Est., 6-12-1827.
FOREMAN, JAS., Est., 12-11-1837.
FOREMAN, JAS., Est., 12-13-1841.
FRANCEWAY, ANN, App., 3-14-1837.
FRANCEWAY, JOS., Will, 11-11-1822.
Dev.: Bushrod, Benj., Bennet, sons; Drusilla, dau.; others.
FRANCEWAY, JOS., Est., 12-14-1829.
FRENCH, CATH., Est., 10-11-1841.
FRENCH, CATHERINE, Est., 9-13-1847.
FRENCH, HENRY, Est., 9-12-1842.
FRENCH, JACOB, Will, 5-8-1826.
Dev.: Henry, John, sons; Mary, Barbery, Rachel, Eliz., Hannah, dau.; Cath., wife.
FRENCH, JACOB, Est., 10-13-1828.
FRENCH, JACOB, Est., 10-12-1840.
FRENCH, JOHN, Est., 7-8-1839.
FRENCH, JOHN, Est., 3-13-1848.
FRENCH, MARY, Will, 2-14-1842.
Dev.: Nancy, Barb., dau.; Chris., Henry, sons.
FRENCH, MARY, Est., 3-11-1844.
FRIEZE, BERN, Est., 2-14-1825.
FRY, JOHN, App., 6-9-1828.
FRYATT, JOHN, Will, 6-8-1829.
Dev.: Tilletson, son; Betsy Tate, Rosanna Brown, Nancy Snodgrass, dau.; others.
FRYATT, JOHN, Est., 12-12-1831.
GAINOR, SAMP., App., 4-11-1842.
GANOL, DAN., Est., 10-9-1826.
GANTT, ERASMUS, Est., 11-13-1848.
GARARD, DAVID, Est., 2-14-1825.
GARARD, DAVID, Est., 7-14-1828.
GARDNER, PETER, Will, 10-11-1847.
Dev.: Jacob M., Peter, sons; Polly, Catherine Ringer, Eliz. An Menghinia, dau.; others.
GARVARD, JOH., App., 11-9-1818.
GATRILL, RICH., Est., 1-13-1817.
GEHR, DAN., Est., 6-12-1843.
GEHR, DANIEL, Est., 4-12-1847.
GERRARD, JON., Sale, 5-12-1818.
GILL, JOHN, Est., 9-14-1846.

GILL, THOM., Est., 1-9-1843.
GORRELL, ABR., Est., 11-14-1836.
GORRELL, JACOB, Will, 7-14-1823.
Dev.: Isabella, wife; others.
GORRELL, JOS., Adm., 3-9-1818.
GORRELL, JOS., Est., 3-8-1824.
GORRELL, WM., Will, 9-13-1841.
Dev.: Isabella, wife; Abr., Levi., Wm., sons; Mary Ann, dau.
GORRELL, WM., Est., 3-11-1844.
GORRELL, WM. B., App., 11-9-1846.
GRANTHAM, WM., Will, 8-14-1838.
Dev.: Susannah, wife; Jos., John, Lewis, Moses, sons; Cath. Winning, Maria French, Eliza Seibert, Lydia, dau.
GRANTHAM, WM., Est., 9-14-1840.
GRAY, JOHN, Will, 7-8-1816.
Dev.: Jane, wife; John E., Jas., sons; Mary Ann, dau.; others.
GRAY, JOHN, Est., 2-14-1825.
GRAY, JOHN, Will, 11-13-1837.
Dev.: Jane, mother.
GRAY, JOHN, Est., 2-13-1837.
GREEN, WM., Will, 2-14-1842.
Dev.: Eliz., wife; others.
GREEN, WM., Est., 3-9-1846.
GREGORY, MARY, App., 7-10-1848.
GRIFFITH, DAVID, Will, 9-12-1831.
Dev.: Wife; Wm., John, sons; Mary Craighill, Amy, dau.
GRIFFITH, DAVID, App., 11-14-1831.
GRIST, GRAVENER, Est., 10-10-1825.
GRISTE, GRAVNER, Will, 11-12-1822.
Dev.: Ruthe, wife; Geo., father; Cath., mother; others.
GROVE, PETER, Est., 1-9-1826.
GRUBER, ELIZ., App., 6-12-1848.
GUSTIN, ALPHEUS, App., 9-9-1816.
GWILLIAMS, RESIN, Will, 3-12-1849.
Dev.: Henry, son; Maria Byers, Sarah, Eliza, Ellen, dau.; wife.
GWILLIAMS, RESIN, App., 6-11-1849.
HAGAMAN, JOS., Est., 11-12-1827.
HAINES, JOS., Will, 10-10-1831.
Dev.: Sarah, wife; others.
HAINS, SARAH, Will, 2-13-1832.
Dev.: Jos. Myers, bro.; slaves; many other bequests.
HAMME, JACOB, App., 9-12-1825.
HAMME, JACOB, SR., Est., 2-13-1826.
HAMME, SAM., Will, 12-9-1822.
Dev.: Eliz., wife; Jacob, son; Lydia Stephens, Louise, Eliz. Long, dau.
HAMMOND, JAS., Adm., 12-8-1817.
HARLAN, JEHU, Will, 6-14-1847.
Dev.: Wife; Silas, Fel. Boyd, Jas. Brown, John Williamson, Wm. Hunter, Scott, sons; Margaret Ann, Martha, Mary, Isabella, Sarah Elisa, dau.
HARLAN, JEHU, Est., 7-9-1849.
HARLAN, JOHN, Est., 1-11-1819.
HARRISON, JOHN, Will, 11-13-1838.
Dev.: Wife; Benj., John, Otho, Napoleon, sons; Sarah, Lucy Anderson, Nancy, dau.; others.
HARRISON, JOHN, Est., 5-13-1839.

HARRISON, DR. JOHN S. JR., App., 7-8-1846.

HARRISON, JOHN, Est., 7-10-1848.

HARTSOOK, WM., Est., 2-14-1825.

HARTSOOK, WM., Est., 11-9-1829.

HASELET, ROBT., Will, 5-13-1822.
Dev.: numerous bequests.

HASLETT, ROBT., App., 6-9-1823.

HASTINGS, ROBT., App., 1-12-1819.

HAVERLEY, GODFREY, Est., 6-14-1830.

HEDGES, HEZEKIAH, App., 12-13-1847.

HEDGES, JOS., Est., 8-9-1824.

HEDGES, JOSHUA, Will, 11-13-1826.
Dev.: John, Josiah, bro.; Eliz. Curtis, Phebe Lemon, Mary, Angelina, sis.

HEDGES, JOSHUA, Will, 4-9-1832.
Dev.: slaves; Southwood, Chaplin, sons.

HEDGES, SAM., Will, 12-9-1822.
Dev.: Nancy, wife; Jos., Jonas, Sam., Seaton, Wm., Baley, John, sons; Eliz., Mary, Everlina, Ann, Isabella, Harriett, Rebeckoh, Sarah, Ellener, Enoch, Lucinda, dau.

HEDGES, SAM., Will, 6-14-1824.
Dev.: Rebecah, wife; Josiah, Joshua, Sam., Hezekiah, sons; Eliz. Morgan, Rebecah Robinson, Phebe, Ruth Robinson, dau.

HEDGES, SAM., Est., 6-12-1826.

HEDGES, SARAH, Will, 8-9-1841.
Dev.: John, Hiram, Josiah, sons; Phebe Lemon, Mary Lingamfelter, Eliz. Curtis, Angeline Cunningham, dau.

HEDGES, SARAH, App., 9-13-1841.

HEDGES, SOL., Will, 10-13-1823.
Dev.: Sarah, wife; Joshua, John, Hiram, Josiah, sons; Eliz. Curtis, Phebe, Mary, Angelina, dau.

HEDGES, SOL., Est., 6-11-1827.

HEFFNER, FRED., App., 2-13-1826.

HELFERSTAY, JOHN, App., 2-8-1847.

HELM, BARB., Est., 2-14-1825.

HENDERSON, JOHN, App., 1-9-1837.

HENRY, JOHN, Est., 5-12-1823.

HENRY, JOHN, Est., 10-12-1829.

HENRY, JOHN B., Est., 2-9-1846.

HENSHAW, ANN, Est., 2-14-1825.

HENSHAW, HIRAM, Will, 8-11-1845.
Dev.: Jas. Wm., Samuel P., sons; Mary C. Morgan, Martha Jane, dau.; others.

HENSHAW, HIRAM, App., 4-12-1847.

HENSHAW, WM., Est., 2-14-1825.

HERBERT, ELISHA, Will, 2-14-1842.
Dev.: Mary Ripple, sis.

HERBERT, ELISHA, Est., 2-12-1844.

HILL, ABR., Est., 9-8-1823.

HILL, GEO., Est., 3-9-1840.

HILL, JACOB, Est., 11-10-1845.

HILL, RACHAEL, Est., 2-9-1846.

HILL, RACHEL, Est., 5-11-1840.

HITE, ROBT., JR., App., 7-13-1818.

HOBERMILE, JOHN, Adm., 12-8-1817.

HOFFMAN, ABR., Will, 11-11-1839.
Dev.: Mary, wife.

HOFFMAN, CATH., Est., 7-13-1840.

HOFFMAN, JOS., Will, 3-13-1849.
Dev.: Several bequests.

HOGE, JOHN, Will, 6-13-1826.
Dev.: to the persons entitled in equity.

HOKE, PETER, App., 8-9-1842.

HOLLINGSWORTH, PARK., App., 3-12-1838.

HOLLINGSWORTH, PARK., Est., 7-13-1840.

HOOK, MICH., App., 2-11-1822.

HOOPER, JOHN, Will, 10-12-1818.
Dev.: Mary, Eliza, dau.; Mary, wife; others.

HOOPER, JOHN, Est., 3-15-1825.

HORN, GEO. SR., Will, 3-14-1827.
Dev.: John, Jacob, Wm., Phil., Thom., sons; Marg. Dugan, dau.; others.

HORN, GEO., Est., 6-9-1829.

HORN, GEO., Est., 7-9-1839.

HORN, JACOB, Est., 4-9-1832.

HORN, PHILIP, Est., 2-13-1832.

HORN, THOM., Est., 3-13-1837.

HORN, THOS., Est., 9-13-1847.

HORN, WM., App., 8-9-1830.

HOUCK, ELIZ., Est., 3-13-1826.

HOUCK, JACOB, Est., 8-14-1820.

HOUCK, JACOB, Est., 2-14-1831.

HOUCK, MARG., Will, 8-14-1820.
Dev.: Eliz. Thurston, Cath. Kesecker, Sally Hite, dau.; Henry, David, Sam., Geo., sons; others.

HOUCK, MARG., Est., 3-11-1839.

HOUCK, MICH., Will, 12-10-1821.
Dev.: Eliz., wife; John, Dan., Sam., Jacob, Henry, Mich., Geo., Adam, sons; Maria, Eliz., dau.; others.

HOUCK, MICH., Est., 1-10-1825.

HOUCK, MICH., Est., 3-11-1839.

HOUCK, WM., Est., 2-11-1839.

HOUKE, MARG., Est., 2-14-1825.

HOUKE, WM., App., 3-12-1838.

HOUSEWORTH, SARAH, Will, 11-13-1843.
Dev.: Nancy Reiley, Marg. Butts, Eliz. Daniels, Mary, dau.; Sol., Valentine, Isaac, Wm., sons.

HOUSEWORTH, SARAH, Est., 9-14-1846.

HOUT, GEO., Will, 3-8-1847.
Dev.: Wife; Catherine, Eliz. Russler, Sarah Crow, Magdalena Horn, Angel Bartis Margaretta, Catherine Price, dau.; others.

HOUTE, GEO., Est., 3-13-1848.

HOVERMALE, JOHN, Will, 3-11-1816.
Dev.: Chris., Fred., sons; others.

HOYLE, JACOB, App., 11-8-1819.

HUBBY, JAY, Est., 12-8-1823.

HUDGEL, RESIN, Est., 9-14-1846.

HUDGEL, RESIN, Est., 3-13-1848.

HUDSON, WM., Will, 2-9-1824.
Dev.: Bridget, wife; Jesse, John, Jas., sons; Cath. Myers, dau.; others.

HUDSON, WM., App., 9-13-1824.

HUFFMAN, CATH., App., 11-12-1838.

HUNTER, DAVID, Will, 4-14-1829.
Dev.: Wife; Louisa, Mary, dau.; Moses, son; other children; slaves.

HUNTER, DAVID, Est., 9-12-1831.
HUNTER, DAVID, Est., 12-11-1837.
HUNTER, DAVID, Est., 1-11-1840.
HUNTER, MOSES, Sale, 12-14-1829.
HYRONIMUS, CONRAD, Will, 6-13-1831.
Dev.: Sarah, wife; others.
IRELAND, GEO., Will, 5-13-1844.
Dev.: Sarah, wife; Presby. Church.
JACK, ISAAC, Est., 2-12-1838.
JACK, ROBT., Est., 8-9-1830.
JACK, WM., & ANN, Adm., 10-13-1817.
JOHNSON, ABR., App., 6-10-1822.
JOHNSON, WM., Est., 1-10-1825.
JOHNSTON, ABR., Est., 2-14-1825.
JOHNSTON, ABR., Est., 6-8-1829.
JOHNSTON, JOS., Est., 11-11-1839.
JONES, PETER, Will, 11-11-1844.
Dev.: Eliz., wife; others.
JORDAN, WM., Est., 2-14-1825.
KANODE, POLLY, Est., 12-13-1841.
KEAN, PERC., Will, 8-12-1816.
Dev.: Eliz., Shiles, dau.; Thom., John,
Wm., sons; others.
KEAN, PERC., App., 2-10-1817.
KEARNEY, JOSIAH, App., 3-12-1844.
KEARNEY, WM., Est., 11-13-1843.
KEESECKER, AND., Est., 8-14-1820.
KEESECKER, ELIZ., Will, 1-13-1845.
Dev.: Matheas, John, Henry, Aaron,
sons; Mary Ann Hill, Eliz. Sellers,
dau.; others.
KEESECKER, ELIZ., App., 2-10-1845.
KEESECKER, JACOB, Est., 3-12-1832.
KEESECKER, JACOB, Est., 3-10-1845.
KEESECKER, MATT., Est., 2-9-1829.
KENDLE, DEVAULT, App., 10-10-1825.
KENNEDY, SAM., Will, 3-9-1818.
Dev.: Eliz., wife; John, Thom., sons;
Jane Murphy, dau.; others.
KEPHART, BERN., App., 5-12-1829.
KERNEY, JACOB, Est., 5-14-1838.
KERNEY, JAS., Est., 3-11-1828.
KERNEY, JAS., Est., 12-13-1841.
KERNEY, WM., Est., 1-10-1848.
KESECKER, AND., Will, 2-10-1817.
Dev.: Susannah, Rachael, Chris. Houk,
Eliz. Basore, Mary Bitzer, dau.; And.,
Mich., sons; others.
KESECKER, MATHIAS, Will, 6-9-1823.
Dev.: Eliz., wife; Mathias, John,
Aaron, Jacob, Henry, sons; Mary,
Eliz., Chris., dau.; Milly, slave.
KILMER, DAVID, Est., 12-14-1846.
KISER, JOS., App., 11-13-1848.
KISINGER, JOHN, Will, 5-13-1839.
Dev.: Susanna, wife; Sam., Otho,
James, John, sons; others.
KISINGER, JOHN, Est., 3-9-1840.
KISINGER, SUSAN, Est., 11-13-1848.
KITCHEN, JOB., Est., 2-9-1819.
KITCHEN, RACHEL, Est., 12-13-1824.
KNUP, CATH., Will, 1-9-1832.
Dev.: Eliz. Moore, Cath. Shall, Ivanny
Houseman, dau.; Geo., John, sons.

KNUP, VAL., Will, 1-12-1824.
Dev.: Cath., wife; Geo., John, sons;
Cath. Shall, Fanny Houseman, Eliz.
Moore, dau.; others.
KNUP, VAL., Est., 2-12-1827.
KRAGALOE, GEO., Est., 12-13-1824.
KREGLOE, GEO. SR., Will, 10-13-1823.
Dev.: Cath. Besr, dau.; John, Geo.,
Jacob, Wm., Peter, sons; Wm., bro.
KREGLOW, GEO., Est., 10-8-1827.
KREGLOW, GEO., Est., 7-9-1849.
KROESEN, WM., Est., 5-8-1848.
KROH, HENRY, Will, 10-13-1823.
Dev.: Barbary, wife; Lemon, Jona-
than, Jacob, Henry, Dan., Simon,
sons; Rebecca Myers, Kath., Polly,
dau.; others.
KROH, HENRY, Est., 12-12-1825.
KYLE, HUGH, Est., 3-15-1820.
KYSER, JOHN, App., 6-11-1821.
LAFEVER, HENRY, Est., 3-8-1830.
LAMON, GEO., Est., 2-11-1828.
LAMON, MARY, Est., 6-12-1838.
LANE, THOM. JR., Est., 5-15-1821.
LATIMER, THOM., App., 5-14-1849.
LAWVER, FRED., Will, 2-14-1831.
Dev.: Polly, wife; others.
LAWVER, MARY, Will, 2-9-1846.
Dev.: Adam Stewart, nephew; Cath-
erine Rhodes, niece.
LAYMASTER, JOHN, Will, 3-14-1825.
Dev.: Nancy, wife; Wm., John, sons;
Eliz. Ann, Marg., Eliza, dau.; others.
LAYMASTER, JOHN, Est., 2-14-1831.
LEE, JOHN, App., 4-11-1825.
LEE, MARY, Est., 3-11-1845.
LEE, SAM., Will, 10-10-1842.
Dev.: Sarah, Mary, sis.; others.
LEE, SAMUEL, Est., 3-8-1847.
LEE, SARAH, Will, 6-?-1845.
Dev.: Numerous bequests.
LEE, SARAH, Est., 1-10-1848.
LEE, THOM., Est., 2-14-1837.
LEFEVER, HENRY, Est., 7-10-1826.
LEFEVER, MARG., Est., 8-9-1830.
LEMASTER, JOHN, Est., 6-11-1827.
LEMASTER, JOHN, Est., 1-11-1836.
LEMON, GEO., Will, 2-13-1826.
Dev.: Mary, wife.
LEMON, THOM., Will, 2-12-1838.
Dev.: Barb., wife; Jos., Wm., Sam.,
James, Robt., Nich., Jacob, sons; Hes-
ter, Virginia, Eliza Billmire, Mary,
dau.
LEMON, THOM., Est., 12-13-1841.
LEMON, WM., Will, 3-11-1822.
Dev.: Eliz., wife; John, Edwin, Wm.,
sons; Harriett, Eliz., Mary Ann, Jane
Hester, Attralinda, dau.
LEMON, WM., Est., 10-10-1825.
LEOPARD, ADAM, App., 6-9-1817.
LEOPARD, BARB., Will, 2-14-1842.
Dev.: John, Geo., Adam, sons; Mary,
Nancy Lechron, Cath., dau.
LEOPARD, BARD., Est., 2-12-1844.
LEOPARD, DAN., Est., 5-10-1824.
LEOPARD, DAN., Est., 2-13-1826.
LEOPARD, MICH., Est., 7-8-1839.

LEOPARD, MICH., Est., 9-11-1843.
LESSLEY, JOHN, Will, 6-16-1825.
Dev.: Jane Mulhall.
LESSLEY, JOHN, Est., 10-11-1830.
LEWIS, MARY, Will, 11-11-1822.
Dev.: Pris. McDonnel, dau.; Lewis, son.
LEWIS, WM., App., 3-12-1844.
LIGHT, ANN, Will, 2-9-1829.
Dev.: Cath. Hoke, Ann Thornburg, Mary Dering, dau.; Sam., Jos., David, sons; others.
LIGHT, ANN, Est., 7-?-1831.
LIGHT, JACOB, Est., 6-13-1837.
LIGHT, JOHN, Will, 2-12-1827.
Dev.: Nancy, wife; Peggy, Eliz., Susanna, Caroline, dau.; Peter, John, Jacob, Hamilton, sons; Charles, Pilberry, slaves.
LIGHT, JOHN, Est., 10-10-1836.
LIGHT, NANCY, Est., 11-9-1840.
LIGHT, PETER, JR., Will, 10-9-1821.
Dev.: Eliz., wife; Jacob, John, Peter, sons; Mary Ann, Nancy, Eleanor Wilson, dau.; other.
LIGHT, PETER, Est., 2-14-1825.
LINGENFELTER, ABR., Est., 2-14-1825.
LINGENFELTER, VAL., Est., 6-14-1819.
LITTLEJOHN, WM., App., 1-9-1816.
LOCKE, MEVERELL, Est., 3-15-1831.
LOCKE, THOM., Will, 5-14-1838.
Dev.: Mererell, grandson; others.
LOCKE, THOM., Est., 10-11-1841.
LONG, JOHN, Est., 5-10-1824.
LONG, JOHN, Est., 3-8-1830.
LONG, MARY, Will, 11-14-1831.
Dev.: Eliz., dau.
LOWRY, JAS., Will, 9-9-1816.
Dev.: Mary, wife; Wm., John, Sam., James, sons; Jane Kennedy, dau.; others.
LUCAS, BASIL, Will, 8-9-1841.
Dev.: Eliz., wife; Lenise, Matilda, dau.; Thornton, Basil, Dennis, Alfred, Barton, Henderson, sons; others.
LUCAS, BASIL, Est., 1-10-1848.
LUCAS, GABRIEL, Est., 1-10-1848.
LUTHEY, JACOB, Est., 7-10-1848.
LUTHY, JACOB, Est., 10-14-1844.
LYLE, JOHN, Est., 5-12-1818.
LYLE, WM. O., Est., 2-8-1847.
LYNCH, DAN., App., 3-14-1842.
MACKEY, MOSES, Will, 11-8-1841.
Dev.: Hester, Mary, Sarah, sis.; others.
MACKEY, MOSES, Est., 5-13-1844.
MACKEY, MOSES, Est., 1-10-1848.
MACKEY, RUTH, Est., 6-13-1836.
MAGAN, JOHN, App., 9-9-1816.
MANOR, SAM., App., 9-11-1848.
MARCHENT, ISAAC, Adm., 11-12-1821.
MARLATT, AB., App., 6-13-1831.
MARLATT, ELIZ., Sale, no date.
MARSHALL, JOHN, Est., 10-13-1823.
MARTIN, GEO., Est., 8-13-1827.
MARTIN, JAPHTA, Est., 4-9-1827.

MARTIN, JEPTHA, Will, 6-14-1824.
Dev.: Levi, Jacob, Nat., John, David, sons; Marg. Thornburg, Eliza Williamson, Mary, dau.
MASON, ALEX., Est., 7-11-1831.
MASON, WM., Est., 7-10-1837.
MATHEWS, ENOCH, Est., 3-12-1838.
MAYHEW, WM., Will, 5-8-1843.
Dev.: Mary Ann, wife; children.
MAYHEW, WM., Est., 1-10-1848.
MCALLISTER, BENJ., Est., 2-14-1825.
MCALLISTER, CHRIS., Will, 6-8-1840.
Dev.: Barb., wife; Geo., Henry, sons; Rosella, Va., dau.; mother; other children.
MCALLISTER, CHRIS., Est., 9-?-1844.
MCCLEARY, JANE, Will, 9-8-1845.
Dev.: John, husband; John, Jos., sons; Matilda, Jane, dau.; others.
MCCLEARY, JOHN, Will, 1-9-1832.
Dev.: John, Wm., And., sons; Rosannah Lock, Angeline, dau.; others.
MCCORMICK, JOHN, Est., 7-9-1849.
MCCOUCH, JAS., Est., 12-9-1844.
MCCOY, WM., Est., 5-10-1824.
MCDANIEL, MARY, Will, 6-9-1828.
Dev.: Hannah, Nelly Pitzer, Polly Pitzer, dau.; Jared, Alex., Cleaburgh, John, sons.
MCGOVRAN, ANN., Est., 9-10-1838.
MCGOVRAN, PHIL., Will, 9-8-1823.
Dev.: Nancy, wife; Edmond, son; Ann, Mary Ann, dau.
MCGOVRAN, PHIL., App., 11-14-1836.
MCINTIRE, HENRY, Will, 11-14-1825.
Dev.: Thom., bro.; others.
MCINTIRE, THOM., Est., 7-?-1849.
MCINTIRE, THOS., Will, 11-8-1847.
Dev.: Andrew, son; Mary, Eliz. M., dau.
MCKAY, ABSOLOM, Est., 6-8-1818.
MCKEEVER, ANGUS, Will, 10-9-1837.
Dev.: Cath., wife; John, son; Eliz., Jane Abernathy, dau.; other.
MCKEEVER, DAN., Will, 6-13-1831.
Dev.: Mother; Eliz., sis.
MCKEWAN, MICH., Will, 3-10-1828.
Dev.: Mary, wife; James, Sedwick, Peter, sons; Cath. Dare, dau.; Cath. Church of Martinsburg.
MCKINNEY, JOHN, Est., 4-13-1819.
MCKOWN, ISAAC, Est., 1-10-1820.
MCKOWN, ISABELLA, Will, 6-?-1845.
Dev.: John, George, Warner, Samuel, sons; Mary, Jane Gold, Sarah, Isabella, dau.
MCKOWN, ISABELLA, Est., 3-9-1846.
MCKOWN, JOHN, Will, 10-14-1839.
Dev.: Marg., wife; Morgan, Hiram, Edmund, Jos., sons; Mariah, dau.
MCKOWN, JOHN, Est., 12-13-1842.
MCKOWN, SAM., Will, 10-9-1837.
Dev.: Isabella, wife; Sam., John, Geo., Warner, sons; Jane Gold, Mary Ann, Sarah, Isabella, dau.
MCKOWN, SAM., Est., 3-11-1844.
MCQUILKIN, JACOB, Est.; 11-13-1848.
MEANOR, SAM., Est., 7-9-1849.
MENDENHALL, JAS., Est., 8-9-1819.

MENDENHALL, JAS., Est., 6-11-1827.

MENSER, GEO., Will, 1-13-1840.
Dev.: John, son; Emily, dau.

MENSER, GEO., Est., 11-14-1842.

MERCHANT, ISAAC, Est., 2-10-1845.

MERCHANT, NANCY, Est., 11-13-1843.

MERCHANT, WM., Will, 9-13-1830.
Dev.: Hannah, wife; Wm., son; Rody, Nancy, dau.

MERCHANT, WM., App., 3-14-1831.

MILES, LLOYD, App., 2-12-1816.

MILES, LLOYD, Est., 2-12-1816.

MILES, LLOYD, Sale, 2-12-1816.

MILES, RUTH, Est., 2-12-1816.

MILES, RUTH, Sale, 2-12-1816.

MILES, RUTH, App., 2-19-1816.

MILLER, ABR., Est., 7-9-1849.

MILLER, ABS., Sale, 11-12-1827.

MILLER, BARB., Est., 2-8-1836.

MILLER, BARB., App., 3-14-1836.

MILLER, CHRIS., Will, 2-10-1823.
Dev.: several bequests.

MILLER, DAVID, Est., 10-9-1827.

MILLER, DAVID, App., 3-8-1830.

MILLER, DAVID, Sale, 3-8-1830.

MILLER, DAVID, Est., 6-14-1830.

MILLER, DAVID, Est., 2-14-1831.

MILLER, DAVID, Est., 11-14-1831.

MILLER, DAVID, Est., 8-12-1839.

MILLER, DAVID, App., 9-10-1827.

MILLER, DAVID, Est., 12-13-1841.

MILLER, ELLEN, Est., 2-12-1844.

MILLER, ELIZ., Est., 1-13-1840.

MILLER, ELON, Inv., 4-10-1820.

MILLER, ELON, Will, 1-10-1820.
Dev.: Chris, wife; slaves; others.

MILLER, ELON, App., 9-13-1824.

MILLER, ELON, Sale, 9-13-1824.

MILLER, ELON, Est., 12-12-1825.

MILLER, ELON, Est., 3-10-1828.

MILLER, ESTHER, Sale, 2-14-1825.

MILLER, GEO., Est., 2-14-1825.

MILLER, HENRY, SR., Will, 3-10-1817.
Dev.: Henry, Jacob, Geo., Adam, John, sons; Rosanna Hout, Eliz. Job, Mary Choppert, Hannah, Cath. Dall., dau.; others.

MILLER, HENRY, SR., Inv., 1-10-1825.

MILLER, HENRY, SR., Est., 1-10-1825.

MILLER, HENRY, SR., Sale, 1-10-1825.

MILLER, HENRY, Est., 9-8-1817.

MILLER, HENRY, Will, 3-14-1842.
Dev.: Molly, Cath., Eliza, Rosannah, Mariah, dau.; Tobias, Henry, Jacob, Wm., sons.

MILLER, HENRY, App., 2-12-1844.

MILLER, HENRY, Sale, 2-12-1844.

MILLER, HENRY, Est., 3-11-1844.

MILLER, HESTER, App., 2-14-1825.

MILLER, JACOB, App., 2-13-1832.

MILLER, JAMES, Est., 1-14-1822.

MILLER, JAMES, App., 2-14-1825.

MILLER, JAMES, Sale, 2-14-1825.

MILLER, JAS., Will, 11-13-1837.
Dev.: Ann, niece.

MILLER, JAS., App., 1-8-1838.

MILLER, JAS., Sale, 3-12-1838.

MILLER, JOS., Will, 12-11-1820.
Dev.: Marg., wife; Wm., Jas., David, Jos., sons; Mary Jane, Nancy Eliz., dau.

MILLER, JOS., Sale, 8-12-1823.

MILLER, JOS., Est., 3-14-1825.

MILLER, MARY, App., 2-8-1836.

MILLER, MARY, Sale, 2-8-1836.

MILLER, MICH., Est., 8-14-1818.

MILLER, WM., Will, 9-13-1824.
Dev.: Sarah, wife; David, son; other children.

MILLER, WM., Sale, 2-14-1825.

MILLER, WM., Est., 3-13-1826.

MILLER, WM., Est., 9-10-1827.

MILLER, WM., Sale, 9-10-1827.

MILLER, WM., Est., 8-11-1829.

MILLER, ZACH., Adm., 3-10-1817.

MILLER, ZACH., App., 3-10-1817.

MINGHINI, BENEDICT, Will, 12-12-1831.
Dev.: Chas., bro.; Dr. Rich. McSherry, trustee for mother.

MINGHINI, JOS., Sale, 6-12-1827.

MINGHINI, JOS., Est., 6-13-1827.

MINGHINI, JOS., App., 6-12-1827.

MINGHINI, JOSIPPI, App., 7-10-1848.

MINGHINI, JUSEPPA, Est., 11-10-1830.

MIXWELL, ADAM, App., 2-13-1837.

MIXWELL, ADAM, Sale, 2-13-1837.

MIXWELL, ADAM, Est., 2-11-1839.

MONG, GEO., Est., 3-14-1837.

MONG, JOHN, Will, 3-11-1844.
Dev.: Mary, wife; Cath. Seibert, Eliz. Hawk, Mary Seibert, Marg. Gladden, Sarah Small, Susan Stewart, dau.; Geo., Wm., sons; others.

MONG, JOHN, App., 6-10-1844.

MOON, DEBORAH, Will, 12-11-1837.
Dev.: Jane, Rachel, Nancy, dau.; Hiram, son.

MOON, DEBORAH, App., 1-8-1838.

MOON, JEAN, Will, 6-10-1817.
Dev.: Martha, granddau.

MOON, SIMON, Est., 12-13-1824.

MORGAN, ELIZ., Est., 9-12-1840.

MORGAN, JEPHTHA, Est., 11-13-1848.

MORGAN, LEVI, Est., 10-12-1840.

MORGAN, LUCINDA, App., 5-10-1841.

MORGAN, MARY, Est., 1-10-1825.

MORGAN, MARY, Will, 7-12-1830.
Dev.: Mariah, Lucinda, sis.

MORGAN, MORGAN, Est., 2-12-1827.

MORGAN, MORGAN, Est., 9-12-1836.

MORGAN, OLIVIA, Will, 11-13-1843.
Dev.: Dan., Jacob, bro.; Eliz. Ranson, sis.; others.

MORGAN, PRIS., Will, 10-14-1822.
Dev.: numerous bequests.

MORGAN, PRIS., Est., 6-14-1824.

MORGAN, RAWLEIGH, Est., 8-14-1826.

MORGAN, RAWLEIGH, Est., 9-12-1831.

MORGAN, SAM., Will, 12-13-1824.
Dev.: Morgan, Josiah, Levi, Wm., bro.;
Maria, Rebeckah, Mary, Eliz. Ann,
Lucinda, sis.

MORGAN, SAM., Est., 6-9-1828.

MORISON, ABIGAIL, Will, 12-12-1836.
Dev.: Hannah Page, dau.; Wm., son.

MORISON, WM., Will, 6-14-1836.
Dev.: Abigail, wife; Dan., Wm., sons;
Hannah, dau.

MORRISON, HANAH, Est., 6-11-1827.

MORRISON, JESSEE, Will, 1-8-1849.
Dev.: Sally, wife; Polly Crim, Sally,
dau.; Nat., Rich., James, Andrew, David, sons.

MORRISON, RICH., Est., 3-12-1832.

MUMMA, JACOB, Will, 11-13-1848.
Dev.: Eliz. Miller, Mary Miller, dau.;
Sam., son; Barb., wife; others.

MURLEY, ARANDLE, Est., 11-10-1845.

MURPHY, PHILIP, Est., 11-13-1848.

MURPHY, WM., Est., 6-10-1839.

MURPHY, WM., Est., 1-10-1848.

MURQUART, NICH., App., 6-8-1840.

MURRAY, ZACH., Will, 3-14-1821.
Dev.: numerous bequests.

MURRAY, ZACH., Est., 3-10-1828.

MYERS, CATH., Est., 5-9-1842.

MYERS, HENRY, Est., 6-10-1839.

MYERS, JOHN, Will, 5-9-1836.
Dev.: John, Henry, Jacob, sons; Eliz.
Hensell, Cath. Seibert, dau.; others.

MYERS, JOHN, Est., 6-13-1837.

MYERS, JOHN, Est., 5-9-1842.

MYERS, MARTIN, Will, 9-11-1820.
Dev.: Cath., wife; Jacob, bro.; children.

MYERS, MARY, Est., 5-9-1842.

MYERS, TETER, Est., 3-9-1840.

NACE, HENRY, Est., 11-11-1816.

NADENBOUSCH, JAS., App., 4-13-1846.

NADENBOUSCH, MARY ANN, Will, 11-
9-1830.
Dev.: Eloisa, Eliz., sis.; John, Phil.,
Jas., bro.

NEAD, DAN., Will, 6-9-1823.
Dev.: Mathias, Dan., Peter, John,
sons.

NEWBROUGH, WM., Will, 9-15-1847.
Dev.: Ann, wife.

NEWKIRK, GEO., Est., 2-14-1825.

NEWKIRK, JAS., Will, 8-11-1817.
Dev.: Martha, wife; Eliz., Rose, dau.

NEWKIRK, JAS., Est., 8-11-1823.

NEWKIRKE, GEO., Will, 1-13-1823.
Dev.: Martha, wife; Marg., Mary, dau.;
James, son.

NEWSON, ALEX., App., 4-16-1828.

NICHOLAS, AMOS, Will, 4-9-1821.
Dev.: Rebeckah, wife; John, son; Eliz.
Morgan, Rebeckah Robinson, Ruth
Robinson, Phebe Hedges, sis.

NICHOLS, AMOS, Est., 3-13-1826.

NICHOLS, ELIZA, App., 6-14-1830.

NICHOLS, JOHN, Est., 3-8-1830.

NICHOLS, TERRISSA, Will, 12-11-1826.
Dev.: Eleanor Ford, sis.; others.

NIPE, GEO., Will, 2-14-1842.
Dev.: Mary, wife; James, son; other
children.

NIPE, GEO., Est., 3-11-1844.

NOLAND, OBED, Est., 6-11-1838.

NOLL, ANN, Will, 5-14-1849.
Dev.: Godleib, son; slaves; others.

NOLL, GEO., Est., 2-13-1837.

NOLL, GEO., Est., 11-11-1839.

NOLL, HENRY, Est., 4-13-1846.

ODEN, ALEX., Will, 2-8-1836.
Dev.: Martha, wife.

ODEN, ALEX., Est., 6-11-1838.

ODEN, ELIAS, App., 3-12-1832.

OLLEBAUGH, JOHN, Est., 8-14-1843.

OLLER, PETER, Will, 4-?-1823.
Dev.: Cath., wife; Peter, Jacob, Geo.,
sons; Eliz. Barber, Cath. Marley, dau.;
others.

OLLER, PETER, Est., 5-14-1827.

ORR, WM., Est., 9-13-1847.

ORRICK, ANN, Est., 9-14-1840.

ORRICK, CHAS., Est., 1-8-1838.

ORRICK, MARY, Est., 2-14-1825.

ORRICK, WM., Est., 2-14-1825.

ORRICK, WM., Est., 6-15-1830.

OSBORN, JOS., Est., 11-15-1825.

PAGE, JOHN, Est., 3-8-1830.

PAGE, THOM., App., 2-18-1816.

PAINTER, JACOB, SR., Will, 6-14-1824.
Dev.: Eve Cath., wife; John, Jacob,
sons.

PAINTER, JACOB, SR., Est., 3-12-1832.

PAINTER, JACOB, Will, 3-8-1841.
Dev.: John, Geo., bro.; Mary Mong,
Cath. Watters, Eva Swarts, Marg. Wal-
ter, sis.; others.

PAINTER, JACOB, Est., 11-10-1845.

PALMER, JACOB, Est., 12-11-1826.

PARKE, JOHN, Est., 2-14-1842.

PATTON, WM., Est., 5-9-1825.

PAULL, AND., Est., 11-9-1829.

PAULL, HUGH, Est., 3-10-1828.

PAULL, WM., Est., 3-13-1826.

PAYNE, MARTIN, Will, 5-13-1822.
Dev.: freed all slaves.

PAYNE, MARTIN, Est., 11-12-1827.

PAYNES, WM., Est., 11-9-1829.

PEAKER, RICH., Will, 9-10-1827.
Dev.: Aley, dau.; other.

PEARL, JOHN, App., 3-15-1836.

PEARL, JOHN, Sale, 3-16-1836.

PENDLETON, WM., Will, 4-14-1817.
Dev.: Sarah Wigginton, Mary Orrick,
Lucy Ferguson, Betty Cunningham,
Ann Porterfield, Eleanor Walker, Em-
ily, dau.; Nat., Benj., Wm., sons;
others.

PENDLETON, WM., Est., 2-14-1825.

PERRELL, JOHN, Est., 3-11-1839.

PERRILL, JOHN, Est., 7-10-1837.

PHILIPS, RUTH, App., 11-12-1838.

PITZER, ELIZ., Will, 7-10-1826.
Dev.: Mary Clark, mother.

PITZER, JOHN, Est., 11-12-1827.

PITZER, MATHIAS, Will, 6-10-1816.
Dev.: Marg., wife; James, Sam., And., Conrad, John, Mathias, Wm., Mich., Jacob, sons.

PITZER, MATHIAS, App., 10-14-1816.

PITZER, MICH., App., 11-12-1822.

PLOTNER, DAN., Will, 4-13-1840.
Dev.: Christeena, wife; children.

PLOTNER, DAN., Est., 3-14-1842.

PLUMMER, JOS., Est., 6-11-1827.

POISAL, JACOB, App., 3-10-1840.

POISAL, JACOB, Sale, 3-10-1840.

PORTER, JOHN, Will, 12-11-1848.
Dev.: Nancy, wife; John, son.

PORTER, JOHN, App., 6-11-1849.

PORTERFIELD, ARCH., Est., 3-13-1837.

PORTERFIELD, ARCH., Est., 3-15-1842.

PORTERFIELD, CHAS., Will, 1-10-1826.
Dev.: John, neph.; others.

PORTERFIELD, CHAS., Est., 4-9-1838.

PORTERFIELD, ELIZ., Adm., 10-13-1817.

PORTERFIELD, GEO., Est., 2-8-1830.

PORTERFIELD, GEO., Will, 9-12-1842.
Dev.: Rachel, wife; Juliana, Martha Oden, Jane Morrison, dau.; others.

PORTERFIELD, GEO., Est., 8-14-1843.

PORTERFIELD, GEO., Est., 3-13-1848.

PORTERFIELD, JOHN, Will, 3-13-1826.
Dev.: Rachel, wife; Sam, slave; others.

PORTERFIELD, JOHN, Est., 3-12-1828.

PORTERFIELD, JOHN, Est., 2-8-1830.

PORTERFIELD, NANCY, Will, 10-11-1819.
Dev.: John, husband; other.

PORTERFIELD, WM., Will, 6-11-1821.
Dev.: Chas., Wm., James, Geo., sons; Mary Harlan, Eliz. Robinson, dau.

PORTERFIELD, WM., Est., 2-14-1825.

POTORF, AND., Will, 6-13-1825.
Dev.: Mary, wife; others.

POTTORF, AND., Est., 1-14-1828.

POWELL, ARCH., Will, 8-12-1844.
Dev.: Brothers and sisters; others.

POWELL, ARCH., App., 3-11-1845.

POWELL, ROBT., Est., 12-8-1823.

QUIGBY, JOHN, Est., 8-8-1817.

QUIGLEY, ELIZ., Est., 2-14-1825.

QUINN, JAS., Est., 11-12-1816.

RAMSBERGER, HENRY, Adm., 8-?-1817.

RAMSBERGER, HENRY, Est., 3-12-1827.

RAMSEY, SAM., Est., 6-10-1822.

RAINFELT, JOHN, Est., 4-9-1816.

RANDALL, ROGER, Adm., 6-12-1821.

RAY, SAM., SR., App., 8-13-1822.

RAY, SAM., Est., 8-8-1825.

REEL, ELIZ., Will, 10-11-1819.
Dev.: Dan., John, Jacob, Abr., sons; Mary, Sarah, Susanna, dau.

REEL, ELIZ., Est., 8-10-1824.

REEL, PETER, App., 1-11-1820.

REEL, PETER, Adm., 10-15-1822.

REES, ELLIS, Will, 7-14-1845.
Dev.: Jacob, Daniel, Samuel, bro.; Lydia Morgan, Lydia Rose, sis.; others.

REES, JACOB, Will, 10-10-1825.
Dev.: Ruth, wife; Jacob, Sam., sons; Jane, dau.

REES, JACOB, Inv., 3-14-1827.

REES, THOM. SR., Will, 8-9-1819.
Dev.: Marg., Jane, dau.; Joel, son; others.

REES, THOM. SR., Est., 3-13-1832.

REES, THOM., Est., 10-11-1824.

RICHARDS, LUCY, Will, 9-12-1825.
Dev.: numerous bequests.

RICHARDS, LUCY, App., 6-11-1828.

RINER, HENRY, App., 4-11-1836.

RIPPEE, MATT., Will, 10-15-1822.
Dev.: David, John, Jos., Sam., Matt., sons; Jane Lowry, Betsey, Nancy Sanks, Rebecca, Eliz. Hoge, dau.; others.

RIPPEY, MATTHEW, Will, 5-14-1838.
Dev.: Nancy Sank, Rebecca, sis.

RIPPEY, MATTHEW, Est., 3-8-1847.

RIPPEY, REBECCA, Will, 12-13-1847.
Dev.: Eliz. Hoge, sis.; others.

RIPPEY, REBECCA, App., 2-14-1848.

ROBBINS, CATH., Est., 11-13-1843.

ROBENS, JOB, Est., 6-13-1837.

ROBERTS, BOYD, Will, 9-11-1848.
Dev.: Geo., son; Rhoda Pultz, dau.; others.

ROBERTS, BOYD, App., 12-11-1848.

ROBERTS, SAM, Will, 1-9-1837.
Dev.: Josiah, Jos., sons; Nanny, dau.; wife; other children.

ROBERTS, SAM., Est., 3-8-1841.

ROBINSON, GEO., Will, 5-8-1820.
Dev.: Susan, wife; Hannah, Sarah, Chris., Susan, dau.; others.

ROBINSON, GEO., Est., 12-13-1824.

ROBINSON, ISRAEL, Will, 10-13-1828.
Dev.: Jane, wife; James, Wm., Israel, sons; Jane, Nancy, Eliz., dau.

ROBINSON, ISRAEL, Est., 3-15-1836.

ROBINSON, ISRAEL, Est., 2-12-1844.

ROBINSON, JAMES, Est., 12-13-1841.

ROBINSON, JANE, Will, 4-13-1846.
Dev.: Eliz., Nancy, dau.; Wm., Israel, sons.

ROBINSON, JANE, Est., 5-8-1848.

ROBINSON, JAS., Est., 6-13-1837.

ROBINSON, JAS., Est., 7-9-1849.

ROBINSON, JOSH., App., 8-13-1827.

ROBINSON, JOSH., Est., 5-12-1828.

ROBINSON, THOM., Will, 12-11-1837.
Dev.: James, Robt., sons; Jane, Sarah, Hannah Vinsonheller, Susan Cox, Eliz. Ganed, Lydia Saturfield, dau.

ROBINSON, THOM., Est., 12-13-1841.

ROONEY, MICH., Will, 12-11-1837.
Dev.: Martha, wife; slaves; Mich., Geo., Henry, sons; Mary Ryner, dau.; other.

ROONEY, MICH., Est., 7-13-1840.

ROPP, MARY, App., 12-14-1840.

ROPP, MARY, Est., 6-13-1842.

ROPP, SOL., Est., 5-13-1839.

ROPP, SOL., Will, 8-8-1842.
Dev.: Mary Ann, wife; others.

ROPP, SOL., Est., 8-12-1844.

ROSS, ANN, Will, 2-13-1843.
Dev.: Christian Gain, Marg. Baley.

ROSS, ANN., App., 4-10-1843.

ROUSH, AND., Est., 9-11-1826.

ROUSH, ANDREW, Est., 6-14-1830.

ROUSH, GEO., App., 4-12-1841.

ROUSH, NICH., JR., Adm., 6-15-1819.

ROUSH, NICH., JR., Est., 6-9-1823.

RUNNER, WM., App., 2-13-1837.

RUSH, ABR., Est., 4-9-1816.

RUSH, JACOB, Est., 8-12-1823.

RUSH, JACOB, App., 4-10-1848.

RUSH, SARAH, Est., 5-14-1827.

RUSH, SARAH, Est., 8-11-1828.

RUSH, WM., Will, 12-11-1820.
Dev.: Leo., Wm., sons; Sarah, wife;
Eliza, Sarah, Sidney, Sarah Turner,
dau.; others.

RUSH, WM., App., 8-9-1824.

RUSSELL, JAS., Est., 8-12-1839.

SACKMAN, ANTHONY, App., 5-12-1845.

SANKS, NANCY, Will, 9-14-1846.
Dev.: Rebecca Rippey, sis.

SATTLEMYER, CASP., App., 2-14-1825.

SCHOFFERD, PHIL., Will, 3-10-1823.
Dev.: Eliza., wife; Geo., Adam, Jacob,
sons; Cath., Eliz., Mary, Susannah,
Barb., dau.

SCHOPPERT, NICH., Will, 11-8-1824.
Dev.: Agnes, wife; Eliz. Ward, Marg.,
Chris. Anderson, dau.; Jacob, son.

SCHOPPERT, NICH., Est., 7-13-1829.

SCHRODE, JOHN, App., 3-8-1819.

SCHRODE, SOL., App., 8-11-1824.

SCHRODE, SOL., Est., 8-11-1824.

SECHMAN, ANTHONY, Est., 5-12-1845.

SECHMAN, BARB., Est., 4-10-1837.

SECHMAN, BENJ., App., 8-11-1823.

SECHMAN, BENJ., Est., 2-14-1825.

SECKMAN, CATHERINE, App., 5-12-1845.

SECKMAN, CATHERINE, Est., 5-12-1845.

SECKMAN, CATHERINE, Sale, 5-12-1845.

SEIBERT, GEO. B., Est., 8-9-1830.

SEIBERT, JACOB, Est., 12-12-1836.

SEIBERT, JACOB, Est., 12-13-1841.

SEIBERT, JOHN, Will, 2-10-1823.
Dev.: Cath., wife; Henry, John, sons;
Cath. Strayer, sis.

SEIBERT, JOHN, Est., 1-10-1825.

SEIBERT, JOHN, Est., 6-15-1830.

SEIBERT, JOHN, App., 11-14-1831.

SEIBERT, JOHN S., Will, 9-13-1830.
Dev.: Eliza, wife; others.

SEIBERT, MICH., App., 9-11-1848.

SELLERS, MARTIN, App., 3-13-1837.

SETTLEMIRE, CAS., Will, 11-8-1819.
Dev.: Mary, Sarah, dau.; Eliza, adopted dau.; Mary, wife; Geo., bro.

SHAFFER, PETER, Est., 11-9-1818.

SHAFFER, PETER, App., 11-9-1818.

SHARP, THOM., Est., 4-13-1819.

SHARTLE, JACOB, Adm., 3-12-1822.

SHEERER, RACH, Est., 2-14-1825.

SHEERER, THOM., Est., 2-14-1825.

SHERRARD, JOS., Est., 1-8-1827.

SHERRARD, JOS., Est., 4-13-1830.

SHEWALTER, ELIZ., Will, 10-12-1840.
Dev.: Jos., Jacob, sons; Jane, Harriett
Wysong, Eliza Fishburn, Caroline
Compton, Ann Kelly, dau.; others.

SHEWALTER, ELIZ., Est., 5-9-1842.

SHIELDS, MARY, Will, 8-10-1824.
Dev.: Charity Hedges, dau.

SHIELDS, SALLY, Will, 3-12-1832.
Dev.: Eliz. Harper, Nancy Yates, sis.;
Presby. and Meth. church.

SHIELDS, SARAH, Est., 2-13-1837.

SHIELDS, WM., Will, 2-13-1832.
Dev.: Sally, Eliz. Harper, Nancy Yates,
Charity Cunningham, Janny Robin-
son, dau.

SHIMP, JOHN, Will, 10-10-1836.
Dev.: Barbary, Eve, Salome Albright,
dau.; John, Jonas, sons; Eve, wife;
others.

SHIMP, JOHN, Est., 5-13-1839.

SHOCKEY, JACOB, Will, 1-12-1818.
Dev.: Ann, wife; John, Bazel, Jacob,
sons; Polly, Nancy, Susanna, Cath.,
dau.

SHOCKEY, JACOB, App., 4-8-1822.

SHOEFSTALL, JOHN, Adm., 6-13-1820.

SHOFESTOLE, GEO., Will, 5-13-1818.
Dev.: Ann Morris.

SHOOK, JOHN, App., 4-10-1837.

SHOPPERT, NICH., App., 4-11-1825.

SHOPPERT, NICH., Sale, 4-11-1825.

SHOPPERT, PHIL., Est., 5-9-1825.

SHOPPERT, PHIL., App., 5-9-1825.

SHOWALTER, JOS., Est., 6-14-1830.

SHOWALTER, JOS., Est., 7-13-1840.

SHOWATTER, JOS., App., 4-14-1829.

SHRODE, SOLLOMAN, Will, 8-12-1822.
Dev.: Mary, wife; Solloman, Geo.,
David, sons; Rosanna, Susanna, Han-
nah, Cath., dau.; others.

SIDWELL, JAMES, Will, 5-13-1816.
Dev.: Amy, wife; Lydia, wife; Marg.
Stephson, dau.; others.

SIGLER, JOHN, App., 5-13-1844.

SIGLER, JOHN, Sale, 5-13-1844.

SILER, JOHN, App., 1-8-1849.

SILER, MARG., App., 3-10-1823.

SILER, MARG., Est., 2-14-1825.

SILER, PHIL., Will, 12-13-1841.
Dev.: Benj., son; widow.

SILER, PHIL., Est., 8-14-1843.

SILVER, MARY, Will, 5-9-1825.
Dev.: Nancy, Bershaba Hettyford, Lu-
cetta, dau.; Sam., Ed., Geo., Jos.,
Thom., sons.

SILVER, MARY, Est., 5-10-1830.

SLAUGHTER, AMEALA, App., 6-9-1823.

SLAUGHTER, AMELIA, Will, 11-11-1822.
Dev.: Thom., Wm., Geo., sons; Cath.
Askew, Mary, Jane, Millie, Fanny,
dau.

SLAUGHTER, FRANCES, Will, 4-8-1839.
Dev.: Jane, Amelia Eichelberger, sis.;
David Eichelberger, neph.

SLAUGHTER, GEO., Est., 11-13-1848.

SLAUGHTER, MARY, Will, 2-13-1843.
Dev.: Amelia Eichelberger, Jane, sis.

SLOAN, JAMES, Est., 4-12-1841.

SMALL, GEO., Est., 1-9-1826.

SMALL, GEO., Est., 10-8-1827.

SMALL, HENRY, Will, 8-13-1827.
Dev.: Elenor, wife; Wm., John, Adam, sons; Nancy Paull, Polly, dau.

SMALL, HENRY, Est., 3-9-1829.

SMALL, JACOB, Est., 9-10-1838.

SMALL, JACOB, Est., 5-8-1848.

SMALL, WM., Sale, 6-15-1842.

SMITH, CASPER, Est., 1-10-1826.

SMITH, JACOB, Est., 10-12-1829.

SMITH, JESS, Will, 12-10-1827.
Dev.: Eve, wife; her heirs.

SMITH, JESSE, Est., 3-14-1831.

SMITH, THOM., Will, 8-14-1843.
Dev.: Isabella, wife; Ann Hunter, dau.; others.

SMITH, THOM., Est., 10-14-1844.

SMITH, THOS. C., Est., 9-8-1845.

SNIDER, ABR., Will, 5-12-1845.
Dev.: Catherine, wife; Jacob, Jas., Daniel, Christian, sons; Maria Myers, Sharlotte Miller, Eliz. Jane, dau.

SNIDER, ABR., App., 4-12-1847.

SNODGRASS, CATHERINE, Est., 6-9-1845.

SNODGRASS, ROBT. SR., App., 7-11-1825.

SNODGRASS, ROBT. SR., Est., 11-14-1836.

SNODGRASS, ROBT., Will, 12-13-1830.
Dev.: Catherine, wife; Sarah Ann, Eliz. Hodges, Mary Evans, dau.; Jos., son.

SNODGRASS, ROBT., Est., 11-15-1836.

SNODGRASS, STEP., Est., 11-14-1836.

SNODGRASS, WM., Adm., 5-11-1818.

SNODGRASS, WM., Est., 6-11-1838.

SNODGRASS, WM., Est., 5-8-1848.

SNOWDEEL, PETER, Est., 11-10-1828.

SNOWDEEL, PETER, Est., 3-9-1830.

SNOWDEEL, PETER, App., 11-10-1828.

SNOWDEEL, PETER, Sale, 11-10-1828.

SNOWDEIL, GEO., Sale, 3-14-1836.

SNYDER, GEO., Est., 2-12-1844.

SNYDER, JOHN, Will, 11-11-1816.
Dev.: Jacob, bro.; two churches.

SOISTER, DAN., Est., 9-12-1831.

SOUTHWOOD, ED., Will, 12-13-1824.
Dev.: Ed., son; Frances Burns, Susan Hite, dau.; others.

SPECK, PETER, Will, 6-14-1830.
Dev.: Christena, wife; Benj., son; Eliz., dau.; others.

SPECK, PETER, Sale, 1-9-1842.

SPERO, GEO., App., 5-9-1831.

SPERO, GEO., Est., 10-8-1838.

SPEROW, GEO., Est., 11-10-1845.

SPEROW, SARAH, Will, 1-14-1839.
Dev.: Sarah Trammel, Rebecca, dau.; David, Geo., Wm., son; others.

SPERWO, SARAH, Est., 6-14-1841.

SPICKNALL, BAZIL, Will, 3-11-1822.
Dev.: Eliz., wife; Darkus, Eliz., dau.; Clement, John, Bazil, sons.

STANLEY, JOHN, Will, 3-8-1847.
Dev.: Numerous bequests.

STANLEY, JOHN, Est., 7-9-1849.

STARRY, CON., Est., 10-8-1838.

STEEL, JOHN, App., 8-8-1825.

STEEM, ROBT., Est., 2-14-1825.

STEEN, ROBT., Will, 1-8-1821.
Dev.: sister's children.

STEIDLEY, FRED., Will, 3-12-1832.
Dev.: Eliz., wife; Sol., John, son; Eliz., Cath., Abalona, dau.; other.

STEPHENS, JOHN, Will, 9-11-1848.
Dev.: John, Geo. Washington Stephens.

STEVENS, THOM., App., 2-14-1842.

STIPP, FRANCES, App., 4-9-1849.

STOUT, PHIL., Will, 2-10-1817.
Dev.: Bart., Phil., sons; Ann Baker, Eliz. Tedrick, Rebecca Anderson, Mary Wolfe, Sarah Tedrick, Cath. Smith, dau.; John McDonal, orphan, others.

STOUT, PHIL., Est., 2-13-1819.

STRAYER, ADAM, Will, 11-9-1818.
Dev.: Mary, wife; John, Adam, son; Cath., mother.

STRAYER, JACOB, Est., 10-13-1828.

STRODE, JAMES, Est., 11-10-1828.

STRODE, JOHN, Sale, 2-14-1820.

STOCKEY, JACOB, Est., 3-9-1846.

STUCKEY, JOHN, App., 9-14-1840.

STUCKEY, JOHN, Est., 12-13-1842.

SUBER, PETER, Est., 2-12-1827.

SWANEY, JOHN, Inv., 8-11-1817.

SWARTZ, MATHIAS, Will, 1-9-1843.
Dev.: Maria, wife; Frederica Fuss, dau.

SWARTZ, MATHIAS, App., 12-11-1843.

SWEARINGEN, HEZ., Will, 2-10-1840.
Dev.: Isabella, wife.

SWEARINGEN, HEZ., Est., 12-9-1844.

SWEARINGESS, THOM., Adm., 8-12-1818.

SWENEY, MARY, Will, 5-10-1847.
Dev.: Sarah, Maria Maddox, dau.; Jeremiah, Andrew, Alexander, Samuel Johnston, John, sons; others.

SWIMLEY, JACOB, Will, 3-8-1824.
Dev.: Cath., wife; Cath. Thomas, Dorathy, dau.; John, Jacob, Geo., Lewis, Henry, Martin, Jos., sons.

SWIMLEY, JACOB, Est., 3-13-1826.

SWIMLEY, JACOB, Est., 6-10-1839.

SWINGLE, BENJ., Will, 11-13-1848.
Dev.: Eve, wife; Mary Coleman, Rachel, Bell, Cath., Bowers, Eliz., Sybole, dau.; Benoni, son; others.

SWIFT, GODWIN, Est., 3-11-1816.

SWIFT, MARTHA, Will, 6-14-1825.
Dev.: Lewis and Robt. Willis, Elijah, Elisha, and Leroy Swift, sons; slaves.

SWIFT, MARTHA, Est., 7-9-1827.

SYBERT, FRED., Inv., 12-11-1815.

SYBERT, GEO., App., 6-9-1828.

SYESTER, DAN., Will, 10-12-1829.
Dev.: Hannah, wife; Caty, second
wife; Nancy, Sally, Sophia, Betsey,
Susannah, Polly, Peggy, dau.; Elias,
John, Dan., David, Jacob, sons.

SYESTER, DANIEL., App., 4-12-1830.

SYLER, JOHN, Est., 2-10-1817.

TABB, ED., Will, 1-11-1819.
Dev.: Wife; others.

TABB, ED., Inv., 6-14-1819.

TABB, GEO., SR., Will, 11-9-1829.
Dev.: Ann, wife; Bailey, Seaton, sons;
Mary, Eliz., Mildred, Harlot Ann, dau.

TABB, GEO., SR., Est., 5-14-1832.

TABB, JOHN, Will, 12-13-1847.
Dev.: Arabella, wife; Matthews Wal-
ton, Edw. Franklin Tabb, Geo. Wash-
ington, John Turner Walker, Harrison
Noble, Robt. Elliot White, sons; Eliz.
Brown, Ruth Va. Walker, Dorcas Su-
san Mitchell, Mary Evaline Jenney,
Annabella Ellen Snodgrass, dau.

TABB, JOHN, App., 7-10-1849.

TABB, THOM., App., 3-12-1832.

TABLER, ADAM, Will, 12-11-1837.
Dev.: Wife; Julia, Phebe Bands, Cath.
Claycomb, Mary, Susan Helferstay,
dau.; Chris., Adam, Wm., sons; others.

TABLER, ADAM, Est., 11-11-1839.

TABLER, GEO., Will, 11-12-1827.
Dev.: Polly Rutherford, dau.; Henry,
Chris., Mich., Wm., sons; others.

TABLER, GEO., Est., 10-12-1829.

TABLER, GEO., Est., 6-13-1837.

TABLER, HENRY, Sale, 3-13-1837.

TABLER, HENRY, App., 3-13-1837.

TABLER, PHEBE, Est., 12-13-1841.

TABLER, WM., Will, 6-12-1847.
Dev.: Rosannah Frevill, Mary Peter-
man, Elisa Nedler, Eliz. Hudgel, Sarah
Myers, dau.; Wm. F., Jas., Christian
W., Thos. H., sons; others.

TATE, DAVID, Will, 7-11-1836.
Dev.: Mary, wife.

TATE, ELIZ., Est., 12-13-1841.

TATE, ELIZ., Est., 5-8-1843.

TATE, JOHN, SR., Will, 6-15-1819.
Dev.: Mary, Eliz., Rachel, Rosannah
Sally Calvin, dau.; John, And., Sam.,
sons.

TATE, JOHN, SR., Est., 9-13-1824.

TATE, MAGNUS, Est., 11-15-1826.

TATE, MAGNUS, Est., 7-13-1829.

TATE, MAGNUS, Est., 11-15-1831.

THARP, NAT., Will, 2-13-1826.
Dev.: Easther, wife; Hannah Thatcher,
Mary Everhart, Abbigail Everhart,
dau.; Wm., son.

THARP, NAT., Est., 1-14-1828.

THATCHER, JON., Will, 4-10-1848.
Dev.: Hannah, wife; Sarah Walters,
Hannah Smith, Mary McCuley, dau.;
Jon., Sam., Mark, Absolum, sons; oth-
ers.

THATCHER, JON., App., 8-15-1848.

THOMPSON, CORN., Sale, 8-13-1816.

THOMPSON, CORN., Est., 12-11-1820.

THOMPSON, CORN., Est., 5-14-1838.

THOMPSON, ELISHA, Est., 11-12-1822.

THOMPSON, JOHN, Will, 8-10-1818.
Dev.: John, Elton, sons; Ann Pierce,
Dourris Commyges, dau.; others.

THOMPSON, JOHN, Est., 11-12-1822.

THROCKMORTON, JOB, Est., 6-11-1827.

THROCKMORTON, ROBT., Est., 8-12-
1823.

TOOLE, JAS., Est., 12-11-1820.

TURNER, JESSE, Est., 5-12-1845.

TURNER, JOHN, Est., 3-8-1830.

TURNER, SIMEON, Est., 1-12-1829.

TURNER, RUTH, Est., 3-8-1830.

UNGER, NICH., Will, 4-14-1817.
Dev.: Geo., Dan., bro.

VAIL, ELIZ., App., 6-11-1844.

VAIL, WINIFRED, App., 5-12-1823.

VAIL, WINIFRED, Est., 5-10-1824.

VANMETER, ISABELLA, App., 3-9-1818.

VANMETER, JOHN, Will, 10-12-1818.
Dev.: Ezra, John, Thornton, sons;
Cath., Eliza, Josina, Maria, Nancy Al-
burtus, dau.; Hannah, Johnson, slaves.

VANMETER, JOHN, SR., App., 2-14-1825.

VANMETER, NAT., Est., 10-11-1824.

VANMETER, NAT., Est., 12-11-1826.

VANMETRE, ABR., SR., Est., 3-13-1837.

VANMETRE, ABR., SR., Est., 11-13-1839.

VANMETRE, ISAAC, Will, 2-11-1828.
Dev.: Mary, wife; Jos., Van, John,
Jacob, Evans, Wm., Abr., Isaac, sons;
Isabella, Mary, Marg., dau.; John,
grandson.

VANMETRE, ISAAC, Est., 12-13-1830.

VANMETRE, ISAAC, Will, 3-14-1831.
Dev.: Mother; Jacob, Evans, Wm.,
Van, Jos., John, Abraham, bro.; Isa-
bella, sis.

VANMETRE, ISAAC, Est., 12-11-1837.

VANMETRE, JACOB, Est., 6-10-1816.

VANMETRE, JOHN, Est., 4-15-1828.

VANMETRE, JOS., Est., 3-13-1837.

VERNER, PAUL, App., 6-10-1816.

VERNER, PAUL, Est., 5-12-1823.

VINSONHELLER, JOHN, Will, 11-13-
1826.
Dev.: Geo., John, sons; Sarah Hedges,
dau.; heirs of other children.

VINSONHELLER, JOHN, Est., 5-12-1829.

VINSONHELLER, JOHN, Est., 6-13-1837.

VINSONHELLER, PHIL., App., 7-12-
1841.

VINSONHELLER, PHIL., Est., 7-12-1841.

VIOLETT, THOM., Adm., 5-12-1819.

WAGGONER, AND., Est., 9-15-1818.

WAGGONER, AND., Est., 10-10-1831.

WAITE, HARRISON, App., 11-9-1846.

WALKER, JAMES, Est., 12-10-1827.

WALKER, JAS., Sale, 2-14-1825.

WALTERS, JOHN, Est., 1-10-1848.

WALTERS, MICH., Will, 1-9-1843.
Dev.: Marg., wife; Harrison, Geo.,
Mich., Jacob, sons; Sarah Diffenderfer,
Cath. Young, Eliz. Fryatt, dau.

WANDLING, JONATHAN, Est., 8-10-
1846.

WARD, AQUILLA, Est., 5-14-1827.

WARD, JACOB, Est., 6-13-1837.
WARD, JACOB, Est., 12-14-1846.
WARD, JAS., App., 3-13-1820.
WARD, JOEL, Will, 2-13-1837.
Dev.: Eliz., wife; Nich., son; Nancy Holmes, Eliz. Lamon, dau.; numerous other bequests.
WARD, JOEL, Est., 7-8-1839.
WARD, JOS., App., 1-13-1840.
WARD, JOS., Est., 3-9-1840.
WARD, WM., Est., 4-8-1839.
WATSON, REV. JOHN, Est., 7-13-1840.
WATSON, JOHN, Est., 2-10-1845.
WEAVER, JACOB, Will, 9-9-1844.
Dev.: Jacob, Geo., Casper, John, sons; Helena, Mary, dau.
WEAVER, JOHN, Est., 2-14-1825.
WEAVER, JOS., Est., 5-14-1832.
WELSH, MICH., Est., 8-13-1827.
WENDLE, JOHN, Est., 12-8-1823.
WEVER, JOS., App., 2-14-1831.
WHITE, JOHN, Est., 2-14-1825.
WHITE, JOHN, Est., 3-9-1829.
WHITENECK, HEN., Sale, 7-12-1819.
WHITING, CHAS., HENRY, Will, 11-8-1847.
Dev.: Sarah, wife; Harold, Norman, sons; Ella, dau.; others.
WHITING, DR. C. H., App., 3-?-1849.
WICKERSHAM, ELIZA, Will, 6-14-1830.
Dev.: orphans of Johnathan Wickersham.
WICKERSHAM, FRANCES, Will, 6-14-1830.
Dev.: orphans of Johnathan Wickersham.
WICKERSHAM, JANE, Will, 6-14-1830.
Dev.: orphans of Jonathan Wickersham.
WICKERSHAM, JAS., Will, 6-14-1830.
Dev.: orphans of Johnathan Wickersham.
WICKERSHAM, JON., Will, 5-10-1824.
Dev.: Mary, wife; Ed., James, sons; Maria, Narina, dau.
WICKERSHAM, JON., Est., 8-15-1826.
WICKERSHAM, REBECA, Will, 6-14-1830.
Dev.: orphans of Johnathan Wickersham.
WIDDESS, THOS., Est., 2-?-1846.
WILEN, NICH., Will, 5-8-1843.
Dev.: Marg., wife.
WILHELMS, JOHN, Will, 9-11-1826.
Dev.: John, David, Sam., Henry, Jacob, Umphrey, sons; Eliz., Mary, dau.
WILHELMS, JOHN, App., 2-12-1827.
WILLIAMS, BARB., Est., 5-14-1838.
WILLIAMS, CHAS., Est., 12-12-1831.
WILLIAMS, ED., Est., 8-10-1825.
WILLIAMS, MARTHA, Will, 5-14-1832.
Dev.: Adam Cockburn, half-bro.; to Presby. Church after his death.
WILLIAMS, MARTHA, Est., 6-14-1836.
WILLIAMSON, JOHN, Will, 4-13-1843.
Dev.: Marg., wife; Mary Nolan, dau.; Jacob, Wm., Leonard, sons; others.

WILLIAMSON, JOHN, Est., 9-13-1847.
WILSON, ELIJAH, Est., 7-12-1830.
WILSON, HENRIETTA, Will, 4-12-1841.
Dev.: Julia Stephen, sis.; others.
WILSON, HENRIETTA M., Est., 9-13-1847.
WILSON, ISABELLA, Est., 3-8-1841.
WILSON, ISABELLA, Est., 5-8-1843.
WILSON, CAPT. JAS., Est., 2-10-1817.
WILSON, CAPT. JAS., App., 2-10-1817.
WILSON, JAS., Est., 9-10-1827.
WILSON, JOHN, Will, 4-12-1841.
Dev.: Isabella, dau.
WILSON, JOHN, Est., 12-13-1841.
WILSON, JOHN, Est., 7-9-1849.
WILSON, JOS., App., 6-15-1819.
WILSON, MARY, Est., 3-8-1841.
WILSON, MARY, Est., 5-8-1843.
WILSON, ROBT., Will, 5-13-1818.
Dev.: Henrietta, wife; Charlotte, dau.
WILSON, SAM., JR., Will, 8-12-1816.
Dev.: Wm., son; Mary Gammon, Ann, dau.; others.
WILSON, SAM., Sale, 5-13-1817.
WILSON, SAM., Est., 11-9-1829.
WILSON, SAM., Est., 10-11-1841.
WILSON, WM., SR., Est., 6-10-1844.
WILSON, WM., Will, 6-13-1831.
Dev.: Mary, wife; Isabella, Mary Coe, dau.; John Park, son; others.
WILSON, WM., Will, 5-10-1841.
Dev.: Mary, Nancy Manford, dau.; Hiram, John, Sam., Robt., sons; others.
WILSON, WM., App., 1-11-1847.
WINDER, JAS., App., 6-12-1837.
WINDLE, JOHN, Est., 2-12-1827.
WINNING, JOHN, Will, 11-10-1817.
Dev.: Phebe, wife; Jane, Sarah, dau.; James, son.
WINNING, JOHN, Est., 8-15-1821.
WINNING, PHEBE, App., 11-11-1828.
WINNING, PHEBE, Est., 11-12-1828.
WINNING, SAM., Est., 12-13-1841.
WITHROW, JOS., App., 2-14-1842.
WITHROW, JOS., Est., 11-9-1846.
WIZENBERGER, GEO., Will, 12-8-1817.
Dev.: Cath., wife; John, Jacob, Geo., sons; Susanna, Eliz., Cath., dau.
WIZENBERGER, GEO., Est., 10-11-1819.
WOLFF, CHRIS., Will, 9-11-1837.
Dev.: Eliz., wife; children.
WOLFF, CHRIS., Est., 1-13-1840.
WOLFF, CHRIS., Est., 6-10-1843.
WOLFF, GEO., Will, 4-14-1845.
Dev.: Eliz., wife; Bernard C., John G., sons; Ann Maria Doll, Catherine Doll, dau.; others.
WOLFF, GEO., Est., 7-10-1848.
WOODFORD, MARY, Will, 2-11-1839.
Dev.: numerous bequests.
WOODWARD, THOM., App., 3-8-1841.
WOODWARD, THOS., Est., 3-10-1845.
WRIGHT, JAS., App., 12-11-1837.
WYNKOOP, ADRIAN, Est., 3-8-1824.
WYNKOOP, SARAH, App., 6-13-1825.

YARNELL, JOS., Will, 12-8-1817.
  Dev.: Rachael, wife; Jeppe, Jos., sons; Henrietta, dau.
YARNELL, JOS., Adm., 5-11-1818.
YEATES, AND., Est., 4-15-1817.
YINGLING, MARY, Est., 6-9-1823.
YOEL, ANNA EVE, Will, 10-11-1819.
  Dev.: Cath. Ellis, dau.; others.
YOEL, ANNA EVE, App., 11-8-1819.
YOUNG, HENRY, Est., 8-12-1816.

ZACHMAN, ANTH., Will, 4-10-1837.
  Dev.: Cath., wife; other.
ZIMMERMAN, CATH., Will, 9-14-1818.
  Dev.: And., Mich., Geo., Henry, Jacob, Eli, sons; Chris., Cath., Eliz., Polly, dau.
ZIMMERMAN, CATH., Est., 11-14-1825.
ZIMMERMAN, MICH., Est., 2-14-1825.
ZINN, DAN., App., 3-14-1825.
ZUCK, JOHN, Est., 10-13-1828.

West Virginia Estate Settlements

In 1936 and 1937, the West Virginia Commission on Historic and Scenic Markers, the Works Progress Administration, and the Federal Emergency Relief Administration compiled court records of the various counties, such as Births, Deaths, Marriages, and Wills. Under Wills were grouped subjects pertaining to Estate Settlements, including Wills, Inventories, and Appraisements. Copies of these county records were filed at the Department of Archives and History, Charleston; the Library of West Virginia University, Morgantown; and the DAR Library, Washington.

Believing that there would be particular interest on the part of the general public in the Estate Settlements in the older counties, the West Virginia Historical Society has undertaken to abstract the Estate Settlement Records, as filed in the State Department of Archives and History, and offer them for publication in the *West Virginia History Quarterly*. (No responsibility can be assumed as to the accuracy of the copies made from the original county records.

There are 13 counties which were formed prior to 1800, and it has been agreed to arrange these counties in chronological order, and to print their records from the earliest date to 1850. The formation dates of these counties are as follows: Hampshire—1753; Berkeley—1772; Monongalia—1776; Ohio—1776; Greenbrier—1778; Harrison—1784; Hardy—1786; Randolph—1787; Pendleton—1788; Kanawha—1788; Brooke—1797; Wood—1798; and Monroe—1799.

Monongalia County, Formed 1776

Abbreviations used in this material include: Acc.—account; Adm. — administrator; App. — appraisement; Bro. — brother; Dau. — daughter; Dev. — devisees; Guard. — guardian; Inv. — inventory; S. B.—sale bill; Set.—settlement; Sis.—sister; —Ven. vendue.

ALTON BENJ., Will, 6-1849. Dev.: Jane, Marg., Harriet, Kath., Hannah, Eliz., Mary, dau.; Jesse, Sam., David, Jos., Miller, sons.

AMOS, HENRY, Will, 8-29-1828. Dev.: James, Henry, John, Geo., sons; Miriam, Mary, dau.; others.

AMOS, STEPHEN, Will, 8-1824. Dev.: Eliz., wife; Jane, Milly, Nancy, Mary Ann, dau.; James, Peter, Alpheus, sons.

AMOS, STEPHEN, Inv., 8-1825.

AMOS, STEPHEN, Set., 10-1825.

AMOS, STEPHEN'S HEIRS, Set., 6-16-1827.

AMOS, STEPHEN'S HEIRS, Set., 8-27-1830.

ANDERSON, JOHN, S. B., 10-9-1813.

ARCHER, STEPHEN, Will, 7-1824. Dev.: Martha, wife; Eliz., Peggy, Mary, dau.; James, stepson.

ARNETT, ANDREW, Will, 4-1824. Dev.: Eliz., wife; And., John, Sol., Thom., sons; Mary, Eliz., Casandra, Sara, dau.

ARNETT, AND., Inv., 5-1825.

ARNETT, DAN., Inv., 12-1-1825.

ARNETT, DAN., S. B., 9-1826.

ATHEY, ANN W., S. B., 6-21-1831.

ATHEY, ANN W., Inv., 6-30-1831.

ATHEY, ELISHA, Inv., 6-10-1823.

ATHEY, ELISHA, S. B., 8-1823.

ATRIDGE, JAMES, Inv., 1-8-1825.

ATRIDGE, JAMES, Set., 6-1826.

AUSTIN, JOHN, Will, 1-1849. Dev.: Sarah, wife; Emily, Hannah, Rebecca, dau.; David, Jos., Jas., Corn., John, Hugh, Dan., Wm., Jesse, sons.

AUVEL, DAN., Will, 2-1838. Dev.: Susanna, wife; Dan., Geo., John, Elias, sons; Lydda, Harriet, Anna, dau.

BAILEY, ELIAS, Will, 3-1841. Dev.: Eleanor, wife; Nancy, Hester, Sarah, dau.; Asher, Jesse, Reuben, sons; others.

BAKER, GEO., Will, 9-1844. Dev.: Eliz., wife; children.

BAKER, PRIS., Set., 2-12-1825.

BALLAH, AGUSTA, Set., 4-3-1810.

BALLAH, ANN, Will, 6-19-1834. Dev.: Cath., Mary, Eliz., Rach., dau.; Enoch, Hiram, sons.

BALLAH, AUGUSTA, App., 10-19-1807.

BALLAH, AUGUSTUS, Inv., 10-30-1807.

BALTZELL, GEO., Will, 3-1816. Dev.: Mary, wife.

BARKER, JAS., Will, 1-1823. Dev.: Amelia, wife; Imly, son; Nancy, Mary Ann, Anarah, dau.

BARKER, JAMES, Inv., 1-29-1823.

BARKER, JAMES, S. B., 2-1823.

BARKER, JAMES, Set., 11-19-1824.

BARKER, JOHN, Will, 5-1825. Dev.: Mary, wife; Jos., Dan., Jas., sons.

BARKER, JOHN, Inv., 6-16-1826.

BARKER, JOHN, Set., 9-24-1827.

BARKER, PRIS., Inv., 8-31-1822.

BARKER, PRIS., S. B., 9-10-1822.

BARNES, HENRY, Inv., 7-13-1808.

BARNES, HENRY, S. B., 7-30-1808.

BARNES, HENRY, Add. Inv., 2-11-1809.

BARNES, HENRY, Set., 9-29-1810. ,

BARNS, HENRY, Inv., 11-6-1826.

BARNS, THOM., SR., Will, 10-1836. Dev.: Wm., John, Thom., Jas., sons; Mary Ann, Phebe, Sally, dau.; others.

BARNS, UZ, Will, 5-1833. Dev.: Nat., Jas., Uz, sons; Cath., Phebe, Rach., dau.; others.

BARRICKMAN, JOHN, App., 1-10-1805.

BARTLY, JOHN, Will, 6-1826. Dev.: Wm., son; Eliz., dau.

BASNET, BOAZ, Will, 9-1826. Dev.: Mary, wife; children.

BASNETT, MARY, Will, 5-1838. Dev.: Ann, dau.; Boaz, son.

BATTIN, THOM., Will, 9-16-1821. Fayette Co., Pa. Dev.: John, son; Rach., Anna, Polly, Hannah, Betsey, dau.; others.

BAYLES, JESSE, Will, 4-1807. Dev.: Wm., Jesse, David, Adin, sons; Peggy, Mary, Tietsy, Phebe, dau.

BEARD, MOSES, App., 5-1816.

BEATTY, GEO., Will, 12-1823. Dev.: Mary, wife; Mary, dau.; John, Wm., Sam., Robt., sons.

BEESON, JACOB, Will, 12-22-1818. Fayette Co., Pa. Dev.: Eliz., wife; Jonas, Jacob, Henry, sons; Rebecca, Lydia, Jane, Ann, Agnes, Rachel, Mary, dau.; others.

BENNETT, MARY, Inv., 1-30-1818.

BENNETT, MARY, S. B., 1-31-1818.

BERKSHIRE, JOHN, Will, 3-1832. Dev.: Eliz., wife; Ralph, Wm., Corn., sons.

BERRY, THOM., App., 6-1802.

BERRY, THOM., Will, 6-1802. Dev., Rachel, wife; Curtes, John, Nat., Sam., Thom., Jos., sons; Marg., Sarah, Eliz., Rach., dau.

BILLINGSLEY, SYRUS, Inv., 2-4-1819.

BILLINGSLEY, SYRUS, S. B., 2-5-1819.

BILLINGSLY, SIAS, Will, 1-1819. Dev.: Hannah, wife; Wm., Sam., Fran., sons; Mary, Marg., Alex., dau.; others.

BLACKISTON, GEO., Will, 5-1836. Dev.: Sarah Inghram, niece; James Inghram, neph-in-law.

BLACKSHIRES, EBEN., Will, 12-1834. Dev.: Elis., wife; Fran.; Elias, sons; Sarah, Pris., dau.

BLASNET, JOS., Will, 1810. Dev.: Francis, bro.; others.

BOGGESS, ROBT., Will, 6-1839. Dev.: slaves; Sam., Rich., Fielding, Caleb, Geo., Albertes, Alonzo, bro.

BONNER, JOHN, Set., 2-10-1812.

BOWLBY, JAS., Will, 6-1842. Dev.: Williampee, Eliz., Caty., dau.; Robt., John, sons; others.

BOYERS, JACOB, Will, 2-1836. Dev.: Eliz., wife; Cath., July Ann, Eliz., dau.; Josiah, Wm., Jeff., Hezekiah, Simon, sons; others.

BOYLES, CHAS., Will, 11-1826. Dev.: Lettice, wife; Joshua, son; Mary, Eliz., Nancy, Marg., dau.

BOYLES, CHAS., Inv., 12-29,1826.

BOYLES, CHAS., Set., 12-22-1828.

BOYLES, CHAS., S. B., 3-1829.

BOYLES, CHAS., Set., 4-25-1831.

BOYLS, CHAS., SR., 11-1813. Dev.: Patience, Sarah, Marg., dau.; Mich., Chas., Gil., sons.

BRADLEY, JOHN, Will, 4-1831. Dev.: Williamiah, wife; Jeremiah, Jas., David, Asa, John, Benj., Wm., sons; Eliz., dau.

BRAND, GEO., Will, 8-1849. Dev.: Martha, wife; Wm., Jas., Chas., sons; Jane, Julia Ann, dau.; others.

BRAND, JAS., Will, 5-1836. Dev.: Mary, wife; Jos., Sam., John, sons.

BRAND, JAS., Will, 11-1844. Dev.: Eliz., wife; Alex., son; other children.

BRAND, JOHN, Will, 2-1834. Dev.: Jane, wife; Geo., James, John, sons; Mary, Jane, Nancy, dau.

BREWER, CHRIS., SR., Will, 1-1846. Dev.: Anna, wife; Rach., Barb., Mary, dau.; Chris., Enoch, sons.

BRIGHT, ALKANE, Will, 8-1835. Dev.: Aaron, son; Susanna; Mary Morris.

BRITTON, ANN, Will, 1-1838. Dev.: Eliz., Cath., Mary, dau.

BROCK, WM., Will, 6-1838. Dev.: Marg., wife; Simeon, Wesley, sons.

BROOKE, THOM. F., Will, 11-1836. Dev.: Mary, wife; Rich., Ed., Benj., Jas., Theo., sons; Sarah, Rach., Mary, Pris., dau.; Servants.

BROUGHMIRE, HENRY, Will, 12-1811. Dev.: Chris., wife; Marg., Chris., Eliz., Susanna, Mary, Amelia, dau.; Henry, John, Sam., sons; others.

BROWN, ADAM, Inv., 3-2-1825.

BROWN, ADAM, S. B., 12-1825.

BROWN, ADAM, Inv., 6-1826.

BRUMAGE, REBECCA, Will, 10-1837. Dev.: Nelson, Allen, sons; Casander, Amandy, Matilda, Minerva, dau.

BRUMMAGE, JOS., Inv., 9-18-1829.

BRUMMAGE, JOS., S. B., 9-18-1829.

BRUMMAGE, JOS., Set., 3-1831.

BUNNER, CASPAR, Will, 9-1820. Dev.: Reuben, son; Sarah, wife; Mary, Rebecca, Ara, Sara, Eliza, Emmy, Nancy, Anne, dau.

BUNNER, JOHN, Will, 10-8-1810. Dev.: Martha, wife; Rebecca, Mary, Rach., dau.; Enoch, Jos., John, Jas., Amos, Reuben, sons; others.

BUNNER, JOHN, Inv., 11-7-1810.

BUNNER, JOHN, S. B., 11-16-1810.

BUNNER, JOHN, Set., 9-4-1820.

BUNNER, JOHN, Inv., 9-5-1829.

BUNNER, JOHN, S. B., 9-14-1820.

BUNNER, JOS., Will, 11-1828. Dev.: Mary, Cath., Eliz., Marg., Rutha, dau.; Jos., John, Gasper, Henry, sons.

BUNNER, JOS., SR., Inv., 12-1828.

BUNNER, JOS., SR., S. B., 12-4-1828.

BUNNER, JOS., SR., Set., 4-19-1831.

BUNNER, JOS., Will, 6-1847. Dev.: Chris., wife; heirs.

BUNNER, MARTHA, S. B., 2-13-1819.

BURCHINAL, THOM., Inv., 1-1827.

BURNS, BENJ., Will, 4-9-1847. Dev.: Marg., wife; Jas., John, Gideon, David, sons; Mary, Martha, dau.

BURROUGHS, CHAS., Inv., 6-10-1818.

BURROUGHS, ELIJAH, Will, 3-23-1798 Dev.: John, Chas., Wm., sons; Eliz., Cath., Ann, dau.

BURROUGHS, ELIJAH, Inv., 4-19-1798.

BURROUGHS, ELIJAH, Set., 1-26-1802.

BURROUGHS, ELIJAH, Set., 4-14-1806.

BURROUGHS, ELIJAH, Set., 6-13-1808.

BURROWS, ED., Inv., 8-12-1811.

BURROWS, ED., S. B., 2-1812.

BURROWS, ED., Set., 8-1826.

BURROWS, EZEKIEL, Will, 6-1819. Dev.: Prusillah, wife; Mary, Nancy, dau.; others.

BURROWS, JESSE, Will, 12-2-1840. Dev.: Phebe, wife.

BURTON, BENJ., Will, 11-1823. Dev.: Caty, wife; Sam., James, sons; Polly, Susannah, Barb., Nancy, Berry, dau.

BURTON, BENJ., Inv., 7-5-1824.

BURTON, BENJ., S. B., 8-21-1824.

BURTON, BENJ., Set., 11-1827.

BURTON, CATH., Inv., 6-1828.

BURTON, CATH., S. B., 6-1828.

BURTON, CATH., Set., 12-19-1829.

BUSSY, JESSY, Will, 5-1850. Dev.: Sarah, wife; Thom., Jessy, Ed., Edmond, sons; Ruth, Naomy, dau; others.

BUTCHER, ROBT., Will, 5-1832. Dev.: Lydia, wife.

BUTLER, ISAAC, Set., 5-23-1832.

CAIN, RICH., Inv., undated.

CAIN, RICH., S. B., Set., 12-7-1816.

CAMP, ADAM, Will, 2-1842. Dev.: Cath., wife; John, Zenas, sons; Ann, Mary, Eliz., dau.; other children and grandchildren.

CARPENTER, DAVID, Inv., 9-5-1827.

CARPENTER, DAVID, Set., 7-28-1828.

CARPENTER, JOHN, Inv., 7-13-1826.

CARPENTER, JOHN, S. B., 10-21-1826.

CARROL, ANTHONY, Will, 2-1830. Dev.: Temperance, wife; Jas., James Walls, sons; Pegey, Polly, dau.

CHALFANT, REUBEN, Inv., 11-20-1817.

CHALFANT, REUBEN, S. B., 12-25-1817.

CHALFANT, REUBEN, S. B., 2-2-1818.

CHALFANT, SOL., Will, undated. Dev.: Robt., son; Sussanna, Hannah, Jemima, Mary, Lydia, dau.

CHALFANT, S U S A N, Will, 6-1842. Dev.: Eveline, Eliz., dau.; Andrew, Francis, sons.

CHENEY, EZEKIEL, Inv., App., 12-26-1814.

CHIPPS, THOM., App., 5-5-1801.

CHIPPS, THOM., VENDUE, 5-9-1801.

CHIPPS, THOM., Set., 1-4-1804.

CHIPPS, WM., Inv., 6-1828.

CLARE, THOM., Will, 6-1814. Fayette Co., Pa. Dev.: Cath., Cummins, sis.; slaves; others.

CLARK, BART., Will, 4-1811. Dev.: Mary, wife; David, John, Wm., Jonney, Eugenus, sons; Betsy, dau.

CLARK, JAS., Will, 9-1808. Dev.: Eleanor, wife; John, Jas., Isaac, Sam., Robt., sons; Mary, dau.; others.

CLARK, JAMES, Inv., 11-11-1808.

CLARK, JAMES, Set., 8-20-1830.

CLAYTON, JOHN, Set., 6-1830.

CLAYTON, THOM., Inv., 6-2-1821.

CLAYTON, THOM., S. B., 6-1821.

CLAYTON, THOM., Set., 6-22-1822.

CLEGG, ALEX., Inv., 10-8-1829.

CLEGG, ALEX., S. B., 10-22-1829.

CLEGG, ALEX., Set., 11-1832.

CLELAND, JAMES, Vendue, 9-5-1817.

CLELAND, JAMES, App., 9-5-1817.

CLELLAND, JAS., Will, 4-1817. Dev.: Ann, wife: Francis, Alex., Pat., Larkin, Jas., John, sons; Sally, Ann, Peggy, Drusilla, Nancy, Thoda, Polly, Susannah, dau.

COLDRING (COLDREN) J A C O B, Inv., undated.

COLE, COVERDILL, Will, 2-1831. Dev.: Sophia, wife; Esther, Eliz., dau.; Jos., Hynson, Wm., sons; others.

COLE, JOS., Will, 2-1850. Dev.: Eliz., wife; Wm., Coverdale, sons; Eliz., Mary, dau.; others.

COLE, SOPHIA, Will, 3-1837. Dev.: Job, Sally, black man and woman.

COLLINS, ELIZ., Will, 2-1846. Dev.: Mary, dau.; Jos., son; others.

COLLINS, SAM., Inv., 6-1826.

COLLINS, SAM., S. B., 6-2-1826.

COLLINS, SAM., S. B., 3-1827.

COLLINS, SAM., Set., 11-1832.

COLREN, JACOB, S. B., undated.

COMBS, JOS., Will, 12-1839. Dev.: Mary, wife; Rach., Malinda, Joanna, Sarah, dau.; Henry, son.

CONAWAY, CALEB, Will, 2-1850. Dev.: Nancy, wife; children.

CONNOR, JAS., Will, 9-1802. Dev.: Wife: Mrs. Rich. Foreman, Eliz., Grace, dau.; John, Dan., Jas., Robt., sons; others.

CONNER, JAMES, Vendue, 9-28-1802.

CONNER, JAMES, Inv., 11-1832.

CONNER, JOHN, Will, 12-2-1796. Dev.: Mary, wife; Robt., John, Jas., Wm., sons; Eliz., Grace, Sarah, dau.

COOPER, JOHN, Will, 6-1830. Dev.: Sarah, wife; others.

CORE, MICH., Inv., 1-31-1816.

CORE, MOSES, Will, 10-1845. Dev.: Mrs. Core, wife; children.

COSTOLO, WM., Will, 4-1850. Dev.: Charity, wife; Francis, John, Geo., sons; Eliz., Mary, Caro., Nancy, Louise, dau.

COTTON, JAMES, Inv., 9-22-1806.

COURTNEY, JOHN, Will, 11-1839. Dev.: Rebecca, wife; John, Isaac, sons; Rebecca, Elenor, Nancy, Eliz., Jane, Arah, dau.

COURTNEY, M A R Y, Will, 10-1832. Dev.: Isabella, Rebecca, Eliza., Nancy, dau.; Wm., Robt., sons.

COURTNEY, ROBT., SR., Will, 8-1824. Dev.: Wm., Robt., sons; Mary, wife; Jane, Marg., Eliza, Nancy, Rebecca, Isabella, dau.

COURTNEY, ROBT., S. B., 10-26-1824.

COURTNEY, ROBT., Inv., 12-1824.

COURTNEY, ROBT., Set., 11-26-1825.

COURTNEY, ROBT., Set., 4-20-1826.
COURTNEY, ROBT., Set., 12-1830.
COURTNEY, THOS., Will, 9-1811. Dev.:
Isabella, wife; Robt., Thom., Mich.,
John, sons; Eliz., Mary, Anna, dau.
COURTNEY, THOM., Inv., 9-13-1811.
COURTNEY, THOM., Set., 2-1812.
CROSS, DAN., Will, 5-1846. Dev.:
Matilda, wife; children.
CROSS, NICH., Will, 5-1828. Dev.:
Kath., wife; James, Dan., Geo., sons.
CROSS, NICH., S. B., 7-8-1828.
CROSS, NICH., Inv., 4-1829.
CUMMINGS, JOS., Inv., 6-1831.
CUNNINGHAM, GEO., Will, 12-1841.
Dev.: Isaac, son; Marg., Mary, Mar-
gery, dau.; others.
CUNNINGHAM, JOHN, App., 6-15-1799.
CUNNINGHAM, JOHN, Set., 9-21-1815.
CUNNINGHAM, MARG., Will, 5-28-
1799.
Dev.: Marg., Susanna, dau.; Mich.,
Jas., Geo., sons; others.
CUNNINGHAM, MICH., Will, 12-1813.
Dev.: Marg., dau.; Susannah, Marg.,
sis.; James, bro.; others.
CUNNINGHAM, MICH., Inv., 12-28-
1813.
CUNNINGHAM, MICH., Set., 6-30-1815.
CUNNINGHAM., MICH., Set., 4-12-1817.
CUNNINGHAM, MICH., Set., 4-14-1817.
CUNNINGHAM, MICH., Set., 6-25-1818.
CURRY, JOHN, Inv., 8-14-1805.
CURRY, JOHN, S. B., 8-15-1805.
CURRY, JOHN, Set., 3-1807.

DANCER, JESSE, Will, 3-1849. Dev.:
Sary, wife; Jon., Saxton, Elijah,
Byard, Jesse, sons; Clary, Eliz., Sary,
Polly, dau.; others.
DAVIS, BRINKLEY, App., undated.
DAVIS, BRINKLEY, S. B., undated.
DAVIS, BRINKLEY, Set., 5-13-1816.
DAVIS, CHAS., Set., 6-1828.
DAVIS, CHAS., Set., 7-1830.
DAVIS, CHAS., Set., 3-1832.
DAVIS, DAN., Will, 12-1816. Dev.:
Luranah, wife; Isaac, Peter, Ananias,
Jehu, sons; Phebe, Eliz., Mille, Mary,
dau.
DAVIS, DAN., Inv., 12-18-1816.
DAVIS, DAN., Set., 2-1820.
DAVIS, JEHU, Will, 3-1825. Dev.:
Eunice, wife; Mary Waters, Eliz.
Stillwell, Ester Hill, Pheby, Mahala,
dau.; Wm., Peter, Jehu, Jas., Sam.,
sons.
DAVIS, LURANNAH, Inv., 8-24-1819.
DAVIS, LURENNA, Set., 5-1-1824.
DAVIS, LURENNA, S. B., 9-1824.

DAVIS, MATHIAS, Will, 2-1829. Dev.:
John, Robt., Mathias, Jos., sons;
others.
DAVIS, OWEN, Will, 8-3-1810. Fayette
Co., Pa. Dev.: Hannah, wife; Phil.,
Sam., Masech, Enoch, John, Isaac,
James, sons; Mary, Eliz., Hannah,
Anne, dau., others.
DAVIS, PETER, Set., guardian, 2-1827.
DAVIS, PETER, Set., 8-1832.
DAVIS, ROBT., Inv., 9-4-1825.
DAVIS, ROBT., Will, 8-1825. Dev.: John,
Robt., Caleb, sons; Eliz., Watts, Mary
Furbey, dau.; others.
DAVIS, ROBT., S. B., 9-16-1825.
DAVIS, ROBT., Set., 8-30-1826.
DAVIS, ROBT., Set., 6-25-1827.
DAVIS, ROBT., Set., 6-22-1829.
DAVIS, ROBT., Set., 3-23-1831.
DAVIS, UNICE, Will, 9-1837. Dev.:
Mahala Vandervort, Eliz. Stillwell,
Phebe Hayes, dau.; Wm., Jas., sons;
other dau.
DAUGHERTY, JAS., Will, 10-1805.
Dev.: Enos Daugherty.
DEAN, JOHN, Inv., 11-1813.
DEAN, JOHN, S. B., 11-1813.
DERING, HENRY, Will, 2-1846. Dev.:
Fred., son; grandchildren, others.
DERING, SOPHIA, Will, 5-1833. Dev.:
Harriet Lowry, sister.
DEVAULT, JACOB, Will, 9-1827. Dev.:
Mary, wife; Abraham, son; Phebe
Hayhusk, dau.
DICKENS, JOHN, Inv., 11-29-1821.
DICKENS, JOHN, S. B., 6-1822.
DICKENS, JOHN, Set., 8-1824.
DOOLITTLE, MARY, Will, 7-1820. Dev.:
Lucy Wells, dau.
DOOLITTLE, MOSES, Inv., 4-20-1820.
DOOLITTLE, MOSES, S. B., 4-20-1820.
DOOLITTLE, MOSES, Set., 8-20-1824.
DORRAH, ROBT., Will, 11-1848. Dev.:
Joh., Robt., Wm., Henry, sons; Mary,
Ruth, dau.; others.
DORSEY, GEO., Will, 5-1824. Dev.:
Sisson, wife; Rebeccah, Burnes, Pris-
cilla Dearing, dau.; Caleb, Benj., Lar-
kin, John, Geo. Washington, sons.
DORSEY, GEO., Inv., 6-1824.
DORSEY, GEO., Set., 4-1828.
DORSEY, GEO., S. B., 5-1828.
DRAGOO, EPHRAIM, Will, 6-1834.
Dev.: Elis., wife; Evolina, Louisa,
Hannah, dau.; Wm., son.
DUNLAP, JOS., Will, 11-1839. Dev.:
Jane, wife; others.

DUSENBERRY, JOHN, Will, 10-1827. Dev.: Sarah, wife; Sam., Henry, Dan., Corn., sons; Sarah Clark, Lidia Cunningham, Mary, dau.; others.

DUZENBERRY, JOHN, Inv., 11-1827.

EASTBURN, THOM., Will, 11-1843. Dev.: John, Thom., Benj., Jackson, Maria, Marg., illegitimate children by Nancy Wells, housekeeper.

ECKART, MARY ANN, Will, 7-1850. Dev.: Adam, John, sons; others.

EDDY, AZEL, Inv., 8-20-1827.

EIDON, JOS., Will, 9-1846. Dev.: Jos., father; Henry, bro.

EVANS, DUDLEY, Will, 3-1844. Dev.: Rawley, Nimrod, Jas., John, sons; Nancy, Phebe, Marg., Cynthia, dau.; others.

EVANS, JESSE, Will, 3-1843. Dev.: Eliza Wilson, dau.; others.

EVANS, JOHN, Will, 5-1834. Dev.: Rawley, son; others.

EVANS, JOHN, Will, 5-1849. Dev.: Gilly, wife; James, son; Lucy, Marg. Chadwick, dau.; others.

EVANS, NIMROD, S. B., 3-1828.

EVANS, NIMROD, Will, 3-1-1828. Dev.: Mrs. Nancy Britton; slaves; others.

EVANS, NIMROD, Inv., 3-3-1828.

EVANS, NIMROD, Inv., 5-3-1828.

EVANS, NIMROD, Set., 6-27-1831.

EVANS, NOMROD, S. B., 11-22-1828.

EVANS, THOM., Will, 9-1808. Dev.: Kath., wife; Rich., John, Jas., Thos., Evan, David, Benj., sons; Isabella Hoskins, Peggy Hammond, Caty, Polly, dau.

EVERLY, GASPAR, Will, 12-1800. Dev.: wife; Simeon, Sam., Wm., Jesse, sons.

EVERLY, GASPER, Inv., 11-29-1803.

EVERLY, GASPER, S. B., 12-30-1803.

EVERLY, SAM., Will, 5-1842. Dev.: Anna, wife; Jas., Simeon, John, Asberry, Jackson, Van Buren, sons; Phebe, Malenda, Marg., Matilda, Elmira, Maria, dau.; others.

EWELL, THOM., Will, 5-23-1844. Dev.: Cina Griggs, dau.

EWING, ROBT., Inv., 4-13-1804.

EWING, ROBT., Set., 6-1804.

EWING, ROBT., S. B., 6-29-1804.

FAST, ADAM, Will, 2-1840. Dev.: Eliz., wife; Jacob, Adam, Josh, Jonathon, Rich., Allen, sons; Marg. Ferrel, Sarah Robins, Hannah Leyman, Keziah Grubb, Naomi Leyman, Cath. Haun, Margery Malott, Polly, Clarissa, daus.; others.

FERGUSON, JOHN, Will, 12-4-1793. Dev.: Barsheba, wife; Cath. Lanham, Ann Wilson, Rebecca Wilson, Susanna McCrea, Lydia Bell, Marg., dau.; John, son.

FERRELL, GERT., Will, 8-1849. Dev.: Father and mother; Angeline Brand, dau.

FETTY, JOS., Will, 7-1846. Dev.: Eliz., wife; Esaias, Marcus, sons; Mary Barrickman, Delela, daus

FLEMING, BOAZ, Will, 5-1830. Dev.: Clarissa Hamilton, Mary, Sally, Peggy, Joanna, Eliz. Bartlett, Jane Richardson, Derexa, dau.; Wm., David, Lem., sons; others.

FLEMING, BOAZ, Set., 12-27-1830.

FLEMING, THOM., Inv., 7-8-1815.

FORDE STANDISH, Will, 9-24-1832. Dev.: Maria, Eleanor, Marg., Ann, Mary, dau.: Wm., John, Geo., Standish, sons; Mary Groves (mother of Maria and Geo.), Sarah, wife; others.

FORTNEY, DAN., Will, 2-1818. Dev.: Barbary, wife; Dan., Jacob, Henry, John, sons; Cath. Grim, Betsy, Barbary, Christina, Nancy, dau.

FORTNEY, DAN., S. B., 4-15-1818.

FORTNEY, DAN., Inv., 8-11-1818

FORTNEY, DAN., Set., 8-25-1819.

FOSTER, ARON, Inv., 7-2-1820.

FOSTER, FIDELIUS, Will, 6-1800. Dev.: Cath., wife; Rebecca Weaver, Eliz. Stewart, Marg. Ortt, Cath. Stewart, dau.; John, son; others.

FOSTER, FIDELIUS, Vendue, 6-20-1800.

FOSTER, FIDELIUS, Set., 9-29-1818.

FOSTER, FIDELUS, Inv., 6-12-1800.

FOSTER, JOHN, Inv., 4-28-1830.

FOSTER, JOHN, S. B., 5-15-1830.

FOSTER, JOHN, Set., 7-21-1832.

FOWLER, JOHN, Will, 9-1815. Dev.: Susannah, wife; John, Caleb, Reason, Nehemiah, Isaac, Josh., sons; Eliz. Rhodes, Nancy Hall, Sophia Con, Mary, Sarah, dau.; others.

FOWLER, JOHN, App., 3-8-1816.

FOWLER, JOHN, Vendue, 5-1817.

FRALEY, CHRISTINA, Will, 9-1815. Dev.: Hannah Grubb, Sally Campbell, dau.; others.

FRANKLIN, JULIET, Set., 12-6-1830.

FREELAND, AARON, Will, 1-1844. Dev.: Eliza, wife; Martin, son; Martha Ann, dau.

FREELAND, JOHN, Will, 2-1842. Dev.: Wife; Perry, Elijah, sons; Rebecca, Sarah Youst, dau.

FRETWELL, THOM., Inv., 10-15-1808.

FRETWELL, THOM., Set., 9-1809.

GAGE, JAMES, Will, 11-1825. Dev.: Simeon, Abel, Azel, sons.

GALERO, CHRIS., Inv., 10-15-1796.

GALLAHUE, JER., Inv., 6-24-1825.

GALLAHUE, JER., S. B., 6-24-1826.

GALLAHUE, JER., Set., 11-1828.

GALLAHUE, JEREMIAH, Will, 5-1825. Dev.: Ann, wife; Charles, Wm., Henry, Chas., sons; Phebe, Sarah, Cath., Mary, Marg., dau.

GARDNER, DR. JOHN, Will, 2-1805. Dev.: Thom. Powell, Jacob Finney, Wm. Franklin, friends; others.

GARLOW, ANDREW, Will, 8-1842. Dev.: Susanna, wife; Jos., Ephraim, John, sons; Matilda Snider, dau.

GARLOW, CHRIS., Will, 9-2-1796. Dev.: Ann, wife; John, Andrew, Jos., Dan., sons; C h r i s t e e n, Mary, Hannah, Sarah, Eliz., Lavina Garlow, Magdalen Partnes, Ann Partnes, dau.

GARLOW, CHRIS., Set., 6-1826.

GAUGH, THOM., Will, 4-1825. Dev.: Josh.; Thom., Jas., Hiram, Pat., sons; Rachel, wife; Biram, bro.

GEFFS, JAMES, S. B., 11-1828.

GEFFS (JEFFS), JAMES, Inv., 10-26-1827.

GEFFS, JAMES, Set., 11-25-1828, 1-14-1832.

GILBERT, STEPHEN, Will, 11-1820. Dev.: Permela, wife; Stephen, Enoch, Jos., sons; Phoebe, Rachel, Marg., dau.; others.

GILBERT, STEPHEN, Inv., 12-5-1820.

GILBERT, STEPHEN, S. B., 6-1822.

GILBERT, STEPHEN, Set., 11-24-1827.

GILLISPIE, JOHN, Will, 8-1-1814. Dev.: Hannah, dau.; John, son.

GILLISPIE, NEAL, Will, 6-1843. Dev.: Nancy, wife; Eliz. Irwin, Susan Beacher, Mary Krepps, dau.; James, son; others.

GLISSAN, THOM., Will, 7-1815. Dev.: Mary, Marg., Sarah, Cath., Elenor, Ann, dau.; Thom., James, sons; others.

GODWIN, WM., Inv., undated.

GOFF, JOHN, Inv., 4-10-1803.

GOFF, JOHN, Vendue, 7-9-1803.

GOFF, JOHN, Set., 8-18-1821.

GOFF, JOHN, Will, 4-1803. Dev.: Monica, wife; John, Jas., sons; Hannah, Ludie, Joanna, Jane, dau.; others.

GOSSET, JANE, Will, 10-1816. Dev.: Marg. Boid, niece.

GOUGH, JOHN, Set., 2-1823.

GOUGH, JOSH., Will, 5-1820. Dev.: Thom., Byram, Wm., sons; Charity, wife; Ann Jones, Lucy Jones, Eliz. Lewellin, Charity Minear, Polly Lewellin, dau.

GOUGH, JOSH., Inv., 6-3-1820.

GOUGH, JOSH., S. B., 6-17-1820.

GOUGH, JOSH., Set., 3-19-1830.

GRAHAM, JOHN, W i l l, 11-15-1798. Dev.: Rebecca, wife; David, Robt., Ebenezer, sons; Marg., Fanny, Nancy, Jean, Rebecca, dau.

GREGG, THOM., Will, 4-1819. Dev.: Louis, wife; Eliz. Little, Sarah Parker, M a r t h a Crowse, Abba Weaver, Rachel Ferrill, Marg. Burck, Hannah Prewet, dau.

GRIGGS, THOM., Inv., 5-8-1819.

GRIGGS, THOS., Will, 1-1839. Dev.: Sina, wife; Hulda, dau.; Harman, Haymond, Harvey, Henderson, Hamilton, Hillery, sons.

GRUB, JOHN, Inv., undated.

GRUB, JOHN, Will, 1-1817. Dev.: John, Jas., Amos, Enoch, Geo., Sam., sons; Mary, Martha, dau.

GUSEMAN, ABRAHAM, Inv., 1-21-1822.

GUSEMAN, ABRAHAM, S. B., 1-24-1822.

GUSEMAN, ABRAHAM, 1st Set., 5-1-1824.

GUSEMAN, ABR., 2nd Set., 1-22-1827.

GUSEMAN, GODFREY, Will, 3-1838. Dev.: Marg., wife; Amaziah, son; Mary Kern, dau.; Susan Murdock, sis.

GUSTIN, ALPHEUS, Will, 9-1800. Dev.: Mary, wife: Abel, Ashbel, Abiel, Ammoriah, Ammise, Alpheus, sons; Maple Pearce, Mary Stewart, Marg., dau.; others.

West Virginia Estate Settlements
(FROM HALL TO RUBLE)

In 1936 and 1937, the West Virginia Commission on Historic and Scenic Markers, the Works Progress Administration, and the Federal Emergency Relief Administration compiled court records of the various counties, such as Births, Deaths, Marriages, and Wills. Under Wills were grouped subjects pertaining to Estate Settlements, including Wills, Inventories, and Appraisements. Copies of these county records were filed at the Department of Archives and History, Charleston; the Library of West Virginia University, Morgantown; and the DAR Library, Washington.

Believing that there would be particular interest on the part of the general public in the Estate Settlements in the older counties, the West Virginia Historical Society has undertaken to abstract the Estate Settlement Records, as filed in the State Department of Archives and History, and offer them for publication in the *West Virginia History Quarterly*. (No responsibility can be assumed as to the accuracy of the copies made from the original county records.

There are 13 counties which were formed prior to 1800, and it has been agreed to arrange these counties in chronological order, and to print their records from the earliest date to 1850. The formation dates of these counties are as follows: Hampshire—1753; Berkeley—1772; Monongalia—1776; Ohio—1776; Greenbrier—1778; Harrison—1784; Hardy—1786; Randolph—1787; Pendleton—1788; Kanawha—1788; Brooke—1797; Wood—1798; and Monroe—1799.

Monongalia County, Formed 1776

Abbreviations used in this material include: Acc.—account; Adm. — administrator; App. — appraisement; Bro. — brother; Dau.—daughter; Dev.—devisee; Guard.—guardian; Inv.—inventory; S.B.—sale bill; Set.—settlement; Sis.—sister; Ven.—vendue.

HALL, ASA, Inv., 8-24-1815.
HALL, ASA, S.B., 8-31-1815.
HALL, ASA, Set., 1-11-1817.

HALL, ELEANOR, Will, 7-1824. Dev.: Sabea Dawson, Nancy Hoult, sis.; others.

HALL, ELEANOR, Inv., 7-30-1824.
HALL, ELEANOR, Set., 5-1827.
HALL, NAT., Inv., 7-30-1827.
HALL, NAT., S.B., 1-1829.
HALL, NAT., Set., 6-1829.
HALL, JORDAN, Will, 6-1835. Dev.:
Nancy, wife; Rynear, Wm., Jas., sons;
others.
HALL, REYNEAR, Will, 4-1818. Dev.:
Ellenor, wife; Nathan, Allen, Jordan,
bro.; Rebecca, sis.; others.
HALL, RYNEAR, Inv., 5-2-1818.
HALL, RYNEAR, S.B., 5-15-1818.
HALL, RYNEAR, Set., 9-5-1823.
HALL, RYNEAR, Set., 5-15-1827.
HAMILTON, BENJ., Will, 6-1833. Dev.:
Phoebe, wife; Wm., Aaron, Benj.,
Robt., Jacob, sons; Ann, dau.; other.
HAMILTON, THOM., Will, 12-1842.
Dev.: Eliz., wife; others.
HAMILTON, WM., Set., 7-8-1797.
HANEY, BARNEY, S.B., 3-21-1812.
HANEY, BARNEY & REBECCA, Set.,
5-1827.
HANWAY, JESSE, Will, 1-1805. Dev.:
Rachel, wife; Sam., Jesse, John,
sons; Nancy Warman, Eliz., Mary,
Sarah, Rebecca, Martha, daus.
HANWAY, SAM., Will, 6-1834. Dev.:
Sam, John, neph., others.
HARDEN, JOHN, Will, 6-3-1803. Dev.:
Isabella, wife; John, Absolom, Henry,
Hector, Nestor, Geo., Cato, sons; John
(illegitimate son); Mariam, Mary
Ann, Molthea, Alice, daus.; others.
HARP, ABNER, Will, 4-1804. Dev.:
Jane, wife; Rich., son; Eliz., Cath.,
Mary, Martha, daus.
HARR, JOHN, Inv., 3-23-1827.
HARR, JOHN, Will, 2-1827. Dev.: Nun,
Zimri, John, sons; Phebe, dau.; oth-
ers.
HARR, JOHN, Set., 7-25-1829.
HARRIS, JOHN, S.B., 8-19-1808.
HARRIS, JOHN, Inv., 10-1808.
HARRISON, CASS., Will, 8-1829. Dev.:
Susannah Martin, Eliz. Scott, Ann
Seas, daus.; others.
HARRISON, NANCY, Will, 10-1848.
Dev.: Mahala, Julia Ann John, daus.
HARRISON, JOS., Inv., 12-1824.
HARRISON, JOS., S.B., 12-1825.
HARRISON, JOS., Set., 3-17-1828.
HART, BART., Set., 5-24-1824.
HARTLEY, ANTHONY, Will, 3-1812.
Dev.: Amos, son; Lydia, dau.; others.
HASP, ABNER, Set., 10-13-1807.
HASTINGS, JOHN, Inv., 8-8-1814.
HAWTHORN, ALEX., Will, 2-1822.
Dev.: Jane, Isabella, Betty, sis.;
Robt., bro.; others.

HAYHURST, DAVID, Will, 9-1840. Dev.:
Sarah, wife; Michael, Sarah, daus.;
Benj., Jos., Wm., David, John, And.,
Jas., sons.
HAYHURST, JAS., Will, 6-1849. Dev.:
Eliz., wife; others.
HAYMOND, ED., Inv., 5-1826.
HAYMOND, ED., Set., 2-26-1828.
HAYS, CURTIS, Will, 7-1816. Dev.:
Mary, wife; Charles, son.
HECK, JUSTICE, Will, 9-1825. Dev.:
Wife; Geo., Adam, Phil., Justice, Da-
vid, sons; Susannah, Sarah, Rachel,
Eliz., daus.
HELLIN, THOM., Will, 12-25-1797. Dev.:
Anne, dau.; others.
HENDERSON, ELIZ, Will, 4-1837. Dev.;
John, son; Mary, Maria, Nancy, Har-
riet, Julia Hill, daus.; others.
HENKINS, PETER, Will, 9-1849. Dev.:
Susanna, Christina, Marg. Chalfin,
Eliz. Brown, Mary Goodwin, Rebecca
Long, Sarah Morris, Abe Fletcher,
Casandra Dawson, daus.; Elijah, Ab-
raham, sons.
HENNEN, WM., Will, 3-1850. Dev.:
Eliz. Walker, dau.; James, John,
Enoch, Thom., Wm., Alex., sons.
HENRY, AARON, Will, 11-1825. Dev.:
Rebecca, wife; Mary Means, Eliz.
Hess, Rebecca Owens, Jane Cino,
daus.; Otho, Francis, Jos., sons.
HENTHRON, HENRY, Will, 3-1842.
Dev.: Sarah, wife; Mary, dau.; other
children.
HESS, ABRAHAM, Inv., App., 12-14-
1814.
HESS, ABRAHAM, S.B., 12-24-1814.
HESS, ABR., Set., 8-25-1828.
HESS, PETER, SR., Will, 10-1833. Dev.:
Eliz., wife; Jeremia, Peter, Polser,
John, Thom., Wm., sons; Cath. Smith,
Eliz. Barb, daus., others.
HIBBS, WM., Will, 11-1828. Dev.: Marg.,
wife; Jos., Wm., Sam., sons; Mary
Martin, Rachel Wisecarver, Eliz. Ves-
sil, daus.
HIGGINS, JOS., Will, 1-1840. Dev.:
Eliz., wife; Baltus, Dan., Isaac, Jos.,
David, Josh., Levi, sons; Eliz. Hough-
man, Sarah, daus.; others.
HIGHLY, JOHN, Inv., 2-23-1805.
HILL, GEO., Will, 10-1848. Dev.: Julia,
wife; Priscilla, Rebecca, daus.; Robt.,
son.
HILL, REBECCA, Will, 11-1843. Dev.:
Robert Johnston Hill, son; others.
HILL, ROBT., Inv., 2-7-1822.
HILL, ROBT., S.B., 3-1-1822.
HIRADER, JOHN, Will, 1-1807. Dev.:
Mary, wife; Dan., John, sons; others.

HITE, GEO., Inv., 1-1818.
HITE, GEO., Set., 11-16-1819.
HITE, GEO., Set., 6-1824.
HOARD, BART., Inv., 12-27-1823.
HOARD, MARY, Inv., 3-22-1828.
HOARD, MARY, S.B., 3-22-1828.
HOGE, JON., Set., 5-14-1816.
HOGE, JON., Set., 7-23-1821.
HOGE, WM., (infant son of Jon. Hoge, dec. 1814), Set., 8-14-1823.
HOLLAND, BRICE, Inv., 5-1829.
HOLLAND, BRICE, S.B., 5-1829.
HOLLAND, BRICE, Set., 6-9-1830.
HOLLAND, CAPEL, Inv., 12-30-1823.
HOLLAND, CAPEL, Set., 5-19-1824.
HOLLAND, CAPEL, Inv., 6-9-1824.
HOLLAND, CAPEL, S.B., 6-10-1824.
HOLLAND, CAPEL, Set., 3-26-1826.
HOLLAND, JACOB, Will, 10-1838. Dev.: Mary, wife; Phil., Allen, Dan., Wm., Sol., Rich., sons; Eliz., Sarah, daus., others.
HOLLAND, MARY, Inv., 1-5-1831.
HOLLAND, MARY, S.B., 1-6-1831.
HOLLAND, MARY, Will, 5-1832. Dev.: Jacob, Brice, sons; Massa Brown, Eliz. Howell, daus.; others.
HOLLAND, MARY, Set., 9-24-1832.
HOLLAND, RAWLEY, Set., 6-9-1830.
HOSTETLER, DAN., Will, 4-1849. Dev.: Rhody, wife; Dan., Nat., Nich., Isaac, Sam., John, Armstrong, sons; Eliz., Barbary, Rhody, daus.; others.
HOULT, JOHN, Inv., 8-11-1826.
HOULT, JOHN, Set., 5-24-1828.
HOULT, JOHN, Set., 1-1832.
HOULT, JOS., Inv., 1-16-1822.
HOULT, JOS., S.B., 2-16-1822.
HOULT, JOS., Set., 10-20-1826.
HOWELL, GEO., Will, 2-1848. Dev.: Mary, wife; Wm., son; Ann, dau.
HUFFMAN, ISAAC, Inv., 5-1827.
HUFFMAN, ISAAC, S.B., 5-1827.
HUNT, JONAS, Will, 12-1839. Dev.: Jane, wife; James, Billy, Josh., sons; Matilda, Sally, Betty, Mary, daus.
HURLEY, CALEB, Will, 4-1834. Dev.: Sally, wife; Eliza Cole, dau.
HURLEY, SIMEON, Inv., 10-8-1818.
HURRY, JAMES, Will, 1-1831. Dev.: Marg., wife; Rachel, dau.; others.
HURRY, JAMES, Inv., 2-21-1831.
HURST, WM., Will, 7-1802. Dev.: Eliz.
ICE, THOM., Will. 9-1840. Dev.: Drewsilla, wife; Andrew, Isaac, sons; Mary, Sarah, Phebe, Ann, daus.; others.
IRELAND, WM., Inv., 1-31-1823.
IRELAND, WM., Set., 2-24-1825.
JACKSON, SAM., Will, 7-28-1818. Dev.: Rebecca, wife; John, Sam., Josiah,

sons; Susannah, Updegraff, Rebecca, Ruth Dixon, daus.; others.
JANES, JOS., Set., 11-21-1818.
JARRETT, BENJ., Inv., 9-21-1815.
JARRETT, BENJ., S.B., 10-8-1816.
JARRETT, BENJ., Set., 1-24-1818.
JARRETT, JOHN, Will, 6-1840. Dev.: Lurany, wife; Wm., John, Geo., sons.
JEANS, JOS., Inv., 7-5-1813.
JENKINS, BART., Inv., 5-1788.
JENKINS, JOSIAH, App., Inv., 2-24-1798.
JENKINS, JOSIAH, Sale, 3-31-1798.
JENKINS, JOSIAH, Set., 7-7-1798.
JENKINS, LAEL, Will, 1-1839. Dev.: Cartwright, mother; Jas., bro.
JESTER, JOHN, Will, 1-1846. Dev.: Castilda, wife.
JOHN, LEM., Inv., 11-29-1823.
JOHN, LEM., Will, 11-1823. Dev.: Rhuma, wife; other.
JOHN, LEM., Set., 2-14-1827.
JOHN, LEM., Will, 5-1850. Dev.: Susannah; Agnes, Christiana, daus.; Chapman, Pascal, Asbury, Thom., Lanselot, John, sons; others.
JOHN, COL. WM., Inv., 10-1814.
JOHN, COL. WM., S.B., 10-1815.
JOHN, WM., Will, 11-1814. Dev.: Mary, wife; Owen, Wm., Lem., Thom., Lewis, sons; Mary Evans, Jane Miller, Rebecca Miller, daus.
JOHN, WM., Set., 5-13-1816.
JOHNSON, ELIZ., Will, 8-1845. Dev.: Eliz., Lyda, Nancy Polly, gr. dau.; Waitman, gr. son; other.
JOHNSON, JOHN, Will, 7-1828. Dev.: Cath., wife; Susanna, Sarah, Anne, Eliz., daus.; Christian, Henry, sons.
JOHNSON, JOHN, Inv., 8-29-1828.
JOHNSON, JOHN, S.B., 9-27-1828.
JOHNSON, NAT., Will, 11-21-1836. Dev.: Eliz., wife; others.
JONES, ROBT., Set., 5-1810.
JOSEPH, JOS., Inv., undated.
JOSEPH, JOS., Will, 11-13-1796. Dev.: Jemima, wife; Eli, son; Dalilah Atkin, Pethena Simplor, daus.; other.
JOSEPH, WM., Will, 7-1828. Dev.: Sarah, wife; John, Hezekiah, Lem., Nat., Jeremiah, sons; Rebecca, Betsy, Sarah, Fanny, Rosanah, daus.
KELLY, JAMES, Inv., 11-27-1830.
KELLY, JAS., Will, 11-1830. Dev.: Jane, wife; Alex., James, Josh., Matt., sons; Jane, Barrachman, Martha, Nancy, Marg., daus.
KELLY, JAMES, S.B., 12-9-10-1830.
KELLY, MATT., Will, 4-1796. Dev.: Joan, wife.
KELLY, PAT., W.B., 2-1825.

KELLY, PAT., Will, 8-1824. Dev.: Permela, wife; others.
KELLY, PAT., Inv., 2-1825.
KELSO, JOS., Will, 10-1848. Dev.: Eliz., wife; Ed., John (sons of wife Eliz.), Wm., son; others.
KERNS, MICH., Will, 7-1833. Dev.: Barbary, wife; John, Mich., sons; Christiana Jones, dau.; others.
KILSO, JOS., Will, 10-1808. Dev.: Eliz., wife; John and Ed. Bennett (sons of wife Eliz.), Wm., son; other.
KINKAID, WM., Will, 8-1838. Dev.: Mary, wife; Eliz., Mary, Sarah, daus.; Jos., Wm., David, sons.
KIRKHART, ANTHONY, Inv., 4-7-1829.
KIRKHART, ANTHONY, S.B., 4-7-1829.
KIRKHART, ANTHONY, Set., 3-27-1832.
KNIGHT, JACOB, Will, 8-1834. Dev.: Esther, wife; children.
KNIGHT, THOM., Will, 2-1830. Dev.: Barb., sec. wife; Wm., Thom., Seth, sons; Eliz. Thorne, dau.
KRAMER, GEO., Will, 8-1848. Dev.: Frances, wife; Leroy, son; other.
LANCASTER, ELIZ., Will, 12-1843. Dev.: Permilia Minor, Eliz. Tennant, Cinthia Davis, Ziba Smith, daus.; Virgil, son; other.
LANCASTER, WM., Inv., 8-18-1830.
LANCASTER, WM., S.B., 8-19-1830.
LANCASTER, WM., Set., 5-28-1832.
LANCASTER, WM., Will, 11-1832. Dev.: Eliz., wife; Permilia Minor, Eliz. Tennant, Melilda Climon, Syntha Smith, Zyba Smith, daus.; Virgial, John, sons; others.
LANHAM, ARCH., Inv., 10-28-1811.
LANHAM, ARCH., S.B., 11-9-1811.
LANHAM, WM., Will, 11-1830. Dev.: Chas. Morgan, heir of dec. son Alex.; Cath.
LAWLIS, WM., App., 5-1826.
LAWLIS, WM., S.B., 5-1826.
LAZZEL, SAM., Inv., 8-26-1826.
LAZZEL, SAM, S.B., 11-1826.
LAZZEL, THOM., Will, 6-1825. Dev.: Hannah, wife; Wm., son; other children.
LAZZELL, SAM., Set., 1-18-1827.
LAZZELL, THOM., Inv., 8-2-1825.
LAZZELL, THOM., S.B., 9-1825.
LAZZELL, THOM., Set., 2-1827.
LEESON, RICH., Will, 1-1822. Dev.: Nancy, dau.; John, Thom., sons.
LINCH, JOHN, Inv., 7-9-1819.
LINCH, JOHN, 2nd Inv., 10-1819.
LINCH, JOHN, S.B., 10-25-1819.
LINCH, JOHN, Set., 12-1824.
LINN, WM., Will, 2-1809. Dev.: Isabella; Ann, Sally, daus.; Hughey, Gibsen, John, Wm., Sam., sons; other.

LINN, WM., Set., 2-20-1814.
LITTLE, ADONIJAH, Inv., Sale, undated.
LOUGH, JOHN, Will, 4-1814. Dev.: Jean, wife; Sam., Geo., Robt., Thomis, sons; Sarah, Nelly, daus.
LOUGH, JOHN, Inv., 3-15-1816.
LOUGH, JOHN, S.B., 6-1816.
LOUGH, JOHN, Set., 4-1822.
LOUGH, JOHN, Will, 8-1842. Dev.: Jane, July, Mary Jones, Eliz. Cordry, Sarah Cordry, daus.; Anna, wife; Matt., son; other.
LOUGH, JOS., Will, 11-1850. Dev.: Jane, wife; John, Matt., And., Jos., David, sons; Mary, Ann Kelly, Nancy Fleming, Jane Mercer, daus.; others.
LOW, PHILLIP, Will, 11-1845. Dev.: Rebecca, wife; Lucinda Trippett, Lurana, Eliz., Rebecca, Mary, daus.; Lem., Josh., Levi, Phillip, Gustavus, Harrison, sons.
LOWE, ABRAHAM, Will, 4-1798. Dev.: Eliz., wife; James, David, sons; Sarah, dau.
LOWMAN, WM., Inv., 8-7-1820.
LOWMAN, WM., S.B., 8-25-1820.
LOWMAN, WM., Set., 7-20-1822.
LOWMAN, WM., heirs, Set., 9-26-1822.
LOWMAN, WM., Set., 2-12-1825.
LOWMAN, WM., Set., 10-1828.
LOWMAN, WM., Heirs, Set., 1-22-1827.
LUCUS, JOANNA, Will, 3-1828. Dev.: Joanna, Eliz., Hannah Pindle, daus.; Amos, son; others.
LUCUS, JOANNA, Inv., 3-28-1828.
LUCUS, JOANNA, S.B., 4-1828.
LUCUS, JOANNAN, Set., 8-1830.
LYMAN, JACOB, App., 8-6-1814.
LYMAN, JACOB, S.B., 8-25-1814.
LYMAN, JACOB, Set., 4-10-1821.
LYMING, BENJ., Inv., 5-30-1825.
LYMING, BENJ., S.B., 8-1825.
LYNN, WM., Inv., 2-1809.
McBEE, ALEX., Will, 3-1835. Dev.: Taresa, wife; Zadok, Walter, Philip, John, Tillmon, sons; Mary, Eliz., daus.
McBEE, ZADOCK, Will, 10-1819. Dev.: Anne, wife; Wm., Philip, Alex., Walt., Zadock, sons; Mary Pope, Nancy Hamilton, Eleanor Warman, daus.
McCLAIN, JOHN, Will, 11-1823. Dev.: Sarah Moor, Marg. Karr, Mary, dau.; John, Stephen, Wm., James, Jos., sons; others.
McCLEERY, WM., Will, 4-26-1821. Dev.: Esther, wife; others.
McCLEERY, WM., Inv., 7-16-1821.
McCLEERY, WM., S.B., 9-1-1821.
McCOLLUM, JAS., Will, 12-31-1796. Dev.: Eliz., wife; Mary, dau.; Dan., son.

McDADE, STEPHEN, Will, 7-1831. Dev.: Rachel Brown, Sarah Arthely, Eliz. Brown.

McDADE, STEPHEN, Inv., 7-1831.

McDADE, STEPHEN, S.B., 8-13-1831.

McDANIEL, WM., Will, 11-1842. Dev.: Eliz., wife; Nancy, Dorothy, Drusilla, daus.; others.

McGEE, JAMES, Will, 5-28-1821. Dev.: Nancy, wife.

McGEE, JAMES, S.B., 6-25-1821- Morgantown. Wheeling, 2-4-1822

McGEE, JAMES, Inv., 6-1-1822.

McGRANAHAN, JAMES, Set., 1795.

McGRANAHAN, JAMES, Inv., 10-5-1795.

McNEELY, HUGH, Inv., App., 6-1805.

McNEIL, ELIZ., Will, 2-1837. Dev.: Marcus Moore, son; others.

MADERA, CHRISTIAN, Will, 6-1822. Dev.: John, son; others.

MARSHALL, ELI, S.B., 6-10-1828.

MARSHALL, ELI, Inv., 6-16-1828.

MARSHALL, JAMES, Set., 5-24-1817.

MARSHALL, JAS., SR., Inv., 6-23-1815.

MARSHALL, JAS., Will, 8-1815. Dev.: Mary, wife; Hezekiah, Eli, James, sons; others.

MARSHALL, JAS., S.B., 9-9-1815.

MARTIN, ALLEN, Will, 5-1817. Dev.: Athelia, wife; Horatio, Aquilla, Rutner, Sam., John, sons; Athelia, dau.; other.

MARTIN, COL. CHAS., Inv., 4-15-1800.

MARTIN, COL. CHAS., S.B., 5-1800.

MARTIN, COL. CHAS., Set., 5-11-1811.

MARTIN, HENRY, Will, 6-1823. Dev.: Susannah, Mary Underwood, Nancy Fleming, Eliz. Holber, Susannah, Mela, daus.; Henry, Thom., sons; others.

MARTIN, HENRY, Inv., 9-12-1823.

MARTIN, HENRY, S.B., 9-1824.

MARTIN, JESSE, Set., 1808.

MARTIN, JESSE, Inv., 6-17-1809.

MARTIN, JESSE, S.B., 6-10-1810.

MARTIN, JESSE, S.B., 7-8-1811.

MARTIN, JESSE, Set., 2-5-1812.

MARTIN, THOM., Will, 12-1841. Dev.: Mary, wife; Amos, son; other son.

MASSIE, ISHMAEL, Will, 3-1848. Dev.: Caroline, wife.

MASSIE, WELFORD, Will, 4-8-1833. Dev.: Martha, wife; Geo., Oscar, sons; Thom., Bro.; Adela, Elvira, daus., Eliz., mother.

MATTHEW, JONATHAN, Will, 10-1805. Dev.: Rach., dau.; Wm., son; wife; other children.

MAXON, WM., Will, 7-1815. Dev.: Ann, wife; Jesse, Elijah, sons; Mary, Hannah, daus.

MAXON, WM., Inv., 11-6-1815.

MAXON, WM., S.B., 11-17-1815.

MAZZY, BENJ. & ELIZ. (dec. widow), Inv., 1-13-1823.

MAZZY, BENJ. & ELIZ. (dec. widow), S.B., 2-1823.

MEAN, JACOB, Will, 8-30-1837. Dev.: Robt., father; Sarah, Elenor, sis.

MEEKS, THOM., Will, 5-1826. Dev.: Susannah, wife; Susannah Courtney, Eliz. Vinson, Polly Byron, Rebecca Jones, Edith, Casandy, Levina, daus.; Wm., Amos, Matt., Sam., Jos., Josiah, Thom., John, Abraham, Asby, sons.

MERCER, ABNER, Inv., 2-1-1830.

MERCER, ABNER, Set., 2-1-1832.

MERCER, ROBT., Will, 5-1822. Dev.: Eliz., wife; Abner, John, Jos., Robt., Wm., Levi, sons; Eliz., Rachel, Leah, daus.

MEREDITH, DAVIS, Will, 8-1825. Dev.: Ann, wife; Absolom, Thom., Job, Davis, Wm., sons; Hannah, Rebecca, Nelly, Rach., Martha, Elenor Meredith, daus.; Baptist Missionary Soc.

MEREDITH, DAVIS, Inv., 1-1826.

MEREDITH, DAVIS, S.B., 1-1826.

MEREDITH, DAVIS, Set., 9-1826.

MEREDITH, THOM., Inv., 9-3-1825.

MEREDITH, THOM., S.B., 8-1826.

MEREDITH, THOM., Set., 6-23-1827.

MERL, CLEMENT, Will, 12-1804. Dev.: Cath., wife; Cath., dau.

MERRIFIELD, RICH., Will, 12-1798. Dev.: Pheba, wife; Sam., John, sons; Bashela Springer, Mary, Eliz., daus.

MERRIFIELD, RICH., App., 6-8-1799.

MERRIFIELD, RICH., Set., 4-10-1801.

MICHAEL, HENRY, Will, 6-27-1842. Dev.: Ann, wife; Marion, Cyrus, Alvin, John, James, Dan., Felix, sons; Martha, Matilda, Darky, Sarah Boils, Ary Hague, Liza Cowell, daus.

MIERS, JOHN, Will, 10-1845. Dev.: Polly wife; John, Sol., David, Wm., Jacob, Jas., Enos, sons; Anna, dau.

MILLER, AND., App., 11-1-1796.

MILLER, PETER, Will, 5-1838. Dev.: Mary, wife; Jane Wilcots, Eliz. Emos, Dolly Emos, Marg. Hartley, Sarah Evans, Hannah Fleming, Nancy Jackson, Rosanna Brumage, Lucinda Morgan, Ellener Liepper, daus.; Elisha, John, Peter, Henry, sons; others.

MILLER, THOM., Inv., 4-1814.

MILLER, THOM., S.B., 4-1-1814. ,

MILLER, THOM., Set., 6-1817.

MILLER, WM., Will, 10-1825. Dev.: Mary, wife; David, Jesse, Jos., sons; others.

MILLER, WM., Inv., 11-7-1825.

MILLER, WM., S.B., 11-24-1825.

MILLER, WM., Set., 4-25-1828.

MOHAN, ARAH (infant dau. of James), Set., 10-23-1824.

MOHAN, ARAH (ward), Set., 5-1829.

MOHAN, JAMES, Inv., 1-5-1822.

MOHAN, JAMES, S.B., 1-30-1822.

MOHAN, JAMES, Set., 8-17-1824.

MOORE, ABRAHAM, Will, 4-1845. Dev.: Wife; Sarah, dau.; Jackson, Lindzy, Marion, sons.

MOORE, JOSIAH, Inv., 9-13-1822.

MOORE, JOSIAH, S.B., 9-15-1822.

MOORE, JOSIAH, Set., 1-8-1825.

MOORE, JOSIAH, Guardian, 4-15-1826.

MOORE, JOSIAH, Set., Guardian, 3-22-1831.

MORGAN, DAN., Will, 8-1833. Dev.: John, bro.; others.

MORGAN, EVAN, Inv., App., 11-5-1814.

MORGAN, EVAN, S.B., 3-1815.

MORGAN, MORGAN, Will, 9-1829. Dev.: Achilles, M o r g a n, Isaac, James, Aaron, David, Jacob, sons; Drusilla Cochrane, Eliz. Martin, Dorothy Clelland, daus.; others.

MORGAN, PHOEBE, Will, 6-1824. Dev.: Jehu Lash, Hyram Thompson, Illegit. sons.

MORGAN, WM., Inv., 3-2-1797.

MORGAN, WM., Set., 3-14-1798.

MORGAN, ZACK, Inv., 12-6-1795.

MORGAN, ZACK., Vendue, 8-9-1796.

MORGAN, ZACK., Inv., 11-5-1814.

MORGAN, ZACK., Set., 3-1817.

MORGAN, ZACK., S.B., 4-1822.

MORGAN, ZACK., Set., 4-20-1822.

MORGAN, ZACKQUILL, Will, 3-1835. Dev.: Lina, wife; Mary, Melinda, Eliz., Sarah West, daus.; John, David, sons.

MORRIS, JOHN, Will, 10-20-1796. Dev.: Elanor, wife; Jos., Morris, John, Rich., James, sons; Eliz., Elenor, daus.

MORRIS, LEVI, Inv., 11-23-1815.

MORRIS, LEVI, S.B., 2-1816.

MORRIS, LEVI, Set., 5-18-1818.

MORRIS, LURANAH, Will, 6-1827. Dev.: Charity Jenkins, Eliz. Baker, daus.; other.

MORRIS, WM., Will, 6-1825. Dev.: Eliz., wife; Prudence, Horne, Susan, daus.; Wm., Sam., James, Abraham, Jacob, Josh., Rich., John, Elijah, Lewis, sons.

MORTON. SAM., Will, 6-1805. Dev.: Hannah, wife; Benj., Wm., sons; Eliz. Willets, Sarah Roreman, Ann Brandon, S u s a n n a Neil, Hannah, Mary, Rebecca, Phebe, Edith, daus.; others.

MOXLEY, JOHN, App., undated.

MOXLEY, JOHN, Vendue, undated.

MURPHY, HUGH, Will, 8-1814. Dev.: Mother; Sarah, dau.; Gil., bro.; other.

MURRAY, JOHN, Will, 6-1818. Dev.: Henry Henthorn; Wheat Neighbors.

MYERS, MARY, Will, 11-1834. Dev.: Eliz., dau.; others.

MYERS, PETER, Will, 8-1825. Dev.: Jacob, Peter, Jos., John, sons; Sarah Bailey, Eliz. Corbley, Mary, Phoebe, daus.; others.

NEELY, JAS., Will, 8-1834. Dev.: Jos., John, James. Sam., sons; Ann, Eliz., Mary, Sarah, Rachel, daus.

NEWBROUGH, JOS., Inv., 6-13-1822.

NORRIS, WM., Will, 4-1817. Dev.: Mary Hays, Vilendi Neighbors, Martha Deval, Charity Jenkins, daus.; others.

NUZUM, THOM., Inv., 9-18-1817.

NUZUM, THOM., Vendue, 10-3-1817.

NUZUM, THOM., Set., 11-18-1824.

NUZUM, THOM., Set., 6-24-1828.

NUZUM, THOM., Set., 1-25-1830.

OSBORNE, PETER, Will, 10-1831. Dev.: Wife; Peter, son; others.

OSBORN, ZERAH, Will, 5-1836. Dev.: Mary Lewellen, dau.; Thom, son; others.

O'KELLY, BERNARD, Will, 10-1848. Dev.: Eliz. Sabina, dau.; Geo., Asha, Fielding, Charles, Hugh, sons; others.

OSTEN, JOHN, Will, 1-1849. Dev.: Sarah, wife; Emely, Hannah, Rebecca, daus.; David, Corn., John, James, Hugh, Dan., Wm., Jesse, sons.

PARKER, JOHN, Will, 12-1840. Dev.: Mary, wife; Wm., Jos., John, Eli., sons; Riach. Clayton, Eliza, daus.

PARRISH, ED., Will, 6-1813. Dev.: Rachel, wife; Wm., Josh., Rich., Enoch, Ed., Casey, Jesse, Eavins, Isaac, Ephrim, sons; Susannah Perrin, Rachel Cole, Nancy Hamilton, Sinthey, Doliley, Elaner, Dorcus, Sarah, Ruth, Mary, daus.

PARRISH, ED., App., 6-26-1813.

PARRISH, ED., S.B., 7-3-1813.

PARRISH, ED., Set., 3-17-1818.

PARRISH, ED., Set., 8-12-1824.

PATTEN, ROBT., App., 12-22-1815.

PATTEN, ROBT., S.B., 1-2-1816.

PEARSE, ELIAS, Will, 12-1807. Dev.: Amy, wife; Isaac, son; Eliz. Hill, Elenor Hawkins, Drusilla, Sarah, daus.

PEARSE, ELIAS, Set., 9-9-1809.

PEARSE, ELIAS, Set., 9-9-1810. ;

PETTYJOHN, JOHN, Will, 8-1815. Dev.: Sarah, wife; Wm., Amos., sons; Rhoda Bailey.

PETTYJOHN, WM., SR., Inv., 12-4-1799.

PETTYJOHN, WM., S.B., 12-7-1799.

PETTYJOHN, WM., Will, 10-1799. Dev.: Ruth, wife; John, son; Mary Haymond, dau.; others.

PETTYJOHN, WM., Set., 9-5-1801.

PETTYJOHN, WM., Set., 2-1806.

PETTYJOHN, WM., JR., App., 10-13-1796.

PETTYJOHN, WM., JR., Set., 7-1800.

PICKENPAUGH, JOS., Will, 10-1822. Dev.: Jemima, wife; Peter, son; Pleasant, Maria, Sarah, Jemima, daus.

PICKENPAUGH, JOS., Inv., 11-8-1822.

PICKENPAUGH, JOS., S.B., 9-12-1823.

PICKENPAUGH, JOS., Set., 8-15-1825.

PIERCE, ELIAS, Inv., App., 12-23-1808.

PIERPOINT, JOHN, Will, 5-16-1796. Dev.: Ann, wife; Larkin, Zackquill, Francis, John, sons; Ann, Temperance, Sarah Watson, daus.

PIERPOINT, JOHN, App., Inv., 8-31-1796.

PIERPOINT, ZACKQUILL, Will, 7-1840. Dev.: Dorcas, wife; Nancy Stewart, Barsheba Vandevort, Cath. Murdock, Jane, Sarah, Cobun, daus., Lott, son; others.

PILES, DAVID, Will, 6-1841. Dev.: Drusilla, wife.

PILES, ELIJAH, Will, 7-24-1836. Dev.: Jemima, mother.

PILES, JOHN, Will, 1-1801. Dev.: Elijah, David, Hunter, sons.

PILES, JOHN, Inv., 1-24-1801.

PILES, JOHN, Inv., 4-13-1801.

PILES, JOHN, Set., 6-13-1803.

PILES, ZACHARIAH, Will, 11-1840. Dev.: Susannah, wife; Uriah, Josh., Elijah, John, Elisha, Zachariah, sons; Hannah Sine, Rebecca Cordray, Nancy Park, Sarah Eddy, Cath. Stull, daus.

PINDALL, JACOB, Will, 10-2-1828. Dev.: Hannah, wife; Thom., Evan, sons; Hannah, Ruhanah, Susan, Joanna Lawman, Eliz. Coombs, daus.; others.

PINDALL, JACOB, Inv., 5-27-1829.

PINDALL, PHILIP, Will, 1-1804. Dev.: Rachel, wife; others.

PIXLER, CONRAD, Inv., 6-30-1810.

PIXLER, CONRAD, Vendue, 7-7-1810.

PIXLER, CONRAD, Set., 2-9-1816.

PIXLER, JOHN, Will, 8-1839. Dev.: Eliz., wife; children.

POLSLEY, JACOB., Inv., 2-21-1829.

POLSLEY, JACOB, Set., 5-22-1829.

POLSLEY, MARG., Will, 5-1823. Dev.: Marg., wife; John, Dan., sons; Mariah Bellings, Amanda, Paulina, Eliz. Newberry, Rowena Graham, daus.

POLSLEY, MARG., S.B., 4-3-1830.

POLSLEY, MARG., Inv., 2-1831.

POWELL, ISAAC, Will, 3-1819. Dev.: John, Silas, Ellis, Isaac, Jos., Amos, Levi, Bushrod, Chalfant, Jas., sons; Abigail West, Sarah, Hannah, Eliz., Polly, Rebecca, daus.; Eliz., wife; others.

POWELL, ISAAC, Inv., 4-20-1819.

POWELL, ISAAC, S.B., 6-4-1819.

POWELL, SILAS, Will, 8-1840. Dev.: Nancy, wife; Jacob, John, Squire, Isaac, sons; Polly Shuttlesworth, Hannah Stansbury, Rachel, daus.; others.

POWELL, RICH., Set., 12-11-1796.

POYNTER, ESTHER, Will, 3-4-1845. Dev.: Eliz., Ruth, daus.; Wm., Hynson, sons; (Refused to be admitted to record).

PRICE, CALEB, Will, 4-1846. Dev.: Mary, wife; Sarah Hews, Mary, daus.; Jacob, Caleb, John, Nat., Isaac, sons; others.

PRICE, ISAAC, Will, 5-1849. Dev.: Mary, wife; brothers, sisters.

PRICE, NAT., Will, 8-1850. Dev.: Phebe, wife; John, Smith, sons.

PRICKETT, JACOB., S.B., 7-21-1826, 8-4-1826.

PRICKETT, JACOB, Inv., 8-11-1826.

PRICKETT, JACOB, Set., 8-26-1828.

PRICKETT, JACOB, Set., 7-1832.

PRICKETT, JOSIAH, Will, 7-1807. Dev.: Charity, wife; Josiah, John, Job, sons; Susanna Carberry, Ann Dragee, Sarah Morgan, Dot. Morgan, Lydia Ross, Drusilla Jolliffe, daus.

PRICKETT, JOSIAH, Inv., 8-15-1807.

PRICKETT, JOSIAH, S.B., 9-9-1807.

PRICKETT, JOSIAH, Set., 10-29-1808.

PRIDE, WM., Inv., 4-10-1802.

PRIDE, WM., S.B., 11-19-1802.

RABER, WM., Will, 3-1849. Dev.: Cath., wife; Eliz. Everly, Marg. Lemley, daus.; Phillip, Qm., Sam., sons.

RAMSEY, JOHN, Will, 8-1796. Dev.: John, Andrew, sons; Rebecca Sibbony, Mary Simpson, Hannah Haden, daus.; others.

RAMSEY, JOHN, SR., Will, 5-1818.
Dev.: Mary, wife; Sam., Wm., Jesse,
John, Thom., sons; Sarah, Rachel,
Polly, Nancy, daus.

RAMSEY, JOHN, S.B., 8-1818.

RAMSEY, JOHN, Inv., 8-22-1818.

RAMSEY, WM., Inv., 11-11-1822.

RAMSEY, WM., S.B., 1-1823.

RAMSEY, WM., Set., 5-2-1825.

RANDAL, GREENBURY, S.B., & Set.,
9-20-1796.

RAVENSCRAFT, JOHN, Will, 12-1807.
Dev.: Eliz., wife; John, Sam., sons;
Cath., dau.

RAVENSCRAFT, JOHN, Inv., 3-11-1809.

RAVENSCRAFT, JOHN, Set., 2-18-1812.

RAVER, CHRIS, S.B., 5-6-1828.

RAVER, CHRIS., Set., 5-15-1830.

RAY, PAT., Will, 1-28-1839. Dev.: Eleanor, Sarah, Eliz., Julia, Mary, daus.;
Thom., Jas., sons.

RAY, THOM., Will, 10-1841. Dev.: Jennett, wife; Delia, Volander, daus.;
Geo., son; others.

REED, ISAAC, Will, 1-1845. Dev.: Rebecca, wife; Nat., Isaac, Amos, Thom.,
Stephen, sons; Eliz. Wallace, Jemima Faucett, Rebecca, Rachel, daus.

REED, JAMES, Will, 8-1839. Dev.: Lydia, wife; John, Wm., Art. sons;
Mary, Sarah, Jane, daus.

REED, JOHN, Will, 3-1819. Dev.: Wm.,
Jos., James, John, sons; Sara Duna,
Martha Vandevort, daus.

REED, JOS., Inv., App., 11-4-1816.

REED, WM., Will, 10-1846. Dev.: Mary,
wife; James, Sam., Wm., Jos., sons.

REEDER, HEZEKIAH, Inv., 9-1812.

RICH, DAN., Will, 10-1840. Dev.: Hannah, wife; Henry, Rawley, Washington, sons; Lucinda Cannon, Susan
Lemley, Mary Tennant, daus.; other
children.

RIDGWAY, CATH., Will, 1-1830. Dev.:
Lott, Noah, sons; Rachel, Jaco, Patty
Jeffry, Phebe Moore, Sarah Henthorn, Mary Watson, Dorcus Pierpoint, Harriet Foster, daus.

RIEGEWAY, LOTT, Inv., 1-1797.

RIEGWAY, LOTT, Will, 12-1796. Dev.:
Cath., wife; Noah, Joel, sons; six
daughters.

RIGGS, AARON, Inv., 1-24-1815.

RIGGS, CYRUS, Inv., 1-23-1815.

RIGGS, CYRUS, S.B., 2-1815.

RIGGS, SIMEON, Inv., Sale, Undated.

RIGGS, SIMEON, Will, 10-1808. Dev.:
Mercy, wife; Sarah Pick, Rhoda
Grier, Phebe D a u g h e r t y, Cath.
Thomas, Nancy Thomas, daus.; Cy-
rus, Jos., Isaac, Aaron, sons.

RIGGS, SIMEON, Set., 7-1813.

RIX, JOHN, Inv., 6-23-1827.

ROBE, WM., Will, 4-1803. Dev.: Sarah,
wife; David, Robt., Josiah, sons;
Mary Stuart, Sarah Sutton, daus.

ROBERTS, PHILIP, Set., 8-24-1819.

ROBES, SARAH, Will, 4-1804. Dev.:
Mary Stewart, Sarah Sutton, daus.;
David, Robt., Josiah, sons; others.

ROBINS, DAN., Inv., 1-1813.

ROBINS, DAN., S.B., 1-29-1813.

ROBINS, DAN., S.B., 2-26-1813.

ROBINS, DAN., Set., 3-23-1816.

ROBINSON, JAMES, S.B., 10-1804.

ROBINSON, JAMES, App., 12-1804.

ROBINSON, JAMES, Will, 6-1839. Dev.:
Sarah, wife; Marg., Cath., Ann, Sarah,
daus.; James, John, sons.

ROBINSON, JOHN, Will, 10-1846. Dev.:
Delila, wife; others.

ROSE, CHAS., Will, 9-1816. Dev.: Rebecca, wife; Charles, John, Thom.,
Hopkins, sons; Mary, Rose, Rachel,
Rebecca, Aley Connor, Hannah Free-
love, daus.

ROSE, CHAS., Inv., App., 9-21-1816.

ROSURE, JACOB, Inv., 6-7-1828.

ROSURE (ROSER), JACOB, S.B., 6-14-
1828.

ROSURE (ROSER), JACOB, Set., 6-
1830.

ROSURE (ROSER), JACOB, Set., 11-
1831.

ROWAN, JOHN, Will, 4-1831. Dev.:
Marg., wife; Stewart, bro.

RUBLE, JACOB, Will, 10-1841. Dev.:
Josh., illeg. son; other children.

RUBLE, SAM., Inv., & App., 10-19-
1799.

West Virginia Estate Settlements

In 1936 and 1937, the West Virginia Commission on Historic and Scenic Markers, the Works Progress Administration, and the Federal Emergency Relief Administration compiled court records of the various counties, such as Births, Deaths, Marriages, and Wills. Under Wills were grouped subjects pertaining to Estate Settlements, including Wills, Inventories, and Appraisements. Copies of these county records were filed at the Department of Archives and History, Charleston; the Library of West Virginia University, Morgantown; and the DAR Library, Washington.

Believing that there would be particular interest on the part of the general public in the Estate Settlements in the older counties, the West Virginia Historical Society has undertaken to abstract the Estate Settlement Records, as filed in the State Department of Archives and History, and offer them for publication in the WEST VIRGINIA HISTORY QUARTERLY. (No responsibility can be assumed as to the accuracy of the copies made from the original records.)

There are 13 counties which were formed prior to 1800, and it has been agreed to arrange these counties in chronological order, and to print their records from the earliest date to 1850. The formation dates of these counties are as follows: Hampshire—1753; Berkeley—1772; Monongalia—1776; Ohio—1776; Greenbrier—1778; Harrison—1784; Hardy—1786; Randolph—1787; Pendleton—1788; Kanawha—1788; Brooke—1797; Wood—1798; and Monroe—1799.

Monongalia County Formed 1776

Abbreviations used in this material include: Acc.—account; Adm. — administrator; App. — appraisement; Bro. — brother; Dau.—daughter; Dev.—devisee; Guard.—guardian; Inv.—inventory; S. B.—sale bill; Set.—settlement; Sis.—sister; Ven.—vendue.

(From Sanders to Youst)

SANDERS, JOHN, Inv., 9-6-1823.

SANDERS, JOHN, S.B., 9-16-1823.

SANDERS, JOHN, Set., 2-1825.

SANDERS, JOHN, Set., 7-1831.

SAULLARD, ELIAS, Will, 1798. Dev.: Benj., Gabriel, sons; others.

SAYRES, SELEE, Set., Guard., 6-26-1831.

SCOTT, DAVID, Will, 3-1846. Dev.: Mary, wife; Hannah Chesney, Maria Huffman, Rachel Chips, Phebe Hess, Jemima Neely, Kath. Barrickman, Cinthia Fortney, Judity Bouslog, daus. Jeff., Enoch, Jacob, James, sons.

SCOTT, DAVID, Will, 1-1850. Dev.: wife; children; other.

SCOTT, JACOB, Will, 10-1808. Dev.: Cath., wife; Jos., James, Morgan, sons; Phebe, Sarah, daus.

SCOTT, JACOB, Inv., 12-31-1808.

SCOTT, JACOB, Set., 2-22-1812.

SCOTT, JACOB, 2nd Inv., 5-1811.

SCOTT, JAMES, Will, 11-1840. Dev.: Fralix, Benj., Jos., James, sons; Kath. Neely, dau.; other children had received their shares.

SCOTT, JAMES, Will, 7-1848. Dev.: Sandford, Bushrod, Enos, sons; Juliet Hamilton, Caroline Massie, Theresa Shively, daus.

SCOTT, JOS., Set., 10-2-1818.

SCOTT, JOS., (inf.) Set., 2-1825.

SCOTT, ROBT., S.B., 8-7-1819.

SCOTT, WM., Inv., 1-24-1823.

SELBY, McGRUDER, Will, 5-1835. Dev.: wife; James, Leonard, sons; Eliz., Ara, daus.

SEMPLE, MARG., Set., 10-13-1801.

SHEETS, COMROD, S.B., 6-1819.

SHEETS, PHIL., Inv., 2-11-1828.

SHEETS, PHIL., S.B., 5-1828.

SHIVELY, PHILIP, Will, 7-1841. Dev.: Jacob, Philip, Henry, sons; Polly, Betsy, Cath., Abigail, daus.; others received their share.

SHRIVER, ABRAHAM, Will, 12-1837. Dev.: Mary, wife; Adam, Elias, John, Benj., Isaac, Jos., Abraham, sons; Cath. Horner, Christena Core, Daus.; others.

SHRIVER, ABRAHAM, Will, 2-3-1847. Dev.: Massa, wife; James, Abraham, Adam, Lot, sons; Alice, Eliz., daus.

SHRIVER, JACOB, Inv., 11-1825.

SHRIVER, JACOB, S.B., 11-1825.

SHRIVER, JOHN, Will, 5-1814. Dev.: Mary, wife; Jacob, John, Sam., Dan., sons; Susannah, dau.

SHRIVER, JOHN, Inv., App., 5-27-1814.

SHRIVER, JOHN, Set., 8-10-1819.

SHRIVER, JOHN, Will, 4-1847. Dev.: Lucy, wife; Mark, Henry, Abraham, sons.

SHULTZ, CONRAD, App., 9-1815.

SHUMAKER, BAULSER, Will, 9-1809. Dev.: Susannah Shumaker, dau.; John, son; other.

SHUMAN, JOHN, Will, 5-1832. Dev.: Eliz., wife; Mary Kendall, Cath. Kendall, Rachel Fetty, Letty Huffman, Hannah Kendall, Eliz. Floyd, Sophia Shuman, daus.; John, Benj., Josh., sons.

SHUMAN, JOHN, Inv., 5-31-1832.

SIDWELL, HUGH, Will, 8-1831. Dev.: Henry, son.

SIMMS, JOB., Will, 1-1-1797. Dev.: Sarah Simms.

SIMPKINS, CHAS., Will, 9-9-1843. Dev.: Barbary, wife; others.

SISCO, ABRAHAM, Will, 4-1799. Dev.: John, Abraham, Absalom, sons; Mary, wife; Eliz., Mary, Hannah, Rebecca, Sarah, daus.

SMELL, PHILIP, Will, 4-1835. Dev.: Jacob, Michel, Philip, Peter, sons; Cath. Spurgeon, Eliz. Shaw, Mary Gull, daus.

SMITH, ANTHONY, Will, 10-1847. Dev.: Eleanor, wife; Hester, Nancy Irwin, Sarah Price, Hannah Toothman, Acksah Wisman, Mary Brown, Lucinda Watson, daus.; Timothy, Jes., John, sons; others.

SMITH, GEO., Inv., 9-17-1820.

SMITH, GEO., Set., 8-19-1822.

SMITH, HENRY, Will, 12-1842. Dev.: Julia, wife; Paulian, Nancy Hannah, Mary Ann; daus.; Rich., Milton, Laban, sons.

SMITH, JACOB, App., 2-23-1809.

SMITH, JACOB, Vendue, 3-7-1809.

SMITH, JACOB, Set., 5-1810.

SMITH, JOHN, S.B., 11-20-1803.

SMITH, JOHN, Inv., 12-1804.

SMITH, JOHN, Will, 9-1808. Dev.: Sarah, wife; Jos., Sam., Aran, Jonas, sons; Mary, Phebe, Ann, Sarah, daus.

SMITH, WALT., Will, 10-1849. Dev.: Ann Hamilton, Sarah Wilkins, Maria, Amelia Kinkaid, Christiana Pool, daus.

SMITH, WM., Will, 12-1816. Dev.: Ruth, Wm. Byeres, step grandson.

SNIDER, EMMA, Report, 11-22-1824.

SNIDER, PRICE & MARY, Report, 11-22-1824.

SNIDER, HENRY, Inv., 7-2-1805.

SNODGRASS, CHAS., Inv., App., 7-9-1808.

SNODGRASS, CHAS., S.B., 8-2-1808.
SNODGRASS, CHAS., Set., 8-31-1810.
SNODGRASS, JOHN, Inv., 9-11-1812.
SNODGRASS, WM., Will, 5-1832. Dev.:
Barb., wife; Michael, Benj., Nathan,
Wm., Isaac, Francis, sons; Martha
Hawkins, Isabella Satterfield, daus.;
others.
SNYDER, GEO., Will, 3-1829. Dev.: Eliz.
Glasgo, Mary Wolford, Sarah Wol-
ford, Marg. Burris, Reumy Lemley,
Dorcus Turner, Becky Smith, daus.;
Jeremiah, son.
SOULARD, ELIAS, Inv., App., 10-20-
1798.
SOUTH, CATH., Inv., 12-3-1831.
SOUTH, CATH., S.B., 12-3-1831.
SPRINGER, JOHN, Will, 1-1817. Dev.:
Job, Alpheus, Dennis, sons; Bashaba,
wife; daus, unmarried.
SPRINGER, JOHN, Inv., 7-9-1817.
SPRINGER, JOHN, Set., 3-6-1827.
SPURGEON, JAS., Will, 7-1810. Dev.:
Jesse, Jon., sons; Drusilla Glover,
Lenny Castilla, Cath. Kelly, Kiza,
Betty, daus.; two unnamed daus.,
wife.
SPURGEON, JAS., Inv., 8-31-1810.
SPURGEON, JAMES, Vendue, 9-27-1810.
SPURGEON, JAS., Set., 3-18-1811.
SPURGEON, JAS., Inv., 4-28-1812.
SPURGEON, JAS., S.B., 5-1-1812.
SPURGEON, JAS., S.B., 6-5-1813.
SPURGEON, JAS., Set., 6-1813.
SPURGEON, JAS., Set., 8-26-1816.
STAFFORD, JAMES, Will, 10-1826. Dev.:
Lucretia, wife; James, Seth, Nehe-
miah, Thom., Wm., sons; Rebecca
Hennen, Lucinda Neel, Mary Rogers,
Nancy Jenkins, daus.; servants.
STAFFORD, JAS., Inv., 1-1829.
STAFFORD, JAS., S.B., 1-24-1829.
STAFFORD, JAS., Set., 12-28-1829.
STAFFORD, JOHN, Will, 1-1823. Dev.:
Joan, wife; James, Wm., Thom., sons;
Mary Ann, Lida, Nancy, daus.
STAFFORD, JOHN, Inv., 7-26-1823.
STANLEY, JOHN, Will, 7-1801. Dev.:
Hannah, wife; others.
STANLEY, JOHN, App., 7-13-1801.
STANLEY, JOHN, S.B., Set., 8-19-1801.
STATLER, CHRISTENY, Inv., 3-26-1829.
STATLER, CHRISTENY, S.B., 4-3-1829.
STATLER, JOHN, Inv., 5-28-1825.
STATLER, JOHN, S.B., 6-9-1825.
STEEL, JOHN, Will, 11-1822. Dev.:
Marg., wife; John, Thom., Geo., sons;
Mary Devaut, Nancy, Eliz., Martha,
Suzanna, daus.
STEELE, JAMES, Will, 11-1840. Dev.:
Thomas Steele, Sr.; others.

STEELE, JAS. JR., Inv., 11-7-1829.
STEELE, JAS. JR., W.B., 11-30-1829.
STEELE, JAS. JR., Set., 9-1831.
STEMPLE, GODFREY, Set., 4-9-1798.
STEMPLE, MARG., Inv., undated.
STEMPLE, MARG., Will, 4-5-1798. Dev.:
John, Martin, David, sons; Christena,
Cath., Rosanah, Susanah, Eve, Polly,
daus.; dau. Barbary excluded.
STEMPLE, MARG., S.B., 6-1800.
STEPHENSON, HUGH, Will, 5-4-1796.
Dev.: Peggy, wife; John, James, Wm.,
sons; Mary, Liddy, Anny, daus.
STERLING, AND., Will, 11-1814. Dev.:
Mary, wife; John, Philip, Andrew,
Jos., sons; Mary, Eliz., Joanna, daus.;
others.
STERLING, AND., Inv., App., 11-21-
1814.
STERLING, AND., S.B., 2-1815.
STEVENSON, ANN, Inv., 12-1826.
STEVENSON, ANN, S.B., 12-1826.
STEWART, DAN., Inv., 5-1830.
STEWART, JOHN, S.B., undated.
STEWART, JOHN, App., 11-30-1795.
STEWART, JOHN, Set., 8-18-1803.
STEWART, ROBT., Set., 9-1811.
STEWART, WM., Vendue, 3-22-1811.
STEWART, WM., Set., 10-12-1816.
STILES, STEPHEN, Will, 5-1819. Dev.:
Deborah, wife; Job, Aaron, Wm..
John, sons; Eliz. Knight, Ruth Ryn-
hart, Lyddy Long, daus.
STILES, STEPHEN, Inv., 8-23-1819.
STILES, STEPHEN, Set., 3-6-1826.
STILLWELL, JER., Set., 8-27-1832.
STOCKWELL, JOHN, Will, 2-1840. Dev.:
James, Sam., Isaac, Elijah, sons;
Mary Goldwin, Fannie, Eliz., daus.;
others.
STONEKING, ADAM, Will, 3-1848.
Dev.: Adam (son of first wife), Robt.,
Alvy, Wm., sons; Sarah, Malinda,
daus.
STRAIT, JOHN, Will, 9-1833. Dev.:
Eliz.; Ephraym, Augustus, Jacob,
Jonathon, sons; Mary Ann, Dorothy,
Mary, Joonah, daus.
STUART, JOHN, Set., 10-5-1804.
STUART, WM., Will, 3-1811. Dev.: Eliz.,
wife; Alex., Chas., Dan., Robt., sons;
Sarah McKinley, Nancy Park, daus.;
others.
STULL, GODFREY, Inv., 2-1-1822.
STULL, GODFREY, S.B., 2-8-1822.
STULL, GODFREY, Set., 7-8-1823.
SUMMERS, PHIL., Inv., 9-30-1815.
SYPOLE, GEO., Will, 6-1813. Dev.:
Mary, wife; Chris., Nat., Geo., sons.
TAYLOR, WILDY, Vendue, 6-28-1803.
TAYLOR, WILDY, Inv., 10-10-1803.

TENANT, ELIZ., Inv., 3-25-1830.

TENANT, ELIZ., S.B., 11-1830.

TENANT, ELIZ., Set., 11-16-1832.

TENNANT, RICH., Will, 1-1823. Dev.: Eliz., wife; Peter, Rich., Wm., John, Alex., Jos., Adam, Abraham, Jacob, sons; Mary, Eliz. Connor, Cath. Morris, Marg. Verner, daus.; other.

TENNANT, RICH., Inv., 1-31-1823.

TENNANT, RICH., S.B., 2-20 & 21-1823.

TENNANT, RICH., Set., 1-26-1829.

TENNANT, RICH, JR., Inv. 8-30-1824.

TENNANT, RICH, JR., S.B., 6-1825.

THOMAS, BENJ., Will, 8-1825. Dev.: Eliz., wife; Eliz. John, Nancy Sidwell, Lucinda, daus.; John, Benj., Wm., James, Rich., Jos., Elisha, sons; others.

THOMAS, BENJ., Inv., 9-6-1825.

THOMAS, THOMAS, Will, 6-1836. Dev.: Marg. Reeder, Sinthia Miller, Sarah Hull, Matilda Baker, Nancy, Levina, Mary Temperance, daus.; Wm., Garrett, Nat., sons.

THOMPSON, DAN., Inv., 2-1817.

THOMPSON, DAN., Vendue, 4-25-1817, 12-21-1817, 11-11-1817.

THOMPSON, DAN., Set., 11-1818.

THOMPSON, DAN., Set., 11-17-1819.

THOMPSON, THOM., Will, 4-1800. Dev.: Sarah, wife; heirs.

THORN, JOHN, Inv., 2-10-1821.

THORN, JOHN, S.B., 3-10-1821.

THORN, JOHN, Set., 8-24-1822.

THORN, JOHN, Inv., 9-26-1831.

THORN, JOHN, S.B., 10-15-1831.

THORN, THOM., Inv., 9-30-1803.

THORN, THOM., S.B., 4-1804.

TIBBS, FRANCIS, Account, 4-1818.

TIBBS, JAMES, Will, 12-1848. Dev.: Hannah, Hess, dau., Robt., sons; others.

TIBBS, JOHN, Will, 10-1822. Dev.: Martha, wife; Frances, dau.; other children.

TICHENOR, AARON, Will, 5-1826. Dev.: Jonathon, Aaron, Nat., James, Moses, sons; Mary Bird, Easter Rice, Hannah, daus.

TITZARD, LEONARD, Will, 6-1801. Dev.: Chashey, wife; Eliz. Southworth, Sarah Lenah, Susanna, Rachel, Cath., Hanner, Marah, daus.; Isaac, son.

TOBIN, HANNAH, Will, 5-1849. Dev.: Robt. Bell, Jos. Bell, bros.; Martha Bell, sis.; others.

TOBIN, ROBT., Will, 2-1845. Dev.: Hannah Tobin and heirs; Robt. Tobin heirs.

TONCRA, JOHN, Set., 10-6-1827.

TONCRAY, JOHN, Set., 11-1817.

TONCRAY, JOHN, Set., 2-25-1820.

TONERAY, JOHN, Inv., 6-2-1814.

TOOFMAN, CHRIS., Will, 5-1823. Dev.: Phebe, wife; Jacob, John, Geo., Benj., sons; Marg. Maria, Cath., Rachel, Eliz., Drusilla, daus.

TOOFMAN, CHRIS., Inv., 9-27-1823.

TOOTHMAN, TETRICK, Will, 5-1825. Dev.: Barbary, wife; Tetro, Wm., Mich., John, Geo., Andrew, Chria., Adam, sons; Mary Mats, Mary Arnett, Christina Bobs, Eliz. Kerns, Hannah, Cath., Sarah, Barbary, daus.

TRADER, SABRA, Inv., App., 12-1807.

TRAVIS, ROBT., Will, 3-1847. Dev.: Mary, wife; Wm., John, Oliver, Wesley, Jos., Robt., Solomon, Travis, sons; Eliz., Mary, Evaline, daus.; other son.

TRICKETT, JOS., Will, 9-1805. Dev.: Marg., wife; Mary, dau.; John, Wm., Mich., sons; seven younger children.

TROY, SIMON, Will, 7-1799. Dev.: Hannah, wife; James, Chris., sons; Mary, Elizabeth, Eleanor Bromigan, daus.; others.

TUTTLE, ANDREW, Will, 5-1845. Dev.: wife; children.

TUTTLE, JOEL, Will, 5-1845. Dev.: Anne, wife; Dan., Jesse, John, Isaiah, Andrew, Wm., Jeremiah, sons; Mary, Peggy, Betsey, daus.; others.

VAN CAMP, ISAAC, Will, 3-1833. Dev.: Mary, wife; Eliz., Mary, Jamima, Dorcas, Hannah, Rachel, daus.; Adam, Wm., Peter, John, sons.

VANDERGRIFT, EBEN., Inv., 7-14-1827.

VANDERGRIFT, EBEN., S.B., 8-1827.

VANDERGRIFT, EBEN., Set., 4-18-1831.

VANDERGRIFT, JACOB, Inv., 3-25-1830.

VANDERGRIFT, JACOB, S.B., 4, 5, 6, 7-1830.

VANDERGRIFT, JACOB, Set., 5-21-1831.

VANDERVORT, NICH., Inv., 8-13-1813.

VANDERVORT, NICH., S. B., 10-7-1813.

VANDERVORT, NICH., Set., 9-1818.

WADE, ALEX., Will, 6-1803. Dev.: wife; Aaron, Elijah, Alex., Thom., Elisha, Hosea, Geo., sons; Mary, dau.

WADE, ALEX., Inv., 6-21-1803.

WADE, DAN., Will, 10-1837. Dev.: Thom., father; Dorcas, wife; Thom., Wm., Dan., Geo., sons; Clarrey, Marcy, Sary, Jemimy, daus.

WADE, GEO., Will, 11-1848. Dev.: Cassa, wife; Delila, Sela, Abigale, Ary Ann, Rachel, daus.; Oath, Greenberry, Geo., Wenman, sons.

WADE, THOM., Will, 2-11-1841. Dev.: Sally, wife; Thom., Elon, Jethro, Isaac, Ezra, sons; Samantha, Loretta, Mary, daus.; other.

WADE, WENMAN, Will, 7-1838. Dev.: Celly, wife; other.

WALKER, JAS., Inv., 1-20-1830.

WALKER, JAMES, Will, 1-1828. Dev.: Sarah, wife; James, John, Jonathon, sons; Ann Riggs, Mary Cunningham, Eliz. Stateler, Sarah Myers, Susannah, daus.

WALKER, JAMES, S.B., 2-8-1828.

WALKER, JAMES, Set., 5-24-1830.

WALLS, JAMES, JR., Will, 7-1839. Dev.: Grace, wife; Eliz., Marg., Jemima, Grace, Sarah Temperance, daus.; Josh, James, Wm., sons; others.

WARMAN, BART., Inv., 12-16-1826.

WARMAN, BART., S.B., 12-1826.

WARMAN, BART., Set., 11-27-1827.

WARMAN, FRANCIS, Inv., app., 6-6-1800.

WARMAN, FRANCIS, Set., 7-13-1801.

WARMAN, FRANCIS, Will, 6-1838. Dev.

WARMAN, FRANCIS, Will, 6-1838. Dev.: Mary, wife; Thom., Reason, John, Stephen, Francis, Hirgamial, Bartholmew, sons; Marg., Malinda, Sarah, Anne, Lavina, daus.

WATSON, DAVID, Inv., 7-31-1830.

WATSON, DAVID, S.B., 6-1831.

WATSON, JAMES, GREEN, Will, 3-1834. Dev.: Ann, wife; Marg. Cox, Mary, daus.; Henry, James, Thomas, sons; others.

WATSON, JOHN, Inv., 12-8-1809.

WATSON, JOHN, Set., 6-1824.

WATSON, JOHN, Will, 9-1831. Dev.: Geo., son; Mary Freeland, Sarah Yost, Susannah Woods, Priscilla, daus.; others.

WATSON, JOHN, Inv., 12-1831.

WATSON, JOHN, S.B., 12-1831.

WATSON, WM., Will, 6-1809. Dev.: Janey, wife; Jacob, Wm., David, John, sons; 3 unnamed daus.; other.

WATTS, ARCH., App., 10-1805.

WATTS, ARCH., S.B., 10-1805.

WATTS, JOHN, Set., 2-1796.

WATTS, RICH., Will, 4-11-1836. Dev.: wife; John, son; Agnes, dau.; unborn child.

WEAVER, BALDWIN, App., Inv., 6-18-1796.

WEAVER, HENRY, Will, 9-1830. Dev.: Nancy, wife; Barb. Marple, Eliz. Sayne, daus.; John, Jacob, sons; others,

WEAVER, HENRY, Inv., 10-29-1830.

WEAVER, HENRY, S.B., 3-17-1831.

WEAVER, JOS., Will, 11-1827. Dev.: Rebecca, wife; Geo., Jos., John, Jacob, sons; others.

WEAVER, JOS., Inv., 8-1828.

WEAVER, JOS., S.B., 12-25-1827.

WEAVER, JOS., Set., 4-27-1829.

WEBSTER, JAMES (Adrm. of And. Miller, Dec.) Set., 12-7-1827.

WELLS, AUGUSTIN, Will, 9-10-1839. Dev.: Lucy, wife; Ephraim, Moses, Hezekiah, John, Thom., sons; Martha, Lucy, Asenath, daus.; others.

WELTNER, JOHN, App., 11-8-1819.

WELTNER, JOHN, S.B., 11-9-1819.

WELTNER, JOHN, Set., 8-1824.

WERNINGER, AUGUSTUS, Inv., 8-24-1824.

WERNINGER, AUGUSTUS, S.B., 6-1826.

WERNINGER, AUGUSTUS, Set., 6-19-1826.

WERNINGER, AUGUSTUS (heirs), Set., 3-27-1827.

WERNINGER, AUGUSTUS, Set., 11-24-1830.

WERNINGER, AUGUSTUS (Heirs), Set., 4-14-1831.

WEST, JOHN, Inv., 3-6-1832.

WEST, JOHN, S.B., 5-1832.

WHITE, BENJ., Will, 3-1824. Dev.: Marget, wife; Benj., son; Eliz., Nancy, daus.; others.

WHITE, GRAFTON, Inv., 1-1830.

WHITE, GRAFTON, S.B., 1-1830.

WHITE, GRAFTON, Set., 8-28-1832.

WHITE, STEPHEN, Will, 12-1834. Dev.: Mich., bro., others.

WILES, GEO., Will, 8-1811. Dev.: Reganer, wife; Jacob, Geo., Wm., John, sons; Susanna Byanhurst, Marg. Rightinour, daus.

WILES, GEO., Inv., 9-16-1811.

WILES, GEO., S.B., 9-28-1811.

WILES, REGINA, Inv., 6-12-1813.

WILES, REGINA, S.B., 6-19-1813.

WILHELM, PETER, App., 12-12-1809.

WILHELM, PETER, S.B., 12-15-1809.

WILHELM, PETER, Set., 3-10-1826.

WILKINS, JEPTHEATH, Inv., 2-2-1819.

WILKINS, JEPTHA, S.B., 2-12-1819.

WILLEY, LEVEN, Inv., App., 6-30-1815.

WILLEY, MARG., Will, 8-1816. Dev.: James, John, Absolum, Boyd, sons; Nancy Veach, dau.; others.

WILLIAMS, GABRIEL, Will, 2-1828. Dev.: Margrit, wife; Clark, Gabriel, Mark, Otho, sons; Abigail, Eliz., Ruth, Cynthia, daus.

WILLIAMS, GABRIEL, Inv., 1-1830.

WILLIAMS, GABRIEL, S.B., 1-1830.

WILLIAMS, GABRIEL, Set., 3-23-1830.

WILLIAMS, HENRY, Will, 6-1835. Dev.: Sarah, wife.

WILLIAMS, SARAH, Will, 10-1839. Dev.: Joseph, Lewis and Foster Williams, Mary Bennett, Phebe Somers, Rhode Kisner, Sarah Culp.

WILSON, GEO., Will, 9-1816. Dev.: Mary, wife; Wm., Arthur, sons; Hannah, Marg., daus.; others.

WILSON, HUMPHREY, App., 7-2-1814.

WILSON, HUMPHREY, Set., 8-1818.

WILSON, JOHN, Inv., 6-3-1826.

WILSON, JOSEPH, Will, 9-1814. Dev.: Anne, wife; Susannah Beal, Eliza Jones, Perthena, daus.; Jos., John, Sam., James, sons; other.

WILSON, JOSIAH, Will, 8-1821. Dev.: Juliet Muchelroy.

WILSON, REBECCA, Will, 2-1823. Dev.: Bersheba Williams, Vilender Foster, Reckah Haymond, Harriett Evans, Nancy, Ruth, daus,; Josiah, Abraham, sons.

WILSON, REBECCA, Inv., 5-31-1823.

WILSON, REBECCA, S.B., 1-6-1827.

WILSON, REBECCA, Set., 2-2-1827.

WILSON, REBECCA, Set., 9-15-1828.

WILSON, WM., Will, 2-1807. Dev.: Rebecca, wife; Stephen, Geo., Josiah, Abraham, sons; Barsha Williams, Linny, Rebecca, Harriet, Ruth, Nancy, Ellenor, daus.

WILSON, WM., Inv., 5-30-1807.

WILSON, WM., S.B., 10-10-1807.

WILSON, WM., Set., 5-1809.

WILSON, THOM., Inv., 3-2-1826.

WILSON, THOM., S.B., 4-3-1826.

WILSON, THOM., Set., 9-8-1830.

WILYARD, ELIZ., Will, 3-1836. Dev.: Elias, Jacob, Geo., Isaac, sons; Eliz.,

Dolly Jenkins, Charlotte Lowder, daus.; others.

WINDSON, JAMES, Vendue, undated.

WINDSON, WM., Will, 3-1846. Dev.: Parthena, wife; Dudley, son; Sarah Toothman, Eliz., Evans, Ann Evans, Delia Mitchell, daus.; others.

WINDSOR, JAMES, App., undated.

WINSOR, WM., Inv., 3-15-1826.

WINSOR, WM., S.B., 5-1826.

WIREMAN, CHRISTIAN, Will, 5-31-1800. Dev.: Cath., mother, Mary, wife; Jos. Pryer, friend.

WOLCOTT, WM., Inv., 8-6-1825.

WOLF, CHARLOTTE, Will, 9-1844. Dev.: Mary Rhore, Cath. Runner, daus., John, Peter, Lewis, sons; black man.

WOLF, LEWIS, Will, 12-1841. Dev.: Dev.: Sharlotte, wife; Peter, John, Lewis, sons; Cath. Runner, Mary Rhore, daus.; Tom, slave.

WOLF, PETER, Will, 1-1850. Dev.: Eliz., wife; John, Lewis, sons; Mary Ann Weaver, Charlotte Hayder, Marg. Herd, Eliz., Rebecca, Maria Virginia, daus.

WOLVERTON, ELIZ., Will, 8-1826. Dev.: Tillman, Vincent, Rich., sons; Eliza, Anna, Susanna, Priscilla, daus.

WOODRING, ABR., Set., 9-1810.

WOODRUFF, ERASTUS, Will, 8-1849. Dev.: Mary, wife; Abraham, Elias, sons.

WORLEY, EZEK., Inv., 4-1806.

WORLEY, EZEK., S.B., 4-1806.

WORLEY, EZEK., Set., 4-5-1806.

WOTRING, ABR., Inv., 10-25-1809, 12-8-1809.

WOTRING, ABR., S.B., 1-8-1810.

WOTRING, ABR., Inv., 1-1827.

WOTRING, ABR., S.B., 1-1827.

WOTRING, ABR., Set., 6-1828.

YOUST, PETER, Will, 12-22-1849. Dev.: Marg., wife; Washington, John, Nimrod, Geo., Methia, sons; Mary, dau.; others.

West Virginia Estate Settlements

In 1936 and 1937, the West Virginia Commission on Historic and Scenic Markers, the Works Progress Administration, and the Federal Emergency Relief Administration compiled court records of the various counties, such as Births, Deaths, Marriages, and Wills. Under Wills were grouped subjects pertaining to Estate Settlements, including Wills, Inventories, and Appraisements. Copies of these county records were filed at the Department of Archives and History, Charleston; the Library of West Virginia University, Morgantown; and the DAR Library, Washington.

Believing that there would be particular interest on the part of the general public in the Estate Settlements in the older counties, the West Virginia Historical Society has undertaken to abstract the Estate Settlement Records, as filed in the State Department of Archives and History, and offer them for publication in the *West Virginia History Quarterly*. (No responsibility can be assumed as to the accuracy of the copies made from the original records.)

There are 13 counties which were formed prior to 1800, and it has been agreed to arrange these counties in chronological order, and to print their records from the earliest date to 1850. The formation dates of these counties are as follows: Hampshire—1753; Berkeley—1772; Monongalia—1776; Ohio—1776; Greenbrier—1778; Harrison—1784; Hardy—1786; Randolph—1787; Pendleton—1788; Kanawha—1788; Brooke—1797; Wood—1798; and Monroe—1799.

Ohio County Formed 1776

Abbreviations used in this material include: Acc.—account; Adm. — administrator; App. — appraisement; Bro. — brother; Dau.—daughter; Dev.—devisee; Guard.—guardian; Inv.—inventory; S.B.—sale bill; Set.—settlement; Sis.—sister; Ven.—vendue.

ABRAM, STEPHEN, Will, 8-24-1799. Dev.: Stephen Abram.

ALBRIGHT, PHILIP, Will, 5-22-1823. Dev.: Marg., David, John, Sarah, and Mary Albright.

ALLISON, MARY, Will, 8-7-1812. Dev.: James Buchanon, Esther Brown.

ANDERSON, ALEX., Will, 9-16-1802. Dev.: Dolly and James Anderson.

ANDERSON, ELIZ., Will, 1-1848. Dev.: Otho Heiskell, Cath. Norris.

APLIN, ROBT., Will, 10-26-1847. Dev.: Jane Aplin.

ARMSTRONG, ARCHIBALD, Will, 3-8-1848. Dev.: Cath. Armstrong.

ARMSTRONG, WM., Will, 8-21-1847. Dev.: Marg., John, Wm., Ann, Mary, Hanah, and Sarah Armstrong.

ASHLY, ZACH., Will, 11-18-1806. Dev.: John Ashly.

ATKINSON, JOHN, Will, 5-21-1821. Dev.: James, Geo., John, Robt., James, Sarah, David, Hanna, and Rebeckah Atkinson.

AULT, MATHIAS, Will, 2-22-1790. Dev.: Eliz. Ault, Philip Hup, Lazarus Rhyne, Eliz. Smith, Eliz. Fisher.

BAGGS, ANDREW, Will, 3-31-1798. Dev.: Agnes, Martha, Wm., John Baggs, Agnes Denison, And. Martin.

BAGGS, WM., Will, 10-26-1849. Dev.: Mother, Andrew, Mary, Jane, Rebecca, Ann, Levinia, Marg., Ellen, and Sarah Baggs.

BAIRD, THOM., Will, 11-1-1844. Dev.: Sarah, James, Eliz., Cath., and Mary Baird.

BARNS, JAMES, Will, 7-13-1832. Dev.: Mary and James Barns, Emily Butler.

BASSETT, FRANCIS, Will, 3-16-1846. Dev.: Francis and Jane Bassett, Martha and Henry Morrison.

BEAL, ALPHEN, Will, 6-28-1833. Dev.: Easter, Mariah, Harriett Lethe, Alphens Williams.

BEALL, BASIL, Will, 5-24-1815. Dev.: Mary Ann Simms, Mary and Bethann Carter, Ann Williams, Cillan Cregg, Basil, Jos., Ninian, Benj., Citizen Beall.

BEALL, GEO., Will, 2-27-1800. Dev.: James, Joshe, Mary, Wm., Agnes, John Beall.

BECK, JOHN, Will, 3-15-1816. Dev.: John, Wm., Frances, Susanna, Rebecca, and Alex. Beck, Mary Kauch, Rebecca Barns.

BECK, SAM, Will, 7-30-1848. Dev.: Mary Beck.

BEIRD, JOHN, Will, 5-21-1828. Dev.: Jane, Josiah, Jos., Wm., Eleanor, Eliz., John and Jane Beird.

BELL, ANDREW, Will, 10-11-1849. Dev.: Nancy, Cassyann, Sarah, Robt., and Sam. Bell, Nancy and Marg. Wayt.

BELL, HENRY, Will, 10-20-1839. Dev.: Moses and Mrs. Bell.

BELL, JAMES, Will, 3-19-1841. Dev.: Jenny, John, Geo., Mary, Jane, Wm., Edie, and Jos. Bell.

BELL, ROBT., Will, 11-3-1823. Dev.: Sarah, Andrew, and James Bell, Agness Giffen.

BENTLEY, WM., Will, 12-30-1822. Dev.: Rosannah, Jacob, Jos., Wm., Isaac, John, Marg., Sarah, and Ruth Bentley.

BERRYHILL, SAM., Will, 1-17-1823. Dev.: Marian Berryhill.

BILDERBACH, CHAS., Will, 5-5-1789. Dev.: Wife, dau.; Ephriam.

BLANEY, HENRY, Will, 4-21-1838. Dev.: Wm. Harkin.

BLARE, JAMES, Will, 6-1-1824. Dev.: Amealy, Brice, Jos., Geo., Wm., Ezekil, Mary, Lot, Jeremiah Blare, Caty Vandevanter, Deborah Pyles, Sarah Wayman, Ann Robinson, Elenor Dodd.

BOGGS, MATHEW, Will, 1-25-1817. Dev.: Martha Boggs.

BONAR, JOHN, Will, 10-20-1824. Dev.: Mary, Eliz., Rebecca, Martin, David, John, Mathew, and Nancy Bonar.

BONNET, JOHN, Will, 6-21-1816. Dev.: Eve, Benj., Eliz., Lewis and Somon Bonnet.

BONNET, LEWIS, Will, 11-27-1807. Dev.: Eliz., Lewis, and John Bonnet; Mary and Barb Radiffer, Eliz., Lountz, Lewess Hookis.

BOWMAN, MICH., Will, 12-18-1806. Dev.: Josh Bolton.

BRICE, JOHN, Will, 2-25-1811. Dev.: Jean and James Brice.

BROWN, AMIE, Will, 4-9-1827. Dev.: Amie, Eliz., and Dan. Steenrod.

BROWN, AND., Will, 9-26-1807. Dev.: Rodah and Eliz. Brown.

BROWN, JOHN, Will, 3-13-1843. Dev.: Sarah, James, Jos. Brown; Nancy Johnston, Sarah Allen.

BROWN, JOSIAS, Will, 5-12-1819. Dev.: Wm., and Alex. Brown, Marg. Atkinson, Ann and Hannah McCoy, Jane Waddle, Cath. Michel, Ruth Miligin, Elijah Brown.

BRUICE, SAM., Will, 3-1-1793. Dev.: Rebecca, John, Thom., Stephen, Rachel, Mary Bruice.

BUCHANON, JAMES, Will, 1-11-1799. Dev.: Mary Faye, Nancy, Thom., Sam. Buchanon.

BUCHANON, WALTER, Will, 2-14-1844. Dev.: Geo., Wm., Sarah, Marg., Eliza, Mary, John, James, and Sam., Buchanon.

BUCHANON, WM., Will, 1-21-1813. Dev.: Geen Morgin, Marg. and John Strayer, Mary Graham, Anibel Yoho, Rebecca Burton, Eloner Rine, Wm., Jas., Eben. Buchanon; Mary Bratton.

BUCHANON, WM., Will, 6-21-1822. Dev.: Walt., Arch., Jane, and Eliz., Buchanon, Wm. and Sarah Oldham.

BUKEY, JOHN, Will, 10-14-1815. Dev.: Nancy and Wm. Bukey, Jemima Hedges.

BURCH, ZEPHENIAH, Will, 10-19-1828. Dev.: Ruth, Jesse, John, Eleanor and Jamima Burch, Jennett, Ruth, Delila, and Hiram Curtis.

BURKHAM, STEPHEN, Will, 9-2-1840. Dev.: Francis, Sarah, Jane, Elza, Sarah, Wm. D., Wm., Isaac, and Stephen Burkham, Rebecca Criswell, Mary Magill, Sarah Bently.

BURKHEAD, JOHN, Will, 8-19-1802. Dev.: Deborae Burkhead.

BURKITT, JACOB, Will, 1-28-1817. Dev.: Mary and Henry Burkitt.

BURNS, WALTER, Will, 10-25-1848. Dev.: Nancy Burns.

CALDWELL, ELIZA, Will, 4-21-1847. Dev.: Alex. Caldwell, Margaretta, and Eliza Good; Mary Brady.

CALDWELL, JAMES, Will, 4-22-1802. Dev.: John, Sam, James, Alex, Jos. Caldwell, Eliz. Williamson.

CALDWELL, SAM., Will, 3-4-1826. Dev.: Sam. and James Caldwell, John McCraken, Jean Melay.

CAMPBELL, JOESEPH, Will, 4-1-1816. Dev.: James, Sam., and Elisa Campbell.

CARMICHAEL, DAVID, Will, 6-18-1832. Dev.: Jane and Mrs. Carmichael.

CARMICHAEL, JAMES, Will, 6-24-1831 Dev.: Eliz., Wm., and Hugh Carmichael.

CARROLL, GEO., Will, 12-12-1834. Dev.: Thom., Geo., James, John, Eliz., Jacob, Wm., and Mary Carroll; Caleb and Marg. Johnston.

CARTER, ARTHUR, Will, 11-11-1840. Dev.: Bethan, Rich., Thom., Bazil, John and Cil Ann Carter; Lee Ann Boggs, Mary Marlin.

CASKEY, JOS., Will, 2-3-1795. Dev.: John, Sarah Caskey.

CHAMBERS, DAVID, Will, 3-12-1787. Dev.: Sarah, Jos., John, Mary, Sam., Benj., Marg. Chambers.

CHAPLINE, JAMES, Will, 1-7-1815. Dev.: Sam., Alex., Moses, Hamilton, Zane, Henry, John, Moses and Mary Chapline.

CHAPLINE, MARY, Will, 1882. Dev.: Moses, Sam., and James Chapline.

CLARK, HENRY, Will, 6-17-1815. Dev.: Mary, Barnabas, Wm., Hellen, John, Mary, Terrance, Pat., Martha, Ann, Francis, and Laurence Clark; Cath. Patterson.

CLARK, JOB, Will, 1-27-1823. Dev.: Hezekiah, Ebenezer, and Rebeckah Clark.

CLARK, WM., Will, 9-3-1823. Dev.: Wm., Ruth and Henry Clark.

CLEGG, THOM., Will, 4-19-1828. Dev.: James, Sam., Rich., Thom. Clegg.

CLEMENS, JAMES, Will, 10-25-1846. Dev.: Ellen, Mary, Helen, Sherrard, Jacob, and James.

COATES, WM., Will, 11-22-1841. Dev.: Wm., Eliz., Henry, Nathan, and Mrs. Coates, Eliz. Bernard.

COE, PHILIP, Will, 11-6-1815. Dev.: Isaac, Philip, Pam., Perlina, Jane and Abigail Coe; Rachel Jones, Eliz. Hines, Hanah Holdren, Ethel Cisarel, Saral Beeler.

CONCLE, HENRY, Will, 1-12-1815. Dev.: Marg. Concle, Henry Hash.

CONWELL, YATES, Will, 10-15-1783. Dev.: Mrs. Conwell, Jehu, Wm., Rachel.

COOEY, ELIZA, Will, 8-1822. Dev.: Sarah McClure, John and Thom. Cooey.

CORDELL, THOM., Will, 4-21-1824. Dev.: Betsy, John, Harriet, Wm., Allen, Delila, and Isaac Cordell.

COWAN, WM., Will, 5-3-1792. Dev.: Jane, Jean, Alex, John, Hugh, Wm. Cowan, Elender Rankin, Geo. Camble.

COX, GABRIEL, Will, 6-6-1778. Dev.: David, Diana, Peter, Eleanor, Israel Cox, Mary Ann Spencer, Marg. McCoy.

COX, MICHAEL, Will, 6-7-1829. Dev.: Abraham, John, Geo., Jerutha, Thom., Jos., Sam., Isaac, Wm., Eliz., David, and Jane Cox; Ann Hupp, Mahala Brown.

CRAIG, JAMES, Will, 1-22-1813. Dev.: And., Mary Alex., and James Craig, Sarah St. Clair, Martha Rude, Hanah Carlon, Rachel Babbit, Abigail White.

CRANSWICK, RICH., Will, 11-1834. Dev.: Cath. and Rich. Cranswick.

CROTHERS, JOHN, Will, 10-7-1839. Dev.: Hugh and Mary Crothers, Jane Rerlin.

CROUCH, NEHEMIAH, Will, 3-16-1803. Dev.: Eliz., Rease, Isabell, Mary, Wm., Nehemiah Crouch.

CROW, PETER, Will, 3-27-1826. Dev.: Susan, Jacob, Isaac, Abr., Sam., Peter, Sebria, Sufiah, Susanah, and Lueyan Crow; Polly Hagerman, Frances Blane.

CRUGER, DAN., Will, 6-29-1833. Dev.: Sara Metcalf, Hannah Nowell, Christina Taylor, Helen Fowler, Frances and Dan. Strong, Dan. and Eliza Ford.

CURRY, ROBT., Will, 10-17-1807. Dev.: Rach., Sam., Moses, David, Eliz., Martha Curry.

CURTIS, JAMES, Will, 8-30-1831. Dev.: Salathiel, John, and June Curtis; Abigail Caldwell.

CUTLY, WM., Will, 3-12-1802. Dev.: Thom. Cutly.

DAVIS, CEPHUS, Will, 3-10-1848. Dev.: Eliz. and John Davis.

DAVIS, THOMAS, Will, 12-10-1830. Dev.: Nancy Johnston, Eleazer and John Davis, Rebecca Ferrel, Sarah Martin.

DAWSON, NICH., Will, 1-13-1790. Dev.: Vilot Dawson.

DAYLEY, PETE, Will, 2-7-1804. Dev.: Mary, John, Peter, Esau, Jacob, Jesse Dayley.

DEAN, JAMES, Will, 4-4-1836. Dev.: Nancy, Robt., Eliz., and James Dean, John McLure.

DEMENT, Benajah, Will, 3-16-1816. Dev.: Ann Harding, Eliz. Finley, Mary Gilmore, Sarah R o g e r s, Marg. Pickens, Aless Dement.

DENNISTON, ANDREW, Will, 10-20-1840. Dev.: Nancy, Sarah, Nancy, Eleanor, Anne, James, Matthew, And. Deniston; Olsa Morrow.

DICKEY, MARG., Will, 3-21-1804. Dev.: Sam. and James Dickey, Mary Waddle.

DICKEY, WM., Will, 8-30-1822. Dev.: Mary, Jr., Mary, James, John, Ben., and Jasases Dickey.

DONOVAN, LYDIA, Will, 5-20-1809. Dev.: Chizzia Milla, Cath., Lydia, Rebecca, Levi, Dan., Valentine, and Dan Donovan.

DOTY, JOHN, Will, 3-27-1805. Dev.: Micasah Doty.

DOWLER, ED., Will, 6-5-1819. Dev.: Eliz., Mary, and Mrs. Dowler.

DOWNING, WM., Will, 9-28-1812. Dev.: James, Marg., John, Jos., Sam., Wm., David, Alex., Robt., Josh., And., Mary, and Jennet Downing; Rev. Alex McCoy.

DUNN, HEZEKIAH, Will, 10-12-1807. Dev.: Rachel, Eleanor, Matin, and Joe Dunn; Dru. Estep.

EDELEN, MARTHA, Will, 5-8-1835. Dev.: Priscilla, Martha, and Thom., Pentony, John Taylor.

ENNIS'S, WM., Will, 10-5-1848. Dev.: Miles Smith, Sarah Sommers.

EOFF, JOHN, Will, 5-12-1826. Dev.: Susan and John Eoff, Eliz. Woods, Sarah and Eleanor White, Naomi Cecil, Anna and Susan Williams.

ESTEL, ISAIAH, Will, 7-19-1831. Dev.: Cath. Estel, Geo. McAlpin.

EWART, ELIZ., Will, 3-17-1814. Dev.: Robt. and Anne Ewart, Eliz. and Marg. Villers, Mary Williams, Francis Collins.

FAIRCHILD, ABIGAIL, Will, 7-18-1842. Dev.: Abigail Prescott, Martha and Camillus Bishop, Bethiah Booth, Wm. Fairchild, Amily and Camilia Pollock, Abigail Hedges.

FALLOUR, MARY, Will, 10-28-1843. Dev.: Mary, John, Nich., Lewis, and Breaton Fallour.

FARIS, ADAM, Will, 7-24-1838. Dev.: David Faris, Dorratha, Mary, Marg., David and Adam Faris; Mary, Josiah, and Faris Brown.

FARIS, JOHN, Will, 3-5-1838. Dev.: Rosanna, Agnes, Mary, Dorotha, Martha, Nancy, Sally, Jane, Wm., Sam., Davis, Robt., and John Faris.

FARIS, WM., Will, 10-4-1814. Dev.: John, Adam, Mary and Wm. Faris.

FARMER, FRED., Will, 3-11-1842. Dev.: Jame, Sam., Dan., and Washington Farmer; Martha Bukey.

FERREL, MOSES, Will, 12-10-1828. Dev.: John, Gean, Mary, Jos., and Marg. Ferrel.

FINNLEY, JAMES, Will, 3-28-1814. Dev.: Eliz., Wm., Nancy, Sam., Ellis, and Eliz. Finnley.

FINNLEY, SAM., Will, 4-21-1827. Dev.: Eliz., Wm., Sam., Agness, Eliz., Hugh, Elenor, and Marg. Finley, Elenor Harvy.

FOOT, AND., Will, 2-28-1816. Dev.: Marg. Foot.

FOOT, ELIZAH, Will, 4-7-1812. Dev.: Mary, John, Jos., Amos and Andrew Foot.

FORDYCE, JOHN, Will, 10-21-1845. Dev.: Corbly, Jos., James, John Jr., Abner, Bensen, Nancy, Hettie, and Rachel Fordyce.

FORMAN, ELIZ., Will, 3-28-1839. Dev.: Nancy Marshall, John Wesleys, Sarah Hedges, Jane Hedges, Lucy and Emma Forman, W. Curtis, W. Marshal.

FOX, JOSIAH, Will, 11-24-1842. Dev.: Chas. and Francis Fox, Eliz. Chapline; Anna, Robt., and Geo. Curtis, Rebecca Pickering, Sarah Dungan, Mary Updegraff.

FRAZIER, DAVID, Will, 10-10-1834. Dev.: Nancy, John, Sam., James, Wm., Rosanna, Eliz., and Marg. Frazier; Isabella Pierson.

FRAZIER, SAM., Will, 6-7-1828. Dev.: Rosanah, Wm., David, and Sam. Frazier; Marg. Brown.

FRAZIER, SAM., Will, 10-17-1849. Dev.: Sam., Andrew, Wm., James, David, Hamilton, Robinson, Robt., and Mrs. Frazier; Eliz. McCoy, Rosanna Dare, Marg. Bell.

FRENCH, WM., Will, 3-6-1843. Dev.: Eliz., Eliza, Peter, Cath., Sarah, John, David, and Marg. French.

GIBSON, GEO., Will, 11-24-1814. Dev.: Jean, Wm., and Geo. Gibson.

GIFFEN, DAN., Will, 3-24-1841. Dev.: Agnes, John, and Robt. Giffen; Marg. Waddle, Mary Murry, Sarah Meathers, Agnes Frazier.

GILL, JOS., Will, 1-30-1845. Dev.: Wm., Sam., Will, Mary, Nancy, Ann, James, and John Gill; Eliz., James, and Wallace Park; Hugh and Wm. Hannah, Mary Clark, Eliz. Ford, Sarah Stein, Wm. Rankin, John Fox, Jr., Ben Stanton, Sr., Fanny Sen, Eliz. Job, Samm Narris, Harrison Henry.

GLASS, SAM., Will, 2-22-1796. Dev.: Anne, David, Jean, Marg., Susanah Glass.

GORBY, THOM., Will, 3-24-1814. Dev.: Eliz., Jabe, Ely, Jehew, Eben., Jesse and John Gorby, Rebecca Ellit, Faithful Clark, Hanah Parson.

GRAHAM, EDMUND, Will, 12-1826. Dev.: Edmund, Mary, Ann, and Isabella Graham; Geo., St. Peter, and Ann Zinn.

GRAHAM, MICHAEL, Will, 1-15-1819. Dev.: Patience, Deborah, and Jos. Graham.

GRAHAM, PATIENCE, Will, 2-28-1835. Dev.: Deborah Tanner, Jos. Graham.

GRANGER, CHAS., Will, 10-21-1832. Dev.: Jos. Morrison.

GRAY, WM., Will, 8-12-1825. Dev.: Jane, Walt., John, Wm., Eliz., and Jane Gray; Mary Gillaspie.

GREGG, GEO., Will, 3-21-1810. Dev.: Naomi, John, Geo., Assey, and Ruth Gregg; Mary Villars.

GRIFFIN, ROBT., Will, 12-5-1826. Dev.: Geo., Dan., John, and Mrs. Griffin; Eliz. Downing, Jean Farrel.

GRINDSTAFF, JONOTHAN, Will, No date. Dev.: Mother Grindstaff.

GRINDSTAFF, LEWIS, Will, 5-22-1812. Dev.: Rozanah, Moses, Jon., Thom., Mary, Sadie Grindstaff.

GROVES, WM., Will, 7-27-1815. Dev.: Mary and Wm. Groves, Rebecca McConcka.

HAMITT, BENJ., Will, 4-6-1790. Dev.: Ruth, Rhoda, James Hamitt.

HARNESS, MARY, Will, 4-9-1804. Dev.: Eliz. Tomlinson, Robt., Drusilla, Sam., Jos., Isaac, Mary, Lucy, Nat., and Jesse Harness; Sam. Carpenter.

HARRIS, BENJ., Will, 1-10-1818. Dev.: Susanna Crusen.

HARVEY, BENJ., Will, 5-8-1829. Dev.: Cath., Benj., Theo., Ann, and Jane Harvey; Elizh. Duncan, Rachel Pursall, Sarah Bell, Elizh and Jane Holiday.

HASWELL, JOHN, Will, 8-11-1845. Dev.: Mary Ann Haswell.

HEBDEN, SYLVESTER, Will, 10-8-1849. Dev.: Rich, and Frances Hebden.

HEMPHILL, THOM., Will, 12-29-1848. Dev.: Wallace, Thom., Mary, and Jos. Hemphill.

HENDERSON, JAMES, Will, 7-8-1839. Dev.: Kath. and Jos. Henderson, James. King.

HENDERSON, MARY, Will, 11-30-1838. Dev.: James, John, and Sarah Henderson.

HENTHORNE, SUSANAH, Will, 2-2-1799. Dev.: James, Adam, Wm., Sarah, Mary, Eliz. Henthorne.

HERVEY, WM., Will, 2-17-1845. Dev.: Dorotha, Thom., Mary, Wm., James, Andrew, David, John, and Henry Hervey; Jane Dunlap, Martha Parks, Mary Futhy, Marg. Huly.

HESTWOOD, SAM., Will, 3-25-1804. Dev.: Eliz., John, Rossanah, Sarah, and Mary Hestwood.

HOGLAND, DERRICK, Will, 4-16-1790. Dev.: Eliz., Mercy, Mary, Rebecca, Rich., Cath., Isaac, Cynthia Hogland.

HOLLIDAY, JAMES, Will, 1-28-1846. Dev.: John, Nancy, Wm., James and David Holliday; Jane Norris.

HOLLINGSHEAD, Will, 10-13-1842. Dev.: Eliz. and James Dare.

HOLMES, OBEDIAH, Will, 2-18-1794. Dev.: Mary, Wm., Obediah, Abraham, Isaac, Jacob, Jos., Sam. Holmes, Eliz. Pumprey, Marg. Hayes.

HOLMES, SAM., Will, 8-15-1799. Dev.: Mary Holmes.

HORNBROOK, JACOB, Will, 12-5-1840. Dev.: Jacob, Edwin, and Thom. Hornbrook.

HORNBROOK, WM., WELLINGTON, Will, 4-3-1840. Dev.: Sara Hornbrook.

HOSACK, DAVID, Will, 12-15-1814. Dev.: David, Eliz., Thom., Marg., John, and Wm. Hosack.

HOSACK, JAMES, Will, 3-22-1833. Dev.: Mary and Mary Jane Hosack.

HOSACK, JOHN, Will, 3-10-1811. Dev.: Rebecca, Jane, and Wm. Hosack.

HOSACK, MARY, Will, 12-14-1846. Dev.: John and Mary Creighton; Mary Jane Hosack, Jane McClaine, Home Missionary Fund.

HUKIL, JAMES, Will, 10-24-1812. Dev.: James and Rachel Hukil.

HULL, JOHN, Will, 3-1-1809. Dev.: Rebekah and Henry Hull.

HUMPHREY, ROBT., Will, 7-10-1828. Dev.: Martha, Robt., Jos., David, and John Humphrey; Robt. McKee, Jane, Genny, and Ann Dickey; Martha McKee.

HURST, MORGAN, Will, 7-4-1803. Dev.: Rebeccah, Morgan, Mills, Anne, Drusilla, Ruth, and Rachel Hurst.

HUTCHINSON, DAN., Will, 1-20-1844. Dev.: Sarah, Enoch, Sarah Hutchinson, Deborah Cunningham.

HUTCHINSON, JAMES, Will, 12-4-1824. Dev.: Nancy, James, Mary, Rebeckah, Nancy, Sarah, Martha, Jane, John, Marg., and Levina Hutchinson.

JACOB, JOHN, Will, 10-9-1848. Dev.: Mrs. Jacob.

JAMES, JANE, Will, 2-12-1848. Dev.: Wm. Davis.

JAMISON, HENRY, Will, 5-20-1845. Dev.: Mary Jamison.

JAMISON, SAM., Will, 4-23-1816. Dev.: Sally, Mary, Marg., James, and John Jamison.

JEFFERSON, JOHN, Will, 11-23-1831. Dev.: Eliz. and Jane Jefferson.

JEFFERY, JOHN, Will, 2-12-1825. Dev.: Esther, Martha, Thom., and Sam. Jeffery.

JERROME, JOHN, Will, 6-16-1836. Dev.: Emely Jerome.

JOHNSON, JACOB, Will, 11-29-1786. Dev.: David, Thom. Susanah Johnston.

JOHNSTON, JAMES, Will, 11-9-1836. Dev.: Hamilton, Eliz. Thom. Johnston, Martha Mason.

JOHNSTON, JAMES, Will, 6-7-1842. Dev.: Ann Johnston.

JOHNSTON, JAMES, Will, 1847. Dev.: Polly, Washington, and Mrs. Johnston.

JONES, DAVID, Will, 6-2-1818. Dev.: Morgan, Horatis, Eleanor, David, Ann, Mary and Eliz. Jones, Jos., Horatis and Mary Ann McClean; Elisha Garrett, Gaven Murchie.

KARBER, ADAM, Will, 3-5-1832. Dev.: Ann Karber.

KELLER, MARTIN, Will, 7-6-1812. Dev.: Marg., Jacob, and David Keller.

KELLY, ISAAC, Will, 11-18-1823. Dev.: James and Benj. Potter, Narcissa McCullock, Isaac and Nancy Poage.

KELLY, JOHN, will, 8-16-1832. Dev.: Owen Shia.

KEVER, ANN, Will, 11-1-1849. Dev.: Jesse Powell, Nancy Henthorn, Thom. Hood.

KEVER, WM., Will, 8-7-1832. Dev.: Ann Kever, Gane Hood.

KIDD, WM., Will, 9-27-1843. Dev.: Thom., Lawson, Wm., Mary, Eliz., Nancy and David Kidd.

LEE, JANE C., Will, 12-4-1813. Dev.: Eliz. Lee, Sally Chapline.

LEECH, JOHN, Will, 8-12-1844. Dev.: Mary and Mary Ann Leech.

LEPER, JAMES, Will, 9-17-1776. Dev.: Marg. Leper.

LEWIS, EZEKIEL, Will, 12-22-1825. Dev.: Phebe and Edmond Lewis.

LINN, MOSES, Will, 1-14-1793. Dev.: Prudence, Mary, Henry Linn.

LIST, JOHN, Will, 5-5-1825. Dev.: Sarah, Caroline, Thom., and John List; Sarah Nichol, Jeremiah Hays.

LIST, JOHN, Will, 5-17-1848. Dev.: Eugenius, Ann, Hannah, Eliza, Heber, Sarah, Dan., and Henry List; Sarah Hubbars, Sally Nicholas, Caroline Seamon, Mary Morrison.

LOCKWOOD, EPHRAIM, Will, 9-7-1805. Dev.: Susannah, Dave, Jacob, Wm., Josh., Lawrence, and Eliz. Lockwood, Dimees Brown, Rachel Steenrod, Mary Buchanon, Abigiel Steenrod.

MADDIN, MARG., Will, 12-30-1847. Dev.: Henry McMillen, Mary Stoolfire, John Fribberton.

MAGERS, ELIAS, Will, 7-26-1829. Dev.: Jos., Peter, Geo., and Mrs. Magers; Ann Helloms, Analizar Porter, Marg. McKinsey, Mary Durben, Sary Boner, Elizar Hanes.

MARLING, JOHN SR., Will, 7-27-1820. Dev.: Isabel, Mathew, Sam., Moses, Eliz., James, John, Eliza, and Wm. Marling, Sarah Oldham.

MARTIN, JOHN, Will, 1-10-1819. Dev.: Jane, James and John Martin.

MAXWELL, JOHN, Will, 1-18-1814. Dev.: Sally and Mary Roberts, James, Jane, Geo., Thom., And., John, Wm., and Robt., Maxwell.

MAXWELL, JOHN, Will, 1-25-1829. Dev.: John, Thom. Maxwell, Wm. Roberts, Wm. Whitham, Thom. McConn.

McANALL, THOM., Will, 10-6-1846. Dev.: John, Martha, Mary, and Hugh McAnall; Rachel Blany, Marg. Garvin.

McCAMMON, JAMES, Will, 10-22-1827. Dev.: Giny, Nancy, Mary, John, Jane, James, Marg., and Susannah McCammon.

McCLURE, MARG., Will, 6-14-1845. Dev.: Sarah McClure, Sarah Marshall.

McCLURE, RICH., Will, 12-11-1808. Dev.: Rich. Jr., Sam., Susan, Eliz. McClure.

McCLURE, SAM., Will, 11-27-1803. Dev.: Anne, James, and Mary McClure; John Kirkwood.

McCOLLOCH, ABRAHAM, Will, 12-26-1838. Dev.: Sam., James, Wm., Eliz., Sarah, Marg., Abraham, John, Ebenezer, and Rebecca McColloch; John, Nancy, and Eliz. Hair.

McCONN, THOM., Will, 8-16-1845. Dev.: Wm., Thom., Marcus, Eliz., Jane, Mary, Jos., and Isabella McConn.

McCONNELL, JAMES, Will, 2-14-1797. Dev.: Sam., Rebecca, Hugh, James, Mary, and John McConnell; Esther Buchanan, Eliz. Shepherd.

McCONNELL, SAM., Will, 5-5-1814. Dev.: James, Thom., John, Sam., Agnes, and Rachel McConnell; Sam. Finley.

McCOY, ALEX., Will, 12-27-1833. Dev.: Wm., John, and Eliz. McCoy; Mary Craig.

McCOY, ANGUS, Will, 12-18-1848. Dev.: Jane, Dan., and John McCoy; Angus Reed.

McCREARY, JAMES, Will, 6-10-1839. Dev.: Ann McCreary.

McCREARY, THOM., Will, 8-23-1802. Dev.: Margt., Wm., Thom., Mary Jane, and Eliz. McCreary.

McCUTCHEON, HUGH, Will, 3-15-1826. Dev.: Eleoner, John, Wm., and Hugh McCutcheon; Jean and Eleoner Stewart.

McDONALD, ARCH., Will, 5-17-1836. Dev.: John Ruhamah, and James McDonald; Eliz. Faris, Marg. and Cath. Rust, Jane Waddle.

McENTIRE, WM., Will, 12-27-1782. Dev.: Eliz. McEntire.

McFARLAND, JAS., Will, 11-21-1796. Dev.: Martha, John, Moses McFarland.

McFARLAND, JOHN, Will, 5-30-1797. Dev.: James, Marg. Wilson, Robt. Atkinson, Eliz., Sally, Andy, John, Sam., Jos., Ezekial McFarland.

McGREGOR, JOHN, Will, 5-11-1825. Dev.: Mary, James and Alex. McGragor; Mary, Wm., John, Alex., Marg., Russell, Martha, James David, Sam., Mary, Eliz. Bone.

McGUIRE, HUGH, Will, 4-19-1815. Dev.: Rachel, Isreal, Wm., Sarah, James, Hugh, Mary, and Eliz. McGuire.

McKEWAN, PETER, Will, 1833. Dev.: Mary McKewan.

McLURE, DAVID, Will, 5-10-1848, 5-9-1849. Dev.: Adeline Caldwell.

McMAHON, WM., Will, 3-31-1794. Dev.: Anne, Frien, Rich., John, Jos., James, Polly, Susan, Agnes McMahon.

McMECHEN, WM., Will, 6-5-1795. Dev.:
James, Wm., Benj., Sarah, Sid, Jane
McMechen; Agness, Nancy McCul-
loch, David; Francis Broom.
McMULLEN, JOHN, Will, 8-29-1842.
Dev.: Mary McMullen.
MICHELL, MARG., Will, 9-11-1843.
Dev.: Jane and John Wright, Hugh
and Wm. Wallace.
MICHELL, ROBT. Will, 3-8-1805. Dev.:
Christianna McFarland, Jean Blear,
Isabell, Anna, Hannah, John, Gaven,
Robt., Geo., Math. Michell.
MILLER, JOHN, Will, 2-14-1843. Dev.:
Marg., John, Eleanor, Sarah, Mary,
and Geo. Miller, Mary Jamison.
MILLIGAN, JOHN, Will, 4-31-1832.
Dev.: Sarah, Geo., James, John, and
Hugh Milligan; Mary Given, Hannah
Brown, Sarah Morison, Eliz. Dawney,
Ruth Faris, Lydia McCoy.
MILLS, ELIZ., Will, 7-15-1807. Dev.:
Benj., Geo., Lidia Mills; Cath. Rench,
Rach. Pumphrey, Dysulla Ridgely,
Rebeccah Mooran.
MILLS, JOHN, Will, 10-19-1832. Dev.:
Ruth, Moses, and John Mills; Rachel
Wallace.
MILLS, LEVI, Will, 5-14-1805. Dev.:
Eliz., Geo., and Benj. Mills; Cath.
and Dan Rench, Rebecca Moran,
Rachel Pumphrey, Drusilla Ridley.
MILLS, LYDIA, Will, 6-19-1841. Dev.:
Mary Ann Degarms.
MILLS, SAM., Will, 5-13-1847. Dev.:
Andrew Mills, Wm. Wilson.
MILLS, THOM., Will, 7-25-1806. Dev.:
John, Es., and Thom. Mills; Marg.
Zane, Jane Carpenter, Mary Gilken-
son, Rebeccah Williams, Sara Brice-
son, Hanah Zane, Thom. and Ezekial
Howard.
MITCHELL, ALEX., Will, 1840. Dev.:
Martha, Isaac, Jane, Zach., Sam.
Mitchell, Nancy Jacob.
MITCHELL, ANDREW, Will, 2-9-1823.
Dev.: Marg. Mitchell.
MITCHELL, HUGH, Will, 9-12-1833.
Dev.: Susan, And., John, Robt., Willy,
Sarah and Mary Mitchell; Lathena
and Peggy Leffler, Marg. McClure,
Nancy Wilson.
MONTGOMERY, WM., Will, 1-1-1813.
Dev.: Jos., Wm., Eliza, Jane and
John Montgomery.
MOORE, DAN., Will, 12-3-1842, 1-12-
1849. Dev.: Jane, Henry, Dan., Moore,
Hannah Simonson, Marg. Rupell,
Dan., and Rebecca Stockton.

MOORE, JOHN, Will, 2-16-1846. Dev.:
Mary Moore.
MOORE, THOM., Will, 10-22-1849. Dev.:
Elihah and Wm. Moore, Episcopalian
Methodist.
MORGAN, ED., Will, 6-17-1799. Dev.:
John, Jos., Mordecai, Susanah, Mor-
gan; Hannah and Eliz. Gilleland,
Mary Gamble, Rachel Van Metre,
Elce Mounts.
MORGAN, JAMES, Will, 1-4-1840. Dev.:
Jos. Morgan, Hugh Mitchell.
MORRISON, Sarah, Will, 7-6-1847. Dev.:
Janey, Sam., and Wm. Morrison.
NAILOR, SAM., Will, 5-28-1792. Dev.:
Mary, James, Benj. Nailor.
NEELY, HUGH, Will, 2-5-1805. Dev.:
Thom., Rachel, Sarah, and Flovenor
Neeley; Bazeleel Meek, Ealenor Mc-
Carde.
NEELY, RACHEL, Will, 11-14-1830.
Dev.: Hugh Neely, Rachel and Nancy
Catz.
NELLY, FLORENNA, Will, 5-1817. Dev.:
Rach., Hugh, Wm., John, Basil, John
Nelly; and Hugh Harris.
NELSON, JOHN, Will, 8-7-1810. Dev.:
Isabella, John, James, and Jos. Nel-
son; Mary Poak, Isabella Martin,
Frances Caldwell, Marg., Houston,
Eliz. Waddle.
NELSON, JOHN, Will, 4-19-1821. Dev.:
Marg., Robt., Joe., Thom., Benj., Isa-
bella, Marg., Mary and James Nel-
son.
NENSWANGER, CHRISTIAN, Will, 2-
20-1828. Dev.: Abraham, John, Ann,
Susan, Sally and Mary Nenswanger,
Mary Hars.
NEWBERRY, THOM., Will, 5-18-1777.
Dev.: Geo. McColloch, Sr., Rebecca,
Geo. Jr., Silas McColloch.
NICHOLAS, JOHN, Will, 2-9-1800. Dev.:
Rebeccah, Amos, Ed. Mathiah, Ann,
Jos., John Nicholas; Marg. Dover,
Anna White, Mary Foster, Sarah
Brown.
NICKOLDS, REBECKAH, Will, 8-21-
1811. Dev.: Nancy, Jos., John, Amos,
Mathew, Ed., Mathew, and Hannah
Nickolds, Mary Foster, Anna Ham-
met, Marg. Hover.
OLDHAM, ISAAC, Will, 4-1821. Dev.:
Sarah, Wm., Sarah, John, James,
Robt., Sam., Hannah, Isaac, Thom.,
Cath., Mary, Esther, Alley and Eliz.
Oldham.
PATTERSON, JOEL, Will, 2-20-1816.
Dev.: Margara Patterson.

PATTERSON, JOHN, Will, 6-1-1791. Dev.: Marg., Joel, Robt., Sarah, Agnes Susanah Patterson.

PATTERSON, ROBT., Will, 5-7-1822. Dev.: Jane, James, John, Wm., Nancy, Sally, Amy, Elcy, Marg., and Jane Patterson.

PATTERSON, THOM., Will, 8-16-1845. Dev.: John, Nancy, Eliz., Rachel, Sarath, Jos., and Mrs. Patterson.

PAUL, ROBT., Will, 12-9-1820. Dev.: Mary, Wm., John, Jane, Elener, Mary, Eliz., Agness, Rosanna, Andrew and St. Anthony Paul.

PEMBERTON, JAMES, Will, 8-14-1839. Dev.: Hannah, Thom., Adeline, Eliz., Wm., and Sarah Pemberton.

PERRINE, WM., Will, 4-5-1817. Dev.: Ann, Eliz., James, Lewis, and Hannah Perrine.

PERSON, JOHN, Will, 9-12-1817. Dev.: Eleanor, James, David, Henry Pierson; Marg. Musterd, Mary Maxwell.

PETTIT, JAMES, Will, 5-16-1823. Dev.: Wm., Eliz., and James Pettit, Sid. Thompson.

PHIPPEN, DAMARIS, Will, 4-3-1849. Dev.: Mary, Geo., James, and John Phippen, Eliz. Barnard.

PHIPPEN, RICE, Will, 12-20-1842. Dev.: Damaris Phippen.

POGUE, ROBT., Will, 3-14-1830. Dev.: Nancy, Gabriel, Elijah, and Eliz. Pogue.

POLLOCK, HAMILTON, Will, 9-23-1824. Dev.: Thom., Stephen, Cath., Jane, Eliz., Isabella, Mary, Leticia, Isabella, Ham., Ann, Marg., and James Pollock.

POLLOCK, STEPHEN, Will, 4-30-1811. Dev.: Jane and Hamilton Pollock; James Johnston.

POTTER, FREEDOM, Will, 4-5-1828. Dev.: Lucy Potter.

POTTER, PAUL, Will, 4-26-1825. Dev.: Mary Potter.

PURCELL, JAMES, Will, 6-3-1840. Dev.: Nancy, Betsy, and Martha Purcell; Jane, James, John, Dan., and Angus McCoy; Marg. Myers, Nancy and Furgus Smith; Mary Yates.

RALSTON, JAMES, Will, 5-6-1815. Dev.: Mary and Ebenezer Ralston.

RAY, NANCY, Will, 8-19-1845. Dev.: John, Nancy, May and Jos. Ray; Charlotte Clark, Mary Maryland, Sam. Hiram.

RAY, ROBT., Will, 4-1-1834. Dev.: Sarah, Mary, Harvey Jr., Ruth and John.

RAY, THOM., Will, 8-24-1838. Dev.: Nancy, Jos., James, John, Sam., and Hiram Ray; Charlotte Clark, Mary Marlin.

REED, JAMES, Will, 11-2-1820. Dev.: Ann, India, Mary, Clemont, Ann, John, and Rachel Reed.

REED, JAMES, SR., Will, 12-22-1835. Dev.: Wm., John, James, David, and Mrs. Reed. Jane McCament, Marg. Pourter, Nancy Pickens, Isabella McMurrey.

REEVES, CALEB, Will, 4-26-1841. Dev.: Micojoh, Nancy and Cochrene Reeves; Bethan, Mary Jane, Wm., David and Sarah Boggs.

REYNOLDS, WM., Will, 6-28-1839. Dev.: Marg. and James Reynolds, Ann Shnody.

RICHARDS, MARY, Will, 6-21-1842. Dev.: James and Mary Richards; Eliz., Lucy, Hannah, Sarah, Adaline, and Geo. Hogg; Geo., Asa, and Mary Thatcher.

RICHARDSON, THOM., Will, 6-6-1836. Dev.: Marg., Sarah, Cecelia Richardson; Marg. Ainsworth, Louise Branch, Eliz. Little, Marg. Staby, Thom and John Astor.

ROBARDS, WM., Will, 8-28-1783. Dev.: Geo. McCollock.

ROBERTSON, CHAS., Will, 6-30-1812. Dev.: Sarah Robinson.

ROBERTS, CHRISTINA, Will, No date. Dev.: Marg. Chaney, Hannah, Anna, Abner, Thom., and Geo. Roberts; Mary, Ann, David, and Rachel Robertson.

ROBERTS, GEO., Will, 3-7-1816. Dev.: Wm., Anne, Sara, Mary, Marg., and Thom. Roberts.

ROBERTS, JOHN, Will, 1-25-1825. Dev.: Christiana, Abner, Thom., Geo., Jacob, Rich., Marg., David, John, Eliz., Ed., Jeremiah, Anna, Hannah, Rachel Roberts.

ROBINSON, AND., Will, 8-25-1812. Dev.: Eleanor and And. Frazer.

ROBINSON, ED., Will, 1-12-1783. Dev.: Aaron, Ed., Mary Robinson.

ROBINSON, JOHN, Will, 7-28-1830. Dev.: Christian, Rosan, James, Wesley, June, John, and Thom., Robinson; Nancy Fry, Mary Thompson, Eliz. Davison, Ruth Crump.

ROBINSON, REBECCAH, Will, 1-12-1841. Dev.: James, Isaac, Jos., and Jane Mays, Eliza Reed, Rev. Geo. Buchanon, Rev. Wm. Wallace, Thom. Johnston, Isaac Kelly, Alex. Anderson, Dr. John Presley, Home Missions, Theo. Seminary Alleghenytown, Short Creek Congregation.

ROBINSON, SAM., Will, 3-25-1835. Dev.: Rebecca Robinson, Isaac Kelly.

RODGERS, EZEKIAL, Will, 4-4-1846. Dev.: Sarah, Prudence, Nancy, Benj., and Nicolis Rodgers; Jane Meloclin, Socrates Eversole, Polly Rodgers.

RODGERS, NICHOLS, Will, 1-23-1806. Dev.: Mary, Abr., Ezek. Rodgers; Eliz. Stackhouse, Mary Berryhill, Martha Linn, John Rogers, Pru. Rowlana.

ROLFE, JOHN, Will, 1-11-1800. Dev.: James, Jane, Eliz. Rolfe.

RUCHMAN, SAM., Will, 1-10-1832. Dev.: Elenor, Moses, John, James, David, Thom., Sam., Elenor, Eliz., and Marg. Ruchman; Lucinda Strong, Sarah Welling.

SALSBERRY, JAMES, Will, 2-27-1849. Dev.: Eliz., Harry, James, David, Jos., and Wm. Salsberry; Hannah Scott, Sarah Land, Jane Cunningham.

SCHWOPE, JOHN HENRY, Will, 2-17-1841. Dev.: Cath. Schwope.

SCOTT, ANDREW, Will, 5-25-1826. Dev.: James Scott.

SEAMON, JONAH, Will, 1-15-1811. Dev.: Eliz., Robt., Geo., Sarah, Martha, Marg., Hettie, Rebecca, Mary, John, and Jer. Seamon.

SHARPE, JOHN, Will, 6-20-1846. Dev.: Eliz. and Abraham Sharpe.

SHELMERDINE, JOHN, Will, 4-27-1819. Dev.: Edwin and Grafton Shelmerdine; Augusta Cockney, Ann Kilgore.

SHEPHERD, DAVID, Will, 1-20-1795. Dev.: Rachel, Eliz., Moses Shepherd; Sarah Springer, Ruth Mills.

SHIELDS, SAM., Will, 10-23-1813. Dev.: Trusdale, Sarah, Mary, John, Betey, Jane, Geo., Peggy, and Sam Shields.

SIMMS, IGNATIUS, Will, 2-1806. Dev.: Joe Casta, Clement and Rich. Simms; Cath. and Rich. Small; Eliz. Goe.

SKINNERS, WALTER, Will, 3-11-1814. Dev.: Marg., Fred. Jemima, and Dan. Skinners.

SMITH, EMANUEL, Will, 8-13-1803. Dev.: Diana, John, Delilah, Chas., Eliz. Smith.

SMITH, GEO., Will, 5-30-1785. Dev.: Marcilius, Phillip, Henry Smith.

SMITH, JAMES, Will, 12-5-1785. Dev.: Elander Smith.

SMITH, JAMES, Will, 11-15-1790. Dev.: Wife: Henry, Thom., James Smith.

SMITH, JANE, Will, 1830. Dev.: Sam. Smith, Cath. Henderson, Mary Fowler.

SMITH, JOHN, Will, 10-2-1833. Dev.: Eliz. Smith.

SMITH, JOHN, Will, 1-1-1835. Dev.: Martha, Jane, Wm., and Eliz. Smith.

SMITH, MARY, Will, 2-5-1848. Dev.: Henry, John, Geo., David, Jos., Fergus, Mary, Wm., and Henry Smith; Eliz. Keenan, Jane Shively, Pleasant and Mary Millen, Sarah and Mary Ritchey, Mary Williams, Mary Newton, Rebecca and Furgus Roberts.

SMITH, NOAH, Will, 11-9-1801. Dev.: Terssissa, Fanny, Nancy, Laury and Livingston Smith; Terssissa Owens.

SMITH, THOM., Will, 12-14,1806. Dev.: Jerucis, Henry and Jos. Smith.

SMITH, WM., Will, 1844. Dev.: John and Wm. Smith.

SNODGRASS, MARY, Will, 6-22-1796. Dev.: Alex. Leeperson, Thom. Cunningham, Mary Sample, Jeanie, Jos., Alex., Mary, James, Marg. Snodgrass.

SOCKMAN, JOHN, Will, 6-18-1826. Dev.: Cath. and John Sockman.

SPAHR, ANN, Will, 2-20-1833. Dev.: Thom., Amelia, Jos., and Sam. Laws, Eliz. Spahr; Sina McFarland, Rebeccah McFarland.

SPRIGG, ZACH. Will, 5-26-1828. Dev.: Eliz., Sam., H. S., James and Horatio Sprigg; Zach., Jacob, Lucindia Yarnell, Charlotte, Lucindia and Jane Croes, Cynthia Jacobs, Cynthia Lane, Eliza Greathouse.

STEWART, MARY, Will, 1-15-1842. Dev.: Juliet Stewart and Robt. Williamson.

STEWART, ROBT., Will, 10-31-1805. Dev.: Martha, John, Wm., Rossanah, Edie, Robt. Stewart, Agnes Farris, Sarah Watt, Mary Kirkwood, Jenny Bell, Martha Porterfield.

STEWART, ROBT., Will, 4-3-1833. Dev.: Mary, Sam., Nancy, Fleming, Irwin, Thom., John, and Wm. Stewart, Jane Cunningham.

STEWART, ROBT., SR., Will, 8-30-1836. Dev.: Mary, Hugh, Thom., Robt., Jos., and James Stewart; Robt. and Eliz. Waddle; Agnes Williamson, Esther Miller.

STEWART, WM., Will, 5-30-1836. Dev.: Robt., John, Wm., James, Edia, Rebecca, and Jane Stewart; Martha, James, Wm., and Jos. Bell.

STRICKER, GEO., Will, 11-7-1810. Dev.: Eliz. Bueky, John Stricker, Mary Bell.

STRICKER, SID., Will, 11-26-1808. Dev.: Sam. McColloch, Cath., Sid., and Jane Stricker; Ben McMechen, Sarah Boggs, Sis. Barr, Jane Taylor.

STROUP, CONRAD, Will, 5-31-1786. Dev.: Marg., Henry, John, Susanah, Sarah, Cath., Eliz. Stroup.

STUMP, JOHN, Will, 7-9-1829. Dev.: Sarah Stump.

SWEARINGIN, ZACH., Will, 2-19-1799. Dev.: Phoebe, Nancy, Mary Swearingin.

SWEARINGTON, VANN, Will, 11-5-1793. Dev.: Elzey, Zach., Eleanor, Vann, Thom. Swearington; Durcilla, Vann, John Brady.

TANNER, JOS., Will, 12-30-1840. Dev.: Deborah Tanner.

TAYLOR, JOHN, Will, 9-30-1813. Dev.: Martha Patterson, Susanah Hupp, James, Geo., John, Robt., Thom. Wm., David, and Eleanor Taylor.

TERRELL, DAN, Will, 6-10-1844. Dev.: Jane, Jeremiah, Adam, Robt., and Dan. Terrell; Mary Coates, Rebecca Watson, Marg. Thompson, Ruth Hartong.

TERRILL, JURUD, Will, 8-1-1799. Dev.: Sarah, Geo., Jevie, Abner, Eber, Jerud, Cherisa, Rodab, Peter, Dan., Ely, John Terril, Amos Scarmuhom.

THOMPSON, WM., Will, 1-12-1839. Dev.: Geo. Eliz., John, Robt., and Wm. Thompson; Eliz. Steenrod.

TODD, WM., Will, 4-13-1828. Dev.: Eliz., Wm., James, and John Todd.

TOMLINSON, JOS., Will, 10-24-1824. Dev.: Sam., Jos., Robt., Jos., Nat., Eliz., and Jessey Tomlinson; Wm., Eliza, Dru., and Betsy McMahon, Dru. Buky, Mary Kenard, Lucy Riggs.

TUFFORD, JUDETH, Will, 6-16-1832. Dev.: Eliz. Harris.

TURNER, MARY, Will, 3-31-1834. Dev.: Mary Israel, John Parriott.

TUSH, GEO., Will, 7-17-1806. Dev.: Marg., Neriah, Mary, Eliz., and Rachel Tush.

UPDGRAFF, JOSIAH, Will, 6-30-1815. Dev.: Mrs. and Israel Updgraff.

VANDERANTER, NICH., Will, 4-12-1832. Dev.: Clovah, John, Jane, Cornelius, Nich., and Mary Vanderanter; Ann Roberts.

VANMETRE, JOS., Will, 1822. Dev.: Marg., Robt., Sarah, Jos., and Vinc. VanMetre.

VANSCYOE, ABEL, Will, 7-30-1814. Dev.: John, Cornelius, James, Aron, Ann, Mary, Cath., and Ruth Vanschoe.

WADDEL, WM., Will, 4-29-1929. Dev.: Eliz., Wm., John, Benjane and James Waddel.

WADDLE, JOHN, Will, 3-27-1818. Dev.: Jos., John, Robt., Josh., and Mrs. Waddle; Eliz. Neilson, Marg. Atkinson, Mary Platt.

WARD, JOS., Will, 3-3-1825. Dev.: Wm., Jos., Hester, Eliz., John, and Jane Ward; Anne Moore.

WARNOCK, JOHN, Will, 9-10-1839. Dev.: Isabella, Wm., John, Sarah, Robt., and James Warnock; Jane Robb, Isabella McMillan, Rebecca Bigger.

WARNOCK, REBECCA, Will, 12-3-1810. Dev.: David, Wm., and Robt. Warnock; James Farell, Mary McDonald, Martha Stewart.

WASHINGTON, LAWRENCE, Will, 10-30-1823. Dev.: Mary Washington.

WATSON, JOHN, Will, 1-5-1839. Dev.: Mary Watson.

WAYMAN, SAM., Will, 6-1-1845. Dev.: Sarah and Martin Wayman, Eliz. Woodcock.

WAYMAN, THOM., Will, 1-6-1826. Dev.: Saray, Wm., Leonard, John, Zach., and Sam., Wayman; Mary Hughes, Dorcas Welling, Harriet Smith, Mohala Bane.

WAYT, JOHN, Will, 11-18-1817, 3-13-1818. Dev.: Mary, Robt., and Nat. Wayt.

WAYTS, NAT., Will, 12-24-1845. Dev.: Wm., Sarah, Susan, James, John and Andrew Wayts; Polly Pollock, Mendi Messionary Soc.

WELLS, BENJ., Will, 11-26-1790. Dev.: Temperance, Benj., Amos, Caleb, Sarah, Chas., Abraham, Wm. Wells; Temperance Talbot.

WHEAT, CONRAD, Will, 3-14-1781. Dev.: Conrad, Jacob, Marg., Molly Wheat; Martin Coon.

WHITE, ANDREW, Will, 8-18-1821. Dev.: Sol., Ebenezer, Isaac, Eliz., M., Mary, Eliz., and James White; Sarah Howel.

WHITE, ANDREW, Will, 1-17-1849. Dev.: Hester, John and Andrew White.

WHITE, JOHN, Will, 12-25-1825. Dev.: Sally and Andrew White.

WHITE, JOHN, Will, 1-6-1831. Dev.: Eliz., Eliza, John, Thom., Wm., Robt., and Alex. Smith, Marg. Myers.

WHITE, ROBT., Will, 5-3-1803. Dev.: Rebeccah, Rachel, Jos., Anne, Ruth, Leah and Margert White.

WHITE, SAM., Will, 8-9-1778. Dev.: Jemima White, Eliz. Meek, Marg. Rollins.

WHITTAM, JOS., Will, 2-4-1843. Dev.: Peregrine, Wm., John, Jos., Geo., Rachel, and Sarah Whittam; Henry Martin.

WILLCOXTON, HENRY H., Will, 8-22-1792. Dev.: Toccastos and Antony Willcoxton.

WILLIAMS, THOM., Will, 11-9-1802. Dev.: Marg., Jonethen, Pressellir, John, Hugh, Rebecca, Ruth, Thom., Hannery, Cesia, Ellender and Marget Williams.

WILLIAMSON, MOSES, Will, 4-8-1789. Dev.: Jean, John, Thom., Jane Williamson.

WILLIAMSON, WM., Will, 5-8-1849. Dev.: Marg. and Mrs. Williamson.

WILSON, LEWIS, Will, 2-29-1828. Dev.: Rosanna Willson.

WILSON, CATH., Will, 6-8-1848. Dev.: Enoch and Peter Wilson; Mary Mathews.

WILSON, DAVID, Will, 11-11-1843. Dev.: Alex. Wilson.

WILSON, EUGENIUS, Will, 5-21-1831. Dev.: Mary, Edgar, Norvel, Agness, Louisa, Julia, Geo., and Alpheus Wilson; Thom. Ray.

WILSON, FRED., Will, 3-20-1834. Dev.: Wm., Geo., Jacob, Mary, Susan, Jos., Cath., Thom., and Sam. Wilson.

WILSON, GEO., Will, 5-7-1834. Dev.: Rebeckah, Sam., and Jos. Wilson.

WILSON, HENRY, Will, 7-13-1835. Dev.: Eleanor, Senne, Sevnia, and Cath. Wilson; Rebeckah and Terusha Shook, Eliz. Tittle.

WILSON, JOHN, Will, 4-9-1818. Dev.: Rebeckah, Jos., Lewis, Cath., Sarah and Lavinia Wilson; Rebeckah Applegate, Rachel Cully.

WILSON, JOS., Will, 8-7-1823. Dev.: Rachel and Polly Cully; Cath., Lavinia, Rebeckah, Jos., Lewis Wilson; Cath., Dimit, Sarah McColloch, Nancy Dimit, Sarah Pierce, Susan Philips, Hannah Egbert.

WILSON, JOS., Will, 5-17-1825. Dev.: Cath., Jos., James, Wm., Jos., Cath., Thom., Geo., Jacob, Mary, Fred., and Geo. Wilson; Susannah Perkinson.

WILSON, WM., Will, 4-13-1829. Dev.: Sarah, Robt., Mich., Thom., and Rebecca Wilson; James Pearce, Mary Mackall.

WOODS, ANDREW, Will, 2-10-1831. Dev.: Andrew, Robt., and Alf. Woods; Jane Hoge, Marg., and Dr. Archd Todd.

WOODS, ROBT., Will, 8-16-1830. Dev.: Eliz., Robt., And., and Thom. Woods; Robt., Susan, James, Eliza, and Friend Cox.

WORTHINGTON, THOM., Will, no date. Dev.: Cath., Mary Ann, Eliz., Jacob, Wm. Worthington.

WRIGHT, ANN, Will, 12-8-1845. Dev.: Alex. and Ann Jefferson.

WYNKOOP, HANNAH, Will, 12-20-1825. Dev.: Levi and Hannah Gooding.

YATES, THOM., SR., Will, 9-18-1846. Dev.: Thom., Elenor, Mary, And., Wm., Jos., John, Mary, Adam, and Jane Yates; Colonization Soc., Bible Soc., Martha Dunlap, Dorothy, Thom., Mary, Wm., and James Hervey.

YOUNG, HENERY, Will, 7-16-1810. Dev.: Nancy Perris, Moses and Wm. Young.

ZANE, EBENEZER, Will, 8-5-1811. Dev.: Noah, Dan., Eliz. Zane; Rebeckah Clark, Cath. Martin.

ZANE, JOHN, Will, 11-4-1805. Dev.: Eliz. Sprigg, Noah Zane.

ZANE, NOAH, Will, 10-28-1831. Dev.: Mary, Ebenezer, Platoff, Hambdin, Eliz., Cornelia, Sophia, and Mary Zane.

West Virginia Estate Settlements

In 1936 and 1937, the West Virginia Commission on Historic and Scenic Markers, the Works Progress Administration, and the Federal Emergency Relief Administration compiled court records of the various counties, such as Births, Deaths, Marriages, and Wills. Under Wills were grouped subjects pertaining to Estate Settlements, including Wills, Inventories, and Appraisements. Copies of these county records were filed at the Department of Archives and History, Charleston; the Library of West Virginia University, Morgantown; and the DAR Library, Washington.

Believing that there would be particular interest on the part of the general public in the Estate Settlements in the older counties, the West Virginia Historical Society has undertaken to abstract the Estate Settlement Records, as filed in the State Department of Archives and History, and offer them for publication in the *West Virginia History Quarterly.* (No responsibility can be assumed as to the accuracy of the copies made from the original records.)

There are 13 counties which were formed prior to 1800, and it has been agreed to arrange these counties in chronological order, and to print their records from the earliest date to 1850. The formation dates of these counties are as follows: Hampshire—1753; Berkeley—1772; Monongalia—1776; Ohio—1776; Greenbrier—1778; Harrison—1784; Hardy—1786; Randolph—1787; Pendleton—1788; Kanawha—1788; Brooke—1797; Wood—1798; and Monroe—1799.

Greenbrier County Formed 1778

Abbreviations used in this material include: App.—appraisal; Bro.—brother; Dau.—daughter; Dev.—devisees; Inv.—inventory; S.B.—sale bill; Set.—settlement; Sis.—sister; Ven.—vendue.

ADAIR, JAMES, Will, 9-1839. Dev.: Mary, wife; Robt., Wm., James, sons; Jane, Mary Level, daus.

ADAIR, JAMES, App., 11-1843.

AIRY, CUTLIP, App., 11-1822.

ALDERSON, JOS., Will, 8-1845. Dev.: Polly, wife; Polly Lewis, Patsy Feamster, daus.; Geo., Lewis, sons.

ALDERSON, JOS., App., 9-1845.

ALEXANDER, JAMES, Will, 2-1849. Dev.: Marg., wife; Julia Larue, Martha Palinia, Ann, Esthe Johnston, daus.; Robt., Wm., James, sons.

ALLEN, ANSON, App., 3-1839.

ALTHARE, JACOB, App., 11-1832.

ANDERSON, JOHN, Will, 11-28-1817. Dev.: Betsy, wife; others.

ANDERSON, JOHN, App., 12-8-1817.

ANDRICK, CHRISTIAN, Will, 2-27-1816. Dev.: Christian, Jacob, Fred., sons; Martha Cook, Mary Sulser, Nancy Nickle, Eliz. Stars, daus.

ARBAUGH, ADAM, Will, 3-27-1800. Dev.: Mary, wife; John, Mich., Adam, sons; Sophia, Eave Baker, Christian Dozer. Caty Fleshman, Mary Sowards, Eliz. Fleshman, Lucy Claypool, Barb. Miller, daus.

ARBAUGH, JOHN, App., 11-1808.

ARBUCKLE, CHARLES, Will, 4-1846. Dev.: Esther, wife; Charles, son; Rebecca Poage, Frances McPoage, Emily Creigh, Betsy Graham, Mary Feamster, daus.

ARBUCKLE, ESTHER, Will, 12-1846. Dev.: Rebecca Poage, Frances McPoage, Emily Creigh, Mary Feamster, daus.

ARBUCKLE, MATHEW, CAPT., App., 11-20-1781.

ARBUCKLE, MATHEW CAPT., Inv., 11-20-1781.

ARBUCKLE, MATHEW, Inv., 11-23-1786.

ARMSTRONG, JANE, Will, 9-1848. Dev. Sarah Elliott, Ann Walkup, Eliz. Elliott, adopted daus.

ARMSTRONG, JOHN, Will, 8-1846. Dev.: Jane, wife; Archibald, Wm., bro.; Marg., Rebecca, sis.

ARMSTRONG, JOHN, App., 2-1847.

ARMSTRONG, JOHN, S.B., 2-1847.

ARNOLD, JOHN, Will, 3-26-1815. Dev.: Abigale, wife; Jos., son; others.

ARNOLD, JOHN, App., 4-1816.

ATTLEE, JAMES, Will, 6-1800. Dev.: Marg., Sam., Thom. Beard; Robt. Stephen and John Myles, James, Hanna.

BAILEY, MATILDA, Will, 9-1832. Dev.: Ed., bro.; Mary Minter, sis.

BALLENTINE, WM. App., 1-1792.

BALLEWS, LENORD, Will, 11-19-1785. Dev.: Jane, wife; Barb., dau.; John, son; Lenord, grandson.

BARNES, OZIAS, Inv., 8-20-1782.

BARNS, OZIAS, App., 8-20-1782.

BEARD, JANNETT, Will, 8-1819. Dev.: Sam., Wm., Joniah, sons; Mary, Jane Armstrong, daus.

BEARD, JANNETT, App., 9-1819.

BEARD, JOHN, App., 10-1807.

BEARD, JOHN, Will, 9-27-1808. Dev.: Jannett, wife; Agnes, Sabina, Betsey, Jane, Mary, daus.; Wm., Josiah, sons.

BEARD, THOMAS, Will, 11-22-1814. Dev.: Jannat, Wm., and Betsy Beard.

BEARD, THOMAS, App., 12-1815.

BEAZLEY, MARY, Will, 12-1818. Dev.: Ann, sis.

BEDFORD, WM., Will, 6-1820. Dev.: Fanny, wife.

BEDFORD, WM., App., 10-1820.

BENNETT, ELI, S.B., 8-16-1839.

BENNETT, ELI, App., 2-1840.

BENNETT, THOM., Will, 2-1839. Dev.: Eliz., wife; Mary, Caty Persinger, Mary, daus.; Elijah, Jesse, Ely, Sol., John, Aaron, Sam., sons.

BENNETT, THOMAS, App., 2-1840.

BIRD, THOMAS, App., 6-1824.

BLACK, JOS., Will, 11-1843. Dev.: Abigail, wife; Wm., John, Sam., Henderson, sons; Abigail, Rebecca, daus.

BLACK, JOS., App., 12-28-1843.

BLAKE, WM., Will, 10-1831. Dev.: Lewis, Wm., Moses, Chas., sons; Jane, Polly, Eliz., Sally, daus.

BLAKE, WM., App., 3-1832.

BOGGS, JAMES, Will, 2-1806. Dev.: Marg., wife; James, Alex., sons.

BOGGS, JAMES, App., 9-1806.

BOSTICK, MOSES, App., 10-1799.

BOURLAND, WM., App., 9-1832.

BOWEN, ANTHONY, Will, 10-30-1787. Dev.: Ellis, wife; And., Wm., Anthony, James, sons; Susanna, Hanna, Polly, Betsy, daus.

BOWMAN, JOHN, Will, 1-1820. Dev.: Children of brother Peter, and children of sister Kath. Detwider.

BOWMAN, JOHN, App., 2-1820.

BOWYER, WM., Will, 10-1823. Dev.: John, Frances, Henry, Wm., James, Lewis; Mary Caldwell, sis.

BRAND, JOHN, App., 3-1824.

BRIGHT, DAVID, Will, 9-28-1808. Dev.: Mary, wife; Jefse, Mich., David, Geo., sons; others.

BRIGHT, MICHAEL, Will, 9-1833. Dev.: Sarah, wife; David, Jesse, Michael, Kyle, Washington, sons; Eliz., Sarah, Mary, Ann, daus.

BRITT, WM., App., 12-1826.

BROOKS, HARRISON, App., 6-1840.

BROOKS, HARRISON, S.B., 1-1843.

BROWN, JAMES, App., 1-1804.

BROWN, JAS., App., 2-1808.

BROWN, SAM., Will, 12-31-1793. Dev.: Alex., John, bros.; Marg., Sally, Martha, Dorthe, sis; Wm., son.

BROWN, SAM., App., 1-8-1794.

BROWN, SAM., App., 7-1827.

BROWN, SAM., Will, 4-1828. Dev.: Eliz., wife; Nancy Miller, dau.

BROWN, WM., Will, 11-1826. Dev.: Sarah, wife; Sam., John, Geo., Wm., James, sons; Sarah Rogers, dau.

BROWN, WM., App., 3-1828.

BRYANT, MARTIN, App., 8-1823.

BUCKHANNON, CHARLES, App., 9-1804.

BUNGER, FETTY, Will, 9-30-1906. Dev.: Eliz., wife; Carthren, dau.; Jacob, John, sons.

BURGAIN, THOMAS, App., no date.

BURGOIN, THOM., Inv., no date.

BURR, AARON, Will, 8-1834. Dev.: Rebecca, wife; Peter, Aaron, John, sons; Nancy, Lucinda, Isabel, daus.

BURR, JOHN, Will, 4-26-1808. Dev.: Sarah, wife; Abigal Commings, Cloe Shepard, Sarah Gay, Hulda Howdashatt, daus.; Aros, Pete, Stephen, Reubin, sons.

BURR, JOHN, App., 7-1808.

BURR, STEPHEN, S.B., 12-1811.

BURR, T., App. & S.B., 11-1810.

BUSTER, CLAUDIAN, App., 11-1842.

BUTT, THOM., SR., Will, 3-1833. Dev.: Polly, wife; Geo., Ed., Thom., sons; Lydia, dau.

CAHOON, CHAS., Will, 7-1814. Dev.: John, son; Frances Malinda, step-dau.

CAIN, JOHN, App., 3-1822.

CAIN, JOHN, Vendue, 2-1827.

CALHOON, CHARLES, App., 9-1814.

CALLISON, ISAAC, App., 10-1836.

CALLISON, ISAAC, App., 3-1837.

CALLISON, JAMES, App., 6-1792.

CALLISON, JAMES, Will, 7-1827. Dev.: Betsy Morrison, sis.

CALLISON, JAMES, App., 11-1829.

CAMPBELL, JOHN, App., 3-1803.

CAMPBELL, JOHN, Will, 1-25-1803. Dev.: Hannah, Jane, Sarah, Marthe, Mary, Rebecah, daus.

CARAWAY, THOMAS, App., 8-8-1848.

CARLILIS, DAVID, Inv., 8-10-1786.

CARLISLE, DAVID, App., 8-18-1786.

CARRELL, SAM., S.B., 9-1819.

CART, ADAM, Will, 8-1826. Dev.: Cath., wife; Thom., David, Leonard, Conrod, Thom., sons; Marg. Brown, Nancy Parker, Polly, Eve, Susannah, daus.

CART, ADAM, App., 8-1827.

CHAPMAN, BOTTEN, Will, 2-1836. Dev.: Eliz., mother; Polly Thompson, Emily, sisters; Abraham, Geo., Jos., Jacob, John, bros.

CHAPMAN, JOHN, App., 12-1826.

CHAPMAN, JOHN, S.B., 12-1826.

CHRIST, HENRY, Will, 8-1842. No devisees listed.

CHRISTAL, WM., Will, 6-1796. Dev.: Marg., dau.; others.

CHRISTIAN, ELLISON, App., 7-17-1794.

CLARK, ALEX., Will, 10-1794. Dev.: James, Wm., Ralph, Elex., John, Sam., sons; Rebekah, Martha, daus.; Sarah, wife.

CLARK, ALEX., App., 4-1795.

CLAYPOOL, JAMES, App., 4-27-1790.

CLAYPOOL, JOS., Will, 1-20-1785. Dev.: Ephrom, Jos., Jeramiah, James, sons.

CLAYPOOL, JOSEPH, Inv., 4-27-1790.

CLINEBELL, DAVID, App., 5-1849.

CLINEBELL, DAVID, Will, 4-1849. Dev.: Susan, wife; Robt., son.

CLINGMAN, JACOB, App., 7-1829.

COALTER, MARY, Will, 2-1825. Dev.: John, Moses, sons.

COCKBURN, ROBT., Will, 9-1810. Dev.: Isabell, Sarah, Eliz., daus.

COCKE, JESSE, Will, 2-1822. Dev.: Mother, sisters, brothers.

COFFMAN, MICHAEL, Will, 12-1842. Dev.: Mary, wife; John, Sam., Jacob, sons; Mary Hutchison, Anna Lewis, Susan Stuart, daus.

COFFMAN, MICHAEL, App., 1-4-1843.

COFFMAN, MICHAEL, S.B., 1-1843.

COLE, RICHARD, Will, 6-1838. Dev.: Rich., son.

COMBER, WM., App., no date.

COMBS, JOHN, Will, 4-1841. Dev.: James Scott, friend.

COMBS, JOHN, App., 1-1842.

COMBS, JOHN, S.B., 1-1842.

COMER, FRED, Will, 11-1823. Dev.: Anna, wife; Eve, dau.; George, grandson.

CONNER, JOHN, Will, 4-26-1791. Dev.: Eliz., wife; James, John, sons.

CONNOR, JOHN, App., 6-28-1791.

CONRAD, GEO., App., 5-19-1784.

CONRAD, GEO., Set., 8-20-1793.

CONRODS, GEO., Inv., 5-12-1784.

COOK, VALLENTINE, Will, 12-1797. Dev.: Susanna, wife; Jacob, Vallentine, Adam, sons.

COOKE, THOM., Inv., no date.

CORRELL, JOHN, App., 11-1838.

CORRELL, JOHN, Will, 7-1838. Dev.: Sam., Jos., John, Buber, James, sons; Mary Waite, Eliz. Waite, Martha Myles, Agness, Marg., Sarah, daus.

CORRELL, JOHN, S.B., 1-1839.

COTTLE, URIAH, Will, 4-13-1779. Dev.: Wife; Chas., Wm., sons.

COTTLE, URIAH, Inv., 5-17-1786.

COTTLE, URIAH, Set., 5-17-1786.

COULTER, JOHN, Will, 2-22-1814. Dev.: Mary, wife; Geo., son; Hannah Delaney, Polly Brown, Sally Snodgrass, Jean Brown, daus.; John, Robt., John Moses, sons.

COX, JESSE, App., 6-1822.

CRAIG, ROBT., Will, 9-20-1804. Dev.: Nancy, wife; Robt., son; Jane, Betsy, Rebecca, Mary, Nancy, Marg., daus.

CRAIG, ROBT., App., 12-1804.

CRAIG, ROBT., Will, 12-1813. Dev.: John, bro.; Peggy, Rebecca Benson, Ann Benson, Sarah Westlake, sis.

CRAIG, ROBT., App., 3-1814.

CRAIGE, WM., App., 5-1799.

CRANE, JOS., Will, 3-1839. Dev.: Sarah Ann, wife; Mary Jane, dau.; Ed., Wm., Geo., Jos., Benj., James, sons.

CRANE, JOS., App., 8-12-1839.

CRAWFORD, JAMES, Will, 3-1836. Dev.: John, James, Wm., Hiram, sons.

CRAWFORD, JAMES, App., 2-1837.

CRAWFORD, MARY, Will, 2-1828. Dev.: Sam., McClung, son-in-law.

CRAWFORD, WM., App., 2-23-1846.

CREEK, REBECCA, Will, 1-1800. Dev.: John, Jos., Jacob, sons; Ann Cegor, Susannah Cegor, Mary Combs, Eliz. Nicholas, daus.

CREIGH, JENNET, Will, 12-1833. Dev.: Thom., bro.; Jennet, niece.

CREIGH, THOMAS, App., 1-29-1849.

CRIST, HENRY, App., 1-1843.

CRISTALL, WM., App., 9-1797.

CROOKSHANKS, JOHN, App., 10-1822.

CURRY, OLIVER, App., 1-1838.

CURTNER, CATH., Will, 2-1844. Dev.: Phoebe and James Daugherty.

CUTLIP, DAVID, Will, 3-1822. Dev.: Sam., son.

DANGERFIELD, JOS., Will, 10-1840. Dev.: Sally, wife; Wm., Jos., Fauntleroy, sons; Mary, dau.

DARING, COONROD, Will, 5-1841. Dev.: Molly, wife; Adam, James, Jacob, John, sons; Sarah Brown, Hanna Jones, Marg. Suttle, Mary, daus.

DARING, CONROD, App., 9-1841.

DAVID, WM., App., 3-31-1847.

DAVIS, JOHN, Will, 4-1800. Dev.: Jean, wife; Polly, Sally, Jean, Rebecah, Nancy Fear, daus.

DAVIS, WALTER, Will, 9-1800. Dev.: Elioner, wife; Sarah Bracken, Nancy Dixon, sis.; others.

DAVIS, WALTER, App., 10-1800.

DAVIS, WM., App., 3-31-1847.

DEARING, CONROD, S.B., 8-1841.

DECKER, GEO., App., 12-18-1802.

DICKENS, PHOEBIE, Inv., 2-15-1791.

DICKSON, JOHN, Will, 9-26-1809. Dev.: Eliz., wife; Jos., Rich., John, sons; Jane, Eliz., daus.

DICKSON, JOS., Will, 7-1822. Dev.: Nancy, wife; Robt., Jos., John, Geo., Sam., sons; Margrans Nevins, dau.

DIXON, JOSEPH, App., 9-1822.

DOLAN, J. W., Will, 6-1847. Dev.: Margary, Rachael Robinson, sis.; Robt., bro.

DONALDSON, JAMES, Set., 11-1817.

DORAN, JACOB, Will, 9-24-1793. Dev.: Cath., wife.

DORAN, JACOB, App., 1-1794.

DORMAN, JOHN, Will, 8-1839. Dev.: Stephen, Nehemiah, bro.

DORMAN, JOHN, List, 6-27-1844.

DOTSON, THOMAS, S.B., 8-1825.

DOTSON, THOMAS, App., 6-1827.

DOUGHERTY, WM., App., 10-1828.

DOZER, HENRY, App., 10-1846.

DOZER, HENRY, S.B., 10-1846.

DRENEN, LAWRENCE, Inv., 6-18-1784.

DRENEN, LAWRENCE, App., 6-19-1784.

DRINON, LAWRENCE, Inv., 11-7-1784.

DRINEN, LAWRENCE, App., 11-17-1784.

DUFFY, M., App., 8-1827.

DUNBAR, JOHN, Will, 6-17-1794. Dev.: Sarah, wife; Reubin, John, Sam., sons; Eliz. Whitman, Ann Claypool, Sarah Warren, Marg., daus.

DUNBAR, JOHN, App., 7-29-1794.

DUNBAR, MATHEW, App., 4-1797.

DUNBAR, MATT., Set., 4-1807.

DUNCAN, JOHN, App., 12-1825.

DUNN, GEO., App., 7-1848.

DUNN, JOHN, S.B., 6-1843.

DUNN, JOHN, Inv., 6-1843.

DUNN, WM., Will, 8-1821. Dev.: Hanna, wife; Ralph, John, Geo., Wm., sons; Betsey Dunn, Nancy Sharp, daus.

DUNN, WM., App., 4-1822.

EAGLE, ABRAHAM, App., 1-1833.

EAGLE, JOHN, JR., App., 10-1848.

EDGAR, THOMAS, Will, 7-1822. Dev.: Ann, wife; Thom., Archer, sons; Nancy, Eliz., Letitia, Sally, daus.

EDGAR, THOMAS, App., 8-1822.
EDGAR, WM., Will, 8-1848. Dev.: Eliz.,
wife; James, Geo., Wm., Edwin, sons;
Mary, Sarah, Nancy, Tabitha, Sune,
Martha Holt, daus.
ELIOT, JAMES & MARG., Inv., 4-1831.
ELIOTT, JAMES, Will, 6-27-1815. Dev.:
Ann, wife; Wm., Arch., Robt., Thom.,
John, James, sons; Jenny Carreck,
Ann Kincaid, daus.
ELIOTT, JAMES, App., 11-1815.
ELLIOTT, JAMES, Inv., 10-1830.
ELLIS, JAMES, App., 7-1848.
ELLIS, JAMES, S.B., 1-1849.
ELLISON, JAMES, Will, 12-27-1791.
Dev.: James, Jos., John, sons; Asa
Hayns, Ruth, Marey Paul, daus.; John
Paul, grandson; Ann, wife.
ERSKINE, HENRY, Will, 11-1847. Dev.:
Agatha, wife; Eliz. Crocket, Marg.,
Jane, daus.
ERSKINE, HENRY, App., 10-31-1848.
ERSKINE, HENRY, App., 12-1848.
ERVIN, BENJ., Will, 11-1848. Dev.:
Eliz. McClure, Cath., Esther, daus.:
Charles, John, Sam., James, sons.
ERVIN, FRANCIS, App., 11-1843.
ERVIN, JAMES, Will, 1-1831. Dev.:
Sarah, wife; Jinny Brown, Sally
Austin, daus.; Andrew, son.
ERVIN, JOHN, App., 8-26-1791.
ERWIN, FRANCIS, Will, 10-1843. Dev.:
Wm., bro.
ERWIN, WM., Will, 4-24-1804. Dev.:
Mary, wife; Jean, Eliz., Marg., Shus-
ana, daus.; Francis, John, Wm., sons.
ESTILE, WALLACE, Will, 6-1792. Dev.:
Bound, Benj., John, Sam., Wallace,
Isaac, Wm., sons; Rebeckah, Sus-
anah, Abigail, daus.; Mary Ann, wife.
ESTILE, WALLACE, Inv. 4-1792.
ETHEL, JOSEPH, Will, 2-1824. Dev.:
Polly Kible, sis.; John Combs, neph.
EVANS, G., App., 2-1814.
EVANS, ROBT., S.B., 3-1814.

FAUGHT, CASPER, App., 1-1796.
FEAMSTER, SUSAN, Will, 5-1837. Dev.:
Mary McClung, Eliz., sis.
FEAMSTER, THOS., App., 11-1832.
FEAMSTER, WM., App., 12-1801.
FILIN, JAMES, Inv., 10-30-1787.
FLESHMAN, MOSES, Will, 9-1847.
Dev.: Henry, Abraham, Simeon, Geo.,
sons; daus. names not given.
FLESHMAN, MOSES, App., 10-1847.
FLESHMAN, MOSES, S.B., 10-1847.
FLESHMAN, ROBT., App., 3-19-1798.
FLESHMAN, SAM., Will, 5-1819. Dev.:
Caty, wife; Mich., Sam., Emanuel,
Chas., sons; Cathy Rachel, Eliz. Sid-
enstricker, Mary Shouh, daus.

FLESHMAN. SAM., App., 8-1819.
FLINN, JAMES, App., 10-30-1787.
FLINNS, JAMES, Inv., no date.
FORD, ARNOLD, App., 8-1826.
FOX, WM., Will, 10-1845. Dev.: Eliz.,
wife; Mary Davis, Jane Davis, Ruth.
daus.; Sam., Jos., David, Wm., sons.
FRAZER, MARG., Will, 2-1828. Dev.:
James, Marg., Addison, Sarah.
FRAZER, MARG., App., 3-1829.
FRAZURE, THOM., Will, 7-1833. Dev.:
Mary, wife; Alex., son; Ataline, Het-
ty, daus.
FRY, DOMINICK, Will, 6-1846. Dev.:
Christiane, wife; John, Fred., Mich-
ael, Wesley, Jacob, Huffman, Jos.,
Frances, David, Wm., Thom., Mathew,
Andrew, sons; Anna, Selina, Esther,
Mary, Eliz., Christian, daus.
FRY, DOMINICK, App., 8-1846.
FRY, DOMINICK, S.B., 8-22-1846.
FRY, JOHN, App., 2-1848.
FRYER, JOHN, Will, 8-1847. Dev.: Eliz.,
Suttle, Carolina Windon, Jamima
Yeates, granddaus.
FULWIDER, GEO., App., 10-1831.

GARDINER, JOHN, Will, 9-1805. Dev.:
Sarah, wife; Geo., son; Jean, Mary,
daus.
GARDINER, JOHN, App., 11-1805.
GEORGE, THOMAS, Will, 2-1844. Dev.:
Cath., wife; Sally Guinn, Jane Hugg-
man, Betsy Surbaugh, Polly Saffer.
Sinthy Frazer, Malindy Bogess, Peg-
gy Miller, Della McCrey, Cath. Sum-
ner, daus.; Thom., John, Geo., Wm.,
sons.
GEORGE, THOMAS, App., 3-7-1844.
GEORGE, THOMAS, S.B., 4-1844.
GIBSON, LEVIN, App., 8-14-1802.
GIBSON, LEVIN, App., 9-1806.
GILKISON, ISAAC, App., 9-1841.
GILLIAN, ROBT., Will, 9-1830. Dev.:
Malinda, wife; James, Nathan, John.
sons; Sarah, Mary, daus.
GILLILAN, ROBT., Inv., 5-1831.
GRATTAN, CHARLES, Will, 9-1826.
Dev.: Nieces and nephews.
GRATTON, DAN., Will, 10-22-1815.
Dev.: Polly, wife; Thom., son; Eliz.,
Euphy, Mary, daus.
GRATTON, DAN., App., 8-1824.
GRATTAN, THOM., Will, 11-1819. Dev.:
Henry, Polly, Eliz., Uffy, and Mary
McNeal, nieces and neph.
GREEN, PHILIP, Will, 12-1847. Dev.:
Eliz. Legg.
GREENLEE, JOHN, App., 6-1815.
GREGORY, JOHN, App., 2-1803.

GREGORY, JOHN, Will, 6-1825. Dev.:
Marg., wife; John, Sam., James, sons;
Kath., Jane Brown, Ann, Eliz., daus.

GREGORY, JOHN, App., 11-1825.

GREGORY, MARG., App., 6-1830.

GRIFFITH, ABRAHAM, App., 3-1826.

GRIFFITH, THOM., App., 4-29-1789.

GRIFFITH, THOS., Inv., 11-19-1788.

GUINN, MOSES, App., 8-1823.

GUINN, MOSES, App., 1-1824.

GWINN, SAM., Will, 4-1839. Dev.:
Sam., Andrew, Ephriam, Moses, John,
sons; Ruth Garret, Isabella Busby,
Betsy Newsome, Ruth, Jane, Betsy,
Isabella, daus.

GWINN, SAM., App., 5-1-1839.

GWINN, SAM., S.B., 9-1839.

HAMILTON, AND., Will, 6-1796. Dev.:
Ard., son; Wm., bro.; others.

HAMILTON, ANDREW, App., 7-21-1796.

HAMILTON, WM., Will, 12-1825. Dev.:
Isabella, wife; And., Wm., Jacob,
John, sons; Martha Rogers, Sarah
Hunter, Eliz. Skiles, Mary Renick,
daus.

HAMILTON, WM., App., 1-1827.

HANDLEY, ARCH., Will, 7-1796. Dev.:
Jean, wife; Sarah Shanks, dau.;
James, son; others.

HANDLEY, JOHN, Will, 6-1834. Dev.:
Jos., Isaac, Robt., John, Wm., sons;
Mary Livesay, Grezilla Caraway,
daus.

HANDLEY, WM., Will, 9-1838. Dev.:
Archibald, Wm., John, sons; Peggy
Campbell, Polly Shanklin, Sally Wilson, daus.

HANDLY, ARCH., App., 4-1797.

HANDLY, JOHN, App., 2-1810.

HANDLY, JOHN, App., 2-1810.

HANDLY, THOMAS, App., 8-1847.

HANDLY, THOMAS, S.B., 10-1847.

HANNA, JAMES, App., 1-1815.

HANNA, JAMES, Will, 3-1825. Dev.:
Wife; Wm., John, David, Nat., And.,
sons; Jane McMillion, Nancy McCoy,
daus.

HANNA, JAMES, App., 7-1825.

HANNA, JAMES, S.B., 5-1832.

HANNA, JOSEPH, SR., S.B., 3-1836.

HANNA, JOSEPH, SR., App., 3-1836.

HANNA, WM., App., 6-29-1789.

HANNAH, WM., Inv., 3-15-1788.

HAPTONSTALL, ISAAC, Will, 9-1832.
Dev.: John, Abraham, Isaac, sons;
Lancy Knap, dau.

HARIS, DAN., App., 2-1814.

HARIS, DAN., S.B., 2-1814.

HARRAH, CHAS., Will, Marg., wife;
Robt., Thom., Chas., sons; Hannah
Butler, Sarah, Marg., daus.

HARRAH, THOMAS, S.B., 5-1846.

HARRAH, THOMAS, APP., 5-1846.

HARRAH, WM., Will, 11-25-1806. Dev.:
Marg., wife; Robt., Danel, Sam.,
Chas., Wm., James, sons; Mary Osborn, Eliz., Marg., Sarah, Hannah,
daus.

HARROW, WM., App., 1-1808.

HASS, DAN., Will, 12-1813. Dev.:
friends.

HAWVER, ANDREW, App., 2-1847.

HAWVER, MICHAEL, Will, 12-1817.
Dev.: Barb., wife; Mich., Christian,
Geo., sons; Barb. Buren, Magdalin
Judy, Kath. Kipler, daus.

HEDRICK, HENRY, App., 1-3-1801.

HENDERSON, JAMES, App., 2-19-1796.

HENDERSON, JAMES, Will, 4-30-1793.
Dev.: Sarah, wife; Wm., bro.

HENDERSON, JOHN, Will, 6-26-1787.
Dev.: Ann, wife; Sam., John, James,
Wm., sons.

HENDERSON, JOHN, Inv., 7-9-1787.

HENDERSON, JOHN, App., 7-31-1787.

HENDERSON, JOS., Will, 12-1848. Dev.:
Marg., wife.

HENNEY, JOHN, Will, 2-1832. Dev.:
John Littlepage, Jane Cook, James
Hudgeons, Betsy Corron.

HENSON, WM., App., 2-1825.

HICHMAN, JOHN, Will, 4-1827. Dev.:
Nancy, wife; Sarah Young, Peggy,
Betsy Sheaves, Abigail, Jane Benson,
Ann, Polly, daus.; Wm., Lewis,
Thompson, sons.

HILL, PERKINS, App., 9-1839.

HINKLE, JOHN, Inv., 4-1831.

HINKLE, JOHN, Will, 5-1841. Dev.:
Wm., Richard, sons.

HINKLE, JOHN, App., 8-1843.

HINKLE, PHILIP, Will, 9-1835. Dev.:
John, Sam., Jacob, Philip, Abraham,
sons; Clare Shirey, Eliz. Carrell, Polly Brance, daus.

HIRONS, SAM., Will, 9-29-1789. Dev.:
Abigal, wife; Sam., Jos., sons; Sarah,
dau.

HISEY, JOSEPH, App., 10-1828.

HISEY, JOSEPH, S.B., 10-1828.

HOBBLE, GEO., Will, 6-1827. Dev.:
Sophia, wife; Wm., Geo., Jacob,
Mich., sons; Kath., Charinda, daus.

HOBLE, GEO., App., 7-1827.

HOCKMAN, JACOB, Will, 4-1842. Dev.:
Mary, wife; Eliz., Susan, Mary Argenbright, daus.

HOLCOMB, HENRY, App., 12-1846.

HOLCOMB, HENRY, S.B., 12-1846.
HOLESAPPLE, HENRY, App., 11-1813.
HOLLINSWORTH, JOHN, App., 4-1800.
HOLLINSWORTH, JOHN, S.B., 5-1800.
HOLSOPPLE, HENRY, App., 11-1822.
HOOVER, FRED., Will, 12-1837. Dev.:
Geo., John, Dan., Jacob, sons; Eve,
Barb., Rebecca, Polly Page, daus.
HOWVER, MICHALL, Will, 10-1842.
Dev.: Mary, wife; Andrew, son;
Eliz. Crist, Marg. Pinnell, Cath. Kin-
caid, dau.
HUFFMAN, MICH., Will, 3-31-1807.
Dev.: Rosannah, Mary, daus.; Sam.,
Nat., James, sons.
HUFFMAN, MICHAEL, App., 4-1807.
HUFFMAN, REUBEN, Will, 3-1833.
Dev.: Cath., wife; Sol., Eliz., Nelly,
daus.; other children.
HUGARD, JAMES, App., 2-22-1791.
HUGGART, JAMES, App., 1-1812.
HUGGART, JOSEPH, App., 1-1838.
HUGGART, WM., App., 1-1827.
HUGHART, JAMES, Will, 1-25-1791.
Dev.: John, And., Geo., Jos., sons;
Agnes, wife; Agnes, Eliz., Rebecca,
Jane, Mary, daus.
HUGHART, JAMES, Inv., 2-22-1791.
HUMPHREYS, ELIZ., Will, 9-1810. Dev.:
Robt., son; Marg. Reynolds, dau.
HUMPHREYS, JAMES, App., 10-14-
1795.
HUMPHREYS, JOHN, App., 3-1828.
HUMPHREYS, JOHN, App., 3-1839.
HUMPHREYS, RICHARD, Will, 3-26-
1816. Dev.: James, Wm., Rich., Sam.,
sons; Nancy Taylor, Polly, Betsy, Is-
abella, Sally, daus.
HUMPHREYS, RICHARD, App., 5-1816.
HUMPHREYS, ROBT., Will, 12-1846.
Dev.: Mathew, Alex., John, bro.
HUMPHREYS, ROBT., App., 1-1847.
HUMPHREYS, SAM., Will, 8-1821. Dev.:
Grizzel, wife; Robt., Sam., Wm., sons;
Martha Taylor, Ruth, Marg., Issa-
bella, Kathrn, Betsy, daus.
HUMPHREYS, SAM., App., 11-1821.
HUNTER, HENRY, Will, 7-28-1818.
Dev.: John, son; Frances Steele, dau.
HUNTER, HENRY, App., 10-1818.

HUNTER, JOHN, Will, 12-1824. Dev.:
Sally, wife.
HUNTER, MATHEW, Will, 12-1837.
Dev.: Geo., Moses, Mathew, John,
sons; Mary, Eliza, Isabella, Marg.,
daus.
HUNTER, MATTHEW, S.B., 3-1838.
HUNTER, MATTHEW, App., 3-1838.
HUTCHISON, JOHN, App., 10-1796.
HUTSENPILLER, BENJ., S.B., 3-1842.
HUTSENPILLER, BENJ., App., 3-1842.
HYDE, CHARLES, Will, 7-1843. Dev.:
Eleanor, wife; Cyrus, son.

JACKSON, MARGERY, Will, 5-1849.
Dev.: John, James, Alex., bro.; Jane
Robinson, Peggy, sis.
JAMES, DAVID, Will, 1-1823. Dev.:
Jane, wife; John, James, David, sons;
Nancy, Ellen, Sarah, Fanny, Marg.,
Martha, daus.
JAMES, DAVID, App., 3-1823.
JAMES, JOS., Will, 4-26-1808. Dev.:
Sam., John, and John Correll, Jr.
JAMES, JOSEPH, App., 11-1808.
JAMISON, DAVID, App., 9-1819.
JARRETT, JAMES, Will, 7-1822. Dev.:
Rosanna, wife; Delilah, Eveline, Leah
Graham, daus.; Jacob, Morris, Geo.,
James, Vincent, Levi, Wm., Owen,
Isaac, Abraham, sons.
JARRETT, JAMES, App., 11-1824.
JEFFRIES, THOMAS, App., 3-1843.
JOHNSTON, JANE, Will, 10-1825. Dev.:
Geo., Wm.,. Andrew, sons; Polly
Feamster, dau.
JOHNSTON, SAM., Will, 4-1819. Dev.:
Mary, sis.
JOHNSTON, WM., Will, 1-25-1803. Dev.:
Jane, wife; James, Sam., Wm., Geo.,
John, And., sons; Polly, Saley, daus.
JOHNSTON, WM., App., 6-1803.
JOHNSTON, WM., Will, 5-1849. Dev.:
Sarah, wife; James, Neville, Andrew,
sons; Eliz. Huggens, Sophrona Hug-
gens, Clina Meadows, daus.
JONES, LAVINEY, Will, 4-1847. Dev.:
Marg., Nutter, Debitha, daus.; Thom.,
Wilson, sons.

West Virginia Estate Settlements

In 1936 and 1937, the West Virginia Commission on Historic and Scenic Markers, the Works Progress Administration, and the Federal Emergency Relief Administration compiled court records of the various counties, such as Births, Deaths, Marriages, and Wills. Under Wills were grouped subjects pertaining to Estate Settlements, including Wills, Inventories, and Appraisements. Copies of these county records were filed at the Department of Archives and History, Charleston; the Library of West Virginia University, Morgantown; and the DAR Library, Washington.

Believing that there would be particular interest on the part of the general public in the Estate Settlements in the older counties, the West Virginia Historical Society has undertaken to abstract the Estate Settlements Records, as filed in the State Department of Archives and History, and offer them for publication in the *West Virginia History Quarterly*. (No responsibility can be assumed as to the accuracy of the copies made from the original records.)

There are 13 counties which were formed prior to 1800, and it has been agreed to arrange these counties in chronological order, and to print their records from the earliest date to 1850. The formation dates of these counties are as follows: Hampshire—1753; Berkeley—1772; Monongalia—1776; Ohio—1776; Greenbrier—1778; Harrison—1784; Hardy—1786; Randolph—1787; Pendleton—1788; Kanawha—1788; Brooke—1797; Wood—1798; and Monroe—1799.

Greenbrier County Formed 1778

Abbrevations used in this material include: App.—appraisal; Bro.—brother; Dau.—daughter; Dev.—devisees; Inv.—inventory; S.B.—sale bill; Set.—settlement; Sis.—sister; Ven.—vendue.

KAYSER, MARTIN, Inv., 5-2-1789.
KAYSER, MARTIN, Inv., 7-28-1789.
KEARNES, ABR., Will, 8-1828. Dev.:
    Eleanor, wife; Abraham, Thom., sons.
KEENY, E., App., 10-1826.

KEENY, MICHAEL, Inv., 1-31-1791.
KEENY, MICHAEL, App., 2-22-1791.
KEENEY, M. A., App., 11-1843.
KEENEY, MOSES, S.B., 12-1841.
KEELY, NATHANIEL, App., 2-4-1815.

KELLY, THOMAS, Will, 2-1832. Dev.: Lovey, wife; James, Joseph, John, Thom., Morgan, sons; Mary, Marg., Eliz., McCorkle.

KESLER, PETER, Will, 2-1832. Dev.: Cath., wife; Jacob, Fred, sons; Cath., Judy, Susan Dodson, Polly Dodson, daus.

KESLER, PETER, App., 11-1832.

KESSINGER, MATHEW, App., 12-1795.

KILLPATRICK, RODGERS, App., 1-1798.

KILPATRICK, RODGERS, Set., 11-15-1797.

KILPATRICK, ROGER, Will, 10-1797. Dev.: Jean, wife; James, Thom., sons; Nancy Morris, Lattys Paul, Jean, Marg. Bartin, daus.

KINCAID, ANDREW, Will, 5-1811. Dev.: Mary, wife; Andrew, John, Robt., James, Thomas, sons; Sarah Caldwell, Eliz. Miller, Ann Graten, May Wyatt, Marg. Stone, daus.

KINCAID, ANDREW, App., 8-1811.

KINCAID, ANDREW, App., 4-10-1838.

KINCAID, ANDREW, S.B., 9-1838.

KINCAID, ELIZ., App., 3-1843.

KINCAID, JAMES, App., 1-1812.

KINCAID, JAMES, Will, 8-1838. Dev.: Phebe, wife; Eliz., Frances, Agness, Mary Marg. McCollister, daus.; Alex., Wm., sons.

KINCAID, JAMES, App., 9-1838.

KINCAID, JAMES, App., 1-1839.

KINCAID, JAMES, S.B., 1-1839.

KINCAID, JOHN, App., 3-1843.

KINCAID, JOHN, S.B., 3-1843.

KINCAID, SAM., Will, 6-1819. Dev.: Marg., wife; Susannah, Sally Brown, Betty Brown, Ann Kinhead, daus.; Thom., David, Sam., Geo., James, sons.

KINCAID, SAM., App., 3-1830.

KINCAID, THOM., Will, 7-28-1795. Dev.: Mary, wife; Mary, Shusahah, daus.; James, And., sons.

KINCAID, THOM., App., 9-21-1795.

KINGAM, DAVID, App., 7-1828.

KIRKPATRICK, GEO., Will, 8-27-1811. Dev.: Thomas, bro.

KIRKPATRICK, GEO., App., 11-1811.

KIRKPATRICK, THOM., Will, 8-1847. Dev.: Jane Bozwell, Sally Lynch, daus.; Geo. son.

KNAPP, CALEB, Will, 5-1830. Dev.: Betsy, wife; James, Josh., Caleb, Jr., Abraham, Moses, sons; Peggy, dau.

KNAPP, CALEB, App., 3-1831.

KNIGHT, JAMES, Will, 8-1848. Dev.: Marg., wife; And., Cavendish, Geo.,

Thom., Alex., sons; Jane Williams, Polly Hinkle, Aley McMillion, Rebecca Ludington, Nancy Lewis, daus.

KNOWLES, CHARLES, App., 10-1812.

LACY, WM., SR., App., 4-1775.

LANDIS, CHRISTIAN, S.B., no date.

LANDES, CHRISTIAN, App., no date.

LAVINA, JAMES, App., 9-1847.

LEWIS, GEO., Will, 9-1811. Dev.: Febe, wife; Milly, Rachel, Hannah, Nancy, daus.; Hezekiah, Geo., sons.

LEWIS, GEO., App., 4-1813.

LEWIS, GEO., App., 11-1827.

LEWIS, HEZEKIAH, Will, 6-1830. Dev.: Diana, wife; John, Geo., James, Sam., sons; Nancy Prion, Polly Cutlip, Rachel Walker, Betsey Nite, Salley Bruggey, Lidea Lewis, Marrat Dodral, Diana Lewis, daus.

LEWIS, HEZEKIAH, Inv., 2-1831.

LEWIS, JOHN, Will, 4-1787. Dev.: Mary, wife; John, Geo., Robt., Benj., sons; Sarah, Phebe, Agnes Howard, Cath., Keeny, daus.

LEWIS, JOHN, Inv., 5-27-1787.

LEWIS, JOHN, App., 5-29-1787.

LEWIS, JOHN, App., 3-1811.

LEWIS, JOHN, Set., 9-1814.

LING, COMRADE, Will, 11-1817. Dev.: Eliz., wife.

LINSON, ED., Will, 1-1831. Dev.: Anna, wife; Betsy, Nancy, Sally, Polly Neal, daus.; John, Jacob, Geo., sons.

LIPPS, HENRY, Will, 2-1826. Dev.: Rebecca, wife; Jacob, Geo., sons.

LIPPS, HENRY, App., 7-1826.

LIPPS, JOHN, App., 9-1838.

LIPPS, REBECCA, Will, 2-1828. Dev.: Jacob, Danniel, John, Geo., sons; Eliz., dau.

LIVESAY, JOHN, Will, 9-1840. Dev.: Mary; Jos., Charles, John, sons.

LIVESAY, JOHN, App., 1-1847.

LIVESAY, JOS., Will, 9-1841. Dev.: Marry, mother, Charles, bro.

LOCKHART, JACOB, Will, 3-23-1786. Dev.: Mary, wife; Chas., James, John, sons; Agness, Eliz., dau.

LOCKHART, JACOB, App., 7-31-1787.

LOCKHART, WM., Inv., 7-31-1787.

LONGENACKER, JACOB, Will, 3-1822. Dev.: Sybilla, wife; Abraham, David, sons; Magdalene Koontz, Mary Koontz, Rebecca Koontz, Barb. Henchman, Christiana Peters, Eliz. Ellis, daus.

MANN, ROBT., App., 7-1807.

MARA, FRANCIS, Will, 6-9-1791. Dev.: Hanna, wife; Marg., dau.

MARRA, FRANCIS, App., 7-7-1791.

110   West Virginia Estate Settlements

MARY (COLORED), App., 3-1827.
MASSEY, ANN, Will, 6-1834. Dev.:
Nieces and nephews.
MASTERS, CHARLES, Will, 3-1844.
Dev.: Rachel, wife; Sarah, Eliz.,
Marg., daus.; Andrew, Alex., sons.
MASTERS, CHARLES, App., 2-1845.
MASTERS, CHARLES, S.B., 10-16-1846.
MASTERS, RACHEL, App., 9-1847.
MASTERS, RACHEL, S.B., 9-1847.
MASTIN, WM., App., 7-1847.
MATHEWS, ARCHER, Inv., 2-1790.
MATHEWS, GEO., App., 6-1827.
MATHEWS, JOHN, Will, 11-1849. Dev.:
Susan, Ophlia Cary, Ann Brown, Su-
san, daus.
MATHEWS, SAMPSON, Will, 4-1841.
Dev.: Martha, wife; Jacob, Andrew,
sons; Jane Woods, dau.
MATHEWS, SAMPSON, App., 4-1841.
MATHEWS, SAMPSON, S.B., 6-1841.
MATHEWS, TOWNSEND, Will, 9-27-
1808. Dev.: Eliz., wife; Townsend, son;
others.
MATTICS, ALEX., Will, 11-1840. Dev.:
Eliz., dau.; Mathew, Scofield, Thom.,
Alex., John, Washington, Peter, sons.
MAZE, JOHN, App., 11-1836.
MAZE, JOHN, S.B., 7-1838.
MAZE, JOHN JOS., JR., Will, 8-1836.
Dev.: Eliza, Florence, Jane, Eveline,
Amanda, sis.; Charles, bro.
MAZE, JOS., Will, 5-1827. Dev.: Nancy,
wife; Florence, Jane, Eliza, Emeline,
Amanda, daus.; Charles, John, sons.
MCCALLISTER, MARY ANN, Will, 5-
1838. Dev.: John Waren, son-in-law;
Jane, niece.
MCCARTY, THOMAS, App., 1-1802.
MCCLEARY, HUGH, App., 1812.
MCCLENACHAN, JOHN, App., 8-1818.
MCCLENACHAN, JOHN, Will, 6-1837.
Dev.: Eliza, wife; Mildred, mother.
MCCLENECHAN, ELIZA, Will, 12-
1847. Dev.: Joel McPherson, bro-in-
law.
MCCLINTIC, ROBT., Will, 7-1845. Dev.:
Jane, wife; Robt., Jos., Alex., Archi-
bald, Moses, sons; Nancy Beard, Sally
Price, Jane Mann, daus.
MCCLINTIC, ROBT., App., 9-1845.
MCCLINTIC, ROBT., S.B., 9-1845.
MCCLINTICK, ELIZA, Will, 3-1840.
Dev.: Thomas, husband.
MCCLUNG, ALEX., App., 2-1820.
MCCLUNG, CHARLES, Set., 2-1805
MCCLUNG, ED., App., 4-1848.
MCCLUNG, JAMES, Will, 9-28-1790.
Dev.: Nancy, wife; Wm., son; Jane,
Eliz., Nancy, Cath., daus.

MCCLUNG, JAMES, App., 6-1812.
MCCLUNG, JAMES, Will, 9-1824. Dev.:
Sam., Jos., bros.
MCCLUNG, JAMES, Will, 9-1824. Dev.:
Polly, wife; Geo., son.
MCCLUNG, JAMES, App., 11-1825.
MCCLUNG, JOHN, App., 12-31-1848.
MCCLUNG, JOS., Will, 7-23-1849. Dev.:
Eliz., wife; Charles, Jos., Franklin,
sons; Marg. Rader, Nancy Keans,
Jane Bright, Eleanor, Eliz. Bright,
Lucinda, daus.
McCLUNG, SAM., App., 4-1806.
MCCLUNG, SAM., Will, 10-1845. Dev.:
Mary, Susan, Betsy, daus.; Thomas,
Charles, sons.
MCCLUNG, SAM., App., 5-1847.
MCCLUNG, SAM., S.B., 2-1848.
MCCLUNG, WM., Will, 3-1833. Dev.:
John, James, Wm., Alex., Sam., Jos-
eph, sons; Abigail Black, Jane Cav-
endish, daus.
MCCLURE, ARTHUR, Will, 10-1800.
Dev.: Martha, wife; James, Wm.,
Chas., Sam., Arthur, John. sons;
Cath. Furns, Jane Callison, Martha
Stinson, Rebecca Snodgrass. Eliz.,
Mary, daus.
MCCLURE, ARTHUR, App., 2-5-1801.
MCCLURE, ARTHUR, Will, 7-1842.
Dev.: Eliz., wife; Jos., Sam., sons;
Marg., Sarah, Eliz. Nanna, Hannah
Gardner, Rachel Spitser, daus.
MCCLURE, DAVID, Will, 9-1842. Dev.:
Jean Erwin, Eliz. Gibson, Marg. Mc-
Clure, daus.; Robt., Geo., sons.
MCCLURE, DAVID, App., 10-1842.
MCCLURE, GEO., App., 3-1804.
MCCORKLE, SAM., App., 6-1822.
MCCOY, JAMES, Will, 11-21-1780. Dev.:
John, Wm., James, David, sons;
Jane, Sarah, Eliz., Mary, daus.; Jane,
wife.
MCCOY, JAMES, Will, 5-28-1816. Dev.:
Mary, wife.
MCCOY, JOHN, Will, 4-22-1779. Dev.:
James, son.
MCCOY, WM., App., 2-5-1795.
MCDOWELL, WM., App., 8-16-1796.
MCDOWELL, WM., Will, 2-1797. Dev.:
Robt., Wm., Sam., Dan., Josiah, Arch.,
sons; Jeaney, Sarah Thompson, Ann
Boyd, Hannah Rodgers, daus.
MCFERREN, JAMES, Will, 6-1843. Dev.:
Nancy, wife; And., John, James, Wm.,
sons; Sabina Bowen, Polly Brown,
Eliz. Hughart, Adaline Beirne, Nancy,
Rebecca, Sally, daus.
MCLAUGHLIN, JAMES, App., 11-
1830.

MCMILLION, JOHN, Will, 6-1804. Dev.:
Martha, wife; Wm., Jos., sons; Jane,
Cath., Sally, Nancy, Mary, Eliz.,
Patty, Hannah, daus.

MCMILLION, JOHN, Will, 4-30-1848.
Dev.: Rachel, wife; Beverly, Andrew,
John, sons; Ann, Carroline, Hannah
McClung, Jane, Eliz. Neal, Rebecca
Knight, Martha McClung, daus.

MCMILLION, WM., App., 10-1827.

MCNEIL, ARCHIBALD, App., 8-1828.

MCNEIL, POLLY, Will, 1-1845. Dev.:
Henry, bro.; John Coalter, negro boy.

MEALMAN, ANDREW, App., 8-1813.

MENNIS, ROBT., Will, 4-1840. Dev.:
Henry Robertson, Wm. Mennis, nephews; Ann Robertson, niece.

MILLER, THOMAS, App., 6-1815.

MILLOOSE, JOHN, App., 6-1813.

MOORE, SAM., App., 9-1810.

MOOREHEAD, JOHN, Will, 4-1848.
Dev.: John, Robt., Francis, James,
sons; Nancy Nickell, Eliz. Ervin,
Jane McVey, Frances Diddle, Mary
McVey, daus.

MOOREHED, JOHN, SR., App., 6-1849.

MORRISON, ANDREW, Will, 3-1845.
Dev.: Eliz., wife; Wm., Andrew, John,
sons; Thankful Williams, Eliz., Wats,
Rebecca Corn, Jane Roberts, Hannah Perkins, Nancy Cummings, daus.

MORRISON, WIDOW, App., 8-1798.

MORROW, JAMES, Will, 1-1790. Dev.:
Mary, wife; James, Sam., sons; Agnes Craegg, Jane Wymer, daus.

MORROW, JAMES, App., 7-17-1798.

MORROW, WM., Will, 2-1825. Dev.:
Eliz., wife.

MOYERS, GEO., Will, 7-1835. Dev.:
Marg., wife; Adam, son; Barb. Hut-
cheson, dau.

MOYERS, LEWIS, Will, 7-1835. Dev.:
Mary, wife; Andrew, Cherls, sons;
Margarit, Mary, Barb., Eliz., daus.

MURLEYS, DANIEL, Will, 8-22-1781.
Dev.: Marg., wife; two sons.

MUSHBARGER, JOHN, S.B., 8-17-1801.

MUSHBARGER, JOHN, Will, 6-1807.
Dev.: Cath., wife; Chris., P e t e r,
Henry, Dan., Sam., Jacob, John, Jos.,
sons; Lissey, Katey, Barb., Nancy,
daus.

MUSHBARGER, JOHN, S.B., 8-1807.

MYARS, JOHN, Will, 10-1823. Dev.:
John Hess and wife.

MYERS, LEWIS, App., 10-1835.

MYERS, LEWIS, S.B., 10-1835.

MYERS, MARY, Will, 8-1844. Dev.:
Mary, Barb., Eliz., daus.

MYLES, JANE, Will, 8-1848. Dev.: Wm.,

Sam., sons; Jane Byrd, Eliz. Martin,
Annie Neal, Marg. Martin, daus.

MYLES, JOHN, Will, 6-1848. Dev.:
James, Wm., John, Jos., Sam, sons;
Marg. Martin, Eliz. Martin, Jane
Byrd, Anness Neal, daus.

MYLES, JOHN, App., 12-1848.

NEAL, JAMES, App., 11-1819.

NELSON, WM., App., 4-1794.

NEWTON, JAMES, App., 8-1824.

NEWTON, JOS., Will, 5-1812. Dev.:
Wm., James, Kenneth, Anderson,
Thomas, sons; Hannah, Sarah Blake,
daus.; Helena, wife.

NEWTON, JOS., App., 6-1812.

NICHOLAS, GEO., Will, 8-22-1820.
Dev.: Mary, wife; Henry, son; Eliz.
Perkins, dau.

NICHOLAS, GEO., App., 2-1822.

NICHOLAS, GEO., S.B., 2-1822.

NICHOLAS, JOS., Will, 10-1801. Dev.:
sons and daus.

NICHOLAS, JOS., Set., 8-24-1805.

NUNELLY, HENRY, Will, 10-1844. Dev.:
Frances, wife.

NUNLY, HENRY, App., 1-1845.

O'BRIAN, JAMES, App., 11-21-1781.

O'BRYAN, JAMES, Inv., 4-1781.

OCHELTREE, AMANDA, App., 1-1848.

OCHLETREE, DAVID, App., 10-1839.

OCHLETREE, DAVID, App., 3-1840.

OCHLETREE, DAVID, S.B., 10-1841.

OCHLETREE, JONATHAN, App., 2-
1842.

O'NEAL, JOHN, App., 1-1793.

O'NEALE, JOHN, Will, 4-1792.

OSBORN, DAVID, App., 8-1807.

OSBORN, DAVID, S.B., 8-1807.

OSBORN, JOHN, Will, 7-29, 1806. Dev.:
James, John, Jos., Jeremiah, David,
Elijah, Levi, sons; Huldah Kinkead,
Sarah Alderson, daus.

OSBORN, JOHN, S.B., 12-1806.

OSBORN, JOHN, App., 12-1807.

OSBORNE, GEO., Inv., 1-1847.

PATTERSON, JOHN, Will, 6-1844. Dev.:
Eliz., wife; James, Henry, Lewis,
Charles, Wm., John, Thomas, Jos.,
sons; Mary, Cath., Eliz., daus.

PATTON, JOHN, Will, 3-1842. Dev.:
Marg. Hughart, dau.; James, son.

PEARIS, ROBT., App., 2-1830.

PEEBLES, JAMES, Will, 7-1822. Dev.:
Ann, wife; James, David, John, sons;
Mary Ralston, Peggy McLaughlin,
Ann Anderson, Fanny Hamilton (dis-
inherited), daus.

PERKINS, ELI, App., 10-1844.

PERKINS, ELIAS, Will, 6-1843. Dev.:
Mary, wife; Sam., Eli, Thom., David,

James, sons; Polly Griffith, Nancy, Betsy, Caty, daus.

PERKINS, HENRY, Will, 10-24-1815. Dev.: Henry, Wm., sons; Eliz., Jane, Hannah, daus.

PERKINS, JAMES, Will, 5-1825. Dev.: Eliz., wife; James, Thom., Sam., Levin, Masten, Will, And., sons; Eliz. Spencer, Sara Atha, Marian Morisson, daus.

PERKINS, JAMES, App., 6-1825.

PHELPS, ISAAC, App., 11-1806.

PIERCY, CHRISTIAN, Will, 8-1848. Dev.: Eliz., wife; Thom., John, sons; Hannah, Eliz. Carline, daus.

PINNELL, JOHN, Will, 10-1820. Dev.: Eliz., wife; Nancy Henning, Lucy, Jannett, Hannah, Anna, daus.; Thom., Jos., James, Geo., Hezekiah, sons.

PINNELL, JOHN, S.B., 3-1821.

POPE, ADAM, Will, 1-1835. Dev.: Nephews, grandson.

PRICE, JOHN, App., 7-1815.

PRICE, SAM., Inv., 8-1830.

PUCKET, CRAWFORD, Will, 11-1849. Dev.: Sarah, wife; children.

RADER, ANTHONY, Will, 6-1826. Dev.: Eliz., wife; John, Alex., sons; Kath. Meneck, Eliz. McClung, Deborah McClung, Dolly Linson, Polly Conner, daus.

RADER, ANTHONY, Will, 6-1826. Dev.: Eliz., wife; John, Alex., sons; Kath. Meneck, Eliz.

RADER, JAMES, Will, 7-1842. Dev.: Eliz., wife; Mary Ann, dau.; Green, James, Elijah, sons; Abraham, father.

RADER, JAMES, App., 1-1843.

RAINEY, MICHAEL, Will, 11-16-1784. Dev.: Mary, wife; Cath. Sullivan, sis.

RAINEY, MICHAEL, Inv., 3-16-1785.

RALSTON, ANDREW, Inv., 8-26-1782.

RALSTON, ANDREW, App., 9-22-1782.

RAMBO, JAMES, App., 2-1821.

RAMBO, JOS., Will, 1-1821. Dev.: Sarah, wife; Jos., Peter, Reuben, Levi, Wm., Jacob, sons; Jemima, Deborah, Sarah, Drusilla, daus.

READER, GEO., Will, 10-24-1815. Dev.: Marg., wife; Geo., Adam, Alex., sons; Betsy McNell, Mary Bird, Cath. Hefer, Barb. Cratsar, Dolly Hup, Ellan Hup, Sally Hup, Marg. More, Clary Hup, daus.

READER, GEO., App., 2-1817.

REANEY, MICHAEL, App., 3-16-1785.

REID, JAMES, App., 4-1796.

REID, JAMES, Will, 6-1830. Dev.: Peggy, wife; John, James, Alex., Sam., sons; Eliz., Mary, Sarah, daus.

RENICK, GRIGSBY, App., 3-1841.

RENICK, ROBT., Will, 2-1835. Dev.: Grigsby, Franklin, sons; Sally, Frances Frazer, Fanny Leach, daus.

RENICK, WM., Will, 4-25-1815. Dev.: Robt., bro., others.

RICHARD, JOSIAH, Will, 2-20-1787. Dev.: Jane, wife; Josiah, Elijah, sons; Esther, dau.

RICHARDS, JAMES, App., 1-1-1791.

RICHARDS, JAMES, App., 4-26-1791.

RICHARDS, JAMES, Inv., 4-26-1791.

RICHARDS, JAMES, Will, 4-26-1791. Dev.: Zaley, wife; Josiah, Robt., sons.

RICHARDS, JOSIAH, App., 4-21-1787.

RICHARDS, JOSIAH, Inv., 4-21-1787.

RICHESON, FRANCINA, Will, 9-1848-49. Dev.: Valencant, son; Eliza, dau.

RIFFE, FLORENCE, App., 1-1-1848.

ROBINSON, ALEX., Will, 10-1824. Dev.: Mathew, Alex., sons; Mary, dau.

ROBINSON, ALEX., Will, 12-1827. Dev.: Betsy, wife; Wm., John, Alex., Wallace, sons.

ROBINSON, ALEX,, App., 2-1828.

ROBINSON, MATHEW, Will, 10-1843. Dev.: Polly, sister; Mathew Humphreys, nephew.

ROBINSON, MATHEW, Inv., 11-1843.

ROBINSON, MATHEW, S.B., 11-1843.

ROBINSON, ROBT., Will, 8-1825. Dev.: Madge, wife; James, David, Mathew, sons; Peggy Dollan, Madze, Nancy, daus.

ROBINSON, ROBT., App., 10-1825.

ROBINSON, WM., App., 9-1797.

RODGERS, ARCHIBALD, Will, 12-28-1846. Dev.: John, Achilles, Charles, James, sons; Jane Mahan, Nancy Tuckwiller, daus.

RODGERS, ARCH., App., 3-1847.

RODGERS, DAVID, Inv., 3-5-1785.

RODGERS, DAVID, App., 3-16-1785.

RODGERS, JOHN, App., 9-1798.

RODGERS, JOHN, Set., 6-30-1801.

RODGERS, MICHAEL, Will, 5-1846. Dev.: Eli, Dan., Michael, John, James, sons; Aby Shaver, Sally Myers, Rachel McMannan, Cath. Honeker, daus.

RODGERS, MICHAEL, App., 8-1846.

ROGERS, NICKALL, S.B., 12-1846.

RUCKER, DUET, App., 2-1849.

RUPEL, GEO., Will, 6-1824. Dev. Martin, bro.

RUPLE, GEO., App., 8-1824.

SAMMONS, JOHN, App., 1-1838.

SCHAE, ANTHONY, App., 6-21-1785.

SCOTT, ALEX., Will, 11-1849. Dev.: Wm. (son of Rachel Kempinstall).

SCOTT, JOHN, App., 2-1849.
SEA, JOHN, App., 1-10-1795.
SEMMETT, MATHIAS, App., 5-1820.
SEMMETT, MATHIAS, S.B., 5-1820.
SHANKLIN, JAMES, App., 3-1813.
SHANKLIN, ROBT., Inv., 4-26-1781.
SHANKLIN, ROBT., App., 4-26-1791.
SHINDAFFER, GEO., App., 6-1805.
SHOALS, MARTIN, Will, 6-24-1793.
Dev.: Anne, wife; Cath., Anne, daus.
SKEENS, THOMAS, S.B., 5-1824.
SKEIN, JAMES, App., 3-1828.
SKILES, JACOB, App., 1-1817.
SMITH, JAMES, Will, 6-24-1806. Dev.:
Pheby, wife; John, Benj., Sam.,
James, Stapen, sons; Baky Cade, dau.
SMITH, WM., App., 5-1829.
SMITHEE, WM., Will, 10-1825. Dev.:
Wife; Letitia, dau.
SNELL, JOHN, App., 1-1806.
SPOTTS, BARB., Will, 3-1843. Dev.:
David, son; Sally Gibson, Rebecca
Dowd, Sally Witzel, daus.
SPOTTS, ELIZ., Will, 11-1839. Dev.:
Barbara, mother.
SPOTTS, GEO., App., 2-1822.
SPOTTS, JOHN, Will, 4-1838. Dev.:
Mary, wife; Eliza Jane, dau.; John
Geo., son.
SPOTTS, JOHN, App., 5-1838.
STEVENSON, ANN, App., 8-1843.
STEVENSON, ANN, Will, 9-1843. Dev.:
Charles, James, sons; Francis Hand-
ley, dau.
STUART, GEO., App., 12-1824.
STUART, JOHN, Will, 9-23-1823. Dev.:
Agatha, wife; Charles, Lewis, sons;
Marg., Jane Crockett, daus.
SUITER, HIRAM, Will, 8-1846. Dev.:
Marg., dau.
SURBAUGH, ANN, Will, 6-1846. Dev.:
John, Henry, Jacob, David, Wm.,
sons; Polly Hutsonpiller, Cath., daus.
SURBAUGH, DAVID, Will, 9-1823.
Dev.: Anne, wife; Cath. Mary, Bar-
bary, daus.; Henry, Jacob, David,
John, Wm., sons.
SURBOUGH, ANN, App., 8-1846.
SURBOUGH, BARB., S.B., 3-1844.
SURBOUGH, BARBARA, App., 3-1844.
SURBOUGH, DAVID, App., 11-1823.
SYDENSTRICKER, PHILIP, Will, 9-
1833. Dev.: John, Jacob, Philip, Hen-
ry, David, sons; Eliz. Fleshman,
Nancy, daus.
TAGERT, JACOB, App., 1-26-1846.
THOMPSON, ROBT., Will, 4-1840. Dev.:
Martha, Jane Tucker, Elener Mc-
Clung, Mary E., Rebeca, daus.; Robt.,
Geo., John, sons.

THOMPSON, ROBT., App., 4-1841.
THOMPSON, ROBT., S.B., 7-1841.
THOMPSON, T., Set., 8-3-1797.
THOMPSON, THOMAS, App., 7-1795.
THORNTON, JOHN, App., 4-1804.
TUCKWILLER, JOHN, Will, 1-1832.
Dev.: Hanna Hedrick, Eliz. Perkins,
Ester Hedrick, Barb. Wilson, Caty
Fleshman, Nancy Dwver, Rachel,
Mary, daus.; David, John, sons.
TUCKWILLER, JOHN, App., 6-1832.
TUCKWILLER, JOHN, JR., S.B., 10-
1835.
TURPEN, JAMES, Will, 5-5-1777. Dev.:
Mother; Martin, Aron, Sol., bro.
TURPEN, JAMES, App., no date.
TURPEN, JAMES, Inv., no date.
VANANSDAL, CALEB, Will, 1-1827.
Dev.: Cornelias, James, sons; Sarah,
Nancy, Marg., Jane, Patsy Littlepage,
Eliz. Wylie, daus.
VANANSDAL, CALEB, App., 9-1827.
VANOSDOL, SARAH, Will, 1-1825.
Dev.: Rich. Williams, son; Marg.,
granddau.
VANCE, JACOB, App., 6-26-1798.
VARNER, SARAH, Will, 1-1824. Dev.:
Ann Edwards, Eliz. Buckanna, Rach-
ael Johnson, sisters; others.
VENABLE, JAMES, Will, 8-1838. Dev.:
Wm., Dean, sons.
VINEY, JOHN, App., 7-9-1803.
VINEY, JOHN, Will, 6-28-1803. Dev.:
Sarah, wife; John, Abr., Geo.,
Nathan, sons; Rachel Lewis, Liah
Lewis, Sarah McClung, Dinah Lewis,
daus.
WADE, LEONARD, Will, 4-1846. Dev.:
Geo., Leonard, James, sons; Mary,
Matilda, Eliz. Underwood, Susannah
Alderman, daus.
WADE, LEONARD, App., 10-17-1846.
WALKUP, ANN, Will, 9-1823. Dev.:
Wm., Arch., Robt., Thom., John, and
James Elliott, sons; Jinny Cerrich,
Anny Kincaid, daus.
WALKUP, ANN, App., 6-1824.
WALKUP, CHRISTOPHER, Will, 9-1818.
Dev.: Ann, wife; Martha McClure.
Marg. Beard, Rebach Edmisten, Mary
Cravey, Sally Prier, daus.; Jos., John,
Chris., sons.
WALKUP, CHRISTOPHER, App., 2-
1819.
WALKUP, JOHN, S.B., 9-1815.
WALKUP, JOS., App., 5-1840.
WALKUP, MARY, App., 3-1820.
WALKUP, ROBT., Will, 4-1824. Dev.:
James, Nat., Jos., John, sons; Jane
Deitz, Nancy Price, Ann Cutlip, daus.

WALL, JOHN, App., 12-1818.

WALLACE, MOSES, Inv., 11-19-1785.

WALLACE, MOSES, App., 3-21-1786.

WALLACE, ROBT., Will, 8-1838. Dev.: Polly, wife; Sam., Alex., Washington, Robt., Moses, sons; Hetty, Betsy McClung, Nancy Hickman, Susan, Jane, daus.; Caroline, dau. of wife Polly.

WALLACE, ROBT., App., 12-1838.

WALTON, CHARLES, App., 6-1837.

WALTON, JAMES, Will, 10-1810. Dev.: Nancy, wife; Sam., Wm., Sol., Jos., James, Chas., sons; Abigail, Petty, Nancy, Polly, daus.

WALTON, JAMES, App., 9-1811.

WALTON, JOHN, Will, 4-26-1808. Dev.: Ann, wife; Wm., Geo., James, John, Elijah, Elsha, sons; Jane, Nancy, Eliz., Elender, daus.

WALTON, NANCY, App., 2-1820.

WALTON, WM., App., 11-1808.

WATTS, JAMES, Will, 12-1810. Dev.: Mary, wife; James, John, Fetethiah, sons; daughters.

WELCH, ALEX., App., 9-1810.

WELCH, FRANCES, Will, 10-1834. Dev.: James, Thom., Sam., sons; Nancy Reynolds, Frances Bright, daus.

WELCH, JOHN, App., 7-1824.

WELL, CHARLES, App., 9-1820.

WHANGER, JOHN, App., 4-1841.

WHITE, WM., Will, 8-1849. Dev.: Wife; Geo., Rich., Wm., James, Robt., sons; Annis Fenton, Eliz. Snead, daus.

WHITE, WM., S.B., no date.

WILLEY, HENRY, Will, 2-1769. Dev.: Robt., Wm., bros.; Abigail, Jane, sis.; Mary, wife.

WILLIAMS, DAVID, SR., Will, 2-1837. Dev.: Rebeckah, wife; Lucinda Oliver, Marg., Martha, Malinda, Rebeckah, Sally, McCoy, Polly Jeffries, Nancy McPhersen, Eliz. Huggart, daus.; James, John, David, Charles, sons.

WILLIAMS, DAVID, App., 3-1837.

WILLIAMS, DAVID, S.B., 3-1837.

WILLIAMS, JOHN, Will, 12-1830. Dev.: Martha, wife; John, son; Mary Hinkle, Nancy Hinkle, Sarah Butt, Martha Pullin, Ann Kingan, Thomsey Dorset, daus.

WILLIAMS, JOHN, S.B., 1-1833.

WILLIAMS, JOHN, Will, 10-1839. Dev.: Eliz., wife; Henson, Rich., John, Wm., sons; Nancy Mathes, Susan Eagle, Polly Danks, Betsy Rader, Sally Burr, daus.

WILLIAMS, JOHN, App., 12-1840.

WILLIAMS, MARTHA, Will, 2-1846. Dev.: Eliz. Donally, daus.

WILLIAMS, RICH., Will, 7-1843. Dev.: Thankful, wife; Madison, Elijah, Elinah, Andrew, Rich., Wm., Lewis, John, sons; Elizah Guinn, Marg. Guinn, Matilda Hedrick, daus.

WILLIAMS, RICHARD, App., 11-1843.

WILLIAMS, RICHARD, S.B., 11-1843.

WILLIAMS, SAM., Inv., 11-1784.

WILLIAMS, SAM., App., 3-1785.

WILLIAMS, SAM., Will, 10-1818. Dev.: Sally, wife; Rich., son; others.

WILLIAMS, SAM., App., 12-1818.

WILLIAMSON, SAM., Will, 11-16-1784. Dev.: David, Alex., John, bro.; Marg., Ann, sis.

WILSON, JAMES, Will, 8-22-1781. Dev.: Eliz., wife; Dorcus, dau.; And., James, sons.

WILSON, JAMES, Inv., 3-27-1782.

WILSON, JAMES, App., 4-16-1782.

WILSON, JAMES, Will, 8-22-1786. Dev.: Eliz., wife; Dorcas, dau.; Wm., And., James, sons.

WILSON, JOHN, Will, 1-1818. Dev.: James, And., John, Wm., sons; Jane Ellis, Nancy Lee, Eliz. Guinn, Polly Jarrett, Rebecca Jarrett, daus.

WILSON, JOHN, App., 6-1818.

WITHROW, JAMES, Will, 12-1843. Dev.: Mary Jane, Letitia, Maria, Marg., Lucy, daus.; John, Wm., James, sons.

WOODS, WM., Will, 4-12-1775. Dev.: Shusanna, wife; Peter, Mich., Wm., Adam, Arch, John, Andrew, sons; Mary, Eliz., Hanna, Sarah, daus.

WYATT, ED., App., 7-31-1787.

WYATT, ED., Inv., 7-31-1787.

WYLIE, JAMES, App., 3-1838.

WYLIE, THOMAS, Will, 9-1819. Dev.: Marg., wife; Ranken, Robt., Andrew, James, Wm., Thom., sons.

WYLIE, THOMAS, App., 3-23-1846.

WYLIE, RANKIN, Will, 8-1840. Dev.: Jane, wife; Thom., Rankin, sons; Marg., dau.

WYLIE OR WHILEY, RANKIN, App., 10-9-1840.

WYLIE, OR WHILEY, RANKIN, S.B., 4-1841.

West Virginia Estate Settlements

In 1936 and 1937, the West Virginia Commission on Historic and Scenic Markers, the Works Progress Administration, and the Federal Emergency Relief Administration compiled court records of the various counties, such as Births, Deaths, Marriages, and Wills. Under Wills were grouped subjects pertaining to Estate Settlements, including Wills, Inventories, and Appraisements. Copies of these county records were filed at the Department of Archives and History, Charleston; the Library of West Virginia University, Morgantown; and the DAR Library, Washington.

Believing that there would be particular interest on the part of the general public in the Estate Settlements in the older counties, the West Virginia Historical Society has undertaken to abstract the Estate Settlements Records, as filed in the State Department of Archives and History, and offer them for publication in the *West Virginia History Quarterly*. No responsibility can be assumed as to the accuracy of the copies made from the original county records.

There are 13 counties which were formed prior to 1800, and it has been agreed to arrange these counties in chronological order, and to print their records from the earliest date to 1850. The formation dates of these counties are as follows: Hampshire—1753; Berkeley—1772; Monongalia—1776; Ohio—1776; Greenbrier—1778; Harrison—1784; Hardy—1786; Randolph—1787; Pendleton—1788; Kanawha—1788; Brooke—1797; Wood—1798; and Monroe—1799.

Harrison County, Formed 1784

Abbreviations used in this material include App.—appraisement; Bro.—brother; Dau.—daughter; Dev.—devisee; Inv.—inventory; S.B.—sale bill; Set.—settlement; Sis.—sister.

ADAMS, JACOB, Will, 1-24-1816. Dev.: Eliz., wife; others.

ADAMS, JACOB, Set., 10-12-1821.

ALEXANDER, JESSE, Inv., 8-29-1811.

ALEXANDER, VINCENT, Inv., no date.

ALLEN, BARNES, Will, 2-18-1820. Dev.: Eve, wife; John, Joshua, Israel, Stephen, sons; Cath., Rebecca, daus.

ALLEN, JOSHUA, Inv., 11-23-1810.

ALTOP, JOHN, Inv., 4-28-1836.

ARCHBOLD, JAMES, Will, 8-2-1819. Dev.: Ann, wife; James, Ed., Noah, Sam., Israel, sons; Mary Ann, dau.; Ed., grandson.

ARCHBOLD, JAMES, Inv., 4-12-1826.

ARMSTRONG, CATH., Will, 1-5-1831. Dev.: Maxwell, Ed., Thomas, sons.

ARMSTRONG, GEO., Inv., 6-30-1821.

ARMSTRONG, MAXWELL, App., 5-20-1811.

ARNOLD, GEO., App., no date.

ARNOLD, JOHN, Will, 8-4-1811. Dev.: Jemima, wife; Isaac, Geo., James, Benj., sons; Eliz., Mary, Ritturah, daus.

ASBURY, JANE, Inv., 1-23-1816.

ASBURY, JOHN, S.B., 3-23-1812.

ASH, ADAM, Inv., 5-24-1819.

ASH, ADAM, Set., 2-9-1822.

ASH, CATHERINE, Inv., no date.

ASHCRAFT, Ezekiel, Will, 3-15-1830. Dev.: Hester, wife; Mary, dau.; John, Aaron, sons.

ATKINSON, RICHARD, Inv., 10-8-1828.

BACKAS (BACCHUS), WM., Will, 4-13-1814. Dev.: Mary, wife; Wm., Sanford, Thom., Henry, Thomas, sons; Nancy Swiger, Eleanor Swiger, Sallie, Sarah, daus.

BACKUS, HENRY, Inv., 12-17-1834.

BAILEY, JOSEPH, Inv., 1-24-1826.

BAILEY, JOSEPH, JR., Inv., 10-15-1826.

BAILEY, WM., Will, 6-15-1845. Dev.: Elzira Tracy, Eliz. Brown, Ann Bailey, daus.; Elias, Carr, Silas, Washington, Joseph, sons.

BAIRD, MARG., Will, 5-12-1800. Dev.: Mary Clark, Eliz. Reynolds, Fanny Baird, Peggy Baird, daus.; Jos. Reynolds, Thomas Reynolds, sons.

BAIRD, WM., Will, 12-12-1790. Dev.: Marg., wife; Fanny, Peggy, Ester Little, Ruth Wallace, daus.; Wm., son.

BALDEN, MARIAN, Set., 9-19-1831.

BALEY, JOSEPH, Set., 6-12-1836.

BALL, JOHN, Inv., 3-26-1834.

BARKLEY, JOHN, Cert., 8-12-1790.

BARNES, DANIEL, S.B., 8-22-1821.

BARNES, JAMES, Inv., 2-28-1838.

BARTLETT, BENJ., Will, 3-13-1824. Dev.: Mary Ann, wife; Joshua, Thomas, Benj.; Wm., sons; Mary Ann, Nancy Coplin, Rebecca Wilkinson, Synthia Bartlett, daus.

BARTLETT, BENJ., Inv., 5-27-1824.

BARTLETT, BENJ., Set., 12-18-1826.

BARTLETT, JOHN, Inv., 7-23-1804.

BARTLETT, JOHN, Set., 3-19-1833.

BARTLETT, THOM., Will, 7-5-1802. Dev.: Marg., wife; Thomas, son; grandchildren.

BARTLETT, THOMAS, Set., 6-18-1832.

BARTLETT, WM., Inv., 1-25-1815.

BARTLETT, WM., Inv., 1-9-1826.

BARTLETT, WM., Inv., 7-13-1826.

BARTLETT, WM., SR., Will, 10-5-1825. Dev.: Sarah, wife; John, Robert, Benj., Josiah, James, sons; Sarah Lester, Dortha, Selvey, daus.; Baptist society.

BOND, RICHARD, JR., Inv., 3-1820.

BEATTY, ALEX., S.B., 2-10-1833.

BEATY, JOHN, Will, 11-11-1806.

BELL, ELIZ., Inv., 10-1-1824.

BELL, JOSEPH, Will, no date; Dev.: Abigail, wife; Wm., Simon, sons; Clarrissa, Sarah, Eliz., daus.

BELL, RICHARD, SR., Will, 8-9-1849. Dev.: Richard, Isaac, Aaron, sons; Hannah Paugh, Rebecca Aighbonos, Martha Deerman, Delila Angery, daus.; Heirs of Thos., James, John, sons.

BENNELL, JOHN, Set., 12-7-1826.

BENNETT, DAVID, Will, 9-1-1807. Dev.: Christeena, wife.

BENNETT, DAVID, Sale and Set., 12-12-1814.

BENNETT, JACOB, Inv., 1824.

BENNETT, JACOB, Set., 11-18-1831.

BENNETT, WM., S.B., 3-21-1836.

BETT, RACHEL, Will, 12-24-1808. Dev.: Starks, slave; May Nixon, Rachel Clark, niece.

BIGLER, JACOB, Will, 5-29-1829. Dev.: Hannah, wife; Sarah Rose, Ruth Whiteman, Maria Flowers, Marg. Bigler, Hannah McCauley, daus.; Jacob, son.

BLAIR, ALEX., Inv., 7-13-1830.

BLAIR, ALEX., Set., 11-1838.

BOGGESS, ALONZO, Will, 12-18-1848. Dev.: Geo., Alonzo, sons; Caroline, Angat, Cath., July, Melissa, Accah Coffman, Amelia Robinson, daus.

BOGGESS, JOHN, Inv., 10-23-1815.

BOGGESS, SAM., Inv., no date.

BOGGESS, SAMUEL, Will, 5-1845. Dev.: Wm., Samuel, Frederick, Susan, Mary, children.

BOLLEN, MARY ANN, Inv., 3-12-1824.

BOND, MARY, S.B., 8-1825.

BOND, RICHARD, S.B., no date.

BONIT (BONNETT), SAMUEL, Inv., 12-17-1789.

BONNELL, JOHN, Inv., 1-24-1824.

BOOCHER (BUTCHER), JOHN, Inv., 8-11-1806.

BOOHER, HENRY, Will, 2-15-1841. Dev.: Cath., wife; Eliz., Barbary, Sarah Piles, Cath. Baker, Hannah Booker, daus.; Conrad, son.

BORING, JAMES, Will, 6-12-1836. Dev.: Jaret, Absolam, sons; Mary, Rebecca Johnson, daus.; Sarah, wife.

BOULTON, ABRAHAM, Will, 7-18-1847. Dev.: Noah, Peter, sons; Barbary Miller, sister; Rose Anna, wife.

BOWERS, JACOB, S.B., 5-16-1800.

BRAY, JOHN, Will, 1-10-1834. Dev.: Ellen, wife; others.

BROWN, JABEZ, Inv., 12-14-1816.

BROWN, JOHN J., SR., Will, 10-1-1807. Dev.: Eleanor, wife; Mary Flesher, dau.; other children; John Meguming; Fanny, slave.

BUCKLEW, GEO., Will, 11-15-1815. Dev.: Sarah, wife; Elias, son; Jane, Ellinder, Ann, Tabetha, daus.

BURNSIDE, WM., Inv., 5-5-1820.

BURNSIDE, WM., Set., 9-22-1825.

BUSH, ADAM, Inv., 1-1-1805.

BUSH, MARY, S.B., no date.

CALDWELL, DAVID, Inv., 9-6-1820.

CAMPBELL, THOMAS, Set., 9-4-1826.

CAMPBELL, WM., Will, 8-12-1823. Dev.: Perygrine, James, Joseph, sons; Harriet, Eliz., Marie, daus.

CANHORN, JOB, Set., 10-24-1823.

CARDER, MURIAH, Will, 1-17-1820. Dev.: Milly, Mary, Susannah, Fanny, Lucy, daus.; Wm., son.

CARDER, THOMAS, Inv., 9-19-1833.

CARPENTER, NICHOLAS, Will, 1791. Dev.: Mary, wife; John, Nicholas, David, Christopher, Joseph, David, John, sons; Daus.

CARR, JOSHUA, Set., 8-9-1825.

CARR, SAM., Will, 3-22-1824. Dev.: Marg., wife; Andrew, John, Richard, Seborn, Walter, Joshua, Benj., sons; Eliz., Providence, daus.

CARSWELL, SAM., Will, 9-1831. Dev.: Marg., wife; Mary Ann Ely, Margaretta, daus.; Sam., Matthew, sons; others.

CASTER, DAVID, Will, 8-26-1822. Dev.: Mary, wife; Marg., Dursilla, Delethe, daus.; Wm., James, Lewis, Sam., sons.

CASTOR, DAVID, Set., 9-15-1828.

CATHER, MARG., Inv., no date.

CATHERWOOD, CHARLES, Will, 2-29-1817. Dev.: Eliz., wife; Eliz., dau.

CATHERWOOD, CHARLES, Set., 5-23-1821.

CHALLE, PETER, Will, 6-10-1804. Dev.: Rhosana, wife.

CHAMBERLAIN, JOHN, Inv., no date.

CHAPIN, NANCY, Will, 2-19-1844. Dev.: Ruaham, Eliz., Sophronia, CS, daus.

CHAPMAN, WM., Set., 8-19-1795.

CHASE, SAM., Set., 9-18-1828.

CHEUVRONT, JOSEPH, Will, 2-2-1832. Dev.: Aaron, Amos, John, Thomas, Gideon, Caleb, Enoch, sons; Cassandra, Mary, Eliz., Presilla, daus.; wife.

CHIDESTER, HOLDRIDGE, Inv., 8-4-1835.

CHILDERS, WM., Inv., 12-5-1839.

CLARK, ALISON, Inv., 3-22-1813.

CLARK, ALLISON, Set., 6-24-1830.

CLARK, ROBERT, Will, 7-21-1808. Dev.: Jane, wife.

CLARK, WATSON, Inv., 12-25-1804.

CLEMANS, ABLE, Will, 6-20-1806. Dev.: Mother; Isaac, bro.

COBERLY, DAN., Inv., 12-18-1838.

COFFMAN, GEO., Inv., 2-8-1836.

COLE, WM., Will, 7-10-1818. Dev.: Eliz., wife; Wm., Joshua, sons; Heziah Stephens, Sarah Corder, Ealse Glassok, Johanah, daus.

COLE, WM., Inv., 7-3-1820.

COMPBELL, ANDREW, Will, 8-5-1823. Dev.: Mary, wife; Polly, Ann Umble, Hannah Michael, daus.; Wm., Robert, Thomas, sons.

CONLEY, JEREMIAH, Will, 10-13-1824. Dev.: Miriah, wife; James, Peter, sons.

COON, ABRAHAM, Inv., S.B., 9-4-1835.

COON, CONROD, Inv. 1-23-1818.

COPLIN BENJ., SR., Will, 3-27-1835. Dev.: Drusilla, wife; Johnthan, David, sons.

CORNEILOUSON, JOHN, SR., Set., 9-15-1818.

CORNELISON, PETER, Set., no date.

CORNELISSON, PETER, Inv., 6-17-1819.

COTTRILL, ANDREW, Inv., 7-3-1813.

COTTRILL, ANDREW, S.B., 9-24-1813.

COTTRILL, NOTLEY, Inv., 1-5-1840.

COTTRILL, THOMAS, Inv., 2-22-1823.

COVERT, MORRIS, Will, 1-8-1832. Dev.: Nancy, wife.

CRIM, WM., Inv., 8-7-1837.

CRISLIP, JACOB, Set., no date.

CRISLIP, JACOB, Will, 4-14-1821. Dev.: Nancy, wife; Wm., Abrahm, Sam., Isaac, Geo., Jacob, John, sons; Mary, Nancy Ours, Patsy, Sally, daus.

CRISS, LEWIS, Inv., 1-28-1805.

CROSS, JOSEPH, App., 3-15-1803.

CROUCH, JONATHAN, Inv., 5-4-1736.

CRUSEN, LEVI, Inv., 3-25-1839.

CUNNINGHAM, ADAM, Inv., no date.

CUNNINGHAM, ADAM, Will, 7-5-1849. Dev.: Roann, Emily, daus.; Christopher, son.

CUNNINGHAM, ED., Will, 12-4-1800. Dev.: Sarah, wife; Jos., Benj., Wm., Adam, Thomas, Enaith, sons; Leah, Rachel, Ann, Mary, Eliz., Kettery, daus.

CUNNINGHAM, JOSEPH, Inv., 9-15-1837.

CUNNINGHAM, MARY, Inv., 10-29-1818.

CUTRIGHT, HENRY, Will, 6-3-1823. Dev.: Sarah, wife; Abraham, brother.

DALLAM, WM., Will, 3-29-1834. Dev.: Thomas, John, Wm., Francis, Henry, sons; Mary, dau.

DANBURY, ABRAHAM, Set., no date.

DAVIS, CALEB, Will, 12-2-1816. Dev.: Leah, wife; Mary Bryon, Arisminty Koon, daus.; Robt., John, Clement, Henry, Caleb, Dan., sons.

DAVIS, CALEB, Set., 9-13-1823.

DAVIS, JACOB, Will, 7-5-1793. Dev.: Mary, wife; Jacob, Sam., Crandal, Zebulon, sons; Lydia, Mary, Eliz., daus.

DAVIS, JESSE, Inv., 2-2-1825.

DAVIS, JOSHUA, Inv., 8-31-1839.

DAVIS, JOSIAS, Will, 1-1-1833. Dev.: Martha, wife.

DAVIS, NATHAN, Inv., 10-24-1804.

DAVIS, OWEN, Will, 6-3-1806. Dev.: Mary, wife; Notley, John, Henry, Jacob, Philip, sons; Mary Cottrill, Eliz. Husteas, Mary Goodwin, daus.

DAVIS, THOMAS, Will, 5-1-1794. Dev.: Henry, John, sons; Barthany; Pritchard, dau.

DAVIS, WM., Inv., no date.

DAVISSON, DAN., Will, 7-16-1810. Dev.: Lemuel, Geo., Nat., Henry, sons; Edith, Cath. Armstrong, Eliz. Wilson, Patsy Wilson, Prudence Coplin, daus.

DAVISSON, DAN., Set., 9-18-1833.

DAVISSON, GEO., Inv., 7-14-1837.

DAVISSON, HENRY, Will, 8-26-1824. Dev.: Lemuel, bro., Prudence Coplin, sister.

DAVISSON, HEZEKIAH, Will, 4-15-1794. Dev.: Ann, wife; Ithamer, son; Marg., Lucinda, Eliz., Ann, daus.

DAVISSON, JESSE, Inv., 1823.

DAVISSON, JOSEPH, Inv., 4-27-1815.

DAVISSON, L. E., Set., 5-30-1834.

DAVISSON, LEMUEL HEIRS, Set., 3-24-1832.

DAVISSON, WM., Will, 11-24-1824. Dev.: John, bro.

DAWSON, WM., Inv., 4-15-1832.

DAWSON, WM., Set., 6-12-1834.

DEAKINS, FRANCIS, Will, 9-24-1804. Dev.: Elinor, wife; others.

DEAKINS, NANCY ANN, Will, 12-4-1832. Dev.: Ann Caussin, niece.

DENNISON, JOHN, Set., 5-14-1827.

DENNISON, JOHN, Inv., 11-30-1824.

DEVILBISS, JOHN, Inv., 1823.

DICK, ROBERT, Will, 4-6-1803. Dev.: Benj. Wilson, executor.

DICKINSON, JOHN, Will, 9-20-1810. Dev.: Barbary, wife; Hannah, Mary, daus.; Dan., son.

DICKS, JOB, Inv., 2-18-1833.

DICKS, JOB, Set., 11-8-1834.

DIX, DAVID, Inv., 3-9-1821.

DOUGLASS, LEVI, Inv., 8-4-1787.

DUFFIELD, ISAAC, Inv., 11-19-1795.

DUNKIN, JOHN, Will, 4-11-1836. Dev.: Phebe, wife; John, Geo., Asbyry, Dan., sons; Ameties, dau.

DUVALL, LEWIS, Will, 4-3-1831. Dev.: Sary, wife; Evan, Geo., sons; Mary Ann Maddox, dau.

DUVALL, SARAH, Set., no date.

DUVALL, SARAH, Inv., 9-2-1833.

EARIT, SAM., Inv., no date except 1833.

EAST, ROBERT, Inv., 3-3-1809.

EASTER, THOMAS, Set., 11-16-1813.

EIB, JACOB, Will, 12-17-1825. Dev.: Jacob, son; Susan Bond, dau.; Modelina, dau.-in-law.

ELBERT, VALENTINE, Will, 10-16-1816. Dev.: Cath., wife; Adam and Mary Keller, grandchildren; Cath. Bierly, Susannah Hardman, Ulinanne, daus.; Frederick, Elbert, John, Valentine, sons; others.

ELSWORTH, MOSES, Will, 7-10-1794. Dev.: Mary Eliz., wife; Jacob, Wm., Moses, sons.

ELY, HUGH, Will, 5-10-1849. Dev.: Ruth, wife; Eliz., Randolph, Elias, children.

EMERICK, SIMON, Will, 4-30-1832. Dev.: Mary, wife; Samuel, son; Rachel Godrey, dau.

ESTLACK, THOMAS, Inv., 8-27-1822.

ESTLACK, THOMAS, Set., 12-22-1828.

ESTLACK, THOMAS, Inv., 1-1-1835.

EVANS, JOHN, Will, 2-19-1824. Dev.: Abigail, wife; others.

EVERRETT, WALTER, Will, 6-10-1802. Dev.: Mary, wife; Nathan, Walter, sons; Ruth, Bythiah, daus.

EVICK, FRANCIS, Will, 7-14-1814. Dev.: Son of Caty Evick; others.

EVICKS, CHRISTIAN, Inv., no date.

FAIR, THOMAS, Inv., 8-29-1829.

FERGUSON, ELIZA ANN, Will, 9-8-1833. Dev.: Dolly, mother; sisters.

FERGUSON, SAM., Set., 8-1830.

FINDLEY, WM., Inv., 10-21-1808.

FINDLEY, WM., Will, 5-27-1836. Dev.: Sarah, wife.

FISHBURN, DANIEL, Set., 8-8-1832.

FITZRANDOLPH, SAM., Will, 6-11-1822. Dev.: Marg., wife; Jesse, Salem, David, sons; Hulana Bonnell, dau.

FLEMING, EDWARD, Inv., 1-12-1825.

FLEMING, EDWARD, Set., 3-10-1827.

FLEMING, JAMES, Will, 12-20-1823. Dev.: Mary, wife; Emrack, son.

FLEMING, JAMES, Set., 2-6-1836.

FLEMING, NATHAN, Will, 2-7-1823. Dev.: Lydia, wife; Archibald, Nathan, Thomas, Wm., Joseph, sons; Eliz. Hays, Rachel Hart, Lydia, Mary, Jane, daus.

FLEMING, NATHAN, Inv., 7-21-1825.

FLESHER, HENRY, Will, 11-26-1802. Dev.: Eliz., wife; Andrew, Peter, Henry, John, sons; Ann, Eliz., Mary, Susannah, daus.

FLESHER, PETER, Inv., 3-7-1815.

FLING, ELIZ., Will, 1-29-1816. Dev.: Heirs of Jane Bucklew, Nancy Morrison, Eliz., Marg. DeWitt, Rebekah, daus.

FLUHARTY, STEPHEN, Inv., no date.

FORD, PETER, S.B., no date.

FORINASH, CHARLES, Set., 9-11-1823.

FORRINGASH (FORINASH) CHARLES, Inv., 8-29-1815.

FRANKLIN, RICHARD, Inv., 4-25-1832.

FREEL, JEREMIAH, Inv., 7-27-1817.

GAWTHROP, THOMAS, Inv., 4-18-1833.

GAWTHROP, THOMAS, Set., 9-23-1834.

GILLESPIE, SILAS, Will, 11-26-1795. Dev.: Sarah, wife; Enos, Andrew, Richard, sons; Mary Phillips, Anne, daus.

GILLIS, WM., Inv., 1-21-1828.

GOFF, MARTHA, Inv., 5-25-1829.

GOODWIN, JOHN, Will, 12-19-1842. Dev.: Eliz., wife; Zepporah, Zadock, Comfort, Tabitha, John, Polly, Nancy, Wm., Geo., children.

GOSS, HAMILTON, Will, 3-21-1839. Dev.: James Gawthrop, John Reynolds, Samuel Wes.

GOSS, MARTHA, Will, 4-1-1811. Dev.: John Reynolds, nephew.

GOSS, SARAH, Will, 6-19-1848. Dev.: Rebecca Hansel, Marg. Lancaster, dau.

GOULDER, JOHN, Will, 4-12-1816. Dev.: Milly, wife; Willis, Henry, John, sons; Liny, dau.; others.

GREATHOUSE, GABRIEL, Inv., 12-18-1813.

GREATHOUSE, GABRIEL, Set., 9-17-1836.

GREATHOUSE, JOHN, Will, 5-12-1838. Dev.: Milly, wife; Stephen, Enos, Jacob, Augustin, sons.

GREATHOUSE, MILLY, Inv., 9-7-1839.

GREATHOUSE, WM., Will, 3-25-1791. Dev.: Barbary, wife; John, Frederick, Gabriel, Wm., sons; Mary, Caty Hartset, Anna McCarty, daus.

GREEN, GEORGE, Will, 10-1842. Dev.: Frances, Susan, Malinda, daus.; Jesse, James, Geo., sons.

GREEN, ROBERT, Will, 9-21-1789. Dev.: Wife; Jesse, Amos, Robert, Silas, sons; Mary Chalfant, sister; Lot, son; Abigail Hollingsworth, Rachel, Rebecca, daus.

GREGORY, JOSEPH, Inv., 11-24-1822.

GREGORY, JOSEPH, Set., 6-19-1830.

GRIFFIN, ABNER, Will, no date. Dev.: May, wife; Mary, dau.; Geo., grandson.

GRIFFIN, HENRY, Will, 12-7-1813. Dev.: Rachel, wife; Henry, son; Sally, dau.; expected child.

GRIFFIN, HENRY, Inv., 5-17-?

GRIFFITH, STEPHEN, Will, 3-23-1801. Dev.: Eliz., Hannah, Mary, Rachel, daus.; Jane Evans.

GRUBB, ENOCH, Will, 11-16-1835. Dev.: Thomas Rhea, John, Amos, bro.

HALL, DAVID, S.B., 10-11-1828.

HALL, HENRY, Inv., 4-8-1815.

HALL, JORDAN, Set., no date.

HALL, JORDAN, Will, 9-5-1834. Dev.: Matilda, wife; Edgar, Eugenus, Joseph, sons.

HALL, SAM., Inv., 9-29-1836.

HALL, SAMUEL, Will, no date. Dev.: Eliz., wife; John, James, sons; Rebecca, Nancy, daus.

HALL, WILLIAM, Will, 8-23-1828. Dev.: Wm., Vincent, Richard, Sam., sons; Betsy, Sally White, Malinda Bigson, daus.; Mary, wife.

HANEY, JOHN, Inv., 1-11-1820.

HARBERT, SAMUEL, Will, 3-15-1847. Dev.: Ruhama Carothers, Eliz. Sarah, Rebecca Harvey, Mary Randall, daus.; Bassel Harvey, friend.

HARBERT, THOMAS, Inv., 11-17-1818,

HARDY, ANN, Will, 3-21-1821. Dev.: Louisa, dau.

HARPOLE (HARPOLD), ADAM, Will, 6-24-1802. Dev.: Marg., wife; Nicholas, Daniel, John, Adam, Solomon, Absalom, sons; Susan, Barbary Bonnett, dau.

HART, JOHN, Will, 2-1-1803. Dev.: Deborah, wife; James, John, Wm., sons; Eliz., dau.

HARTMAN, GEO., S.B., 6-1-1799.

HARTMAN, GEO., Will, 7-2-1818. Dev.: Sarah, wife; James, Gainer, sons; Hannah, Abigail, Marg., Sarah, Nancy, daus.; Geo., son.

HARVEY, BASIL, Will, 1-7-1836. Dev.: Mary, wife; Lewis, Benj., Pruet, Basil, sons.

HARVEY, JOSEPH, Inv., 11-24-1831.

HASTINGS, JOSEPH, Will, 5-15-1796. Dev.: Nancy, wife; Abner Stout, Noah Stout, Abner Davisson, step-sons.

HAYMOND, WM., Will, 11-10-1821. Dev.: Mary, wife; Dick, Cyrus, sons.

HAYMOND, WM., Inv., 3-9-1822.

HAYS, JOHN, Will, 5-23-1815. Dev.: Eliz., wife; Sam., son.

HELDRITH, FRAZIER, Inv., 8-3-1831.

HENLIN, JAMES, Set., 2-4-1830.

HICKMAN, ADAM, Will, 8-7-1826. Dev.: Marg., wife; Cath. Lochery, Mary Sommerville, Judith Henry, Marg. Coffman, daus.; Adam, John, Abraham, sons.

HICKMAN, ELIZ., Will, 9-17-1792. Dev.: Joshua, son; Ann White, dau.

HICKMAN, SOTHA, Inv., no date.

HILL, WM., Will, 6-14-1805. Dev.: Philip, Wm., Abraham, Jacob, James, sons; Cath., dau.; Mary, wife.

HINKLE, LEONARD, Inv., 9-30-1839.

HITCHCOCK, WM., Inv., 7-29-1819.

HITE, MATHIAS, Inv., no date.

HOFF, ABRAHAM, Inv., 9-10-1839.

HOLDEN, BENJ., Will, 11-9-1831. Dev.: Marg., wife; Charles, Alex., Peter, Benj., Thomas, Pearson, sons; Arominer, Grace, Jemima, daus.; Judson, Sarah, grandchildren.

HOLDEN, BENJ., Set., 9-21-1835.

HOKDEN, BENJ., Will, 9-21-1835.

HORNBACK, JONATHAN, Inv., 3-5-1831.

HOUGH, THOMPSON, Inv., 12-13-1834.

HUFFMAN, MOSES, App., 7-7-1813.

HUFFMAN, MOSES, Inv., 2-2-1814.

HUFFMAN, MOSES, Set., 3-7-1823.

HUGHES, DUDLEY, Inv., 7-27-1820.

HUGHES, JOHN, Inv., 11-27-1839.

HUMPHREY, DAN., Inv., 2-1816.

HUSTEAD, MOSES, Will, 6-9-1835. Dev.: Marg., wife; Wm., son.

HYDE, JAMES, S.B., 12-23-1811.

HYDE, JAMES, Set., 10-8-1831.

INGRAM, ABRAHAM, Will, 8-19-1817. Dev.: Eliz., wife; Jacob, son; Comfort, dau.; other children.

INNIS, WM., Will, 12-5-1813. Dev.: Robert, son; Esther, Mary, Eliz., daus.

IRELAND, Alex., Sr., Inv., 9-21-1816.

IRELAND, ANN, Will, 12-18-1819. Dev.: Ann, Sarah Madden's heirs, Eliz. Giner, Mary Bailey, Jennie Waterman, Maryann Baccus, Pressley Cann, daus.

IRELAND, ANN, Inv., 8-22-1820.

IRELAND, JONATHAN, Inv., 7-7-1798.

ISRAEL, BENONE, Will, 6-1841. Dev.: Methodist Missionary Society, others.

ISRAEL, BENONI, Inv., 5-1841.

ISRAEL, JACOB, Will, 4-16-1783. Dev.: Priscella, wife; young son; Isaac, bro.

JACKSON, ED., Will, 5-7-1807. Dev.: Wife; Stephen, Jacob, Wm., Sam., sons; Sarah Fletcher, Mary Flint, Jemima Arnold, Lucia, Phebe, daus.

JACKSON, EDWARD, Will, no date. Dev.: Eliz., wife; Maria, Flora, Virginia, daus.; Geo., Alfred, sons.

JACKSON, EDWARD, Set., 6-29-1821.

JACKSON, GEO., Will, 1-26-1831. Dev.: Wife; Lucy, Sophia, Sarah Kincheloe, Cath. Williams, Prudence Arnold, Mary Seely, daus.; Andrew, Geo., Wm., John, sons.

JACKSON, JOHN, S.B., 3-23-1826.

JACKSON, JOHN, Will, 9-2-1801. Dev.: Sophia, Eliz. Reager, daus.; Eliz., wife.

JACKSON, JOHN G., Inv., 7-18-1825.

JACOBS, JACOB, Will, 3-3-1803. Dev.: Wm., Jacob, sons; Rebecca Frazer, Mary Gifford, Sarah Plum, Caty Bennett, Hannah Harbert, daus.

JAMES, HUGH, Will, 4-21-1848. Dev.: Lydia, wife; Daniel, Lydia, Ashbell, Oliver, Wm., Sinderella, Hugh, Mima, James, children.

JONES, ENOCH Inv. 7-21-1804.

JONES, GEO., Set., 5-9-1840.

JONES, JOHN, Inv., 10-27-1834.

JONES, JOHN, Set., 6-21-1838.

JOHNSON, JACOB, S. B., 8-30-1795.

JOHNSON, JAMES, Inv., 4-25-1835.

JOHNSON, PETER, Inv., 12-1-1840.

JOHNSON, WM., Inv., 2-17-1795.

KARSHNER, JOHN, Will, 1-28-1825. Dev.: Rebecca, sister.

KAYSER, JACOB, Will, 2-20-1833. Dev.: Permelia, wife.

KAYSER, PAMELIA, Will, 11-1844. Dev.: Mary Kayser, dau.-in-law.

KEEPER, HENRY, Will, 7-10-1822. Dev.: Mary, wife; Wm., John, Andrew, sons; Sarah, Peggy, Petsy, daus.

KENNEDY, JAMES, Will, 7-1845. Dev.: James, Wm., Lois Knisly, Job, Marg., children; Sarah, wife.

KERSHNER, JOHN, Inv., 11-18-1825.

KEYS, WM., Set., 4-24-1834.

KEYS, WM., Inv., 2-1-1838.

KILLIE (KELLY), JOHN, Will, 5-21-1796. Dev.: Ann, wife; John, Geo., sons; Mary, dau.

KING, ELIJAH, Inv., 6-24-1829.

KNIGHT, BAILEY, Will, 7-14-1839. Dev.: Sarah, wife; James, Peter, Isaac, Benj., sons; Mary Ann, Sally, Frances Curry, daus.

KNIGHT, WM., Will, 4-19-1834. Dev.: Agnes, wife; Thornton, son; Benj., son; Sarah Stark, Mildred Atchison, daus.

KNIGHT, WM., Inv., 9-1-1834.

LACY, THOMAS, Inv., 1-25-1802.

LAKE, VINCENT, Inv., 10-30-1815.

LAKE, WM., Will, 3-22-1824. Dev.: Wm., Geo., Nimrod, Ila, Jeremiah, Vincent, sons; Susanne Norris, Mary Cross, Jemy Neal, daus.; grandchildren.

LAMBERT, JONATHAN, Inv., 10-15-1805.

LANG, JOHN, Inv., 3-15-1837.

LANG, NANCY, Will, 7-29-1836. Dev.: Dau. of deceased dau., Sarah Bailey; James, John, Henderson, Lemuel, sons; Nancy, Aseneth, daus.

LANHAM, ALEX., Inv., no date.

LANHAM, ALEX., Set., 9-22-1812.

LANHAM, FRANCIS, Will, 6-8-1824. Dev.: Frances, wife; Dennis, son; Nancy, Celia, Lydia, Eliz., Areas, daus.

LATHAM, JOHN, Will, 5-17-1843. Dev.: Winny, wife.

LEWIS, ASHER, Inv., 6-17-1814.

LEWIS, REBECCA, Will, 5-2-1829. Dev.: Charles, husband; Ruhama, Jester Jane, daus.

LINDSAY, WALTER, Will, 6-15-1820. Dev.: Mary, wife; Walter, grandson.

LINK, HANNAH, Will, 12-29-1829. Dev.: Mariah Bartlett, Cath., Emiline Robinson, daus.; Ed., son.

LINK, PETER, Will, 10-29-1819. Dev.: Hannah, wife; Emiline, Mariah, Cath., daus.; Ed., Wm., sons.

LIONS (LYONS), ANDREW, Inv., 3-7-1815.

West Virginia Estate Settlements

(Harrison County, from Lockard to Zumbro)

LOCKARD, AARON, Inv. 3-29-1820.

LOFFTUS, WASHINGTON, Inv., 6-13-1814.

LONG, DAN., Will, 7-18-1821. Dev.: Eliz., wife; Christian, Daniel, Jacob, John, sons; Polly Lapole, Susan, daus.; Cath. Fetre, housekeeper.

LOUDIN, JOHN, Will, 11-11-1822. Dev.: Sary, wife; Thomas, John, Walter, sons; Mary, dau.

LOUDIN, JOHN, Will, 8-17-1845. Dev.: Eliz., wife; Nicholas, son; Sarah Rider, dau.

LOWE, ROBERT, Inv., 4-10-1809.

LOWE, ROBERT, Set., no date.

LOWTHER, THOMAS, Will, 5-19-1816. Dev.: Cath. Switzer, Jesse, Elias, Wm., sons; Peggy, Nancy, daus. and children of Cath. Switzer.

LOWTHER, WILLIAM (Guardian), Inv., 8-18-1790.

LOWTHER, WM., COL., Inv., 12-23-1814.

LOWTHER, WM., Set., no date.

LUCAS, BASIL, Will, 2-1-1820. Dev.: Joanna, wife; John, son.

LUCAS, JOHN, Will, 1-18-1847. Dev.: Mary, wife; Wm., John, Basil, Geo., sons; Mary Glowers, dau.

LUCAS, Mary, Will, 9-20-1847. Dev.: Bazsil, step-son.

LYNCH, PETER, Inv., no date.

LYNCH, PETER, Inv., 10-29-1834.

LYNN, ROBT., Will, 1-31-1832. Dev.: Cath., wife; Sarah, Nancy, Priscella, Louisa, daus.; Robert, Benj., sons.

LYON, ALEX., Inv., 5-29-1817.

LYONS, JOHN, Inv., 4-11-1836.

MARKWELL, JOS., Inv., 6-22-1810.

MARSH, ELIJAH, Inv., 10-29-1839.

MARTIN, GEO., Will, 10-9-1825. Dev.: John, Jacob, brothers.

MARTIN, JACOB, Will, 6-1842. Dev.: John Martin, brother; Anderson Jones, friend.

MARTIN, JOEL, Inv., 5-16-1799.

MARTIN, WM., Inv., 7-24-1809.

MARTIN, WM., Will, 4-22-1848. Dev.: Templeton Martin.

MARTIN, WM., Set., no date.

MASON, THOMAS, S.B., 4-17-1830.

MASTERS, DAVIS, Inv., 6-12-1823.

MAXON, EPHRAIM, Will, 8-12-1795. Dev.: Wife; Jess, son; Amey, Sally, Prudence, Piety, Charity, daus.

MAXON, THOMAS, Will, 10-8-1822. Dev.: Ina Vanhorn, dau.; Timothy, son.

MAXON, ZEBULON, Will, 10-8-1822. Dev.: Mary, wife; John, Gideon, sons; Cath. Davis, dau.

MAXWELL, ALEX., Inv., 11-28-1839.

MAXWELL, BEDWELL, Will. 9-1845. Dev.; Nancy, wife; Amos, Eli, sons.

MAXWELL, DAVID, Will, 11-29-1819. Dev.: Mary, wife; Bonnell, Armstrong, sons.

MAXWELL, ROBERT, Will, 5-1845. Dev.: Melisent Carter.

McCANN, THOMAS, Will, 1-15-1828. Dev. Martha, wife; Thomas, James, Wilson, sons; Sarah, dau.

McCULLOUGH, JAMES, Will, 9-2-1798. Dev.: Rachel, wife; Jane Adams, dau.; John, son.

McCULLOUGH, JAMES, Inv., 10-16-1812.

McCULLOUGH, JOHN, Inv., 11-4-1831.

McCULLOUGH, JOHN, Set., 5-10-1837.

McDESSETT, CHARLES, Inv., no date.

McGEE, THOMAS, Inv., no date.

McGLOTHLIN, HENRY, Inv., 11-29-1822.

McINTIRE, ANDREW, Will, 12-29-1815. Dev.: Pamelia, wife; Elexander, mother; Sam., Charles, James, Wm., bro.

McINTIRE, CHARLES, Will, 7-17-1843. Dev.: John, Wm., Andrew, Charles, sons; Celia, Mary, Sarah, daus.; Hannah, wife.

McINTIRE, JAMES, Will, 9-21-1845. Dev.: Elias, Allison, sons; Delila Miller, Sarah, Seneth, Barnes, daus.

McINTIRE, JOHN, Inv., no date.

McINTIRE, PAMELIA, Will, 10-13-1819. Dev.: Ledoe McIntire.

McINTIRE, SAM., Will, 10-30-1825. Dev.: Eliz., wife; Wm., son.

McKINLEY, THOMAS, Inv., 9-16-1836.

McKINNEY, GEO., Set., 8-1831.

McKINNEY, GEO., Set., 1-19-1837.

McKINNEY, MICHAEL, Inv., 7-6-1837.

McPHERSON, JAMES, Will, 5-10-1839. Dev.: Eliz., wife; John, Jesse, Wm., Gary, Stephen, Sam., James, Dan., sons; Sarah Romein, Ruth McPherson, Eliz., Mary Chidister, Ann Paugh, Rachel, Ruth, Eliz., daus.

McRAE, FAUQUER, Will, 1-15-1829. Dev.: Susan Milling, dau.; Susan, wife of son Alex.

McWHORTER, THOMAS, Inv., no date.

McWHORTER, THOMAS, Set., 8-26-1826.

MINEAR, Wm., Will, 10-16-1842. Dev.: Eliz., wife; children.

MONTGOMERY, GEO., Will, 11-2-1815. Dev.: James, Wm., sons; Nancy, dau.; Ann, wife.

MOOR (MOORE), RICHARD, Will, 4-11-1815. Dev.: Marg., wife; Richard, son; Ann Robinson, Sarah and Aseny Cunningham, daus.

MOORE, RICHARD, Will, 2-15-1841. Dev.: Polly, Rush, Jeptha, Wm., Richard, Rebecca Webb, Ann Sandy, children.

MOORE, RICHARD, SR., Inv., 2-23-1841.

MOORE, SAM., Inv., 7-24-1822.

MOORE, SAM., Set., 9-17-1828.

121

MOORE, SARAH, Will, 1-1844. Dev.: Mary Haymond, Hannah Adams, sisters.

MORRIS, ISAAC, Will, 7-3-1830. Dev.: Joseph, Sam., Levi, sons; Ruth, Carolina, daus.; Ruth, wife.

MORRIS, RUTH, Will, 3-13-1839. Dev.: Grandchildren.

MORROW, ELIZ., Will, 3-2-1831. Dev.: Mary Fowler, James Fowler.

MUEREHEAD (MUIRHEAD), GEO., Will, 2-6-1812. Dev.: Martha, wife; Rebecca Nutter, dau.; Geo., son; Ephraim, grandson.

MUIRE, JOHN, Inv., 4-9-1803.

NAY, JOHN, JR., Will, 3-3-1840. Dev.: Phebe, wife; Isaac, Henry, Elias, Joseph, Alfred, sons; Matilda Tetrick, Sarah Tetrick.

NEAL, CHARLES, Inv., 3-13, 1810.

NEALE, CHARLES, Set., no date.

NEALE, JAMES, Inv., 10-30-1828.

NEEL, JAMES, Set., 11-15-1834.

NEWLON, Sarah, Inv., 1827.

NEWLON, THOM., Will, 7-7-1813. Dev.: Wm., John, James, sons; Sarah, wife; Sarah, dau.; Susannah, Peyton, other children.

NEWLON, THOMAS, Inv., 5-15-1814.

NEWLON, WM., Inv., 12-31-1816.

NICHOL, JOHN, Will, 2-15-1847. Dev.: Eliz., wife; Calvin, John, Eliza., Sally, Jos., Martha, Amanda, Eliz., children.

NIXON, BENJ., Inv., 7-15-1815.

NIXSON (NIXON), JONATHAN, Will, 6-10-1799. Dev.: Sarah, wife; Geo., Robert, Jesse, Sam., Jonathan, sons; Mary Tucker, Hannah, Eliz., Sarah, Ellender, Anne, Rachel, daus.

NUTTER, JAMES, Will, 5-8-1833. Dev.: Jacob, David, Shelton, Andrew, Christopher, Geo., sons; Nancy, dau.

NUTTER, JAMES, Set., 8-15-1835.

NUTTER, JOHN, Will, 4-28-1808. Dev.: Esther, wife; Christopher, John, sons; Sarah Glaspy, dau.

NUTTER, THOMAS, Inv., 8-6-1802.

NYHOFF, GEVARDUS, Will, 9-20-1800. Dev.: Gevardus, son; Henry Weaver.

ODLE, JOSHUA, Inv., 1-15-1827.

ODLE (ODELL), JOSHUA, Set., 4-12-1841.

OGDEN, ANN, Inv., 8-10-1825.

OGDEN, JONATHAN, Will, 8-13-1807. Dev.: Ann, wife; Thomas, Sam., Wm., Nathan, sons; Mary Robey, Tobitha, Sarah Martin, Susannah Sigler, Nancy Richardson, daus.

OGDEN, THOMAS, Will, 4-7-1830. Dev.: Eliz., wife; Jonathan, Sam., Nathan, Wm., sons; Anna Barnes, dau.

ORR, NICHOLAS, Will, 10-17-1842. Dev.: Anne, wife; Nicholas, John, Eliz., Ann, Matthew, Robert, Jane, Susannah, Sarah, Amanda, children.

ORTON, AURORA, Inv., no date.

OSBERN, JOSEPH, Will, 8-1845. Dev.: Mary, wife.

PARKS, JOS., Inv., 4-15-1815.

PARRIMORE, MATHEW, Will, 7-3-1816. Dev.: Mathew and Ezekiel Parrimore, nephews.

PARSONS, EDWARD, Inv., 8-15-1811.

PATTERSON, JOHN, S.B., 9-2-1834.

PATTON, FRANCIS, Will, 3-30-1797. Dev.: Ruth, wife; Andrew, John, Israel, Robert, sons; Phebe, dau.

PATTON, JOHN, JR., Inv., 8-27-1834.

PATTON, WM., Inv., 12-11-1826.

PEARCE, ISAAC, Inv., no date.

PEPPER, PARKER, Inv., no date.

PERRY, JAMES, Set., 8-22-1838.

PETERSON, WM., Inv., 8-19-1815.

PEYTON, LAKE, Inv., no date.

PHELPS, OLIVER, Will, 5-30-1823. Dev.: Karem, wife; children.

PHILLIPS, SARAH, Set., 10-19-1824.

PHILLIPS, THOMAS, Will, 10-7-1798. Dev.: Mary, wife; Thomas, Reynolds, Robert Bartlett, grandsons.

PINDALL, JAMES, Will, 11-12-1825. Dev.: Ruhamah, wife.

PINDALL, RUHAMAH, Will, 5-3-1828. Dev.: Nancy Chapin, sister.

PLANT, SAM, Inv., 3-1-1832.

PLUMER, MARG., Set., 10-4-1834.

PLUMER (PLUMMER), ROBERT, Will, 10-30-1817. Dev.: Jane Critchfield, Mary Mackie, Afe McDaniel, daus.; Joel, son; Peggy, wife.

PLUMMER, HANNAH, Inv., 6-11-1808.

PLUMMER, JOHN, Will, 1-22-1822. Dev.: Jesse Fitzrandolph, good friend.

PLUMMER, MARG., Inv., no date.

PLUMMER, ROBERT, Set., 2-24-1826.

POLING, MARTIN, Will, 1-23-1814. Dev.: Sam, Wm., sons; Peggy, Elenor, Sarah, daus.; Eliz., wife.

POLSLEY, PAULINA, Set., 10-10-1834.

POOL, RICHARD, Will, 1-1-1838. Dev.: Nancy, wife.

POST, GEO., Will, 8-9-1849. Dev.: Eliz., wife; Geo., Jacob, Enoch, sons; Eliz. Summerville, Mary Gaston, daus.

POWEL (POWELL), HENRY, Inv., 7-6-1804.

POWELL, HENRY, Inv., 8-30-1825.

POWELL, REUBEN, Inv., 10-10-1832.

POWERS, JOHN, Will, 2-10-1823. Dev.: Wm. Powers, John Davis.

POWERS, MAJOR, Will, 2-26-1786. Dev.: Wm., Nehemiah, John, sons; Noemy, dau.

PRICE, WASHINGTON, Inv., no date.

PRUNTY, JOHN, Inv., 4-29-1823.

QUEEN, ARMSTEAD, Inv., 8-10-1827.

RADABAUGH, GEO., Inv., 6-13-1815.

RADCLIFF, JOHN, Will, 12-30-1812. Dev.: John, Jonathan, Benj., James, sons; Susannah, dau.; Cath., wife.

RAMAGE, WM., Inv., 3-26-1839.

READ, JOHN, Inv., 5-22-1799.

READ, JOHN, Will, 5-16-1825. Dev.: Esther, wife; Thomas, Francis, sons; Eliz. Vanhorn, dau.

REAGER, HENRY, Will, 4-24-1806. Dev.: Susannah, wife; Anthony, Henry, Saul, sons; Rachael, dau.; Anna Reager, sister.

REAGER, JACOB, Inv., no date.

REED, THOMAS, Inv., no date.

REEDER, BENJ., Will, 2-21-1843. Dev.: Sophia, Nancy, Mary, Benj., Elisha, grandchildren.

REEDER, JOHN, Inv., 10-6-1835.
REEDER, JOSEPH, Will, 7-2-1798. Dev.: John, Joseph, Abel, Thomas, sons; Eliz., wife; Ann, Mary, Eliz., daus.
REEDS, STEPHEN, Will, 12-1841. Dev.: Cath., wife.
REES, JACOB, Will, 4-23-1789. Dev.: Hannah. wife; children.
REYNOLDS, CORNELIUS, Will, 7-17-1848. Dev.: Mary, wife; Geo., son; Angelina, Polly Hazelton, daus.
RHITTENHOUSE (RITTENHOUSE), ISAAC., Inv., 3-7-1814.
RICE, AMON, Will, 7 - 7 - 1825. Dev.: Jemima, wife; Abner, Hezekiah, Wm., Thomas, sons; Sarah, Eliz., daus.
RICHARDSON, JOHN, Inv., 4-14-1825.
RICHARDSON, SAM., Will, 3-17-1848. Dev.: Wife; John, son.
RICHMOND, DAN., Assignment, 10-15-1799.
RIFFLE, JACOB, Inv., 9-26-1817.
RIGHTER, JOHN, Will, 11-24-1808, Dev.: Sarah, wife; Maria, dau.; Jacob, John, Abraham, Peter, sons.
RIGHTER, JOHN, Inv., 2-12-1821.
RILEY, LAWSON, Inv., 9-4-1820.
RITTENHOUSE, ISAAC, Will, 6-7-1834. Dev.; Mary, Eliz., Nancy, daus.; Sam., Bennett, sons.
RITTENHOUSE, ISAAC, Set., 6-16-1835.
ROADS, JOHN, Will, 11-16-1840. Dev.: Sarah, wife; Wm., John, Jas., Washington, sons; Nancy, Martha, Eliz., Sarah, Nancy Richcreek, Eleanor, daus.
ROBERTS, ELIJAH, Inv., 8-19-1837.
ROBEY, JEREMIAH, Will, 1-12-1835. Dev.: Henderson, son.
ROBEY, PATRICK, Inv., no date.
ROBINSON, ABSALOM (WARD), Set., 7-31-1819.
ROBINSON, BENJ., S.B., 6-16-1832.
ROBINSON, BENJ., Set., 9-22-1835.
ROBINSON, CATH., Will, 4-5-1820. Dev.: Eliz. Shinn, Jemima Wood, Mary Cunningham, Rebecca Wood, sisters; Abner, Job, Absalom, brothers.
ROBINSON, ELIZ., Set., 7-31-1819.
ROBINSON, JOB., Inv., 6-26-1819.
ROBINSON, JOB., Set., 10-20-1825.
ROBINSON, JOHN, Will, 1-7-1807. Dev.: Abner, Absalom, Joab, sons; Mary Cunningham, Rebecca Wood, Eliz., Jemima, Cath., Sarah, daus.
ROBINSON, JOHN, Inv., 1-30-1807.
ROBINSON, JOHN, Set., no date.
ROBINSON, WM., Inv., 1-29-1799.
ROBINSON, WM., Will, 11-1840. Dev.: Eliz., wife; Caleb, Sam., John, Lott, sons; Leah, Rachel, Grissy, Ann, Sarah, Rebecca Mary, daus.
ROBINSON, WM., Inv., 11-28-1840.
ROMINE, JACOB, Will, 8-16-1847. Dev.: Israel Davis, friend.
ROMINE, JOSEPH, Will, 2-19-1849. Dev.: Catharine, wife; Majerly, Villa, Eliz. Reed, Nancy Young, daus.; Jos., Jacob, Geo., Lemuel, sons.
ROSS, ALEXANDER, Will, 6-28-1824. Dev.: Sally, Rosanna, daus.; Robert, Lewis, Geo., sons; Mary Ann, wife.

ROSS, CYRUS, Inv., 7-19-1828.
ROSS, JOHN, S.B., 7-21-1828.
ROSS, JOHN, Will, 5-10-1835. Dev.: Mathew, son; Eliz., wife; Sarah, Patty, Levina, Mary, daus.
RUNYAN, JOHN, S.B., no date.
RYLAND, NICHOLAS, Will, 10-7-1825. Dev.: Sarah, wife.

SEHON, JOHN, Will, 5-19-1847. Dev.: Fanny, wife; John, Edwin, Geo., James, sons; Eliz McMechen, dau.
SHARP, JOHN, Inv., no date.
SHARPLESS, JOHN, Inv., 12-14-1838.
SHAVER, JOHN, App., 10-8-1791.
SHIELDS, WM., Will, 6-24-1833. Dev.: Marg., wife; Harrison, Dan., sons; Jane, dau.; John, son.
SHINN, BENJ., Will, 3-11-1791. Dev.: Ann, wife; Isaac, Samuel, sons; Deborah, Lucretia, Ama, daus.
SHINN, CLEMENT, Will, 12-3-1805. Dev.: Ruth, wife; Joseph, Moses, Daniel, Clement, Ed., Sam., sons; Hepzibah, Ackey, daus.
SHINN, ELIZ., Inv., 10-16-1813.
SHINN, ISAAC, Will, 8-1845. Dev.: Deborah Davisson, Lucretia, Agnes Bartlett, Susan Berkley, Rachel Wilkinson, dau.; Sam., Isaac, sons.
SHINN, JONATHAN, Will, 6-1817. Dev.: Levi, Asa, Smasa, sons; Eliz., Hannah, Ruth, Sarah, daus.; Sarah, wife.
SHINN, LEVI, Inv., 1-25-1808.
SHINN, SAM., Will, 2-14-1831. Dev.: Isaac, Francis, sons; Sarah Norris, Hanna Wilkinson, Eliz. Ogden, daus.; Sarah, wife.
SHREVE, JOS., Will, 9-8-1811. Dev.: Nephews and others.
SIGLEY, GEO., Inv., 6-21-1823.
SILMAN, JOSEPH, Inv., 6-1837.
SINCEL, ELIJAH, Inv., no date.
SINCLAIR, NATHAN, Will, 6-27-1831. Dev.: John, Henry, Thomas, sons; children of son Wm.; Nancy, dau.
SLEETH, JOHN, Inv., 10-25-1794.
SMITH, AARON, Will, 5-14-1826. Dev.: James, Aaron, Joshua, Levi, Moses, Timothy, Isaac, Wm., sons; Elias, son; Sarah, wife.
SMITH, DAVID, Inv., 10-17-1828.
SMITH, EPHRAIM, Will, 3-6-1803. Dev.: Charity, wife; Benj., Hezekiah, sons; Rachel Bockover, Hannah, Massey Carpenter, Sarah, Eliz., daus.
SMITH, JAMES, Inv., 6-10-1835.
SMITH, JOHN, Inv., 11-9-1815.
SMITH, JOHN, Inv., 2-18-1824.
SMITH, JOS., S.B., 10-12-1820.
SMITH, JOSEPH, Inv., 9-28-1820.
SMITH, SARAH, Will, 9-3-1833. Dev.: Joshua, James, Levi, Moses, Timothy, Jacob, Wm., Elias, Barnes, sons; Eliz., dau.
SMITH, THOM., App., 7-1795.
SNYDER, CONRAD, Will, 1-4-1810. Dev.: Marg., wife; Dan., son; Marg., Eliz., Hannah, Cath., Sarah, daus.

SOMMERVILLE, ALEX., Will, 6-5-1837. Dev.: Eliz., Charity, sisters; Jane Haymond, Matilda Bartlett, sisters; Geo., brother.

SOMMERVILLE, JAMES, Inv., 8-10-1821.

SOMMERVILLE, JAMES, S.B., no date.

SOMMERVILLE, JOHN, Set., 4-22-1825.

SOMMERVILLE, JOS., Inv., no date.

SOMMERVILLE, MAXWELL, Will, 6-1842. Dev.: Mary, wife; James, infant, son.

SOMMERVILLE, ROBT., ANN, THOMAS., Set., 12-1-1838.

SPICER, RANDOLPH, Will, 1-9-1821. Dev.: Randolph, son.

STALNAKER, JACOB, Bond, 2-18-1786.

STEALEY, JACOB, Will, 10-1841. Dev.: Eliz., wife; John, Edmund, James, sons; others.

STEEL, ELIZ., Will, 4-2-1828. Dev.: Martha, Mary Linsey, Eliz. Brown, daus.; Sam., son.

STEIR, MOSES, Will, 4-13-1810. Dev.: Eliz., wife; Benj., Kohn, sons; Marg. Randolph, Mary Nutter, Sarah Nutter, Ann Eliz., daus.; Moses, son.

STEPHENS, GEO., Inv., 2-24-1804.

STOUT, AMOS, Will, 3-8-1849. Dev.: John, Andrew, Aaron, sons; Rachel, wife; Ruth, Priscilla, Sarah, Lucinda, Rebecca, Lucina, daus.

STOUT, BENJ., Will, 11-20-1843. Dev.: Lovey, wife; John, James, Thomas, sons.

STOUT, BONHAM, Set., 3-13-1791.

STOUT, DAN., Will, 7-8-1808. Dev.: Cath., wife; Dan., Hezekiah, sons, daus.

STOUT, DAN., Will, 7-6-1809. Dev.: Cath., wife; Dan., Hezikiah, sons; daus.

STOUT, DAVID, Will, 12-31-1825. Dev.: James, Samuel, brothers; Deliverance, dau.; Jamina Stout; Eleanor Davis.

STOUT, EZEKIAL, Will, 9-12-1795. Dev.: Sarah, wife; Dan., Benj., Hezekiah, sons; daus.

STOUT, JIRAH, Inv., 2-21-1831.

STOUT, JOB, Will, 12-3-1834. Dev.: Marg., wife; Abner, Margin, Job, Joseph, Noah, sons; Rebecca, Mary, Matilda, Nancy, Sarah, Martha, Susan, daus.

STOUT, JONATHAN, Inv., no date.

STOUT, NOAH, App., 1-24-1814.

STOUT, NOAH, Set., 11-24-1826.

STOUT, RACHEL, Will, 9-5-1809. Dev.: Nathaniel, brother.

STRUM, ISAAC, Will, 7-4-1840. Dev.: Marg., wife; John, son.

SUMMERVILLE, THOMAS, Will, 6-15-1835. Dev.: Alex., Geo., John, sons; Eliz., Charity, Jane Hay, Matilda Bartlett, daus.

SWICK, ANTHONY, Will, 5-15-1839. Dev.: Thomas, James, sons; Polly, dau.; wife.

SWIGER, FIELDING, Inv., 6-10-1826.

SWIGER, FIELDING, Inv., 3-22-1829.

SWIGER, JACOB, Will, 6-1842. Dev.: Nancy, wife; Geo., Zacckous, Thomas, Jacob, sons; Susana, dau.

SWIGER, JOHN, Will, 2-21-1821. Dev.: Rachel, Nancy Burton, Hannah Bridwell, daus.

TANNER, ED., Inv., no date.

TAYLOR, JOHN, Will, 7-14-1816. Dev.: Hannah, wife; Mary, Eliz., Hannah, Sarah, Aheble, daus.; Benj., David, Henry, sons; Phebe, dau.

TEAT, WM., Will, 7-17-1843. Dev.: Jane Williams, Lydia Davisson, daus.; Thompson, Hugh, sons.

TETRICK, ANN, Inv., 11-28-1833.

TETRICK, ANN, Set., 2-23-1836.

TETRICK, JOSIAH, Inv., 9-20-1837.

THARP, BENJ., Inv., 6-24-1804.

THOMAS, EVAN, Inv., 2-27-1840.

THOMAS, GEO., Inv., 3-21-1811.

THOMAS, GEO., Set., 2-12-1825.

THOMPSON, ASAIAH, Inv., 12-11-1839.

THOMPSON, BENONI, App., 2-8-1815.

THOMPSON, ISRAEL, Inv., 12-11-1839.

THOMPSON, JAMES, Will, 9-25-1817. Dev.: Jane, wife; John, Hugh, Sam., sons; Marg., dau.

THOMPSON, SAM., Will, no date. Dev.: Jane, mother; Hugh, bro.; Jane Lynch, Peggy Reynolds, sis.

THOMPSON, URIAH, Inv., 12-25-1825.

THOMPSON, WM., Will, 1-14-1812. Dev.: Eliz., wife; Wm., Hezekiah, Moses, sons; Rachel, Mitchell, Eliz. Mitchell, Sarah Thompson, Polly Neal, daus.

THOMPSON, WM., Inv., 10-7-1818.

THREHELD, JOHN, Inv., 12-1-1840.

THRELKELD, JOHN, Will, 7-23-1833. Dev.: Patsy, wife; Henry, John, sons; Dolly, Martha, Matilda, Adaline, daus.

TOLBERT, COTTRILL, Inv., 10-19-1802.

TOLBERT, COTTRILL, S.B., 10-20-1826.

TOWERS, GEO., Inv., 8-16-1816.

TRAPNAL, ANDREW, Inv., 12-1-1834.

TRUMAN, ROBT., Will, 3-27-1810. Dev.: Jane, wife; Job, son.

TUCKER, SAM., Will, 9-1-1806. Dev.: Rebekah, wife; Michael, Jeremiah, Sam., Boothe, sons; Charity, Sarah, Eliz., Marah, Bashabe, Rebekah, daus.

TUCKER, WM., Inv., 4-13-1807.

TYSON, ENOS, Inv., 4-13-1819.

TYSON, ENOS, Set., 5-6-1825.

VANHORN, ABRAHAM, Inv., 8-31-1820.

VANHORN, ABRAHAM, Set., 1-9-1824.

VANHORN, JOB, Inv., no date.

VANHORN, WM., Will, 8-25-1807. Dev.: Sarah, wife; Job, Wm., sons; Eliz., Mary Barnard, Abigail, Anna, daus.

VANHORN, WILLIAM, Will, 8-17-1831. Dev.: Sarah, wife; Moses, Wm., Bennett, sons; Eliz., Sarah, Mary, Dianne, Anna, Rebecca, Eliz., daus.

VANHORN, WM., Inv., 9-29-1840.

VINCENT, ELIZ., Set., 11-13-1812.

WALBORN, JOHN, Will, 12-20-1820. Dev.: Ed., John, sons; Cath., wife; Patsy, dau.; Polly, Betsy, stepdau.

WALBURN, JOHN, S.B., 5-8-1821.

WALDO, PHIPPS, Inv., 7-31-1832.

WAMSLEY, DAVID, Will, 3-8-1849. Dev.: Sophia, slave; Mary Smith, Eliz. Woods, Tabitha Boggess, Hannah Bartlett, Rebecca Robinson, daus.

WAMSLEY, SAM., Inv., 2-5-1811.

WAMSLEY, SAM., Set., 8-15-1829.

WARD, JOB., Will, 5-8-1831. Dev.: Talitha, wife; Rachel Davis, Sarah Casto, Hannah Crislip, Phebe Christ, daus.; Acquilla, James, sons.

WARDER, HENRY, Inv., 7-14-1834.

WARREN, KISIAH, Inv., 10-23-1828.

WASHBURN, ISAAC, SR., Inv., 11-22-1834.

WASHBURN, ISAAC, JR., Inv., 7-20-1835.

WASHINGTON, LEEWISH, Inv., 11-28-1828.

WASH'T-FETTERMAN, Will, 12-21-1840. Dev.: Sarah, wife; Gilbert, Geo., Gertrude, Wilfred, Francis, children.

WEAVER, HENRY, Inv., 4-26-1821.

WEAVER, HENRY, Set., 11-8-1824.

WEAVER, HENRY, Set., 8-1-1838.

WEBB, ELIZ., Will, 3-12-1837. Dev.: Ann, dau.

WEBB, JOHN, Inv., 3-9-1833.

WEBB, JOHN, Set., 3-16-1836.

WEBB, SARAH, S.B., no date.

WEBB, THOMAS, Will, 6-17-1820. Dev.: Dan., James, Nathan, Thomas, David, sons; Sarah, wife; Sarah Jane, Phebe, Mary, Prudence, Nancy Robinson, Eliz. Johnson, daus.

WEBB, THOMAS, Set., 8-15-1825.

WEBB, THOMAS, Inv., 5-13-1835.

WEBB, MRS. THOMAS AND MRS. JONAS, Set., 6-13-1840.

WELCH, WM., Will, 6-8-1837. Dev.: Nancy, wife.

WELLS, ELISHA, Inv., 2-28-1822.

WEST, EDMOND, Will, 10-10-1784. Dev.: Edmond, Jr., John, Thomas, Alex., sons; Betsy, dau.; wife.

WEST, EDMUND, Will, 2-24-1814. Dev.: Cath., wife; Moses, John, Edmund, sons; Mary, dau.

WEST, JOSEPH, App., 2-10-1810.

WHEELER, CLEMENT, Will, 1834. Dev.: Sarah, wife; Nancy Hawkins, Sarah, Lucinda, Eleanor, Amanda, daus.; Wm., John, Bennett, sons.

WHITE, ALEX., S.B., 4-27-1815.

WHITE, ALEX., S.B., 4-27-1825.

WHITE, JOS., Inv., 5-25-1828.

WHITE, WM., Will, 6-1-1823. Dev.: Dorcas, wife; Wm., Henry, James, sons; Rachel, Amy, dau.

WHITE, WM., Inv., 8-30-1825.

WHITE, WM., Set., 7-20-1836.

WHITEMAN, AMOS, Inv., no date.

WHITEMAN, DAN., Set., 9-4-1829.

WILKINSON, GABRIEL, Inv., 7-12-1790.

WILKINSON, JOS., Will, 8-29-1789. Dev.: Mary, wife; Sam., Jos., Thomas, Nathan, sons; Eliz., Massa, Ann, daus.

WILKINSON, JOSEPH, Will, 1-9-1821. Dev.: Jane, wife; Geo., Ephraim, Wm., Joseph, John, Jeremiah, Jedediah, Benj., sons; Nancy, Eliz., Amy, Mary Ann, daus.

WILKINSON, NATHAN, Will, 1-8-1821. Dev.: Charity, wife; Sarah, Mary, daus.; Joseph, Ezekiel, Lemuel, David, Cicero, sons.

WILKINSON, NATHAN, Inv., 9-13-1821.

WILKINSON, SAM., Will, 5-11-1795. Dev.: John, son; Marg., wife; Sarah, Mary, Marcy, Marg., Ann, daus.

WILKINSON, WM., Will, 7-1842. Dev.: Nancy, wife; Marg., Emily, daus.; Hinkel, John, sons.

WILLIAMS, CORNELIUS, Will, 6-22-1833. Dev.: Hannah, wife; Elija, Enoch, Isaac, sons; Rebecca, Polly Sillivan, daus.

WILLIAMS, WM., Will, 11-1843. Dev.: Mark, Geo., Isaac, John, Wm., Thomas, Jeremiah, sons; Susan, Ruth, Polly, Rebecca, Nancy, daus.; Sophia, wife.

WILLIAMSON, JOHN, Inv., 12-23-1835.

WILLIS, WM., Inv., 11-21-1823.

WILLIS, WILLIAM, Set., 11-15-1830.

WILSON, BENJ., SR., Will, 3-20-1827. Dev.: Wm. Stephen, Benj., John, Cornelius, Thomas, Josiah, sons; Mary, Sarah, Ann, Edith, Eliz., Deborah, daus.; Archibald, Noah, Philip, David, James, Dan., sons; Margaret, Phebe, Martha, Juliann, Harriet, Rachel, daus.

WILSON, DAVID., Will, 2-10-1828. Dev.: Daniel, brother; Phebe, Marg., Martha, Juliane, Harriet, Rachel, sisters; Phebe, Mother; Josiah, brother.

WININGS (WINANS), ISAAC, Inv., 10-9-1812.

WINNINGS, ISAAC, Set., 2-17-1826.

WIRE, DANIEL, Inv., 8-12-1815.

WISEMAN, BENJ., Inv., 1-20-1815.

WISEMAN, BEN J., Set., 7-16-1831.

WISEMAN, GEO., Will, 5-11-1816. Dev.: Hannah, wife; Nancy, Jack, Mary McKinley, Rachel Daniel, Rebecca Carder, daus.; Thomas, Jonathan, sons.

WOLF, MICHAEL, Will, 1-30-1838. Dev.: Madaline, wife; Isaac, son, Jacob, John, Geo., Caty Cottrill, Peggy Cottrill, Sarah Sullivan.

WOLLARD, LUDWIG, Will, 2-26-1821. Dev.: Susan, wife; John, son.

WOOD, BENJ., Will, 1-5-1839. Dev.: Sarah Rogers, dau.; children of Eliz. Robinson; Thomas, son.

WOODARD, ANN, Will, 3-31-1837. Dev.: Mary Ann Fox, Hannah Moore, daus.; John, son; children of Ann Sommerville, dau.

WOODWARD, JOHN, Will, 12-24-1824. Dev.: Eliz., wife; John, James, sons; Eliz. Carpenter, dau.

WOODYARD, LOUIS, Inv., 4-20-1817.

WOOLCOTT, JOS., Inv., 6-2-1815.

WRIGHT, DAVID, Inv., 9-14-1812.

WRIGHT, GEO., Will, 3-9-1810. Dev.: Eliz. Deacon, step-dau.

YATES, LEWIS, Inv., 7-1-1829.

YATES, MARTIN, Inv., 10-23-1826.

YATES, WM., Inv., 3-2-1827.

ZINN, ALEX, Inv., 4-10-1824.

ZUMBRO, GEO., Will, 9-19-1842. Dev.: Marg., wife; Polly, Cath. Grove, Eliz. Spindle, Marg., daus.; John, Adam, sons.

West Virginia Estate Settlements

In 1936 and 1937, the West Virginia Commission on Historic and Scenic Markers, the Works Progress Administration, and the Federal Emergency Relief Administration compiled court records of the various counties, such as Births, Deaths, Marriages, and Wills. Under Wills were grouped subjects pertaining to Estate Settlements, including Wills, Inventories, and Appraisements. Copies of these county records were filed at the Department of Archives and History, Charleston; the Library of West Virginia University, Morgantown; and the DAR Library, Washington.

Believing that there would be particular interest on the part of the general public in the Estate Settlements in the older counties, the West Virginia Historical Society has undertaken to abstract the Estate Settlements Records, as filed in the State Department of Archives and History, and offer them for publication in the *West Virginia History Quarterly*. No responsibility can be assumed as to the accuracy of the copies made from the original county records.

There are 13 counties which were formed prior to 1800, and it has been agreed to arrange these counties in chronological order, and to print their records from the earliest date to 1850. The formation dates of these counties are as follows: Hampshire—1753; Berkeley—1772; Monongalia—1776; Ohio—1776; Greenbrier—1778; Harrison—1784; Hardy—1786; Randolph—1787; Pendleton—1788; Kanawha—1788; Brooke—1797; Wood—1798; and Monroe—1799.

Randolph County, Formed 1787

The Abbreviations used in this material include App.—appraisement; Bro.—brother; Dau.—daughter; Dev.—devisee; Inv.—inventory; S.B.—sale bill; Set.—settlement.

ALBERT, PETER, App., Nov. 1828.
ALBERT, PETER, Set., Mar. 1829.
ALEXANDER, ELIAS, Will, Apr. 1825. Dev.: Grewsylah, wife; Elias, son; Amey, Dorcy, daus.; others.
ATKENS, JOHN, App., 2-5-1798.
ATKENS, JOHN, Set., 2-5-1798.

BALL, SAMUEL, App., May 1820.
BALL, SAMUEL, S.B., May 1822.
BALL, SAMUEL, Set., May 1822.
BALL, SAMUEL, Set., Aug. 1824.
BENNETT, ASA, App., Jan. 1816.
BOND, ISAAC, Will, April 1818. Dev.: Sarah, wife; Joshua, son.
BOND, ISAAC, App., July 1818.
BOND, SARAH, Will, June 1832. Dev.: Joshu, son.

BOND, SARAH, App., Feb. 1833.
BOND, SARAH, S.B., Feb. 1833.
BOND, SARAH, Set., Apr. 1835.
BOND, SARAH, Set., May 1839.
BONEFIELD, SAMUEL, Will, Aug. 1826. Dev.: Elizabeth, dau.; Thornton, William, sons; others.
BONNIFIELD, GREGGORY, S.B., Mar. 1814.
BONNIFIELD, GREGGORY, Set., Mar. 1814.
BONNIFIELD, GREGGORY, Set., Dec. 1815.
BONNIFIELD, SAMUEL, App., Dec. 1826.
BONNIFIELD, SAMUEL, S.B., Dec. 1826.
BONNIFIELD, SAMUEL, Set., Aug. 1828.
BOOTH, DANIEL, App., 6-4-1795.

BOOTH, DANIEL, S.B., 12-24-1795.
BOOTH, DANIEL, Set., 1797.
BOOTH, DANIEL, Add'l. S.B., Nov. 1824.
BOOTH, DANIEL, Set., May 1844.
BOOTH, DANIEL, 2nd., S.B., July 1824.
BOOTH, DANIEL, SR., App., July 1827.
BOOTH, DANIEL, SR., S.B., July 1827.
BOOTH, DANIEL, JR., App., July & Nov. 1824.
BOOTH, DANIEL, JR., Set., Sept. 1825.
BOOTH, DANIEL, JR., Set., 5-27-1839.
BOYLES, GILBERT, Will, Dec. 1835. Dev.: Elenor, wife; James, Michael, Gilbert, Charles, Andrew, sons; Marian, Margaret, Sarah, Edes, daus.; others.
BOYLES, GILBERT, App., Sept. 1836.
BOYLES, GILBERT, S.B., Sept. 1836.
BOYLES, GILBERT, Set., March 1838.
BOYLES, JOHN, Will, March 1840. Dev.: Richard, Michael, bros.; others.
BRIGGS, WILLIAM, Will, Aug. 1845. Dev.: Mary, wife; Susan Ryan, Sarah Hart, daus.
BRIGGS, WILLIAM, App., 11-24-1845.
BRIGGS, WILLIAM, S.B., Feb. 1846.
BUCKEY, PETER, App., Aug. 15, 1950.
BUCKEY, PETER, S.B., 8-15-1850.

CANFIELD, DANIEL, App., June 1833.
CANFIELD, DANIEL, Set., 3-28-1836.
CANFIELD, TITUS, App., June 1833.
CANFIELD, TITUS, Set., March 22, 1836.
CANFIELD, TITUS, Set., Dec. 1848.
CARLOCK, CATHERINE, Will, 1-5-1802. Dev.: Catherine Whitman, Mathew Whitman, grandchildren.
CARR, ENOCH, App., Nov. 1845.
CARR, ENOCH, S.B., Nov. 1845.
CARR, ENOCH, Set., July 1847.
CASEBOTT, ASHEAL, App., 4-18-1815.
CASEBOTT, ASHEAL, S.B., Aug. 1815.
CASEBOTT, ISAAC, Set., Aug. 1817.
CHANNEL, JERIMIAH, Will, Jan. 1798. Dev.: Nancy, wife; Jeremiah, son.
CHENOWETH, JOHN, Will, 6-28-1831. Dev.: Mary, wife; Robert, William P., John I., Jehu, Gabriel, sons; Nellie Hart, dau.; other.
CHENOWETH, JOHN, App., July 1831.
CHENOWETH, JOHN, S.B., Nov. 1832.
CHENOWETH, JOHN, Set., Jan. 1833.
CHENOWETH, JOHN K., Will, May 1848. Dev.: Sarah, wife; Mary Ann, Elithea, Catharine, daus.; Jacob, Marshall, Coffman, sons.
CHENOWETH, JOHN K., App., June 1848.
CHENOWETH, JOHN K., S.B., June 1848.
CHENOWETH, MARY, Will, Feb. 1849. Dev.: Mary Stalnaker, Eleanor Hart, daus.; John I., son; Poll, servant.
CHENOWETH, MARY, App., 3-3-1849.
CHENOWETH, MARY, S.B., 3-3-1849.
CHENOWETH, MARY, Set., Oct. 1849.
CLARK, JOHN, App., Jan. 1826.
CLARK, JOHN, S.B., Jan. 1826.
CLARK, JOHN, Set., Oct. 1829.

CLARK, MARY, App., Nov. 1841.
CLARK, MARY, S.B., Nov. 1841.
CLARK, MARY, Will, Oct. 1841. Dev.: John, James, sons; Louiza, dau.; others.
COBBERLY, JESSE, Set., Dec. 1835.
COBBERLY, JESSE, Set., Nov. 1836.
COBERLY, JESSE, App., Sept. 1832.
COBERLY, JESSE, S.B., Sept. 1832.
COLLETT, SOLOMON, Will, June 1836. Dev.; Edith, wife; Edmund D., John S., William B., Charles C., sons; Martha J., Mary Ellen, Phebe, daus.; other.
COLLETT, SOLOMON, App., Sept. 1836.
COLLETT, SOLOMON, S.B., Sept. 1836.
COLLETT, SOLOMON, Set., Mar. 26, 1838.
COLLETT, SOLOMON, Additional Inv., March 1838.
COLLETT, THOMAS, App., Oct. 1823.
COLLETT, THOMAS, SR., Set., July 1826.
COLLEY, BENJAMIN S., App., June 1842.
COLLEY, BENJAMIN S., Set., Feb. 1844.
CORLEY, WILLIAM, App., Feb. 1826.
CORLEY, WILLIAM, Sup. S.B., Nov. 1826.
CORLEY, WILLIAM, S.B., Feb. 1827.
CRANE, JONAS, App., Dec. 1849.
CRANE, JONAS, App., Feb. 1850.
CRANE, JONAS, S.B., Feb. 1850.
CROUCH, ABRAHAM, App., Nov. 1849.
CROUCH, ABRAHAM, S.B., Nov. 1849.
CROUCH, ELIZABETH, App., April 1850.
CROUCH, ELIZABETH, App., Aug. 26, 1850.
CROUCH, ELIZABETH, S.B., Aug. 1850.
CURRENCE, WILLIAM, Will, 11-27-1848. Dev.: Nancy, wife; Jonathan, William H., John, sons; Elizabeth Chenoweth, dau.
CURRENCE, WILLIAM, S.B., Feb. 1849.
CURRENCE, WILLIAM, SR., App. 3-25-1848.
CURRENCE, WILLIAM, SR., App., Feb. 1849.

DAY, GIDEON, App., Sept. 1837.
DAY, GIDEON, S.B., Sept. 1837.
DAY, GIDEON, SET., April 1840.
DOOMIRE, RICHARD OR RINEHART, Set. Oct. 1833.
ENGLAND, JAMES, Set., Jan. 1831.
FANSLER, HENRY, App., Feb. 1844.
FANSLER, HENRY, S.B., Feb. 1844.
FANSLER, HENRY, Set., June 1846.
FINK, HENRY, App., 1790.
FRIEND, THOMAS, S.B., 12-22-1814.
FRIEND, THOMAS, S.B., July 1815.
FRIEND, THOMAS, Set., Aug. 1818.
FURGESON, ELLIS, App., Oct. 1846.
FURGESON, ELLIS, S.B., Oct. 1846.
FURGESON, ELLIS, Set., July 1849.
GOFF, JOHN T., Inv., 1806.
GOFF, SALATHIAS, Will, 9-16-1791. Dev.: Elizabeth, wife; Hiram, John, George, sons; Ann, Elizabeth, Mary Ann, daus.; others.
GOFF, SALATHIEL, App., 2-25-1792.
GOFF, SALATHIEL, Inv., April 1806.

GOFF, SALATHIEL, Inv., 4-28-1806.
GOFF, SALATHIEL, Set., April 1806.
GRIMES, JONAS, App., Nov. 1825.
GRIMES, JONAS, S.B., Nov. 1825.

HADDAN, DAVID, Will, 12-26-1791. Dev.:
Rebecca, wife; David, son; Margaret,
Elizabeth, daus.
HAIGLER, JACOB, App., Aug. 1842.
HAIGLER, JACOB, App., Nov. 1842.
HAIGLER, JACOB, S.B., Nov. 1842.
HARDEN, JOHN, Will, March 1811. Dev.:
Isabella, wife; John, Absolom, Hector,
sons; Moliha, Alice, daus.; others.
HARDIN, NESTER, Will, Nov. 1839. Dev.:
Absolem, Alsy, Nester, Jr., sons; Agnes
Boyles, Sarah Kittle, Isabel Coffman,
Catherine Boyles, Lyda Hardin, Jula
Mole, daus.; others.
HARDIN, NESTER, App., June 1840.
HARDIN, NESTER, S.B., June 1840.
HARDIN, NESTER, Set., Dec. 1842.
HART, EDWARD, Will, Oct. 1812. Dev.:
Nancy, wife; John, Edward, Joseph, Eli-
jah, sons; Susanah, Deborah, Elizabeth,
daus.
HART, EDWARD, App., 12-24-1812.
HART, EDWARD, Set., 12-25-1837.
HART, ELIJAH, App., Nov. 1819.
HART, ELIJAH, S.B., Nov. 1819.
HART, ELIJAH, Set., Aug. 1821.
HART, ELIJAH, Set., March 1825.
HEATER, DANIEL, App., June 1850.
HEATER, DANIEL, S.B., June 1850.
HEATER, JOHN, App., July 1818.
HEATER, JOHN, S.B., July 1818.
HEATER, JOHN, App. 1819.
HEATER, JOHN, S.B., 1819.
HEATER, JOHN, Set., May 1819.
HELMICK, JACOB, July 1815, Will. Dev.:
Abraham, Adam, John, Jacob, sons; Han-
nah, Elizabeth Westfall, Sarah Boers,
Molly Buffington, Barbara Clark, daus.;
other.
HILL, JOHN, Will, June 1839. Dev.: Bar-
bary, wife; Frederick, William, Jacob,
George, John, sons; Elizabeth, Catrena,
Eanez, daus.; other.
HIXSON, WILLIAM, Will, Oct. 1841. Dev.:
Mary Tedrick, Catharine Vanscoy, daus.;
John, son.
HIXSON, WILLIAM, App., 9-26-1842.
HIXSON, WILLIAM, S.B., 9-26-1842.
HOGAN, EDWARD, App., July 1849.
HOGAN, EDWARD, S.B., July 1849.
HOLDER, MARY, App., Feb. 1825
HOLDER, MARY, S.B., Feb. 1825.
HOLDER, THOMAS, App., July 1814.
HOLDER, THOMAS, S.B., July 1814.
HOLDER, THOMAS, Will, Feb. 1814. Dev.:
Margaret, wife; Jacob, son; others.
HOLDER, THOMAS W., App., Dec. 1828.
HOLDER, THOMAS W., S.B., Dec. 1828.
HORNBACK, BENJAMIN, S. B., June
1831.
HORNBACK, BENJAMIN, S.B., June 1831.
HORNBACK, LYDIA, Will, Sept. 1845.
Dev.: Sarah Channel, Polly Wood, Ann
Carr. Susannah Slagle, daus.; others.
HORNBACK, LYDIA, App., March 1846.
HORNBACK, LYDIA, S.B., March 1846.
HORNBECK, BENJ., Will, Apr. 1827. Dev.:
Lyda, wife; Sarah Channel, Anne Carr,
Susannah Slagle, Polly Wood, Lyda Van-
scoy, daus.; William Moses, Jonathan,
Joseph, John, sons.
HUFFMAN, JOHN, App., May 1827.
HUFFMAN, JOHN, S.B., May 1827.
HUFFMAN, JOHN, Set., April 1828.

INGLAND, JAMES, Will, June 1829. Dev.:
Elizabeth, wife; Polly, James, Elizabeth,
Susana, Satty, Elizabeth, Margaret, Delity,
Jemimy, daus.; Henry, John, sons.
ISNER, JACOB, App., June 1816.
JENKS, ABNER, Will, June 1842. Dev.:
Sarah, wife; Brown, William, Levi, sons;
Sarah Smith, dau.; others.
JOHNSON, BENJAMIN, App., Sept. 1828.
JOHNSON, BENJAMIN, S.B., Sept. 1828.
JOHNSON, BENJAMIN, Set., Nov. 1830.
KALER, JACOB, App., Nov. 1828.
KALER, JACOB, S.B., Nov. 1828.
KALER, JACOB, Set., Jan. 1830.
KEES, ALEXANDER, App., Feb. 1825.
KEES, ALEXANDER, S.B., Feb. 1825.
KELLEY, EBENEZEER T., Will, May
1816. Dev.: Rachel, wife; Mary, Eunis,
Rebeccah, Osee, Anna, Jane, daus.; John,
Jack, Isaac, Samuel, Johnston, sons.
KELLEY, EBENEZER, App., Jan. 1817.
KETTLE, ISAAC, S.B., June 1817.
KINNAN, JOSEPH, App., 6-26-1793.
KINNAN, JOSEPH, S.B., 6-26-1793.
KINNAN, JOSEPH, Set., 6-26-1793.
KITTLE, ABRAHAM, JR., S.B., July 1814.
KITTLE, ABRAHAM, Set., March 1816.
KITTLE, ABRAHAM, Will, Sept. 1816.
Dev.: Mary, wife; Jacob, Richard, John,
George, Daniel, Abraham, sons; others.
KITTLE, ABRAHAM, SR., App., 1816.
KITTLE, ABRAHAM, SR., S.B., June
1817.
KITTLE, ABRAHAM, SR., Set., Sept. 1818.
KITTLE, ABRAHAM, SR., Set., Oct. 1818.
KITTLE, ISAAC, Will, Feb. 1816. Dev.:
Sarah, wife; Rachel, Clara Ann, daus.;
Martin D., Nestor H., sons.
KITTLE, ISAAC, App., March 1816.
KITTLE, ISAAC, S.B., March 1816.
KITTLE, ISAAC, Set., Aug. 1817.
KITTLE, JACOB, Will, Jan. 1843. Dev.:
Anne, dau.; Benjamin W., son; others.
KITTLE, JACOB, App., Feb. 1844.
KITTLE, JACOB, S.B., March 1844.
KITTLE, JACOB, Set., May 1845.
KITTLE, MOSES, App., March 1826.
KITTLE, MOSES, S.B., March 1826.
KITTLE, MOSES, Set., June 1827.
KITTLE, RICHARD, Will, Jan. 1831. Dev.:
Margaret, wife; others.
KITTLE, RICHARD, App., Nov. 1832.
KITTLE, RICHARD, S.B., Nov. 1832.
KITTLE, RICHARD, Set., 7-27-1835.

LIGHT, JOHN, Will, Dec. 1834. Dev.:
Elizabeth, wife; John, Martin, sons; Mary
Hornbeck, Agnes Hornbeck, Elizabeth
Wamsley, Catharine, Susanna Currence,
Phebe, Sarah, Jane, daus.
LIGHT, JOHN, App., July 1835.
LIGHT, JOHN, S.B., July 1835.
LITLE, ROBERT, App., Sept. 1849.
LITLE, ROBERT, S.B., Sept. 1849.
LONG, JOHN, App., Jan. 1939.
LONG, JOHN, S.B., Jan. 1839.
LONG, JOHN, Set., 2-9-1841.
LOUGH, GEORGE, App., 1818.
LOUGH, GEORGE, S.B., 1818.

MACE, HENRY, Set., March 1811.
MACE, HENRY, Set., 8-27-1811.
MARSH, VINCENT, Will, 11-2-1802. Dev.:
Darkey Bonnefield, Elizabeth Dammerel,
aunts.
MARTENEY, CHARLES, App., 9-28-1807.
MARTENEY, CHARLES, Admr's. Acct.,
10-16-1807.
MARTENEY, MARY, App., April 1811.
MARTENEY, MARY, S.B., April 1811.

MARTENEY, MARYANN, Will, Feb. 1811. Dev.: five daus. (not named); Henry.
MARTENEY, MARY ANN, Set., Aug. 1814.
MARTENEY, WASHINGTON G., App., March 1840.
MARTENEY, WASHINGTON G., S.B., July 1849.
MARTENEY, WASHINGTON G., Set., July 1849.
MARTENEY, WM., Will, July 1847. Dev.: Nancy, wife; Sally Wilmoth, Crescy Bell, Jane Dolbear, daus.; Daniel, William, sons; others.
MARTENEY, WILLIAM, App., June 1848.
MARTENEY, WILLIAM, S.B., June 1848.
MARTENEY, WILLIAM, Set., 7-24-1849.
MARTENEY, WILLIAM, S.B., Aug. 1849.
MASE, HENRY, Will, 1807. Dev.: Annie, wife; John, son; others.
MASE, HENRY, App., 7-17-1807.
MASE, HENRY, Set., 10-24-1807.
MCCLURG, JAMES, Will, Mar. 1833. Dev.: Elizabeth Wikham, dau.; others.
MCLAIN, JAMES, Will, Aug. 1820. Dev.: Dorcas, wife; John, Abner, sons.
MCLEAN, NOAH, Will, Feb. 1842. Dev.: Julian, wife; children (not named).
MCMULLEN, ANDREW, Will, Feb. 1788. Dev.: none.
MIDDLEBROOK, STEPHEN, Will, Oct. 1849. Dev.: Susan, dau.; Nancy, wife; Elijah, Robert, Stephen, sons; unborn child.
MILLER, MARTAIN, App., April 1814.
MILLERS, JOHN, Will, June 1814. Dev.: Janet, wife; Andrew, Martain, sons; Sarah Mace, dau.
MINEAR, DAVID, App., Jan. 1839.
MITCHELL, GEORGE, Will, Feb. 1822. Dev.: Mary, wife.
MITCHELL, GEORGE, App., April 1822.
MOORE, DANIEL, Will, Jan. 1843. Dev.: Deborah, wife; Martin, William, Daniel, Richard, Joseph, Samuel, sons; Rachel Helm, Mary Gross, Deborah, Margarett, daus.
MOORE, DANIEL, S.B., March 1844.
MOORE, DANIEL, Set., May 1845.
MOORE, WILLIAM, App., July 1836.
MOORE, WILLIAM, S.B., July 1836.
MOORE, WM., Set., May 1839.
MORRELL, SAMUEL, Will, Nov. 1840. Dev.: Elizabeth, wife; Sary, Polly, Sally Ann, Elizabeth, daus.; John, Samuel, Lair D., Abel, sons.
MORRIS, MARY, Will, Oct. 1845. Dev.: Thomas, Henry, sons; others.
MORRIS, ROBERT, Will, Oct. 1845. Dev.: Mary, wife; Robert, Thomas, Henry, sons; Hetty Marshall, Maria Nixson, daus; other.
MORRISON, ROBERT, Will, Oct. 1842. Dev.: Clancy, wife; Luiza, dau.
MORRISON, ROBT., App., March 1843.
MORRISON, ROBT., S.B., March 1843.
MORRISON, ROBT., Set., Nov. 1843.
MYERS, CHAS., Will, Aug. 1813. Dev.: Molly, wife; Adam, John, Jacob, sons.

NEILSON, CHARLES, App., Sept. 15, 1795.
NEILSON, CHARLES, S.B., 9-15-1795.
NEILSON, CHARLES. Set., 6-2-1797.
NELSON, JAMES, Will, Feb. 17, 1842. Dev.: Priscilla, wife; John, William Davis, Thomas, sons; unmarried daus. (not named)
NESTER, JACOB, JR., App., Jan. 1816.
NESTER, JACOB, JR., Set., Mar. 1820.

PANE, HENRY, Will, Aug. 1839. Dev.: Elizabeth, wife; children. (not named)

PARSONS, CATHERINE, App., June 1848.
PARSONS, CATHERINE, Set., Feb. 1849.
PARSONS, CATHERINE, S.B., July 1850.
PARSONS, CATHERINE, Set., Aug. 1850.
PARSONS, DAVID, App., March 1835.
PARSONS, DAVID, S.B., March 1835.
PARSONS, WILLIAM, Will, Sept. 1829. Dev.: Catherine, wife; Job, Solomon, sons; Elizabeth Tygart, Anna Parsons, Nancy Daniels, Annes Miles, Malinda Parsons, daus.
PARSONS, WILLIAM, App., Oct. 1829.
PARSONS, WILLIAM, Set., Nov. 1835.
PAXTON, CATHERINE, App., May 1826.
PAXTON, CATHERINE, S.B., May 1826.
PAXTON, CATHERINE, Set., Feb. 1827.
PAXTON, EZEKIEL S., App., Dec. 1819.
PAXTON, EZEKIEL S., S.B., Dec. 1819.
PAXTON, EZEKIEL S., Set., Aug. 1824.
PETRO, HENRY, Will, Jan. 1834. Dev.: Elizabeth, wife; Susan Butcher, Christine Evans, Nancy, Nancy Colett, daus.; others.
PETRO, HENRY, App., March 1835.
PETRO, HENRY, S.B., March 1835.
PETRO, HENRY, Set., 1-25-1836.
PETRO, JOHN, App., Jan. 1830.
PETRO, JOHN, S.B., July 1830.
PETRO, JOHN. Set., June 1837.
PHARAS, ROBERT, App., Jan. 1824.
PHARAS, ROBERT, S.B., Jan. 1824.
PHARAS, ROBERT, Report App., Oct. 1824.
PHARES, ROBERT, Will, Oct. 1823. Dev.: Susan, wife; William, Jesse, Abel, Benjamin, Johnson, John, sons; Nancy, Elizabeth, Susan, daus.
PHILLIPS, CATHERINE, App., Nov. 1821.
PHILLIPS, CATHERINE, S.B., Nov. 1821.
PHILLIPS, CATHERINE, Set., July 1822.
PHILLIPS, JOHN, Will, Aug. 1815. Dev.: Catherine, wife; Rachel, Elizabeth Weese, Mary Weese, Catherine, Sophia, daus.; George, John J., sons.
PHILLIPS, JOHN, App., Sept. 1815.
PHILLIPS, JOHN, S.B., Sept. 1815.
PHILLIPS, JOHN, Set., 5-27-1817.
PHILLIPS, JOHN G., App., Dec. 1832.
PHILLIPS, JOHN G., S.B., July 1833.
PHILLIPS, JOHN G., Set., 5-19-1834.
PHILLIPS, JOHN G., Set., Sept. 1842.
PHILLIPS, JOSEPH, App., June 1838.
PHILLIPS, JOSEPH, S.B., June 1838.
PHILLIPS, JOSEPH, Set., 9-16-1839.
PHILLIPS, LEVI W., App., June 1849.
PHILLIPS, LEVI W., S.B., June 1849
PHILLIPS, THOMAS, Will, Aug. 1810. Dev.: Susannah, wife; Moses, Benjamin, Henry, Isaac, Joseph, John, Thomas, William, sons.
PHILLIPS, THOMAS, App., 9-22-1810.
PITMAN, JOSEPH, App., May 1832.
PITMAN, JOSEPH, S.B., May 1832.
PITMAN, JOSEPH, Set., April 1833.
PITTMAN, JOSEPH, Will, Jan. 1832. Dev.: Nancy, wife; Joel, John, sons; Susannah, Easter, Juda, Abbey, daus.; others.
POLIN, WILLIAM, Will, Sept. 1838. Dev.: Rachel, wife; Henry, John, Barnett, Martin, William, Daniel, sons; Margarett, Mary, Rachel, daus.; others.
POLING, ISAAC, Will, Oct. 1834. Dev.: Eve. wife: children. (not named)
POLING, ISAAC, App., Jan. 1835.
POLING, ISAAC, S.B., Jan. 1835.
POLING, ISAAC. Set., June 1846.
POLING, MARTAIN, Will, Jan. 1820. Dev.: Elizabeth, Deborah Moore, Sally, Rachel, Margaret Holsberry, Madeline Nestor, daus.; Samuel, Martin, Roger, William, sons.

POLING, MARTIN, SR., App., May 1820.
POLING, MARTIN C., Will, 6-18-1819.
Dev.: Lilason, wife; Mary, Rachel, Milley
Nestor, Sarah McHenry, daus.; John,
Jonas, Amos, David, sons.
POLING, MARTIN C., App., Aug. 1819.
POLING, MARTIN G., S.B., Aug. 1819.
POLING, SAMUEL, Will, Aug. 1840 Dev.:
Margaret, wife; John, Martin, Daniel,
William, Samuel, sons; Elizabeth Keller,
Sarah Bolyard, Poly Kittle, daus.; others.
POLING, SAMUEL M., App., Sept. 1840.
POLING, WILLIAM R., App., May 1842.
POLING, WILLIAM R., S.B., May 1842.
PONNELL, JOSEPH, Will, June 1831.
Dev.: Sarah, wife; others.

RORABAUGH, JOHN, Will, July 1842.
Dev.: Nancy, wife; Anna, Gerusha Batt,
Drusilla Mitchell, Deliley, Matilda Po-
land, Rutha, Linda, daus.; Jehu, Phillip,
Nathan, Nathaniel, Anthony, sons.
RORABAUGH, JOHN, App., Oct. 1842.
RORABAUGH, JOHN, S.B., Oct. 1842.
RORABAUGH, JOHN. Set., March 1844.
ROSECRANCE, HEZEKEAH, Will, Apr.
1819. Dev.: Nancy, wife; Catherine, Mary,
Margarett, Susannah, Prudence, daus.;
Eli, Levi, Hezekiah, John, James, sons.
ROSECRONCE, HEZEKIAH, App., Sept.
1819.
ROSECRONCE, HEZEKIAH, S.B., Sept.
1819.
ROSECRONTS, HEZEKIAH, Set., lAug.
1822.
ROSECRONTS, ELY, Will, Feb. 1826.
Dev.: mother, not named; William,
Hezikeah. Levi, John, bros.
ROY, JOSEPH, JR., App., Nov. 1845.
ROY, JOSEPH, JR., S.B., Nov. 1845.
ROY. JOSEPH, JR.. Set., July 1847.
RUNNER, ISAAC, Will, Feb. 1812. Dev.:
wife (not named).
RUNNER, ISAAC, App., April 1812.
RUSH, JOHN, Will, Apr. 1831. Dev.: Eve,
wife; others.
RUSH, JOHN, App., June 1831.
RUSH. JOHN, S.B., June 1831.
RYAN, JAMES, App., Oct. 1831.
RYAN, JAMES, S.B., Oct. 1831.
RYAN, JAMES, Set., Aug. 1835.
RYAN, SOLOMON, App., June 1840.

SCHOONOVER, BENJAMIN B., Will,
Sept. 1844. Dev.: Catharine, wife.
SCHOONOVER, BENJAMIN, S.B., Sept.
1847.
SCHOONOVER, BENJAMIN, Set., Dec.
1847.
SCOOT, JOHN, S.B., Oct. 1804.
SCOTT, BENJAMIN T., Will, Aug. 1838.
Dev.: Jane, wife; Homan, John, Wil-
liam, Thomas B., sons; Mary Crawford,
Katherine, Melia, Elizabeth, Virginia,
daus.
SCOTT, BENJAMIN T., App., July 1839.
SCOTT, BENJAMIN T., S.B., July 1839.
SCOTT, BENJAMIN T., Set., 2-28-1840.
SCOTT, BENJAMIN T., Set., July 1843.
SCOTT, WILLIAM, App., April 1844.
SCOTT, WILLIAM, S.B., Sept. 1844.
SEE, ADAM, App., Dec. 1840.
SEE, ADAM, S.B., Dec. 1840.
SEE, ADAM, Set., Dec. 1840.
SEE, GEORGE, App., March 1833.
SEE, GEORGE, S.B., Mar. 1834.
SEE, GEORGE, Set., 3-13-1834.
SEE, GEORGE, Add. Set., 10-9-1835.
SEE, GEORGE, Set., Jan. 1845.

SIMON, CHRISTIAN, Will, 11-28-1848.
Dev.: Rebecca, wife; James D., John D.,
Isaac, Job, Christian, sons; Catharine
Warner, Comfort Post, daus.; other.
SIMON, CHRISTIAN, App., Jan. 1849.
SLAGLE, JACOB, Will, June 1832. Dev.:
Jacob, Isaac, George, sons; Elizabeth Hix-
on, Mary Cunningham, Jemimah Hart,
Susan Marsh, Nancy Tolbert, Catherine
Slagle, daus.
SLAGLE, JACOB, App., Nov. 1832.
SLAGLE, JACOB, Set., June 1833.
SMITH, ANTHONY, App., Oct. 1803.
SMITH, ANTHONY, S.B., Oct. 1803.
SMITH, ANTHONY, Set., Oct. 1804.
SMITH, HENRY, App., 2-11-1836.
SMITH, HENRY, S.B., 2-12-1836.
SPINNER, MARY, App., July 1823.
SPINNER, MARY, S.B., Dec. 1823.
SPINNER, MARY, Set., April 1839.
SPRINGSTONE, ABRAHAM, App., 6-22-
1807.
SPRINGSTONE, ABRAHAM, S.B., 6-22-
1807.
SPRINGSTONE, ABRAHAM, Set., Jan.
1811.
SPROWL, JOHN, Will, Mar. 1837. Dev.:
Esther, wife; others.
STALNAKER, ADAM, Will, Apr. 1815.
Dev.: Naomi, wife; Randolph, Daniel
sons; Maria, Elenor, daus.
STALNAKER, ADAM, App., June 1815.
STALNAKER, ADAM, S.B., June 1815.
STALNAKER, ADAM, Set., March 1826.
STALNAKER, ANDREW, Will, Dec. 1840.
Dev.: Catharine, wife; Archibald, Wash-
ington, Marshal, sons; Catharine See,
Mary Coffman, Elizabeth Bush, Sarah
Chenoweth, daus.
STALNAKER, ANDREW, App., Jan. 1841.
STALNAKER, BOSTON, Will, Feb. 1826.
Dev.: Margaret, wife; Warwick, Alex-
ander, Hambleton, Ferdinand, sons; Polly
White, Betsy Crouch, Dorcas Mace, Ka-
tharine, Eliza, daus.
STALNAKER, BOSTON, App., March
1826.
STALNAKER, BOSTON or SEBASTIAN,
Set., June 1826.
STALNAKER, FERDINAN, Will, Aug.
1841. Dev.: Sarah, wife; Absolem, John
Y., William L., Alexander F., sons; Rachel
Jane, Emitine, Margaret Catherine, daus.;
others.
STALNAKER, FERDINAND, App., Nov.
1841.
STALNAKER, FERDINAND, S.B., Feb.
1843.
STALNAKER, FERDINAND (Heirs), Set.,
Mar. 1846.
STALNAKER, FERDINAND, Set., Nov.
1850.
STALNAKER, GEORGE W., App., Feb.
1844.
STALNAKER, GEORGE W., S.B., 4-24-
1846.
STALNAKER, GEORGE W., Set., April
24, 1846.
STALNAKER, JACOB, SR., App., Dec.
1834.
STALNAKER, JACOB, Will, Aug. 1792.
Dev.: Elizabeth, wife; Andrew, son.
STALNAKER, JACOB, Inv., Dec. 1796.
STALNAKER, SEBASTIAN, App., Jan.
1824.
STALNAKER, VOLUNTINE, Will, Dec.
1833. Dev.: Lucy, wife; Abraham, Jacob,
sons.
STALNAKER, VOLUNTINE, App., Feb.
1834.

STINEBAUGH, JOHN, App., April 1830.
STOUT, SAINT LEDGER, Will, April 1806. Dev.: Anna, wife; John, Leonard, sons.
STOUT, ST. LEDGER, App., 6-18-1806.
STOUT, ST. LEDGER, Set., June 1809.
SUMMERFIELD, JOSEPH, Will, May 1828. Dev.: Abigail, wife; Thomas, Jesse, sons; Betsy White, Sarah Roy, Mary Snider, Margaret Wolford, daus.; others.
SUMMERFIELD, JOSEPH, App., Sept. 1828.
SUMMERFIELD, THOMAS, Will, Apr. 1821. Dev.: Martha, wife; Thomas, son; other.

TALBOTT, BENJAMIN, Will, May 1846. Dev.: William, Benjamin I., Francis D., Thomas, James, sons; others.
TALBOTT, BENJAMIN, App., Oct. 1846.
TALBOTT, BENJAMIN, S.B., Oct. 1846.
TAYLOR, ISAAC, App., July 1835.
TAYLOR, ISAAC, S.B., July 1836.
TAYLOR, ISAAC, Set., Aug. 1837.
THORN, FREDERICK, Inv., Jan. 1810.
TOMIRE, RINEHART, Will, Apr. 1831. Dev.: Louie, wife; others.
TOOMIRE, RINEHART, App., April 1832.
TOOMIRE, RINEHART, S.B., April 1832.
TRACY, JAMES, Will, July 1845. Dev.: Lettice, wife; Sarah Wilmoth.
TRACY, JAMES, App., Jan. 1846.
TRACY, JAMES, S.B., Jan. 1846.
TRACY, JAMES, Set., Dec. 1847.
TRACY, LETTICE, App., May 1848.
TRACY, LETTICE, S.B., May 1848.
TRIPLETT, MOSES, App., Aug. 1849.
TRIPLETT, MOSES, S.B., Jan. 1850.
TROUTWINE, FREDERICK, App., Aug. 1829.
TROUTWINE, FREDERICK, S.B., Aug. 1829.
TROUTWINE, FREDERICK, Will, June 1829. Dev.: Barbary, wife; others.
TROUTWINE, FREDERICK, Set., 4-3-1839.
TRUBY, JOHN, App., April 1801.
TRUBY, JOHN, S.B., April 1801.
TRUBY, JOHN, Set., 7-23-1804.

VANDEVENTDER, WILLIAM, App., 1801.
VANDEVENTDER, WILLIAM, S.B., 12-14-1801.
VANDEVENTDER, WILLIAM, Set., 9-27-1808.
VANSCOY, AARON, SR., S.B., Oct. 1849.
VANSCOY, AARON, SR., Set., 10-22-1849.
VANSCOY, AARON, App., March 1843.
VANSCOY, AARON, S.B., Jan. 1843.
VANSCOY, AARON, Will, Oct. 1845. Dev.: Jane, wife; Sarah, dau.; Jesse, Joshua, sons; others.
VANSCOY, AARON, S.B., 11-24-1845.
VANSCOY, AARON, App., Nov. 1845.

WAMSLEY, SAMUEL, Will, Mar. 1848. Dev.: John C., Andrew M., Samuel L., Jacob S., sons; Sally Crouch, Mary Harper, Judith, Rebecca, daus.
WAMSLEY, SAMUEL, App., June 1848.
WAMSLEY, WILLIAM, App., March 1844.
WAMSLEY, WILLIAM, Set., May 1847.
WARD, JACOB, Will, Sept. 1834. Dev.: Elizabeth, wife; Washington, William, Levi, Jesse, Anonijah, Jacob, Whitman, sons. Will contested.

WARD, ELIZABETH, App., 8-26-1850.
WARD, GEORGE, Will, 2-6-1791. Dev.: Margaret, wife; David, George, sons; Mary, dau.
WARD, GEORGE, S.B., 5-16-1791.
WARD, JACOB, S.B., 11-1849.
WARE, RICHARD, Will, June 1834. Dev.: Matilda, Lucinda, Elizabeth, daus.; Richard Brooks, Geo. Washington, James Randolph, Jacob See, John Newton, Benoni T., sons.
WARE, RICHARD, App., 9-5-1834.
WARE, RICHARD, S.B., 9-5-1834.
WARE, RICHARD, Set., Feb. 1844.
WARTHEN, RAPHAEL, Will, Feb. 1798. Dev.: Margret, wife; Catharine, Clotilda, daus.
WARTHEN, RAPHAEL, App., 3-1-1798.
WEECE, JACOB, Will, June 1826. Dev.: Catherine, wife; Jacob, Daniel, John, sons; Christena Wilfong, Mary Wells, daus.; others.
WEES, JACOB, Will, July 1832. Dev.: Sarah, wife; Absolem, Jacob, John, Jesse, Eli, sons; Catharine Daniels, Hannah McLain, Sarah, daus.
WEES, JACOB, App., Aug. 1832.
WEES, JACOB, S.B., Aug. 1832.
WEES, JACOB, Set., Feb. 1834.
WEESE, JACOB, App., Aug. 1826.
WEESE, JACOB, S.B., Aug. 1826.
WESTFALL, ISAAC, App., Sept. 1804.
WESTFALL, ISAAC, S.B., Sept. 1804.
WESTFALL, ISAAC, Set., 1806.
WESTFALL, JACOB, App., 1801.
WESTFALL, JACOB, Add. Inv., 2-23-1801.
WESTFALL, JACOB, Sup. Inv., 1803.
WESTFALL, JACOB, S.B., 2-17-1804.
WESTFALL, JACOB, Set., 4-23-1804.
WESTFALL, JACOB'S HEIRS, Set., Feb. 1812.
WESTFALL, JACOB'S HEIRS, Set., Jan. 1814.
WESTFALL, JOSIAH, App., June 1803.
WESTFALL, JOSIAH, S.B., Sept. 1809.
WESTFALL, JOSIAH, Set., Sept. 1809.
WESTFALL, JOSIAS, Will, July 1802. Dev.: Cornelius, Jonathan, bros.
WESTFALL, WILLIAM, App., Sept. 1821.
WESTFALL, WILLIAM, S.B., Sept. 1821.
WESTFALL, WILLIAM, Set., Sept. 1825.
WHITE, THOMAS, Will, Sept. 1804. Dev.: Abagail, wife; William, Thomas, David, sons.
WHITMAN, MATTHEW, Will, July 1836. Dev.: Katharine, wife; Betty Ruthanian, daus.; other.
WHITMAN, MATTHEW, App., April 1837.
WHITMAN, MATTHEW, S.B., April 24, 1837.
WHITMAN, MATTHEW, Amended S.B., 11-28-37.
WHITMAN, MATTHEW, Set., Aug. 1838.
WHITMAN, MATTHEW, Add. App., Nov. 1838.
WHITMAN, MATTHEW, Set., Aug. 1840.
WILLIAM, THOMAS O., Will, 4-26-1849. Dev.: Susannah, wife; all his children (not named); others.
WILLIAMS, THOMAS O., App., 1850.
WILLIAMS, THOMAS O., S.B., 1850.
WILMOTH, ANDREW, Will, Nov. 1835. Dev.: Lucinda, wife; John W., Wilson, bros.

WILMOTH, ANDREW, App., April 1836.
WILMOTH, ANDREW, S.B., April 1836.
WILMOTH, JACOB, App., 8-30-1844.
WILMOTH, JACOB, S.B., Oct. 1844.
WILMOTH, JACOB, Set., 4-27-1846.
WILMOTH, JOHN, App., Feb. 1834.
WILMOTH, JOHN, S.B., Feb. 1834.
WILMOTH, JOHN, Set., April 1837.
WILSON, JASPER, App., 2-7-1845.
WILSON, JASPER J., S.B., 2-8-1845.
WILSON, MOSES, App., Dec. 1843.
WILSON, MOSES, S.B., Dec. 1843.
WOLFORD, JOHN, SR., S.B., July 1847.
WOLFORD, JOHN, SR., Set., July 1847.

WOLFORD, JOHN, Will, Sept. 1839. Dev.:
   Mare, wife; all children (not named).
WOLFORD, JOHN, App., Sept. 1840.
WOOLF, NICHOLAS, App., 1800.
WOOLF, NICHOLAS, S.B., 7-4-1800.
WOOLF, NICHOLAS, Set., Dec. 1804.
WOOLF, NICHOLAS, Set., Jan. 1805.

YEAGER, GEORGE, App., March 1824.
YEAGER, GEORGE, S.B., March 1824.
YEAGER, GEORGE, Set., June 1824.
YEAGER, GEORGE, Set., 3-20-1835.
YOAK, JOHN, App., Feb. 1844.
YOAK, JOHN, S.B., Feb. 1844.
YOAK, JOHN, Set., 11-24-1845.

West Virginia Estate Settlements

In 1936 and 1937, the West Virginia Commission on Historic and Scenic Markers, the Works Progress Administration, and the Federal Emergency Relief Administration compiled court records of the various counties, such as Births, Deaths, Marriages, and Wills. Under Wills were grouped subjects pertaining to Estate Settlements, including Wills, Inventories, and Appraisements. Copies of these county records were filed at the Department of Archives and History, Charleston; the Library of West Virginia University, Morgantown; and the DAR Library, Washington.

Believing that there would be particular interest on the part of the general public in the Estate Settlements in the older counties, the West Virginia Historical Society has undertaken to abstract the Estate Settlements Records, as filed in the State Department of Archives and History, and offer them for publication in the *West Virginia History Quarterly*. No responsibility can be assumed as to the accuracy of the copies made from the original county records.

There are 13 counties which were formed prior to 1800, and it has been agreed to arrange these counties in chronological order, and to print their records from the earliest date to 1850. The formation dates of these counties are as follows: Hampshire—1753; Berkeley—1772; Monongalia—1776; Ohio—1776; Greenbrier— 1778; Harrison—1784; Hardy—1786; Randolph—1787; Pendleton —1788; Kanawha—1788; Brooke—1797; Wood—1798; and Monroe—1799.

Hardy County, Formed 1786

(From Alfree to Lynch)

The abbreviations used in this material include App.—appraisement; Bro.—brother; Dau.—daughter; Dev.—devisee; Inv.—inventory; S.B.—sale bill; Set.—settlement.

ALFREE, ABRAHAM, Inv., 5-3-1828.
ALFREE, ABRAHAM, S.B., 5-19-1829.
ALKIRE, MICHAEL, Inv., 3-10-1819.
ALLFREE, JOSEPH, Inv., 5-17-1825.
ALMOND, SUSAN, Inv., 7-1-1850.
ALT, ADAM, Will, 3-4-1850. Dev.: Daniel, bro.
ANGELLS, JOHN, Inv., 7-10-1799.
ARMANTROUT, HENRY, Inv., 6-19-1833.
ARMANTROUT, ISAAC, Inv., 11-4-1844.
ARMANTROUT, ISAAC, Inv., 11-14-1844.
ARMANTROUT, JOB, Inv., 11-6-1837.
ARMANTROUT, SUSANNA, Will, 5-10-1814. Dev.: Henry, son; Mary, Susanna, daus.
ARMANTROUT, SUSANNA, Inv., 9-5-1842.
ARMENTROUT, JOHN, Inv., 10-11-1809.
ARMENTROUT, MARY, Will, 4-1-1850. Dev.: Christopher, bro.; nieces and nephews.

ARMINTROUT, MARIA, Inv., 2-10-1829.
ARNOLD, MOSES, Inv., 4-14-1819.
ARNOLD, ROBERT, Inv., 7-31-1848.
ATHEY, THOMAS, Inv., 4-12-1831.
AULT, HENRY, Inv., 12-16-1818.

BABB, PETER, Will, 9-10-1822. Dev.: Cath., wife; John, Peter, Dan., Wm., Sam., Levi, sons; Lydia, dau.
BAKER, ABRAHAM, Inv., 9-14-1830.
BAKER, ANTHONY, SR., Will, 10-4-1816. Dev.: Barb., wife; Anthony, son; Eliz., Harness, Cath. See, Barb. Frontwine, daus.; others.
BAKER, ANTHONY, Inv., 3-17-1835.
BAKER, JACOB, Will, 10-16-1821. Dev.: Jemima, wife; John, Aaron, Jacob, Levi, Cornelius, Abraham, sons; Rebecca Row, Mary Baker, daus.; others.
BAKER JEMIMA, Inv., 10-12-1830.
BAKER, JESSE, Inv., 4-11-1815.

BAKER, MARY, Will, 7-13-1837. Dev.: Samuel, Wm., Moses, sons; Mary Maycock, dau.; others.

BAKER, MOSES, Inv., 9-5-1805.

BAKER, SAM., Will, 9-13-1809. Dev.: Jacob, Wm., Jesse, James, Solomon, sons; Mary Hill, dau.; others.

BAKER, WM., Will, 6-10-1793. Dev.: Sarah, wife; Wm., James, sons; Rachel, Marg. Paine, Mary, Lydia, Sarah, daus.

BAKER, WM., Will, 9-16-1832. Dev.: Mary, wife; Sam., Moses, Wm., sons; Mary, Eliz. Cherry, Magdalena Burch, Rhoda Downing, Elinor Chrisman, Rebecca Stewart, daus.

BARKDOLL, NICHODEMUS, Will, 9-13-1831. Dev.: Jacob, Jonathan, John, sons; daus., not named.

BASON, JACOB, Will, 2-18-1834. Dev.: Phebe, wife; Jacob, Wm., John, sons; Eliz. Thomas, Mary Grimm, Saraha Kite, Phebe Michael, Hannah Thomas, Nancy Ailsey, daus.

BEAN, BENJ., Will, 5-13-1828. Dev.: Geo., John, Jesse, sons; Priscilla Carr, Eliz. Ferris, daus.

BEAN, BENNETT, Inv., 2-10-1829.

BEAN, JAMES, Will, 4-4-1842. Dev.: Robert, Joshua, Geo., Bennett, sons; Casandra, Marg.; Ann Shepler, Rebecca Ryan, daus.; others.

BEAN, JESSE, Inv., 6-13-1826.

BEAN, ROBERT, Will, 2-7-1791. Dev.: Marg., wife; John, Wm., Geo., Thos., Robt., Bennett, James, sons.

BEAN, THOMAS, Inv., 2-11-1807.

BEAN, THOMAS, Will, 1-4-1847. Dev.: Horatio, Samuel, Richard, sons.

BENNETT, HENRY, Inv., 1-15-1800.

BERGDALL, JACOB, Will, 5-3-1847. Dev.: Isaac, Abraham, Jacob, Aaron, Gideon, sons: Susannah, Clara, Christina, daus.

BERGDOLL, BARB., Inv., 12-6-1847.

BERK, JOHN, Inv., 10-13-1795.

BISHOP, GEORGE, Will, 4-1-1839. Dev.: Eli, Jacob, Wm., Arthro, Thomas, Geo., sons; Eliza Peer, Marie Levi, daus.

BISHOP, JOHN, Inv., 7-5-1847.

BOGARD, ELIZ., Will, 8-1785. Dev.: Ann Mace, Eunice Harness, daus.

BOND, THOMAS, Inv., 9-1-1834.

BONNETT, HENRY, Inv., 7-14-1829.

BOOTS, ADAM, Will, 9-14-1803. Dev.: Barbary, wife; Garret, Adam, Martin, sons; others.

BORROR, JACOB, Will, 7-11-1804. Dev.: Magdalene, wife; Martin, Jacob, Solomon, Isaac, sons; Christina, Ann, daus.

BOUGHMAN, ANDREW, Will, 2-1-1807. Dev.: Cath., wife; Jacob, Isaac, Abraham, Henry, sons; Cath., Christina, Magdalene, Barbara, daus.

BOWMAN, JACOB, Inv. 10-12-1819.

BRADFORD, JOHN, Inv., 1-18-1833.

BRAKE, CATH., Will, 4-9-1816. Dev.: Michael, son.

BRAKE, JACOB, Inv., 9-13-1809.

BRANSON, AMOS, Inv., 6-10-1793.

BRANSON, JONATHAN, Will, 6-12-1827. Dev.: Mary Ann, wife; Susan, dau.; Rebecca, mother; Sally, sis.

BRANSON, JONATHAN, Inv., 6-10-1829.

BRANSON, LIONEL, Will, 4-10-1810. Dev.: Rebeckah, wife; Wm., Jonathan, sons; Eliz. Welton, Rebecca, Sally, Caty Allen, daus.

BRIGHT, JOHN, Inv., 8-11-1824.

BROUGHTON, WM., Inv., 10-11-1797.

BRUCE, ANDREW, Inv., 10-5-1836.

BRUCHER, PHILIP, Inv., 4-13-1796.

BUFFENBERG, DANIEL, Will, 2-24-1826. Dev.: Solomon, bro.; Balinda, sis.; others.

BUFFENBERGER, SOLOMON, Inv. 2-1-1841.

BUFFENBURGER, PETER, Will, 11-11-1817. Dev.: Mary, wife; Daniel, Peter, Solomon, Wm., Elijah, Lindel, Geo., sons; Clary, Linder, Eliz., Moses, Susannah Peterson, daus.; others.

BUFFINBARGER, MARY, Inv., 1-13-1829.

BURCH, JOHN, SR., Will, 1-4-1841. Dev.: Robert, Hezekiah, John, sons; Mary Ann, Marg., Polly Ann Huffman, daus.; others.

BURCH, THOMAS, Inv., 4-4-1842.

BYRNS, ANDREW, Will, 4-11-1820. Dev.: Eliz., wife; Wm., Morgan, Felix, Jarvis, Aaron, sons; Cath., Susannah Heishman, daus.

BYRNS, MORGAN, Will, 8-9-1825. Dev.: Mary, wife; Andrew, son.

BYRNS, WILLIAM, Inv., 6-5-1837.

CALDWELL, FURGESON, Inv., 2-1-1847.

CALHOON, ANN, Will, 4-10-1810. Dev.: John Dunbar, bro.; Elonar How, Martha Jackson, Marg. Claypool, sis.; others.

CALHOON, WM., Inv., 2-2-1795.

CALLENDER, MICHAEL, Will, 11-9-1813. Dev.: Ruth, wife; Hannah, dau.

CARR, CONRAD, Inv., 5-14-1821.

CARR, MICHAEL, Will, 2-5-1844. Dev.: Mary, wife; Mathew, son; Jane Hogeland, Sarah, Eliz., Susan Bean, Mary Bayer, Cath. Wigle, Christina Cratty, Phebe Deldine, daus.; others.

CASEY, BENJ., Inv., 3-14-1815.

CASEY, PETER, Will, 7-9-1787. Dev.: Nicholas, son; Philip Ross, son-in-law; Sarah, Cath., Rebecca, daus.

CASEY, PETER, Will, 7-9-1788. Dev.: Sons and daus.

CHILCOTT, ELIHU, Inv., 9-18-1832.

CHILCOTT, LYDIA, Will, Isaac, son.

CHRISMAN, ISAAC, Will, 4-13-1819. Dev.: Leah, wife; Isaac, John, sons; Rebecca, dau.

CHRISMAN, JACOB, Inv., 11-1-1846.

CHRISTIAN, JACOB, Will, 5-10-1809. Dev.: Isaac, Jacob, sons; others.

CHRISTIE, JAMES, Will, 4-15-1795. Dev.: Nansy, wife.

CLAGGET, JOSIAH, Inv., 1-14-1807.

CLAGGET, JOSIAH, Inv., 4-15-1807.

CLARK, HENRY, Inv., 12-6-1841.

CLARKE, ABRAHAM, Will, 4-13-1808. Dev.: Sarah, wife; children of wife; Watson, son; Nancy, Mary, daus.

CLAYPOLE, JAMES, SR., Will, 12-7-1789; Dev.: John, James, Joseph, Geo., Jesse, sons; Mary Smith, Betty Ozborn, Sarah Viney, daus.; others.

CLAYPOOL, JAMES, Will, 9-10-1811. Dev.: Marg., wife; Abraham, Isaac, Jacob, sons; Marg. Thomas, Hannah Evans, Esther Jacobs, Ruth Denton, Eliz. Wollard, Teijah Blizzard, daus., others.

CLAYPOOL, JOHN, Will, 9-9-1823. Dev.: Nancy, wife; James, John, David, Stephen, Geo., Wm., Aaron, Philip, sons; Mary Metcalf, Elinor Slater, James Osborn, Marg. Osborn, Sarah Slater, Rachel Baker, Hannah Gray, Eliz., Bradigum, Leah Chrisman, Nancy Sinnate, Priscilla Chilcott, daus.

CLIFFORD, ISAAC, Inv., 11-10-1831.

COBY, HEZEKIAH, Inv., 3-15-1826.

COKONOUR, JOSEPH, Will, 4-9-1800. Dev.: Mary, wife; John, Jacob, sons; Sarah, Magdalene, Barbara, Cath., daus.

COLER, HENRY, Will, 3-14-1820. Dev.: Marg., wife; Isaac, John, David, Geo., sons; Eliz., Doratha, Mary, daus.

COMBS, FRANCES, Will, 6-10-1817. Dev.: Nancy, wife; Frances, Henry, Joshau, Charles, Peter, sons; Tracy, Cassa, Lilly, Pyos, Christene, Drucilla Jarbo, Eliz. Bren, daus.

CONRAD, JOHN, Will, 5-6-1805. Dev.: Jacob, Jos., Geo., John, sons; Eliz. Butler, Rebecca Brown, Susanna Willis, daus.

CONRAD, JOHN, Will, 3-13-1821. Dev.: Madgalene, wife; Adam, Isaac, Jacob, Geo., John, Henry, sons; May Bayley, Madleny Kimble, daus.

COOPER, VALENTINE, Will, 5-19-1835. Dev.: John, Samuel, Jonas, Ely, sons; Eliz. Strater, Cath. Hinkle, Clara McConkey, daus.; others.

CORNELL, JOHN, SR., Will, 3-21-1837. Dev.: Jennet, wife; Wm., Joseph, Jacob, John, Archibald, sons; Marg. Wolfe, daus.; others.

COSNER, JACOB, Inv., 4-13-1824.

COSNER, PHILIP P., Will, 5-11-1819. Dev.: Cath., wife; Christian, Jacob, Adam, Philip, John, sons; Eliz., dau.

COUCHMAN, ADAM, Will, 3-17-1781. Dev.: Wife.

COUCHMAN, ADAM, Will, 3-17-1782. Dev.: Wife.

COUCHMAN, PHEBE, Will, 9-25-1832. Dev.: Adaline, Kitty and Jacob Craigen; Evaline Taylor, Susan Baker.

CRAIGEN, JOHN, Will, 1-9-1827. Dev.: Mary wife; Geo., Jacob, sons; Evalina, Susan Perrin, Kitty, Adeleana, daus.

CRITES, JACOB, Inv., 11-12-1828.

CRITES, PHILIP, Inv., 11-9-1823.

CROOSE, CHRISTIAN, Will 2-10-1814. Dev.: Barbara, wife; Michael, Adam, sons; Eliz., dau.

CROSBY, THOMAS, Inv., 12-3-1849.

CROSE. ADAM, Inv., 11-9-1830.

CUNNINGHAM, ELIJAH, Will, 4-1-1850. Dev.: Wilber. James, sons.

CUNNINGHAM, JAMES, Will, 1-13-1829. Dev.: Elijah, James, John, sons; Rebecca, Hannah Pendleton, Phebe Hutton, daus.; others.

CUNNINGHAM, JESSE, Inv., 11-22-1823.

CUNNINGHAM, JOHN, Will, 1-13-1829. Dev.: Rebecca, wife; Wm., Chas., sons; Juliet. Emily Shultz., daus.

CUNNINGHAM, ROBT., Will, 4-14-1802. Dev.: Wife and children.

CUNNINGHAM, ROBT.. Will. 4-14-1802. Dev.: Prudence, wife; Robt., Isaac, sons; Frankey, Miney, Eliz., Nancy, daus.

CUNNINGHAM, SOLOMON, Inv., 6-12-1823.

CUNNINGHAM, WM., Will, 7-8-1828. Dev.: Jemima See, wife; Solomon, Wm., Geo., sons; Hannah VanMeter, Sallie VanMeter, daus.

CUNNINGHAM, WM., Inv., 2-28-1842.

CUNNINGHAM, WM., Inv., 9-4-1843.

DARCUS. MICHAEL, Inv., 3-3-1845.

DARLING, WM.. Inv., 11-16-1786.

DASHER. CHRISTIAN, Will, 9-13-1831. Dev.: Eliz., wife; Isaac, son; Christian, dau.: Reuben. step-son.

DASHER, ELIZ.. Inv., 6-18-1833.

DASHER. LEONARD, Inv.. 3-7-1843.

DAVIS, HANNAH, Inv., 3-8-1825.

DAVIS. JAMES, Will, 7-15-1801. Dev.: Comfort, wife; John, James, Wm., sons; Jane. Comfort, daus.; others.

DAVIS, JAMES, Inv., 2-11-1817.

DAVIS, THOMAS. Inv., 6-10-1793.

DAVIS, WM., Will, 9-15-1835. Dev.: Eliz., wife; Levi, Robt., John, sons; Sarah, Mary, Nancy, daus.

DELAPLAIN, OWEN, Inv., 5-19-1835.

DELAWDER, ABRAHAM, Will, 11-1-1841. Dev.: Barb., wife; Philip, Sam., Jacob, John, David, Abraham, sons; Christena, Polly, Peggy, Civilla, Sally, Kath., Madlin, daus.

DELAWDER, LAURENCE, Inv., 1-17-1837.

DENTON, JANE, Will, 4-9-1787. Dev.: Jacob, Thomas, John, sons; Marg. Robinson, Sarah Williams, Eliz. Crow, daus.

DEVAULT, JOHN, Will, 9-13-1809. Dev.: Wife; Sary, dau.; Jeremiah, son.

DIDIWICK, JACOB, Will, 9-5-1842. Dev.: Cath., wife; Henry, son; Susan Cline, dau.

DOLL, JACOB, Will, 12-12-1798. Dev.: Wife; John, Jacob, sons; others.

DOOGAN, ALEX., Will, 4-12-1790. Dev.: Ann, wife; James, Thomas, sons; Sarah and Mary Chennowith.

DOOGAN, JAMES, Will, 10-1792. Dev.: Sarah, wife; Nancy, dau.; Thomas, son.

DOOLEY, WM.. Inv., 3-27-1837.

DORAN, ELIZ., Will, 9-30-1844. Dev.: Mary Bason, sis.

DORAN, FELIX, Will, 12-11-1810. Dev.: Wm., James, Alex., Peter, sons; Mary, Eliz., Jane Likens, Agness Patterson, Sally Ryan, Isabella Smith, daus.

DOUD, NANCY, Will, 11-3-1840. Dev.: Nancy Craig, granddau.

DOUGLASS, CATH., Will, 1-3-1842. Dev.: Parker, Sally, Cath, Seymour.

DREW, LONDON, Inv., 3-1830.

DYER, ELIAS, Inv., 8-12-1823.

DYER, JOHN, Inv., 8-12-1823.

ELDER, JEMIMA, Will, 3-31-1847. Dev.: Ed., nephew; Balinda Hutton, niece.

ELSWICK, THOMAS, Inv., 2-11-1801.

ERMONTROUT, CHRISTOPHER, Will, 7-10-1805. Dev.: Susannah, wife; Henry, John, Christopher, sons; Mary, Susannah, daus.

EVANS, CATH., Inv., 7-9-1822.

EXLINE, GEO., Will, 3-13-1832. Dev.: Elihah Godfrey.

FISHER, ADAM, Inv., 6-11-1816.

FISHER, ADAM, Inv., 1-12-1830.

FISHER, GEO., Inv., no date.

FISHER, JACOB, Will, 2-4-1839. Dev.: Geo., son; Eliz., Mary Ann Johnson, daus.

FISHER, JEMIMA, Inv., 10-9-1827.

FISHER, JOHN, Inv., 4-1-1839.

FISHER, MICHAEL, Inv., 3-15-1826.

FITZGERRALD, ELIZ., Inv., 8-10-1830.

FITZWATER, ISAAC, Inv., 2-4-1839.

FOLEY, JOHN, Inv., 7-11-1815.

FORGASON, ROBERT, Inv., 7-11-1791.

FOUT, FREDERICK, Inv., 7-15-1801.

FOWLER, WM., Inv., 9-8-1818.

FRAVEL, ANN, Inv., 12-13-1841.

FRAVELL, BENJ., Inv., 9-12-1826.

FRAVELL, HENRY, Inv., 6-12-1827.

FRAVELL, JOSEPH, Will, 6-10-1817. Dev.: Ann, wife; Reuben, Joseph, Benji., sons; Cath. Wilkins, Ann Branson, Eliz., Rebecca, Polly, Amanda, Lidia, daus.

FRAVELL, JOSEPH, Inv., 4-18-1837.

FRAZIER, JOHN, Inv., 4-2-1838.

FREEMAN, ANN, Will, 8-10-1831. Dev.: Ben, Moses, Floro, Jane, slaves.

FRY, WM., Inv., 10-8-1822.

FRYE, HENRY, Will, 6-11-1811. Dev.: Hannah, wife; Henry, Benj., sons; Polly, Frances, Sarah, Rebecca, Eliz., daus.

FRYE, JOHN, Inv., 9-30-1844.

GEORGE, DAVID, Inv., 3-9-1825.

GEORGE, JEREMIAH, Inv., 10-6-1845.

GEORGE, JOSEPH, Inv., 6-1-1840.

GIBONY, JOHN, Inv., 5-18-1831.

GILLIAM, WM., Inv., 7-31-1848.

GILMER, ROBERT, Inv., 1-9-1799.

GOCHENOUR, MARY, Will, 11-30-1846.
Dev.: John, Elisha, Elijah, bro.; Rebecca
Silvy, Rosanna Dolby, Mercy Marshall,
sisters; others.
GODLOVE, FRANCIS, Inv., 6-16-1835.
GOURLEY, WM., Inv., 5-14-1816.
GRAY, JAMES, Will, 4-23-1838. Dev.:
Mary, wife; children.
GREEN, JONES, Will, 7-2-1849. Dev.:
Agnes, dau.
GREEN, LEWIS, Inv., 4-10-1787.
GREEN, MARY, Inv., 12-15-1787.
GROVER, SOLOMON, Inv., 8-10-1824.

HAGGARTY, ADAM, Will, 10-15-1806.
Dev.: Eleanor, wife; Thomas, son; Eliz.,
dau.; others.
HAGLER, SEBASTIAN, Will, 1-15-1802.
Dev.: Eve, wife; Jacob, Leonard, sons;
daus.
HALL, JAMES, Inv., 12-2-1850.
HALTERMAN, CHRISTIAN, Inv., 9-10-
1816.
HALTERMAN, CHRISTOPHER, Will, 2-3-
1845. Dev.: Mary, wife; Geo., Henry,
John, Aaron, Chrisley, sons; Cath. Sny-
der, Mary, Eliz. Koon, daus.
HAMILTON, HENRY, Inv., 1-11-1820.
HANLINE, ELINOR, Inv., 3-5-1845.
HANLINE, MARTIN, Inv., 12-4-1848.
HANNABEL, BENJ., Inv., no date.
HARLISS, JOHN, Will, 5-12-1829. Dev.:
Isaac, Joseph, John, Geo., sons; Eliz.,
Marg., daus.; others.
HARMAN, DAVID, Will, 4-11-1791. Dev.:
Wife; Jacob and Abraham Hinkle.
HARMAN, DAVID, Will, 4-11-1791. Dev.:
Barb., wife; Jacob Hinkle, son; Abraham
Hinkle.
HARNESS, ELIZ., Will, 9-6-1802. Dev.:
Eliz., Mary, Sarah, daus.; David, John,
sons.
HARNESS, EUNICE, Will, 11-11-1823.
Dev.: Eliz. Welton, Jemima Cunningham,
Susan Cunningham, Hanna Hill, daus.;
others.
HARNESS, GEO., JR., Will, 10-4-1816.
Dev.: Rebeckah, wife; John, Geo., sons;
Sarah, Fanny Turley, daus.
HARNESS, GEO., SR., Will, 5-13-1823.
Dev.: Eliz., wife; Adam, Geo., sons;
Dorothy Renick, Martha Renick, Eliz.
Hutton, Pamela Carper, daus.
HARNESS, JOHN, Will, 6-12-1810. Dev.:
Unice, wife; Adam, Joseph, sons; Jemi-
mah Cunningham, Eliz. Welton, Hannah
Hull, Sarah Cunningham, daus.; others.
HARNESS, JOHN, Inv., 11-14-1823.
HARNESS, REBECCA, Inv., 7-13-1824.
HARRIS, DANIEL, S.B., 11-27-1827.
HARRIS, DANIEL, Inv., 5-20-1828.
HARRIS, JAMES, Will, 5-18-1824. Dev.:
Sara, wife; Wm., James, Geo., John,
Anthony, sons; Mary Nancy, Phebe,
Francis McNemar, daus.; Eliz. Shell.
HARRIS, WILLIAM, Will, 1-14-1823. Dev.:
Eliz., wife; James, Wm., Alesey, John,
Geo., step-sons; Mary, Phebe, Hannah,
Eliz., Sarah, Nancy, step-daus.
HARRISS, JOHN, Will, 2-13-1821. Dev.:
Geo., Simon, bros.; Mary, sis.
HATLER, JOHN, Inv., 12-5-1842.
HAYS, JAMES, Inv., 1-23-1824.
HEATH, WM., Will, 2-18-1834. Dev.: Jane,
wife; Chas., Wm., Johathan, sons; others.
HENLINE, ANDREW, Inv., 5-3-1841.
HERSHEY, WM., Will, 11-18-1834. Dev.:
Eliz., wife; John, Wm., James, Henry,
sons; Cath., Rebecca, Eliz., daus.; others.
HICKEY, JOHN, Inv., 9-14-1796.
HICKLEY, JOHN, Inv., 4-6-1846.
HIDER, ADAM, Will, 6-8-1789. Dev.: Wife
and children.

HIDER, ADAM, Will, 6-8-1789. Dev.:
Christina, wife; Michael, Adam, Isaac,
sons; Lydia, Sarah, Cath. Seymour, Mary
Neavill, Eliz., daus.
HIDER, ISAAC, JR., Inv., 12-1-1845.
HIDER, MICHAEL, Will, 8-2-1841. Dev.:
Wife; Hampton, son; Betsy McNeill, Ann
Taylor, Clementian, Cath., daus.; others.
HIGGINS, JOHN, Will, 1-15-1802. Dev.:
Hannah, mother; Elinor Williams, sis.;
Peter, bro.
HILKEY, CHRISTIAN, Will, 6-7-1842.
Dev.: Barbara, wife; Jacob, son; other
children.
HILL, ANN, Will, 4-14-1818. Dev.: Abra-
ham Baker, cousin.
HILL, DANIEL, Will, 4-15-1807. Dev.:
Mary, Anne, daus.; Thos., son.
HILL, MARY, Will, 5-20-1834. Dev.: Mar-
tin and Moses Baker, neph.; Sarah Moore,
Temperance Selby, niece.
HILL, THOMAS, Inv., 4-13-1814.
HINES, JOHN, Will, 2-21-1837. Dev.: Geo.,
John, Joseph, sons; Sarah, Cath. Harness,
Margaret Cooper, Barb. Cooper, daus.
HINKELBAGER, GEO., Inv., 12-12-1798.
HIRE, ANNA MARIA, Will, 11-16-1790.
Dev.: Rudolph, son.
HIRE, LEONARD, Will, 6-16-1786. Dev.:
Mary, wife; Leonard, John, Jacob, Lewis,
Peter, Michael, Rudolph, sons; Mary, dau.
HIRE, LEWIS, Inv., 8-13-1794.
HIRE, PETER, SR., Inv., 10-12-1826.
HITE, GASPER, Inv., 1-15-1833.
HITE, JONATHAN, Inv., 2-21-1837.
HITE, SARAH, Inv., 5-18-1835.
HOBOUGH, MICHAEL, Will, 3-14-1820.
Dev.: Magdalena Waldeberry, widow;
friends.
HOGBIN, JOHN, Will, 7-11-1804. Dev.:
Mary, wife; Joseph, son.
HOGG, DAVID, Will, 10-13-1786. Dev.:
Wm. Rennick, son of widow, Eliz. Ren-
nick.
HOGUE, DAVID, Will, 10-13-1786. Dev.:
Wm. Renneck.
HOLEY, BURCH, Inv., 7-12-1796.
HOMAN, JOHN, Inv., 2-13-1805.
HOMAN, SYCKMAN, Will, 9-8-1812. Dev.:
Madgalena, wife; Peter Hire, John Light,
Martin Power, Matildy Lewis, Jene Lewis,
Benj. Thickson, adopted children.
HORNBACK, ANTHONY, Inv., 9-26-1787.
HOUSE, JACOB, Will, 2-14-1795. Dev.:
Barbara, wife; children.
HOUSE, PETER, Inv., 3-25-1816.
HUFFMAN, ANTHONY, Will, 5-4-1840.
Dev.: Milley, wife; Elemuel, Lefenton,
Harrison, sons; Matilda, Emily, daus.
HUFFMAN, WM., Inv., 4-6-1846.
HUGHES, JAMES, Will, 7-14-1802. Dev.:
Mary, wife; Aaron, Jonathan, John, Levy,
Wm., Isaac, sons; Rebecah Ogden, Susan-
nah Steward, Eliz. Ely, Mary, Rachel,
Leah, daus.
HUGHES, SUSAN, Will, 4-11-1791. Dev.:
Wm., James, Hugh, Johathan, Evan, sons;
Mary, Hannah, daus.; others.
HULBE, GEO., Will, 9-14-1830. Dev.: Su-
san, wife; four sons and 5 daus. not
named.
HUNT, THOMAS, S.B., 11-1826.
HUTTEN, ISAAC, Inv., 4-9-1811.
HUTTEN, MOSES, Will, 7-9-1806. Dev.:
Abraham, Peter, Jacob, Isaac, Johnathan,
sons; Mary Welton, Rebecca Seymour,
Eliz. Seymour, daus.
HUTTON, ABRAHAM, Will, 2-8-1831.
Dev.: Phebe, wife; Moses, Job, sons.
HUTTON, ELIZ., Inv., 8-2-1841.
HUTTON, JOHN, Inv., 6-18-1833.
HUTTON, MOSES, Inv., 8-16-1836.

HYRE, JACOB, Will, 6-1-1846. Dev.: Enoch, Saul, sons; Mahala Welton, Rebecca Judy, Mary Shobe, daus.
HYRE, PETER, JR., Will, 1-10-1826. Dev.: Susannah, wife; Isaac, Elijah, Geo., Jacob, Peter III, sons; Hannah Ben, Susannah McFarland, Eliz. Vandevender, daus.
HYSHMAN, JOHN, SR., Will, 2-10-1829. Dev.: Magdalena, wife; Joseph, Philip, John, Andrew, sons; Cath., Barbara Sager, Magdalena Myers, Mary Baughman, Christena, daus.
IDLEMAN, CONRAD, Will, 7-13-1830. Dev.: Eliz., wife; Francis, John, Lewis, Jacob, sons; Cath. Cosner, Eliz. Rohabaugh, Mary Powell, daus.
INSKEEP, ABRAHAM, Will, 10-14-1823. Dev.: James, Wm., Jeremiah, John, Abraham, Jr., Isaacs, sons; Sarah Wilson, dau.
INSKEEP, ABRAHAM, Will, 12-3-1844. Dev.: Eliza, Mary Fox, daus.
INSKEEP, ISAAC, Will, 12-2-1844. Dev.: Ann, wife; Susan, Rebecca, daus.
INSKEEP, JEREMIAH, Will, 1-5-1846. Dev.: Scotta, wife; Abraham, Henry, sons; Mary Ann Branson, Sally, Rachel Hupp, daus.

JAMISON, ROBERT, Inv., 12-10-1800.
JEFFERSON, LUKE, Inv., 4-16-1801.
JOHNSON, JOHN, Inv., 5-14-1822.
JONES, DOCTOR, Inv., 4-9-1800.
JONES, REV. ED., Inv., 10-11-1797.
JONES, HENRY, Will, 3-5-1838. Dev.: Rachael, wife; Edmond, son.
JUDY, GEORGE, Inv., 2-8-1830.
JUDY, HENRY, SR., Will, 6-8-1824. Dev.: Magdalene, wife; Henry, Martin, Geo., John, Jacob, sons; Eliz. Drainer, Barb., Susanah Goldizen, daus.; others.
JUDY, JACOB, Inv., 8-11-1818.
JUDY, MARTIN, Will, 12-10-1822. Dev.: Mary, wife; Susannah, dau.

KEDNER, GEO., Inv., 6-10-1806.
KEDNOR, GEO., Inv., 5-10-1809.
KELLER, CASPER, Inv., 4-19-1822.
KERNS, NANCY, Inv., 1-10-1814.
KERRAN, PETER, Inv., 9-11-1799.

KETTERMAN, JOHN, Inv., 9-13-1831.
KYLE, FREDERICK, Inv., 6-26-1829.
LAIRD, ALEX,, Will, 9-12-1815. Dev.: Alex. Smith, friend.
LAMB, ELIZ., Inv., 6-5-1837.
LANCISKO, HENRY, Will, 9-10-1799. Dev.: Flory, wife; children.
LANCISKO, MRS. HENRY, Inv., 10-15-1800.
LANDUS, JACOB, Inv., 9-10-1811.
LEHEN, ELI, Inv., 5-3-1847.
LEWIS, MARY, Inv., 4-11-1804.
LIKENS, JOHN, Will, 5-12-1829. Dev.: Market, Rosanna Crossmuck, Barbara Hoover, Sara Hoover, Dolly, Rebecca, daus.
LIKENS, MICHAEL, Will, 1-31-1842. Dev.: Cath. wife; children.
LIKENS, RICHARD, Inv., 3-19-1787.
LILLER, SAM., Inv., 9-8-1818.
LINTHICUM, HEZEKIAH, Will, 7-3-1837. Dev.: Mary, wife; Wm., John, Jesse, sons; Ann, dau.
LINTON, HATHAWAY, Will, 12-10-1806. Dev.: Zach., Lawson, bros.
LITTLER, ABRAHAM, Inv., 7-27-1848.
LITTLER, ISAAC, Inv., 6-11-1822.
LITTLER, JOHN, Inv., 6-6-1842.
LITTLER, MAGDALENE, Inv., 2-13-1827.
LITTLER, THOMAS, Will, 3-11-1818. Dev.: Magdalina, wife; Abraham, Isaac, John, sons.
LIVER, ELIZ., Inv., 1-9-1827.
LORANCE, MARY, Inv., 9-30-1818.
LORENCE, JOHN, Will, 7-8-1817. Dev.: Mary, wife; John, Philip, Andrew, Isaac, Abraham, Daniel, sons; Cath. Pancake, Eliz. Bennett, Mary, daus.
LORENCE, MARY, Will, 7-14-1818. Dev.: John, Philip, Andrew, Abraham, Isaac, Daniel, sons; Eliz., Mary, Cath., daus.
LOUDERMAN, ELEANOR, Inv., 12-4-1848.
LOUDERMAN, PETER, Will, 3-11-1830. Dev.: Eleanor, wife.
LOUTHER, GEO., Inv., 4-9-1787.
LOWREY, JOSEPH, Inv., 10-31-1807.
LYNCH, PATRICK, Will, 5-5-1803. Dev.: Felix, son; others.

West Virginia Estate Settlements

In 1936 and 1937, the West Virginia Commission on Historic and Scenic Markers, the Works Progress Administration, and the Federal Emergency Relief Administration compiled court records of the various counties, such as Births, Deaths, Marriages, and Wills. Under Wills were grouped subjects pertaining to Estate Settlements, including Wills, Inventories, and Appraisements. Copies of these county records were filed at the Department of Archives and History, Charleston; the Library of West Virginia University, Morgantown; and the DAR Library, Washington.

Believing that there would be particular interest on the part of the general public in the Estate Settlements in the other counties, the West Virginia Historical Society has undertaken to abstract the Estate Settlements Records, as filed in the State Department of Archives and History, and offer them for publication in the West Virginia History Quarterly. No responsibility can be assumed as to the accuracy of the copies made from the original county records.

There are 13 counties which were formed prior to 1800, and it has been agreed to arrange these counties in chronological order, and to print their records from the earliest date to 1850. The formation dates of these counties are as follows: Hampshire—1753; Berkeley—1772; Monongalia—1776; Ohio—1776; Greenbrier—1778; Harrison—1784; Hardy—1786; Randolph—1787; Pendleton—1788; Kanawha—1788; Brooke—1797; Wood—1798; and Monroe—1799.

Hardy County, Formed 1786

(From Mace to Young)

The abbreviations used in this material include App.—appraisement; Bro.—brother; Dau.—daughter; Dev.—devisee; Inv.—inventory; S.B.—sale bill; Set.—settlement.

MACE, ELIZ., Will, 6-3-1844. Dev.: Betsy Ann Parson and her heirs.

MACE, NICHOLAS, Will, 2-15-1804. Dev.: Nicholas, son; Ann, wife.

MACHIR, DAN., Will, 11-2-1814. Dev.: Jane, sis.; John Hopewell, Job Hutton, John Machir, nephs.

MACHIR, DANIEL, Inv., 10-22-1829.

MACHIR, JAMES, Inv., 5-13-1828.

MARQUESS, REBECKAH, Inv., 3-10-1829.

MARQUIS, SARAH, Inv., 2-12-1822.

MARQUISS, JAMES, Will, 6-10-1828. Dev.: Rebeckah, wife; Wilson, John, Wm., Smith, James, sons; Rebecca Harriess, Marg. Martin, Nancy Shell, daus.; others.

MARSHALL, BENJ., Will, 4-21-1835. Dev.: Eliz., wife; Sam., Homer, Thomas, sons; Mary Tucker, Miley, Eliz., daus.

MARSHALL, SAM., Inv., 5-30-1850.

MARSHALL, THOMAS, Will, 6-3-1850. Dev.: Ann, Mary, daus.; others.

MARTIN, CHRISTOPHER, Will, 4-11-1820. Dev.: Mary, wife; John, James, Henry, sons.

MASTERS, EZEKIEL, Inv., 4-9-1816.

MATHIAS, BARBARA, Inv., 7-12-1825.

MATHIAS, JOHN, Will, 10-12-1819. Dev.: Barbara, wife; Barbara Hushame, dau.; others.

MCAFEE, MARK, Inv., 10-10-1842.

MCBRIDE, FRANCIS, Inv., 9-11-1800.

MCCARTY, MARY, Inv., 6-15-1815.

MCCONKEY, JACOB, Will, 4-27-1795. Dev.: Will, Sam., John, bro.; Hannah Mathews, Mary Ramsay, sis.

MCCORD, MARY, Inv., 10-11-1825.

MCDEVITT, ROSANNAH, Inv., 9-12-1821.

MCGEE, RAMSEY, Will, 10-10-1791. Dev.: Wm., son; Mary, dau.-in-law.
MCGUIRE, MARY ANN, Will, 10-9-1827. Dev.: Asneath, dau.
MCKINLEY, ALEX., Inv., 6-8-1819.
MCMECHEN, ELIZ., Will, 11-1-1847. Dev.: Sam., son; Cath. Maslin, Marg. McNeill, Eliz. Timberlick, Susan, Almand, daus.; Sarah Wolf, Agnes Lambert, step-daus.
MCMECHEN, JAMES, Inv., 5-4-1846.
MCMICHEN, SAM., Will, 8-20-1833. Dev.: Wife; Seymour, Sam., James, Abel, sons; Caroline Yarger, Agnes Lambert, Sarah Wolf, Eliz., Marg., Susan, daus.
MCNAMORROW, JOSEPH, Will, 2-12-1800. Dev.: Eliz., wife; John, Bryant, Joseph, sons; Eliz., Francis, Nancy, daus.
MCNEILL, DANIEL, Will, 6-17-1806. Dev.: Eliz., wife; Dan., John, Strother, Rees, Benj., Corbin, sons; Sarah Stienburger, Sidney, Doman, daus.
MCNEILL, DANIEL, Will, 7-9-1806. Dev.: Eliz., wife; Dan., John, Strother, Rees, Benj., Corbin, sons; Sarah Steenberger, dau.; other.
MCNEILL, DANIEL, JR., Inv., 10-18-1827.
MCNEILL, DANIEL, Will, 12-2-1844. Dev.: Daniel, Benj., Wm., sons; Cecily, Jane, Juliet Rennick, Rebecca Williams, daus.
MCNEILL, JAMES, Will, 2-14-1810. Dev.: Isaac Pancake.
MCNEILL, JOHN, Will, 3-16-1809. Dev.: Amy, wife; James, Strother, Jonathan, Isaac, sons; Polly, Amy, Anna, Jenny, Sidney, daus.
MCNEILL, STRAWDER, Inv., 3-9-1819.
MCNEMAR, PHILIP, Inv., 8-10-1824.
MICHAEL, GEO., Inv., 2-28-1842.
MICHAEL, NICHOLAS, Inv., 3-5-1838.
MILES, JAMES, Will, 5-4-1846. Dev.: Weston, Samuel, David, James, John, Robert, sons; Rebecca, dau.
MILES, JOHN, Will, 10-4-1847. Dev.: Clementine, wife; Wm., son.
MILLER, ANTHONY, Will, 10-11-1830. Dev.: Eliz., wife; Michael, Andrew, Abraham, Isaac, Jacob, John, sons; Marg. Littler, Rebecca Claybough, daus.; other.
MILLER, CHARLOTTA, Will, 8-31-1840. Dev.: Hiram, John, Marry Day, sons; Nancy, dau.
MILLER, ELIZ., Inv., 6-5-1848.
MILLER, JACOB, Will, 7-11-1787. Dev.: Barbara, wife; Anthony, Jacob, sons; daus.
MILLER, JACOB, Inv., 3-23-1837.
MILLER, MICHAEL, Inv., 12-16-1834.
MONEY, BRYAN, Inv., 9-12-1786.
MONGOLD, DAVID, Inv., 12-7-1843.
MONGOLD, GEO., Inv., 8-8-1820.
MOORE, BENJ., Will, 11-5-1849. Dev.: Abraham, son; Nancy Bishop, Marg. Swisher, Mercy Fry, Rachael Cosner, Mary Ann Smoot, daus.; others.
MOORE, CONRAD, Will, 4-9-1800. Dev.: Philip, John, Michael, brothers; Mary, Margget, Susanna, sis.; children of these bro. and sis.
MOORE, JAMES, Will, 11-11-1823. Dev.: Thos., Jacob, bros.; others.
MOORELAND, ELISHA, Inv., 6-14-1824.
MOORELAND, HENRY, Inv., 6-6-1842.
MORELAND, WM., Inv., 6-10-1817.
MORROW, JAMES, Will, 10-15-1800. Dev.: Wife; Thomas, Robert, James, David, sons.
MOUSE, DANIEL, Will, 7-13-1830. Dev.: Rebecca, wife; Jacob, Michael, Joshua, Adam, sons; Phebe, Teany, Rebecca, Mary Ann, daus.

MOYERS, JOHN, Will, 9-6-1808. Dev.: Wife; Jacob, John, Geo., sons; Mary, Betsy, Rosina, daus.
MOYERS, ROSANNA, Inv., 9-18-1832.
MULFORD, JAMES, Will, 3-12-1817. Dev.: James, son; John Leyman, friend.
MURPHY, AMAN, Inv., 8-18-1832.
MURPHY, HUGH, Will, 5-8-1801. Dev.: Polly, dau.; Hugh, son; others.
MURRY, JOHN, Inv., 3-9-1850.
MYARS, HENRY, Will, 4-8-1793. Dev.: Lydia, wife.

NAVE, ADAM, Inv., 8-21-1849.
NEFF, ELIZ., Will, 5-12-1816. Dev.: Geo., son.
NEFF, GEO., Will, 11-30-1840. Dev.: Enoch, Elizah, Peter, Geo., sons; Eliz. Wilson, dau.; others.
NEFF, HENRY, Inv., 4-16-1801.
NEFF, JACOB, Will, 2-5-1849. Dev.: Isaac, John, Jacob, Washington, Abraham, sons; Susan, Eliz., Marg., Ann Graigen, daus.
NEFF, MICHAEL, Inv., 11-14-1826.
NEVILL, JOS., Will, 4-13-1819. Dev.: Jethro, John, Geo., Joseph, sons; Amealy, dau.; others.
NEWHOUSE, ELIZ., Inv., 7-2-1849.
NEWMAN, CATESBY, Inv., 6-18-1833.
NEWMAN, ROBT., Will, 2-8-1814. Dev.: Eliz., wife.
NORTON, JOHN, Will, 4-10-1805. Dev.: Mary Ann, wife; John, Nathaniel, sons; Eliz. Clagett, Nancy Davis, Sarah Coomes, daus.; others.

O'BANNON, JOSEPH, Inv., 7-12-1825.
OGDEN, ABRAHAM, Inv., 5-12-1829.
OGDEN, DAVID, Will, 1-15-1833. Dev.: Rebecca, wife; James, David, Abraham, Isaac, Elijah, Jackson, sons; Lucinda, Leah, Rachael, Polly Switzer, daus.
OGDEN, DAVID, Inv., 3-19-1833.
OGDEN, JESSE, Inv., 10-4-1816.
OLDAEN, WM., Will, 6-11-1811. Dev.: Isaac Oldaen, bro.
OLDAKER, JACOB, Inv., 8-7-1841.
ORNDORFF, PARMENEUS, Inv., 5-4-1849.
OVERMAN, EULICE, Will, 8-1-1836. Dev.: Polly, wife; Abraham, John, Geo., sons; Mary Ann, Marg., Amanda, daus.

PANCAKE, CATH., Will, 1-15-1800. Dev.: Dolly Tevebough, Cath. Harness, daus.; David, John, sons; others.
PARSON, SARAH, Will, 4-1-1850. Dev.: Adam, son; Betsy Ann, Cath., daus.; other.
PARSONS, GEO., Inv., 1-10-1826.
PARSONS, CAPT. JAMES, Will, 4-13-1813. Dev.: Rebeccah, wife; James, Isaac, Solomon, sons; Jonathan, step-son; Betsy, Amanda, Rebecca, dau.
PARSONS, JAMES, Inv., 6-28-1839.
PARSONS, JONATHAN, Inv., 6-14-1797.
PARSONS, THOMAS, Will, 12-12-1804. Dev.: Else, wife; Wm., Isaac, Geo., James, Miles, Thomas, sons; Sarah, Hester, Marg., Annas, Cath., Rebecca, Hilda, Susannah, Hannah, Mary, Jane, Pamelia, Prudence, Eliz., daus.
PATCH, NATHANIEL, Inv., 12-1-1845.
PAUL, CATHERINE, Will, 6-9-1829. Dev.: Sisters and brothers; others.
PEARSON, ALEX., Will, 5-8-1810. Dev.: Eliz., wife; Robt., son; Mary Linthicum, Ann Cartmill, Effa, daus.
PECK, JOHN, Will, 7-19-1836. Dev.: Phebe, wife; three sons, two daus.

PECK, PHILIP, Will, 11-3-1845. Dev.:
Hannah, wife; others.
PETERSON, JACOB, Will, 2-14-1815. Dev.:
Jacob, son; Mary, Eliz., Sally, Eve, Phe-
be, daus.
PORTER, ROBT., Will, 3-12-1816. Dev.:
Peggy Martin, niece; others.
POWELL, ROBERT, Inv., 1-11-1804.
POWER, VALENTINE, Jr., Inv., 5-21-
1833.
POWERS, VALENTINE, SR., Will, 8-12-
1823. Dev.: Mary, wife; Valentine, Jr.;
son; other.
PRIEST, BARBARY, Inv., 6-14-1831.
PUGH, EVAN, Inv., 9-1799.
PUGH, JACOB, Will, 9-13-1816. Dev.:
Jacob, Robt., James, sons; Priscillia
Thomas, Hanna Harris, Lucretia Old-
aker, Rebecca Fry, daus.; others.
PUGH, JESSE, Inv., 6-14-1797.

RADABOUGH, PETER, Inv., 5-6-1839.
RAINS, ROBERT, Will, 11-19-1833. Dev.:
Sarah, wife; John and James Pack,
friends.
RANDALL, ABEL, Will, 9-10-1792. Dev.:
Felix, Jacob, Alex., sons; Mary, Cath.,
daus.
RANDALL, ALEX., Inv., 11-14-1815.
RANDALL, JACOB, Will, 2-1-1841. Dev.:
Amelia, wife; Abel, Silas, sons; Eliz.
Cowgar, Ruth Cowgar, Marg. Dasher,
Rebecca Dasher, Amelia See, Asenith
See, Jemima Page, Mary Britton, Tabitha,
daus.
RANKINS, GEO., Inv., 5-9-1815.
REAGER, MARTIN, Inv., 2-15-1797.
REDMAN, AARON, Inv., 11-13-1828.
REDMAN, JAMES, Inv., 3-2-1840.
REDMAN, JOHN, Inv., 1-17-1837.
REDMAN, WM., Inv., 9-11-1827.
REDSLEEVES, MICHAEL, Inv., 4-7-1788.
REED, ANTHONY, Will, 8-10-1819. Dev.:
Mary, wife; Benj., Anthony, sons; Deb-
orah, Dolly, Patsy, daus.
REED, WM., Inv., 6-6-1848.
REEL, DAVID, Will, 2-4-1840. Dev.:
Susannah, Jane, Marg., daus.
REIGHMAN, JOHN, Inv., 7-13-1808.
RENICK, WM., Will, 7-15-1807. Dev.:
Ann, wife; Felix, Thos., sons; Margret,
Caty, Mary Ann, Rachael, daus.
REYNOLDS, JOHN, Will, 2-11-1807. Dev.:
Eliz., wife; youngest child.
RICHARDSON, JOSEPH, Inv., 5-11-1803.
RICHARDSON, WM., Inv., 3-10-1812.
RIGHMAN, ELIZ., Inv., 11-9-1819.
ROBERTS, ARCHIBALD, Inv., 2-21-1837.
ROBERTS, JACOB, Inv., 2-21-1837.
ROBERTS, JOSHUA, Inv., 10-12-1794.
ROBERTS, THOMAS, Inv., 1-13-1807.
ROBERTSON, BLAZE, Inv., 9-19-1810.
RODABOUGH, MARY M., Inv., 2-2-1845.
RODES, JACOB, Inv., 6-11-1787.
ROGERS, WM., Will, 9-5-1808. Dev.: Wm.,
James, sons; Eliz., Marg., daus.; others.
ROHRABOUGH, JOHN, Will, 11-13-1821.
Dev.: Anthony, John, sons; Barb. Simon,
Magdalena Spohr, Eliz. Harness, Anna
Myers, Susannah Idleman, daus.
ROHRBOUGH, HENRY, Will, 2-11-1823.
Dev.: John, Christian, Geo., sons; Chris-
tina, Cath., Susan, Eliz., Susannah, daus.;
others.
ROHRBOUGH, HENRY, Will, 11-6-1848.
Dev.: Barbara, wife; Henry, Samuel, Sol,
James, Daniel, sons; Fanny, Malinda,
Hannah, Eve Strader, Jemima Stonestreet,
daus.
ROHRBOUGH, JOHN, Will, 11-3-1840.
Dev.: Assenitt, wife.

RORABOUGH, CONROD, Inv., 5-1-1848.
ROTRUCK, ABRAHAM, Will, 2-5-1838.
Dev.: Hepsibah, wife; children, not
named.
RYAN, JAMES, Will, 10-8-1816. Dev.:
James, John, sons; Eliz. Hanks, Mary
Crose, Sarah Long, Kitty Thompson,
Nancy Corn, Jane Dolohon, Elsey Byan,
daus.
RYAN, MARG., Will, 10-9-1818. Dev.:
David, Joshua, Stephen, Tichnel, sons;
Marg.; Abigail, Jane Tichnel, daus.

SAGER, CONRAD, S. B., 11-7-1827.
SAGER, CONRAD, Inv., 5-19-1829.
SAGER, JOHN, Will, 4-16-1833. Dev.:
John, Wm., Philip, Peter, Abraham,
Adam, sons; Cath. Miller, Ann Rosen-
berger, Eliz. Riggleman, Mary Weaver,
Sallie Kohn, Lydia Landakar, daus.;
others.
SAGERS, ABSOLEM, Inv., 6-5-1848.
SAGERS, JOHN, Inv., 8-2-1847.
SALTERS, THOMAS, Inv., 7-10-1827.
SCOTT, ALEX., Inv., 1-4-1841.
SCOTT, BENJ., Will, 9-13-1790. Dev.:
Benj., John, Alex., Samuel, sons; Eliz.,
Nancy, Hannah, daus.
SCOTT, JAMES, Inv., 10-7-1811.
SCOTT, JANE, Inv., 8-11-1824.
SCOTT, JOHN, Inv., 2-11-1807.
SCOTT, REBECCAH, Will, 11-11-1817.
Dev.: Phebe, Jeane, daus.
SEE, ANN, Will, 11-3-1840. Dev.: Henry,
husband; Chas. C., bro.-in-law.
SEE, ELIZ., Inv., 9-2-1844.
SEE, GEO., Inv., 6-14-1797.
SEE, GEO., Will, 6-10-1828. Dev.: Marg.,
wife; Jacob, John, Absolem, Geo., Nim-
rod, Aaron, Edmon, sons; Marg., dau.
SEE, GEORGE, Will, 6-11-1811. Dev.:
Christiana, wife; Adam, Geo., sons; Mary
Craiger, Phebe, Couchman, Cathy Paul,
Eliz. Stump, daus.; others.
SEE, HENRY, Will, 11-3-1840. Dev.: Ann,
wife; C. C., bro.
SEE, JACOB, Inv., 3-4-1850.
SEE, JOHN, Inv., 4-13-1790.
SEE, JOHN, Inv., 2-9-1803.
SEE, KEZIA, Inv., 2-18-1824.
SEE, MICHAEL, Inv., 3-13-1796.
SELLERS, MARG., Will, 4-15-1801. Dev.:
Fred., John, sons; Susanna, dau.; others.
SEYMOUR, ABEL, Will, 9-9-1823. Dev.:
Ann, wife; Garrett, Felix, Richard, Isaac,
Wm., Van, sons; Cath. Cunningham,
Marg. Welton, Ann, Nancy, Mary, Re-
becca, Polly, daus.; James, bro.; other.
SEYMOUR, ANN, Will, 11-13-1828. Dev.:
Richard, Wm., sons; Nancy, Polly, Mary,
Cath. Cunningham, Rebecca Cunningham,
Eliz. McMechin, daus.
SEYMOUR, JAMES, Will, 1-2-1843. Dev.:
Eliz., wife; John, Jonathan, Thomas,
Felix, sons; Margret Welton, Ann Wel-
ton, Rebecca Hutton, Jane Coyner, daus.;
others.
SEYMOUR, MOSES, Inv., 5-20-1823.
SEYMOUR, RICHARD, Inv., 3-11-1812.
SHANOR, FREDERICK, Inv., 7-9-1806.
SHEARS, SOLOMON, Inv., 9-13-1831.
SHEPLER, CATH., Will, 6-5-1837. Dev.:
Mary Ann, dau.; others.
SHEPPERD, JOHN, Will, 9-15-1802. Dev.:
Sarah, wife; Jonathan, James, Robt.,
Sam., Wm., sons; Ann, Eliz. Talbert,
Sarah Brown, Elisanna Manning, daus.
SHIRK, HENRY, Will, 8-10-1819. Dev.:
Mary Catie, wife; John, Jonathan, Jacob,
Henry, Adam, Job, Absolem, sons; Sue-
annah, Eliz., Mary, Patsy, daus.

SHOBE, ABRAHAM, Will, 1-8-1837. Dev.: Jesse, son; Jane Waltson, dau.; others.
SHOBE, JACOB, Inv., 2-14-1798.
SHOBE, JACOB, Will, 12-13-1831. Dev.: Frances Day.; other children.
SHOBE, LEONARD, Will, 12-13-1831. Dev.: Wife; Martin, Jacob, sons; Eliz., Sarah Ward, daus.
SHOBE, MAGDALINE, Will, 2-5-1849. Dev.: Isaac, son; Eliz. Alkire, Mary Judy, Alony Judy, daus.
SHOBE, MARTIN, Will, 7-1792. Dev.: Eliz., wife; Rudolph, Leonard, Jacob, sons.
SHOBE, MARTIN, Inv., 3-14-1815.
SHOBE, MARTIN, SR., Will, 4-30-1849. Dev.: Jemima, wife; Wm., Adnige, Henry, Amos, sons; Polly Armentrout, Eliz. Gilmor, Hakor Elye, Susannah Armentrout, Clairsey Armentrout, Rebecca, Dafney Stoinspring, Magdalene, Sarah, daus.
SHOBE, RUDOLPH, Will, 5-13-1829. Dev.: Magdalena, wife; Isaac, Solomon, Samuel, Daniel, sons; Eliz. Alkire, Mary Judy, Clory Judy, daus.; others.
SHOEMAKER, GEO., Will, 6-11-1811. Dev.: Cath., wife Geo., Michael, John, sons; Cath. Busby, dau.
SHOEMAKER, JOHN, Will, 10-14-1807. Dev.: Eliz. Michael.
SHOOK, HERMAN, Will, 6-8-1789. Dev.: Wife; Wm., John, Hermonous, David, sons; daus.
SHOOK, HARMONIUS, Inv., 9-14-1824.
SHOOK, JOHN, Will, 12-13-1790. Dev.: Eliz., wife; Mary, dau.; Wm., Peter, Harmon, David, bros.
SHROUT, PETER, Will, 1-12-1804. Dev.: Geo., son; Hannah Bradford, Peggy, Mary Richardson, daus.
SIMON, CHRISTIAN, SR., Will, 8-20-1833. Dev.: Barbara, wife; Christian, Geo., Abraham, Jacob, sons; Magdalena Smith, Barbara Campbell, Cath., daus.
SIMON, GEO., Will, 4-11-1804. Dev.: Mary, wife; Geo., Benj., Jacob, Christian, sons; Eliz. Rodabough, Cath. Rodabough, Mary Kessell, daus.
SIMON, JACOB, Inv., 2-6-1843.
SIMPSON, ALEX., Will, Eliz., wife; James, John, Jonathan, Isaac, sons.
SIMPSON, ELIZ., Will, 3-9-1830. Dev.: Jeremiah Veatch.
SIMS, ELIJAH, Inv., 4-13-1809.
SITES, DANIEL, Will, 8-2-1847. Dev.: Mary, wife; Gideon, Daniel, Solomon, Abraham, Jacob, sons; Magdalena, Barbara, Eleanor, daus.
SITES, FREDERICK, Will, 6-8-1830. Dev.: Eliz., wife; children.
SITES, FREDERICK, Inv., 6-7-1838.
SITES, GEO., Will, 12-7-1790. Dev.: Wife; Frederick, son; others.
SLATER, SAMUEL, Inv., 9-12-1799.
SMITH, ALEX., Will, 9-24-1833. Dev.: Eliz., James, Jacob, Philip, Wm., Jonathan, sons; Delila, Rachael, daus.
SMITH, JOHN, Inv., 10-14-1801.
SMITH, JOHN, Inv., 6-12-1821.
SNODGRASS, JAMES, S. B., 4-21-1831.
SNYDER, JACOB, Will, 8-12-1841. Dev.: Cath., wife; Geo., Jacob, Isaac, Henry, Charles, sons; Leah Fout, Sarah Wilkins, daus.
SNYDER, JOHN, Inv., 10-4-1841.
SPOHR, DAVID, Will, 11-9-1843. Dev.: David and Charlotte Fisher.
SPOHR, JOHN, Will, 2-14-1815. Dev.: Judah, wife; Edward, Gideon, Mathias, David, Anthony, Philip, sons; Nancy Harness, Eliz. Morrow, daus.

SROUT, GEO., Inv., 5-8-1827.
STEPHENS, WM. J. N., Inv., 8-1828.
STERRETT, A. M., S.B., 9-21-1836.
STERRETT, JAMES, Inv., 10-18-1833.
STERRETT, JAMES, S.B., 10-19-1833.
STEWARD, JAMES, Will, 10-14-1817. Dev.: Cloe, wife; John, James, Charles, Jeremiah, Reason, sons; Nancy, Cloe, Lucy Hughes, Nelly Musgrave, Miller Steward, daus.
STEWARD, JOSEPH, Will, 4-10-1810. Dev.: Nieces and nephews; James, bro.
STOMBOCH, PHILIP, Will, 6-9-1812. Dev.: Catty, wife; Jacob, Peter, John, Henry, sons.
STONE, JAMES, Will, 3-9-1819. Dev.: Rebeckay, wife; Thomas, Geo., James, Sam., Wm., sons; Mary David, Marg. Johnson, Sarah Baker, Rebeckah Myers, daus.
STOOKY, ABRAHAM, Inv., 12-10-1816.
STOOKY, JACOB, Will, 4-14-1802. Dev.: Nieces and nephews.
STRAWDERMAN, JOHN, Inv., 6-14-1814.
STRICKLER, JOSHUA, Will, 7-13-1796. Dev.: Ann, wife; others.
STROTHER, CATH., Will, 4-30-1849. Dev.: Nancy Johnson, Abel Randall, Jos. Doughards, James Miles.
STUMP, CATH., Will, 12-4-1783. Dev.: Cath. Brake, Eliz. Welton, Magdaline, daus.; Leonard, Michael, sons.
STUMP, GEO., Will, 5-8-1805. Dev.: Eliz., wife; Geo., John, sons; Emilia, Magdalene, Cath. Cook, Eliz. Nicholas, Sarah Alcaire, Charlotte Philips, daus.
STUMP, GEO., Inv., 11-14-1829.
STUMP, CAPT. LEONARD, Inv., 12-2-1826.
STUMP, LEONARD, Will, 2-10-1829. Dev.: Adam, son; Ann Barnett, Cath. Harness, Hannah Dyre, Christena Perril, Mary Ann Hutten, daus.; others.
STUMP, MICHAEL, Inv., 7-10-1799.
STUMP, SARAH, Will, 2-12-1822. Dev.: James, Leonard, Jesse, sons; Cath. Whitecotton, Sarah Simon, daus.
SUFFOLK, SARAH, Inv., 11-9-1825.
SWISHER, MICHAEL, Will, 6-3-1844. Dev.: Mary Magdalena, wife; Jos., Abraham, Henry, sons; Rebecca Burch, Eliz. Bean, Cath. Wise, Barb. Bryan, daus.
SWITZER, DANIEL, Inv., 4-12-1833.
SWITZER, NICHOLAS, Will, 3-8-1814. Dev.: Philip, Jacob, Simon, Valentine, sons; Filly, dau.

TAYLOR, HIRAM, Inv., 11-3-1845.
TAYLOR, JOHN, Inv., 4-8-1817.
TETERIG, JOHN, Will, 7-11-1826. Dev.: Barb., wife; Daniel, Jacob, John, Philip, Adam, Peter, sons; Mary, Cath., Barbary, Susanna, daus.
TEVEBOUGH, DANIEL, Will, 2-11-1801. Dev.: Solomon, John, Geo., Dan., sons.
TEVEBOUGH, DANIEL, Will, 9-9-1828. Dev.: Martha, wife.
THARP, JOHN, Inv., 8-2-1841.
THOMAS, JOHN, Inv., 2-21-1837.
THOMAS, JOHN, Inv., 10-15-1845.
THOMAS, MORRIS, Will, 1-13-1796. Dev.: Owen, Oswald, Elisha, John, David, sons; Rachel Deny, Eliz. Deny, Sarah, Susanna, daus.
THOMAS, OWEN, Inv., 5-6-1839.
TOLER, MATHEW, Inv., 7-17-1832.
TUCKER, AARON, Inv., 11-13-1821.
TUCKER, ABSOLEM, Inv., 5-4-1840.
TUCKER, ASA, Inv., 2-1-1847.
TURNER, WM., Will, 2-14-1810. Dev.: Dan. McNeill, friend.

UPDYRAFF, JOS., Will, 5-7-1814. Dev.:
Hattie, wife; Emily, dau.; other children.
VANMETER, ABRAHAM, Will, 9-9-1823.
Dev.: Eliz., wife; Joe, servant.
VANMETER, ELIZ., Will, 8-31-1840. Dev.:
Hannibal, Bruce, Charles, George, Jacob,
Solomon, Isaac, Milly, Mary, Rebecca,
servants.
VANMETER, GARRETT, Will, 7-7-1788.
Dev.: Ann, wife; Isaac, Jacob, sons; Ann
Seymour, dau.
VANMETER, ISAAC, Will, 12-14-1757.
Dev.: Annah, wife; Henry, Jacob, Gar-
rett, sons; Sarah Hickman, Cath., Rebecca
Hite, Hellita, daus.
VANMETER, ISAAC, Will, 12-14-1757.
Dev.: Henry, Jacob, Garrett, sons; Cath-
erine, dau.; Abraham Hite, son-in-law.
VANMETER, ISAAC, Will, David Garrett,
John, sons; Sallie, Ann Gibson, Eliz.
Inskeep, daus.; others.
VANMETER, JACOB, Inv., 9-13-1808.
VAN METER, JACOB (COL.), Will, 10-
13-1829. Dev.: Tabitha, wife; Abraham,
Garrett, Isaac, sons; Hannah, Ann, Re-
becca, Susan, Sally, daus.
VEATCH, HANSON, Will, 1-19-1836. Dev.:
Eliz., wife; Patrick, Elijah, Thomas, sons;
Polly, Sallie, daus.; others.

WALKER, JOSEPH, Inv., 9-17-1836.
WALLACE, MARY, Inv., 5-3-1847.
WALTON, JOHN, Will, 1-11-1809. Dev.:
Nancy, wife; Wm., son.
WARDEN, BENJ., Inv., 8-3-1846.
WARDEN, SARAH, Will, 10-13-1829. Dev.:
Magdalena, Mary, Sally, Scota, daus.;
John, James, Jacob, Benj., sons.
WARDEN, WM., Will, 10-14-1823. Dev.:
Sarah, wife; Jacob, Benj., John, James,
sons; Sarah, Magdalina, Mary, Scottie,
daus.
WARDEN, WM., Set., 9-26-1832.
WEBB, JOHN, Inv., 9-13-1808.
WELTON, AARON, Will, 6-1-1840. Dev.:
Mary, wife; Wm., Archibald, Simon, Abel,
sons; Eliz. Seymour, Sarah, daus.; others.
WELTON, DAVID, Will, 12-12-1815. Dev.:
Jesse, son; Rachel, Eliz. Rennick, Re-
becca Moducett, daus.
WELTON, ELIZ., Will, 3-4-1839. Dev.:
Cyrus, son; Belinda Hutton, dau.
WELTON, FELIX, Will, 9-12-1815. Dev.:
Eliz., wife; Werten, son; Maria, Eliza,
daus.
WELTON, ISAAC, Inv., 4-14-1818.
WELTON, JESSE, Inv., 2-10-1829.
WELTON, JESSE, Inv., 11-19-1835.
WELTON, JOB., Will, 11-14-1820. Dev.:
John, Aaron, Job, sons; Eliz. Clark,
Nancy Hutton, daus.; others.
WELTON, JOHN, Will, 11-4-1844. Dev.:
Rachel, wife; Felix, Job, Martin, sons;
Amanda, Eliz., Sarah Seymour, Mary
Chambers, Eliza Fisher, daus.
WELTON, PHEBE, Inv., 1-13-1829.
WELTON, WM., Inv., 12-10-1816.
WELTON, WM., Inv., 1-4-1841.
WESTFALL, JOHN, Will, 4-13-1789. Dev.:
Sarah, wife; Isaac, Jacob, Abell, John,
Cornelius, Abraham, sons.
WESTFALL, SARAH, Will, 11-9-1791.
Dev.: Isaac, Jacob, sons; others.
WHEELER, THOMAS, Will, 10-15-1800.
Dev.: Jane Condell (mother of his child-
ren); Benj., Thos., Wm., sons; Eleanor,
Dolly, Ruth, Jinney, Sarah, Rachael,
Eliz. Amy, daus.
WHETZEL, NICHOLAS, Will, 9-13-1816.
Dev.: Eliz., wife; John, son.

WHITLEY, WM., Inv., 1-10-1798.

WILKINS, GEO., Inv., 2-12-1822.
WILKINS, GODFREY, Inv., 3-22-1836.
WILKINS, JOSEPH, Inv., 10-5-1840.
WILKINS, MATHIAS, Inv., 10-12-1803.
WILKINS, SARAH, Will, 10-31-1842. Dev.:
Aaron, Archibald, Silas, Pharoh, Mathias,
Moses, Job, sons, Marg., Cath., daus.
WILLIAME, ELEANOR, Will 1-8-1822.
Dev.: Thos. Hagerty, son; Eliz. Hilton,
dau.; others.
WILLIAMS, EBENEZAR, Will, 4-14-1818.
Dev.: Rachel, wife; David, Geo.; Eb-
enezar, James, sons; Abigail, Mary,
Nancy, Rachel, Susan Marg., daus.
WILLIAMS, EDWARD, Will, 5-10-1831.
Dev.: Mortimer, Washington, Joseph,
sons; Mary Toler, Nancy McMichen,
Amelia Seymour, Caroline, Rebecca, Eliz.
Gamble, daus.; others.
WILLIAMS, SARAH, Inv., 8-10-1830.
WILLIAMS, VINCENT, Will, 9-15-1802.
Dev.: Rebekah, wife; Isaac, bro.
WILLIAMS, VINCENT, Inv., 5-7-1819.
WILLIS, JACOB, SR., Will, 11-14-1826.
Dev.: Abraham, Jacob, John, sons; other
children.
WILSON, CHARLES, Will, 8-9-1815. Dev.:
Easter, wife; John, Charles, Isaac, Joseph,
sons; Sarah, Rebecca Fowler, Rachel
Neff, Jane Neff, Jane Neff, Mary, daus.
WILSON, DAVID, Will, 9-6-1805. Dev.:
Mary, wife; Jacob, John, Geo., Job, Isaac,
Abel, Jesse, Enoch, sons; Barb., Sarah,
Marg., daus.
WILSON, ESTER, Will, 7-1-1850. Dev.:
Charles, David, Jos., grandsons.
WILSON, HENRY, Will, 9-5-1805. Dev.:
Martha, wife; John, Thomas, Crawmore,
David, sons; Margret, Eliz., Ann, daus.
WILSON, JOHN, Will, 9-6-1847. Dev.:
Susan, wife; John, Heydon, David, Isaac,
sons; Mary Wilkins, Scotia, Rebecca,
Ellen Chilcott, Nancy Baker, Lydia Kohn,
Sarah Ann Hulver, Susan Hulver, Cath.
Varmuse, Amanda Pergley, daus.
WILSON, JOSEPH, Inv., 6-3-1844.
WILSON, MARTHA, Will, 11-18-1826.
Dev.: Moses, Wilson, grand-son.
WILSON, RACHAEL, Will, 9-3-1850. Dev.:
Wm., Jacob, sons; Martha Wimer, Sarah
Hose, daus.
WILSON, WILLIAM, Will, 9-9-1801. Dev.:
Eliz., wife; Benj., Archibald, Wm., John,
David, Solomon, James, sons; Eliz. Clay-
pole, Marg. Ruddle, daus.; others.
WIMER, DANIEL, Inv., 5-31-1847.
WISE, ELIZ., Inv., 9-14-1830.
WISE, FREDERICK, Inv., 4-9-1823.
WISE, WM., Inv., 12-10-1822.
WOLLERD, JOHN, Will, 1-10-1810. Dev.:
Marg., wife; John, Henry, sons; Mary
Smith, Christina Shaver, Chataraina Hen-
jhiner, Eliz. Shineman, Susanna Wollerd,
Magdalena, daus.
WOOD, PETER, Inv., 7-10-1805.
WYCOFF, SAM., Will, 9-14-1814. Dev.:
Martha, wife; Simon, Wm., sons; Ann,
dau.

YOAKUM, GEO., Will, 4-13-1789. Dev.:
Cath., wife; Eliz. Harness, Cath., Mary,
Marg., Magdaline, daus.; others.
YOAKUM, JACOB, Will, 11-7-1838. Dev.:
Sandfor and Sally Simmons; grand-
children.
YOKEM, PHILIPP, Will, 12-9-1807. Dev.:
Geo., Philipp, Michael, Jacob, John, sons;
Eliz. Renick, Barbara Starr, Cath. Beves-
ly, daus.
YOUNG, JOHN, Will, 4-13-1808. Dev.:
Marg. Hunter, Mary Doyl, daus.; James,
John, sons; others.

West Virginia Estate Settlements

In 1936 and 1937, the West Virginia Commission on Historic and Scenic Markers, the Works Progress Administration, and the Federal Emergency Relief Administration compiled court records of the various counties, such as Births, Deaths, Marriages, and Wills. Under Wills were grouped subjects pertaining to Estate Settlements, including Wills, Inventories, and Appraisements. Copies of these county records were filed at the Department of Archives and History, Charleston; the Library of West Virginia University, Morgantown; and the DAR Library, Washington.

Believing that there would be particular interest on the part of the general public in the Estate Settlements in the other counties, the West Virginia Historical Society has undertaken to abstract the Estate Settlements Records, as filed in the State Department of Archives and History, and offer them for publication in the *West Virginia History Quarterly*. No responsibility can be assumed as to the accuracy of the copies made from the original county records.

There are 13 counties which were formed prior to 1800, and it has been agreed to arrange these counties in chronological order, and to print their records from the earliest date to 1850. The formation dates of these counties are as follows: Hampshire—1753; Berkeley—1772; Monongalia—1776; Ohio—1776; Greenbrier—1778; Harrison—1784; Hardy—1786; Randolph—1787; Pendleton—1788; Kanawha—1788; Brooke—1797; Wood—1798; and Monroe—1799.

Pendleton County, Formed 1788

The abbreviations used in this material include App.—appraisement; Bro.—brother; Dau.—daughter; Dev.—devisee; Inv.—inventory; S.B.—sale bill; Set.—settlement.

ADAM, LOSS, Will, 12-5-1789. Dev.: Barbara, wife.

ANDERSON, JAMES, Will, 6-24-1850. Dev.: Catherine, Polly, Elizabeth, sisters; others.

ARBAGAST HENRY, Will, 2-23-1844. Dev.: Levi, George, Benjamin, Henry, Aloynd, Andrew, sons; Nelly, Patsy, Catherine, Mary, Phebe, Sophie, Hester, Elizabeth, daus.

ARMSTRONG, WILLIAM, Will, 3-7-1806. Dev.: Jane, wife; William, James, sons; Mary, Margaret, Elizabeth, Sarah, Ann, daus.

BENNETT, JOSEPH, Will, 5-7-1808. Dev.: Hannah, wife; Jacob, John, Elijah, sons.

BENNETT, JOSEPH, Will, 8-24-1850. Dev.: Susannah, Agnes, Catherine, Amanda, daus.; James, William, Jacob, Mortimore, Isaac, Joseph, Moses, Aaron, John, Marton, Henry, sons.

BEVRIDGE, DANIAL, Will, 4-22-1818. Dev.: Catherine, wife; Jacob, Peter, sons.

BIBLE, GEORGE, Will, 12-16-1833. Dev.: Henry, John, Adam, George, William, Jacob, Philip, Samuel, sons; Susannah, Elizabeth, Barbara, Eve, daus.; others.

BLAND, HENRY, Will, 6-24-1850. Dev.: Wife (name not given); Parry, Stuard, sons; Daughters not named.

BODKIN, JOHN, Will, 7-10-1791. Dev.: Mary, wife; William, son; Margret, dau.

BORREN, THOMAS, Will, 4-17-1801. Dev.: Catherine, wife; Peter, Adam, Abraham, sons.

BORRER, CHARLES, Will, 1-3-1841. Dev.: Elizabeth, dau.; Martin, John, Solomon, Daniel, sons; others.

BOYERS, LEONARD, Will, 2-11-1815. Dev.: Nancy, dau.; Anthony, son.

143

CALHOON, JOHN, Will, 3-26-1850. Dev.: John, William, sons; others.

CAMPBELL, ALEXANDER, Will, 3-17-1845. Dev.: Rachel, wife; Thomas, Hanson, Samuel, Azarah, Milton, sons; Laura, dau.

CAZENOVA, OCTAVIUS, Will, 2-18-1841. Dev.: William, bro.

COIL, JACOB, Will, 2-23-1810. Dev.: Margaret, wife; Henry, son.

CONROD, MAGDALENA, Will, 3-12-1850. Dev.: Catherine, Phebe, Barbra, Hannah, daus.; Adam, son; others.

COONROD, JACOB, Will, 12-25-1838. Dev.: Medlean, wife; Adam, son; Catherine, dau.; others.

COYLE, GEORGE, Will, 2-18-1793. Dev.: Hannah, wife; George, Jacob, John, sons; Catherine, Elizabeth, Barabara, Hannah, daus.

CROMMET, CHRISTOPHER, Will, 4-27-1814. Dev.: Frederick, Conrod, George, sons; Flora, Margaret, Catherine, Rebecca, Molly, daus.

CURRY, JAMES, Will, 5-14-1836. Dev.: Mrs. Curry, wife; William, Robert, James, Edward, John, sons; Elizabeth, Jean, Jennie, daus.

CURRY, MARY, Will, 5-13-1841. Dev.: Edward, Benami, John, Nephs.

DAUGLES, THOMAS, Will, 11-28-1792. Dev.: Elizabeth, wife; John, Thomas, William, Robert, sons; Susa, Elizabeth, Sarah, daus.

DEVERICK, JOHN, Will, 7-30-1840. Dev.: Mary, wife; John, William, sons; others.

DICE, GEORGE, Will, 7-26-1841. Dev.: Catherine, wife; Elizabeth, dau.: Jacob, son; others.

DICE, MATHIAS, Will, 3-19-1799. Dev.: Catherine, wife; Mathias, William, Jacob, Philip, John, George, sons; Barbary, Pheba, Mary, Anna, Catherine, Elizabeth, daus.

DICE, PHILLIP, Will, 9-28-1801. Dev.: George, John, Jacob, Mathias, William, bros.: Elizabeth, Catherine, Christena, Barbia, Pheuba, daus.

DOLLY, JOHN, Will, 11-17-1838. Andrew, John, George, sons; Catherine, Phebe, Christina, Mary, Anna, Eve, daus.

DUNKLE, JOHN, Will, 2-7-1801. Dev.: Elizabeth, wife; Elizabeth, dau.

DUNKLE, JOHN, Will, 9-21-1813. Dev.: Margaret, wife; George, John, William, Samuel, Rheuban, sons; Margret, Mary, Sarah, daus.

DYER, MATHEW, Will, 9-4-1829. Dev.: Rebecca, wife.

DYER, SUSANNA, Will, 11-25-1833. Dev.: Mary, Elizabeth, Ruth, daus.; others.

DYER, SUSANNAH, Will, 11-25-1833. Dev.: Mary, Elizabeth, Ruth, Hannah, daus.; others.

DYER, WILLIAM, Will, 5-14-1842. Dev.; Margaret, wife; Rebecca, dau.; James, Roger, sons; others.

DYER, ZEBULAN, Will, 6-5-1845. Dev.: divide among heirs.

EAGLE, CHRISTIAN, Will, 4-28-1841. Dev.: Jane, wife; Samuel, George, Christian, sons; Martha, Celia, Lucinda, Elizabeth, Margaret, Jane, Lydra, Ann, Sally, Catherine, Susanna, daus.

ECKORD, ABRAHAM, Will, 2-26-1816. Dev.: Philip, John, bros.; Magdalene, Mary, sis.

EDMON, THOMAS, Will, 3-13-1837.Dev.: Matilda, wife; Carolin, dau.; others.

ERRIVIN, GEORGE, Will, 11-3-1841. Dev.: Deborah, wife; Israel, John, Jared, sons; Martha, Margaret, Ingabo, Serenia, Barbara, Joannah, Algina, daus.

ERVIN, CATHERINE, Will, 8-5-1814. Dev.: Ruth, dau.

EVIC, EVE, Will, no date. Dev.: George, son.

EYE, CHRISTIAN, Will, 6-16-1846. Dev.: Elizabeth, wife; William, Christian, Henry, Jacob, Reuben, sons; Elizabeth, Sally, Susan, Phebe, daus.; others.

EYE, CHRISTOPHER, Will, 2-21-1797. Dev.: Katrine, wife; Bantriana, Elizabeth, Mary, Rachel, daus.; Fredrick, George, sons.

EYE, FREDERICK, Will, 5-24-1849. Dev.: John, son; Elizabeth, Mary, daus.; other.

FISHER, JOHN, Will, 1-19-1835. Dev.: John, Zebulon, William, sons; Phebe, Elizabeth, daus.; Anna, wife.

FLEISHER, CONARD, Will, 8-21-1797. Dev.: Sophia, wife; Peater, bro.

GALL, GEORGE, Will, 12-6-1810. Dev.: John, son; others.

GAUL, GEORGE, Will, 12-6-1802. Dev.: John, son.

GIBSON, SAMUEL, Will, 6-3-1841. Dev.: Mrs. Gibson, wife; Sarah, Margaret, daus.; Samuel, son; others.

GUM, ADAM, Will, 12-30-1846. Dev.: Peter, Adam, sons; Netty, Susannah, Eliza, daus.: wife's name not given.

HAKLER, DANIEL, Will, 5-5-1845. Dev.: Jacob Hinkle.

HAMMER, BALSER, Will, 9-3-1835. Dev.: Elizabeth, wife; Sarah, Catherine, Fanny, Magdoline, Mary, Elizabeth, Susannah, daus.; others.

HAMMER, GEORGE, Will, 12-4-1797. Dev.: Susanna, wife; George, Henry, Jacob, sons; Susanna, Elizabeth, daus.

HANNACOST, MITCHEL, Will, 8-6-1805. Dev.: Elizabeth, wife.

HARDWAY, GEORGE, Will, 11-5-1811. Dev.: Susanah, wife.

HARMAN, JOSHUA, Will, 3-5-1849. Dev.: Eve, wife; Joel, John, George, Isaac, sons; Eve, Catherine, Phebe, Elizabeth, Mahulda, daus.

HARPER, NICHOPAS, Will, 2-17-1818. Dev.: Henry, Peter, George, sons; Barbara, Ann, Elizabeth, Catherine, Mary, Sarah, Susanna, daus.

HARPER, PHILIP, Will, 1-11-1793. Dev.: Jacob, Philip, sons.

HARPMAN, HENRY, Will, 11-20-1846. Dev.: Jobe Moser, son-in-law; others.

HAYS, SARAH, Will, 9-30-1815. Dev.: George, William, sons; Nancy, Peggy, daus.; others.

HEATON, EPHRAIM, Will, 3-15-1811. Dev.: Mrs. Marton, wife.

HEAVNER, FREDERICK, Will, 11-16-1816. Dev.: William, George, sons; Catherine, Elizabeth, Mery, daus.; others.

HEDRICK, BARBARA, Will, 1-31-1850. Dev.: Samuel, husband.

HEDRICK, CHARLES, Will, 6-11-1849. Dev.: Mary, Hannah, Elizabeth, Leveinda, daus.; Zebulon, son.

HEDRICK, JOHN, Will, 5-20-1839. Dev.: Tina, Barabara, Eve, Elizabeth, daus.; Charles, Adam, sons; other.

HELMICK, ADAM, Will, 8-31-1844. Dev.: Catherine, wife; Abel, Corelins, Moses, Nathaniel, Elihue, Thomas, sons; Anny, Elizabeth, daus.

HENRY, SYBERT, Will, 3-21-1795. Dev.: Rachel, wife; Jacob, son.

HERBERT, MARY, Will, 1-31-1850. Dev.: Ruth, Hannah, Susan, Elizabeth, sisters; others.

HEVENER, JACOB, Will, 12-18-1810 Dev.: Daniel, Michell, Samuel, Peter, John, sons; Mary, dau.

HICKLIN, JAMES, Will, 3-13-1839. Dev.: Sarah, wife; others.
HINER, JOHN, Will, 7-12-1813. Dev.: Ester, wife; Jacob, John, Joseph, Harman, sons; Ester, Jane, Mary, Agnes, Elizabeth, daus.
HINER, JOSEPH, Will, 11-29-1849. Dev.: Jane, wife; George, William, Samuel, Joseph, sons; Magdalene, Nancy, Margaret, Jane, Sarrah, daus.; others.
HINKLE, ABRAHAM, Will, 12-8-1814. Dev.: Cathirine, wife; Mary, Elizabeth, Susanna, Cathirine, daus.; Lenard, Mickael, Isaac, sons; others.
HINKLE, JUSTICE, Will, 11-16-1793. Dev.: Christina, wife; George Ketterman, son-in-law.
HIVELY, CHRISTRAN, Will, 6-13-1837. Dev.: Sally, wife; John, son; Martha, dau.
HOLLINGSWORTH, LEVI, Will, 1-24-1821. Dev.: Hannah, wife; Paschall, Henry, sons; others.
HOOVER, MICKAEL, Will, 12-28-1830. Dev.: Susannah, wife; Mary, dau.; John, Sebastan, George, Mickael, Thomas, sons; others.
HOPKINS, ELIZABETH, Will, 5-5-1844. Dev.: Thomas, son; others.
HOPKINS, JOHN, Will, 6-16-1842. Dev.: Elizabeth, wife; Cyrus, John, sons; others.
HOW, HENRY, Will, 4-18-1813. Dev.: Mary, wife.
HUFMAN, MARY, Will, 3-25-1844. Dev.: Susanna, dau.
HULL, JACOB, Will, 3-11-1815. Dev.: Jane, wife; Henry, Jacob, Welton, sons; Mary, Jane, daus.
HULL, PETER, Will, no date. Dev.: Barbara, wife; Henry, Peter, Adam, Jacob, William, sons; Susanna, Barbara, daus.; others.

JAMES, WILLIAM, Will, 4-25-1801. Dev.: Margret, wife; Nelle, Elizabeth, Margret, daus.; Henry, John, William, Edward, sons.
JOHNS, ISAAC, Will, 8-22-1797. Dev.: William, James, Jaremeah, Zachariah, sons; Mary, Elizabeth, daus.
JOHNSTON, MARY, Will, 3-3-1843. Dev.: Sarah, Lydie Scott, daus.
JORDAN, ANDREW, Will, 4-7-1818. Dev.: Letty, wife; William, Harrison, John, Andrew, sons; Elizabeth, Rachel, Letty, daus.
JUDY, NANCY, Will, 5-3-1848. Dev.: Ursula, Roxana, Virginia, Nancy; others.

KEE, AARON, Will, 8-9-1813. Dev.: Catharine, wife; James Boggs, McCreery.
KEISTER, FREDRICK, Will, 8-10-1806. Dev.: Hannah, wife; Fredrick, George, James, sons.
KINKADE, THOMAS, Will, 11-25-1844. Dev.: Betsy Ann, Margret, daus.; Peter, John, William, sons.
KYLE, ABRAHAM, Will, 6-27-1843. Dev.: Susanna, wife.

LAMBERT, GEORGE, Will, 10-17-1840. Dev.: Nelly, wife; George, Noah, John, Harrey, Arnold, sons; Mary, dau.
LANTZ, JOSEPH, Will, 2-14-1817. Dev.: Susannah, wife; Jonas, Benjamin, Joseph, sons; Sosanna, Barbara, Mary, Catharine, daus.
LANTZ, JOSEPH, Will, 4-22-1850. Dev.: Joseph, Levi, Abraham, Michael, sons; Martha, Rachel, Hannah, Catherine, daus.

LIFE, MARTIN, Will, 4-5-1797. Dev.: Annie, wife; Martin, son.

MALCOM, JOHN, Will, 9-24-1834. Dev.: Jane, wife; others.
MANUS, RICHARD, Will, 8-19-1799. Dev.: Joseph Teeter, Marveal Teeter.
MARTEN, WILLIAM, Will, 3-31-1845. Dev.: Emaline, wife.
MAUZY, MICHAEL, Will, 3-6-1846. Dev.: David, James, Joseph, sons.
MAYERS, MARTIN, Will, 9-27-1839. Dev.: Sally, wife; Betsy, Polly, Catherine, Sally, Fanny, Peggy, Susan, daus.; James, Samuel, sons.
McCOY, JOHN, Will, 8-20-1796. Dev.: Sarah, wife; Elizabeth, Sara, Jemina, Jane, daus.; Robert, Oliver, William, John, Bengamin, Joseph, James, sons.
McCLURE, JOHN, Will, 1-25-1847. Dev.: John, son; others.
McCULLEN, DRUNCAN, Will, 6-26-1810. Dev.: Phebe, wife; Darid, son; Duncan, grd. son.
McCULLON, ROBERT, Will, 10-9-1823. Dev.: Thomas, Robert, Joseph, sons; Prudence, Eleanor, daus.
MICHELL, FUSELL, Will, 4-12-1796. Dev.: widow (name not given).
MILLER, GEORGE, Will, 5-14-1845. Dev.: Samuel, George, John, Adam, sons; Eve, Mary, daus.
MILLER, JOHN, Will, 9-6-1848. Dev.: Margaret, wife; others.
MILLER, STEPHEN, Will, 10-19-1789. Dev.: Rashel, wife; George, Abraham, sons.
MILLER, THOMAS, Will, 2-16-1799. Dev.: Mickael, son.
MILLER, THOMAS, Will, 12-16-1847. Dev.: Catherine, wife; others.
MITCHELL, JOHN, Will, 2-27-1850. Dev.: Jessee, Leonard, John, William, sons; Mary, Ann, daus.
MORAL, JOHN, Will, 1-23-1795. Dev.: Sarrah, wife; Hannah, Mary, Sarrah, daus.
MOUSE, ADAM, Will, 2-20-1841. Dev.: Michael, bro.; Becky, sis.
MOUSE, MICKAEL, Will, 9-3-1814. Dev.: Michael Mouse, neph.; Adom Mouse, bro.
MOWERY, LEONARD, Will, 7-5-1846. Dev.: Susannah, wife.
MULLENAX, JOHN, Will, 6-3-1809. Dev.: Jane, Mary, daus.; James, Archibolt, Samuel, sons.
MUMBERT, JACOB, Will, 3-17-1815. Dev.: Magdalene, wife; George, son.

NELSON, ELIGAH, Will, 8-31-1838. Dev.: Margaret, wife; Elizabeth, Margaret, Mary, Hannah, Jane, Sarah, Susanna, daus.; Samuel, John, Eligh, Solomon, Jonathon, Jacob, sons.

PHARES, SARAH, Will, 5-16-1840. Dev.: Elizabeth, Abagail, Mary, daus.; Andrew, William, sons; others.
POBE, PETER, Will, 7-22-1831. Dev.: Catherine, wife; John, son; Catherine, dau.; others.
PROPST, JOHN, Will, 1-19-1785. Dev.: Catherine E.
PROPST, JOHN, Will, 3-8-1846. Dev.: Dorothea, Sarah, Mary, daus.
PROPST, SAMUEL, Will, 11-3-1845. Dev.: Ann Elizabeth, wife; William, Daniel, Elias, sons; Polly, Alley, Elizabeth, Sarah, Barbery, Malenda, Frany, Parbany, daus.; others.

PROPST, SARAH, Will, 6-11-1846. Dev.: Solomon, bro.
PULLENS, WILLIAM, Will, 11-16-1841. Dev.: Thomas, bro.; and wife.

RAY, JOSEPH, Will, 8-13-1798. Dev.: Josey, wife; William, Joseph, John, sons; Sarah, Elizabeth, Pamelia, Mary, Dianah, daus.
REDMAN, SAMUEL, Will, 2-21-1804. Dev.: Margaret, wife; Samuel, Henry, Eli, John, sons; Margaret, Jannet, daus.
REXROTH, ZACHARIAS, Will, 4-26-1798. Dev.: Mrs. Rexroth, wife.
RICHARD, SAMUEL, Will, 11-28-1795. Dev.: Rachel, wife; John Smith; Mary Hancel.
ROOT, JACOB, Will, 8-30-1812. Dev.: Nathian, son.
RYMER, GEORGE, Will, 12-13-1845. Dev.: Delilah, wife; Elizabeth, Margaret, Eleanor, daus.; George, Silas, James, William, Thomas, sons; others.

SHREVE, JOHN, Will, 2-25-1843. Dev.: Eliza, wife; Kitty, dau.; Benjamin, son.
SIMMONS, GEORGE, Will, 4-14-1810. Dev.: Eve, wife; Jacob, son; Margaret, dau.; others.
SIMMONS, GEORGE, Will, 4-5-1839. Dev.: Mrs. Simmons, wife; Jacob, Jackson, Eli, Mickael, sons; Susannah, Ann, daus.; others.
SIMMONS, GEORGE, Will, 2-5-1850. Dev.: Mary, wife; Henry, son; Sarah, Barbara, Katherine, Jennie, Mary Ann, Susan, Margaret, daus.
SIMMONS, JOHN, Will, 12-24-1825. Dev.: Mary, wife; Daniel, John, George, David, Joseph, Mark, Henry, sons; Mary, Catherine, Barbara, daus.; others.
SIMMONS, LEONARD, Will, 4-1-1805. Dev.: Lerra, wife; John Cook, son-in-law.
SIMPSON, WILLIAM, Will, 5-15-1840. Dev.: Abel, son.
SIMS, SILAS, Will, 5-10-1845. Dev.: John, Kial, sons; Margaret, dau.; Sarrah, wife.
SIRON, JOHN, Will, 2-19-1836. Dev.: Easter, wife; Jacob, Johnathon, Joseph, John, sons; Sarah, Jane, Jemina, Elizabeth, Magdalene, Easter, Ann, daus.
SITES, JACOB, Will, 7-7-1849. Dev.: Catherine, wife; Sampson, William, sons; Barbary, Margaret, Elizabeth, Eve, daus.
SKIDMORE, JOHN, Will, 9-16-1809. Dev.: Mary, wife; James, John, Levi, Eligah, Andrew, Isaac, Ede, sons; Hanna, Pheabe, Nanie, Barbra, Mary, Rachel, daus.
SKIDMORE, JOSEPH, Will, 10-20-1806. Dev.: Elizabeth, wife; James, son; Barba, Sarah, daus.; others.
SKIDMORE, RACHEL, Will, 3-3-1841. Dev.: William, son; others.
SKIDMORE, RACHEL, Will, 5-18-1843. Dev.: Mary, Phebe, Sarrah, daus.; Jessee, son; others.
SMITH, CHRISTIAN, Will, 4-2-1850. Dev.: Susannah, wife; Immanuel, Christian, sons; others.
SMITH, JOHN, Will, 3-31-1838. Dev.: Sally, dau.; Henry, Samuel, Joseph, Jack, John, Daniel, Peter, Christian, sons.
SMITH, JOHN, Will, 11-9-1846. Dev.: Jane, wife.
SNYDER, HENRY, Will, 4-21-1838. Dev.: Christian Snyder and his heirs.

STEPHENSON, JAMES, Will, 5-8-1813. Dev.: Rachel, wife; Esther, Janie, Margaret, Rebecca, Cyntha, daus.; Adam, James, sons.
STEPHENSON, JOHN, Will, 1-3-1799. Dev.: Margaret, wife.
STONE, MARY, Will, 6-4-1842. Dev.: Catherine, Molly, daus.; Jacob, Daniel, sons.
SWADLEY, HENRY, Will, 3-2-1845. Dev.: Peter, Marks, Nicholas, Jacob, sons; Eliza, Lorina, Sally, Mary, Maemy, Hessy, daus.
SWADLEY, MARY, Will, no date. Dev.: Catherine, dau.; others.
SYBERT, NICHOLAS, Will, 8-10-1812. Dev.: George's and Henry's children; others.

TAR, ABRAHAM, Will, 4-8-1848. Dev.: Sarah, dau.; Philip, son.
TETER, GEORGE, Will, 11-28-1795. Dev.: Anna, wife; Poret, Jacob, Joseph, Isaac, George, sons; Susanna, Mary, Barbara, daus.
TETER, JOHNETHON, Will, 8-9-1845. Dev.: Elizabeth, wife; Leban, Benjamin, sons; Huldah, dau.; others.
TETER, PHILIP, Will, 9-28-1813. Dev.: Reuben, Moses, sons; Sarah, Esther, Elizabeth, daus.
TETER, SAMUEL, Will, 3-31-1841. Dev.: Jull, Jonathen, Elias, Henry, Samuel, Joshau, bros.; others.
TRUMBO, ANDREW, Will, 6-28-1828. Dev.: Mary, wife; Salsberry, son; Elizabeth, Malenda, Margaret, Sarrah Ann, Mary, daus.
TRUMBO, ANDREW, Will, 9-20-1839. Dev.: Salsberry, son; others.
TRUMBS, ESTER, Will, 7-7-1844. Dev.: Jacob, Hendren, David, Vandevanter, sons; Dolly, Hannah, daus.; others.
TURNEPSEED, JOHN, Will, 4-12-1801. Dev.: Elizabeth, wife.

VANNIMON, PETER, Will, 7-27-1807. Dev.: Moses Thompson, Sariah Norton.
VINT, JAMES, Will, 3-16-1843. Dev.: William, John, sons; Elizabeth, Jane, Cyntha, daus.; others.

WAGGONER, LEWIS, Will, 12-15-1783. Dev.: Adom, son.
WAGGONER, MICKAEL, Will, 10-1-1836. Dev.: Christina, wife.
WALDREN, GEORGE, Will, 11-21-1814. Dev.: William, son; Sarah, dau.; others.
WALKER, GEORGE, Will, 4-17-1810. Dev.: Sarah, wife; John, son.
WALLO, ANN MARY, Will, 2-2-1839. Dev.: Magdelena, Margret, Sarrah, sis.; George, Leonard, Michael, Henry, bros.; others.
WARNER, JOHN, Will, 3-27-1800. Dev.: Anna, wife; Sarah, Katherine, Jane, Milly, daus.; James, son.
WILEONG, REGINA, Will, 5-19-1841. Dev.: Catherine, dau.
WILFONG, HENRY, Will, 1-9-1838. Dev.: Mary, wife; Henry, Jacob, Mickael, Daniel, Eli, Joseph, George, sons; others.
WILFONG, JACOB, Will, 8-7-1834. Dev.: Regina, wife; Elizabeth, Polly, Sally, Susannah, Amanda, Catherina, daus.; Henry, George, John, Adam, Jacob, Noah, Abel, Eli, Zebulan, sons.

WILFONG, JOHN, Will, 1814. Dev.: Catherine, wife; Henry, father; Esabeth, child.

WILFONG, SOPHIA, Will, 12-15-1808. Dev.: Mary, dau.

WILLIAM, CLIFTON, Will, 5-10-1796. Dev.: Barbra, wife; John, son.

WILSON, ELI, Will, 10-27-1842. Dev.: Hannah, wife; Elizabeth, Ruth, Jane, Polly, daus.; Eli, John, Abram, William, sons; others.

WILSON, JAMES, Will, 6-12-1810. Dev.: Elizabeth, wife; Elizabeth, Martha, Eleanor, daus.; William, Ralph, Isaac, George, James, Samuel, Eli, sons.

WILSON, WILLIAM, Will, 4-13-1813. Dev.: Mary, wife; Samuel, Robert, sons.

WILSON, WILLIAM, Will, 4-13-1847. Dev.: Andrew, James, William, Henry, George, Wesley, Eli, John, Samuel, sons; Henrietta, Lucinda, Martha, Mary Ann, Dorthy, Elizabeth, daus.; Jane, wife.

WIMER, PHILIP, Will, 8-13-1839. Dev.: Elizabeth, dau.; others.

West Virginia Estate Settlements

In 1936 and 1937, the West Virginia Commission on Historic and Scenic Markers, the Works Progress Administration, and the Federal Emergency Relief Administration compiled court records of the various counties, such as Births, Deaths, Marriages, and Wills. Under Wills were grouped subjects pertaining to Estate Settlements, including Wills, Inventories, and Appraisements. Copies of these county records were filed at the Department of Archives and History, Charleston; the Library of West Virginia University, Morgantown; and the DAR Library, Washington.

Believing that there would be particular interest on the part of the general public in the Estate Settlements, the West Virginia Historical Society has undertaken to abstract the Estate Settlements Records, as filed in the State Department of Archives and History, and offer them for publication in the *West Virginia History Quarterly*. No responsibility can be assumed as to the accuracy of the copies made from the original county records.

There are 13 counties which were formed prior to 1800, and it has been agreed to arrange these counties in chronological order, and to print their records from the earliest date to 1850. The formation dates of these counties are as follows: Hampshire—1753; Berkeley—1772; Monongalia—1776; Ohio—1776; Greenbrier—1778; Harrison—1784; Hardy—1786; Randolph—1787; Pendleton—1788; Kanawha—1788; Brooke—1797; Wood—1798; and Monroe—1799.

Kanawha County, Formed 1788

The abbreviations used in this material include: App.—appraisal; Bro.—brother; Dau.—daughter; Dev.—Devisees; Inv.—inventory; S.B.—sale bill; Set.—settlement; Sis.—sister; Ven.—vendue.

ABSTON, JESSE, App., 1850.
ADKINS, JOHN, App., 1837.
AGNEW, THOMAS J., App., 1849.
ALDERSON, GEORGE, Will, 1805.
ALDERSON, GEORGE, Will, 6-12-1805.
Dev: Sarah, wife; Mary, Catherine Morris, daus.; John, Levi, George, Joseph, sons; other.
ALEXANDER, ROBERT, Will, 1846.
ALLEN, CHAS., App., 1850.
ALLEN, POLLY, App., 1828.
ANDERSON, JAMES, Will, 1838.
ANDERSON, JAMES, Will, 8-2-1838. Dev.: Thomas, Andrew, Isaac, John, sons; Anna, Almira, Amanda, Milvina, Sarah Bowman, Nancy Melton, Mary Bess, daus.
ANDERSON, JAMES, App., 1841.
ARCHER, JOSEPH, will, 10-1-1841. Dev.: Sarah Archer, aunt, others.
ARMSTRONG, ANDREW, App., 1826.
ATKESON, JOHN, App., 1839.
ATKINSON, JOHN, S.B., 1839.
AULSE or AULTS, ADAM, App., 1831.
AUSTIN, JOHN, Will, 1823.
AUSTIN, JOHN, Will, 1-13-1823, 3-11-23.
Dev.: Archebold, James, Thomas, Frances, sons; Sally Hubbard, Mary Ferris, Susaner

Lang, Elizabeth Morgan Aires, Zebia Barker Welch, daus.
AUSTIN, JOHN, App., 1826.
AUSTIN, JOHN, S.B., 1826.

BAGBY, JOHN, Will, 1835.
BAGBY, JOHN, App., 1835.
BAGBY, JOHN, S.B., 1936.
BAGLY, JOHN, Will, 11-10-1828. Dev.: Susanah Spencer, Mildred Chaiborn, Elizabeth Parkey, daus.; John, James, sons; others.
BAILEY, ISBAM, Will, 6-11-1817, Dev.: Isban Jr., son.
BAILEY, ISHAM, App., 1835.
BAILEY, ISHAM, S.B., 1835.
BAILEY, ISHAN, Will, 1817.
BAILEY, PLEASANT, App., 1847.
BAILEY, PLEASANT, S.B., 1847.
BAILEY, WILLIAM, Will, 3-13-1837. Dev.: Sarah, wife; Samuel, William, John, Ruben, James, sons; Nancy Phillips, Elizabeth Grimes, Martha Langham, daus.
BALEY, WILLIAM, Will, 1837.
BALEY, WILLIAM, App., 1837.
BALEY, WILLIAM, S.B., 1837.
BEAUMONTE, SAMUEL, Will, 1838.

148

BEAUMONTE, SAMUEL, Will, 3-13-1838.
Dev.: John, son; Amelia, Fanny, daus.
BEST, LEVI, App., 1840.
BEST, LEVI, S.B. 1840.
BICKETTS, JOHN, App., 1836.
BIXBY, GRACE, Will, 1849.
BIXBY, GRAVE, Will, 1-8-1849. Dev.: William A. Quarrier; Mrs. Caroline W. Quarrier.
BLAINE, WILLIAM, App., 1825.
BLAKE, JAMES, App., 1833.
BLAKE, JAMES, App., 1835.
BRADFORD, NOYES, Will, 2-19-1850. Dev.: Harriet, wife; James, son; other children not named.
BREAM, JAMES, Will, 1842.
BREAM, MARY, Will, 1845.
BRIANT, RICHARD, Will, 1850.
BROWN, CHARLES, Will, 1849.
BROWN, CHARLES, Will, 1-8-1849. Dev.: wife, Tallyrand, Charles, sons; Virginia Campbell, Mary Campbell, daus.
BROWN, MATHEW, Will, 8-4-1846. Dev.: George W., son; others.
BRUEN, MATHIAS, Will, 6-20-1848. Dev.: Harman, Alexander, George, sons; Eveline Harriet Whitehouse, dau.; others.
BRYAN, JAMES, Will, 4-12-1793. Dev.: James, father; Elizabeth Brown, Catherine George, Margaret Lewis, sisters; John, half-bro.; others.
BRYANT, RICHARD, Will, 1850.
BRYANT, RICHARD, Will, 1-21-1850. Dev.: Martha, wife; Polly, Peggy, Dolly, Martha, Rebecca Hayslet, Sally Cobb, daus.; Andrew, William, sons; others.
BULLET, SOPHIA C., Will, 1-2-1804. Dev.: Frederick, David, Anthony, sons; Joan, dau.; others.
BULLET, THOMAS, Will, 2-23-1778. Dev.: Joseph, bro.; Seth Combs, sis.; others.
BULLETT, CUTHBERT, Will, 1791.
BULLETT, CUTHBERT, Will, 10-3-1791. Dev.; wife; Thomas, son; Frances, Sarah, Helen, Sophia, daus.; others.
BULLETT, SOPHIA, Will, 1804.
BULLETT, THOMAS, ESQ., Will, 1776.
BURCH, VINCENT, Inv., 1824.
BURCH, VINCENT, App., 1824.
BURDETTE, ELIAS, App., 1848.
BURDETTE, ELIAS G., S.B., 1848.
BUSTER, MARY, Will, 12-28-1818; 2-23-1819. Dev.: Thomas, Samuel, Joseph, sons; Dorcas, Philipi, Polly, daus.
BUSTER, MARY, Will, 1819.
BUSTER, THOMAS S., App., 1826.

CABELL, JOHN J., App., 1835.
CABELL, JOHN J., Add. App., 1835.
CALVERT, MILLS W., App., 1850.
CALVERT, MILLS W., S.B., 1850.
CARR, MOSES, App., 1844.
CARTMILL, DAVID, Will, 9-27-1820 Dev.: Nancy, wife.
CARTMILL, DAVID, App., 1826.
CARTMILL, DAVID, S.B., 1826.
CARTMILL, HENRY, App., 1825.
CARTWELL, DAVID, Will, 1820.
CASEY, SAMUEL, App., 1822.
CASEY, SAMUEL, S.B., 1823.
CAVENDER, JOHN, App., 1830.
CAVENDER, JOHN, S.B., 1830.
CHADDOCK, CALVIN, App., 1823.
CHADDOCK, CALVIN, S.B., 1823.
CHAMBERS, MARTHA, App., 1837.
CHAMBERS, MARTHA, S.B., 1837.
CHANDLER, AMOS, Inv., 1822.
CHARLESSON, JOHN, Will, 1840.
CHILDRESS, ROBERT, Will, 1848.
CHILDRESS, ROBERT, Will, 6-11-1848, 7-10-1848. Dev.: Mary, wife; children.

CHILTON, LUCINDA (Mrs.), App., 1838.
CHILTON, SAMUEL, Will, 1834.
CHILTON, SAMUEL, S.B., 1837.
CHILTON, SARAH E., Will, 1835.
CHILTON, SARAH ELIZA., Will, 1-11-1836. Dev.: Frances E., dau.
COATS, ALDEN, Inv., 1823.
COBB, GEORGE B., Will, 1848.
COBB, GEO. B., Will, 7-10-1848, 9-11-1848. Dev.: William, John Archibal, Emily, sons; Nancy Taylor, Eliza Harper, Jane Nicholas, Eliza, Rebecka, daus.
COBB, LEONARD, App., 1835.
COBB, SILAS A., App., 1850.
COBB, WILLIAM, App., 1825.
COBB, WILLIAM, S.B., 1826.
COBBS, FLEMING, Will, 1846.
COLQUITT, SUSANNA, Will, 6-2-1845. Dev.: Wm. H., son; Catherine Curtis, Anna, daus.; others.
COMPTON, ABEL, App., 1841.
COMPTON, ABEL, S.B., 1847.
COON, HENRY, App., 1841.
COOPER, GEORGE L., S.B., & App., 1849.
COOPER, JOHN, App., 1823.
COOPER PHILIP, S.B., 1824.
COX, ISAAC P., App., 1848.
COX, WILLIAM R., Will, 1843.
COX, WILLIAM R., App., 1843.
COX, WILLIAM R., Dower Assignment, 1843.
CRAWFORD, GEORGE, App., 1828.
CUNNINGHAM, JONATHAN, App., 1826.

DAGGS, SQUIRE, App., 1840.
DAVIS, CYNTHIA, (Not given), 1845.
DAVIS, CYNTHIA, S.B., 1845.
DAWSON, JOHN R., App., 1848.
DEETER, DANIEL J., App., 1834.
DEETER, DANIEL J., S.B., 1834.
DERRICK, JONATHAN, Will, 1846.
DERRICK, JONATHAN, App., 1847.
DICKINSON, JOHN, Will, 1799. Dev.: Martha, wife; Mary Shrewsbury, Martha Shrewsbury, Nancy Kincaid, Gean Dickinson, Catherine Humphreys, daus.; Adam, John, sons; others.
DIXON or DICKSON, JOHN, App., 1836.
DIXON or DICKSON, JOHN, App., 1837.
DIXON or DICKSON, JOHN, Add. App., 1837.
DIXON or DICKSON, JOHN, S.B., 1837.
DONALLY, ANDREW, Will, 3-18-1832. Dev.: Major, wife; Van Bibber, Drydon, Andrew, Wm., James, Lewis, sons; others.
DONALLY, ANDREW, Will, 1850.
DOWLING, JAMES, Will, 1846.
DUBOIS, FRANCES, Will, 1807.
DUDDING, JOHN, App., 1842.
DUDDING, JOHN, Will, 1842.
DUNLAP, JOHN, App., 1833.

EAGLES, ED., Will, 1804.
EAGLES, ED., Will 6- 1804, Dev.: Milanda; Enic, son; Sarah, dau.
ELLIS, ALFRED, Gdn. Sett., 1824.
ELLIS, JAMES, Will, 1809.
ELLIS, JAMES, Will, 11-14-1809. Dev.: Sabra Ella, Ella Ellis, Polly, Elizabeth McClung, daus.; Simon, James Eliaghiah, Alfred, sons.
ESTILL, WILLIAM C., S. B., 1826.
ESTILL, ZECHARIAH F., Will, 10-8-1832. Dev.: Elizabeth Mays, dau.; Thomas Mathew Mays, Edmund Morris Mays, John Dickens Mays, sons.

FANT, ELIAS, F., Will, 1843.
FIFE, THOMAS A., App., 1824.
FLANAGAN, NICHOLAS, Will, 1823.
FLANAGAN, NICHOLAS, Will, 3-10-1823. Dev.: George, son.

FORQUERAN, MARY, App., 1827.
FORQUERAN, MARY, S.B., 1827.
FORQUERAN, WILLIAM, App., 1837.
FORQUERAN, WILLIAM, S.B., 1838.
FRY, THORNTON, Will, 1823.
FRY, THORNTON, App., 1824.
FRY, THORTON, Will, 12-8-1823, 1-12-1824. Dev.: Eliza, wife; children.
FUNK, JOHN, App., 1842.

GARREAW, GABRIEL, App., 1847.
GARREAW, GABRIEL, Will, 1847.
GEBHART, LAWRENCE, App., 1850.
GEIBLEY, JACOB, Will, 8-8-1838. Dev.: French, dau.; Lewis, son.
GEIGLEY, JACOB, Will, 1838.
GILLASPY, SAMUEL, Will, 8-11-1812. Dev.: Elizabeth, wife; Theophelius, Samuel, Billy, John, sons; Peggy Williams, Nelly Lain, Jean, Betsy, Sally, daus.
GILLESPY, SAMUEL, Will, 1812.
GIVEN, JOHN, App., 1837.
GIVEN, JOHN, S.B., 1837.
GLOVER, SOLOMON, Will, 8-31-1838. Dev.: Catherine Sherman, Joanna Birch, Mary Ann Grover, Balusia Foot, Maria Beach, Huldah Clark Danberry, daus.; Ziba, son; others.
GORMAN, PETER, App., 1825.
GOSHORN, GEORGE, App., 1846.
GOSHORN, GEORGE, S.B., 1846.
GREGORY, WILSON, Will, 1849.
GRIFFITH, BENJAMIN, App,m 1836.
GRIFFITH, BENJAMIN, S.B., 1836.

HAMMACK, MARTIN, App., 1839.
HAMMACK, MARTIN, S.B., 1839.
HAMMOND, MILDRED G., Will, 1805.
HAMMOND, MILDRED G., Will, 2-13-1805. Dev.: Thomas, husband; mother, others.
HANSFORD, JOHN, Will, 1850.
HANSFORD, JOHN, Will, 10-21-1850. Dev.: Hiram, William, Morris, Felix, John Carrol, Chas., Alva, Marshall, Gallitum, Milton, sons; others.
HANSFORD, JOHN, App., 1850.
HANSFORD, JOHN, Add., App., 1850.
HARMAN, HENRY, App., 1824.
HARMON, HENRY, S.B., 1824.
HARMON, HENRY, Dowry Assignment, 1825.
HARRIMAN, JOHN, Will, 1840.
HARRIMAN, JOHN, Add. App., 1840.
HARRIMAN, JOHN, Add. App., 1841.
HARTWELL, EPHRIAM, App., 1825.
HARTWELL, EPHRIAM, S.B., 1825.
HARTWELL JONAS H., Will, 6-12-1837. Dev.: William, bro.; Lydia Maria, Mary Augustine, sisters.
HARTWELL, JONES H., Will, 1837.
HARVEY, JOHN, Will, 1849.
HARVEY, JOHN, App., 1849.
HARVEY, JOHN, Will, 9-17-1849. Dev.: Ruth, wife; Mary Painter, Saline Hill, Virginia, Fanny, daus.; Lewis, Morris, sons.
HARVEY, JOHN, S.B., 1849.
HAYZLET, JANE, Will, 8-2-1833. Dev.: Maylard, wife.
HAYZLETT, JAMES, Will, 1833.
HAYZLETT, JAMES, App., 1834.
HAYZLETT, JOHN, Will, 1830.
HAYZLETT, JOHN, App., 1830.
HAZLET, JOHN, Will, 11-8-1830. Dev.: Anne Day, wife.
HAZLETT, JOHN, Will, 11-8-1830. Dev.: Washington T., son.
HENDRICK, BENJ., App., 1843.
HENRY, SAMUEL, Will, 12-11-1821. Dev.: Samuel Gillaspie, son; Jenny, wife.
HENRY, SAMUEL, Will, 1830.
HERSHBARGER, JOSEPH, App., 1832.

HICKS, JOHN, App., 1848.
HILL, JAMES, App., 1824.
HILL, MORRIS, App., 1835.
HOGUE, WILLIAM, App., 1825.
HOLSTINE, JOHN, App & S.B., 1846.
HOLSTINE, JOHN, Will, 1846.
HORTON, WILLIAM, App., 1824.
HUBBARD, THOMAS, App., 1835.
HUBBARD, THOMAS, S.B., 1835.
HUDDLESTON, NATHAN, App., 1821.
HUDSON, DAVIS, Will, 5-27-1844. Dev.: bros.; sis.; others.
HUDSON, MORRIS, Will, 1832.
HUFF, JOHN, App., 1824.
HUGHES, EDWARD, App., 1839.
HUGHES, EDWARD, Will, 1839.
HUGHES, EDWARD, S.B., 1840.
HUGHES, THOMAS, SR., Will, 1794.
HUGHES, THOMAS, Will, 1794.
HUGHES, THOMAS, Will, 6-27-1794. Dev.: Edward, Thomas, sons.
HUNTER, CHARLES, Will, 1848.
HUNTER, CHARLES, App., 1848.
HUNTER, CHARLES, Will, 7-10-1848. Dev.: Polly Ferqueron, Mildred Simms, Patsey Childers, daus.; George, James, sons; others.
HUNTER, CHARLES, S.B., 1849.
HUTCHINSON, ANDREW, Will, 1815.
HUTCHINSON, ANDREW, Will, 11-16-1815. Dev.: Silinea, wife; Augustus, Archible, sons.
HUTCHINSON, EUSEBUIS R., Will, 1838.
HUTCHINSON, EUSELUIS, R., 5-14-1838. Dev.: David, Junius, sons; Jerimah H., Bare, dau.; others.

IRVIN, BENJ., F., App., 1850.

JAMES, JESSE, App., & S.B., 1846.
JARRETT, ABRAHAM, Aprsrs, Aptd., 1850
JARRETT, ABRAHAM, Will, 1850.
JARRETT, ABRAHAM, Will, 4-19-1850. Dev.: Nancy Wilson, dau.; David Sea, Jacob, Peter, sons; others.
JARRETT, JAMES, Will, 1840.
JARRETT, JOHN, App., 1829.
JARRETT, JOHN, S.B., 1829.
JAVINS, DANIEL, Inv., of S.B., 1826.
JONES, CHARLES, Will, 1842.
JONES, JOHN, Will, 1838.
JONES, JOHN, App., 1838.
JONES, JOHN, Will, 3-12-1838. Dev.: Frances, wife; Gabriel, William, Edmund, John, Hillary, Benj., sons; Nancy Huddleston, Cynthia Spinks, daus.; others.
JONES, LYDIA, Will, 1835.
JONES, LYDIA, App., 1836.
JONES, LYDIA, Will, 8-10-1835. Dev.: John, David, Thomas, Lewis, bros.
JONES, NICHOLAS, Will, 3-10-1823. Dev.: Lydia, sister; John, Thomas, David, Lewis, bros.
JONES, NICHOLAS, Will, 1835.
JONES, THOMAS, Will, 1846.
JONES, THOMAS, App., 1847.
JOPLING, RALPH, App., 1820.

KELLY, JACOB, App., 1829.
KELLY, JACOB, Will, 1829.
KELLY, JACOB, Will, 3-9-1829. Dev.: Wife; Reuben, Thornton, James, Wm., Jacob, John, Jermiah, sons; Nancy Johnson, Polly Light, Elizabeth Huddleston, Peggy Johnson, Susana, Sally, daus.
KELLY, JACOB, Will, 1829.
KELLY, JACOB, App., 1829.

KELLY, JACOB, Will, 3-9-1829. Dev.:
Wife; Reuben, Thornton, James, Wm.,
Jacob, John, Jermiah, sons; Nancy John-
son, Polly Light, Elizabeth Huddleston,
Peggy Johnson, Susana, Sally, daus.;
others.
KELLY, JACOB, Will, 3-28-1829. Dev.:
Jermiah, wife; Reuben, Thorton, James,
William, Jacob, John, sons; Polly Light,
Elizabeth Hudleston, Peggy Shannon, Su-
sannah, Sally, Percilla, daus.
KELLY, WILLIAM, App., 1846.
KING, SAMUEL, App & S.B., 1844.

LACY, JOHN, Will, 1842.
LACY, JOHN, Will, 6-13-1842. Dev.: Sally,
Elizabeth, Dicy, Susan, Moses, Anne, Re-
becca, Polly, daus.; Jordon, Adam, sons.
LASLEY, MANOAH, App., 1835.
LASLEY, MANOAH, S.B., 1835.
LEONARD, JAMES, Will, 1846.
LETT, ROBERT, Will, 1848.
LETT, ROBERT, App., 1848.
LETT, ROBERT, S.B., 1848.
LEWIS, JANE, Will, 1846.
LEWIS, MILES, App., 1832.
LEWIS, MILES, S.B., 1832.
LEWIS, THOMAS, Will, 1801.
LEWIS, THOMAS, Will, ___ ___ 1801. Dev.:
Sally Thorton, wife; Thomas, Andrew, Wil-
liam, Samuel, sons.
LEWIS, WM., App., 1837.
LIGON, MARTHA E., Will, 1837.
LIKENS, JOHN, Will, 1819.
LIKENS, JOHN, Will, 7-13-1819. Dev.:
Mary, wife; Jesse Fredway.
LITT, ROBERT, Will, 7-10-1848. Dev.:
grandchildren.
LOVELL, JOSEPH, Will, 1835.
LOVELL, JOSEPH, Will, 12-14-1835. Dev.:
Betty Washington Lovell, wife; children.
LYKENS, JOHN, App., 1825.

MARSH, FARNHAM, App., 1831.
MARSH, FARNHAM, S.B., 1831.
MARTIN, JAMES, Will, 11-14-1816. Dev.:
Wife; William, Tipson bros.
MARTIN, JAMES, Will, 1816.
MARTIN, JOB., Will, 1839.
MARTIN, NATHAN, App., 1828.
MAY, WILLIAM, Will, 9-10-1824. Dev.:
Elizabeth, wife; William, John, Jacob, Reu-
ben, James, Thomas, sons; Mary Pettery,
Hannah May, daus.; others.
MAY, WILLIAM, Will, 1827.
MAZE, JAMES, Will, 9-10-1799. Dev.: Eliz-
abeth, wife; Joseph, James, Jonathan,
Benati, sons; Jenny, dau.
MAZE, JAMES, Will, 1799.
McCALLISTER, JOHN, App., 1831.
McCALLISTER, JOHN, S.B., 1831.
McCALLISTER, MARGARET, App. &
S.B., 1846.
McCALLISTER, RICHARD, App., 1826.
McCALLISTER, RICHARD, S.B., 1826.
McCLANAHAN, BENJAMIN, App. & S.B.,
1831.
McCOWEN, MALCOM, Will, 1813.
McCOWN, MALCOM, Will, 12-12-1813.
Dev.: Nellie, wife; John, Mathew, Mal-
colm, George, Febias, Joseph, Savilster,
William, sons; Peggy Casdorp, Nancy Mc-
Callister, Frances, daus.
McCOWN, MATTHEW, App., 1821.
McCOY, JOHN, Will, 1-13-1823. 3-10-1823.
Dev.: Eliz. Grinston, dau.; others.
McCOY, JOHN, Will, 1823.
McCOY, JOHN, App., 1825.
McCOY, JOHN, S.B., 1825.
McCOY, SAMUEL, App., 1847.
McCOY, SAMUEL, S.B., 1848.

MEEKS, WM., Will, 8-11-1813. Dev.: wife;
children (not named).
MEEKS, WILLIAM, Will, 1813.
MELTON, ELISHA, App., 1830.
MELTON, SAMUEL, App., 1841.
MIDKIFF, SAMUEL, Will, 9-10-1827. Dev.:
Elizabeth, wife; Ezuqua, Eli, Samuel, sons.
MIDKIFF, SAMUEL, Will, 1827.
MILAM, JAS. L., App., 1843.
MILAM, JAS. L., S.B., 1846.
MILAM, SIMON, App., 1846.
MILAM, SIMON, S.B., 1846.
MILLER, JOHN, Will, 5-9-1836. Dev.: Eliz-
abeth, wife.
MILLER, JOHN, Will, 1836.
MILLER, ROBERT H., App., 1833.
MORRIS, BENJAMIN, Will, 8-20-1829.
Dev.: Nancy, wife; Akilliss, son; Frances
Shelton, Virginia, daus.
MORRIS, BENJAMIN, Will, 1829.
MORRIS, BENJAMIN, App., 1829.
MORRIS, CATHERINE, App., 1823.
MORRIS, CATHERINE, Will, 1823.
MORRIS, EDMUND, App., 1834.
MORRIS, FRANCIS, S.B., 1849.
MORRIS, HUDSON, Will, 8-8-1831. Dev.:
sons and daughters.
MORRIS, HUDSON, Will, 1831.
MORRIS, JOSHUA, Will, 9-13-1824. Dev.:
Francis, wife; William, John, Edmund,
Henry, sons; Elizabeth, Lucy Chapman,
Nancy Chapman, daus.; others.
MORRIS, JOSHUA, Will, 1824.
MORRIS, JOSHUA, App., 1825.
MORRIS, JOSHUA, S.B., 1825.
MORRIS, JOSHUA, App., 1848.
MORRIS, KATHERINE, Will, 9-8-1823.
Dev.: Jane Hansford, Cythia Noice, daus.;
Katherine Venerable.
MORRIS, LEONARD, Will, 1831.
MORRIS, LEONARD, Will, 7-11-1831. Dev.:
Peggy, wife; Lenord, Charles, Joshua, Hi-
ram, sons; others.
MORRIS, LEONARD, App., 1831.
MORRIS, LEONARD, S.B., 1831
MORRIS, LEVI, App., 1834.
MORRIS, LEVI, S.B., 1834.
MORRIS, NANCY, Will, 5-18-1832. Dev.:
Celica Harvey, dau.; other children; others.
MORRIS, WILLIAM, Will, 1793.
MORRIS, WILLIAM, Will, 1-7-1793. Dev.:
William, Henry, Leonard, Josiah, John,
Caleus, Levi, sons; Elizabeth, Frankie,
daus.
MORRIS, WILLIAM, Will, 4 ___ 1803. Dev.:
Katherine, wife; Kathern, Caroll, Cynthia,
daus.; John, William, John Hansford,
sons.
MORRIS, WILLIAM, Will, 1803.
MORRISON, LEWIS, App., 1835.

NEAL, CHARLES, App., 1840.
NEAL, CHARLES, Add. App., 1840.
NICHOLAS, GEO. W., App., 1847.
NICHOLAS, GEO W., S.B., 1847.
NOYES, BRADFORD, App., 1850.
NOYES, BRADFORD, Inv., 1850.
NOYES, BRADFORD, Will, 1850.
NOYES, JOHN, Will, 6-14-1814. Dev.: Isiah,
Bradford, bros.
NOYLES, JOHN, Will, 1814.

PAITT, EDMUND, Will, 10-9-1848. Dev.:
Andrew, David, Joseph, sons; Eliz., wife;
Ann, Jane, Polly, daus.
PARKS, ANDREW, App., 1837.
PARSONS, WILLIAM, Will, 12-4-1835.
Dev.: Jane, stepdaughter.
PARSONS, WILLIAM, Will, 1835.
PARSONS, WM., Will, 1835.

PERSINGER, JOHN, Will, 4-3-1810. Dev.: Wife; Luke, John, sons; Elizabeth Harmon, dau.
PERSINGER, JOHN, Will, 1811.
PHILSON, ROBERT, App., 1821.
POLLY, DANIEL, App., 1826.
POWELL, JONAH, App., 1827.
PRICE, ARCHIBALD I., Will, 1832. Dev.: Sear, wife; Calvin, Edward, sons.
PRICE, EDMUND, Will, 9-13-1847. Dev.: Rebecca, wife; Milanda, Nancy, Jane, Elizabeth, Louise, Merida, Sarah, Mary, daus.; Vincent, Squire, sons.
PRICE, EDMUND, Will, 1847.
PRICE, EDWARD, Will, 8-13-1822. Dev.: Elizabeth, wife; Jane, dau.; grandchildren.
PRICE, EDWARD, App. & S.B., 1833.
PRICE, EDWARD, Will, 1832.
PRIOR, JAS. P., Aprsr. Rep., 1832.
PRITT, EDMUND, Will, 1848.
PROVINCE, SARAH, Will, 7-26-1796. Dev.: Joseph, Benjamin Wright, sons; others.
PROVINCE, SARAH, Will, 1796.

QUARRIER, ALEXANDER, Will, 9-10-1827. Dev.: Sarah, wife; Alexander, Monroe, James Wright, sons.
QUARRIER, ALEXANDER, Will, 1827.

RANEY or RENEY, JOHN G., App., 1835.
RANEY or RENEY, JOHN G., S.B., 1835.
RAUSH, THOS. F., App., 1847.
RAY, JOHN, App., 1844.
RAY, JOHN, S.B., 1848.
REABURN, ISSAC, Will, 9-9-1832. Dev.: Susan, wife.
REABURN, ISSAC, App., 1833.
REABURN, ISSAC, Will, 1833.
REYNOLDS, CHAS. G., App., 1847.
REYNOLDS, SILAS, App., 1815.
REYNOLDS, SILAS, Add. App., 1816.
REYNOLDS, WM., App., 1835.
RIDGEWAY, ELIZABETH, Will, 1842.
ROBERTS, JAS., App., 1843.
ROBERTSON, GEO., App., 1833.
ROBERTSON, GEO, S.B., 1833.
ROCK, MALAY M., Will, 1850.
ROCK, MALOY MASON, Will, 5-4-1850. Dev.: Mary A. Rock, wife; (children not named).
ROGERS, HENRY, Will, 4-10-1837. Dev.: Wife; Lenora, Mary Ruffner, Maria Chusman, daus.; James, son; others.
ROGERS, HENRY, Will, 1837.
ROSSER, JOHN, App., 1826.
ROSSER, JOHN, S.B., 1826.
ROYCE, AUSTIN E., App., 1835.
ROYCE and CHAPEL, App., 1835.
RUCKER, JOEL, Will, 1837.
RUFFNER, ANDREW L., App., 1850.
RUFFNER, DAVID, Will, 4- 1803. Dev.: Wife; Joseph, David, Tobias, Daniel, Samuel, Abraham, sons; Eve, dau.
RUFFNER, DAVID, Will, 1803.
RUFFNER, DAVID, Will, 1843.
RUFFNER, TOBIAS, Will, 11-10-1834. Dev.: Isez, Silas, John, Benj., sons; Susan, dau.
RUFFNER, TOBIAS, Will, 1834.
RUFFNER, Wm. M., App., 1835.
RUSSELL, SAMUEL, App., 1848.
RUST, BENJAMIN, App., 1824.
RUST, BENJAMIN, S.B., 1824.
RYAN, JAS., App., 1828.
SAMUELS, GREENBERRY, Will, 6-8-1850. Dev.: John, son; Rachel, Patsey, Sarah, Polly, Nancy, Rebecca, daus.; others.
SAVORY, JOHN, Will, 11- 1814, copy 7-11-1825. Dev.: Robert Alexander, bro.
SAVALY, JOHN, Will, 11- 1814. Dev.: Robert Alexander, son.
SAVARY, JOHN, Will, 1825.
SAVARY, JOHN, Will, 1832.

SESSON, JAMES, Will, 7-10-1837. Dev.: Mary, wife; John, Allen, Henry, James, sons; Eliza, Sarah Ann, Caroline, Mary, Nancy, daus.
SHELTON, ALBERT H., App. & S.B., 1846.
SHEPHERD, WM. P., Will, 1841.
SHEWMAN, TOUSAINT, App. & S.B., 1834.
SHEWSBURY, JOEL, App., 1850.
SHREWSBURY, JOHN, Will, 12-14-1835. Dev.: Samuel, son; Martha Gearneal, dau.; others.
SHREWSBURY, JOHN, Will, 1835.
SHREWSBURY, JOHN, App., 1836.
SHREWSBURY, JOHN D., App., 1829.
SHREWSBURY, JOHN D.,Will, 1846.
SIMMS, RICHARD M., App., 1847.
SIMONTON, ALEXANDER, App., 1848.
SISSON, ALLEN G., App., 1847.
SISSON, JAS., Will, 1837.
SISSON, JAS., App., 1837.
SISSON, JAS., Add. App., 1839.
SISSON, JAS., S.B., 1839.
SITT, ROBERT, Will, 7-10-1848. Dev.: John, son; Polly Albert, Mary F., daus.; others.
SITT, ROBERT, Will, 1848.
SLAUGHTER, ELIZ., Will, 1821.
SLAUGHTER, ELIZ., JAMES, Will, 7-8-1822. Dev.: Goodrich Slaughter, bro.; nieces.
SLAUGHTER, REUBEN, App., 1845.
SMALLWOOD, GEORGE, App., 1845.
SMITH, DANIEL, S.B., 1830.
SMITH, DANIEL, App., 1831.
SMITH, JONATHAN, S.B., 1839.
SMITH, JONATHAN, App., 1840.
SMITH, LEMUEL, Admr. Rep., 1833.
SMOOT, ELIPHALET, App., 1838.
SNYDER, DANIEL, App., 1826.
STARKE, JOHN, App., 1834.
STARKE, JOHN, S.B., 1834.
STEELE, JAS., App., 1838.
STEELE, JAS., App., 1839.
STEELE, JAS., S.B., 1839.
STEELE, JAS., S.B., 1840.
STEELE, JOHN, Will, 1-9-1823. Dev.: Nancy, wife; James, son; Mary Smith, dau.
STEELE, JOHN, Will, 10-9-1826. Dev.: daus.; bros.: sister: others.
STEELE, JOHN, Will, 1826.
STEELE, JOHN, Will Pro., 1827.
STEELE, JOHN ROWAN, Will, 4-9-1849. Dev.: Eli, John, sons; Eliza M. Boone, Ann Buchanan, Alice B. Wakefield, Elizabeth Hughes, daus.; others.
STEELE, WILLIAM, Will, 12- 1826. Dev.: Wife; Agnes Wingfield White, dau.; Jane, Sally, daus.: others.
STEWART, ALLEN, Inv. & App., 1831.
STEWART, ALLEN, Will, 1831.
STEWART, ALLEN, Will, 3-11-1833. Dev.: Nancy Stewart, dau.-in-law; grandchildren.
STRATTON, JOS. D., App., 1845.
SULLIVAN, JOHN, App. & S.B., 1832
SUMMERFIELD, ABSALON, App., 1850.
SUMMERFIELD, ABSALON, S.B., 1850.
SUMMERS, ALBERT S., App., 1825.
SUMMERS, GEORGE, Will, 4-14-1818. Dev.: Nancy F., wife; Elizabeth Lawson, Jane, Sylenia, daus.; Albert, Sidney, sons.
SUMMERS, GEORGE, Will, 1818.
SUMMERS, LEWIS, Will, 1843.
SUMMERS, SAMUEL, Will, 1845.
SUMMERS, SAMUEL, App., 1847.
SUMMERS, WM. S., App., 1835.
SUMMERS, WM. S., S.B., 1835.
SWEAR, WM. P., App., 1848.

SWAN, JAMES, Will, 5-7-1831, 2-10-1834.
Dev.: Katie Sargent, Sallie Webb Sullivan,
daus.; others.
SWAN, JAS., Will, 1833.
SWINDLER, JAS. F., App., 1849.
SWINDLER, JAS. F., S.B., 1849.

TANNER, THOS., App., 1825.
TANNER, THOS., WILL, 1825.
TANNER, THOMAS, Will, 3-15-1825. Dev.:
Mother; Lewis Smith, son.
TAYLOR, THOS. O., Will, 1839.
TEASE, STEVEN, Will, 5-12-1823. Dev.:
Wife; John, James, sons; Katie Thomas,
dau.
TEAYS, MARY, Will, 1834.
TEAYS or TEAYES, MARY, App., 1834.
TEAYS, STEPHEN, Will, 1823.
TEAYS, THOS., App., 1836.
TEMPLETON, EDW., App., 1842.
TEMPLETON, EDW., S.B., 1842.
THOMAS, MATHEW, App., 1840.
THOMAS, JOS., Aprsrs. Aptd., 1839.
THOMAS, JOS., Will, 1839.
THOMAS, JOS., App., 1848.
THOMAS, JOS., App., 1848.
THOMAS, REBECCA, App., 1848.
THOMPSON, NATHANIEL W., App., 1826.
THOMPSON, NATHANIEL W., S.B., 1826.
THOMPSON, PHILIP R., Will, 1837.
THOMPSON, PHILIP R., App., 1839.
THOMPSON, PHILLIP ROATES, Will,
11-16-1837. Dev.: Sarah, wife; Berkett,
Phillip, John, Robert, Francis, Benj., Wil-
liam, sons; Eleanor Brown Thornton, Eliz-
abeth Roates Frye, Sarah, daus.; others.
THOMPSON, WM., Will, 1840.
THOMPSON, WM., App. & S.B., 1841.
TODD, MINERVA B., Will, 1837.
TODD, MINERVA B., App., 1836.
TODD, MINERVA B., Will, 8-8-1837. Dev.:
Lethe Todd, dau.
TODD, PHILIP G., App., 1831.
TONEY, POINDEXTER, App. & S.B., 1835.
TRUSLOW, JAS., App., 1830.
TULLY, JASPER A., App., 1847.
TULLY, JASPER A., S.B., 1847.
TUPPER, EDWARD, Will, 3-6-1835, 5-9-
1836. Dev.: Bertha S., wife; others.
TUPPER, EDWARD W., Will, 1836.
TURLEY, JACK, Will, 1848.
TURLEY, JACOB, Will, 6-12-1848. Dev.:
Betsy, wife; Beatrice, Lilly, Mary, Martha,
daus.; Jermena, David, Washington, Hez-
iah, Jiles, sons.
TURLEY, ZACHARIAH, App., 1833.
TURNER, ROBERT, Will, 9-9-1833. Dev.:
William Wilson Hudson.
TURNER, ROBERT S., Will, 1833.

VAN BIBBER, JOHN, App., 1821.
VAN BIBBER, JOHN, Division of Property,
1823.
VENABLE, CHARLES, Will, 1842.
VENABLE, CHARLES, App., 1843.
VINCENT, JOS., App., 1821.

VINCENT, JOS., Will, 1821.
VINCENT, JOS., App., 1836.
VINCENT, JOS., S.B., 1836.

WARD, JEREMIAH, App., 1824.
WARD, JEREMIAH, Gdn. Sett., 1826.
WARD, JERMIAH, Will, 11- 1808. Dev.:
Polly, wife; Nancy Anne Sanders Ward,
dau.; Washington Woodson, Moses Fugua,
sons.
WARD, JERIMIAH, Will, 1808.
WARD, JEREMIAH, Inv., 1828.
WARD, JOS., Will, 1822.
WARD, JOS., App., 1823.
WARD, JOS., S.B., 1823.
WARD, WASHINGTON W., App., 1827.
WASHINGTON, GEORGE, Will, 9-19-1803.
Dev.: Martha, wife; Samuel, Charles,
bros.; others.
WASHINGTON, GEORGE, Will, 1803.
WASHINGTON, SAMUEL, Aprsrs. Rep.,
1832.
WATSON, JAS., App., 1824.
WATSON, JAS., S.B., 1824.
WATSON, JAS., S.B. (Add.), 1830.
WELCH, JACOB, Will, 8-10-29. Dev.: Eliz-
abeth Griffith, Lucinda Welch, grandchil-
dren.
WELCH, JACOB, Will, 1829.
WELCH, JOHN, Will, 8-10-1829. Dev.:
Grandchildren.
WELCH, LEVI, App., 1850.
WESTLAKE, THOMAS, Will, 4-13-1824.
Dev.: Ann, wife; Nancy, Polly, Minerva,
Sarah Ann, daus.; William, Siras, sons.
WESTLAKE, THOS., Will, 1828.
WHITE, BUFORD, App., 1850.
WHITE, BUFORD, S.B., 1850.
WHITE, WM., App., 1824.
WHITTAKER, LEVI, App., 1826.
WHITTAKER, LEVI, S.B., 1826.
WHITTINGTON, STARK, Inv., 1824.
WHITTINGTON, STARK, S.B., 1825.
WIATT, MARIE, Will, 1846.
WILLIAMS, ISAAC, App. & S.B., 1847.
WILSON, GREGORY? (WILSON GREG-
ORY), Will, 10-19-1849. Dev.: Lucinda,
wife; William, Isher, Henry, sons; Jo-
sephene, dau.; others.
WILSON, GREGORY, Will, 1849.
WILSON, JAMES, Will, 10-26-1835. Dev.:
Lewis, son; others.
WINDSON, JOSEPH, Will, 2-13-1821, Dev.:
Wife, children.
WINDSON, JOSEPH, Will, 1821.
WINDSOR, BENJAMIN, App., 1830.
WOOD, HENRY, Will, 10-11-1814. Dev.:
Mary Ann Williams, wife; Valentine,
Henry, David I., sons.
WOOD, HENRY, Will, 1814.
WOOD, BAZIL A., Will, 1844.
WOOD, NEHEMIAH, App., 1826.
WOOD, NEHEMIAH, S.B., 1826.
WOOD, WM. A., App., 1833.

YOUNG, MATHIAS, App., 1845.

West Virginia Estate Settlements

In 1936 and 1937, the West Virginia Commission on Historic and Scenic Markers, the Works Progress Administration, and the Federal Emergency Relief Administration compiled court records of the various counties, such as Births, Deaths, Marriages, and Wills. Under Wills were grouped subjects pertaining to Estate Settlements, including Wills, Inventories, and Appraisements. Copies of these county records were filed at the Department of Archives and History, Charleston; the Library of West Virginia University, Morgantown; and the DAR Library, Washington.

Believing that there would be particular interest on the part of the general public in the Estate Settlements, the West Virginia Historical Society has undertaken to abstract the Estate Settlements Records, as filed in the State Department of Archives and History, and offer them for publication in the *West Virginia History Quarterly*. No responsibility can be assumed as to the accuracy of the copies made from the original county records.

There are 13 counties which were formed prior to 1800, and it has been agreed to arrange these counties in chronological order, and to print their records from the earliest date to 1850. The formation dates of these counties are as follows: Hampshire—1753; Berkeley—1772; Monongalia—1776; Ohio—1776; Greenbrier—1778; Harrison—1784; Hardy—1786; Randolph—1787; Pendleton—1788; Kanawha—1788; Brooke—1797; Wood—1798; and Monroe—1799.

BROOKE COUNTY, FORMED 1797

The abbreviations used in this material include: App.—appraisal; Bro.—brother; Dau.—daughter; Dev.—Devisees; Inv.—inventory; S.B.—sale bill; Set.—Settlement; Sis.—sister; Ven.—vendue.

ACKLEY, URIAH, Inv., 7-3-1818.
ADAM, WM., Inv., 7-1847.
ADAMS, DAVID, Inv., 9-1850.
ADAMS, SAMUEL, Will, 1-1813. Dev.: Wife children
ADAMS SAMUEL, Will, 8-1815. Dev.: William, Samuel, sons; Ann Buchanan, Barbara Foute, Mary, daus.
ADAMS WM., Will, 5-1828. Dev.: Nancy, wife; Wm., son; Jane Park, Ruth Miller, Masy Kinberly, daus.; others.
ADAMS, WM., Will, 5-1847. Dev.: Jane, Betsy, Marg., daus.; Wm., son; others.
AGNEW, JOHN, Will, 6-1838. Dev.: Mary, wife; John, son; Ann, Susan, Rebecca Mary Alvilda, daus.; other.
AGNEW, JOHN, Inv., 7-10-1838.
ALLISON, JAMES, Inv., 12-29-1822.
ANDERSON, AGNESS, Will, 10-1845. Dev.: Marg., Polly, Jane, Isabell, daus.; John, James, Andrew, Robert, Alex., sons.
ANDERSON, JAMES, Will, 3-1816. Dev.: Martha, wife; Thomas, son; Lydia, dau.
ANDERSON, WM., Inv., 5-1849.

ANDOVER, CHRISTOPHER, Will, 10-31-1831. Dev.: Grandchildren.
ANDREWS, JEREMIAH, Will, 11-26-1832. Dev.: Susannah, wife; Mathew, Jeremiah, Joseph, John, sons; Nancy, Eliz., Cath., daus.; other.
ANDREWS, MARTIN, Will, 9-19-1849. Dev.: Margaree, dau.; John, son; Jacob, John, bros.; others.
ANDREWS, MATHEW, Inv., 10-7-1842.
ANDREWS, WM., Inv., 10-5-1838.
APPLEGATE, JOSEPH, Inv., 8-31-1822.
ARCHER, EBENEZER, Will, 4-1814. Dev.: Betsy, wife; Sam., son; other children.
ARCHER, ELIZ., Will, 9-1845. Dev.: Eliz., Nancy, Mary, Sarah, Eleanor, Easter, Martha, daus.; Ebenezer, David, Samuel, sons; others.
ARCHER, ELIZ., Inv., 12-1845.
ATKINSON, ASA, Inv., 2-1846.
ATKINSON, GEORGE, Will, 3-1822 Dev.: Thomas, James, sons; Mary, Marg.; Elenor, Sarah, Martha, Ruth, Eliz., daus.
ATKINSON, GEO., Inv., 4-1822.

154

ATKINSON, JOHN, Will, 11-1841. Dev.:
Eliz., wife; Joseph, Wm., Geo., Thomas,
James, Ephraim, sons; Nancy, Sarah,
Martha, daus.
ATKINSON, JOHN, Inv., 10-19-1842.
ATKINSON,THOMAS, Inv., 11-21-1823.
ATKINSON, WM., Inv., 5-30-1823.

BAILY, MILINDER, Inv., 11-4-1819.
BAKER, JOHN, Will, no date. Dev.: wife;
Rachel, dau.; other children.
BAKER, NATHAN, Will, 10-1843. Dev.:
Marg., wife; Christian, Nancy, daus.;
others.
BAKER, NATHAN, Inv., 4-1845.
BANE, JOHN, Inv., 6-19-1846.
BARSHEARS, BRICE, Inv., 3-1839.
BAXTER, WM., Will, 2-28-1842. Dev.:
Wm., Richard, sons; Mary, Marg., Ruth,
Susannah, Eliz., Nancy, Rachel, daus.
BAXTON, JACOB, Inv., 10-1836.
BEALL, JANE, Inv., 1-19-1848.
BEALL, JANE, Inv., 4-22-1850.
BEALL, NINIAN, Will, 10-10-1831. Dev.:
Mary, wife; Sam., Bethiam, John, Fasell,
George, James, sons; Nancy, Annalijai,
Eliza. Mary Hammond, Mary Ann Cash,
daus.
BEALL, NINIAN, Inv., 10-10-1831.
BEALL, PHILIP, Will, 11-1844. Dev.:
Jane, wife; Cyrus, Hiram, sons; Eliza,
Leanora, Theadora, daus.
BEALL, PHILLIP, Inv., 1-1845.
BEALL, SAMUEL, Will, 5-27-1833. Dev.:
Bazel, John, bro.; others.
BEARD, WM., Will, no date. Dev.:
children of brothers and sisters; others.
BEDWELL, SAMUEL, Inv., 12-7-1819.
BELL, MARY, Will, 8-1812. Dev.: Philip,
son; Ruth, dau.; others.
BELL, WM., Inv., 9-6-1837.
BLACKMORE, CHARLES, Will, 6-1847.
Dev.: Betsy, wife; Benoni, Thomas, sons;
Mary, dau.
BLAIR, JAMES, Inv., 2-28-1820.
BLAIR, RANDEL, Inv., 12-2-1823.
BLAIR, RUNNEL, Will, 12-18-1812. Dev.:
Charity, wife; John, Daniel, James,
Robert, sons; Jennett, Mary, Eliz., daus.
BONER, WM., Will, 8-30-1830. Dev.:
Jane, wife; Geo., Greenbury, James,
David, sons; Tobitha, Cath., Rebecca,
Eliz., daus.
BONER, WM., Inv., 9-27-1830.
BOWEN, JOSEPH, Inv., 1817.
BREEN, GEO., Will, 1-1821. Dev.: Mary,
wife; sons, daus.
BRIDGELY, WM., Inv., 4-1848.
BROWN, ——, Will, 3-31-1828. Dev.:
Martha, wife.
BROWN, BARB., Will, 10-1845. Dev.: Al-
lice, Honour, Marg., Elisabeth, Nancy,
daus.; James, Jacob, John, Geo., sons;
grandchildren.
BROWN, BARB., Inv., 10-1846.
BROWN, HONOR, Will, 4-1816. Dev.:
Richars, son; others.
BROWN, JOHN, Inv., 4-10-1828.
BROWN, JOHN, Will, 3-31-1834. Dev.:
Wm., bro.; Barb., sis.; others.
BROWN, JOHN, Will, 6-29-1835. Dev.:
Grandchildren.
BROWN, JOHN, Inv., 8-10-1835.
BROWN, JOHN, Will, 4-1847. Dev.: Geo.,
son; others.
BROWN, JOHN, Inv., 6-1847.
BROWN, JOSEPH, Will, 4-1808. Dev.:
Mary, wife; Thomas, Wm., Joseph,
Robert, Samuel, Esebeler, Alexander, sons;
Agnes, Mahela, Hannah, daus.; others.
BROWN, RICHARD, Will, 2-1811. Dev.:
Honor, wife; Rachel Wells, Marg. Mad-

den, daus.; others.
BROWN, RICHARD, Will, 8-29-1842. Dev.:
Honor, Eliz., Marg., Nancy, Alice, daus.;
Barb., wife; John, Geo., sons.
BROWN, SAMUEL, Will, no date. Dev.:
Eliz., wife; Sarah, dau.
BROWN, Wm., Will, 7-30-1832. Dev.:
James, Robert, Joseph, John, sons; Sally,
Ann, daus.; wife.
BROWNING, JEREMIAH, Will, 5-26-1834.
Dev.: Casandra, wife; Lewis, Joseph,
Jeremiah, sons; Eliz., Casandra, Rachel,
daus.
BROWNING, JEREMIAH, Inv., 5-28-1834.
BUCHANAN, JOHN, Will, 5-31-1830.
Dev.: Marg., wife.
BUCHANAN, MARG., Will, 8-25-1834.
Dev.: four sons.
BUCHANAN, MARG., Inv., 9-5-1834.
BUCHANAN, ROBERT, Inv., 2-1850.
BURK, JOHN, Inv., 1-26-1827.
BURT, JAMES, Inv., 7-1842.
BURT, JOHN, Will, 2-28-1842. Dev.: Mary,
wife; Mother; Samuel, bro.
BURT, WM., Inv., 6-1849.
BUSKERT, LAWRENCE, Will, 6-1801.
Dev.: John, Lewis, sons; Mary, dau.;
Rebeckah, wife.
BUTLER, WM., Inv., 6-1842.

CAIN, WALTER, Inv., 3-1831.
CAIN, WALTER, Will, 2-28-1831. Dev.:
Mary, wife; Walter, Jr., son; others.
CALDWELL, JAMES, Inv., 9-5-1826.
CALLENDINE, DANIEL, Inv., 2-12-1822.
CALLENDINE, DANIEL, Will, no date.
Dev.: Martin, Daniel, Abraham, Henry,
sons; Wife; Marg. Vincent, Eliz., daus.;
others.
CALLENDINE, MARTIN, Inv., 4-29-1828.
CALWELL, ROBERT., Will, 11-1815. Dev.:
heirs.
CAMPBELL, ELIZA ANN, Will, 11-1840.
Dev.: A. Campbell, father.
CAMPBELL, JAMES, Will, 10-1840. Dev.:
Marg., wife; John, Bartyl, James, Archi-
bald, sons; Heriet, Nancy, Marg., daus.
CAMPBELL, JAMES, Inv., 5-26-1845.
CAMPBELL, JAMES, Inv., 10-29-1848.
CAMPBELL, JAMES, Will, no date. Dev.:
Patience, wife; James, Alex., Archibald,
Robert, sons; Ann Capes, Marg. Lank-
ford, daus.; others.
CAMPBELL, JAMES, Will, 3-1845. Dev.:
Rebecca, wife; Samuel, Andrew, Joseph,
Wm., sons; Mary, Jane, Cath., daus.
CAMPBELL, JAS., Inv., 11-24-1850.
CAMPBELL, JANE, Will, 3-1847. Dev.:
Wm., Freshwater.
CAMPBELL, JOHN, Inv., 2-6-1823.
CAMPBELL, JOHN, Inv., 2-9-1837.
CAMPBELL, JOSEPH, Inv., 12-8-1824.
CAMPBELL, JOSEPH, Inv., 5-19-1827.
CAMPBELL, PATIENCE, Will, 11-1809.
Dev.: Anna Capes, Marg. Langfit, daus.
CAMPBELL, ROBERT, Inv., 2-1836.
CAPBELL, JAMES, Inv., 3-1845.
CARIENS, MARY, Will, 1-1846. Dev.:
Eleanor, Jemima, daus.
CARLE, NATHANILE, Inv., 12-17-1840.
CARRENS, Mary, Inv., 3-1846.
CARRENS, WM., Inv., 3-1846.
CARRIENS, ELLIOTT, Inv., 8-1846.
CASNELER, JAMES, Inv., 6-1842.
CASNER, JAMES, Will, 8-29-1842. Dev.:
Eley, wife; children.

CHAMBERS, JOHN, Will, 2-1838. Dev.:
Mary, wife; David, James, John, Wm.,
sons; Hulda, dau.
CHAMBERS, SARAH, Will, 5-1814. Dev.:
Samuel, David, John, James, sons; Marg.
Patterson, dau.; others.

CHAPMAN, GEO., Will, 6-1812, Dev.: Johannah, wife; Geo., Wm., Thomas, Hugh, sons; Martha, Jean, Eliz., daus.

CHAPMAN, JOANNA, Inv., 2-1844.

CHAPMAN, JOHN, Inv., 8-1847.

CHAPMAN, THOMAS, Will, 7-1845. Dev.: Alfred, James, Bazzeell, Jackson, sons; Assa, Rachel, Ellen, daus.; others.

CHAPMAN, THOMAS, Inv., 7-1846.

CLARK, WM., Inv., 8-16-1827.

CLAYTON, STEPHEN, Inv., 4-3-1832.

CLAYS, DAVID, Will, no date. Dev.: Anna Brown, Mother; Marg. Meek, Lusannas Chambers, sis.; others.

CLENDENNAN, SAMUEL, Inv., 6-1817.

CLINDINEN, MARY, Will, 11-24-1834. Dev.: Jane, dau.; Wm., son; others.

CLINTON, CHARLES, Inv., 11-5-1820.

COLEMAN, NATHANIEL, Inv., 10-13-1818.

CONGLETON, MOSES, Inv., 12-11-1838.

CONNELL, JAMES, Inv., 5-30-1838.

CONNELL, JOHN, Inv., 7-1831.

CORNELIUS, DANIEL, Will, 10-29-1832. Dev.: Eliz., Elender, daus.; Elijah, Benj., John, sons.

CORNELIUS, DANIEL, Inv., 11-14-1832.

COULTER, RICHARD, Inv., 12-3-1818.

COWAN, HUGH, Will, 3-1815. Dev.: Isabella, wife; Marg., dau.

COX, GEO., Will, 12-25-1837. Dev.: Susanah, wife; John, Joseph, Isaac, James, Geo., Friend, sons; Nancy, Susanah, daus.; others.

COX, ISRAEL, Inv., 5-1846.

COX, JONATHAN, Inv., 5-12-1823.

CRAWFORD, ALEX., Will, 12-1812. Dev.: Josiah, son; Marg. Steel, Isabel, Mary Henry, daus.; others.

CRAWFORD, JAS., Inv., 4-30-1838.

CRAWFORD, JOHN, Inv., 10-1-1824.

CRAWFORD, JOS., Inv., 10-2-1834.

CRAWFORE, JAS., Inv., 9-17-1836.

CRESWELL, MARY, Inv., 10-1823.

CRISWELL, JAMES, Inv., 11-24-1820.

CRISSWELL, JAMES, Will, 9-1816. Dev.: Mary, wife; Robert, John, Samuel, James, sons; Jane, Marg., Mary, Betty, daus.

CRITSER, HENRY, Will, 10-1807. Dev.: Wife; Peter, John, sons; Laney, Hannah, Kitty, Leah, Mary, Charity, Sarah, Agnes, daus.

CROLL, WM., Will, 2-1808. Dev.: Eliz., wife; Children.

Crossan? CROPAN, WM., Will, 10-1807. Dev.: John, Samuel, Robert, bros.; Marey, Jane, Ann, sis.; others.

CROW, JOHN, Inv., 1817.

CROW, PHILIP, Inv., 10-29-1822.

CULLEY, ELIZ., Will, 4-1820. Dev.: Mary, sis.

CUNNINGHAM, GEO., Inv., 11-5-1817.

CUNNINGHAM, SAM., Inv., 9-9-1841.

CUMMINS, ROBERT., Inv., 12-19-1838.

CUMMINS, ROBERT, Will, 8-1839. Dev.: Eliz., Jane, Rebecca, Marg., Martha, daus.

CUPPEY, JOHN, Will, 9-1801. Dev.: Marg., wife; three sons.

CUPPY, ABRAHAM, Inv., 2-25-1819.

CUPPY, MARG., Inv., 4-27-1818.

DAVID, CATH., Will, 12-1818. Dev.: Rachel, Nancy, Carrie, Susanna, Jemina, Honor, daus.; Joshua, Benj., Nathaniel, sons; others.

DAVIS, CATH., Inv., 1-6-1819.

DAVIS, WM., Will, 11-1811. Dev.: Rebecca, wife; David, James, Wm., Evan, sons.

DECAMPS, JACOB, Inv., 2-1842.

DICKSON, SUSANNA, Will, 7-1840. Dev.: Temperance, sis.; Francis, Robert, bros.; others.

DOLEY, PETER, SR., Will, 11-1817. Dev.: Martha, wife; Sarah, Cath. Solomen, Mary, daus.; John, Abraham, Peter, sons.

DONALDSON, JEEDES, Inv., 6-1826.

DOTY, PETER, Inv., 11-28-1818.

DOUBLAZER, HENRY, Inv., 6-1845.

DOUBLAZIER, HENRY, Will, 1-1838. Dev.: Nancy, wife; Susan, dau.

DUNLAP, WM., Will, 4-1820. Dev.: Mary, wife; Sam., Adams, Wm., Josiah, Alex, John, sons; Sary Hegges, Prudence Hegges, daus.; others.

DUNLAP, WM., Inv., 7-19-1819.

DUVALL, GABRIEL, Inv., 11-1849.

DUVALL, ISAAC, Inv., 8-24-1828.

DUVALL, ISAAC, Will, 7-28-1828. Dev.: Wife; children.

DUVALL, ISAAC, Inv., 12-16-1833.

EDGINGTON, DRUSILLA, Will, 3-1817. Dev.: Mary Verie, sis.; Geo.; bro.; Mother; slaves.

EDGINGTON, JOHN, Inv., 6-22-1820.

EDGINGTON, THOMAS, Will, 2-1814. Dev.: Jesse, John, Thomas, sons; Martha, wife.

EDIE, JOHN, Will, 3-28-1842. Dev.: Samuel, Alex., David, Wm., sons; Easther, Jane, Lydia, daus.

ELLIOTT, GEO., Inv., 3-1822.

ELLIOTT, JAMES, Inv., 5-1846.

ELLIOTT, WM., Inv., 9-20-1825.

ELLS, ELIJAH, Inv., 4-1831.

ELLSON, HENSON, Inv., 4-5-1830.

ELSON, HENSON, Will, 3-29-1830. Dev.: Richard, John, sons; Sarah, Mary, Ruth, daus.; wife.

ELSON, RICHARD, Will, no date. Dev.: Rich., Wm., sons; Mary, wife; other.

EVERITT, JOSHUA, Inv., 7-26-1830.

FARNSWORTH, CALVIN, Inv., 9-1822.

FARQUAR, JOHN, Will, 8-25-1828. Dev.: Harriet, wife; Thomas, Isaac, Elisa, Clark, John, sons.

FERGUSON, JAMES, Inv., 10-26-1822.

FETTER, GEO., Inv., 10-1817.

FITZPATRICK, JAS., Inv., 4-8-1840.

FLING, JOHN, Inv., 3-1-1817.

FOLK, JACOB, Inv., 2-15-1822.

FORD, WM., Inv., 4-1849.

FOSTER, BENJ., Inv., 3-2-1827.

FOUT, ANDREW, Will, 9-1808. Dev.: Ann, wife; David, Leman, Andrew, Allen, Jacob, Wm., Alefailemm, Sebastian, Jacob, sons; Jemina, Ann, Mary, Sarah, daus.

FOWLER, JOHN, Will, 8-1814. Dev.: Christiana, wife; Johnsey, sons; other children.

FOWLER, JOSEPH, Will, 3-1840. Dev.: Richard, nephew.

FOWLER, WM., Will, 10-1836. Dev.; Wife; Daniel, Wm., sons.

FOWLER, WM., Will, 12-1849. Dev.: children, grandchildren.

FOWLER, WM., SR., Inv., 2-1850.

FOWLER, WM., JR., Inv., 9-1849.

FREE, ELISHA, Inv., 5-16-1836.

FREEL, ELISHA, Will, 8-30-1830. Dev.: Sarah, Mary, Charlotte, daus.; John, Alex., McDowell, sons; Father and mother.

FREEL, ELISHA, Inv., 9-1-1830.

FRESHWATER, FANNY, Will, 4-1811. Dev.: Wm., Geo., Reuben Christopher, David, sons; others.

GAMBLE, ALLEN, Inv., 7-31-1824.
GAMBLE, MARY, Inv., 4-29-1830.
GARDNER, JOHN, Will, 2-15-1821. Dev.:
Wm., John, James, David, Samuel, sons;
Wife; others.
GASTON, WM., Inv., 10-1829.
GERRIEN, SAM., Will, no date. Dev.:
Hanna, wife.
GIBSON, WM., Will, 2-1818. Dev.: Agnes,
sis.; Mary, niece.
GIBSON, WM., Inv., 4-1818.
GIBSON, WM., Inv., 11-18-1820.
GIST, CORNELIUS, Will, 10-26-1830.
Dev.: Clara, wife; Cornelius, Wm.,
Geo.; Joshua, Joseph, sons; Louisiana,
Emelina, daus.
GIST, GEO., Will, 6-30-1834. Dev.:
Emeline, Louisiana, Camelia, sis.; Corne-
lius, Joshua, Joseph, Wm., bros.
GIST, JOSEPH, Will, no date. Dev.:
James, Sam., Geo., sons; Eliz., wife.
GLADMAN, JOHN, Inv., 7-6-1826.
GLAP, ROBERT, Inv., 11-29-1822.
GLASS, JOHN, Will, 4-1812. Dev.: Ester,
wife; Geo., John, sons; Hannah, dau.
GRAHAM, THOMAS, Inv., 8-9-1825.
GRANT, ALEX., Inv., 6-9-1821.
GRAY, CHARLES, Inv., 8-8-1822.
GREEN, GEO., Inv., 3-30-1821.
GREEN, HUGH, Inv., 3-11-1833.
GREEN, HUGH, Inv., 10-1834.
GREEN, MARY, Inv., 4-4-1826.
GRIFFITH, JAMES, Will, 6-1812. Dev.:
Jemima, wife; Mary, dau; others.
GRIFFITH, WM., Will, 9-1808. Dev.:
Nancy, wife; Wm., Alex., John, sons;
Michael, dau.; other daus.
GRIMES, THOMAS, Will, 7-1848. Dev.:
Jane. wife; Thomas, James, sons; Eliza.,
Mary, Marg., dau.
GRIMES, THOMAS, Inv., 9-1848.
GRUMBY, MARY, Will, 9-1839. Dev.:
Mary, dau.

HAGAN, ANDREW, Inv., 6-1841.
HAGAN, JANE, Inv., 3-1842.
HAGAN, JOHN, Inv., 11-29-1824.
HAGEN, ANDREW, Will, 6-1840. Dev.:
Jane, wife; Ann, mother; John, Wm.,
Henry, Thomas, bro.; Sally, sis.
HAGEN, JANE, Will, 2-28-1842. Dev.:
Sarah, dau.
HAGEN, JOHN, Inv., 11-10-1823.
HAMILTON, JAMES, Will, 1-1806. Dev.:
Nancy, wife; children.
HAMILTON, J. HAILTON, Inv., 1-1845.
HAMILTON, JOSEPH, Inv., 9-25-1819.
HAMILTON, SUSANNAH, Inv., 4-1-1826.
HAMMOND, ELIZ., Will, 9-26-1831. Dev.:
Nancy, Cath., Eliza, daus.; Henry, son.
HAMMOND, GEO., Will, 7-1814. Dev.:
Harry, Shandy, Resin, Thomas, Talbot,
Charles, sons; Rebeckah, dau.
HARRIS, JOHN, Will, 11-1812. Dev.: Eliz.,
wife; Wm., James, Warren, John, sons;
Mary Ellis, Eleanor Snediker, Charity
Snediker, Sally Parsons, daus.
HARTFORD, MATHEW, Will, 4-1814.
Dev.: heirs.
HARTFORD, MATHEW, Inv., 1-25-1825.
HARTFORD, ROBERT, Inv., 7-26-1824.
HARTFORD, ROBERT, Inv., 7-26-1824.
HARVEY, CATH., Inv., 11-1842.
HARVEY, CATH., Will, 6-1843. Dev.:
Mary, Cath., daus.; Wm., Philip, Geo.,
sons.
HAZE, SAM., Inv., 12-8-1831.
HAYS, AGNES, Will, 6-1840. Dev.: Jane,
Lettice, Agnes, daus.; Henry, Robert,
James, Andrew, Wm., sons; others.
HAYS, AGNES, Inv., 12-15-1840.

HAYS, JOSEPH, Will, 4-1845. Dev.:
Marg., wife; children.
HAYS, ROBERT, Inv., 2-24-1819.
HAYS, ROBERT, Will, 5-1819. Dev.:
Eliz., Mother; Ester, Jane, Polly, sis.;
John bro.
HAYS, SAMUEL, Will, 11-28-1831. Dev.:
Jane, Lettie, daus.; David, son; Wife.
HEADINGTON, NICHOLAS, Will, 7-3-
1837. Dev.: Eliz., wife; Samuel, Wm.,
John, Greenberry, Labun, sons; Mary,
Marg., daus.
HEADINGTON, NICHOLAS, Inv., 4-1848.
HEDGES, CHAS., Inv., 5-1838.
HEDGES, JOSEPH, Will, no date. Dev.:
Marg., wife; R. Meeks, C. Story, J.
Cash, Frazear, daus.; Silas, Wm.,
Abraham, Joseph, Sam., sons.
HEDGES, JOSEPH, Inv., 11-10-1821.
HEDGES, JOSEPH, Will, 6-1849. Dev.:
Lotho, Charles, sons; Rebecca, Jane,
Sally, daus.; others.
HEDGES, JOSEPH, Inv., 7-1849.
HEDGES, SOLOMON, Will, 1-1802. Dev.:
Marg., wife; Silas, Joseph, sons; Re-
beckah, dau.; others.
HENDERSON, JAS., Will, 9-29-1838.
Dev.: Isabelle, Rachael, Polly, daus.;
Matthew, Samuel, James, sons.
HENDRICKS, GEO., Inv., 3-16-1836.
HENDRICKS, JOHN, Will, 6-1847. Dev.:
Cath., Rebecca, Charity, daus.; Edward,
Tobias, sons.
HENRY, JAMES, Will, 10-31-1831. Dev.:
Eliz., wife; Jane, Marg., Mary, daus.;
others.
HENRY, JAMES, Inv., 11-8-1831.
HENRY, WM., Inv., 11-4-1823.
HENRY, WM., Inv., 4-15-1824.
HERVEY, HENRY, Will, no date. Dev.:
Marg., wife; Wm., James, John, David,
Henry, sons; Jane Eleson, Mary, Marg.,
daus.
HERVITT, WM., Inv., 10-31-1823.
HIBBITT, WM., Inv., 9-15-1824.
HILL, THOMAS, Will, no date. Dev.:
John, sons; grandchildren.
HINDMAN, JAMES, Will, 3-1848. Dev.:
Samuel, John, sons; Eliz., Eleanor,
Ruemina, daus.; others.
HINDMAN, JAMES, Inv., 12-1848.
HINDMAN, JOHN, Will, 1810. Dev.:
Francis, James, bro.; others.
HOFFMAN, BENJ., Inv., 5-4-1833.
HOLMES, THOMAS, Will, 3-26-1832. Dev.:
Annie, wife; Isar, Thomas, sons; Marg.,
Jane, Anne, Izebele, Pricilla, Eliz., daus.
HOOKER, RICHARD, Will, 10-31-1831.
Dev.: Richard, Geo., Emanuel, Tallman,
sons; Nancy, wife; Eliz., Nancy, Mary,
Jane, daus.; others.
HOOKER, RICHARD, Inv., 11-2-1831.
HUDSON, WM., Will, 3-1808. Dev.: Wife;
John, Lewis, sons; Sarah, dau.; other
children.
HUFFORD, RUDALPH, Inv., 9-14-1830.
HUFFORD, RUDOLPH, Will, 8-31-1830.
Dev.: Cath., wife; Geo., son; others.
HUGES, THOS., Inv., 3-28-1838.
HUGHES, HENRY, Inv., 6-26-1821.
HUGHES, THOMAS, Will, 6-25-1838. Dev.:
John, Wm., Watson, Thomas, James,
Robert, sons; Ann, Polly, Eliza, daus.;
Mary, wife.
HUNT, THOS., Inv., 5-7-1834.
HUNT, THOMAS, Will, 4-1839. Dev.:
Jane, wife; Marg., Polly, Nancy, sis.
HUNTER, JOHN, Inv., 4-1846.

IRWIN, ALEX., Inv., 6-1828.
IRWIN, JAMES, Inv., 8-14-1819.

JACKSON, DAVID, Inv., 6-1842.
JACOBS, GEO., Inv., 10-10- 1835.
JAMES, ANN, Will, 3-1841. Dev.: John, son-in-law; Nancy, granddau.
JAMISON, HENRY, Will, 12-1847. Dev.: Esther, wife; others.
JAMISON, HENRY, Inv., 7-1848.
JAMISON, MARG., Will, 8-27-1837. Dev.: Jane, sis.; John, bro.; others.
JESTER, ANDREW, Inv., 10-6-1837.
JOHNSON, BENJ., Will, 6-1846. Dev.: Joseph, Wm., Josiah, Elias, bros.; Marg., sis.; others.
JOHNSON, BENJ., Inv., 7-1846.
JOHNSTON, ABLE, Will, 3-1820. Dev.: Rachel, Ann, Eliz., Marg., daus.; Joseph, Benj., Joel, Wm., Josah, Amos, Elias, sons; others.
JOHNSTON, ABLE, Inv., 4-16-1820.
JOHNSTON, JOSEPH, Inv., 3-1839.
JONES, DANIEL, Inv., 8-5-1822.
JONES, DANIEL, Inv., 12-3 1824.
JONES, DAVID, Inv., 6-3-1826.
JONES, ELLIS, SR., Will., 11-1839. Dev.: Mary, Rebecka, Cath., Ann, Jane, daus.; Lewis, son; others.
JONES, GEO., Will, 11-26-1833. Dev.: Elebeth, wife; Bety, Sally, Marg., daus.; others.
JONES, GEO., Inv., 12-10-1833.
JONES, ISAAC, SR., Inv., 6-1845.
JONES, SAMUEL, Will, 7-1837. Dev.: James, Jackson, sons; Nancy wife; Jane, Maria, Martha, Eliz., Harriet, daus.
JONES, SAMUEL, Inv., 9-2-1837.

KELLY, JOHN, Inv., 3-1830.
KELLY, JOHN, Will, 3-29-1830. Dev.: Mary, wife; others.
KERNS, NANCY, Will, 3-14-1808. Dev.: Levi, husband, Wm., Johnson, Sam., sons; others.
KIMBERLAND, JOHN, Will, 4-1849. Dev.: Marg., wife; heirs.
KIMBERLAND, JOHN, Inv., 8-1849.
KINCAID, JAMES, Will, 11-1812. Dev.: Nancy, wife; John, son; Ellinor, Jane, Mary Ann, Lornann, daus.; other children.
KIRK, JOHN, Will, 8-29-1843. Dev.: Mary, dau.; Thomas, son; others.
KIRK, JOHN, Inv., 3-1845.
KRIDER, DANIEL, Will, no date. Dev.: Wife; Obediah, son; Rachel, Eliz., daus.
KRYDER, DANIEL, Inv., 4-15-1822.

LASUR, JOSEPH, Inv., 10-1-1825.
LAUCK, SIMON, Inv., 8-1850.
LAZEAR, JOHN, Will, no date. Dev.: Mother; Jane, Nancy, sisters.
LECKY, ALEX., Will, 1797. Dev.: Hugh, two other sons; wife.
LEDLIE, WM., Inv., 6-23-1831.
LEE, JAMES, Inv., 6-1842.
LEE JANE, Will, 5-29-1843. Dev.: James, Hugh, Robert, Andrew, sons; Mary, dau.
LEE, JOSHUA, Will, 5-30-1831. Dev.: Mary Lee, wife.
LEE, JOSHUA, Inv., 6-11-1831.
LEE, MARY ANN, Will, 6-20-1808. Dev.: S. P. Hughes, sis.; Wm., bro.; others.
LEE, THOMAS, Inv., 12-16-1825.
LEE, WM., Will, 9-1819.. Dev.: Jean, wife; James, Hugh, Andrew, Robert, sons; Polly, dau.
LEE, WM., Inv., 10-27-1819.
LEEPER, JAMES, Will, 3-31-1828. Dev.: Mary, wife; James, Wm., John, sons; Ann, Mather, Jean, daus.
LEEPER, JAMES, Inv., 6-25-1828.

LEEPER, JOHN, Will, 12-1849. Dev.: Martha, Jane, sis.
LEEPER, JOHN, Inv., 2-1850.
LEEPER, MARTHA, Inv., 11-1850.
LEEPER, MARTHA, Will, 6-1850. Dev.: Jane, sis.
LINDSAY, JOSHUA, Inv., 4-1837.
LINDSAY, JOSHUA, Inv., 1-1850.
LLOYD, JAMES, Inv., 3-30-1829.
LOW, ELIZ., Will, 9-1839. Dev.: Ann, sis.; David, husband; others.
LUMON, MARY, Will, 4-1804. Dev.: 2 sons of Jane Brownlee, Archibald Brownlee, Marg. Brownlee, Sarah Lattimore, Martha Carrole.
LYONS, FRANCIS, Inv., 5-19-1838.

MACKALL, SAMUEL, Will, 2-25-1833. Dev.: Eliz., wife.
MAGRUDER, JAMES, Inv., 6-1-1819.
MARKS, ALEX., Will, 4-1816. Dev.: Mary, wife; Mary Marks, Eliz., Matilda; John, Thomas, Samuel, James, Wm., sons.
MARKS, ALEX., Inv., 5-11-1816.
MARKS, JAMES, Will, 11-1837. Dev.: Sarah, wife; Eliz., sis.; others.
MARKS, JAMES, Inv., 3-6-1838.
MARKS, JOHN, Will, 8-819. Dev.: Mary, mother; Eliz., Matilda, sister; Thomas, Sam., bro.
MARKS, JOHN, Inv., 9-25-1819.
MARKS, SAMUEL, Will, 6-1847. Dev.: Mary, wife; Amanda, Alice, Alezana, daus.; Jackson, Alfred, John, Lafayette, Hiram, sons; others.
MARROW, ALEX., Inv., 7-10-1818.
MARSHAL, JAMES, Will, 7-1814. Dev.: Samuel, James, John, sons; Eliz., Rebecca, Mary, Alice, daus.
MARSHAL, JAMES, Inv., 8-29-1818.
MARSHAL, SAM., Inv., 3-11-1833.
MARSHALL, ROBERT, Inv., 4-8-1831.
MATHISON, CHRISTOPHER, Will, 8-27-1838. Dev.: Polly, dau.; Robert, son; others.
McBROOM, THOMAS, Inv., 5-25-1818.
McCamant, AME, Inv., 8-30-1817.
McCAUGHAN, ANN, will, 12-1818. Dev.: Thomas, Samuel, brother; others.
McCLEARY, THOMAS, Will, 11-25-1850. Dev.: Mary, wife; Jane, Sarah, Martha, Julian, daus.; James, Wm., Ewing, Thomas, sons; grandchildren.
McCLEARY, THOMAS, Inv., 12-31-1850.
McCLOUD, DANIEL, Will, 8-31-1829. Dev.: Robert, son.
McCOMBS, JOHN, Inv., 3-10-1841.
McDONNEL, ISABELLA, Will, 9-1840. Dev.: John, Robert, Andrew, Geo., sons; Isabela, Joann, Angaline, daus.
McDOWEL, ALEX., Will, 6-30-1828. Dev.: Nancy, wife; others.
McENTYRE, ANN, Will, 9-1844. Dev.: List with no designation as to relationship.
McENTYRE, ANN, Inv., 8-1846.
McGUIRE, BARB., Will, 1-28-1836. Dev.: Christana, Rebecca, sis.; slaves, others.
McGUIRE, BARB., Inv., 2-9-1836.
McGUIRE, FRANCIE, Will, 10-1820. Dev.: Barbara, wife; slaves; others.
McGUIRE, FRANCIS, Inv., 11-8-1820.
McINTIRE, ROBERT, Will, 2-27-1837. Dev.: Ann, wife; Eliz., Nancy, Rebecca, Massa, Dorcas, Marg., Shorlette, daus.; Jon, Robert, Josephus, sons; Isaac, step-son; others.
McKINLEY, JANE, Will, 8-1849. Dev.: Wm., son; Jame, Sophua, Mary, daus.
McLANE, CELIA, Inv., 4-29-1842.
McNARY, JOHN, Will, 11-1844. Dev.: Wm., bro.; Nancy, sis.; others.

McNARY, WM., Will, no date. Dev.:
Marg., wife; David, Robert, James, Wm.,
John, sons; Agnes, Mary, daus.
McNARY, WM., Inv., 8-31-1821.
MEANS, JAMES, Will, 5-28-1821. Dev.:
Rebecca, sis.; James, nephew.
MEEK, SAM., Inv., 10-17-1838.
MEEK, SAMUEL, Will, 10-4-1838. Dev.:
Thomas, Robert, Joseph, James, Samuel,
Garrett, Wm., sons; Susann, Sally Mc-
Nary, Martha Thawley, Ann, Lydia
Grimes, Mary Headington, daus.; others.
MENDEL, HENRY, Inv., 2-1846.
MENDEL, VALLENTINE, Will, 1-1812.
Dev.: Mary, wife; Valentine, Henry,
Peter, Geo., Jacob, John, sons; Mary,
Eliz., Rachel, daus.
MERRYMAN, ELIZAH, Inv., 7-3-1824.
MERRYMAN, JOHN, Inv., 10-2-1823.
MERRYMAN, JOHN, Inv., 1-1845.
MIERS, CHRIS., Will, 6-1797. Dev.:
Mary, wife; Cath., Mary, daus.
MILLER, DAVID, Will, 5-26-1846. Dev.:
Grandchildren.
MILLER, JOSEPH, Inv., 6-19-1839.
MILLER, WM., Will, 10-5-1841. Dev.:
June, wife; Sarah Kelly, mother; child;
others.
MILLER, WM., Inv., 5-5-1842.
MINOVIN, JEAN, Will, 1-1820. Dev.:
Eliz., dau.; nieces and nephews.
MOBBS, LEONARD, Inv., 10-21-1834.
MOLEN, SAMBON, Inv., 11-6-1822.
MONRO, WILLIAM, Will, 6-1797. Dev.:
Wife; Danice, son; Eliz., dau.
MOONEY, PETER, Inv., 1-19-1832.
MOORE, ISIAH, Inv., 11-1845.
MOORE, JOHN, Will, 3-1814. Dev.: Jane,
wife; James, John, Joseph, Samuel, Ro-
bert, sons; Jame, Sarah, Eliz., Maria,
Michel, daus.
MOORE, JOHN, Inv., 9-25-1824.
MOORE, ROBT., Inv., 4-11-1826.
MOORE, ROBERT, Will, 12-1847. Dev.:
Nancy, wife; Rachel, Anna, Sarah, Mary,
daus.; Thomas, Henry, Joseph, John,
James, Samuel, Robert Abraham, Isaac,
sons.
MOORE, ROBERT, Inv., 9-1850.
MOOREHEAD, CHARLES W., Will, 2-
1812. Dev.: Wm., bro.; Eleanor, Peggy,
sis.
MOOREHEAD, JAMES, Inv., 7-6-1836.
MOOREHEAD, JOHN, Will, 1-1808. Dev.:
Marg., wife; James, Wm., sons; Mary,
dau.; others.
MOOREHEAD, ROBERT, Inv., 4-6-1837.
MOOREHEAD, WM., Will, 5-1819. Dev.:
Mary, sis.
MOREHEAD, JAMES, Will, 6-1836. Dev.:
Eliz., wife; John, son; Mary, dau.
MOREHEAD, WM., Inv., 11-1845.
MORGAN, THOMAS, Inv., 2-10-1821.
MORROW, ALEX., Will, 2-1818. Dev.:
Wm., John, James, Alex., sons; Eliz.,
Nancy Mittow, Marg. Moorehead, daus.
MORROW, ALEX., Inv., 4-1848.
MORROW, ALEXANDRE, Will, 12-1847.
Dev.: Susan, wife; Robert, James, Alex.,
sons; daus.
MORROW, JAMES, Inv., 4-19-1825.
MORROW, WM., Will, 9-1839. Dev.:
Nephews.
MURCHLAND, JACOB, Inv., 4-1836.
MURCHLAND, JAMES, Inv., 12-1846.
MURCHLAND, WM., Will, 3-1812. Dev.:
James, Wm., John, Robert, sons; Mary,
Susannah, Eliz., daus.
MURTHEN, ROBERT, Will, 5-1797. Dev.:
Wm., bro.; Cristen Lauthers, sis.; nieces
and nephews.
MYERS, HENRY, Inv., 5-15-1824.

NELSON, JOSEPH, Inv., 8-21-1820.
NESSLY, JACOB, Will, 11-26-1832. Dev.:
Eliz., wife; Barbara, Lucy, Judith, Alice,
daus.; John, Jacob, sons.
NESWONGER, JACOB, SR., Will, 3-1840.
Dev.: Rachel, wife; Sarah, Eliz., daus.;
Geo., John, Jacob, Elija, sons.
NEWHOUN, WM., Inv., 6-25-1819.
NICEWANGER, JOS., Inv., 5-1840.
NICHOLAS, DANIEL, Will, 9-1804. Dev.:
Amelia, wife; Wm., Themeis, Iscah, sons;
Cafendre, Sarah, daus.
NICHOLLS, JOSIAH, Inv., 9-22-1832.

OGDEN, SAM., Inv., 11-15-1844.
OGEN, SAMUEL, Will, 10-4-1844. Dev.:
Nancy Steart, Rachel Scott, Sarah Ray,
Mary Quigley, Eliz. Bertley, daus.; Lewis,
Robert, Daniel, Samuel, John, sons.
ORLTON, HUGH, Will, 3-1815. Dev.:
Wife; John, son; Rachel Morgan, Jane
Burson, Tamer, daus.
ORR, JOHN, Will, 3-27-1843. Dev.: Han-
nah, Marg., daus.; Thomas, son; others.
OWINGS, ASA, Inv., 6-12-1820.
OWINGS, JOHN, Inv., 8-3-1825.

PARKINSON, ELIZ., Inv., 12-1845.
PARKINSON, GEO., Will, 9-1844. Dev.:
Eliz., wife; David, son; others.
PARKINSON, GEO., Inv., 4-1845.
PARKISON, THOMAS, Will, 4-1808. Dev.:
Peggy, wife; John, James, Thomas, David,
Joseph, sons; Peggy, Patty, Susan, Jane,
daus.; Benj., son.
PARKS, JOS., Inv., 5-1835.
PARKS, ROBERT, Inv., 4-15-1824.
PASCO, ANN, Inv., 5-1850.
PATTERSON, JAMES, Will, 4-1818. Dev.:
Jean, wife; Andrew, Arthur, Robert, John,
Archibald, sons; Hannah, Jean, daus.;
others.
PATTERSON, JAMES, Inv., 10-11-1817.
PATTERSON, JAMES, Inv., 9-10-1818.
PATTERSON, JAMES, Inv., 5-31-1824.
PATTERSON, JOHN, Inv., 6-1850.
PATTERSON, ROBERT, Will, 6-29-1829.
Dev.: Eliz., wife; Eliz., Sarah, daus.; Wm.,
James, Alex., sons; others.
PATTERSON, ROBERT, Inv., 7-14-1829.
PATTERSON, WM., Inv., 8-29-1840.
PELLEY, WM., Inv., 9-1817.
PELLY, WM., Will, 4-1814. Dev.: Lydia,
wife; Colbert, son; Rachel, Sally, Nancy,
daus.
PENNINGTON, WM., Inv., 9-29-1823.
PETERSON, CONRAD, Inv., 9-1847.
PETERSON, THOMAS, Will, 8-31-1835.
Dev.: Conrade, Peter, sons; Phebe, daus.;
grandchildren.
PETERSON, THOS., Inv., 9-24-1835.
PERRY, JAMES, Will, 1-1810. Dev.: Wife;
Wm., John, sons; Eliz., Tabitha, Mary,
Jemima, daus.
PITTINGEN, WM., Inv., 11-11-1820.
PITTINGER, WM., Will, 1-1821. Dev.:
Wife, children.
PITTINGER, WM., Inv., 4-26-1821.
PLATTENBURG, GEO., Will, 6-1841. Dev.:
Mary, dau.; Jacob, son; wife.
PLATTENBURGH, WM., Inv., 12-1823.
PLUMBER, JEROME, Will, 7-1807. Dev.:
Geo., son; Eliz., dau.; others.
PORTER, ROBERT, Inv., 10-1848.
PORTER, WM., Inv., 3-1850.
PORTERFIELD, JAMES, Inv., 7-26-1819.
POTTER, JANE, Will, 9-26-1831. Dev.:
James, John, bros.; nieces.
POTTS, JAMES, Inv., 10-13-1831.
PRATHER, CHARLES, Will, 10-1810.
Dev.: Eliz. Wells, dau.; Henry, John, sons.
PRATHER, HENRY, Inv., 12-3-1835.

PRATHER, JOHN, SR., Will, 11-27-1737.
Dev.: Mary, wife.
PRATHER, JOHN, SR., Inv., 6-1838.
PRATHER, MARY, Inv., 10-29-1846.
PRATHER, MARY, Will, 1-1847. Dev.:
Charles, bro.; Cath., sis.
PREFTON, DAN., Will, no date. Dev.:
Ann, wife; Dan., son; Susanna, Jean, Ann,
daus.
PRICES, ABRAHAM, Will, 5-27-1834.
Dev.: Martha, wife; Rebecca, Constantia,
Mary, Ann, Martha, Eliz., Sarah, daus.;
Stephen, Nehermiah, Joseph, Wm., sons.
PROPER, JONATHAN, Inv., 12-3-1822.
PUGH, HUGH, Inv., 4-18-1818.
PUMPHREY, BEAL, Will, 4-29-1844. Dev.:
Mary, Nancy, daus.; Bazellel, Greenberry,
Absolom, Isaac, sons; others.
PUMPHRY, ANN, Will, 3-1815. Dev.:
Richard Boone, nephew; Ann, niece,
Rachel, slave.
PUMPHRY, REASON, SR., Will, 11-1812.
Dev.: Nickolas, Caleb, Wm., Joseph,
John, sons; Ann, wife; Rody Reason, dau.

QUICKSOTTE, DON CARLOS, Will, no
date. Dev.: Prime Prather.

RALLSTON, SAMUEL, Inv., 9-11-1824.
RALSTON, ANDREW, Inv., 6-1842.
RALSTON, DAVID, Inv., 8-5-1836.
RALSTON, JOSEPH, Inv., 5-1-1843.
RALSTON, JOSEPH, Will, 3-27-1843. Dev.:
Sarah, wife; Joseph, Robert, Alex., Sam-
uel, John, Wm., James, Geo., Resin,
Jeremiah, sons; Jean, Anne, Malinda,
Eliz., daus.
RALSTON, JOSEPH, Inv., 4-1847.
RALSTON, JOSEPH, Will, 7-1846. Dev.:
Isaac, Thomas, Wm., sons; Mary, Caro-
lin, daus.
RALSTON, MARTHA, Inv., 12-10-1839.
RALSTON, MARTHA, Will, 6-1839. Dev.:
Eliza, dau.; other children.
RALSTON, MCCREADY, Inv., 12-1842.
RALSTON, ROBERT, Inv., 2-1848.
RALSTON, ROBERT, Will, 11-1847. Dev.:
Wilson, Joseph, sons; Nancy, Sarah,
Deantha, daus.
RAMSEY, SAMUEL, Will, 12-1812. Dev.:
Polly, wife; six daus.
RAY, JOSEPH, Will, 6-1845. Dev.: Per-
melia, wife.
REED, JOHN, Inv., 2-10-1832.
REED, JOHN, Will, 1-28-1833. Dev.: La-
vina, wife; others.
REED, JOHN, Inv., 2-10-1833.
REEVES, ELIZ., Will, 3-1839. Dev.: Na-
thon, Reason, sons.
REEVES, JOSHIAS, Inv., 8-2-1832.
REYNOLDS, JOSEPH, Inv., 10-1829.
RIDGELY, ABSALOM, Will, 7-1850. Dev.:
Absalom, Benj., sons; Eliz., Mahala, Dru-
silla, daus.
ROBENSON, JOHN, Will, 1-1821. Dev.:
Betsy, wife; Nelly, Martha, daus.; Samuel,
Ebenezer, sons.
ROBERTS, DANIEL, Inv., 11-13-1823.
ROBINSON, AARON, Inv., 4-6-1826.
ROBINSON, ELIJAH, Inv., 12-1846.
ROBINSON, ELIZAH, Will, 2-1846. Dev.:
John, Wm., sons; Eleanor, Sarah, May,
Matildah, daus.
ROBINSON, GEO., Inv., 2-5-1837.
ROBINSON, JAMES, Inv., 4-29-1835.
ROBINSON, JAMES, Will, 3-30-1835. Dev.:
Sarah, wife; Amanda, Mary, Providence,
Sarah, Eliz., daus.; Nicholas, Aaron, Is-
rael, Joseph, Aman, sons.
ROBINSON, JOHN, Inv., 2-3-1821.
ROBINSON, JOHN, Will, 7-1845. Dev.:
Nancy Harvey.

ROBINSON, JOHN, Inv., 5-27-1822.
RODGERS, ABRAHAM, Inv., 10-15-1837.
RODGERS, ABRAHAM, Will, 10-30-1837.
Dev.: Wm., Nicholas, Ezekiel, Benj., sons;
Sarah, Polly, Emily, Sarah, Marg., daus.
ROWLAND, JOSEPH, Inv., 4-6-1831.
RUPELL, JAMES, Inv., 9-4-1823.
RUSSELL, PHILIP, Inv., 2-1845.
RUSSELL, PHILIP, Will, 1-1845. Dev.:
Maria, wife; Oliver, John, Edward, sons;
Julia, dau.
RUSSEL, WM., Inv., 12-1850.

SANDERS, BENJ., Will, 5-25-1835. Dev.:
Nancy, wife; James, Samuel, sons; others.
SANDERS, BENJ., Inv., 10-7-1835.
SANDERS, EDWARD, Inv., 3-27-1820.
SANNIHILL, JAMES, Inv., 11-12-1822.
SCOTT, ALEX., Inv., 10-27-1817.
SCOTT, OBED, Inv., 2-6-1840.
SCOTT, ROBERT, Inv., 10-2-1849.
SEAMAN, ELIZ., Will, 9-29-1834. Dev.:
Robert, Geo., sons; Hester, Mary, Re-
beckah, Marthe, daus.
SEAMAN, ELIZA, Inv., 11-12-1834.
SHRYER, JOHN, Inv., 10-5-1839.
SILVER, JANE, Inv., 1-8-1840.
SILVERS, JANE, Will, 12-1839. Dev.:
Francis, son; Jane, Marg., Sarah, daus.;
others.
SILVERTHORN, HENRY, Inv., 1-1846.
SILVERTHORN, HENRY, Will, 10-1846.
Dev.: Mary, wife.
SILVERTHRON, SAM., Inv., 4-28-1841.
SMITH, FERGUSON, Will, 2-1815. Dev.:
Eliz., wife; Mary, Eliz., Lydia Sutherton,
daus.; Fergus, Wm., Hennery, Geo., sons.
SMITH, JOHN, Inv., 2-1823.
SMITH, JOHN, Inv., 8-15-1829.
SMITH, PEROW, Will, 4-1820. Dev.: Han-
nah, wife.
SMITH, WM., Will, 3-1848. Dev.: Andrew,
son; Sally, Cath., daus.; others.
SNEDIKER, GARRET, Inv., 10-31-1826.
SNEDIKER, GARRET, Inv., 4-5-1831.
SNEDIKER, GEO., Will, 2-1839. Dev.:
Susan, wife; John, Geo., sons; Mary,
Eliz., Sarah, Nancy, daus.
SNEDIKER, GEO., Inv., 3-14-1839.
SNEDIKER, GERET, Will, 3-26-1832. Dev.:
Wm., James, Isaac, Garret, sons; Eleanor,
wife; Eliz., Sarah, Alley, Anne, daus.
SNODEN, JOSEPH, no date. Dev.:
Wm., John, sons; Wife; Sarah, Rachel,
daus.
SNYDER, DAVID, Inv., 7-1846.
SPARKS, MARY, Will, 4-1811. Dev.: Wm.,
Solomon, sons.
SPEER, RICHARD, Will, 7-1804. Dev.:
Wife.
SPIVY, JOHN, Will, 4-1816. Dev.: Ber-
sheba, wife, John, Geo., Lewis, sons;
Marg. Middleworth, Mary Middleworth,
Rebecca, Wilcoxon, daus.
STRAIN HANNAH, Will, 3-1850. Dev.:
Ebenezer, son; Rebecca, Nancy, daus.;
others.
STRAIN, HANNAH, Inv., 4-1850.
STRAIN, JOHN, Will, 6-27-1842. Dev.:
Marg., dau.; Wm., Andrew, Robert, John,
sons.
STRAIN, JOHN, Inv., 8-1842.
STRAIN, WM., Will, 5-30-1831. Dev.:
Hannah, wife; Ebenezer, son; Ester, Han-
nah, Rebecca, Nancy, daus.
STRAIN, WM. Inv., 7-1850.
STEPHENS, WM., Will, 1-1838. Dev.: Wm.,
son; Marg., wife; Anna, Mary, Eliz.,
Martha, daus.
STEVENSON, DAVID, Inv., 6-1-1821.
STEVENSON, JOSEPH, Inv., 6-29-1818.

STEWART, GEORGE, Will, 8-20-1800.
Dev.: Susannah, wife; Geo., John, David,
Joseph, Robert, Charles, Samuel, Wm.,
Benj., James, sons; Mary, dau.
STEWART, JAMES, Inv., 12-1845.
STOBRIDGE, JEFE, Inv., 5-25-1834.
STOBRIDGE, JESSE, Will, no date.
Dev.: Eliz., wife; Wm., Jesse, Robert,
sons; Ann, Violette, daus.
STOWBRIDGE, JESSE, Inv., 5-25-1822.
STOWBRIDGE, JESSE, Inv., 11-1826.
STRONG, SAMUEL, Inv., 6-21-1819.
SWEARINGEN, DANIEL, Inv., 10-21-1822.
SWEARINGEN, G. D., Inv., 10-24-1822.
SWEARINGEN, G. O., Inv., 11-27-1829.
SWEARINGEN, GEO., Inv., 10-17-1822.
SWEARINGEN, JOHN, Will, 9-24-1832.
Dev.: Fanny, wife; Blanch, Benourn, Dor-
sey, daus.; Nicholas, Thomas, Geo., John,
sons; others.

TALBOTT, RICHARD, Inv., 4-1848.
TARR, PETER, Will, 5-6-1839. Dev.: Mary,
wife; Jackson, Wm., Samuel, Camel,
Conle, David, sons; Ameda, Sarah, Mary,
daus.
TARR, PETER, Inv., 5-5-1840.
TAYLER, JAMES, Will, no date. Dev.:
Andrew Tayler, James Griffith.
TAYLOR, ELIZ., Will, 7-1811. Dev.: Dau.
of sister Marg.; others.
TELAN, WM., Will, 6-1836. Dev.: Jane,
Eleanor, daus.; Samuel, husband.
TELAN, WM., Inv., 7-5-1836.
THAIR, NATHAN, Will, 3-1837. Dev.:
Sarah, wife; Nathan, James, sons; Phil-
euia. Alzina. Anne, Violette, daus.
THAIR, NATHAN, Inv., 5-7-1837.
THAYER, NATHAN, Inv., 9-1842.
THOMPSON, GILES, Inv., 1-5-1836.
THORELY, SAMUEL, Inv., 5-1850.
THORP. REBECKAH, Will, 1-1820. Dev.:
Grandson and granddau.
THORP, WM., Will, 12-1818. Dev.: Re-
beckah, wife; Alice, dau.
TIBBY, WILLIAM, Will, 8-1845. Dev.:
Eliz., wife.
TIBBY, WM., Inv., 8-1847.
TIERNAN, MICHAEL, Will, 4-1846. Dev.:
Eliz., wife; Marg., Eliza, daus.; Seth,
John, Michael, sons; others.
TILLINGHAST, NICHOLAS, Will, 7-1809.
Dev.: Patience Vilette, Sarah Hammond,
daus.; others.
TODD, JAMES, Will, 6-1841. Dev.: Wm.,
Thomas, James, sons; Nancy, wife; Matty,
Mary, sis.
TORREYSON, JOS., Inv., 10-6-1835.
TRIMBLE, MATHEW, Will, 7-1849. Dev.:
Eliz., wife; Mathew, John, Samuel, Rob-
ert, sons; Maria, Jane, daus.

VALLAHER. JOHN, Inv., 5-1841.
VANMATRE, JOHN, Will, no date. Dev.:
Jeminah, wife; Sarah, dau.; Abraham,
Isaac, sons.

WALKER, ANDREW, Inv., 5-7-1822.
WALKER, JACOB, Inv., 5-1842.
WALKER, JACOB, Will, 5-1840. Dev.:
Eliz., Mary, Marg., Sarah, daus.; John,
son.
WALLACE, WM., Inv., 2-8-1825.
WARTENBY, WM., Inv., 3-26-1822.
WARTENBE, WM., Will, 5-1821. Dev.:
Katharine, wife; Wm., Francis, Isaac,
Joseph, sons; Marg. Baker, Mary Hally,
Sarah Hally, Jane Smith, Susannah, daus.

WAUGH, RICHARD, Will, 12-1844. Dev.:
Sarah, mother; Sally, sis.; Jane Moore,
mother-in-law; Eliza, wife; Richars,
James, Joseph, David, Samuel, sons;
Maria, Martha, Eliza, Frances, Sarah,
daus.
WAUGH, RICHARD, Inv., 11-1846.
WELLS, AARON, Inv., 8-11-1829.
WELLS, ABSALOM, Will, no date. Dev.:
Wife Dorinda; dau.; others.
WELLS, ABSOLOM, Inv., 2-1-1821.
WELLS, ALEX., Will, 12-1812. Dev.: Leah,
wife; others.
WELLS, AMON, Will, 7-27-1829. Dev.:
Ruth, wife; Achsha, Susana, Temperance,
daus.; Downend, Robert, Francis, sons;
others.
WELLS, HENRY, Will, 2-1814. Dev.:
Jemimah, wife; Darius, Nathaniel, sons;
Airy Pumpry, Eliz. Owings, Editha Pum-
phry, Minerva, Leah, Miranda, daus.
WELLS, JESSE, Will, 3-1841. Dev.: Susan,
wife; Nancy, Eady, daus., James, Na-
thaniel, sons.
WELLS, RICHARD, Will, 10-31-1831. Dev.:
Jesse, son; Jemima, dau.
WELLS, ROBERT, Inv., 12-30-1828.
WELSH, ROBERT, Inv., 10-1842.
WHEELER, THOMAS, Inv., 5-1849.
WICOFF, JOACHAM, Will, 9-1841. Dev.:
Nancy, Hannah, Mary, daus., Peter, Cor-
nelius, sons; others.
WIGGINS, CHARITY, Inv., 8-7-1832.
WIGGINS, CHARITY, Will, 7-30-1832.
Dev.: Edw., son; Agnes, Marget, Neary,
Charity, Eliz., daus.
WILCOXEN, JOHN, Will, 1-28-1833. Dev.:
Eliz., wife; Henry, Jesse, sons; Patsy,
Love, Eliz., daus.; others.
WILCOXEN, MARY, Inv., 4-1840.
WILCOXON, GEO., Inv., 12-11-1821.
WILCOXON, HENRY, Inv., 11-1-1832.
WILCOXON, JOHN, Inv., 11-8-1828.
WILCOXON, JOHN, Inv., 2-7-1833.
WILEY, ELIZ., Will, 9-29-1834. Dev.:
Teiporch, Aseneth, Tersy, daus.
WILL, THOMAS, Inv., 4-16-1822.
WILLER, _____ Will, 3-1839. Dev.: Eliz.,
Polly, Cath., Nancy, Sarah, daus.; Jacob,
Peter, sons.
WILLIAMS, HANNAH, Will, 8-1850. Dev.:
Nieces and nephews.
WILLIAMS, JOHN, Will, 4-1845. Dev.:
Eliz., Mary, Emma, daus.; Hannah, Sarah,
sis.
WILLIAMS, JOHN, Inv., 5-1845.
WILLIAMS, MARG., Inv., 11-1842.
WILLIAMS, MARG., Will, 6-1843. Dev.:
Hannah, dau.; John, son.
WILLIAMS, ROBERT, Inv., 3-1836.
WILLIAMSON, WM., Will, . 10-4-1837.
Dev.: Wm., son; Charity, granddau.
WILLSON, ALEX., Will, 12-1810. Dev.:
Adam, Sam., sons.
WILSON, ADAM, Inv., 11-3-1823.
WILSON, ALEX., Inv., 6-29-1822.
WILSON, SAM., Inv., 2-1839.
WILSON, SAM., Inv., 4-1848.
WILSON, SAMUEL, Will, 1-1839. Dev.:
Samuel, John, Andrew, Wm., Alex.,
Adam, Reeves, sons; Nancy, wife; Jane,
Eliz., Narcissa, daus.
WILSON, SARAH, Inv., 12-1847.
WILSON, WM., Inv., 1-25-1821.
WINDON, THOMAS, Inv., 7-25-1820.
WINDSOR, THOMAS, Will, no date. Dev.:
Ann, wife; Eliza., dau.; Sam., Joshua,
sons.
WORK, DAVID, Inv., 10-14-1834.
WORK, DAVID, Will, 10-6-1834. Dev.:
Elizabeth, dau.

WORRELL, EDWARD, Will, 10-1838. Dev.: Marg. Evans and son; Sabra Gardner and son; others.
WORTHINGTON, NICH., Inv., 6-1841.
WORTHINGTON, NICHOLAS, Will, 3-1841. Dev.: Mary, wife; Samuel, Ellis, Nicholas, Caleb, David, Wm., sons; Rebecca, Eliz., daus.
WOODROW, JOSEPH, Inv., 3-14-1839.
WOODS, THOMAS, Inv., 9-15-1830.

WYLIE, JOHN, Inv., 4-1842.
WYLIE, JOHN, Will, 10-1840. Dev.: John, Andrew, Daniel, David, sons; Martha, Mary, daus.
WYLIE, ROBERT, Inv., 11-1841.
WYNN, MOSES, Inv., 3-25-1820.
YOUNG, ANDREW, Inv., 9-3-1834.

ZIELLY, JOHN, Inv., 12-1842.

West Virginia Estate Settlements

In 1936 and 1937, the West Virginia Commission on Historic and Scenic Markers, the Works Progress Administration, and the Federal Emergency Relief Administration compiled court records of the various counties, such as Births, Deaths, Marriages, and Wills. Under Wills were grouped subjects pertaining to Estate Settlements, including Wills, Inventories, and Appraisements. Copies of these county records were filed at the Department of Archives and History, Charleston; the Library of West Virginia University, Morgantown; and the DAR Library, Washington.

Believing that there would be particular interest on the part of the general public in the Estate Settlements, in the other counties, the West Virginia Historical Society has undertaken to abstract the Estate Settlements Records, as filed in the State Department of Archives and History, and offer them for publication in the *West Virginia History* Quarterly. No responsibility can be assumed as to the accuracy of the copies made from the original county records.

There are 13 counties which were formed prior to 1800, and it has been agreed to arrange these counties in chronological order, and to print their records from the earliest date to 1850. The formation dates of these counties are as follows: Hampshire—1753; Berkeley—1772; Monongalia—1776; Ohio—1776; Greenbrier—1778; Harrison—1784; Hardy—1786; Randolph—1787; Pendleton—1788; Kanawha—1788; Brooke—1797; Wood—1798; and Monroe—1799.

WOOD COUNTY, FORMED 1798

The abbreviations used in this material include: App.—appraisement; Bro.—brother; Dau.—daughter; Dev.—Devisees; Inv.—inventory; S.B.—sale bill; Set.—Settlement; Sis.—sister; Ven.—vendue.

ALLEN, ARGY, Will, 7-1830. Dev.: Junney, wife.
ALLEN, SAMUEL, Will, 5-1827. Dev.: Lydia Bartlet, Eliza, Mary, daus.; Wm., Jason, Geo., sons.
ANDERSON, JAMES, Will, 1842. Dev.: Eliz., wife.
BAILEY, ABRAHAM, Will, 1831. Dev.· Wife; Millery Combs, Allpie, Ida, Elnor Pickens, Eliz., daus.; Wm., John, Joseph, Geo., Sam., Martin, Caleb, sons.
BAILEY, ABSOLEM, Will, 8-1830. Dev.: Wife; Milly, Alpie, Ida, Elenor, Eliz., daus.; John, Joseph, Geo., Sam., Martin, Colet, sons.
BALDWIN, CHARLES, Will, 1839. Dev : Ann Eliz., wife; sons.
BARNES, ZEKIAL, Will, 1811. Dev.: Nelly, wife; Gater, Zekiel, Noah, sons.
BARRETT, JAMES, Will, 1842. Dev.: John, bro.
BARRETT, SAM., Will, 1838. Dev.: Jefferson, Wm., Henry, John, sons; others.
BARTLETT, AMOS, Will, 1815. Dev.:

Mary, wife; Hannah, Amos, Jacob, Selinda, sons.
BEASON, JACOB, Will, 12-22-1821. Dev.: Eliz., wife; Jonas, Jacob, sons; Rebecca, dau.
BEAUCHAMP, WM., Will, 10-26-1807. Dev.: Rachel, Eliz., daus.; Wife; Wm., Manlove, David, sons.
BIBBEY, ISAAC, Will, 12-1823. Dev.: Cynthia, wife; children.
BOOKER, JOHN, Will, 1842. Dev.: Mary, wife; others.
BUKEY, DRUSILLA, Will, 1850. Dev.: Eliz., dau.; Isaac, son.
BUTCHER, SAM., Will, 1844. Dev.: Thomas, son; Susan, dau.; others.

CAINES, JOHN, Will, 1827. Dev.: Rebecca, wife; Sally, Mary, Fanny, daus.
CALDWELL, JAMES, Will, 1825. Dev.: Eliz., wife; Wm., Edwin, sons; Jane, Harriet, daus.; others.
CALDWELL, JAMES, Will, 8-18-1847. Dev.: Eliz., wife; Wm., Edwin, sons; Jane; dau.; others.

COMPTON, CATH., Will, 10-18-1841. Dev.: Polly, Eliz. West; Jane Harness, daus.; Geo., son.

COOK, BENNET, Will, 1842. Dev.: John, son; Nora, wife.

COOK, JOHN, Will, 1827. Dev.: Marg., wife; Eliz., Prudence, Mary, Cath., Rayal, Ann, Rhoda, daus.; Tillinghast, John, Jos., sons.

COOK, JOHN, Will, 4-1827. Dev.: Marg., wife; Eliz., Prudence, Mary, Cath., Ann, Rhoda, daus.; Tillinghast, Royal, John, Jesse, sons.

COOK, JOSEPH, Will, 11-1824. Dev.: Rhoda, wife; Bennett, John, Joseph, Tillinghast, Pardon, sons; Phebe, Nancy, Sally, Bathsheba, Prudence, daus.

COONRAD DANIEL, Will, 1833. Dev.: Casa, wife; Barnes, son.

COOPER, HENRY, Will, 1844. Dev.: Henry, Lemiel, Benj., James, John, sons; Matt., slave.

CORNELL, JOHN, Will, 1835. Dev.: Mary, Eliz., daus.; Sheppard, Yates, Cornell, John, Geo., sons.

CORNELL, WM., Will, 1830. Dev.: Jane, wife.

CREEL, GEO., Will, 1825. Dev.: Mary, wife; Mary, dau.; Thomas, David, Alex., Geo., John, sons.

DARNEL, JOSHUA, Will, 10-21-1839. Dev.: Mary, wife; Joshua, son; Rheuhana, Hannah, Artinatice, Malissa, Ann, Willimine, daus.

DAVIS, ALLEN, Will, 5-1836. Dev.: Robert, Allen, Isaac, Geo., sons; Marg., Nancy, Betsey, daus.; Mary, wife; others.

DAVIS, JONATHAN, Will, 1849. Dev.: Thomas, Benj., Wm., sons; Eliz., dau.

DEWEY, JOSEPH, Will, 1850. Dev.: Jane, wife; Mary Brown, Milessa Wells, Olivia, Hectona, sis.; Joshua, Ward, Hiram, sons.

DILLS, PHILIP, Will, 8-3-1800. Dev.: Wm., John, sons; Amy, Eliz., Mary, daus.; Mary, wife.

DOLANS, MARY, Will, 1832. Dev.: Ellen, sis.; Mary Ann, Joann, daus.; others.

DONUREL, JOSHUA, Will, 1838. Dev.: Mary, wife; Rhubanna, Malissa, daus.

DUPERTY, ESTHER, Will, 11-1817. Dev.: Nancy Echols, dau.; Henry, Joshua, Wm., sons.

DYER, ED., Will, 12-1821. Dev.: Wife; Andrew, Wm., sons; Eliz., Susannah, Mary, daus.

EASTBORN, ESTHER, Will, 1812. Dev.: Rachel, dau.; grandchildren.

EDELIN, ROBERT, Will, 1849. Dev.: Jane David, Eliz., Logan, Frances Shaw, Mary Keen, daus.; Benj., son; others.

EDELIN, ROBERT, Will, 5-21-1849. Dev.: John, son; Lucydea Kincheloe, Frances, Mary Keen, daus.; others.

ESKRIDGE, HECTOR, Will, 5-1823. Dev.: Susan, wife; Thomas, Richard, Hamlet, sons.

FLAHERTY, JOHN, Will, 10-5-1801. Dev.: Hannah, Ruth, Martha, Michael, daus.; John, Jacob, James, Abraham, sons; others.

FOLEY, JAMES, Will, 1808. Dev.: Mary, wife; Fanny, Agnes, daus.; Bernard, Scartil, James, sons; others.

FOLEY, JAMES, Will, 5-1808. Dev.: Mary, wife; John, Gross, Barnet, sons; Fanny, dau.; Sam., father; others.

FOUGHTY, GEO., Will, 1807. Dev.: Wm., Jacob, John, sons; Eve, wife.

FOUGHTY, GEO., Will, 12-1807. Dev.: Wm., John, Isaac, sons; Eva, wife.

GARD, JOHN, Will, 1823. Dev.: Ann, wife; Samuel, Nathan, Ephram, Seth, John, Richard, Jeremiah, sons; Hannah, Rachel, Eliz., Keseah, daus.

GOFF, JAMES, Will, 1837. Dev.: Eliz., wife; John, Geo., Robt., Wm., sons; Moneca, Mary, Selby, Eliz., daus.

GRIFFIN, EBENEZER, Will, 1848. Dev.: Garret, Thomas, sons; Mary, Kesiah Dotson, Maria Roe, Aphus, daus.

GUINN, ELIZ., Will, 1850. Dev.: Thomas, Sam., Wm., bro.; Marg., wife; Polley, Lesstie, Sally, Nelly, daus.

HARNESS, SOLOMON, SR., Will, 9-27-1850. Dev.: Sarrah Rolston, Tabitha Foley, Hannah, Eliza, Fanny, Cath., daus.; wife; Granville, Geo., Solomon, sons.

HARWOOD, JOHN, Will, 1848. Dev.: Eliz. Bailey, Henrietta, daus.; Galsway, James, Geo., John, sons; others.

HENDERSON, RICHARD, Will, 4-4-1843. Dev.: Fenton, Robert, Thomas, Wm., Henry, John, sons; Mary, Garnett, Jarrett, Anne, Sally, daus.; Ora, wife.

HILL, JOHN, Will, 1-1823. Dev.: Agnes, wife; Wm., son; Sarah, Agnes, Marg., daus.

HILL, WM., Will, 10-20-1847. Dev.: Moses, Henry, John, Drastus, sons; Ledora, Malinda, daus.; other.

HILL, WM., Will, 1847. Dev.: Malinda, Lorena Kincheloe, daus.; Darestes, John, sons; others.

HOWARD, JOSEPH, Will, 2-9-1847. Dev.: Marg., Cath., daus.

HUTCHINSON, OLIVER, Will, 1846. Dev.: Harriet, wife; Geo., son; others.

HUTCHISON, OLIVER, Will, 3-20-1848. Dev.: Harriet Elliot, Sarah Vanlare, Adaline Bibby, daus.; Nathan, Geo., sons; others.

JAMES, ABEL, Will, 1848. Dev.: Jane, wife; Lemuel, son; Susannah, dau.

JOSEPH, JOSEPH, Will, 1838. Dev.: Nancy, wife; John, son; Marg., Charlotte, Nancy, Matilda, daus.; others.

KEEN, WM., Will, 1841. Dev.: Wm. Keen.

KEEN, WM., Will, 2-23-1842. Dev.: Susan, wife.

KELLER, FRANCES, Will, 10-1821. Dev.: Isaac, Elias, sons; Patsy, Barbary, Hannah, Eliz., Sallie, Riggs, Nancy Pugh, Rebecca Pugh, daus.

KELLEY, ST. CLAIR, Will, 8-1822. Dev.: Mary, wife; Charles, St. Clair, sons.

KINCHELOE, DANIEL, Will, 8-4-1834. Dev.: Nester, Daniel, Elijah, sons; Jane, wife; other.

KINCHELOE, ELIJAH, Will, 1842. Dev.: Daniel, son.

KINNAIRD, DAVID, Will, 1850. Dev.: Rachael Page, Martha, daus.; Geo., son; John, Jose, sons; Lavina, wife.

KINNAIRD, DAVID, Will, 1850. Dev.: Rachael Page, Martha, daus., Geo., son; Linna, wife; others.

KINNAIRD, JOHN, Will, 1848. Dev.: Mary, wife; Rufus, Alfred, sons; Mary, Gardner, dau.; others.

KINNAIRD, JOHN, Will, 5-20-1850. Dev.: Mary, wife; Rufus, Alfred, sons; Mary Server, daus.; others.

LEACH, BARTLETT, Will, 5-1824. Dev.: Marg., wife.

LEACH, FEIDING, Will, 1840. Dev.: James, Amilin, bro.; Mary, Jane, daus.; Thobe, son; others.

LEACH, JOHN, Will, 1835. Dev.: James, Thomas, John, Levi, Wm., sons.
LEACH, MARG., Will, 1825. Dev.: Friends.
LEE, HANNAH, Will, 11-20-1844. Dev.: Jesse, Peter, sons; Hanah, Sarah, daus.
LEE, JESS, Will, 6-1823. Dev.: Hannah, wife; children.
LEE, JOHN, Will, 1830. Dev.: wife; Thomas, bro.; Peter, grandson.
LEE, RICHARD, Will, 1838. Dev.: Nancy, wife; Amy Brown, Rhoda, Nancy, daus.; Wilson, son.
LEE, WILLIAMS, Will, 1827. Dev.: Jacob, sons.
LEWIS, GEO., Will, 1811. Dev.; Friends.
LEWIS, O. P., Will, 1850. Dev.: Wm., father; Mary, mother; Mary, sis.; Alfred, Ed., Francis, bros.
LOCKHART, JOHN, Will, 1832. Dev.: Christina, wife; Allas, Sarah, Eliz., Nancy, Mary, daus.; John, Wm., Isaac, sons.
LOGAN, HENRY, Will, 1845. Dev.: Eliz., wife; Susan, Anna, Marg., Martha, daus.; Wm., Henry, Albert, Randolph, John, Sam., sons.
LYNCH, WM., Will, 1787. Dev.: Wife; others.

MANN, JOHN, Will, 1833. Dev.: Polly, Parson, daus.
MAYBERRY, JOHN, Will, 1848. Dev.: Lucy, wife; Geo., son; others.
MAYHUGH, RICHARD, Will, Walker, John, Hiram, Richard, Freeman, sons.
McCALL, ROBT., Will, 1850. Dev.: nieces and nephews.
McFARLAND, ____, Will, 1846. Dev.: Eliz., dau.; Alfred, Thomas, John, sons.
McGLOUTHLIN, THOMAS, Will, 1841. Dev.: Hannah, wife; David, Edward, Thomas, sons; Martha McKane, Mariah Taylor, Sarah Gibson, daus.
McKENZEY, ANN, Will, 7-7-1812. Dev.: Rebecca, dau.; Benj., son.
McKENZIE, JOHN, Will, 1841. Dev.: Marg., wife; Alex., son; Isabella, Mary, Jane, Eliz., Sophia, daus.
McKINZEY, ANN JANE, Will, 1812. Dev.: Ann Rebecca, dau.; Robert, Benj., sons.
MEAD, MARY, Will, 12-1821. Dev.: Mary, dau.; nieces and nephews.
MILLER, NICHOLAS, Will, 1826. Dev.: Nicholas, Henry, Geo., sons; Cath. Taylor, friend.
MILLS, MARY, Will, 1849. Dev.: Jane Simpson, Ann Fairfax, Ruth Wood, sis.; Peyton, bro.
MILLS, MARY, Will, 1-22-1850. Dev.: Jane Simpson, Ann Fairfax, Rugh Woof, sis.; Peyton Mills, bro.
MITCHELEE, BENJ., Will, 1834. Dev.: Nancy, wife; Elisha, John, Yancy, Henry, sons; Frances, Rebecca, daus.
MORRISON, WM., Will, 1843. Dev.: Marg. Brookover, Sophie Owens, Isabella Morrison, Nancy Evans, Eliz. McClain, Rebecca Steponey, daus.; David, son.

NEAL, JAMES, Will, 1848. Dev.: Lewis, John, sons; Mary Ann, Sarah, Va. Murdock, daus.
NEALE, JAMES, Will, 4-1821. Dev.: Mary; dau.; James, son; Cath., niece.
NEALE, RICHARD, Will, 1839. Dev.; Eliz., wife.

ODDEN, NOAH, Will, 1849. Dev.: Daniel, Lewis, Silas, sons; Eliz., wife.

OTT, LEWIS, Will, 1833. Dev.: Joseph, Feddellis, John, sons; Kath., Casper, Susan, daus.
OWEN, JOHN, Will, 1826. Dev.: Owen, Michael, Ruhana, Neater, sons; Eliz. Seals, Mary Ponders, daus.
OWENS, JOHN, Will, 11-1826. Dev.: Owen, John, Michael, sons; Hannah, wife; Eliz. Seals, Mary Pounder, Ruhanna Moris, Nester Dunbar, Hannah Athey, daus.
OWINGS, THOMAS, Will, 2-1824. Dev.: Ruth, wife; Sam., Thomas, Isaac, Levi, David, sons; Betsy, Susannah, Ann, Matilda, daus.; others.

PADGET, CHARLES, Will, 1847. Dev.: Sonetta, James, sons; Sarah, Mary Ann, daus.
PENNYBACKER, D., Will, 1817. Dev.: Eliz., wife; Hannah, dau.
PILCHER, MOSES, Will, 9-1822. Dev.: Sarah, wife; Stephen, Alex., sons; Cazanda, Eliz., Hulda, daus.
POLK, WM., 1791. Dev.: Leah, wife; Leah Andrews, Sally, Ammy, daus.; Robt., son.
PREYMORE, WM., Will, 4-1819. Wife; grandchildren.
PROVANCE, JOSEPH, Will, 3-20-1846. Rachel, wife; Elisha, Uriah, Nassua, Salina, Rachel, daus.; David Benj., Jesse, Theron, Wm., Simon, sons; others.

RADCLIFF, WM., Will, 1827. Dev.: Susahhan Strahon, Cath. Gillispy, Sarah Carpenter, Martha Bonnett, Jane Stahon, Deborah Badgley, daus.; John, Stephen, sons.
RAQUET, CLADIUS PAUL, Will 1-1825. Dev.: Lydia, wife; children.
RAQUET, NICHOLAS, Will, 1-1825. Dev.: Cladius Paul, bro.
RAWSON, DAVID, Will, 1828. Dev.: Eliz, wife; Stephens, Elliot, James, John, David, sons.
REED, PHILIPS, Will, 1834. Dev.: Mary, wife; Nancy, dau.; John, Posey, Parkerson, sons.
REED, SAM., Will, 1847. Dev.: Arch., son; Ann, Emley, daus.
REED, SAM., Will, 9-17-1849. Dev.: Arch., Sam., Paul, Wilson, Mathew, sons; Annie, Emily, daus.; Susan, wife.
RHODES, WM., Will, 1849. Dev.: Susan, wife.
ROBINSON, JAMES, Will, 5-13-1850. Dev.: Mary Stagg, Prisila, daus.; Thomas, Edmond, sons, others.
ROCHOLD, CHARLES, Will, 10-1830. Dev.: Permilia, wife; Eliz. Corbitt, Sarah Copen, Louisa, Minerve, Saboah, daus.; Ezekiel, Charles, Geo., Maynard, Benj., John, sons. Maryan, dau.
ROCHOLD, MARYNARD, Will, 1814. Dev.: Selby, wife; Charles, son; Elnor, Eliz., Jemima, daus.
ROGERS, DANIEL, Will, 4-4-1825. Dev.: Eliz., wife; Anna, Martha, sis.; John, Henry, sons; Father; Eliz. Slade, Hannah, daus.; others.
ROWELL, WM., Will, 11-1816. Dev.: Hannah, wife.
RUBLE, MARY, Will, 1815. Dev.: Henry, John, sons; Heirs of Wm.; Ann Tyon, Eliz., Mary Dean, daus.
RUBLE, MARY, Will, 12-1815. Dev.: Lewis, Wm., sons; Anna Lyons, Eliz. Stephens, Mary Dean, daus.

SAMS, JONATHAN, Will, 2-4-1847. Dev.: Wife; James, Jonas, John, Jonathan, Daniel, Wm., David, sons.

SAMS, JONATHAN, Will, 2-4-1847. Dev.:
Wife; James, John, Jonas, Jonathan,
Daniel, Wm., sons.
SANDERS, NIMROD, Will, 1842. Dev.:
Sarah, wife.
SCHULTZ, C., Will, 1828. Dev.: Nancy,
wife; Marie, dau.; Michael, bro.
SCHULTZ, CHRISTIAN, Will. 4-17-1830.
Dev.: Nancy, wife; Marie, dau.; Michael,
husband of sister.
SHULTZ, CHRISTINA, Will, 1818. Dev.:
Nancy, wife: Marie, Nancy, daus.
SCHULTZ, MARIE MATILDA, Will, 1839.
Dev.: Nancy, mother.
SMITH, JOHN, Will, 8-11-1838. Dev.:
Eliz., wife; Ann, Sarah, Mary, Marg.,
Eliz., Susan, Jane, daus.; Thomas, Levi,
John, sons; Robert, bro.
SPENCER, JAMES, Will, 1826. Dev.:
Reuben Spencer.
STANFORD, JOHN, Will, 1818. Dev.:
Marg., wife; Marie, Sarah, Eliz., Alma,
Phoebe, daus.; Lewis, Reuben, sons.
STEPHENSON, THOS., Will, 1850. Dev.:
James Leach, gr. son, Sally Stephens,
niece.
STOKLY, _____ Will, 1790. Dev.: John
Conwell, friend.

TAVENNER, THOMAS, Will, 1850. Dev.:
Franklin, Thomas, Isaac, sons, others.
TAVENNER, THOMAS, Will, 1850. Dev.:
Franklin, Thomas, Isaac, Wm., sons;
Eliz., dau.; others.
TEMPLE JOHN, Will, 1812. Dev.: Family.
TIMMS, ELISHA, Will, 1842. Dev.: Phobe,
wife; Frances Buffington, dau.; others.

TRIPLETT, ROBERT, Will, 1843. Dev.:
Thoda, wife; Francis, Alfred, John,
sons; Benedicts, Frances, Ann, daus.
UHL, DAVID, Will, 1817. Dev.: Wife;
Ann Wolfe, Cath. Cradebough, daus;
Jacob, David, Geo, sons.
UHL, DAVID, Will, 1o-1818. Dev.: La.,
wife; Ann Woolf, Susanah Garner,
Cath., Cradelbough, daus.; Jacob, Geo.,
sons.
UHL, DAVID, Will, 1845. Dev.: Wil-
helmenia, wife; Geo., Peter, sons; Sarah,
dau.
UHL, DAVID, Will, 7-20-1846. Dev.: Wil-
berine, wife; Geo., Peter, sons; Sarah
Casey, Phoebe, Eliz., daus.

VANDIVER, LEWIS, Will, 3-1814. Dev.:
Thomas, Abraham, Archibald, Sam, sons;
Eliz., Nancy, Susan, Rashel, Joyce, daus.
VANLEER, ANDREE, Will, 1838. Dev.:
Mary, wife.
WELLS PHINEAS, Will, 1825. Dev.: Jane,
wife; Jane, Bertha, Hannah, Lydia, daus.,
David, Daniel, James, Wm., sons.

WILKINSON, JOSEPH, Will, 6-1824. Dev.:
Nancy, wife; Ezekiel, Calvin, sons.
WILLIAMS, ISAAC, Will, 11-1820. Dev.:
Rebecca, wife; Lucitice, sis.
WILLIAMSON, REBECCA, Will, 9-11-
1825. Dev.: J. A. Kinnard, nephew.
WOODYARD, PRESLEY, Will, 1838. Dev.:
Ann, wife; Richard, Jermot, sons; Ann,
Hanson, daus.

West Virginia Estate Settlements

In 1936 and 1937, the West Virginia Commission on Historic and Scenic Markers, the Works Progress Administration, and the Federal Emergency Relief Administration compiled court records of the various counties, such as Births, Deaths, Marriages, and Wills. Under Wills were grouped subjects pertaining to Estate Settlements, including Wills, Inventories, and Appraisements. Copies of these county records were filed at the Department of Archives and History, Charleston; the Library of West Virginia University, Morgantown; and the DAR Library, Washington.

Believing that there would be particular interest on the part of the general public in the Estate Settlements, in the older counties, the West Virginia Historical Society has undertaken to abstract the Estate Settlements Records, as filed in the State Department of Archives and History, and offer them for publication in the *West Virginia History* Quarterly. No responsibility can be assumed as to the accuracy of the copies made from the original county records.

There are 13 counties which were formed prior to 1800, and it has been agreed to arrange these counties in chronological order, and to print their records from the earliest date to 1850. The formation dates of these counties are as follows: Hampshire—1753; Berkeley—1772; Monongalia—1776; Ohio—1776; Greenbrier—1778; Harrison—1784; Hardy—1786; Randolph—1787; Pendleton—1788; Kanawha—1788; Brooke—1797; Wood—1798; and Monroe—1799.

MONROE COUNTY, FORMED 1799

The abbreviations used in this material include: App.—appraisement; Bro.—brother; Dau.—daughter; Dev.—Devisees; Inv.—inventory; L.S.—List of Sales; Set.—Settlement; Sis.—sister.

ABBOTT, JOHN, Inv., 11-1830.
ABBOTT, JOHN, L.S., 1-1833.
ADAIR, WILLIAM, Will, 3-1849. Dev.: Robert, James, nephews; wife; others.
ALDERSON, JOHN, Will, 5-15-1821. Dev.: John, son; Sally, wife; Peggy Smithson, dau.; others.
ALEXANDER, CHARLES, Will, 6-22-1841. Dev.: James H., bro.; Elizabeth Keenan, Harriet, sis.; others.
ALEXANDER, CHARLES, Set., 2-1848.
ALEXANDER, ELIZABETH, Inv., 8-1850.
ALEXANDER, ELIZABETH, L.S., 11-1850.
ALEXANDER, HENRY, Inv., 9-7-1814.
ALEXANDER, HENRY, Set., 12-1827.
ALEXANDER, ISABELLA, Inv., 9-7-1814.
ALEXANDER, ISABELLA, Will, 11-1834. Dev.: Henry, Andrew, sons; Mary Chapman, Jane Dunlap, Catherine Shanklin, Elizabeth Byrnside, daus.; others.
ALEXANDER, ISABELLA, L.S., 8-1836.

ALEXANDER, JAS., 7-1814. Dev.: Isabella, wife; Andrew, Michael, Henry, Mathew, sons; Jane Dunlap, Catherine Shanklin, Elizabeth Byrnside, Mary Chapman, daus.; others.
ALEXANDER, JAMES, Inv., 9-7-1814.
ALEXANDER, JANE, Will, 8-1833. Dev.: Samuel, James, Mathew, sons; Margaret, Susannah, Mary, Jane, daus.; others.
ALEXANDER, JOHN, Inv., 10-1830.
ALEXANDER, MATHEW, Inv., 9-7-1814.
ALEXANDER, MATHEW, Will, 8-1825. Dev.: Mathew, John, James, Andrew, sons; Jane, wife; others.
ALEXANDER, MATHEW, L.S., 10-1829.
ALEXANDER, MATHEW, Will, 5-1831. Dev.: wife; children.
ALEXANDER, MATHEW, Gdn. (James M. Byrnside), Set., 2-1832.
ALEXANDER, MATHEW, Set., 11-1843.

ALFORD, JOHN, Will, 6-1810. Dev.: John, James, Thomas, sons; Margaret, Sarah, Jane, daus.; Jane, wife.
ALFORD, JOHN, Inv., 7-1834.
ALFORD, JOHN, L.S., 10-1834.
ALFORD, JOSEPH, Inv., 7-20-1819.
ALFORD, JOSEPH, Inv., 2-1839.
ALFORD, JOSEPH, L.S., 12-1840.
ALFORD, JOSEPH, Set., 6-16-1845.

BAKER, DAVID, L.S., 4-1837.
BAKER, DAVID, Will, 9-1840. Dev.: Jacob, Madison, sons; Ann, Catherine Ragland, daus.
BAKER, FREDERICK, Will, 8-1830. Dev.: John, Joseph, Frederick, sons; Sally Piles, Betsy Givings, daus.; Elizabeth, wife.
BAKER, FREDERICK, L.S., 9-1830.
BALDWIN, CLARA, Gdn., Set., 8-1849.
BALDWIN, ELIZABETH, Gdn., Set., 8-1849.
BALDWIN, HARRIET, Gdn., Set., 8-1849.
BALDWIN, WILLIAM H., Gdn., Set., 8-1849.
BALL, REUBEN, Inv., 11-1839.
BALLARD, JABIN, Will, 2-19-1822. Dev.: Patsy, sis.; Squire, bro.; others.
BALLARD, WM., Will, 4-15-1800. Dev.: Betty, wife.
BALLENGER, JEAN, Will, 2-19-1805. Dev.: Elizabeth, Susan, Jane, Florence, daus.; George, Isaac, Henry, sons.
BASFORD, JOHN, Inv., 6-20-1815.
BATTERCUP, WM., Set., 2-1830.
BEAMER, PHILIP, Set., 1-1848.
BECKNER, JOHN, Inv., 3-1833.
BECKNER, JOHN, L.S., 4-1833.
BECKNER, MARY, Will, 6-1849. Dev.: Amanuel, Mathew, sons; Rachael, Sarah, daus.; others.
BEEMER, PHILLIP, Will, 12-17-1838. Dev.: Elizabeth, wife; George, John, Benjamin, Joseph, Phillip, Michael, Henry, sons; Sarah Crosier, dau.; others.
BEIRNE, ANDREW P., Inv., 9-1843.
BEIRNE, ANDREW, L.S., 7-1844.
BEIRNE, ANDREW, Will, 8-1845. Dev.: Andrew, Jr., George, Oliver, sons; Mary D. Steenberger, Susan Patten, Nancy McFarland, Elen, daus.; others.
BEIRNE, COL. ANDREW, Set., 10-1849.
BEIRNE, GEORGE, Inv., 12-29-1832.
BEIRNE, GEORGE, L.S., 1-1835.
BEIRNE, MICHEAL, Gnd., Set., 11-1846.
BEIRNE, MICHEAL A., Gnd., Set., 2-1848.
BEIRNE, OLIVER, Gnd., Set., 2-1848.
BEIRNE, OLIVER F., Gnd., Set., 7-1849.
BENSON, ERVIN, Will, 10-20-1818. Dev.: Mary, wife; Nelly Clark, Jane Carruthers, Margaret Erskine, Elizabeth, daus.; others.
BENSON, MATHIAS, L.S., 2-11-1809.
BiCKETT, MICHAEL, Inv., 11-15-1814.
BICKETT, MICHAEL, L.S., 8-25-1814.
BICKETT, MICHAEL, Set., 8-1829.
BINSON, MARTRIAS, Inv., 2-11-1809.
BLACK, WILLIA, Inv., 5-21-1822.
BLAND, JESSE, Will, 8-1835. Dev.: Henry Hoke.
BOGGESS, SAMUEL, Inv., 6-1848.
BOGGESS, SAMUEL, L.S., 6-1848.
BOGGESS, SAMUEL, Set., 8-1848.
BOGGESS, SETH, Will, 5-1833. Dev.: Edith, wife; Samuel, Andrew, Benjamin, Thompson, sons; Polly Caldwell, Betsy Smith, daus.
BOGGESS, SETH, L.S., 6-1833.
BOGGESS, THOMAS, Will, 1-1832. Dev.: Mary, wife; Seth, Enoch, Elisha, Nimrod, Abraham, sons; Mary Ann Berry, Phebe Pinnell, Judith Fife, Martha Morgan, daus.

BOGGESS, THOMAS, L.S., 3-1832.
BOWDEN, JOHN, Will, 1-16-1821. Dev.: Katherine, wife; James, John, sons; Eleanor, Katherine, Sarah, Mary, Nancy, Seleny, Margaret, daus.
BOWYER, ABRAHAM, Inv., 1-1836.
BOWYER, ADAM, Will, 4-15-1800. Dev.: Christina, wife; Jacob, Isaac, Reuben, sons; Liza Koontz, Barbary King, Susy Arnot, Sally, Margaret Bowyer, Magdaleen Bowyer, daus.
BOWYER, ADAM, L.S., 9-15-1800.
BOWYER, CHRISTINA, Inv., 1-1826.
BOWYER, CHRISTINA, L.S., 1-1826.
BOYD, ELEANOR, Will, 9-1847. Dev.: William, son.
BOYD, ELEANOR, L.S., 10-1847.
BOYD, JAMES, Will, 5-1846. Dev.: Florence, wife; Thomas, John, Nathan, sons; Jane McDowell, dau.
BOYD, JAMES, L.S., 9-1847.
BOYD, JAMES, Set., 6-1849.
BOYD, PATRICK, Will, 3-1835. Dev.: Ann, wife; Robert, Porterfield, sons; Jane Hawkins, Esther Foster, Nancy Bickett, Peggy Hill, Nelly, daus.; others.
BOYD, PATRICK, Inv. 4-1835.
BOYD, PATRICK, L.S., 2-1837.
BOYD, PATRICK, Set., 12-1844.
BROWN, ALEXANDER, Will, 9-17-1822. Dev.: Thomas, John, Samuel, sons; Polly, dau.
BROWN, ALEXANDER, Set., 11-1839.
BROWN, JOHN, Set., 3-1827.
BROWN, WILLIAM, Will, 6-1806. Dev.: John, Alexander, William, sons; Mary, Jane, Sarah, Peggy, Rosey, daus.; others.
BROWN, WILLIAM, L.S., 10-20-1818.
BROWN, WILLIAM, Inv., 2-1824.
BROYLES, AARON, Will, 1-1837. Dev.: Lyddy, wife; John, son; Lucy, dau.; others.
BROYLES, AARON, L.S., 1-1838.
BROYLES, DANIEL, Inv., 9-16-1823.
BROYLES, DANIEL, L.S., 1-1824.
BROYLES, PETER, Will, 6-1824. Dev.: John, Aaron, Zachariah, Solomon, Ephraim, Absolem, Jacob, sons; Peggy Campbell, dau.; others.
BROYLES, PETER, L.S., 8-1825.
BUDD, MARY, L.S., 2-1846.
BUDD, UNDREL, Will, 5-1844. Dev.: Wife.
BULLEY, URIAH, Will, 12-1835. Dev.: America, wife; James, St. Clair, Edwin, sons; Amanda, Belinda, Hetty, Jane, daus.
BURDETTE, ARCHIBALD, Will, 7-1834. Dev.: Margaret, wife; James, Archibald, sons; Elizabeth Holmes, Margaret, Polly, daus.
BURDETTE, GILES, Inv., 2-1830.
BURDETTE, GILES, L.S., 11-1830.
BURNS, MAGNESS, Inv., 10-1838.
BURNES, MAGNESS, L.S., 10-1838.
BURNS, THOMAS, Will, 8-1849. Dev.: Phillip Collins, nephew; others.
BUTTERCUP, WM., L.S., 11-1829.
BYRNSIDE, JOHN, Will, 10-15-1817. Dev.: Elizabeth, wife; James, John, Isaac, sons; Elizabeth, Jane, Juliana, daus.
BYRNSIDE, JOHN, Will, 5-1836. Dev.: Elizabeth, mother, others.
BYRNSIDE, JOHN, L.S., 11-1836.
BYRNSIDE, JOHN, Set., 9-15-1845.

CALDER, ALCER, Will, 9-1849. Dev.: Christian Robertson, sis.; others.
CALLAWAY, ZACHARIAH, Will, 11-19-1816. Dev.: Ellender, wife; Andrew, James, Charles, Joshua, sons; Patty, Peggy, Nancy, Sally, Betsey, Priscilla, daus.

CALLAWAY, ZACHARIAH, L.S., 1-21-1817.

CALLAWAY, ZACHARIAH AND ELEANOR, Set., 11-1849.

CAMPBELL, ARCHIBALD, Inv., 12-1836.

CAMPBELL, ARCHIBALD, L.S., 10-1838.

CAMPBELL, DALILAH, Gdn., Set., 7-1849.

CAMPBELL, JOHN, Will, 8-4-1837. Dev.: Wife; John, son; Margaret, dau.

CAMPBELL, JOHN, L.S., 6-1840.

CAMPBELL, ROBERT, Will, 6-1847. Dev.: Andrew, Caperton, Mathew, Lewis, Robert, Isaac, sons; Jane Holsapple, Sarah Skaggs, Mary Patton, daus.; others.

CAMPBELL, SAMUEL, Will, 1-1814. Dev.: Margaret, wife; Samuel, Isaac, William, sons; Mary D. Ellisen, Jene, Sarah Steel, Rebeckah, daus.

CAMPBELL, WM., Will, 5-1827. Dev.: James, William, Thomas, Alin, Sires, sons; Sarah Hutchinson, wife; Polly Caldwell, Matty Chandler, Emily, daus.

CAMPBELL, WILLIAM, L.S., 7-1827.

CANTLEY, SAMUEL, Inv., 5-28-1810.

CAPERTON, HUGH, Inv., 9-30-1816.

CAPERTON, HUGH, Set., 9-18-1821.

CAPERTON, HUGH, Will, 2-1847. Dev.: Lewis, Allen, William, John, Hugh, George, sons; Mary Jane Echols, Sarah Ann, Elizabeth Rude, daus.; others.

CAPERTON, HUGH, Set., 5-1849.

CARDEN, JOSEPH, Will, 4-21-1818. Dev.: Mary, wife; Isaac, John, Allen, Robert, Joseph, sons; Rachael, Mary, Nancy Reed, Elizabeth Wray, Jane Walker, daus.

CARLILE, ROBERT, Will, 6-17-1823. Dev.: Mary, wife; John, Joseph, Samuel, James, sons; Nancy, Mary, Peggy, Jane Graham, Betsy Hawkins, daus.

CARLISLE, ROBERT, L.S., 6-1824.

CARNIFAX, WILLIAM, Will, 6-1836. Dev.: Jerry, Judy, Mary, Adaline, Sabra, slaves.

CARNIFAX, WILLIAM, L.S., 7-1836.

CARR, JOHN, Inv., 3-1832.

CARR, JOHN, L.S., 3-1832.

CHAMBERS, JAMES, Will, 11-1823. Dev.: Janie, wife; others.

CHAMBERS, ROBERT, Will, 11-1836. Dev.: Jacob, Richard, James, William, sons; Katherine, Anna Ballard, daus.; others.

CHAPMAN, SUSANNA, L.S., 12-6-1829.

CHAPMAN, SUSANNA, Inv., 2-1830.

CHARLTON, ALLICE, Will, 11-1836. Dev.: John, bro.; Ann R. McLaughlin, Mary Perry, Lattice, Isabela Humpreys, sisters; others.

CHARLTON, ALLICE, L.S., 1-1837.

CHARLTON, JOSEPH, Gnd., Set., 2-1848.

CHARLTON, LATTICE, Will, 12-1837. Dev.: Eleanor Charlton, Mary Perry, Ann McLaughlin, nieces; others.

CHARLTON, THOMAS, Will, 4-1819. Dev.: Thomas, Joseph, sons; Isabella Humphrey, dau.

CHARLTON, THOMAS, Will, 6-21-1841. Dev.: Polly, wife; Joseph T., Thomas, sons; others.

CHARLTON, THOMAS, L.S., 6-1843.

CHARLTON, THOMAS, Set., 2-1848.

CHEWNING, KELLIS, Will, 8-1845. Dev.: Nancy, wife; Burwell, John, Walter, sons; Polly Morgan, Sarah Hubart, Elizabeth Baber, daus.

CHEWNING, KELLIS, L.S., 9-1846.

CHEWNING, KELLIS, Set., 10-1849.

CHISTY, JAMES, Will, 3-16-1840. Dev.: Catherine, wife; Robert, James, sons; Isabel Bealey, dau.; others.

CLARK, ALEXANDER, L.S., 6-1849.

CLARK, ALEXANDER, Set., 6-1849.

CLARK, RALPH, Will, 7-1829. Dev.: Elizabeth, wife; John, Alexander, James, Robert, sons; Elizabeth Lou, Rebecca Riffe, Sarah Ann, Agnes, daus.

CLARK, RALPH, Inv., 6-1830.

CLARK, RALPH, L.S., 6-1830.

CLARK, SARAH, Will, 12-1809. Dev.: James, William, Ralph, Alexander, John, Samuel, sons; Rebecah Cantley, Martha, Campbell, daus.; others.

CLARK, JAMES, Will, 8-18-1801. Dev.: Sarah Laferty, dau.; Alexander, John, sons; wife.

COLLINS, JAMES, Will, 12-17-1820. Dev.: Jno. McNutt, Ruth McNutt, friends.

COMER, AUGUSTINE, Set., 5-1826.

COMER, FREDERICK, Inv., 2-1849.

COMER, FREDERICK, L.S., 2-1849.

COMER, WILLIAM, Will, 6-1849. Dev.: Mitchell, Amanda, Mary Jane.

COMER, WILLIAM M., L.S., 11-1849.

COOK, JACOB, Will, 5-1844. Dev.: Rachael, wife; Riley, Ward, Jacob, Lewis, John H., Lorenzo, sons; Polly Bell, Nancy Walker, Caroline, Sarah, daus.

COOK, JACOB, L.S., 8-1845.

COOK, JACOB, Set., 12-1846.

COOK, WILLIAM, Inv., 7-17-1821.

COOK, WILLIAM, Set., 1-1825.

CORNWILL, EDWARD, Will, 9-1808. Dev.: Clary, Frances, Mary, Jane, daus.; Samuel C., son.

CRAWFORD, ARCHIBALD, Inv., 12-1815.

CRAWFORD, GIDEON, Inv., 10-1831.

CRAWFORD, GIDEON, L.S., 10-1831.

CROMWELL, ELIJAH, Inv., 6-1805.

CROW, JAMES, Will, 3-20-1821. Dev.: John, Joseph, sons; Fanny Brown, Jane Broun, Polly Mills, daus.; others.

CUMMINS, ROBERT, Will, 6-21-1841. Dev.: Wife; Charles, Gordon, John, sons; Fanny Ellis, Polly Paul, Betsey Gibson, daus.; others.

CUMMINS, ROBERT, Set., 1-1844.

CUMMINS, ROBERT, Set., 9-1844.

CURRY, JOHN, Inv., 1-16-1821.

CURRY, JOSIAH, Inv., 8-1848.

DAVIS, JOHN, Inv., 3-1833.

DAVIS, JOHN, L.S., 5-1833.

DAVIS, WILLIAM, Will, 11-18-1815. Dev.: Mary, wife; Editha, dau.; Jacob, son.

DEBOY, JOHN, Will, 6-1829. Dev.: Betsey, wife; Uley Cox, Caty Inchminger, Margaret Cook, daus.

DEBOY, JOHN, L.S., 8-1829.

DEBOY, JOHN, Set., 8-1833.

DERIEUX, WILLIAM, Inv., 6-1838.

DETEMORE, CHRISTIAN, Will, 3-1849. Dev.; Lucinda, wife.

DEW, BETTY, Inv., 8-19-1817.

DICKASON, JOHN, Will, 1-1840. Dev.: Jesse, Samuel, Charles, Jacob, Reubin, sons; Elizabeth Stodghill, Margaret Thompson, daus.; others.

DICKASON, JOHN, L.S., 6-1840.

DICKASON, LEVI, L.S., 11-1826.

DICKASON, LEVY, Inv., 8-1826.

DICKASON, THOMAS, Inv., 6-20-1815.

DICKSON, RICHARD, Will, 6-1814. Dev.: Isabella, wife; Richard, John, sons; Elizabeth, dau.; others.

DICKSON, RICHARD, Inv., 4-29-1817.

DILLION, GREGOR, Inv., 3-1849.

DILLION, GREGOR, L.S., 3-1849.

DIXON, JOSEPH, Inv., 12-26-1805.

DONNELLY, PATRICK, Will, 3-1850. Dev.: Andrew, James, sons; others.

DOREN, CATHERINE, Will, 8-1821. Dev.:
Catherine Johnson, Christen Ellis, Mary
Garrod, Hannah Chambers, daus.
DRUMMOND, GEO., Inv., 6-1824.
DRUMMOND, GEORGE, L.S., 5-1832.
DRUMMOND, GEORGE, Set., 6-1832.
DUNLAP, ALEXANDER, Will, 4-19-1841.
Dev.: James A., Addison, Benjamin,
Alexander, sons; Mary Jane, dau.; others.
DUNLAP, JAMES A., Will, 9-1843. Dev.:
Frances, wife; Addison, Alexander, Ben-
jamin, bros.; Mary Jane, Isabella Haynes,
sis.; others.
DUNLAP, JAMES A., L.S., 5-1844.
DUNLAP, JOHN R., Gdn. Set., 3-1849.
DUNLAP, ROBERT, Inv., 1-1831.
DUNLAP, ROBERT, L.S., 1-1831.
DUNN, JOHN, Will, 3-19-1822. Dev.: Is-
abella, wife; William, Harrison, sons;
Betsy, Susay, Anna, Polly, Nancy, daus.
DUNN, JOHN, Inv., 10-1823.
DUNN, REUBEN, Inv., 5-1844.
DUNN, REUBEN, L.S., 8-1844.
DUNN, THOMAS, Will, 8-1837. Dev.:
Mary, wife; John, James, Joseph, Madi-
son, Westley, Harrison, sons; Elizabeth
Phillips, Louisa Jane, Nancy Karnes,
Polly Dunn, daus.
DUNN, WM. T., Set., 4-11-1827.
DUNN, WILLIAM, Set., 8-1830.
DUNSMORE, JAMES, Will, 12-17-1838.
Dev.: James, William, Joseph, sons.

EAGAN, JOHN, Will, 5-21-1816. Dev.:
Elizabeth, wife; Polly Smith Elleanor
Ellis, Elizabeth Ellis, daus.; others.
ELKINS, WILLIAM, Inv., 6-20-1815.
ELKINS, WILLIAM, L.S., 6-20-1815.
ELLIS, JACOB, Set., 12-1830, 2-1835, 3-
1839.
ELLIS, JOHN, L.S., 1-1825.
ELLIS, JOHN, Will, 11-1825. Dev.: Joseph,
son.
ELLIS, JOSEPH, L.S., 6-1830.
ELLIS, JOSEPH, Inv., 6-1830.
ELLISON, ABRAHAM, L.S., 11-1839.
ELLISON, ABRAHAM, Set., 3-1841.
ELLISON, JAMES, Will, 2-18-1839. Dev.:
Elizabeth, wife; Francis, Joseph, sons;
Massy Cantly, Nancy Halstead, Elizabeth
Shumate, Ruth Smith, Polly Wilson, daus.;
others.
ELLISON, JANE, L.S., 12-1832.
ELLISON, JANE, Inv., 3-1833.
ELLISON, JOHN, Will, 7-21-1845. Dev.:
Joseph, John, James, Jesse, sons; Eliza-
beth, Ruth, Eleanor, Nancy, Hannah,
Jaley, daus.
ELLISON, MATT, Inv., 1-1831.
ELLISON, MATT, L.S., 5-1831.
ENSMINGER, PHILLIP, Will, 4-1807.
Dev.: Cally, wife; Susan Miller, Cathy,
Platts, Elizabeth Hunter, Mary M. Vance,
daus.; Andrew, Joshua, Henry, Elijah,
Anthony, Phillip, sons.
ERSKINE, MICHAEL, Will, 9-1812. Dev.:
Margaret, wife; Michael, William, Alex-
ander, Henry, sons; Jane Caperton, dau.,
others.
EWING, JAMES, Inv., 1-1834.
EWING, JAMES, L.S., 4-1834.
EWING, JAMES, Set., 1-1846.
EWING, JOSEPH, Inv., 1-21-1823.
EWING, JOSEPH, Set., 2-1835.
EWING, OLIVER, Will, 6-1823. Dev.:
Oliver Ewing, Sidney; others.
EWING, OLIVER, L.S., 3-1824.
EWING, OLIVER, Will, 12-1847. Dev.:
Frances, Sidney Nelson, sisters; Joseph,
John, bros.

EWING, OLIVER, Set., 7-1850.
EWING, ROBERT, Set., 1-1831.
EWING, SAMUEL, Inv., 6-20-1815.
EWING, SAMUEL, L.S., 10-15-1816.
EWING, SAMUEL, Set., 3-21-1822.
EWING, WILLIAM, Will, 3-17-1818. Dev.:
Joseph, bro.; others.

FARLEY, FRANCIS, Inv., 1-1802.
FARRELL, WM., Will, 3-9-1818. Dev.:
Caty, wife; John, son; Mary, Lucy, Eliza-
beth, Nancy, daus.
FISHER, ISAAC, Will, 7-1824. Dev.: Polly,
wife; Isaac, William, sons, Isabella, Rach-
ael, Polly Crawford, daus.
FISHER, ISAAC, L.S., 6-1825.
FLANNAGAN, GEORGE, Inv. 10-1850.
FLESHMAN, JOHN, Inv., 5-19-1845.
FLESHMAN, JOHN, L.S., 6-16-1845.
FLESHMAN, MICHAEL, Will, 12-1826.
Dev.: Mary, wife; John, Thomas, Elijah,
Abraham, sons; Mary, Sarah, Mina,
daus.; others.
FLESHMAN, MICHAEL, L.S., 7-1828.
FLESHMAN, MICHAEL, Set., 4-1842.
FLESHMAN, PETER, Will, 3-1814. Dev.:
Hannah, wife; John, Benjamin, sons;
Elizabeth, dau.
FLESHMAN, PETER, L.S., 8-15-1815.
FORD, JOHN, L.S., 7-1835.
FORELANDER, LEWIS, L.S., 1-1827.
FORLANDER, LEWIS, Inv., 3-26-1825.
FORS, JOHN, Will, 5-1833. Dev.: Ben-
jamin, son.
FRAMBROUGH, JAMES, Will, 3-1-1818.
Dev.: William, bro.; others.
FRIEND, CHARLES, Inv., 11-21-1816.
FRIGG, STEPHEN, Inv., 5-20-1807.

GABBART, WM. H. & SARAH E., Set.,
11-1849.
GABBERT HEIRS, Gnd., Set., 2-1848.
GALAHORN, EDWARD, Will, 10-15-1800.
Dev.: Temperance, wife; Edward, John,
sons; Betsey, dau.
GARTEN, CHARLES, Set., 3-1830.
GARTEN, GRIFFITH, Set., 11-1844.
GARTEN, ZACHARIAH, L.S., 1-1815.
GARTIN, CHARLES, Inv., 2-1828.
GARTIN, CHARLES, L.S., 2-1828.
GARTIN, GRIFFITH, Will, 7-1835. Dev.:
Children; others.
GARVIN, SAMUEL, L.S., 3-19-1816.
GARVIN, WESTTLEY, Will, 2-1832. Dev.:
Mother; Jane Ellison, Margaret Byrnside,
Phede Garvin, sisters.
GARVIN, WESTLEY, 3-1833.
GATLIFF, MARTHA, Will, 7-16-1799.
Dev.: Charles, son; Mary Pine, Leah
Toney, Hannah Neelly, Happy Willey,
Abby, Tremble, daus.; others.
GIBSON, HENRY, Will, 9-1808. Dev.:
Deecy, wife; Betsey, Rebecca, Nancy,
Priscella, daus., Jonathan, son.
GIVEN, SUSAN, Will, 5-1841. Dev.:
Mother; father; bro.; Nancy Irons, sis.;
others.
GLENN, JAMES, Will, 11-1841. Dev.:
James Young, nephew; others.
GORDON, CHARLES, Inv.: 6-18-1807.
GRAHAM, DAVID, Inv., 12-2-1818.
GRAHAM, DAVID, L.S., 9-16-1823.
GRAHAM, ELIZABETH, & SUSAN, Gdn.
Set., 6-1842.
GRAHAM, FLORENCE, Will, 12-1824.
Dev.: William, son; Jane Garrett, Eliza-
beth, Stodghill, Florence Stodghill, daus.;
others.
GRAHAM, FLORENCE, L.S., 12-1826.

GRAHAM, JAMES, Will, 2-1813. Dev.: Florence, wife; William, David James, Lanty, Samuel, sons; Elizabeth Stodghill, Jane Garrah, Rebeckah, Florence Taylor, daus.
GRAHAM, LANTY, Inv., 6-1840.
GRAHAM, LANTY, L.S., 10-1840.
GRAHAM, LANTY, Set., 6-1844.
GRAHAM, SAMUEL, Inv., 6-1824.
GRAHAM, SAMUEL, L.S., 6-1824.
GRAHAM, SAMUEL, Inv., 7-1834.
GRAHAM, WILLIAM, Will, 7-1836. Dev.: Katherine, wife; William, James, sons; Betsy, dau.
GRAHAM, WILLIAM, L.S., 6-1837.
GRAY, ARCHIBALD, L.S., 1-1831.
GRAY, ARCHIBALD, Inv., 3-1831.
GRAY, JOHN SR., Will, 11-18-1801. Dev.: John, James, Archibald, sons, Jennett, wife; others.
GRAY, JOHN, Will, 2-19-1822. Dev.: Mary, wife; James, Henry, John, Archibald, sons, Margaret, Jenny, Elizabeth, Mary, Rebecca, daus.
GREEN, DANIEL, Inv., 2-1813.
GREEN, JESSE, Will, 10-1824. Dev.: George, Benjamin, Whitson, Thos., Elija, sons; Penelope Campbell, Nancy Shumate, Elizabeth Larew, daus.
GREEN, JESSE, L.S., 12-1824.
GREEN, JESSE, Set., 1-1833.
GREGORY, JAMES, Will, 3-19-1822. Dev.: Jane, wife; others.
GRIFFITH, WILLIAM, Inv., 5-1805.
GRIFFITH, WILLIAM, L.S., 1-2-1807.
GULLETT, WILLIAM, Will, 3-20-1805. Dev.: Jean, wife; George, William, sons; Peggy, Polly Leach, Elizabeth Whorton, daus.
GWINN, ROBERT, Will, 5-17-1841. Dev.: Sarah, wife; James, Robert Thompson, sons; Margaret Viney, Salithiel, Elizabeth, daus.; others.
GWINN, ROBERT, L.S., 9-1841.
GWINN, ROBERT, Set., 12-1844.
GWINN, WILLIAM, Inv., 10-15-1822.

HALL, JOHN, Will, 8-20-1822. Dev.: Children.
HALL, JOHN, Inv., 11-19-1822.
HAM, JOSEPH, Will, 10-15-1799.
HANAH, DANIEL, Inv., 5-1807.
HANDLEY, JAMES, Set., 11-1844.
HANDLEY, JOHN, Will, 2-1811. Dev.: William, John, Isacc, Alexander, Archibald, Samuel, James, sons; Margaret Clark, Sarah Keys, Nancy Aken, Betsy Walker, daus., others.
HANDLEY, JOHN, L.S., 6-18-1816.
HANDLEY, LOUISA, Will, 3-1844. Dev.: John Gill, Zenas Handley, bros.
HANDLEY, MARY ANN, Will, 12-1844. Dev.: Henrietta, Elizabeth, Williams, daus.; James Burke, others.
HANDLEY, WILLIAM, Will, 9-1840. Dev.: Margaret, wife; Zena, John, Jabez, Logan, Henderson, Constantine, sons; Ruthy Lindy, Betse Polly, Lenny, daus.; others.
HANDLY, JAMES, Inv., 2-1847.
HANDLY, WILLIAM, Set., 1-1844.
HANK, JOHN, Will, 9-1831. Dev.: Rebecca, wife, Thomas, son; Eliza Jane, Margaret Susannah, daus.
HANLY, JAMES, Will, 11-1840.
HANLY, MARY ANN, L.S., 5-19-1845.
HARPER, HANNAH, Gnd. New Set., 2-1826.
HARPER, JAMES, Inv., 5-27-1817.
HARPER, JOHN, Will, 7-1819. Dev.: Samuel, son; Polly Bowers, dau.; others.
HARRIS, NANCY, Inv., 6-16-1845.
HARRIS, NANCY, L.S., 2-1847.

HARRIS, ZEPHENIAH, Will, 2-17-1840. Dev.: Booker S. Peck.
HARVEY, NICHOLAS, Will, 12-1826. Dev.: John, James, sons, Sally, wife.
HARVEY, NICHOLAS, Set., 1-1840.
HAYNES, JOSEPH, Will, 2-1847. Dev.: Henry, John, sons; others.
HAYNES, JOSEPH, L.S., 6-1848.
HAYNES, JOSEPH, Add. Inv., 12-1849.
HAYNES, WILLIAM, Will, 5-1819. Dev.: Magdalen, wife; Agnes Erskine, dau.; James, Andrew, William, Thomas, sons; others.
HEATLY, JAMES, Will, 8-1809. Dev.: Henry, bro.; others.
HERBERT, JOHN, Will, 2-1841. Dev.: Martha, wife; Williams, John W., sons; Margaret Beckner, Eleanor D. Stone, daus.
HICKENBOTTOM, MARY, Will, 11-19-1816.
HICKENBOTTOM, MOSES, Will, 2-19-1805. Dev.: Mary, wife; Andrew, James, sons.
HIGGINBOTHAM, JANE, L.S., 12-1850.
HIGGINBOTHAM, THOMAS, L.S., 3-1847.
HIGGINBOTHAM, THOMAS, Will, Dev.: Jane, wife; Moses, son; Catherine Surgeon, Margaret, daus.; others.
HILL, JAMES, Inv., 9-1843.
HILL, JAMES, L.S., 9-1843.
HILL, WILLIAM, Will, 4-1829. Dev.: Wife; John, son; Rachael, Elizabeth, daus.
HILL, WILLIAM, Inv., 4-1829.
HILL, WILLIAM, L.S., 7-1830.
HINCHMAN, JOHN, Will, 2-1844. Dev.: Even, wife; William, Joseph, James, John, Andrew, sons; Cynthia, Malinda, daus.; others.
HINCHMAN, JOHN, L.S., 10-1845.
HINCHMAN, William, Will, 6-21-1815. Dev.: Elizabeth, wife; William, John, sons; Elizabeth, dau.; others.
HINCHMAN, WILLIAM, Exr., Gdn. Set. 7-1844.
HINDS, Will, 2-21-1804. Dev.: Margot, wife; William, Henry, sons.
HOGSHEAD, CHARLES, Will, 4-1843. Isabella, Sally Ann, daus.; others.
HOGSHEAD, JOHN, Will, 5-1819. Dev.: Mary, wife; Eliza Erskine, Ann McPherson, daus.; John, James, Charles, Benjamin, Henry, Percivall, sons.
HOGSHEAD, JOHN B., Inv., 3-1848.
HOGSHEAD, JOHN B., L.S., 3-1848.
HOKE, JOHN, Inv., 11-19-1816.
HOKE, JOHN, L.S., 1-1833.
HOLLRIN, WILLIAM, Set., 6-7-1830.
HOLMES, JOHN, L.S., 1-1840.
HOLMES, JOHN, Set., 4-1842.
HOLRAIN, WILLIAM, Inv., 7-1829.
HONAKER, JACOB, Inv., 8-1838.
HONAKER, JACOB, L.S., 8-1838.
HONICKER, FREDERICK, Will, 12-1824. Dev.: John, Isaac, Jacob, Frederick, sons; Rachel, Sarah, Anna, Letty, Betsey Saunders, Magdaline Cantly, Mary Davis, Peggy Campbell, daus.
HONICKER, FREDERICK, L.S., 2-1825.
HUMPHREYS, JAMES, Will, 11-17-1817.
HUMPHREYS, JAMES, Inv., 8-20-1823.
HUMPHREYS, JAMES, Set., 3-1824.
HUMPHREYS, JOHN, Will, no date. Dev.: John, James, William, Samuel, Richard, Robert, sons, Isabella, Elizabeth, Peggy, Martha, daus.; Catherine, wife.
HUMPHREYS, JOHN, L.S., 9-1825.
HUMPHREYS, JOHN, Inv., 5-1847.
HUMPHREYS, JOHN, D., L.S., 5-1847.
HUMPHREYS, JOHN, Set., 4-1850.

HUMPHREYS, ROBERT, Will, 9-1809.
Dev.: Elizabeth, wife; Robert, James,
John, sons; Rebecca Wilson, Elizabeth
Vineyard, Jane Underwood, Nancy Fenton, Margaret Reynolds, daus.
HUMPHREYS, SAMUEL, Inv.: 4-9-1817.
HUNT, SAMUEL, Will, 7-1833. Dev.:
Rhonda, wife; Sam'l Thompson, son;
others.
HUNTER, JAMES, Will, 11-1850. Dev.:
Mary E., wife; Joseph, Philip, William,
sons; Catherine Nelson, Mary Carter,
Elizabeth Francis, Julia Skaggs, daus.
HUNTER, JAMES, L.S., 11-1850.
HUTCHISON, ALEX., Will, 8-1834. Dev.:
Sarah, wife; Thomas, James, Beniah
Bams, Isaac Newton, sons.
HUTCHISON, ALEX, L.S., 1-1835.
HUTCHISON, SAMUEL, Inv., 1-18-1808.

INSMINGER, CATHERINE, Inv., 6-19-1812.
INSMINGER, CATHERINE, L.S., 7-1813.
INSMINGER, PHILLIP, L.S., 7-1813.

JAMES, CLARK, L.S., 10-10-1801.
JARRELL, DANIEL, Will, 2-21-1804. Dev.:
Mary, wife; children.
JARRETT, SUSANAH, Will, 5-1839. Dev.:
Sarah Blain, dau.; others.
JOHNSON, A. J., Inv., 3-1850.
JOHNSON, CHARLES, Inv., 10-1850.
JOHNSON, RICHARD, Inv., 3-1845.
JOHNSON, RICHARD, L.S., 8-1845.
JOHNSON, RICHARD, Set., 10-1849.
JOHNSON, ROBERT, Will, 5-15-1820, Dev.:
Catherine, wife; Caleb, Samuel, James,
William, Jacob, Barnabas, Robert, sons;
Polly, Betsy, Catherine Graham, Jane
Mann, daus., others.
JOHNSON, THOMAS, Will, 1-1826. Dev.:
Mary, wife; Richard, John, James,
Thomas, sons; Mary Beirne, Nancy, Peggy,
Elizabeth Clark, daus.; other.
JOHNSON, THOMAS, L.S., 3-1828.
JONES, DANIEL, Inv., 12-17-1816.
JONES, DANIEL, L.S., 3-17-1818.
JONES, JAMES, Inv., 6-1847.
JONES, JAMES, L.S., 6-1847.
JONES, JESSE, Will, 5-1849. Dev.: Mary,
wife; Francis, William, Eli, Samuel, Uriah,
John, James, sons; Susan Campbell, Polly
Fife, Betsy, daus.; others.
JONES, JAMES, Inv.: 8-1849.
JONES, JAMES, L.S., 8-1849.
JONES, JOHN, Inv., 8-1848.
JONES, JOHN, L.S., 8-1848.
JONES, JOHN, Set., 7-1850.
JONES, ROBERT, Inv., 6-1833.

KEATLEY, FRANCIS, Will, 1-1825. Dev.:
James, Thomas, William, sons; Ann, Caty,
Hannah, Elizabeth, Polly, daus.; others.
KEATLEY, FRANCIS, L.S., 11-17-1829.
KEATLEY, FRANCIS, Set., 12-1829.
KEATLEY, JESSE, Will, 6-1846. Dev.:
Lydia, wife; James, John, Joseph, Wilson,
Henry, sons; Harrietta Right, Nancy Landers, Emily Halstead, Mary Ann, Adeline,
daus.
KEATON, ANDERSON, Inv., 9-1838.
KEENAN, CHARLES, Will, 12-1843. Dev.:
Anne, wife; Andrew, Michael, sons;
Nancy, Leannah, daus.
KELBURN, ISAAC, L.S., 2-1840.
KELLAR, CONRAD, Will, 8-1836. Dev.:
John, Philip, Henry, David, Abraham,
sons; Katherine Land, Sally Magert, Susanna Hanger, Rachel Gwinn, Elizabeth,
daus.
KELLY, HENRY, Inv., 6-1833.

KELLY, HENRY, L.S., 6-1833.
KELLY, JAMES, Inv., 12-1837.
KELLY, JAMES, L.S., 3-1838.
KILBURN, A., L.S., 8-1835.
KILBURN A., Will, 6-1835. Dev.: Mother;
wife; others.
KILBURN, ISAAC, Will, 3-19-1821. Dev.:
Amos, Isaac, John, sons; wife; Elizabeth,
Hannah, Phebe Wiseman, daus.
KILBURN, ISAAC, Inv., 6-1839.
KINSLEY, THOMAS, Will, 6-1838. Dev.:
George Kinsley, nephew.
KIRBY, WILLIAM, Set., 8-1849.
KITCHEN, JOSEPH W., Will, 7-1829. Dev.:
Agnes Kitchen, mother; Henry C., bro.
KITCHEN, MARGARET, Will, 6-18-1822.
Dev.: Henry, Jos., grandsons.

LAFERTY, WILLIAM, Will, 4-22-1818.
Dev.: William, John, James, Robert,
Ralph, sons; Nancy, Mattie P., Elizabeth Jane, Rebeckky Massey, daus.
LAKE, NICHOLAS, Set., 5-1831.
LAREW, PETER, Will, 5-1840. Dev.: Anne,
wife; John, Jacob, sons; Martha Jane,
Rebecah, Ann, Peggy, Polly, Nancy, Sally,
Betsy, daus.
LAREW, PETER, L.S., 12-21-1840.
LAROWE, DANIEL, Inv., 2-20-1803.
LAURENCE, WILLIAM, Will, 5-1834.
Dev.: Elizabeth, wife: James, William,
John; others.
LAURENCE, WILLIAM, Inv., 1-1835.
LAWHORN, DANIEL, Inv., 12-1831.
LEACH, WILLIAM, Will, 4-1808. Dev.:
Susan, wife; Reuben, John, William,
James, Mathew, Joshua, Edward, Edmond,
Eason, sons; Molly Jones, Elizabeth
Shewmate, daus.
LEACH, WILLIAM, L.S., 5-1809.
LEAKE, NICHOLAS, Will, 11-1825. Dev.:
Jane, wife; Daniel, son; Isabell, Marget,
Betsy Jones, Molly Brown, Jane, Marcome, Nancy Hoke, Eleanor Erskine,
daus.; others.
LEAKE, NICHOLAS, L.S., 3-1829.
LEGG, THOMAS, Will, 9-1808. Dev.:
Elizabeth, wife.
LEGG, THOMAS, L.S., 5-1812.
LEGG, WILLIAM E., Inv., 10-1844.
LEGG, WILLIAM, L.S., 10-1844.
LEMAYEUR, JOHN, Will , 10-28-1806.
Dev.: John Davis, friend.
LEMONS, ANDREW, Gnd. Set., 6-1848.
LEMONS, JOHN, Will, 5-15-1841. Dev.:
Mary, wife; Jacob, Abraham, James,
William, George, John, sons; Mary Burditt, daus.
LEMONS, JOHN, Inv., 2-1844.
LEMONS, JOHN, L.S., 2-1844.
LEMONS, JOHN JR., Will, 5-1844. Dev.:
Matilda, wife; William, Robert, Lewis,
John, sons; Pelina Agnes, Sarah Jane,
Matilda C., daus.
LEMONS, JOHN JR., L.S., 6-18-1845.
LEMONS, MATILDA, Inv., 11-1850.
LEWIS, SAMUEL, L.S., 8-16-1811.
LEWIS, SAMUEL, Inv., 12-18-1815.
LEWIS, THOMAS, L.S., 10-16-1805.
LEWIS, THOMAS, Inv., 11-27-1806.
LEWIS, WILLIAM, Will, 11-18-1818. Dev.:
Anne, wife; Charles, John, Thomas, William, sons; Margaret, Agatha, Elizabeth,
daus.; others.
LINTON, EUPHEMIA, Will, 7-1830. Dev.:
Jno. Barton, James Nisbett, Seth Harrison,
sons.
LINTON, JAMES, N., Inv., 7-1849.
LINTON, JAMES N. L. S. 7-1849.
LINTON, WILLIAM, Will, 6-20-1815. Dev.:
Euphimia, wife; John Barton, James Niesbett, Seth H., sons; Elizabeth H., dau.

LIVELY, BENJAMIN, Will, 4-1840. Dev.:
Loyd, Joseph, William, Benjamin, sons;
Nancy Ann, Frances, Sarah, Mary I.,
daus.
LIVELY, BENJAMIN, L.S., 9-1840.
LIVELY, BENJ., Set., 4-1842.
LIVELY, COTRELL, Will, 12-17-1838.
Dev.: Wife; Wilson, Joseph, Thomas, William, John, sons; Judith McGhee, Polly,
Laomi Pack, Jane Pack, Sally Smith,
daus.; others.
LIVELY, COTRELL, L.S., 12-21-1840.
LIVELY, GODERAL, Set., 10-1843.
LIVELY, JOSEPH, Inv., 11-1846.
LIVELY, JOSEPH, Set., 9-1850.
LIVELY, SARAH, Will, 9-16-1839. Dev.:
William, James, Thomas, Wilson, John,
sons; Jane Pack, Sally Smith, Judith McGhee, Polly, daus.; others.
LOWE, POLLY, Inv., 2-1828.
LOWE, POLLY, Inv., 11-1841.
LOWE, POLLY, L.S., 11-1841.
LOWE, WILLIAM, Will, 3-1838. Dev.:
Joshua, bro.; Sally, sis.; Zadock Lowe,
father.
LOWE, WILLIAM, L.S., 4-1840.
LOWE, ZACHARIAH, Inv., 6-1825.
LOWE, ZACHARIAH, L.S., 6-1825.
LYNCH, JNO., Set., 1827.

MADDY, JAMES, Will, 10-1824. Dev.:
Irma, wife; Thomas, Henry, Andrew,
Wilson, sons; Susannah Luster, Polly Gartin, Jane, Juda, daus.
MADDY, JAMES, L.S., 5-1825.
MADDY, JOHN, Will, 4-1840. Dev.: Barbara, wife; Charles, William, James, Jacob, John, sons.
MADDY, JOHN, L.S., 3-1842.
MADDY, WILLIAM, Inv., 7-21-1845.
MADDY, WILLIAM, L.S., 7-21-1845.
MADDY, WILLIAM, Set., 8-1848.
MADDY, WILLIAM, Set., 10-1849.
MAGGERT, HENRY, Will, 3-1843. Dev.:
John, Samuel, Jacob, James, sons; Elizabeth, Polly, daus.; others.
MAHON, JOHN, Inv., 7-1843.
MAHON, JOHN, L.S., 7-1843.
MAHON, JOHN, Set., 3-1847.
MAILES, JOHN, Inv., 1-1831.
MAMM, JACOB, Inv., 5-16-1815.
MANN, ADAM, Will, 8-1840. Dev.: Polly,
wife; William, James, Joseph, Henry,
Adam, John, sons; Sally Cummins, Jane
Harvey, Coe Gibson, daus.; others.
MANN, JAMES, Will, 12-1835. Dev.:
Nancy, wife; Robert, Alexander, sons;
Betsy Agness, daus.
MANNAX, JOHN, Inv., 5-1807.
MANNIX, JOHN, L.S., 2-27-1809.
MARSHALL, JULIA ANN, Inv., 8-1847.
MARSHALL, JULIA ANN, L.S., 7-1848.
MARSHALL, JULIA A., Set., 9-1849.
MATHEWS, JONATHAN, Will, 4-1841.
Dev.: Hannah, wife; David, George, Alford, sons; Margaret Mitchell, Sally Johnson, Miriam Fluke, Nancy, Lucy, Elizabeth, Susan, daus.
MAYS, PIERCE W., Inv., 3-1824.
MAYS, PIERCE, Inv., 12-1829.
MCCALLISTER, JAMES, Inv., 7-1834.
MCCALLISTER, JAMES, L.S., 7-1834.
MCCALLSTER, JAMES, L.S., 7-1834.
MCCLANAHAN, JOHN, Inv., 8-27-1814.
MCCORMAC, JEREMIAH, L.S., 11-1848.
MCDANIEL, HENRY, Will, 6-1819. Dev.:
Caty, wife; Peggy, Nancy, Patsy, Ann,
daus.; Isaac, James, John, William, David,
sons.
MCDONALD, RHODICEY, Inv., 7-1848.
MCDONALD, RHODICEY, L.S., 7-1848.

MCDOUGLE, JOHN, will, 1-15-1805. Dev.:
Patrick Duncan, Donal, Dougle, bros.;
others.
MCDOUGLE, JOHN, L.S., 6-1808.
MCDOWELL, ARCHIBALD, Will, 8-1813.
Dev.: Catherine, wife; Watty, John, William, James, sons; Hannah Martin, Fanny
Stuart, Peggy Gullet, daus.; others.
MCDOWELL, CATHERINE, Will, 2-1842.
Dev.: James, Witty, sons, Jane Stewart,
Peggy, Gullet, daus., others.
MCDOWELL, CATHERINE, Inv., 5-1844.
MCDOWELL, CATHERINE, L.S., 5-1844.
MCDOWELL, HANSON, Will, 8-22-1805.
Dev.: Mary Atkins, dau.; Elizabeth Atkins, grandchild.
MCDOWELL, HENSON, L.S., 1-1813.
MCGHEE, COTTRELL, Will, 7-1844. Dev.:
James, Caperton, Harvey, bros.
MCGHEE, JOHN, Set., 11-1827.
MCGHEE, JOHN, Will, 4-1841. Dev.: Sally, wife; Joel, James, Harvey, Caperton,
sons; Catherine, Jane, daus.; others.
MCGLAMRY, MATHIAS, Will, 7-15-1817.
Dev.: Lydia, wife; Sarah, Bathshaba, daus.
MCLAUGHLIN, ANDREW, Set., 3-1853.
MCMACHEN, JOHN, Will, 8-1829. Dev.:
James Jacob, John, Stephan, Jessy, William, Cornelius, Washington, sons; Peggy,
Jean, daus.; wife.
MCMAHON, JANE, L.S., 10-20-1837.
MCMAHON, JOHN, L.S., 10-1837.
MCMAHON, WILLIAM, Inv., 3-1814.
MCMAHON, WILLIAM, L.S., 3-1814.
MIDDLEKOFF, ELIZABETH, Inv., 4-1840.
MIDDLEKOFF, ELIZABETH, L.S., 4-1840.
MIDDLEKOFF, ELIZABETH, Set., 9-1848.
MILBOURN, NATHAN, Will, 9-1808, Dev.:
Sally, wife; Jacob, Nathan, Isaac, sons;
Radhael, Polly, Sally Shewmate, daus.
MILBOURNE, NATHAN, L.S., 11-1808.
MILBOURNE, NATHAN, Will, 9-1836.
Dev.: Bros.; sisters; others.
MILBOURNE, NATHAN, L.S., 1-1838.
MILHOLLEN, WILLIAM, Will, 2-1837.
Dev.: Ellaner, wife; others.
MILLER, ADAM, Will, 2-1844, Dev.:
Letha, wife; William, Samuel, Adam,
John, sons; Elizabeth, Mary Jane, Nancy,
daus.
MILLER, ELIZABETH, Will, 4-1840. Dev.:
Issac, Michael, sons; Elizabeth, Sally,
Hannah, daus.
MILLER, JACOB, Will, 7-1808. Dev.: Margaret, wife; Joseph, Jacob, John, George,
Peter, sons; Elizabeth Caperton, Mary
Price, Catherine Walker, Barbara Maddy,
Margaret, Sally, Rhoda, daus.
MILLER, JACOB, L.S., 7-29-1808.
MILLER, JOHN, Will, 6-1936. Dev.: Barbara, wife; John, Adam, Michael, George,
Henry, Daniel, Moses, Jacobs, sons.
MILLER, JOSEPH, Will, 6-17-1823. Dev.:
Dolly, wife; Brice, John, David, sons;
Jane, Elizabeth, Hannah, Rachel, Margaret Shanklin. daus.; others.
MILLER, JOSEPH, L.S., 1-1825.
MILLER, MICHAEL, Will, 8-1834. Dev.:
Elizabeth, wife; Michael, Isaac, John,
sons; others.
MILLER, MICHAEL, L.S., 7-1835.
MILLER, THOMAS, Inv., 5-1842.
MILLER, THOMAS, L.S., 2-1842.
MILLER, THOMAS, Set., 12-1843.
MITCHELL, JOSHUA, Will, 5-1847. Dev.:
Thomas, James, Joseph, sons; Elizabeth
Miller, Sally Cummins, Polly Comber,
Catherine Miller, Nancy Cox, Susan Ellis,
Peggy Cox, Jane Comber, Lucy Fips, daus.
MITCHELL, JOSHUA, Set., 5-1849.
MITCHELL, THOMAS, Inv., 3-1845.
MITCHELL, THOMAS, L.S., 3-1845.

174   West Virginia Estate Settlements

MONTGOMERY, ELIZABETH, Will 5-22-1805. Dev.: Margaret Kitchen, sis.
MURDOCK, JAMES, Inv., 8-1846.
MURDOCK, JAMES, L.S., 8-1846.

NEAL, ANN, Will, 6-1839. Dev.: Nancy Burns, niece.
NEEL, OWEN, Will, 7-1828. Dev.: Isabella, wife; Abner, Owen, John, Joseph, William, sons; others.
NEEL, OWEN, L.S., 6-1829.
NEEL, ROBERT, L.S., 6-18-1805.
NEEL, WALTER, 12-19-1801.
NEELE, RICHARD, Will, 1-1831. Dev.: Nancy, wife; others.
NELSON, JAMES, Set., 2-1837.
NELSON, THOMAS, Inv., 9-1842.
NELSON, THOMAS, L.S., 9-1842.
NETTLE, FELIX, Inv., 6-1838.
NETTLE, FELIX, L.S., 6-1838.
NETTLE, SUSANNAH, Will, 7-1847. Dev.: Jane Nettle, James A. Nettie, Ardealia Nettle, others.
NETTLE, SUSANNAH, Set., 3-1850.
NEWMAN, JONATHAN, Inv., 1-1825.
NICKEL, JOHN, L.S., 3-1827.
NICKELL, ANDREW, Will, 8-19-1839. Dev.: Robert, son; Mary Ann, wife; Percillah, Prushia, Martha, Elizabeth, Anny M., daus.
NICKELL, ANDREW, L.S., 9-1841.
NICKELL, ANDREW, Set., 6-16-1845.
NICKELL, ANDREW, Will, 11-1845. Dev.: Mary, wife; Christopher, Washington, Caperton, Thomas, Andrew, Henderson, William, Edward, Hiram, sons; Melinda, Eliza, Ellin, daus.; others.
NICKELL, ANDREW, L.S., 3-1847.
NICKELL, ANDREW, Inv., 7-1849.
NICKELL, ANDREW, Set., 11-1849.
NICKELL, ANDREW, Set., 5-1850.
NICKELL, ANDREW, Gnd., Set., 11-1847.
NICKELL, BARBARA, Inv., 2-1849.
NICKELL, EDWARD, Set., 9-1849.
NICKELL, ELIZABETH, Will, 4-1849. Dev.: Polly, Nelly, sisters, others.
NICKELL, FRANCIS, Inv., 6-1828.
NICKELL, FRANCIS, Set., 10-16-1837.
NICKELL, FRANK, L.S., 6-1828.
NICKELL, GEORGE, Inv., 12-1836.
NICKELL, GEORGE, L.S., 2-1837.
NICKELL, GEORGE, Set., 10-1844.
NICKELL, GEORGE, Gdn., Set., 2-1848.
NICKELL, GEO., W., Gdn., Set., 6-1850.
NICKELL, ISAAC, Will, 10-1839. Dev.: Polly, Ann Lewis, Elizabeth Craige, Barbarah, Nancy Cottle, Susanah Irvin, Sally McAlister, daus.; others.
NICKELL, ISAAC, Gdn., Set., 10-1847.
NICKELL, ISAAC, Set., 2-1849.
NICKELL, ISAAC, Inv., 3-1849.
NICKELL, ISAAC, L.S., 3-1849.
NICKELL, JAMES, Inv., 5-1849.
NICKELL, JAMES, L.S., 5-1849.
NICKELL, JOHN, Inv., 6-1829.
NICKELL, JOHN, Inv., 10-1844.
NICKELL, JOHN, Set., 12-1845.
NICKELL, JOSEPH M., Gdn., Rep., 7-1849.
NICKELL, MARGARET, Will, 12-1825. Dev.: Elinor Dyer, Elizabeth King, sisters; others.
NICKELL, MARGARET, Inv., 5-1841.
NICKELL, MARGARET, Set., 7-1844.
NICKELL, MARGARET, Set., 11-1850.
NICKELL, MARTHA M., Gdn., Set., 10-1844.
NICKELL, ROBERT, Will, 11-1813. Dev.: wife; Susannah, sis.; Joseph, Isaac, Andrew, bros.; others.
NICKELL, ROBT., Inv., 12-17-1816.
NICKELL, ROBERT, L.S., 12-1850.

NICKELL, ROBERT, Will, 8-1850. Dev.: Dilne, wife; Samuel, Marion, Feamster, sons; others.
NICKELL, THOMAS, L.S., 11-1811.
NICKLE, JOHN, L.S., 6-1842.
NICKLE, JOHN, Inv., 6-1842.
NICKLE, JOHN, L.S., 9-1843.
NICKLE, THOMAS, Will, 3-17-1807. Dev.: Jane, wife; John, Thomas, Robert, George, Andrew, James, sons; Margaret, Barbara, Jane, Elizabeth, Mary, daus.

PACK, BARTLEY, Will, 4-1834. Dev.: Wife; Josephus, son; Polly, dau.
PACK, BARTLEY, L.S., 5-1838.
PACK, JOHN, Inv., 12-1829.
PACK, JOHN, L.S., 11-17-1829.
PACK, SAMUEL, Will, 7-1833. Dev.: Samuel, Matt. Bartley, William, Anderson, Loame, sons; Betsey, Jennet, Polly, daus. others.
PACK, SAMUEL, Set., 11-1847.
PACK, WILLIAM, Will, 5-1837. Dev.: Wife; children.
PARKER, JESSE, Inv., 3-1848.
PARKER, JESSE, L.S., 3-1848.
PARKER, JOSEPH, Will, 6-1819. Dev.: Jenny, wife; Andrew, James, Thomas, Jesse, Joseph, sons; Jenny Polly, Rachael, daus.; others.
PARKER, JOSEPH, Gnd., Set., 1-1837.
PARKER, JOSEPH, Gnd., Set., 5-1850.
PARKER, JOSEPH'S heirs, Add. Set., 1825.
PARKER, JOSEPH'S, heirs, Set., 6-1827.
PARSONS, GEORGE, Inv., 9-25-1805.
PARSONS, GEORGE, L.S., 5-1807.
PATERSON, MATHEW, Will, 12-1802. Dev.: Jennett, wife; Robert, bro.; Sarah Stephenson, sister; Isabella Byrnside, dau.
PATTERSON, JEAN, Will, 7-1830. Dev.: Olover Ewing, William Ewing, nephews; others.
PATTERSON, JEAN, L.S., 1-1831.
PATTON, ROBERT, L.S., 4-12-1805.
PATTON, ROBERT, Inv., 10-1808.
PATTON, ROBERT, Will, 1823. Dev.: Jean, wife; William, Mark, Tristram, sons; Margaret, Jean Cornwell, Mary Ann Nickell, daus.; others.
PATTON, ROBERT, Set., 3-1837.
PATTON, TRISTRAM, Inv., 4-1844.
PATTON, TRISTRAM, L.S., 9-1844.
PATTON, TRISTRAM, Set., 11-1849.
PECK, BENJ., Inv., 8-1841.
PECK, BENJAMIN, L.S., 8-1841.
PENCE, JACOB, Will, 6-9-1821. Dev.: Wife; David, Henry P., Geo. Wash., Moses, sons; Katherine Dickson, Juliana, Elizabeth, Agnes, daus.
PENCE, JACOB, Set., 8-1824.
PENCE, JACOB, Set., 3-1836.
PETERS, CONRAD, Will, 5-1850. Dev.: Clara, wife; Mary, Rhoda J., Angeline, Sarah Larew, daus.; others.
PETRIE, FREDERICK, H., Will, 7-1843. Dev.: Harriet Baldwin, Elizabeth Dunlap, daus.
PETRIE, FREDERICK, Inv., 10-1843.
PHILLIPS, NEHEMIAH, Inv., 6-16-1845.
PHILLIP, NEHEMIAH, L.S., 6-16-1845.
PINE, JAMES, Inv., 1803.
PINE, JAMES, L.S., 6-18-1816.
PINE, ROBERT, Will, 12-1849. Dev.: Nancy, wife.
PRITT, WILLIAM, Will, 6-1814. Dev.: Nancy, wife; Betsey, Patsy, Polly, daus.; Robert, Thomas, John, William, Fetty, James, sons.
PRITT, WILLIAM, Inv., 3-18-1823.
PRITT, WILLIAM, L.S., 3-1824.

RAGLAND, JAMES, L.S., 2-1850.
RAGLANDS, JAMES P., Inv., 2-1850.
RAINS, WILLIAMS, Inv., 6-1848.

RALSTEN, JAMES, Will, 6-1849. Dev.:
Mary, wife; James, Mathew, sons.
RALSTON, MATHEW, L.S., 11-1840.
RALSTON, MATHEW, Will, 10-1840. Dev.:
Jas. W., Mathew, nephews; Melindy
Walker, Ann P., Margaret, Mary J.,
nieces.
RALSTON, MATHEW, Set., 6-16-1845.
RAMSEY, RICHARD, Will 7-1824. Dev.:
Elizabeth, wife; George, John, William,
Joel, Daniel, Bartholamew, sons; Letty
Wikle, Margaret Wiseman, Jane, Sarah,
Mary, Betsey Rice, daus.
RAMSEY, RICHARD, L.S., 7-1828.
REABURN, JOHN, Will, 11-1824. Dev.:
John, Charles, Henry, Isaac, sons; Eliza-
beth, wife; Margaret Tracy.
REED, BENJAMIN, L.S., 9-1830.
REED, BENJAMIN, Inv., 10-1829.
REED, BENJAMIN, Set., 10-1831.
REED, ROBERT, Will, 1-1824. Dev.: Eliza-
beth, wife; John, son; Molly Hickenbot-
tom, Betty Hickenbottom, daus.
RIFFE, JOHN, Inv., 8-1843.
RIFFE, JOHN, L.S., 8-1843.
RIFFE, JOHN, Set., 7-1845.
RINER, JOHN, Inv., 6-17-1823.
RINER, JOHN, L.S., 3-1824.
ROACH, JONATHAN, Will, 7-1840. Rutha,
wife; Isaac, John, Lanty, Elijah, sons;
Rebecah Fleshman, Rhoda Meadows,
Rachel Perry, Letha Handley, Caty Mc-
Neer, Mary Handley, daus.
ROACH, MICKLEBERRY, Inv., 7-15-1815.
ROBERTS, ELIZABETH, Will, 11-19-1817.
Dev.: Thomas Trackwell, nephew.
ROLAND, JAMES, Inv., 5-29-1817.
ROWAN, CHARLES, Inv., 3-1835.
ROWAN, CHARLES, L.S., 4-1841.
ROYALL, WILLIAM, Will, 2-1813. Dev.:
Ann, wife; Wm. Archer.
RUTH, JOSEPH, Will, 9-1825. Dev.: Wil-
liam, son; others.

SCOTT, JAMES, Will, 3-1828. Dev.: Mar-
garet, wife; William, John, James, David,
Mathew, sons; Nancy, Elizabeth, Jane
Burdett, Mary Foster, daus.; others.
SCOTT, JAMES, L.S., 10-1829.
SCOTT, JAMES, Set., 6-3-1839.
SCOTT, WILLIAM, Inv., 5-1831.
SEVAIN, ABRAHAM, Will, 12-10-1803.
Dev.: Lydia, wife; Nancy, Lydia, Polly
Wade. Kity Spichard, Betsy Smith, Susan-
nah Carper, daus.; Henry, son.
SEVAIN, ABRAHAM, Inv., 8-10-1803.
SEWARD, ISAAC, Will, 9-1803. Dev.:
Milstone, wife; Isaac Jr., Thomas, Grif-
fin, sons; Ruth, Milstone, Rebakia, Nelly,
daus.
SHANKLIN, RICHARD, Will, 8-1841.
Dev.: Catherine, wife.
SHANKLIN, RICHARD, L.S., 8-1842.
SHANKLIN, WILLIAM, Will, 5-1848. Dev.:
Catherine, wife; children.
SHANKLIN, WILLIAM, Set., 9-1850.
SHANTON, ROMAN, Will, 6-19-1799. Dev.:
John Champ, grandson; others.
SHAVER, CHARLES, Inv., 11-29-1822.
SHAWVER, JACOB, Inv., 3-1829.
SHAWVER, SEBASTEN, Will, 10-15-1816.
Dev.: Jacob, George, John, Christopher,
sons; Elizabeth Hambarger, Barbara Ro-
wen, Sally, daus.; others.
SHAWVER, SEBASTIAN, Inv., 8-22-1823.
SHAWVER, SEBASTIAN, L.S., 8-22-1823.
SHIELDS, JOHN, Inv., 8-16-1815.
SHIELDS, JOHN, L.S., 8-15-1815.
SHIRES, RICHARD, Will, 6-1808. Dev.:
Thomas, John, sons: Polly Blan, dau.
SHIREY, MARTIN, Will, 7-16-1838. Dev.:
John, son; Polly, Sarah, Eve Hips, Eliza-
beth Hoover, daus.; others.

SHIREY, MARTIN, L.S., 9-1841.
SHUMATE, DANIEL, Will, 8-1826. Dev.:
Milly, wife; Silas, Daniel, John Tollison,
sons; Nancy, Peggy, Rhoda, Malinda,
Rachael, Betsey, daus.; others.
SHUMATE, DANIEL, L.S., 12-1827.
SKAGGS, ISAAC, Will, 1803. Dev.: Nan-
ny, wife; Ebby and Nanny Cashada.
SMITH, BRUTEN, Will, 6-1809. Dev.:
Catherine, wife; Jeramiah, son; Sally,
Polly, Elizabeth, Nancy Kilpatrick, daus.;
others.
SMITH, BRUTEN, L.S., 12-1814.
SMITH, CHRISTIAN, Will, 2-20-1816. Dev.:
Betsey, wife; George, Jacob, Joseph, Wil-
liam, sons; Mary, Barbarah, daus.
SMITH, JOHN, Will, 5-1809. Dev.: Cather-
ine, wife; Christopher, Charles, Samuel,
James, George, William, Joseph, sons;
Margaret, dau.
SMITH, JOHN, Inv., (no date).
SMITH, JOHN, Set., 1-19-1819.
SMITH, MADISON, Inv., 7-1847.
SMITH, MADISON, L.S., 7-1847.
SMITHSON, THOMAS, Will, 8-1832. Dev.:
Sally, wife; others.
SPADE, GEORGE, L.S., 6-1835.
SPADE, GEORGE, Will, 1-1835. Dev.:
Father; mother; others.
SPANGLER, JOHN, Inv., 6-1846.
SPANGLER, JOHN, Inv., 3-1849.
SPANGLER, JOHN, L.S., 3-1849.
SPAR, GEORGE, Will, 5-26-1823. Dev.:
Sally, wife; John, bro.; others.
SPAR, SARAH, Will, 6-1847. Dev.: Eliza
Legg, Sophy McCallister, daus.; others.
SPARR, SARAH, L.S., 12-1847.
SPROWL, MARGARET, Will, 12-18-1815.
Dev.: James, son; Mary Rice, dau.; others.
SPROWL, MARGARET, Inv., 2-20-1816.
STANTON, GARLAND, Will, 1-1837. Dev.:
Ann, wife; children.
STANTON, GARLAND, L.S., 6-1838.
STEELE, THOMAS, L.S., 6-1846.
STEELE, THOMAS, Will, 2-1846. Dev.:
Daughter; others.
STEPENSON, JAMES, Will, 1802. Dev.:
Ann, wife; Samuel, William, sons.
STEVENS, JEREMIAH, W., Inv., 4-1848.
STEVENS, JEREMIAH, Set. 4-1850.
STEVENS, W. P., L.S., 4-1848.
STEVER, HENRY, Inv., 12-18-1813.
STEVER. HENRY, L.S., 3-19-1818.
STODGHILL, JAMES, Will, 5-1836. Dev.:
Mary, wife; William, Samuel, bros.; Mar-
garet, dau.
STODGHILL, JAMES, Inv., 8-1837.
STODGHILL, JAMES G., L.S., 8-1837.
STODGHILL, JOEL, Will, 11-1844. Dev.:
Elizabeth, wife; William, Samuel, Joel,
sons; Rhoda Mann, Nancy Pence, Flora
Dunn, daus.; others.
SULLIPHAN, TIMETH, Will, 5-19-1801.
Dev.: Ketty, wife, Margaret Miller, Ketty
Swoope, daus.; others.
SULLIVAN, NATHANIEL, Will, 3-19-1839.
Dev.: Robert, James, sons; Lydia, dau.;
others.
SULLIVAN, NATHANIEL, L.S., 6-1841.
SULLIVAN, NATHANIEL, Set., 12-1843.
SULLIVAN, NATHANIEL, Set., 10-1850.
SWINNEY, JAMES, Will, 9-1836. Dev.:
Wife; Vincen, James, William, Martin,
sons; Mary, Rachel, Delilah, Delina, Ann
Susan, Elizabeth, daus.
SWOPE, ADAM, Will, 12-17-1849. Dev.:
Jonathan, Samuel, Ephraim, sons; Susan,
Eliza, Catherine, daus.
SWOPE, CATHERINE, Will, 3-22-1822.
Dev.: Joseph, Joseph Casebolt, grand-
sons; Katherine Burdette, Katherine Rife,
Katherine Swope, Katherine Baker, grand-
daughters.

SWOPE, JOSEPH, Inv., 7-17-1821.
SWOPE, JOSEPH, Inv., 6-16-1823.
SWOPE, MICHAEL, Will, 5-1839. Dev.:
John, James, Michael, sons; Mary Thompson, Leah Paul, Nancy Wilson, Peggy Scaggs, Ann Harvey, daus.; others.
SYMMS, SAMUEL, Will, 5-15-1821. Dev.:
Margaret, wife; John, son; Betsy, Agnes Young, Susannah Thomas, Mary Hinchman, daus.

TACKET, NIMROD, Will, 6-1837. Dev.:
James, Isaac, John, Ignatious, Nimrod, sons; Aney, wife; Rhoda Wylie, Elizabeth Fleet, Mary Fifer, Rachael, Nancy, Rebecka, daus.
TAPSCOTT, JAMES, Will, 10-24-1807.
Dev.: Susannah, wife; Robert, Albtion, Warner, Baleas, Newton, sons; Louisa, Caroline, Chichester, daus.
TAYLOR, JOHN, Inv., 11-20-1812.
TAYLOR, JOHN, L.S., 1-1813.
TAYLOR, MARY, L.S., 8-20-1811.
TAYLOR, MARY, Inv., 11-1824.
TAYLOR, NOTLIFF, Inv., 7-6-1808.
TAYLOR, NOTLISS, L.S., 8-1808.
THOMAS, ADAM, Will, 1-1843. Dev.:
Adam Thomas, Henry Thomas, nephews; others.
THOMAS, ADAM, Set., 5-1846.
THOMAS, BENJAMIN, Inv., 3-17-1801.
THOMAS, THOMAS, Will, 3-1836. Dev.:
Thomas, Richard, John, sons; Rebecca, wife; Rebecca, Sarah Johnson, daus.
THOMPSON, JOHN, Inv., 11-1823.
THOMPSON, JOHN, L. S., 11-1823.
THOMPSON, JOHN, L.S., 7-1837.
THOMPSON, JOHN, Set., 9-1825.
THOMPSON, JOHN, Inv., 9-1835.
THOMPSON, SAMUEL, Inv., 2-1832.
TIFFANY, HUGH, Will, 5-1849. Dev.:
Wife; Hugh, James, Charles, John, sons; Mary Ann, Margaret, daus.; others.
TOFFER, JOHN, Will, 6-10-1807. Dev.:
Sally, others.
TOFFER, JOHN, Set., 9-1825.
TOFFER, JOHN, Set., 3-1831.

VAWTER, WILLIAM, Will, 12-17-1822.
Dev.: Peggy, wife; children; others.

WALKER, BENJAMIN, Inv., 6-1831.
WALKER, BENJAMIN, L.S., 7-1831.
WANTZ, ADAM, Inv., 6-1829.

WATERS, JOHN, Inv., 1-19-1819.
WEST, GEORGE, Will, 1-19-1819. Dev.:
Mary, wife; Lucy Taylor, Polly Foster, daus.
WHITE, JOHN, Will, 5-1826. Dev.: Jean, wife; children.
WHITE, JOHN, L.S., 2-1829.
WHITE, THOMAS, Inv., 10-1814.
WHITE, THOMAS, L.S., 10-1814.
WHITE, WILLIAM, Will, 9-1802. Dev.:
Robt., bro.; others.
WIATT, THOMAS, Will, 4-1824. Dev.:
Rachael, wife; James, John, Edward, Thomas, Reuben, Mathew, Isaac, sons; Peggy, Eliza, Sarah Pack, daus.
WICKLINE, ADAM, Inv., 7-1836.
WICKLINE, ADAM, L.S., 6-1841.
WICKLINE, JACOB, Inv., 11-19-1822.
WILLEY, ROBERT, Will, 1799. Dev.:
Sarah, wife; John, Thomas, Robert, William, sons; others.
WILLIS, HENRY, Will, 3-1812. Dev.:
Elizabeth, wife.
WILLIS, HENRY, L.S., 7-28-1812.
WINDLE, SAMUEL, W., Inv., 12-1848.
WINDLE, SAMUEL, W., L.S., 1-1849.
WYATT, RACHAEL, L.S., 6-1827.
WYATT, RACHAEL, Inv., 6-1827.
WYLIE, JOHN, Will, 2-1810. Dev.: Martha Fisk, Margaret Shaver, Mary Smith, Jane Smith, daus.; John, Robert, James, sons.

YOUNG, JAMES, Will, 3-19-1822. Dev.:
Wife; Robert, James, Joseph, sons; Margaret, Betsy, Lydia, Nancy, Susannah, Hannah, daus.
YOUNG, JAMES, L.S., 7-1837.
YOUNG, JAMES, Gnd., Set., 8-1848.
YOUNG, JANE, L.S., 2-1839.
YOUNG, JANE, Will, 1-2-1839. Dev.:
Andrew, son; Sarah Ann, dau.
YOUNG, JANE, Set., 8-1848.
YOUNG, ROBERT, Inv., 3-1804.
YOUNG, ROBERT, L.S., 3-1804.
YOUNG, ROBERT, L.S., 3-19-1816.
YOUNG, WILLIAM, Will, 2-1-1802. Dev.:
Jean, wife; William, James, sons; Sarah, Betsey, Jean Cook, daus.; others.
YOUNG, WILLIAM, L.S., 8-1808.
YOUNG, WILLIAM, Will, 3-1830. Dev.:
Mary, wife; John Nettle.
YOUNG, WILLIAM, L.S., 9-1840.
YOUNG, WILLIAM, Set., 3-1844.